Microprocessor
Systems Design

THE PWS-KENT SERIES IN ELECTRICAL ENGINEERING

Microprocessor Systems Design

**68000 Hardware,
Software, and Interfacing**

Alan Clements
Teesside Polytechnic, England

PWS-KENT Publishing Company
Boston

PWS-KENT
Publishing Company

20 Park Plaza
Boston, Massachusetts 02116

Library of Congress Cataloging-in-Publication Data

Clements, Alan, 1948–
    Microprocessor systems design.

    Bibliography: p.
    Includes index.
    1. Motorola 68000 (Microprocessor) 2. System
design. I. Title.
QA76.8.M6895C54   1987   004.16   86-25488
ISBN 0-87150-095-7

Printed in the United States of America

        89 90 91 — 10 9 8 7 6

Sponsoring Editor: Robert Prior
Production Coordinator: Robine Storm van Leeuwen
Production: Santype International Limited
Interior Design: Julie Gecha
Cover Design: Robine Storm van Leeuwen
Cover Photo: Mark Eberhart/Unique Photo Arts, Inc., Atlanta, Ga.
Typesetting: Santype International Limited
Cover Printing: New England Book Components, Inc.
Printing and Binding: The Maple-Vail Book Manufacturing Group

For Karl and Ethel Amatneek,
Lance Leventhal,
and Nick Panos

Preface

The microprocessor revolution, which placed a central processing unit (CPU) on a single chip, has turned the computer into a handful of chips and has handed these chips over to the electronic engineer—that is, an electronic engineer can now take a microprocessor and design it into a system whose complexity may vary from the trivial to the sophisticated. *Microprocessor Systems Design: 68000 Hardware, Software, and Interfacing* shows how a microprocessor is transformed into a system capable of performing its intended task. It concentrates on the interface between the microprocessor and the other components of a microprocessor system.

Microprocessor Systems Design is written for two audiences. The first is Engineering and Computer Science students who have to study the design of microprocessor systems in order to get the qualification that frees them to design real systems in industry. For them, therefore, this book is written to support a typical course in microprocessor systems design. The second audience is practicing engineers who do not have exams to pass but who must produce an actual system to their employer's specification.

To address both audiences, I have included more practical information than is normally found in textbooks on microprocessor systems design. In particular, I have placed great emphasis on the timing diagram and on the analysis of microprocessor read/write cycles. An understanding of the timing requirements of a microprocessor is vital to the engineer.

Although I am writing about the design of microprocessor systems, I have included a section on programming a microprocessor in assembly language. This inclusion has been made because many of the small educational microprocessor systems can be programmed only in assembly language and because the peripherals appearing in this book are described at the physical level and are best programmed in assembly language.

Anyone writing a book about the practical design of microprocessor systems must choose a real microprocessor to illustrate the techniques involved. I have selected the 68000. The 68000 is one of several 16-bit devices currently available and has been chosen because of its powerful but relatively simple instruction set, its sophisticated interfacing capabilities, and its ability to strongly support multitasking.

Do not think that 8-bit microprocessors are now superfluous! Because they are cheaper than 16-bit microprocessors, 8-bit microprocessors will be around for many years and can often be used in simpler systems. However, 16-bit microprocessors, such as the 68000, are more relevant to teaching because they have all the features of 8-bit devices plus many new features not found on the older chips.

The following paragraphs briefly describe the contents of *Microprocessor Systems Design*. Chapter 1 introduces the basic building blocks of a microprocessor system and provides a framework within which a real system can be discussed. Chapter 2 provides a general introduction to the architecture and programming of the 68000 microprocessor. Sufficient detail of the 68000's assembly language is given to enable the reader to follow the fragments of assembly language appearing elsewhere in the text. Chapter 3 is devoted to program design techniques, including an overview of some of the topics closely related to the design of software for embedded microprocessor systems. In Chapter 4 we examine the basic hardware characteristics of the 68000, including the concepts of the timing diagram and the relationship between the 68000 and random access memory.

Chapter 5 looks at the memory subsystem and is divided into two distinct sections: address decoding and the design of static memory arrays. Chapter 6, which covers exception handling, is especially valuable, given the 68000's wealth of exception-handling facilities. In Chapter 7, we are concerned with the design of more sophisticated microprocessor systems. Multimicroprocessor systems, dynamic memories, memories capable of detecting and automatically correcting errors, and memory management systems are all discussed. The operation of the parallel interface and a description of the 68230 PI/T and the direct memory access (DMA) controller are outlined in Chapter 8.

Chapter 9 deals with the serial interface between a microcomputer and a peripheral. This chapter also covers the international standards used to define the electrical characteristics of a serial data-link. In Chapter 10 we examine the buses linking together the functional modules of a microprocessor system. The characteristics of buses are dealt with under various headings, including timing and protocols, electrical properties, and bus control in microprocessor systems. The popular VMEbus is covered. The final chapter, Chapter 11, presents a practical discussion of some issues involved in microprocessor systems design. Beginning with adequate specifications and moving through design, construction, testability, and maintainability, this chapter concludes with a worked example of a 68000-based microcomputer.

Acknowledgments

I would like to thank all those who helped me with the production of this book. Indeed, if it were not for Karl Amatneek, Nick Panos, and Lance Leventhal in San Diego, this book would not have been written! I had originally intended to write a book on the 6809 microprocessor. These three assaulted me verbally until I agreed to write about the 68000. In particular, I would like to thank Karl for his help in organizing my three visits to the United States, Nick for the time he spent with me discussing the 68000, and Lance for his constructive criticism of my manuscript.

During my third visit to the United States in 1985, I met many of the reviewers of my manuscript as I traveled from PWS Publishers in Boston to San Diego. I thank all my reviewers: George Brown, Rochester Institute of Technology; Ray Doskocil, Motorola, Phoenix, Arizona; Frederick Edwards, University of Massachusetts; Lance Leventhal, Emulative Systems Co., Inc.; Mark Manwaring, Washington State University; David Poplawski, Michigan Technological University; Clara Serrano, Motorola, Austin, Texas; and Marvin Woodfill, Arizona State University.

I must single out two of the reviewers for special praise. Clara Serrano at Motorola in Austin and Ray Doskocil at Motorola in Phoenix are both very busy engineers who spent considerable time working on my manuscript and who gave up even more time to chat with me about my book.

I would also like to thank those at PWS Publishers who helped and guided me through the many stages in the production of this book. A special thanks to my wife, Sue, who read the draft manuscript and provided much useful feedback.

Finally, I would like to thank my employers, Cleveland County Council, who gave me sabbatical leave from Teesside Polytechnic in 1983/1984. It was during this period that I carried out the research and planning for this book. Equally, I must thank Dr. John Darby, my former department head, who supported my application for the sabbatical and who provided considerable assistance with my research.

I encourage readers to send me suggestions and comments regarding this book through PWS Publishers in Boston.

Technical data relating to the MC68000 and other associated products described in this publication is reproduced by kind permission of Motorola Semiconductors.

Contents

4 The 68000 CPU Hardware Model   103

5 Memories in Microcomputer Systems   151

6 Exception Handling and the 68000   220

7 The 68000 in Larger Systems   272

8 The Microprocessor Interface   341

Chapter 1

The Microcomputer

In this chapter we introduce the microcomputer and identify the characteristics of its major component parts. Once we have introduced these parts and described the functions they perform in a microcomputer, we are in a better position to deal with them in detail in later chapters. However, before we can continue, we need to determine exactly what we mean by the terms *microcomputer* and *microprocessor*.

A microcomputer is defined as a stand-alone system based on a microprocessor. A stand-alone system is one that is able to operate without additional equipment. It should be distinguished from the individual functional parts of a microcomputer (the memory, the CPU, the interfaces, and the power supply). Therefore, an understanding of how a microprocessor is interfaced to other components is necessary to the engineer who wishes to design a microcomputer. The term *microprocessor system* should be regarded as meaning the same as *microcomputer* throughout this book.

The microprocessor is a central processing unit (CPU) on a single chip, and is entirely useless on its own. To create a viable computer requires memory components, interface components, timing and control circuits, a power supply, and a cabinet or other enclosure. This book shows how these other components can be connected to a microprocessor to produce a microcomputer.

The applications of a microcomputer are legion and hardly need elaborating on today. Broadly speaking, the microcomputer falls into one of two categories: the general-purpose digital computer and the embedded computer. The general-purpose digital computer is what most people understand by the word *computer*. It has all the necessary memory and peripherals required by a user to execute a wide range of applications programs.

An embedded computer is one dedicated to a specific application and is normally transparent (or "invisible") to the user of the system in which it is located. A typical embedded microcomputer lies at the heart of an automatic bank teller. A customer inserts a credit card in a slot and the microcomputer reads the relevant details from its magnetic strip. The customer keys in an identity code; the microcomputer validates the code and then invites the customer to perform a transaction. Once the transaction has been completed, the microcomputer updates the data in the magnetic strip and operates the mechanical subsystem that returns the card to its owner. The user of the automatic teller is entirely unaware of the embedded computer and of its function.

The fundamental difference between an embedded computer and a general-purpose computer is the optimization of the former to suit a single function. Typically, an embedded computer contains only the components strictly necessary for it to execute its allocated task. In contrast, a general-purpose computer is highly likely to have sufficient memory and peripherals for it to be able to handle a broad range of tasks. In particular, the general-purpose computer almost always has facilities for expansion, thereby enabling the user to add more memory or peripherals at a later date.

1.1 Microprocessor Systems

In this book we examine the design of two types of microcomputer: the single board computer (SBC) and the modular computer, which is composed of a number of separate units linked by a bus. The single board computer is usually associated with the embedded computer, where it is designed to execute a single, fixed task.

The modular computer based on a bus is frequently a general-purpose digital computer and has a degree of sophistication not normally found on an SBC. When we come to design modular microcomputers, we will discover that their design must be flexible so that they can be adapted to a wide number of different applications.

The block diagram of a possible modular, general-purpose, digital computer based on a 16-bit microprocessor is given in figure 1.1. This system consists of a number of modules linked together by a bus. Figure 1.2 provides a photograph of a typical rack-mounted modular system. Although the words *card* and *module* are frequently interchangeable, a card may not necessarily constitute a module in the same sense as in the concept of "modular design and modularity."

Information is moved between the cards by means of a bus, labeled SYSTEM_BUS in figure 1.1, to distinguish it from buses within the individual cards. A bus existing only within a card is termed a LOCAL_BUS. A system bus allows cards to be added to or removed from a microprocessor system. A microcomputer can, therefore, be built out of standard building blocks: the cards. The advantage of a modular approach is that a manufacturer can produce a sufficiently large range of cards to permit any user to construct a microcomputer to his or her own specifications. Furthermore, once this trend begins, a number of independent manufacturers soon start to sell special-purpose cards. This process can most readily be seen in the case of some popular personal computers.

Of course, manufacturers begin to make their own cards for sale only when the market is sufficiently large. The size of the market depends on the widespread acceptance of a particular system bus and of standard size cards that can be plugged into it. Standards for buses were once generated in an ad hoc fashion by

FIGURE 1.1 Block diagram of a possible modular microcomputer

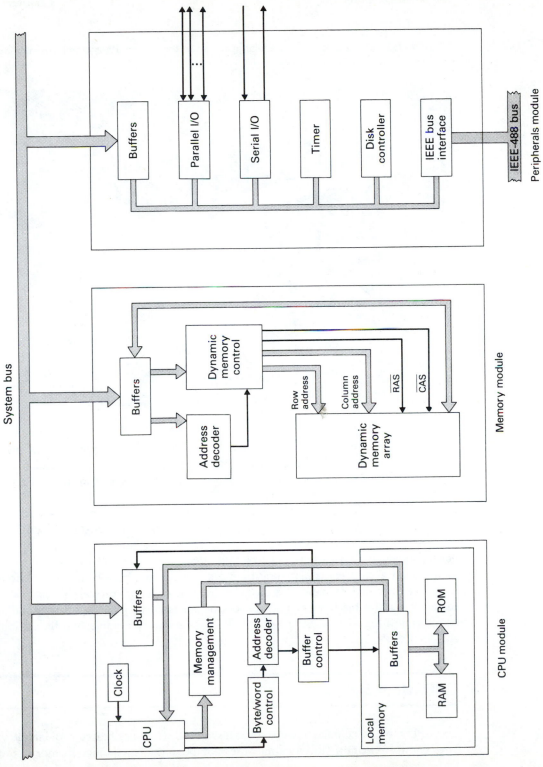

FIGURE 1.2   Photograph of a modular microprocessor system. Photograph supplied by courtesy of BICC-Vero.

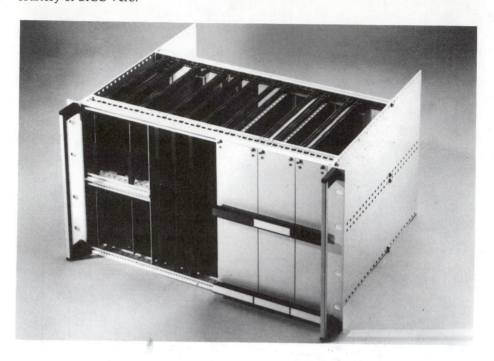

some manufacturer or entrepreneur and later adopted by an international committee. In the case of the 68000, Motorola first created the Versabus, which was later modified by committees to become the VMEBus. Now it is in the process of becoming an international standard.

In the block diagram of figure 1.1, three modules are connected to the system bus: a CPU module, a memory module, and a peripherals module. In practice, there is no reason why these functions cannot be distributed among the various modules of a system. For example, it is quite normal to locate a block of memory on a card containing one or more peripherals. However, the functions have been divided between the modules here in order to provide a reasonable sequence for the teaching of microprocessor systems design. The three modules comprising this system are the CPU module, the memory module, and the peripherals module.

CPU Module

The CPU module contains the microprocessor and its associated control circuitry. The control circuitry includes all the components (excluding memory and peripherals) that must be connected to a microprocessor to enable it to function. Most microprocessors do not contain sufficient circuitry on-chip to allow them to be connected directly to memory components. Generally speaking, the more sophisticated the microprocessor, the greater the demand for additional control circuitry. The following functions are some of those performed by the CPU module.

Clock and CPU Control Circuits

The clock provides the sequencing information needed by the microprocessor to control its internal operations. Modern 16-bit microprocessors require a very simple clock circuit generating a continuous square wave with a frequency of between 4 and 16 MHz. This clock is a master clock and is normally distributed to all modules in the system. Other control circuitry includes the power-on-reset circuit, which forces the microprocessor to execute a start-up routine shortly after the system has been powered up.

Address Decoder

The primary function of the address decoder is to divide the memory space of the CPU into smaller units and to allocate these to individual memory components. The CPU module is usually provided with some local memory that is not accessed from the system bus. This feature enables the CPU module to be tested independently of the rest of the microprocessor system. The address decoder also distinguishes between a memory access to local memory and one to memory situated on another module.

Address and Data Bus Buffers

The microprocessor or any other device distributing information throughout the system cannot normally provide sufficient electrical drive to cater for the loading on the bus from other elements. Special integrated circuits, called *buffers* or *bus drivers*, act as an interface between the microprocessor and the bus. Additional circuitry is needed to control the bus drivers, as only one device may drive the bus at any instant.

Buffer Control

The buffer control logic determines the mode of operation of the bus drivers and receivers on the CPU module. For example, during an access to local memory, the buffers driving the system bus must be disabled.

Although 16-bit microprocessors are designed to operate on 16-bit words, there are occasions when the microprocessor wishes to operate on an 8-bit entity. If memory were organized as 16-bit words, the CPU could not deal with transfer of a single 8-bit word between itself and memory. Most memories in 16-bit microcomputers are byte organized, so that a 16-bit word is stored as two 8-bit words, each independently accessible. Byte/word control logic is required to enable the microprocessor to access either a single byte or both bytes of a 16-bit word.

Bus Arbitration Control

In some microcomputers, the microprocessor has sole control of the system bus and determines the nature of each and every bus access, that is, a read from memory or a write to memory. In other microcomputers, more than one device may access the bus. It may be a DMA (direct memory access) controller, which is used to transfer data directly between a peripheral and memory without the active intervention of the CPU, or it may be another microprocessor. The latter case arises in a multiprocessor environment in which two or more microprocessors can operate independently on separate data. Clearly, if more than one device is able to control the system bus, a set of rules (i.e., a protocol) is needed to determine which can access the bus at any instant and to ensure that every bus controller gets fair access to the bus. The action of determining which device gets access to the bus is called arbitration and is normally carried out by hardware, as software arbitration would be unacceptably slow.

Memory Management

If there is one thing that separates the world of the 16-bit microprocessor from that of the 8-bit microprocessor, it is memory management. Memory management is a generic term and is applied to all those techniques that translate the address of information generated by the computer (i.e., an address that may fall anywhere within its address space) into the address of that information within the available system memory. Most 8-bit and many 16-bit microcomputers do not use memory management techniques. The address generated by the CPU corresponds exactly to the actual location of information in the microprocessor's random access memory. One form of memory management is associated with the term *virtual memory*, and can be employed to make a small random access memory appear to the CPU as if it were much larger than it really is. This form of memory management is performed by holding part of the program or data in high-speed random access memory and the rest of it on disk. Whenever the CPU cannot find the data it requires in the high-speed memory, it moves more data from the disk to the high-speed memory.

Memory management is a rather complex topic and is best introduced by an analogy. Many newspapers have a page containing classified advertisements. The reader replies to an advertisement by writing to the address provided in the paper. This is the physical address of the advertiser. Sometimes the advertisements have box numbers instead of actual (physical) addresses. The reader writes to the newspaper quoting the box number, and the paper forwards the letter to the appropriate advertiser. The paper is performing the action of memory management. It is translating a box number, which we can call a logical address, into the physical address of an advertiser.

The advantage of the above arrangement is that the reader does not care where the advertiser actually lives. The advertiser may live in the street next to the newspaper offices or in another country. The advertiser may move from one office to another. All this is irrelevant to the reader, who simply writes to the box number, leaving it up to the newspaper to perform the address translation.

In computer terms, the address generated by a programmer when his or her program is executed on a microcomputer is called a logical address and corresponds to the box number in the above analogy. The address of information in memory is called its physical address and corresponds to the address of the advertiser. One of the purposes of memory management is to free programmers from all worries about where their programs and associated data are to lie in memory. As mentioned above, virtual memory techniques allow data to be moved between fast RAM and slower disk-based memory with the memory management unit keeping track of the data automatically. Another function is to monitor all memory accesses and to provide a user program with protection from modification by another program.

Memory Module

The memory module of a microcomputer contains the bulk of the random access memory accessible from the system buses. The term *bulk* is used because there may well be small quantities of memory on modules other than the memory module. The memory on the memory module may be read/write random access memory or read-only memory. Read/write memory can be read from or written to and is frequently called simply RAM in computer literature. Read-only memory (ROM) can be read from but not written to under normal conditions. Consequently, ROM is used to hold programs and data that change infrequently, if at all. Typically, ROMs hold interpreters for languages, such as BASIC or FORTRAN, operating systems, and bootstrap programs. A bootstrap program is the first program run when a computer is switched on and is used to start up a system. It is a minimal program designed to read the operating system from mass storage, transfer it to the system's random access memory, and then initiate the execution of the operating system.

When we come to chapter 5, dealing with memories, we will find that a range of memory components is available to the designer. The actual memory component chosen for any given application represents a trade-off between the desirable characteristics of the component and its cost.

The component selected for the memory module in figure 1.1 is called dynamic memory. Dynamic memory is the cheapest form of read/write random access memory available and is frequently chosen as the means of implementing large memories. Unfortunately, dynamic memory is somewhat more complex to use than other forms of read/write memory, and a dynamic memory module must be carefully designed. Chapter 7 deals with the design of memory systems using dynamic memory components.

Peripherals Module

The peripherals module contains the circuits that form an interface between the microcomputer and the rest of the world. For example, a serial input/output interface enables the microcomputer to communicate with any of the CRT terminals currently available. The serial port moves data from point to point one bit at a time.

A parallel port moves data between the microcomputer and an external device, such as a printer, one byte at a time. A parallel port often performs sundry other tasks, such as checking that the printer has accepted the data transmitted to it.

A timer is the general name for an integrated circuit that performs a variety of functions associated with the measurement of time. The actual facilities provided by individual timer chips vary from manufacturer to manufacturer. In general, the timer is able to generate single or repetitive sequences of pulses. It can measure the period or frequency of incoming pulses and is able to interrupt the microprocessor at fixed intervals. The latter operation permits the implementation of multitasking systems in which the computer switches from one job (task or program) to another each time it is interrupted.

The disk controller forms an interface between the microcomputer and a mass storage device, which may be a floppy disk drive or a hard disk drive. Most disk controllers are exceedingly sophisticated devices and often rival microprocessors themselves in complexity. The principal function of the disk controller is to translate the data from the microcomputer into a format suitable for storing on the disk, and vice versa.

The IEEE-bus controller forms an interface between the microcomputer and the popular IEEE-488 bus. Conceptually, the IEEE-488 bus behaves in a way very similar to the system bus. Hewlett-Packard originally devised it and intended it to link together programmable instruments in a laboratory or industrial environment. By controlling test equipment and measuring devices from the IEEE-488 bus, implementing an automatic testing station is possible. A system under test is connected to the test equipment and measuring devices. The computer configures (i.e., sets up) all the equipment via the IEEE-488 bus and then reads the test results from the same bus. Today, the IEEE-488 bus is also used to link peripherals, such as printers or disk drives, with microprocessor systems. The advantage of this bus is that it is now an international standard and is (theoretically) device and manufacturer independent.

The above peripherals represent some of the most popular functions obtainable in the form of a single chip. In a real system, the various peripheral interfaces are likely to be distributed between the modules of the microcomputer.

1.2 Examples of Microprocessor Systems

Before we begin to examine the design of actual microprocessor systems, looking at two generic applications is instructive and will give us an idea of some of the factors involved in microprocessor systems design.

Example 1. Morse Code Transmitter

All radio amateurs once transmitted Morse code by tapping out the dots and dashes on a Morse key (i.e., a simple on/off switch). It is now relatively easy to design a circuit with a conventional keyboard that generates a single Morse character each time a key is depressed.

Figure 1.3 gives the block diagram of a possible Morse code generator. This is a truly basic computer and has the absolute minimum number of components needed to execute its *single* function. The CPU is connected to three major components: a parallel I/O port that detects a keystroke and generates the Morse

FIGURE 1.3   Microprocessor-controlled Morse code generator

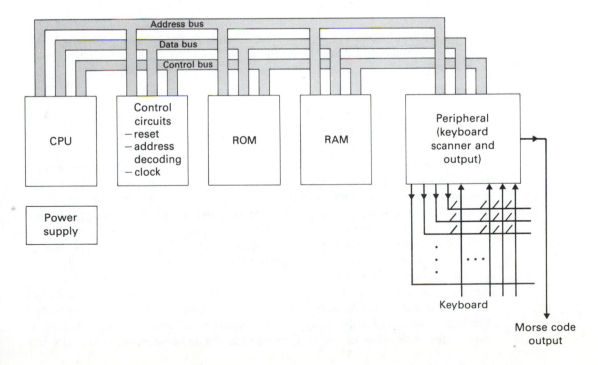

code output, a read/write memory that holds temporary variables, and a read-only memory that contains the program to generate the Morse code. In the vast majority of systems, a few gates and other components are needed to perform certain system functions and to "glue" the CPU to its memory and peripherals.

Figure 1.3 represents the simplest form of microcomputer. It is simple because it has a low component count and does not employ many of the powerful features found on some microprocessors. It is, of course, a single board computer and may be embedded within a radio transmitter. There are relatively few major design decisions in the production of the type of system of figure 1.3, as there are so few components to deal with. In general, the design decisions are often largely economic and depend of the scale of production of the system.

Example 2. Personal Computer

Figure 1.4 provides the block diagram of a possible general-purpose personal computer. In this type of computer there are more functional blocks than in the basic computer presented in figure 1.3 because the general-purpose personal microcomputer is fairly complex and has many different functions to perform. It must be able to input data from several sources (e.g., a keyboard or an external data-link), be able to store and retrieve data from some mass storage device, and be capable of outputting data to a CRT terminal or to its own TV display.

Most of the functions in figure 1.4 are as complex as the whole system of figure 1.3. The designer has to juggle with the conflicting requirements of each module and has to produce a compromise. Much of this book is concerned with the type of computer of figure 1.4 and with the decisions the designer must make.

Summary

This chapter has set the stage for our course in microprocessor systems design. We have introduced the microprocessor around which the microcomputer is to be built. Later chapters show how the microprocessor is connected (i.e., interfaced) to external memory and to input/output devices. Although a microcomputer can be built from a handful of components on a single board, it can also be a very complex arrangement of modules that communicate with each other by means of a bus. When the basic principles of microcomputer design have been presented, we will return to the design of buses for microcomputers.

One of the most important concepts introduced in chapter 1 is that of *modularity*. Modern systems are invariably designed as a number of largely independent modules that work together to achieve the desired effect. Only by decomposing the design of a complex microcomputer into the design of a collection of less complex subsystems can we create highly reliable and sophisticated products. The electrical highway, or bus, which is introduced in this chapter, is one of the main tools of the engineer producing modular subsystems. The bus

FIGURE 1.4   Block diagram of a personal computer

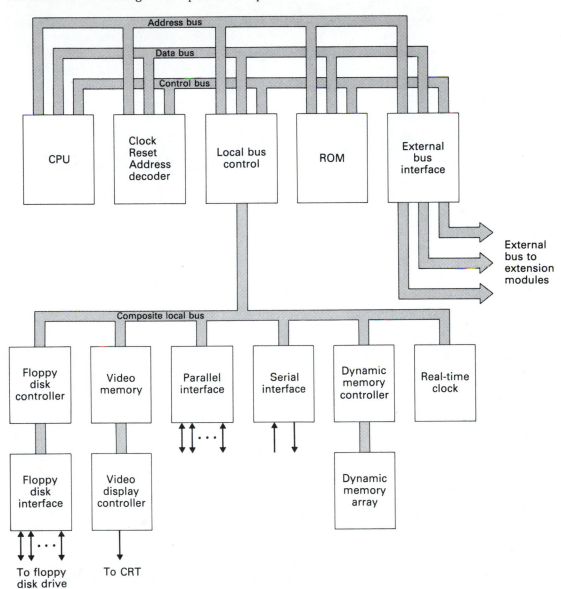

provides the means of linking modules together. Modularity is not limited to the realm of hardware. When we come to the design of software in chapter 3, we will see that this statement is as true for the design of software as it is for the design of hardware.

Chapter 2

Programming

the 68000 CPU

In this chapter we describe the architecture and programming model of the 68000 microprocessor. The instruction set and the addressing modes of the 68000 are treated at an elementary level to enable the student to understand the assembly language programs in later chapters. A prerequisite is a basic knowledge of computer architecture so that, for example, the concepts of a program counter, a Boolean operation, a conditional test, and a stack are familiar. We begin with a look at typical assembler directives. This is followed by an introduction to one of the 68000's most powerful features—its wealth of addressing modes. The final part of this chapter provides an overview of the 68000 instruction set.

2.1 Assembly Language Programming and the 68000

Assembly language is a form of the native language of a computer in which machine code instructions are represented by mnemonics and addresses and constants are written in symbolic form (just as they are in high level languages).

Before we can discuss the instruction set of the 68000, we must define some of the conventions adopted in writing assembly language programs. An assembly language is made up of two types of statement: the executable instruction and the assembler directive. An executable instruction is one of the processor's valid instructions and is translated into the appropriate machine code form by the assembler. Assembler directives tell the assembler something about the program. Basically, they link symbolic names to values, allocate storage, set up predefined constants, and control the assembly process. The assembler directives to be dealt with here are: TTL, EQU, DC, DS, ORG, SECTION, and END. Real assemblers have very many more directives, but most of these often control the format of the output and are not relevant here.

Because assembly language is concerned with the "native processor" itself, it is, therefore, strongly dependent on the architecture of the processor. This situation contrasts strongly with high level languages that are, theoretically, independent of the system on which they run.

First of all, it is necessary to define the size (in bits) of the units of data manipulated by the 68000. The 68000 permits 8-, 16-, and 32-bit operations. A 32-bit entity is called a longword, a 16-bit entity a word, and an 8-bit entity a byte. To avoid confusion, longword, word, and byte will always refer to 32-, 16-, and 8-bit values, respectively, throughout this book.

To provide the reader with an idea of what one looks like, an example of an assembly language program follows.

```
                TTL        Program to input text into a buffer
BACK_SPACE      EQU        $08                    ASCII code for back space
DELETE          EQU        $7F                    ASCII code for delete
CARRIAGE_RET    EQU        $0D                    ASCII code for carriage return
*
                ORG        $004000                Data origin
LINE_BUFFER     DS.B       64                     Reserve 64 bytes for line buffer
*
*    This procedure inputs a character and stores it in a buffer
*
                ORG        $001000                Program origin
                LEA. L     LINE_BUFFER, A2        A2 points to line buffer
NEXT            BSR        GET_DATA               Call subroutine to get input
                CMP.B      #BACK_SPACE, D0        Test for back space
                BEQ        MOVE_LEFT              If back space then deal with it
                CMP.B      #DELETE, D0            Test for delete
                BEQ        CANCEL                 If delete then deal with it
                CMP.B      #CARRIAGE_RET, D0      Test for carriage return
                BEQ        EXIT                   If carriage return then exit
                MOVE.B     D0, (A2)+              Else store input in memory
                BRA        NEXT                   Repeat
                 .                                Remainder of program
                 .
                 .
                 .
                 .
                 .
                 .
                 .
                 .
                 .
                 .
                 .
                END
```

Do not worry about understanding the preceding program. It is intended only to show what an assembly program looks like. A word beginning in the leftmost column is a label and is used by the assembler as a symbolic reference to that line. Commands and assembly language directives consist of a word followed by an optional parameter followed by an optional comment field. These may begin anywhere except in column 1. A line beginning with an asterisk is a comment and is entirely ignored by the assembler. The following assembler directives are of greatest interest to us here. Note that any instruction or assembly directive may be followed by a comment field.

Assembler Directives

TTL   TTL means "title" and gives the program a user-defined name that it puts at the top of each page of the listing when the program is printed.

EQU   The equate directive simply links a name to a value, making programs much easier to read. For example, it is better to equate the name CARRIAGE_RETURN to $0D and use this name in a program than to write $0D and leave it to the reader to figure out that $0D is the ASCII value for carriage return. Consider the following example of its use:

```
STK_FRAME   EQU 128                     Define a stack frame of 128 bytes
          ⋮
            LINK A1, − #STK_FRAME   Reserve 128 bytes for local storage
```

Not only is STK_FRAME more meaningful to the programmer than its numerical value of 128, but it is easy to modify the numeric value by changing the EQU 128 that appears at the head of the program.

DC   This directive means "define a constant" and is qualified by .B, .W, or .L, depending on the length (8, 16, or 32 bits) of the constant to be defined. The constant defined by this directive is loaded in memory at the "current" location. The following examples show how DC is applied:

```
ORG   $001000         Start of data region
DC.B  10, 66          The values 10 and 66 are stored in consecutive bytes
DC.L  $0A1234         The value $000A1234 is stored as one longword
DC.B  'April 8 1985'  The ASCII characters are stored as 12 bytes
DC.L  1, 2            Two longwords are set up with the values 1 and 2
```

The effect of the above directives can be illustrated by a memory map:

ADDRESS	MEMORY CONTENTS		
001000	0A	42	DC. B 10, 66
001002	00	0A	DC. L $0A1234
001004	12	34	
001006	41	70	DC. B 'April 8 1985'
001008	72	69	
00100A	6C	20	
00100C	38	20	
00100E	31	39	
001010	38	35	
001012	00	00	DC. L 1, 2
001014	00	01	
001016	00	00	
001018	00	02	

Note that successive *words* have even addresses that are called "word boundaries."

Constants are automatically aligned on a word boundary if they are either a word or a longword (. W or . L). The operand field of a define constant directive may be a decimal value, a hexadecimal value (prefixed by $), or an ASCII string enclosed by single quotes. Alternatively, the operand may be an expression that is evaluated by the assembler. For example, the assembler directive DC.L 3∗BASE+OFFSET would cause 3∗BASE+OFFSET to be calculated and that value to be stored as a longword in memory.

DS   The define storage directive, DS, reserves storage locations. Its effect is similar to that of DC, but no information is stored in memory—that is, DC is used to set up constants that are to be loaded into memory before the program is executed, whereas DS reserves memory space for variables that will be generated by the program at run-time. DS is also qualified by . B, . W, or . L and its operand defines the size of the storage area. Consider the following examples:

	DS.B	4	Reserve 4 bytes of memory
	DS.B	$80	Reserve 128 bytes of memory
	DS.L	16	Reserve 16 longwords (64 bytes)
VOLTS	DS.W	1	Reserve 1 word (2 bytes)
TABLE	DS.W	256	Reserve 256 words

A label in the left-hand column equates the label with the first address of the defined storage. The label references the lowest address of the defined storage value. In the above example, TABLE refers to the location of the first of the 256 words reserved (or allocated) by the DS directive.

ORG   The "origin" assembler directive defines the value of the location counter that keeps track of where the next item is to be located in the target processor's memory. The operand following ORG is the absolute value of the origin. An ORG directive can be located at any point, as the following example illustrates:

```
            ORG     $001000         Origin for data
TABLE       DS.W    256             Save 256 words for "TABLE"
POINTER_1   DS.W    1               Save one word for "POINTER_1"
POINTER_2   DS.W    1               Save one word for "POINTER_2"
VECTOR_1    DS.L    1               Save one longword for "VECTOR_1"
INIT        DC.W    0, $FFFF        Store two constants ($0000, $FFFF)
SETUP1      EQU     $03             Equate "SETUP1" to the value 3
SETUP2      EQU     $55             Equate "SETUP2" to the value $55
ACIAC       EQU     $008000         Equate "ACIAC" to the value $8000
RDRF        EQU     0               RDRF = Receiver Data Register Full = 0
PIA         EQU     ACIAC+4         Equate "PIA" to the value $8004
*
            ORG     $018000         Origin for program
ENTRY       LEA.L   ACIAC, A0       A0 points to the ACIA
            MOVE.B  #SETUP, (A0)    Write initialization constant into ACIA
*
GET_DATA    BTST.B  #RDRF, (A0)     Any data received?
            BNE     GET_DATA        Repeat until data ready
            MOVE.B  2(A0), D0       Read data from ACIA
*
```

The first occurrence of ORG (i.e., ORG $001000) defines the point at which the following instructions and directives are to be loaded. The four lines after ORG define four named storage allocations of 260 words in all. Following these, two words, $0000 and $FFFF, are loaded into memory. The address of the next free location is $00120C. The three EQUs define constants for use in the rest of the program. Thus, whenever the name SETUP1 is used, the assembler replaces it by its defined value, 3. Note that it is possible to write an expression at any point in the assembler where a numeric value must be provided. For example, PIA EQU ACIA+4 causes the word PIA to be equated to the value ACIA+4 (=$008000 + 4 = $008004).

The second ORG (i.e., ORG $018000) defines the origin from which the following instructions are loaded. It is not necessary to allocate separate regions of memory for data and instructions in this way: the first instruction would have been located at $00120C had the second ORG not been used.

SECTION   This directive sets the program counter to zero as if it were equal to ORG $000000. The purpose of SECTION is to force the assembler to generate program counter relative addressing modes in order to make the resulting code position independent. The meaning of these terms is made clear later in the text. Note that this definition of SECTION is a simplified version of that found in 68000 assemblers.

END   The "end" directive simply tells the assembler that the end of a program has been reached and that there are no further instructions or directives to be assembled.

2.2 Programmer's Model of the 68000

The first step in examining a microprocessor is to look at its on-chip (i.e., internal) storage. Programmer-accessible registers fall into three groups (data, address, and special-purpose registers) and are dealt with in turn. Figure 2.1 shows the arrangement of the 68000's internal storage. This diagram is slightly simplified as there are really two A7s (we will discuss this concept more fully later).

Because the 68000 has address and data registers and address and data pins, there is some danger of confusing registers and pins when writing about them. To avoid this confusion, data and address registers are always denoted by a letter and a single digit (i.e., D0 to D7 and A0 to A7) and data and address bits are always denoted by a letter and two digits (i.e., D_{00} to D_{31} and A_{00} to A_{31}).

Data Registers

From an information storage point of view, the 68000 is internally organized like a 32-bit machine; its registers are, therefore, 32 bits wide. The 68000 has eight general-purpose data registers, D0 to D7, and most operations involving the manipulation of data act on the contents of these registers.

The eight data registers are entirely general in the sense that any operation permitted on Di is also permitted on Dj. Some microprocessors restrict certain operations to specific registers. This restriction is undesirable because it forces the programmer to remember "what can be done to what."

As computers with 16- or 32-bit data wordlengths are less than ideal for the manipulation of text with its byte-oriented characters, microprocessor manufacturers have attempted to improve the efficiency of a 32-bit machine by allowing 8-bit operations to take place on part of the contents of 16- or 32-bit registers. In figure 2.1, the data registers are split into two words by a line of long broken dots and the lower-order words are in turn divided into two bytes by a line of short dots.

Operations on longwords, words, and bytes are denoted by the addition of . L, . W, and . B, respectively, to mnemonics. For example, the operation ADD.L D0,D1 adds the 32-bit contents of data register D0 to the 32-bit contents of D1 and puts the 32-bit result in D1. The operation ADD.B D0,D1 adds the

FIGURE 2.1   Programming model of the 68000

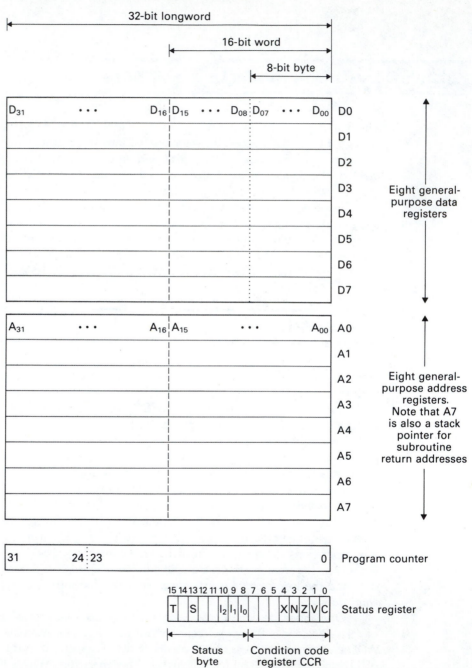

least-significant 8 bits of D0 to the corresponding 8 bits of D1 and puts the result in D1. Note that when a subsection of a data register is operated on, the remainder of the register is unaffected. For example, ADD.B D0,D1 does not affect bits 8 through 31 of register D0 or D1. It should be appreciated that, when a subsection of a data register takes part in an operation, the subsection is always the lowest-order unit of the register—that is, bits 0 through 7 or bits 0 through 15.

Address Registers

The 68000 has eight address registers, designated A0 to A7 in figure 2.1. These registers should be regarded as pointer registers, because they hold addresses specifying the location of data in memory. All address registers are 32 bits wide, and operations performed on their contents affect the whole longword. Byte operations on bits 0 through 7 of an address register are not permitted.

The contents of an address register represent a single entity and the idea of separate address fields has no meaning. Therefore, an operation on the low-order word of an address register always affects the entire contents of that register—that is, if the low-order word of an address register is loaded with a 16-bit operand, the sign bit of the operand is extended into bits 16 through 31 of the high-order word. This happens because the contents of address registers behave like signed two's complement values. For example, if the low-order word of an address register is loaded with %1010 0000 0000 0111 ($A007), the address is sign extended to give the longword %1111 1111 1111 1111 1010 0000 0000 0111 ($FFFFA007). Programmers must be aware of this fact.

Do not be alarmed by the idea of negative (i.e., two's complement) addresses! Suppose A1 contains the value $FFFFFFFA (representing -6) and A2 contains the value $000010000. If we add A1 to A2 we get $FFFFFFFA + $00001000 = $00000FFA (in 32-bit arithmetic), which is six locations *back* from the address pointed at by A2. In other words, a negative address means "backward from the current location."

As in the case of the data registers, an operation on Ai can also be applied to Aj. However, A7 is a special-purpose address register and has an additional role to those of A0 to A6. It acts as the stack pointer used by subroutines to store return addresses in memory. Figure 2.1 is a simplified diagram. One of the simplifications introduced is existence of two A7 registers, each of which is associated with a particular mode of operation of the 68000. For the time being, only one A7 is assumed, as the operating modes of the 68000 are entirely irrelevant to the current discussion. It is sufficient to state that one mode is called the user mode and the other is called the supervisor mode. In general, the supervisor mode is devoted to the operating system; and the user mode, to programs running under the operating system. In all descriptions of the 68000 and its programs, it is perfectly legal to write either A7 or SP. When we need to be explicit, the supervisor stack pointer is written SSP and the user stack pointer is written USP.

The designers of the 68000 have, in effect, said, "Let there be address registers and data registers." Such a view has committed them to a philosophy that treats addresses and data separately. Some microprocessors have registers whose contents may contain data or the address of data. Such microprocessors allow all arithmetic and logical operations to take place on addresses and data values alike.

However, addresses and data are used in entirely different ways and, therefore, should not be treated in the same way. Consequently, designers have created two sets of registers, each with its own rules. One rule is that a word or byte operation on a data register does not in any way affect the bits of the register not taking part in the operation. The same rule does not, of course, apply to the contents of an address register.

When the 68000 was first introduced, there was some debate about whether it was a 16-bit or a 32-bit computer. As stated earlier, the 68000 has 32-bit internal registers and can carry out 32-bit operations on data or addresses. It is, however, interfaced to external systems by a 16-bit address bus, thereby forcing all 32-bit accesses to be implemented as two consecutive 16-bit accesses. Moreover, the external address bus of the 68000 is only 24 bits wide and address bits A_{24} through A_{31} have no effect on the address leaving the chip. Consequently, addresses (and the contents of address registers) are frequently written as six hexadecimal characters (i.e., 24 bits), as the 8 most-significant bits of an address have no meaning as far as the system connected to a 68000 is concerned.

It should be appreciated that, although the 68000 is a word-oriented (16-bit) device with certain 32-bit facilities, its memory is byte addressable—that is, it can address both 16-bit and 8-bit quantities with equal ease. A byte address may be odd or even. In byte addressing, the byte represented by bits D_{00} to D_{07} is the odd byte at the odd address, and the byte represented by bits D_{08} to D_{15} is the even byte at the even address. When the 68000 programmer refers to a longword, its address is defined as the address of the high-order 16 bits of the longword. The next even address holds the low-order 16 bits of the longword. Figure 2.2 illustrates the way in which the 68000's memory is arranged.

Special-Purpose Registers

The 68000 has two special-purpose registers: the program counter (PC) and the status register (SR). The program counter is 32 bits wide and contains the address of the next instruction to be executed. (This description is a simplification of the true state of affairs. The 68000 is a processor that is able to "look ahead" and to fetch instructions before they are needed. Therefore, the 68000 program counter does not always point to the *next* instruction to be executed.) It is a conventional PC with only one quirk. In order to fit the 68000 into a 64-pin package, the external address bus is restricted to 24 bits, which gives an addressing range of 8M words. Bits 24 through 31 of the program counter are not directly accessible in the 68000. The 68020 has a full 32-bit address bus.

FIGURE 2.2   Manner in which the 68000 stores bytes, words, and longwords in its memory space

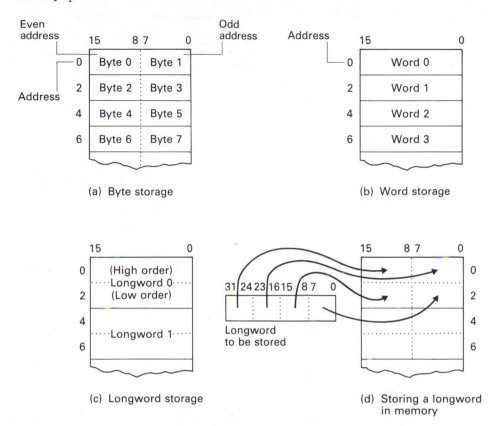

(a) Byte storage

(b) Word storage

(c) Longword storage

(d) Storing a longword in memory

The 16-bit status register (SR) is divided into two logical fields. The 8 most-significant bits are called the "system byte" and control the operating mode of the 68000. The importance of the system byte is dealt with in later chapters. All that need be done here is to introduce its five bits: T (the trace mode bit), S (the user/supervisor mode bit), and I_0, I_1, and I_2 (the interrupt mask bits). The system byte cannot be modified by the programmer when the 68000 is running in the user mode.

The least-significant 8 bits of the SR constitute the condition code register (CCR), and indicate certain things about the nature of each arithmetic and logical operation executed by the 68000. The position of the bits of the CCR is defined in figure 2.3.

The carry bit is conventional, as are the V, Z, and N bits, and represents the carry-out of the most-significant bit of an operand during an arithmetic or logical operation. I have used the word *operand* rather than *word* because the 68000 allows longword, word, and byte operations; therefore, the carry bit represents

FIGURE 2.3   *68000 status word*

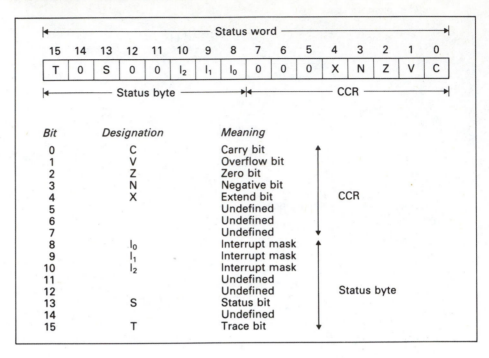

the carry-out from bits 31, 15, or 7, respectively. The example below should clarify the picture.

ADD. B D0,D1

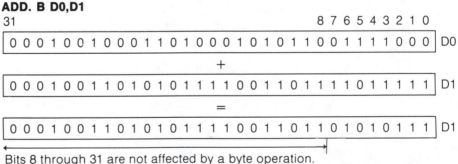

Bits 8 through 31 are not affected by a byte operation.

Carry-out from bit 7 is transferred to the carry bit of CCR.

An add operation such as ADD.B D0,D1 affects only the 8 low-order bits of D1. The carry resulting from the addition is copied into the carry flag, and bits 8 through 31 of D1 remain unchanged. If [D0] = $12345678 and [D1] = $13579BDF, the action of ADD.B D0,D1 results in [D1] = $13579B57 and the carry flag is set to 1. Had we performed a word operation with

ADD.W D0,D1, the carry bit would have been set to the carry-out resulting from bit 15.

Under certain circumstances the X bit, or extend bit, is identical to the carry bit. During an addition, subtraction, negation, or shifting operation, the X bit is made to reflect the state of the carry bit, C. The X bit is included in the condition code byte because it is a "pure extension bit" and is used only when a byte, word, or longword is extended beyond 8, 16, or 32 bits, respectively.

The X bit has been provided because the carry bit is often employed by programmers as a multipurpose test flag. For example, the carry bit is occasionally used to transfer information between subroutines. If C is set following a return from a subroutine, it may indicate that an error occurred in the subroutine. Sometimes the conflict between the use of the C bit as a carry bit acting as the extension bit of the operand during an arithmetic operation and its use as a general-purpose semaphore is inconvenient. For this reason, the X bit is provided exclusively for use in arithmetic operations that generate a true carry-out. Instructions such as CMP, MOVE, AND, OR, CLR, TST, MUL, and DIV affect the state of the carry bit but have no effect on the state of the X bit.

The overflow flag, V, is set if the result of an arithmetic operation, when interpreted as a two's complement value, yields an incorrect sign bit. The zero flag, Z, is set if a result (longword, word, or byte) is zero. The negative flag is a copy of the most-significant bit of a result (longword, word, or byte).

2.3 Addressing Modes of the 68000

In this section, we look at the ways in which the 68000 specifies the address of operands. Most microprocessor instructions have two or three fields. These include the nature of the instruction, the address of the source operand, and the address of the destination operand. The address of an operand can be specified in a number of different ways, collectively called *addressing modes*. The type of sophisticated addressing modes associated with the 68000 provide programmers with a tool for accessing data structures such as tables, arrays, and vectors.

Notation to Define Addressing Modes

Before continuing, we need to develop an unambiguous notation to help us describe information manipulation within the 68000. Such a notation is called *register transfer language* (RTL). Registers are denoted by their name. Square brackets mean "the contents of," so that [D0] means the contents of data register D0. We can therefore write [D4] = 50 to mean that the contents of register D4 is equal to 50.

The base of a number is denoted by a prefix. No prefix indicates decimal, a percent sign (%), binary, and a dollar sign ($), hexadecimal. A 32-bit number is represented by eight hexadecimal characters and a data register holds unsigned integer values in the range $0000 0000 to $FFFF FFFF. For purposes of style, I have left a space between the four least-significant hexadecimal digits of a number and the remaining most-significant digits—except in assembly language programs where numbers must not contain embedded spaces. As stated earlier, addresses are frequently represented by six hexadecimal characters, because A_{24} to A_{31} have no meaning in the system connected to the 68000.

The backwards arrow (←) indicates a transfer of information. Let us consider some examples.

[D4] ← 50	Put 50 into register D4
[D4] ← $1234	Put $1234 into register D4
[D3] ← $FE 1234	Put $FE 1234 into register D3

The following symbols are used in the definition of addressing modes.

SYMBOL	MEANING
M	Location M in the random access memory
[M]	The contents of memory location M
ea	Effective address represents the address of an operand generated by the computer
[M[ea]]	The contents of a memory location specified by ea
Ri(0: 15)	Bits 0 to 15 inclusive of register Ri
Ai	Address register i (i = 0 to 7)
Di	Data register i (i = 0 to 7)
Xi	General register i. Xi may be an address or a data register
⟨ ⟩	The "⟨ ⟩" brackets enclose a parameter required by an expression
d8	An 8-bit signed offset (constant in the range −128 to 127)
d16	A 16-bit signed offset (constant in the range −32K to 32K)

In order to illustrate the action of addressing modes, we introduce two instructions: ADD and MOVE. The ADD operation is defined as

ADD: [destination] ← [source] + [destination]

The contents of "source" are added to the contents of "destination" and the result of their addition becomes the new contents of "destination." Destination and source are both effective addresses. Addressing modes are concerned with the way in which the source and destination of the operands are determined. The assembly language form of ADD is ADD ⟨s⟩, ⟨d⟩.

The second instruction is MOVE, which is the most general instruction found on the 68000 and replaces a whole host of instructions, such as LDA (load accumulator), STA (store accumulator), and PHA (push accumulator) that are associated with many other microprocessors. The MOVE operation is defined as

MOVE: [destination] ← [source]

The contents of "source" are copied into the contents of "destination."

Immediate Addressing

In the immediate (or literal) addressing mode, the actual operand follows the instruction and allows constants to be set up at the time the program is written. For example, the instruction ADD.L #9, D0 adds the number 9 to the contents of data register D0. The "9" is an immediate operand because it forms part of the instruction and the CPU does not have to carry out a further memory access to obtain it. Once a constant is defined in the literal mode, it cannot be changed when the program is running. (The constant can be changed if the technique of using self-modifying code is adopted, but wise programmers should never resort to this practice.)

The hash symbol (#) precedes the operand and indicates to the assembler that the following value is to be used with the immediate addressing mode. The 68000 permits byte, word, and longword immediate operands. The following examples illustrate addressing modes in terms of their assembly language form and define them in RTL.

ASSEMBLY LANGUAGE FORM	RTL FORM	ACTION
MOVE.W #$8123, D3	$[D3(0:15)] \leftarrow \$8123$	The hexadecimal value $8123 is transferred into the lower-order word of register D3.
MOVE.L #$8123, D3	$[D3(0:31)] \leftarrow \$8123$	The hexadecimal value $0000 8123 is transferred into D3.

A typical application of immediate addressing is in setting up control loops. The following example uses immediate addressing several times to preset all the elements of an array of 128 bytes to $FF.

```
        MOVEA.L   #$001000,A0   Load A0 with the address of the array
        MOVE.B    #128,D0       D0 is the element counter (preset to 128)
LOOP    MOVE.B    #$FF,(A0)+    Store $FF in this element and increment pointer
        SUBQ.B    #1,D0         Decrement element counter
        BNE       LOOP          Repeat until all the elements are set
```

Absolute Addressing

Absolute addressing means that the instruction contains the operand's address and is sometimes called *direct addressing*. Absolute addressing is so called because the actual (i.e., absolute) address of an operand is specified at the time the program is written; this address is constant and is not modified in any way by the processor.

The 68000 provides two variants of absolute addressing: absolute short addressing and absolute long addressing. In absolute short addressing, the address of the operand is a 16-bit word following the instruction. This word is sign extended to 32 bits before it is used to access the operand. Consequently, absolute short addresses in the range $0000 to $7FFF are sign extended to $0000 0000 through $0000 7FFF, while absolute short addresses in the range $8000 through $FFFF are sign extended through $FFFF 8000 to $FFFF FFFF; that is, the programmer can use absolute short addressing to access only the top and the bottom 32K bytes of memory space.

Absolute long addressing requires two 16-bit words following an instruction to generate a 32-bit absolute address. This procedure allows the whole of memory to be accessed. The programmer does not have to worry about long and short forms of addressing modes, as the assembler automatically selects the appropriate version. Some examples of absolute addressing are now provided.

ASSEMBLY LANGUAGE FORM	RTL FORM	ACTION
MOVE.L D3, $1234	[M[$1234]] ← [D3(16:31)] [M[$1236]] ← [D3(0:15)]	The contents of register D3 are copied into memory location $1234. Because the 68000's memory is byte organized, locations $1234 to $1237 are required.
MOVE.W $1234, D3	[D3(0:15)] ← [M[$1234]]	The contents of memory location $1234 are moved into the lower-order word of D3.
PTM EQU $FFFFC120 MOVE.L PTM, D2	[D2] ← [M[$FFFFC120]]	The contents of memory location $FFFF C120 are moved into register D2. Note that the address $FFFF C120 is stored as $C120 and is automatically sign extended to 32 bits ($FFFF C120).

Absolute addressing is employed when the address of an operand is known at the time of writing the program. Such an event happens under two circumstances. The first corresponds to memory-mapped input/output, where a given memory address is used as an input or output port address. The second is in programs that will never be relocated; that is, the program and its associated data always occupy the same addresses in memory, irrespective of the machine on which the program is run or of the operating system or whether the system uses memory management. Whenever possible, 68000 programmers should avoid absolute addressing in order to produce position-independent code (PIC). Position-independent code avoids the use of absolute addressing and can be placed anywhere in memory *without* recomputing the address of operands.

Register Direct Addressing

The register direct addressing mode specifies operands (source or destination) that are the contents of the 68000's internal registers. Register direct addressing does not involve a memory access. The effective address of an operand is given by the name of the register (address or data) specified in the instruction. For example, the instruction MOVE. L D0, D3 copies the entire contents of data register D0 into register D3.

Consider the following examples of register direct addressing.

```
MOVE.L  D0, D3   =  [D3] ← [D0]
MOVE.W  D0, D3   =  [D3(0: 15)] ← [D0(0: 15)]
MOVE.B  D0, D3   =  [D3(0: 7)] ← [D0(0: 7)]
MOVE.L  A1, D0   =  [D0] ← [A1]
ADD.L   D1, D2   =  [D2] ← [D2] + [D1]
ADD.L   #12, D2  =  [D2] ← [D2] + 12
```

Note that the general MOVE instruction does not allow the transfer of the contents of a data register into an address register. Thus, while MOVE. L A1, D0 is legal, the inverse operation MOVE. L D1, A0 is not. This philosophy of segregating addresses and data makes it difficult for the programmer to carelessly corrupt an address. We shall soon see that a special instruction, MOVEA, is available for the transfer of information to address registers.

Information within the computer is stored in either memory locations or in registers inside the CPU. Theoretically, it does not matter where data is held, as long as it is manipulated according to the appropriate algorithm. In practice, the storage of data in on-chip registers is preferred because registers can be accessed faster than memory locations.

Address Register Indirect Addressing

Register indirect addressing means that the address of an operand is in a register. This register is called a "pointer register" and is one of the 68000's eight address registers. In RTL terms, the effective address of an operand is specified by: ea = [Ai]. The following examples illustrate the effect of address register indirect addressing. Address register indirect addressing is specified in assembly language form by enclosing the address register in parentheses.

ASSEMBLY LANGUAGE FORM	RTL DEFINITION	ACTION
MOVE.L (A0), D3	$[D3] \leftarrow [M[A0]]$	The contents of the memory location whose address is in A0 are copied into register D3.
MOVE.W D4, (A6)	$[M[A6]] \leftarrow [D4(0:15)]$	The lower-order word of D4 is copied into the memory location whose address is in A6.

As we have already noted, the contents of the address registers cannot themselves be modified by a MOVE operation, because MOVE is explicitly forbidden from acting on the contents of an address register. The instruction MOVEA is provided to move information into an address register. MOVEA ⟨ea⟩, Ai is defined as

$$\text{MOVEA:} \quad [Ai] \leftarrow [\text{source}]$$

For example, MOVEA.L D4,A3 copies the 32-bit contents of D4 into address register A3. Note that MOVEA.W D4,A3 copies the low-order word of D4 into the low-order word of A3 and then copies the sign bit (i.e., bit 15) into bits 16 through 31 of A3. This instruction is almost the same as MOVE, except that the destination address of the operand must be an address register. There are two other differences between MOVE and MOVEA. The more general operation, MOVE, updates the contents of the condition code register. As MOVEA is used only to generate an address, the contents of the CCR are not affected by MOVEA. Another difference is that MOVE permits a byte operation, while MOVEA is defined only for longwords and words (i.e., MOVEA.L, MOVEA.W).

As stated earlier, the two instructions, MOVE and MOVEA, are provided to force the programmer to appreciate the distinction between addresses and data.

However, some assembler writers have circumvented this by allowing the programmer to write MOVE for both MOVE and MOVEA. The assembler itself
automatically chooses the appropriate operation code. The philosophy of segregating addresses and data arouses the same passions in some people as seat-belt
legislation did in others. Some programmers have told me that they resent being
forced to write programs in a "certain" way.

Register indirect addressing provides an efficient method of accessing data
because the address of the operand does not have to be read from memory by the
instruction that accesses the operand. The address is, of course, already in the
CPU in an address register. Consider the following example.

```
                MOVEA.L   #ACIA,A0      Load A0 with the address of
*                                       the ACIA (ACIA is an I/O device)
READ_STATUS     MOVE.B    (A0),D0       Place the contents of the
*                                       location pointed at by A0 in D0
                BTST      #0, D0        Test bit 0 of D0 for data ready
                BEQ       READ_STATUS   Repeat until ACIA ready
                MOVE.B    2(A0),D0      Read the input
```

Note that this addressing mode is efficient only if instruction MOVE.B (A0),D0
is executed several times. MOVE.B ACIA,D0 could have been written, but
such an instruction would require a memory access to read the address of ACIA
every time the instruction is executed. Furthermore, this addressing mode provides a method of generating addresses dynamically during the execution of a
program. For example, if MOVEA.L #ACIA,A0 loads the address register A0
with the address of ACIA, then ADDA.L #16,A0 sets up an address in A0 16
byte locations onward.

Address Register Indirect with Postincrement Addressing

Register indirect with postincrement addressing is a variation of address register
indirect addressing and is also called address register indirect with autoincrementing addressing. The basic operation is the same as address register indirect, except
that the contents of the address register from which the operand address is
derived are incremented by 1, 2, or 4 after the instruction has been executed. A
byte operand causes an increment by 1, a word operand by 2, and a longword by
4. An exception to this rule occurs when the stack pointer, A7, is used with byte
addressing. The contents of A7 are then automatically incremented by 2 rather
than by 1. In this way, the stack pointer always points to an address on a word
boundary. Some examples should make this clear.

ASSEMBLY LANGUAGE FORM	RTL DEFINITION	ACTION
MOVE.L (A0)+,D3	[D3] ← [M[A0]] [A0] ← [A0] + 4	The contents of the memory location whose address is in A0 are copied into register D3. The contents of A0 are then increased by 4.
MOVE.W (A7)+,D4	[D4(0: 15)] ← [M[A7]] [A7] ← [A7] + 2	The 16-bit contents of the memory location whose address is in A7 are copied into the lower-order 16 bits of D4. The contents of A7 are then increased by 2.
MOVE.B (A7)+,D4	[D4(0: 7)] ← [M[A7]] [A7] ← [A7] + 2	The 8-bit contents of the memory location whose address is in A7 are copied into the lower-order 8 bits of D4. The contents of A7 are then increased by 2, rather than by 1, because A7 is the stack pointer.

One application of this addressing mode is accessing a data structure where the individual elements are stored consecutively. For example, consider the following fragment of a program designed to fill a sixteen-element array of longwords (called BUFFER) with zeros.

```
        MOVE.B   #16,D0        Set up a counter for sixteen elements
        MOVEA.L  #BUFFER,A0    A0 points to the first element of the array
LOOP    CLR.L    (A0)+         Clear element and move pointer to next element
        SUBQ.B   #1,D0         Decrement the element counter
        BNE      LOOP          Repeat until the count is zero
```

Address Register Indirect with Predecrement Addressing

This variant of address register indirect addressing is similar to the preceding one except that the specified address register is decremented *before* the instruction is carried out. The decrement is also by 4, 2, or 1, depending on whether the operand is a longword, a word, or a byte, respectively. The two following examples demonstrate how this address mode differs from address register indirect addressing with postincrement.

ASSEMBLY LANGUAGE FORM	RTL DEFINITION	ACTION
MOVE.L −(A0),D3	[A0] ← [A0] − 4 [D3] ← [M[A0]]	The contents of address register A0 are first decremented by 4. The contents of the memory location pointed at by A0 are then moved into register D3.
MOVE.W −(A7),D4	[A7] ← [A7] − 2 [D4(0 : 15)] ← [M[A7]]	The contents of address register A7 are first decremented by 2. The contents of the memory location pointed at by A7 are moved into register D4.

By means of its autoincrementing and autodecrementing modes, the 68000 is endowed with eight stack pointers—A0 through A7. If the stack is considered to grow toward lower addresses, the PUSH operation is implemented by predecrementing and storing and the PULL operation by reading and postincrementing.

The operations necessary to push the entire contents of D0 and the lower-order word of D1 onto the stack pointed at by A4 are

```
MOVE.L   D0,−(A4)
MOVE.W   D1,−(A4)
```

If the contents of the 16-bit word on the top of this stack are to be pulled and stored in D6, the following operation may be used:

```
MOVE.W  (A4)+,D6.
```

Autoincrementing and autodecrementing addressing modes are widely used to deal with data in tabular form (lists or arrays). For example, if sixteen words of data are stored consecutively in memory with their starting address in address register A0, they can be added together by executing the instruction ADD.W (A0)+,D0 sixteen times.

Let us suppose that there are two tables, each *N* bytes long. The following program compares the contents of the tables, element by element, to determine whether they are identical. The "work" is done by a CMPM (A0)+,(A1)+ instruction that compares the contents of the location pointed at by A0 with the contents of the location pointed at by A1 and then increments both pointers. CMPM stands for "compare memory with memory."

```
TABLE_1          EQU      $002000           Location of Table 1
TABLE_2          EQU      $003000           Location of Table 2
N                EQU      $30               Forty-eight elements in each table
                          .
                          .
                          .
                 MOVEA.L  #TABLE_1,A0       A0 points to the top of Table 1
                 MOVEA.L  #TABLE_2,A1       A1 points to the top of Table 2
                 MOVE.B   #N, D0            D0 is the element counter
NEXT_ELEMENT     CMPM.B   (A0)+,(A1)+       Compare a pair of elements
                 BNE      FAIL              If not the same then exit to FAIL
                 SUBQ.B   #1, D0            Else decrement element counter
                 BNE      NEXT_ELEMENT      Repeat until all done
SUCCESS          .                          Deal with success (all matched)
                 .
FAIL             .                          Deal with fail (not all matched)
```

Register Indirect with Displacement Addressing

In the register indirect addressing with displacement mode, the effective address of an operand is calculated by adding the contents of an address register to the sign-extended 16-bit displacement word forming part of the instruction. Remember that "sign-extended" means that the 16-bit two's complement displacement is internally transformed into a 32-bit two's complement number, so that it can be added to the 32-bit contents of an address register. The assembly language form of this addressing mode is d16(An). In RTL form, the effective address of an operand is given by ea = d16 + [Ai]. Two examples should make this clear.

ASSEMBLY LANGUAGE FORM	RTL DEFINITION	ACTION
MOVE.L 12(A4),D3	$[D3] \leftarrow [M[0012 + [A4]]]$	The contents of the memory location whose address is given by the contents of register A4 plus 12 are moved into register D3.
MOVE.W −$04(A1),D0	$[D0] \leftarrow [M[−$04 + [A1]]$	The contents of the memory location whose address is given by the contents of register A1 minus 4 are moved to register D0. The offset, −4, is stored as the value $FFFC.

This addressing mode is roughly equivalent to indexed addressing in 8-bit microprocessors. However, its range is limited because the displacement is only 16 bits, rather than the 32 bits required to provide a comprehensive indexed addressing mode; that is, the offset can specify a location $+32,767$ bytes ahead or $-32,768$ bytes back from the contents of an address register.

Register indirect addressing with displacement is a useful tool for writing position-independent code. An address register is loaded with the starting position of the data in memory. All data accesses are then made with the effective operand address "offset,(Ai)," where Ai points to the data area and "offset" indicates the location of the operand with respect to the start of the table. The monitor in chapter 11 makes extensive use of register indirect addressing to achieve position independence.

Register Indirect with Index Addressing

Register indirect with index addressing takes the register indirect addressing mode one step further. To form the effective address of an operand the contents of the specified address register are added to the contents of a general register, together with an 8-bit signed displacement. The general register may be an address register or a data register and is termed an index register. The assembly language form of this addressing mode is d8(An,Xn.W) or d8(An,Xn.L). In RTL form, the effective address of an operand is given by ea = d8 + [Ai] + [Xj]. The following example shows how an indexed address is computed.

ASSEMBLY LANGUAGE FORM	RTL DEFINITION	ACTION
MOVE.L 9(A1,D0.W), D3	$[D3] \leftarrow [M[9 + [A1] + [D0(0:15)]]]$	The contents of the memory location whose effective address is given by the contents of A1 plus the sign-extended contents of the low-word of D0 plus a constant, 9, are moved into register D3.

This is the most general and most complex form of addressing so far encountered. Some notes are needed to bring out its special features.

1. The 8-bit displacement is a signed, two's complement value, offering a range of -128 to $+127$. An 8-bit displacement is permitted simply because there are only 8 bits in the instruction code left for this purpose after the operation has been specified by the other bits.

2. The contents of the 32-bit index register may be treated as a 32-bit longword or a 16-bit word. For example, MOVE.L 12(A1,D0.L),D3 forms the effective address of the source operand by adding the entire contents of

D0 to A1 plus 12. The instruction MOVE.L 12(A1,D0.W),D3 forms the effective address of the operand by adding the lower-order contents of D0 (i.e., bits 0 through 15, sign extended to 32 bits) to the contents of A1 plus 12.

This addressing mode is used to handle two-dimensional tables. Let us suppose that we need to access the seventh item in a table of records. If the head of the table is pointed at by A0 and the location of the record (from the start of the table) is in D6, the operation MOVE.L 6(A0,D6.L),D0 will access the required item.

Program Counter Relative Addressing

Program counter relative addressing is very similar to register indirect addressing, except that the address of an operand is specified with respect to the contents of the program counter (PC) rather than with respect to the contents of an address register. Two forms of program counter relative addressing are implemented on the 68000: program counter with displacement and program counter with index. The effective addresses generated by these modes are as follows:

        Program counter with displacement: $ea = [PC] + d16$
        Program counter with index: $ea = [PC] + [Xn] + d8$

The assembly language form of these instructions is LABEL(PC) and LABEL(PC,Xi), respectively. Consider the following application of this addressing mode:

```
            MOVE.B      TABLE(PC),D2
                .
                .
                .

TABLE       DC.B        Value1
            DC.B        Value2
```

The assembler uses the offset TABLE in the instruction MOVE.B TABLE(PC),D2 to calculate the difference between the contents of the program counter and the address of the memory location TABLE. The result gives the 16-bit signed offset, d16, required by the instruction MOVE.B TABLE(PC),D2. When the instruction is executed, the offset is added to the contents of the PC to give the address of TABLE and Value1 is loaded into the lower-order byte of D2.

The power of this addressing mode lies in the fact that it allows the programmer to specify the address of an operand with respect to the program counter; that is, if the program is moved (i.e., relocated) in memory, the address of the operand does not have to be recalculated. Therefore, program counter relative addressing enables the programmer to write position-independent code because the operand, Value1, is always d16 locations onward from the instruction that accesses it. An advantage of this addressing mode is that the resulting position-independent code can be placed in read-only memory and located anywhere in a processor's address space.

However, the 68000 permits only source operands to be specified by program counter relative addressing! Consequently, MOVE LIST(PC),D2 is a legal operation, whereas MOVE D2,LIST(PC) is illegal. It has been argued that program counter relative addressing should not be allowed to *modify* a source operand because this would make self-modifying code easy to write. Therefore, program counter relative addressing can only be used to read constants. We will soon discover how the LEA instruction can be used to generate destination operands with program counter relative addresses.

Permitted Addressing Modes

The 68000 has a very regular architecture in the sense that it has no special-purpose data or address registers that can be used only in conjunction with certain instructions (apart from the status register), although it does not have regular addressing modes. Some instructions can be used with almost all the possible addressing modes, while other instructions are limited to one addressing mode. This situation arises as a result of the limited number of op-code/addressing mode combinations possible with a 16-bit instruction. The chip's designers have attempted to provide the most frequently used instructions with the greatest number of addressing modes. I am afraid that there is no simple way to learn which instruction can be used with what addressing modes. Appendix A provides a list of legal addressing modes for each instruction.

The Stack

Because of the 68000's autoincrementing and autodecrementing addressing modes, this CPU has, effectively, eight stack pointers—A0 through A7. Therefore, up to eight stacks can be active at any time. However, when a jump to a subroutine is executed, the return address is saved on the stack pointed at by A7.

The 68000 stack is arranged so that the stack pointer contains the address of the element at the top of the stack. Some processors point to the next free element above the stack. The 68000 stack grows from high to low memory when data is pushed onto it—that is, the stack pointer is decremented before each push. Similarly, the stack pointer is incremented after data has been pulled off the stack. A7 is automatically adjusted by 2 or 4 for word or longword operations, respectively.

A word is pushed on the stack by, for example, MOVE.W Dn,−(A7) and pulled off the stack by MOVE.W (A7)+,Dn. The 68000 also permits a word to be pulled from one stack and pushed on to another in one operation by MOVE.W (A3)+,−(A4). In chapter 3 we show how the stack is used in implementing modules and in passing data between modules.

Earlier we said that there are two A7 registers: the supervisor stack pointer (SSP) and the user stack pointer (USP). The actual stack pointer active at any given instant is determined by the operating mode of the 68000. However, an interrupt or some other exception forces the 68000 into the supervisor mode. Consequently, the return address from exceptions is always stored on the supervisor stack.

2.4 Introduction to the 68000 Instruction Set

It would be impossible to do justice to the power of the 68000 without turning this book into an assembly language manual. Therefore, I have attempted to give an overview of the 68000's instruction set but have omitted much of the fine detail. In particular, greater emphasis is placed on the more interesting or unusual aspects of the 68000, as I assume that most readers are already familiar with basic microprocessor architectures. Definitions of the 68000's instructions are given in the Appendix. As stated earlier, most instructions operate on byte, word, or longword operands and the operand size is specified by a .B, .W, or .L, respectively, after the mnemonic. However, if no size is specified, a .W (word) is taken as the default value.

Instructions can be divided into a relatively small number of groups. One possible grouping is:

Data movement
Arithmetic operations
Logical operations
Shift operations
Bit manipulation
Program control

Other groupings are equally acceptable: some combine logical and shift operations into a single logical group, others split logical operations into a Boolean logical group and a separate group including all shift operations (as I have done), and others include bit manipulation operations within the logical group.

Instructions and the Condition Code Register

After the execution of an instruction, the contents of the condition code byte of the status register (SR) are updated. Table 2.1 shows how the condition code is affected by the 68000's instructions.

TABLE 2.1 Relationship between instructions and the CCR. (Reprinted by permission of Motorola Limited)

MNEMONIC	DESCRIPTION	OPERATION	X	N	Z	V	C
ABCD	Add decimal with extend	(Destination)$_{10}$ + (source)$_{10}$ + x → destination	•	U	•	U	•
ADD	Add binary	(Destination) + (source) → destination	•	•	•	•	•
ADDA	Add address	(Destination) + (source) → destination	—	—	—	—	—
ADDI	Add immediate	(Destination) + immediate data → destination	•	•	•	•	•
ADDQ	Add quick	(Destination) + immediate data → destination	•	•	•	•	•
ADDX	Add extended	(Destination) + (source) + x → destination	•	•	•	•	•
AND	AND logical	(Destination) ∧ (source) → destination	—	•	•	0	0
ANDI	AND immediate	(Destination) ∧ immediate data → destination	—	•	•	0	0
ASL, ASR	Arithmetic shift	(Destination) shifted by ⟨count⟩ → destination	•	•	•	•	•
B$_{cc}$	Branch conditionally	If $_{cc}$ then PC + d → PC	—	—	—	—	—
BCHG	Test a bit and change	~(⟨bit number⟩) OF destination → Z; ~(⟨bit number⟩) OF destination → ⟨bit number⟩ OF destination	—	—	•	—	—
BCLR	Test a bit and clear	~(⟨bit number⟩) OF destination → Z; 0 → ⟨bit number⟩ → OF destination	—	—	•	—	—
BRA	Branch always	PC + displacement → PC	—	—	—	—	—
BSET	Test a bit and set	~(⟨bit number⟩) OF destination → Z; 1 → ⟨bit number⟩ OF destination	—	—	•	—	—
BSR	Branch to subroutine	PC → − (SP), PC + d → PC	—	—	—	—	—
BTST	Test a bit	~(⟨bit number⟩) OF destination → Z	—	—	•	—	—
CHK	Check register against bounds	If Dn ⟨0 or Dn⟩⟨⟨ea⟩⟩ then TRAP	—	•	U	U	U
CLR	Clear an operand	0 → Destination	—	0	1	0	0
CMP	Compare	(Destination) − (source)	—	•	•	•	•
CMPA	Compare address	(Destination) − (source)	—	•	•	•	•
CMPI	Compare immediate	(Destination) − immediate data	—	•	•	•	•
CMPM	Compare memory	(Destination) − (source)	—	•	•	•	•
DB$_{cc}$	Test condition, decrement, and branch	If ~$_{cc}$ then Dn − 1 → Dn; if Dn ≠ − 1 then PC + d → PC	—	—	—	—	—

CONDITION CODES

Continued

TABLE 2.1 *Continued*

MNEMONIC	DESCRIPTION	OPERATION	X	N	Z	V	C
DIVS	Signed divide	(Destination)/(source) → destination	—	●	●	●	0
DIVU	Unsigned divide	(Destination)/(source) → destination	—	●	●	●	0
EOR	Exclusive OR logical	(Destination) $\oplus$ (source) → destination	—	●	●	0	0
EORI	Exclusive OR immediate	(Destination) $\oplus$ immediate data → destination	—	●	●	0	0
EXG	Exchange register	Rx $\longleftrightarrow$ Ry	—	—	—	—	—
EXT	Sign extend	(Destination) sign-extended → destination	—	●	●	0	0
JMP	Jump	Destination → PC	—	—	—	—	—
JSR	Jump to subroutine	PC → − (SP); destination → PC	—	—	—	—	—
LEA	Load effective address	Destination → An	—	—	—	—	—
LINK	Link and allocate	An → − (SP); SP → An; SP + displacement → SP	—	—	—	—	—
LSL, LSR	Logical shift	(Destination) shifted by ⟨count⟩ → destination	●	●	●	0	●
MOVE	Move data from source to destination	(Source) → destination	—	●	●	0	0
MOVE to CCR	Move to condition code	(Source) → CCR	●	●	●	●	●
MOVE to SR	Move to the status register	(Source) → SR	●	●	●	●	●
MOVE from SR	Move from the status register	SR → destination	—	—	—	—	—
MOVE USP	Move user stack pointer	USP → An; An → USP	—	—	—	—	—
MOVEA	Move address	(Source) → destination	—	—	—	—	—
MOVEM	Move multiple registers	Registers → destination (Source) → registers	—	—	—	—	—
MOVEP	Move peripheral data	(Source) → destination	—	—	—	—	—
MOVEQ	Move quick	Immediate data → destination	—	●	●	0	0
MULS	Signed multiply	(Destination) × (source) → destination	—	●	●	0	0
MULU	Unsigned multiply	(Destination) × (source) → destination	—	●	●	0	0
NBCD	Negate decimal with extend	0 − (Destination)$_{10}$ − x → destination	●	U	●	U	●
NEG	Negate	0 − (Destination) → destination	●	●	●	●	●
NEGX	Negate with extend	0 − (Destination) − x → destination	●	●	●	●	●
NOP	No operation	—	—	—	—	—	—
NOT	Logical complement	∼(Destination) → destination	—	●	●	0	0
OR	Inclusive OR logical	(Destination) V (source) → destination	—	●	●	0	0
ORI	Inclusive OR immediate	(Destination) V immediate data → destination	—	●	●	0	0

38

Mnemonic	Description	X	N	Z	V	C	Operation
PEA	Push effective address	—	—	—	—	—	Destination → − (SP)
RESET	Reset external devices	—	—	—	—	—	—
ROL, ROR	Rotate (without extend)	—	•	•	0	•	(Destination) rotated by ⟨count⟩ → destination
ROXL, ROXR	Rotate with extend	•	•	•	0	•	(Destination) rotated by ⟨count⟩ → destination
RTE	Return from exception	•	•	•	•	•	(SP) + → SR; (SP) + → PC
RTR	Return and restore condition codes	•	•	•	•	•	(SP) + → CC; (SP) + → PC
RTS	Return from subroutine	—	—	—	—	—	(SP) + → PC
SBCD	Subtract decimal with extend	•	U	•	U	•	$(Destination)_{10} - (source)_{10} - x \rightarrow$ destination
Scc	Set according to condition	—	—	—	—	—	If cc then 1's → destination else 0's → destination
STOP	Load status register and stop	•	•	•	•	•	Immediate data → SR; STOP
SUB	Subtract binary	•	•	•	•	•	(Destination) − (source) → destination
SUBA	Subtract address	—	—	—	—	—	(Destination) − (source) → destination
SUBI	Subtract immediate	•	•	•	•	•	(Destination) − immediate data → destination
SUBQ	Subtract quick	•	•	•	•	•	(Destination) − immediate data → destination
SUBX	Subtract with extend	•	•	•	•	•	(Destination) − (source) − x → destination
SWAP	Swap register halves	—	•	•	0	0	Register [31:16] ⟷ register [15:0]
TAS	Test and set an operand	—	•	•	0	0	(Destination) tested → CC; 1 → [7] OF destination
TRAP	Trap	—	—	—	—	—	PC → − (SSP); SR → − (SSP); (vector) → PC
TRAPV	Trap on overflow	—	—	—	—	—	If V then TRAP
TST	Test on operand	—	•	•	0	0	(Destination) tested → CC
UNLK	Unlink	—	—	—	—	—	An → SP; (SP) + → An

⊕ Logical exclusive OR
∧ Logical AND
∨ Logical OR
~ Logical complement

• Affected
— Unaffected
0 Cleared
1 Set
U Undefined

NOTE: *The terminology in this table is that of Motorola and differs from the conventions adopted elsewhere in the text.*

39

Data Movement

There are thirteen data movement operations in the 68000's instruction set. A data movement instruction simply copies information from one place to another. Such an instruction is hardly exciting, but it has been reported that 70 percent of the average program consists of data movement operations. The 68000 implements the following data movement instructions: MOVE, MOVEA, MOVE to CCR, MOVE to SR, MOVE from SR, MOVE USP, MOVEM, MOVEQ, MOVEP, LEA, PEA, EXG, SWAP. Some of these instructions have already been encountered in the section on addressing modes, but are included here for completeness. Note that certain instructions that affect the status byte of the SR may not be executed when the 68000 is operating in the user mode.

MOVE, MOVEA   The MOVE instruction copies an 8-, 16-, or 32-bit value from one memory location or register to another memory location or register. All the addressing modes discussed so far can be used to specify the source of the data or its destination, with three exceptions: immediate addressing, address register direct addressing, and program counter relative addressing cannot be used to specify a destination. The V and C bits of the condition code register (CCR) are cleared by a MOVE; the N and Z bits are updated according to the value of the destination operand; the X bit is unaffected. The MOVEA instruction permits all source addressing modes but only the address register direct destination addressing mode. The MOVEA instruction, like all other instructions operating on the contents of an address register, does not affect the CCR.

MOVE to CCR   The MOVE to CCR instruction moves data into the condition code register and is a *word operation*. A MOVE ⟨ea⟩,CCR copies the lower-order byte of the operand at the specified effective address into the CCR. The high-order byte of the operand is ignored. This instruction allows the programmer to preset the CCR.

MOVE to SR, MOVE from SR   The first of these instructions copies a word to the status register. It is a privileged instruction and can be executed only when the 68000 is operating in its supervisor mode. This topic is covered in chapter 6 and is entirely irrelevant to the basic operation of the 68000. The MOVE from SR instruction allows the contents of the processor status word to be examined. Note that this is a privileged instruction in the 68010's instruction set but not in the 68000's. These two instructions are executed only by operating system software and are not required by user (i.e., applications) programmers. Their assembly language forms one MOVE ⟨ea⟩,SR and MOVE SR,⟨ea⟩.

MOVE USP   As already stated, the 68000 has two A7 registers: one associated with the user mode and one with the supervisor mode. These A7s are called USP (user stack pointer) and SSP (supervisor stack pointer), respectively, whenever it is necessary to distinguish between them. When the 68000 is operating in the supervisor mode, the instructions MOVE.L USP,An and MOVE.L An,USP transfer the USP to address register An, and vice versa, thereby allowing the operating system to manipulate the user stack. When the 68000 is in the user mode, the SSP is entirely hidden from the user and cannot be accessed.

MOVEM   The move multiple register instruction offers the programmer a very simple way of transferring a group of the 68000's registers to or from memory with a single instruction. Its assembly language form is MOVEM ⟨register list⟩,⟨ea⟩ or MOVEM ⟨ea⟩,⟨register list⟩. MOVEM operates only on words or longwords. The effect of MOVEM is to transfer the contents of the group of registers specified by the "register list" (described later) to consecutive memory locations or to restore them from consecutive memory locations. Programmers use this instruction to save working registers on entering a subroutine and to retrieve them at the end of the subroutine. The contents of the CCR are not affected by a MOVEM.

The register list is defined as Ai–Aj/Dp–Dq. For example, A0–A4/D3–D7 specifies address registers A0 through A4 and data registers D3 through D7, inclusive.

The instruction MOVEM.L D0–D7/A0–A6, −(SP) pushes all the data registers and address registers A0 through A6 onto the stack pointed at by A7. The instruction MOVEM.L (SP)+,D0–D7/A0–A6 has the reverse effect and pulls the registers off the stack. The autodecrementing addressing mode is used to specify the destinations of the register and the autoincrementing addressing mode is used to specify the source of the registers.

MOVEQ   The MOVEQ (move quick) instruction is intended to move a 32-bit literal value in the range −128 to +127 to one of the eight data registers. The data moved is a byte which is sign extended to 32 bits. Therefore, although this instruction moves an 8-bit value, it yields a 32-bit result. For example, the operation MOVEQ # −3,D2 has the effect of loading the value $FFFF FFFD into data register D2.

MOVEP   The move peripheral instruction copies words or longwords to an 8-bit peripheral. Byte-oriented peripherals are connected to the 68000's data bus in such a way that *consecutive* bytes in the peripheral are mapped onto successive odd (or even) addresses in the 68000's memory space. For example, a peripheral with four internal registers may have the following memory map.

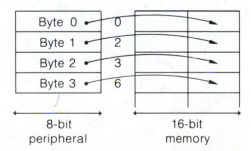

8-bit peripheral   16-bit memory

It is impossible to move more than a byte at a time to an 8-bit peripheral by means of a conventional MOVE. W or a MOVE. L because these move a word or a longword to consecutive bytes in memory. The MOVEP instruction is designed to move a word or a longword between a data register in the 68000 and a byte-wide, memory-mapped peripheral. The contents of the chosen register are moved to consecutive *even* (or odd) byte addresses. For example, MOVEP.L D2,0(A0) copies the four bytes in D2 to the addresses given by [A0 + 0], [A0 + 2], [A0 + 4], [A0 + 6]. Only register indirect with displacement addressing is permitted with this instruction. MOVEP does not affect the CCR. The assembler form of MOVEP is

     MOVEP   Dx, d16(Ay)

or

     MOVEP   d16(Ay), Dx

Data is transferred between a data register and alternate bytes of memory, starting at the location specified and incrementing by two. The high-order byte of the data register is transferred first and the low-order byte is transferred last. If the address is even, all transfers are made on the high-order half of the data bus; if the address is odd, all the transfers are made on the low-order half of the data bus. The following example is of the instruction MOVEP.L D0,(A0).

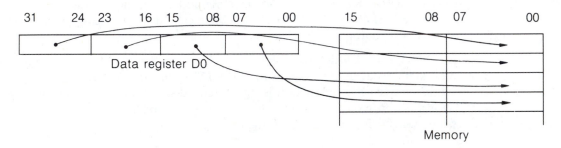

LEA   The load effective address (LEA) instruction calculates an effective address and loads it into an address register. This instruction can only be used with 32-bit operands. The LEA instruction is one of the most powerful instructions provided by the 68000. Two examples of its use are now given.

ASSEMBLY LANGUAGE FORM	RTL FORM	ACTION
LEA $0010FFFF, A5	[A5] ← $0010 FFFF	Load the address $0010 FFFF into register A5.
LEA 12(A0, D4. L), A5	[A5] ← 12 + [A0] + [D4]	The contents of A0 plus the contents of D4 plus 12 are loaded into A5.

In the second example, LEA 12(A0,D4.L),A5, the address evaluated from the expression 12 + [A0] + [D4] is deposited in A5. If the instruction MOVEA.L 12(A0,D4),A5 had been used, the *contents* of that address would have been deposited in A5. The load effective address has been provided to avoid the repeated and time-consuming calculation of effective addresses by the CPU. It is clearly more efficient to put the effective address into an address register by means of a LEA ⟨ea⟩,An instruction than to recalculate the address every time it is used. For example, if the operation ADD. W $1C(A3,D2),D0 is to be repeated many times, it is better to execute a LEA $1C(A3,D2),A5 once and then to repeat ADD.W (A5),D0.

A realistic example of the application of the LEA instruction is given in chapter 3, where we consider the design of a command line interpreter. In that example, a table in memory is pointed to by an address in address register A2. The length of each entry in the table is 6 bytes plus the contents of the first element in the entry. We wish to calculate the address of the next entry. By executing MOVE.B (A2),D1, we can store the length of the current entry (less 6) in D1. Executing a LEA 6(A2,D1.W),A3 then adds the contents of A2 to the contents of the lower-order word of D1 plus 6 and deposits the result in A3—that is, [A3] ← [A2] + [D1(0:15)] + 6. The contents of A3 becomes, of course, the address of the next entry in the table. Note that D1(8:15) must be cleared by CLR.W D1 before carrying out the LEA.

The real importance of the LEA instruction lies in the support it offers for position-independent programming. Remember that program counter relative addressing permits us to use source operands but not destination operands. If we use LEA with program counter relative addressing to generate the address of a destinction operand, this *relative* address is loaded into an address register and can be used with register indirect addressing to achieve position-independent code. The following example shows how this is done.

Case 1	**Case 2**
MOVE.B TABLE(PC),D0	LEA.L TABLE(PC),A0
	MOVE.B D0,(A0)
⋮	⋮
TABLE . . .	TABLE . . .

These examples both generate position-independent code. In case 1, program counter relative addressing is permitted because it is not used to modify a destination operand. In case 2, program counter relative addressing is achieved by loading the relative address into A0.

PEA   The push effective address (PEA) instruction calculates an effective address and pushes it onto the stack pointed at by address register A7. The only difference between PEA and LEA is that LEA deposits an effective address in an address register while PEA pushes it onto the stack. Thus, PEA ⟨ea⟩ is equivalent to LEA ⟨ea⟩,Ai followed by MOVE.L Ai,−(A7).

EXG   The EXG instruction exchanges the entire 32-bit contents of two registers. In RTL terms, [Xi] ← [Xj]; [Xj] ← [Xi], where Xi and Xj represent any data or address registers. Although EXG allows the contents of two data registers to be exchanged, its main application is in transferring a value calculated in a data register to an address register. The CCR is not affected by an EXG.

SWAP The SWAP instruction has the assembler form SWAP Dn and exchanges the upper- and lower-order words of a data register. In RTL terms SWAP is expressed as $[Di(16:31)] \leftarrow [Di(0:15)]$; $[Di(0:15)] \leftarrow [Di(16:31)]$. This instruction has been provided because all operations on 16-bit words act only on bits 0 to 15 of a register. By using a SWAP, the high-order word $Di(16:31)$ can be moved to the low-order word and then operated on by a word-mode instruction. The SWAP instruction affects the CCR in the same way as the MOVE instruction—V and C are cleared, N and Z are updated, and X is unaffected. Note that a byte swap is executed by means of a rotate instruction (see later). ROL.W #8,Dn exchanges the upper and lower bytes of the lower-order word of D0.

Arithmetic Operations

The 68000 has a conventional set of arithmetic operations, all of which are integer operations. Floating-point operations are not directly supported by the 68000. Except for division, multiplication, and operations whose destination is an address register, all arithmetic operations act on 8-, 16-, or 32-bit entities. The arithmetic group of instructions includes: ADD, ADDA, ADDQ, ADDI, ADDX, CLR, DIVS, DIVU, MULS, MULU, SUB, SUBA, SUBQ, SUBI, SUBX, NEG, NEGX, EXT. Note that the 68000 also has three arithmetic operations designed to facilitate calculations in BCD: ABCD (add decimal with extend), SBCD (subtract decimal with extend), and NBCD (negate decimal with extend). Further details of these instructions can be found in Appendix A.

ADD The ADD instruction adds the contents of a source location to the contents of a destination location and deposits the result in the destination location. Either the source or the destination must be a data register. Memory-to-memory additions are not permitted with this instruction. The ADD instruction cannot be used to modify the contents of an address register.

ADDA The ADDA instruction is almost indentical to the ADD instruction and is necessary whenever the destination of the result is an address register. ADDA must, of course, be used only with word and longword operands and has no effect on the contents of the condition code register. For example, ADDA.L D3,A4 adds the entire contents of D3 to A4 and deposits the results in A4.

ADDQ The ADDQ (add quick) instruction is designed to add a literal (i.e., constant) value, in the range 1 to 8, to the contents of a memory location or a register. ADDQ may be used with byte, word, and longword operands. Note that ADDQ can also be applied to the contents of an address register. Some readers might find this a little inconsistent. The term "quick" is employed because the instruction format of ADDQ includes the 3-bit constant to be added to the destination operand. Therefore, an ADDQ #4,D1 is executed faster than the corresponding ADD #4,D1.

ADDI   The add immediate (ADDI) instruction adds a literal value of a byte, word, or longword to the contents of a destination operand and then stores the result in the destination. The destination may be a memory location or a data register. Although ADD #$1234,D4 and ADDI #$1234,D4 are almost equivalent, the ADDI and ADD # instructions are coded differently because ADDI permits a literal to be added to the contents of a memory location. For example, ADDI.W #$1234,(A0) adds the constant $1234 to the memory location pointed at by A0. Some assemblers only permit the use of the ADD # mnemonic and automatically provide the appropriate op-code.

ADDX   The add extended instruction adds the contents of a source location to the contents of a destination location plus the contents of the X bit of the condition code register and deposits the result in the destination location. Only two addressing modes are permitted by ADDX. Both source and destination must be data registers or they must be memory locations accessed by the address register indirect addressing mode with predecrement. The following three examples should make the operation of ADDX easier to understand.

ASSEMBLY LANGUAGE FORM	RTL FORM
ADDX.L D3,D4	$[D4] \leftarrow [D3] + [D4] + [X]$
ADDX.B D3,D4	$[D4(0:7)] \leftarrow [D3(0:7)] + [D4(0:7)] + [X]$
ADDX.L $-(A3),-(A4)$	$[A3] \leftarrow [A3] - 4; [A4] \leftarrow [A4] - 4$
	$[M[A4]] \leftarrow [M[A3]] + [M[A4]] + [X]$

The ADDX instruction is used to perform multiprecision addition. For example, if a 64-bit integer is stored in D0 and D1 (with D1 holding the most-significant 32 bits) and another 64-bit integer is held in D2 and D3 (with D3 holding the most-significant 32 bits), the following operations perform the 64-bit addition.

ADD.L D0,D2	$[D2] \leftarrow [D2] + [D0]$	Add low-order longwords
ADDX.L D1,D3	$[D3] \leftarrow [D3] + [D1] + [X]$	Add high-order longwords together with a carry-in

The first operation, ADD.L D0,D2, adds together the two lower-order 32-bit longwords. Any carry-out from the most-significant bit position (i.e., into bit 32) is stored in the X bit. When the two higher-order 32-bit longwords are added together by ADDX.L D1,D3, the carry-out recorded by the X bit is added to their sum.

CLR   The clear instruction loads the contents of the specified data register or memory location with zero. As no explicit instruction clears the contents of an address register, SUBA.L An,An will clear the contents of An.

DIVS, DIVU These two operations carry out integer division. The assembly language form is DIVU $\langle ea \rangle$,Dn (or DIVS $\langle ea \rangle$,Dn). The 32-bit long word in data register Dn is divided by the 16-bit word at the effective address given in the instruction. The quotient is a 16-bit value and is deposited in the lower-order word of Dn. The remainder is stored in the upper-order word of Dn. DIVU performs unsigned division and DIVS operates on two's complement numbers.

MULS, MULU As with division operations, two multiplication instructions are available. MULS forms the product of two signed (two's complement integers) and MULU forms the product of two unsigned integers. The assembly language forms of these instructions are MULS $\langle ea \rangle$,Dn and MULU $\langle ea \rangle$,Dn. Multiplication is a 16-bit operation that multiplies the low-order 16-bit word in Dn by the 16-bit word at the effective address in the operand. The 32-bit long-word product is deposited in Dn.

SUB, SUBA, SUBQ, SUBI, SUBX These operations are the subtraction equivalents of ADD, ADDA, ADDQ, ADDI, and ADDX, respectively. Each instruction subtracts the source operand from the destination operand and places the result in the destination operand. For example, SUBI.B #$30,D0 is interpreted as [D0(0:7)] ← [D0(0:7)] − $30.

NEG The negate instruction subtracts the destination operand from zero and deposits the result at the destination address. NEG is a monadic operation and has the assembly language form NEG $\langle ea \rangle$. The operand address may be a memory location or a data register but not an address register. This instruction simply forms the two's complement of an operand.

NEGX The negate with extend instruction forms the two's complement of an operand minus the X bit.

EXT The sign extend instruction has the assembly language form EXT.W Dn or EXT.L Dn. The former instruction sign extends the low-order byte in Dn to 16 bits by copying Dn(7) to bits Dn(8: 15). Similarly, the latter instruction sign extends the low-order word in Dn to 32 bits by copying Dn(15) to bits Dn(16:31).

Logical Operations

The 68000 implements four Boolean operations: AND, OR, EOR, and NOT. All logical operations can be applied to longword, word, and byte operands. Additionally, logical operations can, with immediate addressing, be applied to the contents of the status register or the condition code register. Operations on the SR are carried out to alter the mode of operation of the 68000 and are privileged. In general, logical operations are used to modify one or more fields of an operand. A logical AND masks out bits (i.e., clears them), an OR sets bits, and an EOR toggles them (i.e., causes them to change state). The following instructions illustrate the effect of these logical operations. In each case an immediate operand is used. The low-order byte of D0 before each operation is %11110000. Note that the immediate operands of the above instructions use the mnemonics ANDI, ORI, and EORI. The immediate forms of these instructions are able to specify a data register as an operand or a memory location. Logical operations affect the CCR in exactly the same way as MOVE instructions.

ANDI. B	# %10100110, D0	[D0] ← 10100110 . 11110000
		[D0] ← 10100000
ORI. B	# %10100110, D0	[D0] ← 10100110 + 11110000
		[D0] ← 11110110
EORI. B	# %10100110, D0	[D0] ← 10100110 ⊕ 11110000
		[D0] ← 01010110

The actual logical operations supported by the 68000 in terms of their assembly language forms are given below.

AND	⟨ea⟩,Dn	
AND	Dn,⟨ea⟩	
ANDI	#⟨data⟩,⟨ea⟩	
ANDI	#⟨data⟩,CCR	
ANDI	#⟨data⟩,SR	(privileged)
EOR	Dn,⟨ea⟩	
EORI	#⟨data⟩,⟨ea⟩	
EORI	#⟨data⟩,CCR	
EORI	#⟨data⟩,SR	(privileged)
NOT	⟨ea⟩	
OR	⟨ea⟩,Dn	
OR	Dn,⟨ea⟩	
ORI	#⟨data⟩,⟨ea⟩	
ORI	#⟨data⟩,CCR	
ORI	#⟨data⟩,SR	(privileged)

An operation labeled "privileged" can be executed only when the 68000 is operating in its supervisor mode (see chap. 6). Note that logical instructions are not entirely symmetric. For example, the operation EOR ⟨ea⟩, Dn is not permitted!

Shift Operations

In a shift operation, all bits of the operand are moved one or more places to the left or right, subject to the variations described below. The 68000 is moderately well endowed with shift operations.

All shifts can be categorized as logical, arithmetic, or circular. In a logical shift, a zero enters at the input of the shifter and the bit shifted out is clocked into

FIGURE 2.4   68000's shift and rotate instructions

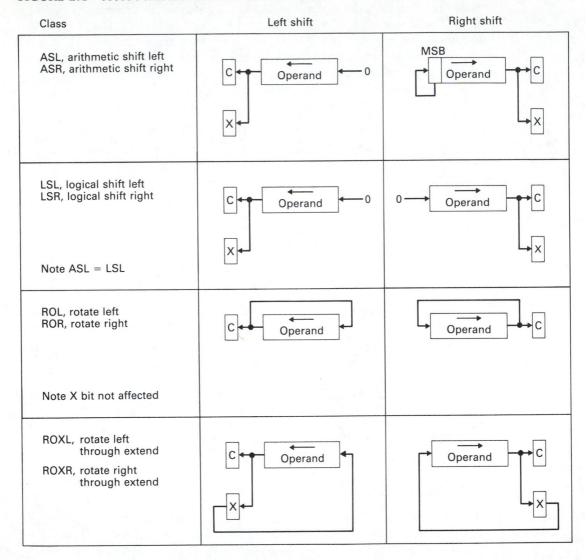

the carry flip-flop. An arithmetic shift left is identical to a logical shift left, but an arithmetic shift right causes the most-significant bit, the sign bit, to be propagated right. This action preserves the correct sign of a two's complement value. For example, if the bytes 00101010 and 10101010 are shifted one place to the right (arithmetically), the results are 00010101 and 11010101, respectively. In a circular shift, the bit shifted out is moved to the position of the bit shifted in. No bit is lost during a circular shift.

The 68000 has eight shift operations in its instruction set, illustrated in figure 2.4. The symbol C denotes the carry bit of the condition code register; X means the extend bit of the CCR.

Arithmetic shifts update *all* bits of the CCR. The N and Z bits are set or cleared as we would expect. The V bit is set if the most-significant bit of the operand is changed at any time during the shift operation. The C and X bits are set according to the last bit shifted out of the operand. However, if the shift count is zero, C is cleared and X is unaffected. Logical shifts and rotates clear the V bit.

Assembly Language Form of Shift Operations

All eight shift instructions are expressed in one of three ways. These are illustrated by the ASL (arithmetic shift left) instruction.

Mode 1.   ASL Dx, Dy   Shift Dy by Dx bits
Mode 2.   ASL #⟨data⟩, Dy   Shift Dy by #data bits
Mode 3.   ASL ⟨ea⟩   Shift the contents of ea by one place

A shift instruction can be applied to a byte, word, or longword operand, with the exception of mode 3 shifts, which act only on words.

In mode 1, the "source" operand, Dx, specifies how many places the destination operand, Dy, needs to be shifted. Dy may be shifted by 1 to 32 bits. In mode 2, the literal, #⟨data⟩, specifies how many places Dy needs to be shifted; this must be in the range 1 to 8. In mode 3, the memory location specified by the effective address, ⟨ea⟩, is shifted one place. Many microprocessors permit only the *static* shifts of modes 2 and 3. The 68000 permits *dynamic* shifts (i.e., mode 1) because the number of bits to be shifted is computed at run-time.

Bit Manipulation

The 68000 provides four instructions that act on a single bit of an operand rather than on the entire operand. In each of the bit manipulation instructions, the complement of the selected bit is moved to the Z bit of the CCR and then the bit is either unchanged, set, cleared, or toggled. The N, V, C, and X bits of the CCR are not affected by bit operations. Bit manipulations may be applied to a byte or to a longword. Even though bit manipulation instructions act on just one bit, they act on either one bit of a specified byte in memory or on one bit of a longword in a data register. The four instructions in this group are BTST, BSET, BCLR, and BCHG.

BTST   This instruction tests a specified bit of an operand. If the bit is zero, set the Z bit of the condition code register. A bit test does not affect the value of the operand under test in any way.

BSET   The bit test and set instruction causes the Z bit of the CCR to be set if the specified bit is zero and then forces the specified bit of the operand to be set to one.

BCLR   The bit test and clear instruction works exactly like BSET, except that the specified bit is cleared after it has been tested.

BCHG   The bit test and change instruction causes the value of the specified bit to be reflected in the Z bit of the CCR and then toggles the state of the specified bit.

In order to apply these four instructions, two items of information are needed by the assembler: the effective address of the operand and the position of the bit to be tested. All addressing modes are available to these four instructions for the destination operand except immediate addressing, address register direct, and program counter relative addressing. The location of the bit to be tested is specified in one of two ways: it may be provided in an absolute (i.e., constant or static) form in the instruction or given as the contents of a data register. In the following example, BTST is used as an illustration, but any of the members of this group could have been chosen.

The assembly language forms of these instructions are

```
BTST   Dn,⟨ea⟩
BTST   #⟨data⟩,⟨ea⟩
```

If the destination address is a memory location, the source operand is treated as a modulo-8 value. If the destination address is a data register, the source operand is treated as a modulo-32 value. As an example of bit manipulation, consider a subroutine to count the number of ones in a byte. On entry to the subroutine, D0(0:7) contains the byte to be tested and on exit it contains the number of ones in the byte. No other registers must be modified by the subroutine.

```
*   D0 = input/output register (only D0. B modified)
*   D1 = one's counter (not modified by subroutine)
*   D2 = pointer to bit of D0 to be tested (not modified by subroutine)
*
ONES_COUNT   MOVEM.L   D1-D2,-(A7)   Save working registers
             CLR.B     D1            Clear one's counter
             MOVEQ     #7,D2         D2 initially points at msb of D0.B
*
NEXT_BIT     BTST      D2,D0         Test the D2. th bit of D0
             BEQ.S     LOOP_TEST     If zero then nothing more to do
             ADDQ.B    #1,D1         Else increment one's count
LOOP_TEST    SUBQ.B    #1,D2         Decrement bit pointer
             BGE       NEXT_BIT      Repeat until count negative
             MOVE.B    D1,D0         Transfer one's count to D0
             MOVEM.L   (A7)+,D1-D2   Restore working registers
             RTS                     Return
*
```

2.5 Program Control and the 68000

The computational power of all computers lies in their ability to choose between two or more courses of action on the basis of the available information. Without such powers of decision, the computer would be almost worthless.

Compare Instructions

A computer chooses between two courses of action by examining the state of one or more bits in its CCR and associating one action with one outcome of the test and another action with the other outcome. Although the CCR bits are updated after certain instructions have been executed, two instructions can be used to implicitly update the CCR. These are the bit test (defined previously) and the compare.

CMP, CMPA, CMPI, CMPM   The compare group of instructions subtract the contents of one register (or memory location) from another register (or memory location) and update the contents of the condition code register accordingly. The N, Z, V, and C bits of the CCR are all updated and the X bit remains unaffected. The difference between the subtract and compare operation is that a subtraction evaluates $P = R - Q$ and retains P while the compare operation merely evaluates $R - Q$ and does not keep the result. All instructions in this group, except CMPA, take byte, word, or longword operands.

The basic compare instruction, CMP, compares the source operand with the destination operand. The destination operand must be a data register and the source operand may be specified by any of the 68000's addressing modes. For example:

CMP.L	D0,D1	Evaluates [D1] — [D0]
CMP.B	TEMP1,D3	Evaluates [D3(0:7)] — [TEMP1]
CMP.L	TEMP1,D3	Evaluates [D3(0:31)] — [TEMP1]
CMP.W	(A3),D2	Evaluates [D2(0:15)] — [[A3]]

Note that CMP ⟨ea1⟩,⟨ea2⟩ evaluates [ea2] — [ea1] so that the *first* operand is subtracted from the *second*. Some other microprocessors perform this in the reverse order. CMP has three variations on its basic form: CMPI, CMPA, and CMPM. CMPI is used to execute a comparison with a literal and is written CMPI #⟨data⟩,⟨ea⟩. Like the corresponding ADDI, the CMPI instruction allows a literal operation to be performed with the contents of a memory location. Consider two examples of CMPI operations.

CMPI.B	#$07,D3	Evaluates [D3(0:7)] — 7
CMPI.W	#$07,TEMP	Evaluates [TEMP] — 7

CMPA means "compare address" and is necessary whenever an address register is compared with the contents of an effective address. Its assembly language form is CMPA ⟨ea⟩,An and it operates only on word and longword values.

CMPM means "compare memory with memory" and is one of the few instructions that permits a memory-to-memory operation. Only one addressing mode is allowed with CMPM: register indirect with autoincrementing. The assembler form of this instruction is, therefore, CMPM (Ai)+,(Aj)+. This instruction is used to compare the contents of two tables, element by element.

Branch Instructions

The 68000 provides the programmer with a tool-kit containing three instructions for the implementation of all conditional control structures. These instructions are

    Bcc   ⟨label⟩   Branch to label on condition cc true
    BRA   ⟨label⟩   Branch to label unconditionally
    DBcc Dn,⟨label⟩   Test condition cc, decrement, and branch

Of these three instructions, the first two are entirely conventional and are found on all microprocessors. The last instruction is more unusual and is not provided by most microprocessors.

Branch conditionally Fourteen versions of the Bcc d8 or Bcc d16 instruction exist, where cc stands for one of fourteen logical conditions. If the specified condition cc is true, a branch is made to the instruction whose address is d8 or d16 locations onward from the start of the next instruction. The number of locations branched is specified by either an 8-bit value, d8, or a 16-bit value, d16. The displacement, d8 or d16, forms part of the instruction and is an 8- or 16-bit signed two's complement value, permitting a branch forward or backward from the location following the instruction Bcc d8 or Bcc d16. An 8-bit signed offset allows a branch of +127 bytes forward or −128 bytes backward and a 16-bit offset provides a range of +32,767 bytes forward and −32,768 bytes backward.

The assembler sometimes automatically selects the short 8-bit displacement or the long 16-bit displacement according to the distance to be branched. Otherwise the programmer must write Bcc.S d8 to force a short 8-bit branch, as the extension .S selects the 8-bit displacement. Note that the value of d8 or d16 is automatically calculated by the assembler, as the displacement is invariably in the form of a label rather than an address.

Table 2.2 defines the fourteen possible values of cc. After an arithmetic or logical operation is carried out (together with certain other operations), the values of the Z, N, C, and V flags in the condition code register are updated accordingly. These flag bits are then used to determine whether the appropriate logical condition is true or false. For example, BCS LABEL causes the state of the carry bit to be tested. If the bit is set (i.e., 1), a branch to LABEL (i.e., the point in the program

TABLE 2.2 Conditional tests and the 68000

MNEMONIC (cc)	CONDITION	FLAGS TESTED	BRANCH TAKEN IF:
CC	Carry clear	C	$C = 0$
CS	Carry set	C	$C = 1$
NE	Not equal	Z	$Z = 0$
EQ	Equal	Z	$Z = 1$
PL	Plus	N	$N = 0$
MI	Minus	N	$N = 1$
HI	Higher than	C, Z	$\overline{C} \cdot \overline{Z} = 1$
LS	Lower than or same as	C, Z	$C + Z = 1$
GT	Greater than	Z, N, V	$N \cdot V \cdot \overline{Z} + \overline{N} \cdot \overline{V} \cdot \overline{Z} = 1$
LT	Less than	N, V	$N \cdot \overline{V} + \overline{N} \cdot V = 1$
GE	Greater than or equal to	N, V	$N \cdot \overline{V} + \overline{N} \cdot V = 0$
LE	Less than or equal to	Z, N, V	$Z + (\overline{N} \cdot V + N \cdot \overline{V}) = 1$
VC	Overflow clear	V	$V = 0$
VS	Overflow set	V	$V = 1$
T	Always true	None	Always
F	Always false	None	Never

NOTE: Some of these tests are designed to operate on integer values (HI, LS) and some on signed, two's complement values (PL, MI, GT, LT, GE, LE).

labeled LABEL) is made; otherwise the instruction immediately following BCS LABEL is executed.

Information stored and manipulated by the computer is often in an unsigned integer form or in two's complement form. Consequently, some conditional tests are intended to be applied after operations on two's complement values while others are applied after operations on integer (or any other non-two's complement) values. To illustrate this point, consider the following two examples.

Case 1	**Case 2**
ADD.L D0,D1	ADD.L D0,D1
BCS ERROR	BVS ERROR
ERROR ...	ERROR ...

Both of these cases add the contents of D0 to D1 and deposit the result in D1. However, in case 1 the numbers are interpreted as being in unsigned integer form. If, when adding two 32-bit integers, a carry is generated out of the most-significant bit position, the carry flag is set. The instruction BCS ERROR causes a branch to ERROR to be made if a carry-out occurred. The part of the program labeled ERROR can deal with (i.e., recover from) the out-of-range condition.

Case 2 considers both numbers to be in two's complement form. After the addition has been completed, the state of the overflow flag is tested and a branch to ERROR is made if overflow occurred during the addition.

Example 1: Use of Conditional Instructions

As an example of the application of conditional branch instructions, consider the conversion of hexadecimal values to their ASCII character equivalents. Table 9.1 in chapter 9 gives the relationship between ASCII-encoded characters and their binary or hexadecimal equivalents. An excerpt from this table is provided for reference:

ASCII CHARACTER	HEXADECIMAL CODE
0	30
1	31
2	32
3	33
4	34
5	35
6	36
7	37
8	38
9	39
A	41
B	42
C	43
D	44
E	45
F	46

The algorithm for the conversion of a hexadecimal value into its ASCII-encoded equivalent can readily be derived from this table. In the following, HEX represents a single hexadecimal number and CHAR the ASCII-encoded character equivalent. Thus, if HEX = $0A, the corresponding value of CHAR is $41. By inspecting the preceding table, we can derive a relationship between CHAR and HEX:

    CHAR: = HEX + $30
    IF HEX > $39 THEN CHAR: = CHAR + $7.

In terms of 68000 assembly language, this algorithm can now be written as follows.

```
     MOVE.B   HEX,D0     Get HEX value to be converted into D0
     ADDI.B   #$30,D0    Add $30 to it
     CMPI.B   #$39,D0    Test for hexadecimal values in the range $0A to $0F
     BLS.S    EXIT       If not in range $0A to $0F then exit
     ADDQ.B   #$07,D0    Else add 7
EXIT MOVE.B   D0,CHAR    Save result in CHAR
```

Branch unconditionally   The branch unconditional instruction, BRA, causes a branch to the instruction whose address is marked by the label following the BRA mnemonic. An 8-bit or 16-bit signed offset follows the op-code for BRA, providing a branching range of up to 32K bytes. The unconditional branch is equivalent to the GOTO instruction in high level languages. The 68000 also has a jump instruction, JMP, which is functionally equivalent to the branch instruction BRA. The only difference between the two instructions is that BRA uses relative addressing while JMP uses the following addressing modes:

```
JMP    (An)
JMP    d16(An)
JMP    d8(An, Xi)
JMP    Absolute_address
JMP    d16(PC)
JMP    d8(PC, Xi)
```

As an example of the application of an unconditional branch, consider the implementation of the CASE statement that is found in many high level languages. In the program below, the variable TEST contains the integer used to determine which of three courses of action (labeled ACT1, ACT2, ACT3) is to be carried out. If TEST contains a value greater than 2, an exception is raised.

```
CASE        MOVE.B    TEST,D0    Put the value of TEST in D0
            BEQ.S     ACT1       If zero then carry out ACT1
            SUBQ.B    #1,D0      Decrement TEST
            BEQ.S     ACT2       If zero then carry out ACT2
            SUBQ.B    #1,D0      Decrement TEST
            BEQ.S     ACT3       If zero then carry out ACT3
EXCEPTION   ...                  Else deal with the exception
            BRA.S     EXIT       Leave CASE

ACT1        ...                  Execute action 1
            BRA.S     EXIT       Leave CASE

ACT2        ...                  Execute action 2
            BRA.S     EXIT       Leave CASE

ACT3        ...                  Execute action 3
            ...
            ...
                                 (Fall through to exit)
EXIT        ...                  Single exit point for CASE
```

This method of implementing a CASE statement is not unique and would not be used if there were many more possible values of TEST. A better method is to use a JMP with a computed address such as JMP d8(A0, D3), where D3 contains a value that is a function of TEST.

Test condition, decrement, and branch   The DBcc instruction is not found in 8-bit microprocessors and provides a powerful way of implementing loop mechanisms. As in the case of the Bcc instruction, there are fourteen possible

computed values of cc plus the two static (i.e., constant) values, cc = T and
cc = F. When cc = T (i.e., DBT), the tested condition is always true, and when
cc = F (i.e., DBF), the tested condition is always false.

The DBcc instruction has the assembly language form DBcc Dn,⟨label⟩,
where Dn is one of the eight data registers and ⟨label⟩ is a label used to specify a
branch address. When the 68000 encounters a DBcc instruction, it first carries out
the test defined by the cc field. If the result of the test is true, the branch is not
taken and the next instruction in sequence is executed. Note that this has the
opposite effect to a Bcc instruction. The branch is limited to a 16-bit displacement.

If the specified condition, cc, is not true, the low-order 16 bits of Dn are
decremented by 1. If the resulting contents of Dn are equal to −1, the next
instruction in sequence is executed. Otherwise a branch to ⟨label⟩ is made. The
DBcc instruction can be defined as follows.

```
DBcc Dn,⟨label⟩:     If cc TRUE THEN EXIT
                     ELSE
                     BEGIN
                     [Dn] := [Dn] − 1
                     IF [Dn] = −1 THEN EXIT
                                      ELSE [PC] ← label
                     END_IF
                     END
              END_IF
              EXIT
```

Unlike the Bcc instruction, DBcc allows the condition F (i.e., false) to be specified
by cc. For example, DBF Dn, ⟨label⟩ always cause Dn to be decremented and a
branch made to ⟨label⟩ until the contents of Dn are −1. Some assemblers permit
the use of the mnemonic DBRA instead of DBF. The simplest application of DBcc
is the mechanization of a loop. Let us suppose that a loop must be executed *N*
times. The following program achieves this.

```
        MOVE.W   #200,D0     Load D0 with 200
NEXT    ...                  Start of body of loop
                             Body of loop
        DBF      D0,NEXT     Decrement D0 and branch if not −1
```

Register D0 is preloaded with 200 and the D0 loop is entered. The
DBF D0,NEXT instruction causes D0 to be decremented by 1 to yield 199. A
branch is then made to NEXT, the start of the body of the loop. When D0
contains 0, the next execution of DBF D0,NEXT yields −1 and the loop is terminated. Note that the loop is repeated [Dn] + 1 times (i.e., 201). Interestingly,
DBcc Dn,⟨label⟩ works only with 16-bit values in Dn; that is, loops greater than
65,536 cannot be achieved directly by this instruction. This procedure speeds up
the operation of the DBcc, as a 32-bit decrement and test would take longer than
a 16-bit decrement and test because (for some operations) the 68000 is internally
organized as a 16-bit machine and two operations have to be carried out to
implement a 32-bit operation.

The DBcc instruction is designed for applications in which one of two conditions may terminate a loop. One condition is the loop count in the specified data register, and the other is the condition specified by the test. A typical computer application of DBcc concerns the input of a block of data.

Data is received by an application program and processed as a block of 256 words. If the word $FFFF occurs in the input stream, the processing is terminated. The data to be input is stored in a memory location INPUT by some external device. Another memory location, READY, has its least-significant bit cleared to zero if there is no data in INPUT waiting to be read. If the least-significant bit of READY is true, data can be read from INPUT. The act of reading from INPUT automatically clears the least-significant bit of READY. This behavior corresponds closely to real input mechanisms.

```
           MOVE.W    #255,D1        Set up D1 as a counter with maximum block size 256
WAIT       BTST.B    #0,READY       Test bit 0 of READY
           BEQ.S     WAIT           Repeat test until not zero
           MOVE.W    INPUT,D0       Get input and move it to D0
              ⋮                     }Process input
           CMPI.W    #$FFFF,D0      Test input for terminator
           DBEQ      D1,WAIT        Continue for 256 cycles or until true
```

Note that a mistake is very easy to make with the DBcc instruction! The lower-order word of the data register specified by the DBcc is decremented, as explained earlier. Therefore, this register must be set up by a *word* operation. Sometimes, it is easy to think that a .B operation is sufficient if the loop count is less than 255!

2.6 Miscellaneous Instructions

We now briefly introduce some of the 68000's instructions that do not fall neatly into any of the groups described earlier.

Set byte conditionally   This somewhat unusual instruction is not found in most other microprocessors. The assembly language form is Scc ⟨ea⟩, where cc is one of the fourteen logical tests in table 2.2 and ⟨ea⟩ is an effective address. When Scc is encountered by the 68000, it evaluates the condition specified by cc and, if true, sets all the bits of the byte specified by ⟨ea⟩. If the condition is false, all the bits specified by ⟨ea⟩ are cleared. After Scc ⟨ea⟩ has been executed, the contents of ⟨ea⟩ are, therefore, either $00 or $FF.

The best way of looking at Scc is to regard it as doing the groundwork for a deferred test. Let us suppose that an operation is carried out and we need to note, say, whether the result was positive, for later processing. One way of doing this is as follows.

```
          BSR          GET_DATA        Get input to be tested in D0
          CLR. B       FLAG            Clear FLAG
          TST. L       D0              Test result
          BMI. S       NEXT            If negative then exit with FLAG = 0
          MOVE. B      #$FF, FLAG      Else set all the bits of FLAG
NEXT ...                               Continue
```

In the above example, the longword in D0 returned by GET_DATA is to be tested. If the longword is negative, zero is stored in FLAG; otherwise $FF is stored. This operation requires four instructions. By using Scc we can simplify it to the following:

```
          BSR          GET_DATA        Get input to be tested in D0
          TST. L       D0              Test result
          SPL. B       FLAG            If negative then FLAG = 0
                                       else FLAG = $FF
```

The use of SPL saves two instructions and also requires less time to run than the version of the program using a BMI instruction.

CHK   The CHK instruction has the assembly language form CHK ⟨ea⟩,Dn and checks the lower-order word of data register Dn against two bounds. If Dn(0:15) < 0 or if Dn(0:15) > [ea] then a call to the operating system is made; otherwise the next instruction in sequence is executed. Operating system calls are covered in chapter 6.

NOP   The "no operation" instruction has no effect on the CPU other than to advance the program counter to the next instruction. A NOP wastes time and memory space—time because it must be read from memory, interpreted, and executed, and space because it takes up a word of memory space. Some programmers use a NOP to generate a defined time delay. Others use it to patch a program; they insert several NOPs when writing a program, and, if the program has bugs, they replace the NOPs by a jump to the code that fixes the bug. Of course, we know of such programmers—but this is something we would never ever do ourselves, would we?

RESET   RESET is a privileged instruction that, when executed, forces the 68000's RESET* output to active-low for 124 clock periods. The instruction resets any device connected to the RESET* pin but has no effect on the 68000 itself.

RTE   The return from exception instruction is privileged and is used to terminate an exception handling routine in the same way that an RTS terminates a subroutine call.

STOP   The assembly language form of this instruction is STOP #n, where n is a 16-bit word. When a STOP is encountered, the value of n is loaded into the status register and the processor ceases to execute further instructions. Normal processing continues only when a trace, interrupt, or reset exception occurs. STOP is, of course, a privileged instruction.

TAS   The test and set instruction has the assembly language form TAS ⟨ea⟩ and tests the byte specified by the effective address. If the byte is zero or negative, the N and Z flags of the CCR are set accordingly. The V and C flags are cleared and the X flag is unaffected. Bit 7 (the MSB) of the operand is set to one, that is, [ea(7)] ← 1. This instruction requires a read-modify-write cycle because the operand must first be read to carry out the test and then written to in order to set bit 7. The TAS instruction is indivisible because the read-modify-write cycle is always executed to completion and cannot be interrupted by another processor requesting the bus. The purpose of this instruction is to facilitate the synchronization of processors in a multiprocessor system.

TRAPV   If the overflow bit, V, of the CCR is set, executing a TRAPV instruction causes the TRAPV exception to be raised and a call to the operating system to be made. If V = 0, a TRAPV instruction has no effect other than to advance the PC to the start of the next instruction.

2.7 Subroutines and the 68000

Like almost all microprocessors, the 68000 has an on-chip hardware facility to implement subroutine call and return mechanisms. Such a facility is, of course, based on the CPU's supervisor/user stack (A7). The 68000 has a conventional jump to subroutine (JSR) instruction. Executing JSR ⟨ea⟩ causes the address of the next instruction (i.e., the return address) to be pushed on to the stack pointed at by A7 and a jump to be made to the effective address. The addressing modes supported by JSR are register indirect, register indirect with displacement, indexed, absolute, and program counter relative. Note that register indirect with predecrementing or postincrementing is not permitted! (I leave it to you to work out why the previous sentence ends with an exclamation mark.) Thus, JSR LABEL means jump to the subroutine whose absolute address is given by LABEL and JSR (A3) means jump to the address found in address register A3.

In addition to JSR, the 68000 also offers a BSR (branch to subroutine) instruction. The effects of JSR and BSR are the same; the only difference lies in their addressing modes. BSR uses an 8-bit or a 16-bit displacement following the opcode, which is added to the contents of the program counter to create a relative address. In general, programmers choose BSR rather than JSR because its addressing mode is always program counter relative: the displacement following a BSR does not depend on the location of the program in memory. Consequently, the relative branch provided by BSR makes the design of relocatable and reentrant programs very easy. A reentrant program is one that may be interrupted and used by the interrupting routine without corrupting any of the data required by the first user.

Subroutines are normally terminated by RTS (return from subroutine), which loads the return address into the program counter from the top of the stack.

Occasionally, the programmer may wish to restore the contents of the condition code register to its presubroutine value after returning from the subroutine. Saving the condition code register on the stack before the subroutine call can be achieved by MOVE CCR, −(A7). At the end of the subroutine, the instruction RTR (return and restore condition codes) is executed to pull (pop) the contents of the condition code register and then the program counter off the stack.

The following example illustrates the use of RTR.

```
             BSR       GET_DATA
             :
             :
GET_DATA     MOVE.W    CCR, −(A7)               Save CCR on stack
             MOVEM.L   D1–D7/A0–A6, −(A7)       Save working registers on stack
             :
             :
             MOVEM.L   (A7)+,D1–D7/A0–A6        Restore working registers
             RTR                                Restore CCR and return
```

Summary

In this chapter, we have introduced the 68000's internal architecture, instruction set, and addressing modes. Although the 68000 has some powerful new instructions such as the DBcc, its real power lies in its multiple-length data operations (byte, word, longword), its large and regular array of data and address registers, and its wealth of addressing modes. The addressing modes of the 68000 make it very easy to write position-independent code and to handle the complex data structures associated with today's high level languages.

If we wish to converse with French people in their native language, we must learn French, and that means spending hours learning irregular verbs. Programming in assembly language is very much the same as learning a foreign language: we must learn the instruction set and addressing modes of a microprocessor before we can go on to write programs of any reasonable size. In this chapter we have laid the foundation for chapter 3, in which we examine the writing of assembly language programs, and for chapter 11, in which we present a monitor written in 68000 assembly language.

We have introduced the 68000's internal architecture, its instruction set, and its addressing modes. One of the most important features of the 68000 is its great simplicity. We have discovered that, for example, the 68000 MOVE instruction replaces many of the data transfer instructions peculiar to other microprocessors. Even better, we have found out that the 68000 supports byte, word, and longword operations and that the programmer can use them simply by adding the suffix .B, .W, or .L, respectively, to an instruction. What could be easier? Although we have only hinted at their power here, it is the addressing modes of the 68000 that make it so easy to write complex code in a clear and compact fashion. Moreover, these addressing modes allow us to handle both the complex data structures and the position-independent code required by today's sophisticated microcomputers.

Although we have provided only an overview of the 68000 assembly language, the reader should now be in a position to follow the assembly language monitor that we develop in chapter 11.

Problems

1. For the following memory map, evaluate the following expressions, where [N] means the contents of memory location N. The purpose of this problem is to illustrate the calculation and the meaning of effective addresses. Assume that all addresses are decimal.

For example, [3] = 4.

a. [7]
b. [[4]]
c. [[[0]]]
d. [2 + 10]
e. [[9] + 2]

f. [[9] + [2]]
g. [[5] + [13] + 2*[14]]
h. [0]*3 + [1]*4
i. [9]*[10]

00	12
01	17
02	7
03	4
04	8
05	4
06	4
07	6
08	0
09	5
10	12
11	7
12	6
13	3
14	2

2. Each of the following expressions conforms to the 68000 assembler. Assume that all addresses are byte values, expressed in decimal form, and that [D0] = 0, [A0] = 4, [A1] = 2, [PC] = 10. Using the memory map of problem 1, explain the action of the following instructions:

a. LEA   (A0),A3
b. LEA   −2(A0),A3
c. LEA   12(A0,D0),A3
d. MOVE.B   −2(A0,D0),D4
e. MOVE.B   2,D4

f. MOVE.B   2(PC),D2
g. MOVE.B   1(PC,A1),D7
h. ADD.B   12,D0
i. ADD.B   D0,4(A0,A1)

3. All of the following 68000 assembly language instructions are incorrect. In each case, what is the error?

a.	MOVE.L	D2,A4		n.	UNLK	D6
b.	EOR.W	(A2)+,D4		o.	ANDI	D4,D5
c.	ADDQ.L	#12,D2		p.	ASL.L	#9,D3
d.	MOVEA.B	#4,A3		q.	BRA.B	2741
e.	ADDQ.B	#0,A4		r.	EOR	(A3),D4
f.	ANDI.B	#FC,D6		s.	DIVU.B	D4,D5
g.	LEA	(A3)+,A4		t.	LEA.B	#4,A3
h.	LEA	(A3),D3		u.	NOT.W	D3,D7
i.	MOVEA.L	A4,D7		v.	RTS.B	D3
j.	MOVEP.L	#7,D6		w.	DIVU.W	D3,A4
k.	MOVE.B	D2,12(PC)		x.	CLR.L	A2
l.	SWAP	A4		y.	CMPM.B	(A3)+,(A4)
m.	EXG.B	D3,A4		z.	MOVEQ.B	#$42,D7

4. Describe the operation of the stack pointed at by A7. In which direction does it grow as items are pushed onto the stack?

5. Write a program to input a sequence of bytes and store them sequentially in memory, starting at location $00 2000. The sequence is to be terminated by a null byte, $00. Then print the even numbers in this sequence. Assume that an input routine, IN_CHAR at $F0 0000, inputs a byte into D0 and that OUT_CHAR at $F0 0004 outputs a byte in D0.

6. Write a subroutine to sort an array of N 8-bit elements into descending order. On entry to the subroutine, A2 contains the first (i.e., lowest) address of the array and D1 contains the size of the array (i.e., number of bytes).

7. Explain the meaning and significance of each of the following terms:
  a. Position-independent code (PIC)
  b. Self-modifying code
  c. Reentrant code

8. A memory-mapped VDT displays the 1024, 8-bit characters starting at $00 F000 on a CRT terminal as 16 lines of 64 characters. The address of the top left-hand character is $00 F000 and the address of the bottom right-hand character is $00 F3FF.

   Design a subroutine to display the ASCII character in D0 in the next free position of the display. A cursor made up of a row count and a column count points to the next free position into which a character is to be written. As each character is received, it is placed in the next column to the right of the current column counter.

   Certain characters affect the position of the cursor without adding a new character to the display. These characters are as follows:

Carriage return	(ASCII $0D)	Move the cursor to the leftmost position on the current row.
Line feed	(ASCII $0A)	Move the cursor to the same column position on the next row.
Back space	(ASCII $08)	Move cursor back one space left.
Space	(ASCII $20)	Code for space character.

When the cursor is positioned on the bottom line of the display, a line feed causes all lines to move up one row (i.e., scroll up). This action creates a new, clear, bottom line and causes the previous top line to be lost.

Construct a subroutine to implement the above memory-mapped display. On entry to the subroutine, A0 points to the current row position and A1 to the column position.

9. Design a cross-assembler for the hypothetical UNIFORM1 microprocessor to run on the 68000. Test the cross-assembler by assembling a UNIFORM1 program both by hand and by means of your cross-assembler.

The syntax of UNIFORM1 is

OPERATION ⟨ea⟩
OPERATION ⟨ea⟩, Ri

where OPERATION is the operation to be carried out, ⟨ea⟩ is an effective address, Ri is one of eight registers, and ⟨address⟩ is a 16-bit address. The structure of an instruction in UNIFORM1 is

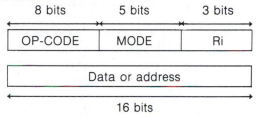

Valid registers are: R0, R1, ... , R7.
Valid addressing modes are

OPERATION	(Rj),Ri	Indexed addressing, modes 0 to 7
OPERATION	#⟨data⟩,Ri	Literal addressing, mode = 8
OPERATION	⟨address⟩,Ri	Absolute addressing, mode = 9
OPERATION	⟨address⟩	Jump, mode = 10
OPERATION	Rj,Ri	Register to register, modes 11 to 18
OPERATION	Ri	Monadic operation on Ri, mode 19
OPERATION	⟨address⟩	Monadic operation on memory, mode 20

The instructions and their op-codes provided by UNIFORM1 are

ADD	$00	CLR	$09
AND	$01	CMP	$0A
ASL	$02	LSL	$0B
ASR	$03	LSR	$0C
BEQ	$04	MOVE	$0D
BNE	$05	NEG	$0E
BCC	$06	OR	$0F
BCS	$07	SUB	$10
BRA	$08		

Chapter 3

Program Design

An engineer armed only with a knowledge of a microprocessor's assembly language would probably design rather poor programs. In this chapter we look at five of the ingredients of good program design: (1) top-down design, (2) modularity, (3) structured programming, (4) testability, and (5) recoverability. An appreciation of these topics allows us to design programs that are both large and reliable. All of these topics are relevant to the design of both assembly language and high level language programs. Indeed, I would argue that these topics are equally relevant to the design of hardware.

One of the greatest difficulties facing the writer of assembly language programs is knowing where to begin. In the second part of this chapter we introduce the program design language (PDL), which is a form of high level language that allows us to express a program algorithmically before we begin to code it into assembly language. We illustrate the application of PDL by providing two worked examples.

A few years ago a friend described the newly emerged microprocessor as "the last bastion of the amateur." He meant that although computer technology (both hardware and software) had come a long way by the mid 1970s, leaving little room in the industry for a sloppy or nonprofessional approach, the microprocessor soon changed that situation. Its very low cost brought it to anyone who wanted to investigate its properties. Therefore people with little or no formal training or experience were using and programming microcomputers. Moreover, the tiny memories available in the 1970s and the lack of development tools forced many people to write programs in assembly language and to develop bad habits such as spaghetti programming. Some were even forced to write programs in hexadecimal machine code form.

Today, the status quo of the 1970s has been resumed and a professional approach to software design for microprocessors is the rule rather than the exception. It is no longer acceptable to throw together assembly language programs. This situation is not because of fashions in programming or sheer snobbishness, but because of the poor results that follow from a blind approach to programming in which the programmer attempts to solve a problem by immediately attempting to code it.

Few people would now argue that there is any intrinsic merit in programming in assembly language. Programmers use it when they do not have a compiler that produces efficient machine code from a high level language. I am including this section on programming in 68000 assembly language because some students may not have a development system that generates 68000 machine code from a high level language. Most students will, however, have access to a system with a 68000 assembler.

In the final part of the chapter we look at the way in which an assembly language program can be constructed by means of a program design language (PDL). A PDL allows a programmer to take advantage of the program design techniques outlined in this chapter. Two examples of program design using PDL are presented.

3.1 Top-Down design

Top-down design or "programming by stepwise refinement" offers a method of handling large and complex programs by decomposing them into more tractable components. Top-down design is an iterative process that seeks to separate the goals of program design from the means of achievement. In other words, we must first decide what we want to do and later think about how to do it. A task is initially expressed in terms of a number of subtasks. Each of these subtasks is, in turn, broken down into further subtasks. Figure 3.1 illustrates this point. At the

FIGURE 3.1   Illustrating top-down design

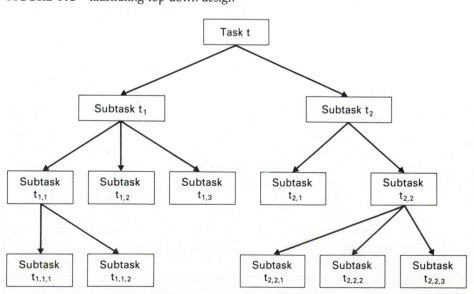

FIGURE 3.2   Example of top-down decomposition

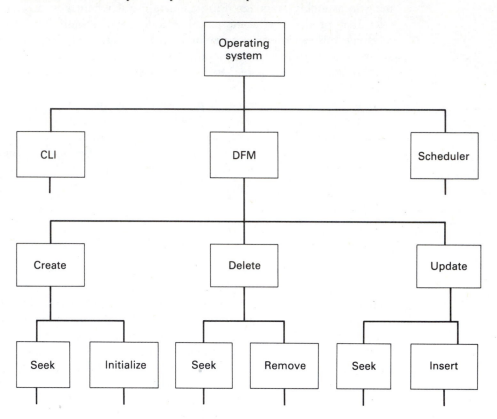

NOTE: For clarity, this diagram is not fully elaborated.

top of figure 3.1 (the highest level of abstraction) is a statement of the problem to be solved. The solution may be broken down into two separate actions, t_1 and t_2. At this level no details about the implementation of these subtasks need be considered. In turn, subtask t_1 may be divided into three further subtasks, $t_{1,1}$, $t_{1,2}$, and $t_{1,3}$. This process is repeated until each subtask has been fully elaborated and is expressed in terms of the most primitive actions available to the designer. Generally speaking, the lowest level of a task is, according to Shooman, "... small enough to grasp mentally and to code at one sitting in a straightforward and uncomplicated manner."

Figure 3.2 shows how this approach can be applied to the design of a disk operating system. The problem has, initially, been split up by a functional decomposition in which each of the subtasks carry out a well-defined function. At the highest level of task definition, the operating system is split into three basic subtasks: a command interpreter, a task scheduler, and a disk file manager (DFM).

Consider the DFM, which can itself be broken down into a number of operations on the data structures stored on the disk, and so on. This approach groups together relevant operations and their associated data at specific levels, and attempts to stop irrelevant detail obscuring the action at a particular level. Thus, the operating system's file utilities manipulate only entire files; they are not interested in the actual organization and structure of the files. These functions belong to the DFM. Equally, the DFM is concerned only with operations on individual records; it relegates any operations involving the disk drive itself to lower level software. An advantage of this approach is that each subtask can be validated independently of its own subtasks. Generally, a program no longer has to be tested as a single entity and its individual components, the subtasks, can be tested independently just like their hardware equivalents. Note that in figure 3.2 some of the subtasks appear several times; for example, the create, delete, and update subtasks each require the same lower level subtask (i.e., seek).

One popular approach to program construction is called "top-down design and bottom-up coding." With this approach the problem is decomposed into levels of abstraction (top-down design), but the system is implemented by coding the lowest levels first (bottom-up coding); for example, when a word processor is coded, the elements dealing with the basic input/output of characters are dealt with first, then the elements that format the input/output, and so on.

System Specification

Before a system can be designed, it must be specified. The specification of a system is a statement of the goals that it must achieve. By setting goals, the specifier of the system gives the designer a method of objectively assessing any system he or she creates. Sometimes the specification can be related to an international standard; for example, a personal computer might have a "serial interface" or a "serial interface conforming to the EIA RS232C standard." In the latter case a copy of the specification can be obtained by the buyer to verify the operation of the system.

A tightly specified system is generally more reliable than a loosely specified system because a tight specification covers all possible eventualities (i.e., operating and input conditions). A loosely specified system may fail if certain input conditions have not been catered for; for example, a command in a machine code debugger may be designed to display the contents of memory location Address_1 through location Address_2. A poorly designed program would start by displaying the contents of Address_1, Address_1 + 1, and so on. A tightly specified system would first check that Address_1 was less than Address_2.

In addition to defining design goals, a helpful procedure is to define "nongoals." In other words, as well as defining what a system should do, we should also state what the system does not attempt to achieve. This action does not mean that obvious nongoals need be stated: there is little point in saying that a personal computer is not intended to fry eggs! A nongoal provides the system with explicit limitations that might otherwise be unclear; for example, a designer may state that security is a nongoal of an interface to store data on a floppy disk. This situation means that the data on the disk is not encrypted and can be read by any other interface without undergoing a decryption process. However, such a process does not mean that the user cannot suitably encrypt the source data before it is presented to the interface for recording on the disk.

3.2 Modular Design

One of the most significant features of modern electronic systems is their modularity. A complex circuit is invariably decomposed into several less complex subsystems, called *modules*. The advantage of such an approach is that the modules can be designed and tested independently of the parent system. A module made by one manufacturer can be replaced by one from another manufacturer, as long as the two modules have the same interface to the rest of the system and are functionally equivalent. In the world of software, modularity is an attempt to treat software like hardware by creating software elements, called modules. The principal requirement of a software module is that it is concerned only with a single, logically coherent task. For example, sin x can be considered as a module—it takes an input, x, and returns a result. It performs a single function and is "logically coherent" because it carries out only those actions necessary to calculate sin x. A module is not just an arbitrary segment of a larger program. An old story is told about the dark ages of programming when a programmer was asked to introduce modularity into his programs. He took a ruler and drew a line after every 75 statements. Those lines were his modules!

A software module is analogous to a hardware element because it has a number of inputs and a number of outputs and can be "plugged into a system." The module processes incoming information to yield one or more outputs. The internal operation of the module is both irrelevant to and hidden from its user, just as the transport properties of electrons in a semiconductor are irrelevant to the programmer of a microprocessor. The advantages of software modules are broadly the same as those of hardware modules. Modules can be tested and verified independently of the parent system and they can be supplied by manufacturers who know little or nothing about the parent system. Figure 3.3 illustrates the concept of a module.

The disk file monitor (DFM), introduced when we were describing top-down design, can be regarded as such a module. It is entered at one point with details of the action to be carried out passed as a parameter to the module. A return is made from the module to its calling point with parameters passed back as appropriate. It is no more reasonable to enter a module at some other point than it is to drill a hole in a floppy disk controller and to attach a wire to the silicon chip. Indeed, the

FIGURE 3.3   Module

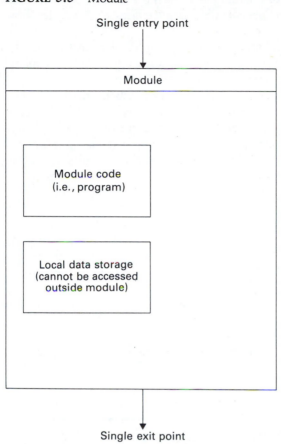

whole point of modular design is to make the design, production, and testing of hardware and software almost identical; for example, the module for sin x takes an input and generates an output, sin x, together with relevant status information. Passing information to the inner working of sin x or getting information from within sin x is quite meaningless to higher level modules.

Module Coupling and Module Strength

A module is sometimes described in terms of two properties: "coupling" and "strength." Coupling, as its name suggests, indicates how information is shared between one module and other modules. Tightly coupled modules share common data areas. This situation is regarded as undesirable because it makes it harder to isolate the action of one module from the action of other modules. We can liken this to a man with pneumonia and liver disease: if he dies, how do you know which illness was the cause?

A module exhibiting loose coupling has data that is entirely independent of other modules. Any data it accesses is strictly private to the module and does not interact with other modules. This condition makes it easier to debug systems because the programmer knows that data associated with a module is not modified by other modules. Therefore, errors can be speedily localized.

The strength of a module is a measure of its "modularity." In the above story about the programmer who divided a program up into units of 75 lines, the resulting modularity is very weak because the modules are entirely arbitrary and functions are distributed between modules in a random fashion.

A strong module is one that performs a single task; for example, the sin x module discussed previously is strong because it does nothing more than calculate the sine of an input x. A weak module performs more than one task; for example, a module dealing with input from the keyboard, a disk drive, and a serial interface is relatively weak. It is a module in the sense that it performs logically related functions (i.e., input), but it is weak because several functions have been grouped together in one module.

The strength of a module is important, because strong modules are relatively easy to test as they perform only one function. Equally, a strong module from one supplier is not difficult to replace with a functionally equivalent module from another supplier. A weak module carries out several tasks, making it more difficult to test.

Passing Parameters to Modules

A module implemented as a subroutine must transfer information between the subroutine and the program calling it. The only exception occurs when a subroutine is called to trigger some event; for example, a subroutine can be designed to ring a bell or to sound an alarm. Simply calling the subroutine causes the predetermined action to take place. No communication exists between the subroutine and the program calling it.

Consider now the application of subroutines to inputting or outputting data. Obtaining a character from a keyboard or transferring one to a CRT terminal requires the execution of a number of actions and is inherently device dependent. Consequently, input and output transactions are frequently implemented by calling the appropriate input or output subroutine.

Suppose a program invokes the subroutine PUT_CHAR in order to display a single character on the CRT terminal. The character is printed by executing the instruction BSR PUT_CHAR and the whole process takes place automatically, due to the processor's stack mechanism, which takes care of the return address. In this example, the program has to transfer just one item of information to the subroutine, namely, the character to be displayed.

In this case, where only a single character is passed to the subroutine, one of the eight data registers serves as a handy vehicle to transfer the information from the calling program to the subroutine; for example, if the character to be displayed is in register D7 and register D0 is used to carry the character to the subroutine, the following code may be written:

```
MOVE.B     D7,D0
BSR        PUT_CHAR
```

The preceding method of transferring data between a program and a subroutine by means of one or more registers is popular and is frequently used where the quantity of data to be transferred is very small or the processor is well endowed with registers. The advantage of this method is that it permits both position-independent code and reentrancy. Position independence is guaranteed because no absolute memory location is involved in the transfer of data and reentrancy is possible as long as the reuse of the subroutine saves the registers employed to transfer the data before they are reused.

The only disadvantage in passing information to and from subroutines via registers is that it reduces the number of registers available for use by the programmer. Moreover, the quantity of information that can be transferred is limited by the number of registers. In the case of the 68000, it is theoretically possible to transfer up to fifteen longwords of data in this way. This total is made up of eight data registers and seven address registers. Address register A7, the stack pointer, cannot itself be used to transfer data.

Mechanisms for Parameter Passing

At this point it is worthwhile mentioning a number of concepts relevant to parameter passing. We need to distinguish between the ways in which parameters are passed and their implementation. The two basic ways of passing parameters are: transfer by value and transfer by reference. In the former, the actual parameter is transferred, while in the latter, the address of the parameter is passed between program and subroutine. This distinction is important because it affects the way in which parameters are handled. When passed by value, the subroutine receives a copy of the parameter. Therefore, if the parameter is modified by the subroutine, the "new value" does not affect the "old value" of the parameter elsewhere in the program. In other words, passing a parameter by value causes the parameter to be cloned and the clone to be used by the subroutine. The clone never returns from the subroutine.

When a parameter is passed by address (i.e., by reference), the subroutine receives a pointer to the parameter. In this case, only one copy of the parameter exists and the subroutine is able to access this unique value because it knows the address of the parameter. If the subroutine modifies the parameter, it is modified globally and not only within the subroutine.

The mechanism by which information is passed to subroutines generally falls into one of three categories: a register, a memory location, or the stack. We have already seen how a register is used to transfer an actual value. A region of memory can be treated as a mailbox and used by both the calling program and subroutine, with one placing data in the mailbox and the other emptying it. However, the stack mechanism offers the most convenient method of transferring information between a subroutine and its calling program.

Passing Parameters by Reference (*i.e., Address*)

Suppose a subroutine is written to search a region of memory containing text for the first occurrence of a particular sequence of characters. The sequence we are looking for is stored as a string in another region of memory. In this example, the subroutine requires four pieces of information: the starting and ending addresses of both the region to be searched and the string to be used in the matching process. Figure 3.4 illustrates this problem.

The information required by the subroutine is the four addresses, $00\ 1000$, $00\ 100D$, $00\ 1100$, and $00\ 1103$. Note that we are passing the parameters by

FIGURE 3.4   Memory map of the string-matching problem

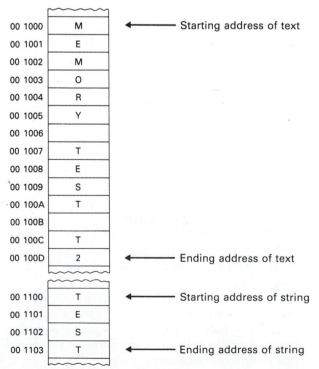

FIGURE 3.5   Passing a block of parameters by their address

00 2000	0000 1000
00 2004	0000 100D
00 2008	0000 1100
00 200C	0000 1103

All that the subroutine needs is
the starting address of the block
of parameters, that is, $00 2000.

reference, because the subroutine receives their addresses; we are not passing the actual parameters (i.e., the text strings) themselves. Eventually, the subroutine returns the value $00 1007. Although it is possible to transfer all these addresses via registers, an alternative technique is to assemble the four parameters into a block somewhere in memory and then pass the address of this block. Figure 3.5 shows how the block is arranged.

The only information required by the subroutine is the address $00 2000, which points to the first item in the block of parameters stored in memory. The following fragment of code shows how the subroutine is called and how the subroutine deals with the information passed to it. In this example, A0 is used to pass the address of the parameter block to the subroutine and A3, A4, A5, and A6 are used by the subroutine to point to the beginning and end of the text and of the string to be matched.

```
        LEA.L     $002000,A0      Set up address of parameter block in A0
        BSR       MATCH           Call string matching subroutine


        .
        .
        .


MATCH   MOVEM.L   A3–A6, – (SP)   Save address registers on stack
        MOVEA.L   (A0) + ,A3      Put starting address of text in A3
        MOVEA.L   (A0) + ,A4      Put ending address of text in A4
        MOVEA.L   (A0) + ,A5      Put starting address of string in A5
        MOVEA.L   (A0) + ,A6      Put ending address of string in A6


        .
        .                         Body of subroutine
        .


        MOVEM.L   (SP) + ,A3–A6   Restore address registers from stack
        RTS
```

In the preceding example, A0 is used as a pointer to the parameter block to obtain the four addresses required by the subroutine. We have passed a parameter by its address (i.e., the address of the parameter block) and have transferred this address in a register (A0). Unfortunately, this method of storing information in a block whose location is fixed in memory cannot always be employed because such a program cannot be used reentrantly. Clearly, if the parameters are stored in a block with a fixed address (i.e., static memory location), any attempt to interrupt the subroutine and to reuse it must result in the parameters being overwritten by new values. A much better approach is to use the stack to pass parameters or pointers to parameters. In this case, if the subroutine is interrupted, the new parameters are pushed onto the stack on top of the old parameters. When the interrupting program has used the subroutine, a return from interrupt is made with the stack in the same condition it was in immediately prior to the interrupt. Chapter 6 deals with interrupts in more detail.

Stack and Parameter Passing

The stack is not only useful for storing subroutine return addresses in such a way that subroutines may call further subroutines but it can also be used to transfer information to and from a subroutine. All that needs to be done is to push the parameters (or their addresses) on the stack before calling the subroutine. The following program fragment shows how this is done for our string-matching algorithm. In this example, we transfer all parameters by reference.

```
              PEA.L     TEXT_START       Push text starting address
              PEA.L     TEXT_END         Push text ending address
              PEA.L     STRING_START     Push string starting address
              PEA.L     STRING_END       Push string ending address
              BSR       STRING_MATCH     Call subroutine for matching
              LEA.L     16(SP),SP        Adjust stack pointer
                .
                .
                .
STRING_MATCH  LEA.L     4(SP),A0         Put pointer to parameters in A0
              MOVEM.L   A3–A6,–(SP)      Save working registers on stack
              MOVEM.L   (A0)+,A3–A6      Get parameters off stack
                .
                .                        } Body of subroutine
                .
              MOVEM.L   (SP)+,A3–A6      Restore working registers
              RTS
```

   In this example, the instruction PEA (push effective address) pushes the effective address of the operands onto the stack, but instead I could have used MOVE.L #TEXT_START,–(SP). The first instruction in the subroutine, LEA.L 4(SP),A0, loads A0 with the starting address of the last parameter pushed onto the stack. We must add 4 to the stack pointer because the return address is at the top of the stack. The instruction MOVEM.L (A0)+,A3–A6 pulls the four addresses off the stack pointed at by A0 and deposits them in address registers

A3 to A6 for use as required. Note that these parameters are left on the stack pointed at by SP after a return from the subroutine is executed.

In the calling program, the instruction LEA 16(SP),SP is executed after a return from the subroutine has been made. This instruction replaces the contents of the stack pointer with the contents of the stack pointer plus 16. Consequently, the stack pointer is restored to the position it was in before the four 32-bit parameters were pushed onto it.

As we have already pointed out, passing parameters on the stack facilitates position-independent code and permits reentrant programming. If a subroutine is interrupted, the stack builds upward and information currently on the stack is not overwritten.

Stack and Local Variables

In addition to the parameters passed between itself and the calling program, most subroutines need a certain amount of "local workspace" for their temporary variables. The word "local" means that the workspace is private to the subroutine and is never accessed by the calling program or other subroutines. In a few circumstances, it is quite feasible to allocate a region of the system's memory space to a subroutine requiring a work area at the time the program is written. The programmer simply reserves fixed locations for the subroutine's variables in a process called *static allocation*. This process is entirely satisfactory for subroutines that are not going to be used reentrantly or recursively.

If a subroutine is to be made reentrant or is to be used recursively, its local variables must be bound up not only with the subroutine itself but with the occasion of its use. In other words, each time the subroutine is called, a new workspace must be assigned to it. Once again, the stack provides a convenient mechanism for implementing the dynamic allocation of workspace.

Closely associated with dynamic storage techniques for subroutines are the *stack frame* (SF) and the *frame pointer* (FP). The stack frame is a region of temporary storage at the top of the current stack. Figure 3.6 illustrates a stack frame.

Figure 3.6 shows how a stack frame is created merely by moving the stack pointer up by d locations. This can be done at the start of a subroutine. Note that the 68000 stack grows toward the low end of memory and therefore the stack pointer is decremented. Reserving one hundred words of memory is achieved by LEA −200(SP),SP. Once the stack frame has been created, local variables are accessed by any addressing mode which uses A7 as a pointer. Before a return from the subroutine is made, the stack frame must be collapsed by LEA 200(SP),SP.

Link and Unlink Instructions

The simple scheme of figure 3.6 has been mechanized in the 68000 by a complementary pair of instructions, LINK and UNLK. These are relatively complex in

FIGURE 3.6   Stack frame

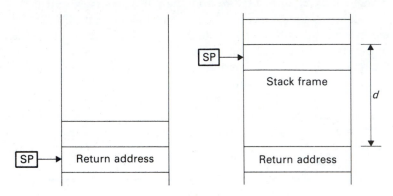

(a) The stack immediately after   (b) The allocation of a stack
    a subroutine call   frame by a subroutine

terms of their detailed implementation, but are conceptually simple. The great advantage of LINK and UNLK is their ability to let the 68000 manage the stack automatically and to make the memory allocation scheme entirely reentrant.

If the stack frame storage mechanism is to support reentrant programming, a new stack frame must be reserved each time a subroutine is called. As each successive stack frame is of a (possibly) variable size, its length must be preserved somewhere. The 68000 uses an address register for this purpose. In the following description of LINK and UNLK, a 16-bit signed constant, d, represents the size of the stack frame. At the start of a subroutine, the registers that must be saved are first pushed on the stack and then the LINK instruction is executed to create the stack frame belonging to *this* subroutine. The following code achieves the desired effect:

```
MOVEM.L   D0–D7/A3–A6,–(SP)   Save working registers on the stack
LINK      A1,#–64             Allocate 64 bytes (16 longwords)
                              of storage on this stack frame
```

In this example, all working registers are saved on the stack, the temporary storage allocation is 64 bytes, and address register A1 is used by LINK. Note that the minus sign is needed because the stack grows toward low memory. The action executed by LINK A1, # −64 is defined in RTL terms as follows:

```
LINK:   [SP]     ← [SP] − 4    Decrement the stack pointer by 4
        [M[SP]] ← [A1]         Push the contents of address register A1
        [A1]     ← [SP]        Save stack pointer in A1
        [SP]     ← [SP] − 64   Move stack pointer up by 64 locations
```

Note that the old contents of A1 are not destroyed by this action: they are pushed on the stack. Similarly, the old value of the stack pointer is preserved in

FIGURE 3.7   Effect of a LINK instruction on the stack

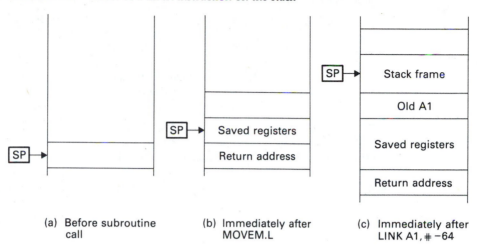

(a) Before subroutine
     call

(b) Immediately after
     MOVEM.L

(c) Immediately after
     LINK A1, # −64

A1. In other words, the LINK destroys no information and, therefore, it is possible to undo the effect of a LINK at some later time. The state of the stack before a subroutine call, after the call and the MOVEM operation, and after a LINK instruction is given in figure 3.7.

After stage (c) in figure 3.7, the stack frame area can be used as required by the programmer; for example, LEA (SP),A2 loads the first free address of the frame into address register A2 and then A2 can be used as an offset in all references to the stack frame. Equally, all data references can be made with respect to the stack pointer. Events become interesting when the subroutine calls another subroutine with its own stack frame. Figure 3.8 depicts this situation.

In figure 3.8 at the initial state (a), subroutine 1 is being executed and has its own stack frame, labeled "Stack frame 1." Let us suppose that a second subroutine is invoked and another LINK A1, # −d executed. The second stack frame can be of any size and is not necessarily related to stack frame 1. This situation is illustrated in figure 3.8 at state (b). Register A1 now contains the value of the stack pointer immediately before the creation of stack frame 2; that is, A1 points to the location of the "old A1." The "old A1" is, of course, a pointer to the base of subroutine 1's stack frame, which holds the "old old A1." Because A1 points to the base (i.e., highest address) of the stack frame, all local variables can be accessed by register indirect addressing with displacement, where A1 is the register used to access them.

The next step is to show how an orderly return from subroutine 2 to subroutine 1 can be made. At the end of subroutine 2, the following sequence is executed:

```
UNLK      A1                      Deallocate subroutine 2's stack frame
MOVEM.L   (SP) + ,D0–D7/A3–A6    Restore working registers from the stack
RTS                               Return to calling point
```

The RTL definition of UNLK A1 is

UNLK: [SP] ← [A1]
        [A1] ← [M[SP]]
        [SP] ← [SP] + 4

We can put this definition more clearly by stating that the stack pointer is first loaded with the contents of address register A1. Remember that A1 contains the value of the stack pointer just before stack frame 2 was created. In this way, stack frame 2 collapses. The next step is to pop the top item off the stack and place it in A1. This process has two effects: it returns both the stack and the contents of A1 to the points where they were located before LINK was executed.

Following the UNLK, the working registers can be pulled off the stack and a return to subroutine 1 made. The execution of subroutine 1 continues from the point at which it left off.

The key to LINK and UNLK is the use of A1 to hold the base of the stack

FIGURE 3.8   Effect of a second call on the stack

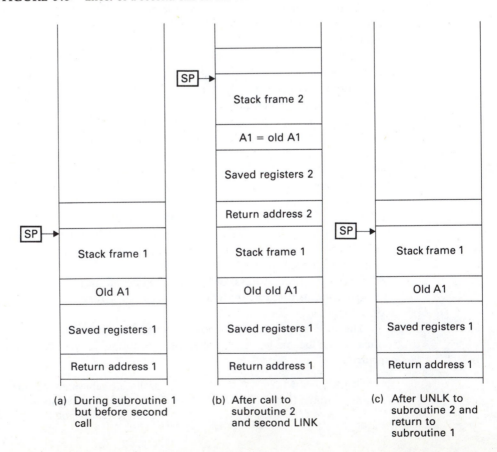

(a) During subroutine 1 but before second call

(b) After call to subroutine 2 and second LINK

(c) After UNLK to subroutine 2 and return to subroutine 1

frame and the storage of the *previous* contents of A1 below the base of the stack frame. The LINK and UNLK instructions have been included to support recursive procedures. A recursive procedure is one that calls itself.

3.3 *Structured Programming*

Structured programming offers a semiformal method of writing programs and avoids the ad hoc methods of program design in widespread use before the late 1960s. The purpose of structured programming is threefold: it improves programmer productivity, it makes the resulting programs easier to read, and it yields more reliable programs. Essentially, structured programming techniques start from the axiom that all programs can be constructed from three fundamental components: the sequence, a generalized looping mechanism, and a decision mechanism. The rise of structured programming is largely attributed to the overenthusiastic use of the GOTO (i.e., JMP) by programmers in the 1960s. A program with many GOTOs provides a messy flow of control, making it very difficult to understand or to debug.

The *sequence* consists of a linear list of actions that are executed in order, one by one. If the sequence is P1, P2, P3, P1 is executed first, then P2, and then P3. The actions represented by P1, and so on, may be single operations or processes. The *process* is similar to the module described previously and has only one entry point and one exit point. Indeed, this very "process" is the one that is expanded into subtasks during top-down design.

The looping mechanism permits a sequence to be carried out a number of times. In many high level languages, the looping mechanism takes the form DO_WHILE or REPEAT_UNTIL. The decision mechanism, which often surfaces as the IF_THEN_ELSE construct, allows one of two courses of action to be chosen, depending on the value of a test variable. By combining these three elements, any program can be constructed without using the GOTO statement.

Note that the pendulum has swung back a little way, and a few people now consider the total banishment of the GOTO to be a little unwise. Sometimes, in small doses, it can be used to good effect to produce a more elegant program than would otherwise result from keeping rigidly to the philosophy of structured programming.

Because of the importance of the decision and the loop mechanisms in structured programming, we will examine their form in high level language and show how they can be implemented in assembly language.

Conditional Structure

The ability of a computer to make decisions can be called *conditional behavior*. As well as showing how the 68000 implements conditional behavior, it is a worthwhile exercise to demonstrate how such behavior appears in high level languages. Consider two entities, L and S. L is a logical expression yielding a single logical value which may be true or false. S is a statement that causes some action to be carried out. In what follows, the term conditional behavior is called control action, the most primitive form of which is expressed as

IF L THEN S.

The logical expression L is evaluated and, if true, S is carried out. If L is false, S is not carried out and the next action following this control action is executed. For example, consider the expression IF INPUT_1 > INPUT_2 THEN OUTPUT = 4. If, say, INPUT_1 = 5 and INPUT_2 = 3, the logical expression is true and OUTPUT is made equal to 4.

A more useful form of the above control action is expressed as

IF L THEN S1 ELSE S2.

Here S1 and S2 are alternative statements. If L is true, then S1 is carried out; otherwise S2 is carried out. There are not circumstances where neither S1 nor S2, or both S1 and S2, may be carried out. Figure 3.9 illustrates the construct in diagrammatic form. For example, now consider the expression IF INPUT_1 > INPUT_2 THEN OUTPUT = 4 ELSE OUTPUT = 7. In this case, if INPUT_1 is greater than INPUT_2, OUTPUT is made equal to 4. Otherwise it is made equal to 7.

The IF L THEN S1 ELSE S2 control action can be extended to a more general form in which one of a number of possible statements, S1, S2, ..., Sn, is executed. As the logical expression L yields only a two-valued result, an expression generating an integer value must be used to effect the choice between

FIGURE 3.9   IF L THEN S1 ELSE S2 construct

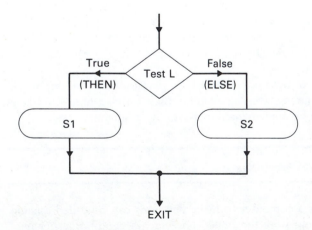

FIGURE 3.10 CASE construct

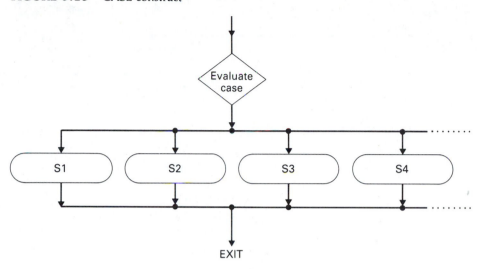

S1, S2, ..., Sn. The multiple-choice control action is called a CASE statement in Pascal or a SELECT statement in some versions of BASIC. Here we use the term CASE statement, which is written:

```
CASE I OF
I1:   S1
I2:   S2
 :    :
 :    :
In:   Sn
END
```

The integer expression I is evaluated and, if it is equal to Ii, statement Si is executed. All statements Sj, where j ≠ i, are ignored. Note that if I does not yield a value in the range I1 to In, an error may be flagged by the operating system. In some high level languages, an exception is raised that provides an alternative course of action called an *exception*. Figure 3.10 illustrates the CASE statement.

In addition to the IF and the CASE statements, all high level languages include a looping mechanism that permits the repeated execution of a statement S. There are four basic variants of the looping mechanism:

1. DO S FOREVER. Here statement S is repeated forever. As forever is an awfully long time, S must contain some way of abandoning or exiting the loop. Typically, an IF L THEN EXIT mechanism can be used to leave the loop. EXIT is a label that identifies a statement outside the loop. Strictly speaking, the IF ... THEN EXIT conditional behavior does not conform to the philosophy of structured programming. However, life without it can be very difficult.

FIGURE 3.11   WHILE construct

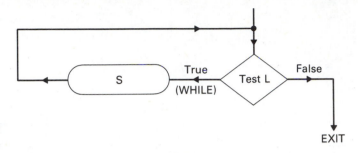

2.   FOR I := N1 TO N2 DO S. In this case, the control variable I is given the successive integer values N1, N1 + 1, ..., N2, and statement S is executed once for each of the N2 − N1 + 1 values of I. This variant is the most conventional form of looping mechanism and is found in most high level languages. Some programmers avoid this construct, as it leads to apparent ambiguity if N1 = N2 or if N1 > N2. In practice, high level languages define exactly what does happen when N1 > N2—but they do not all do the same thing!

3.   WHILE L DO S. Whenever a WHILE construct is executed, the logical expression L is first evaluated and, if it yields a true value, the statement S is carried out. Then the WHILE construct is repeated. If, however, L is false, statement S is not carried out and the WHILE construct is not repeated. Figure 3.11 illustrates the action of a WHILE construct.

4.   REPEAT S UNTIL L. The statement S is first carried out and then the logical expression L is evaluated. If L is true, the next statement following REPEAT ... UNTIL L is carried out. If L is false, statement S is repeated. The difference between the control actions of REPEAT ... UNTIL and

FIGURE 3.12   REPEAT ... UNTIL construct

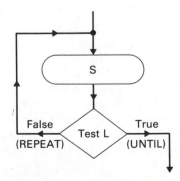

WHILE ... DO is that the former causes S to be executed at least once and continues until L is true, while the latter tests L first and then executes S only if L is true. In other words, the REPEAT ... UNTIL tests the logical expression after executing S, whereas the WHILE ... DO tests the logical expression before executing S. Furthermore, REPEAT ... UNTIL terminates when L is true, but WHILE ... DO terminates when L is false. Figure 3.12 illustrates the REPEAT ... UNTIL statement.

Implementing Conditional Expressions in Assembly Language

All of the preceding high level constructs can readily be translated into assembly language form. In the following examples, the logical value to be tested is in register D0 and is either 1 (true) or 0 (false). The action to be carried out is represented simply by S and consists of any sequence of actions.

```
*               IF L THEN S
*
                TST.B       D0              Test the lower-order byte of D0
                BEQ.S       EXIT            If zero then exit, else continue
                S                           Action S
EXIT
```

```
*****************************************************************

*               IF L THEN S1 ELSE S2
*
                TST.B       D0              Test the lower-order byte of D0
                BEQ.S       ELSE            If zero then S2 (ELSE part)
                S1                          If not zero then S1
                BRA.S       EXIT            Skip past ELSE part
ELSE            S2                          Action S2 (ELSE part)
                :
EXIT
```

```
*****************************************************************

*               FOR I = N1 TO N2
*
                MOVE.B      #N1,D0          D0 is the loop counter
NEXT            S                           Action S (body of loop)
                ADDQ.B      #1,D0           Increment loop counter
                CMP.B       #N2+1,D0        Test for end of loop
                BNE         NEXT            Repeat until counter = N2 + 1
EXIT
```

```
*****************************************************************
```

```
*              WHILE L DO S
*
REPEAT   TST.B      D0          Test the lower-order byte of D0
         BEQ.S      EXIT        If zero then quit loop
         S                      Body of loop (action S)
         BRA        REPEAT      Repeat
EXIT
```

```
**************************************************************
```

```
*              REPEAT S UNTIL L
*
NEXT     S                      Body of loop (action S)
         TST.B      D0          Test the lower-order byte of D0
         BEQ        NEXT        Repeat until true
EXIT
```

```
**************************************************************
```

3.4 Testability

In an ideal world where all stories have a happy ending and toast invariably falls buttered-side upward, design for testability would not be needed. Unfortunately, real-world components sometimes fail, circuits are incorrectly assembled, and the tracks on printed circuit boards break or become shorted together. Therefore, although a microcomputer may have been well designed, when finished it may sit miserably on the bench refusing to do anything.

Manufacturers of microcomputers must test their products. The amount of effort put into testing depends on the application for which the computer is intended and the economics of the situation. A manufacturer churning out ultra low cost microcomputers may perform minimal testing and offer a free replacement policy, as the cheaper alternative may be to replace (say) 1 percent of the computers than to fully test all of them. However, the designer of an automatic landing system for a large jet has to deliver a reliable product; simply letting the consumers do their own testing in the field might have unfortunate consequences.

Design for testability is as important for software components as for hardware elements. The designers of electronic hardware approach testability by providing test points at which the value of a signal can be examined as it flows through a system. Because almost all digital systems operate in a closed-loop mode, the test engineer must break the loop in order to separate cause and effect. Typically, this procedure involves either single stepping the processor or injecting known information into, say, the processor's address pins and observing the effect on the rest of the system. The same tests can be applied to software design. Test points become the interfaces between the modules. Open-loop testing is carried out by breaking the links between software modules, just as is done with hardware. Generally, test points in software are implemented by breakpoints. These are software markers that print out a snapshot of the state of the processor whenever they are encountered during the execution of a program.

Two philosophies of program testing exist: top-down and bottom-up. Bottom-up testing involves testing the lowest level components of a system first. For example, the DFM of figure 3.2 might be tested by first verifying the operation of software primitives such as read/write a sector. When the lowest level components have been tested, the next level up is examined; in this case, "insert module" of the DFM might use the read/write sector primitives that have already been tested.

Bottom-up testing is complete when the highest level of the system has been tested, which is an attractive philosophy because it is relatively easy to implement. A module is tested by constructing the software equivalent of the "fixture" or "jig" used to test hardware in industry. The software fixture provides a testing environment for the module, which cannot stand on its own; for example, a module to read sectors would require software to pass the necessary track and sector addresses to it, examine the returned data, and display the error status at the end of an operation. Note that high level modules may call low level modules during the test, safe in the knowledge that the low level modules have already been tested.

In top-down testing, the highest levels are tested first. This procedure does not require much in the way of a fixture, as the high level modules are tested by giving them the task that the application software is to perform. This philosophy is in line with the top-down design approach and has the advantage that major design errors may be spotted in an early phase. Because high level modules call lower level modules, top-down testing cannot rely on untested lower level modules. In order to deal with this situation, lower level modules are replaced by "stubs." These stubs are dummies that simulate the modules they replace. For example, in testing the DFM, a "read sector" operation must be replaced by a stub that obtains data from an array rather than from the disk drive.

3.5 Recoverability

Recoverability, or exception handling, is the ability of a system to cope with erroneous data and to recover from certain classes of error. Just as students are taught that real gates do not always behave as expected, they should be taught that real software sometimes encounters faulty data. They can then proceed to consider the design of software filters in the same way as the design of hardware filters to remove or to attenuate electrical noise.

The next step is to decide what action to take if a software module fails to achieve the intended results because of faulty software or hardware elsewhere in the system. For example, what does a DFM do if one of the procedures it calls fails to execute an operation such as reading a track? Clearly, permitting the system hang-up in an infinite polling loop is as bad as letting a hardware device hang-up because it has not received a handshake from a peripheral. Designers should always consider the possible forms that recovery may take. Several attempts can be made to read the track to distinguish between a soft and a hard error. If the error persists, a graceful recovery may be attempted. A user who has spent two hours editing a text file would not be very happy if the system collapsed due to a minor error. A better approach would be to save as much of the text as possible and then report the error.

Exception handling is, to some extent, a controversial subject, as a poorly designed or ill-conceived error-recovery mechanism may be far worse than nothing at all. The 68000 provides several exception-handling mechanisms, some at a software level and some at a hardware level.

3.6 Pseudocode (PDL)

This section presents a possible technique for the production of assembly language programs. The history of computer science, like everything else, is two steps forward and one step backward. As the hardware of computers has advanced, a corresponding progress in software has been achieved. The first computers were programmed in machine code. Progress was later made to assembly language, to early high level languages like FORTRAN, and then to block-structured high level languages (HLLs) such as Pascal or Modula2. While a high level language compiled into machine code by an automatic compiler may not execute as rapidly as an equivalent program written by hand in assembly language, few people would argue against the proposition that the HLL greatly improves programmer productivity and program reliability over assembly language programming.

Unfortunately, microprocessor-based machines have traditionally had small random access memories and poor secondary storage facilities. Consequently, relatively primitive languages like BASIC have evolved and these have tended to be interpreted rather than compiled. An interpreted BASIC program is very much slower than either a compiled BASIC or pure assembly language program. This situation has forced those who require low execution times to take the one step backward and return to assembly language programming. Indeed, some applications such as animated graphics or speech processing make assembly language programming almost mandatory.

One of the reasons for the unpopularity of assembly language (at least in professional circles) is the difficulty of writing, debugging, documenting, and maintaining such programs. The productivity of a programmer writing in, say, Pascal is almost certainly far greater than that of one writing in assembly language.

Even though the early 1980s saw a return (by some) to assembly language programming, no excuse exists for developing assembly language programs in a sloppy or ad hoc form. Today's programmers have a great many tools to help them write programs that were not available to their predecessors. One software tool employed by some assembly language programmers is called *pseudocode* or *program development language* (PDL). A PDL offers a way of writing assembly language programs using both top-down design techniques and structured constructs. Unlike real high level languages, the PDL is a personalized pseudo HLL; that is, the programmers may design their own PDLs. The result is that the conventions adopted by one programmer may not be those adopted by another, but as long as any given PDL is self-consistent the end product will not be sloppy.

Characteristics of a PDL

A PDL is nothing more than a convenient method of writing down an algorithm before it is coded into assembly language form; for example, a flowchart could be considered to be one type of PDL. Clearly, a program in PDL form is easier to code than to try and code a problem into assembly language without going through any intermediate steps. The features of a PDL are summed up as follows:

1. A PDL represents a practical compromise between a high level language and an assembly language but lacks the complexity of the former and the "obscurity" of the latter.

2. The purpose of a PDL is to facilitate the production of reliable code in circumstances in which a high level language is not available or not appropriate.

3. A PDL shares some of the features of HLLs but rejects their overall complexity; for example, it supports good programming techniques including top-down design, modularity, and structured programming. Similarly, it may support primitive data structures.

4. A PDL provides a shorthand notation for the description of algorithms and allows the use of plain English words to substitute for entire expressions. This feature gives it its strong top-down design facilities.

5. A PDL is extensible. The syntax of a PDL can be extended to deal with the task to which it is applied.

Using PDL

The best way to introduce a PDL is by means of an example. Consider a 68000-based system with a software module that is employed by both input and output routines and whose function is to buffer data. When called by the input routine, a character is added to the buffer and when called by the output routine, a character is removed from it. The operational parameters of the subroutine are as follows:

1. Register D0 is to be used for character input and output. The character is an 8-bit value and occupies the lowest-order byte of D0.

2. Register D1 contains the code 0, 1, or 2 on entering the subroutine. Code 0 is interpreted as clear the buffer and reset all pointers. Code 1 is interpreted as place the character in D0 into the buffer. Code 2 is interpreted as remove a character from the buffer and place it in D0. We may assume that a higher level module ensures that only one of 0, 1, or 2 is passed to the module.

3. The location of the first entry in the buffer is at $01 0000 and the buffer size is 1,024 bytes. Pointers and scratch storage may be placed after the end of the buffer, as long as no more than 32 bytes of storage are used.

4. If the buffer is full, the addition of a new character overwrites the oldest character in the buffer. In this case, bit 31 of D0 is set to indicate overflow and cleared otherwise.

5. If the buffer is empty, the subtraction of a new character results in the contents of the lower byte of D0 being set to zero and its most-significant bit set as in parameter 4.

6. Apart from D0, no other registers are modified by a call to this subroutine.

Figure 3.13 shows the memory map corresponding to this problem. The map can be drawn at an early stage as it is relatively straightforward. Obviously, a region of 1,024 bytes ($400) must be reserved for the buffer together with at least two 32-bit pointers. IN_POINTER points to the location of the next free position into which a new character is to be placed and OUT_POINTER points to the location of the next character to be removed from the buffer. At the right-hand side of figure 3.13 is the logical arrangement of the circular buffer. This arrangement provides the programmer with a better mental image of how the process is to operate.

The first level of abstraction in PDL is to determine the overall action that the module is to perform. This can be written as follows:

```
Module:  Circular_buffer
             Save working registers
             Select one of:
                              Initialize system
                              Input a character
                              Output a character
             Restore working registers
         End Circular_buffer
```

FIGURE 3.13　Circular buffer

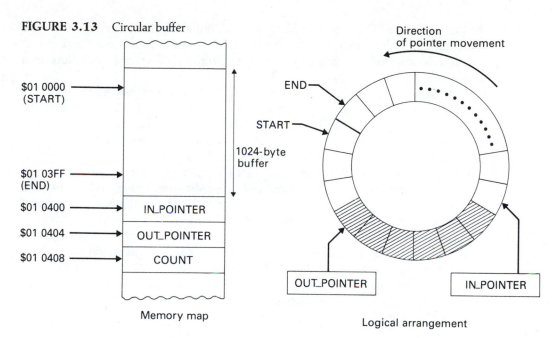

Note that this PDL description is written in almost plain English: any programmer should be able to follow another programmer's PDL. Try doing that in LISP or FORTH! No indication is given of how any action is to be carried out, and the only control structure is the selection of one of three possible functions. The next step is to elaborate on some of these actions.

```
Module: Circular_buffer
        Save working registers
        IF [D1] = 0 THEN Initialize END_IF
        IF [D1] = 1 THEN Input_character END_IF
        IF [D1] = 2 THEN Output_character END_IF
        Restore working registers
End Circular_buffer

Initialize
        Count := 0
        In_pointer := Start
        Out_pointer := Start
End Initialize
Input_character
        Store new character
        Deal with any overflow
End Input_character

Output_character
        IF buffer NOT empty THEN Get_character_from_buffer
                            ELSE return null character
        END_IF
End Output_character
```

At this point, the PDL is getting fairly detailed. Both the module selection and the initialization routines are complete. We still have to work on the input and output routines because of the difficulty in dealing with overflow and underflow in a circular buffer.

Looking at the circular buffer of figure 3.13, it seems reasonable to determine the state of the buffer by means of a variable, COUNT, that indicates the number of characters in the buffer. If COUNT is greater than zero and less than its maximum value, a new character can be added or one removed without any complexity. If COUNT is zero, the buffer is empty and we can add a character but not remove one. If COUNT is equal to its maximum value and therefore the buffer is full, each new character must overwrite the oldest character as specified by the program requirements. This last step is tricky because the next character to be output (the oldest character in the buffer) is overwritten by the latest character. Therefore, the next character to be output will now be the oldest surviving character, and the pointer to the output must be moved to reflect this condition.

Rewriting the entire module in PDL is not necessary, as the first two sections have been resolved into enough detail to allow coding into assembly language. The input and output routines from which the assembly language coding begin are as follows:

```
Input_character
     Store new character at In_pointer
     In_pointer := In_pointer + 1
     IF In_pointer > End THEN In_pointer := Start END_IF
     IF Count < Max THEN Count := Count + 1
                         ELSE
                         BEGIN
                         Set overflow flag
                         Out_pointer := Out_pointer + 1
                         IF Out_pointer > End THEN Out_pointer := Start
                         END_IF
                         END
     END_IF
End Input_character

Output_character
     IF Count = 0 THEN return null and set underflow flag
                         ELSE
                         BEGIN
                         Count := Count − 1
                         Get character pointed at by Out_pointer
                         Out_pointer := Out_pointer + 1
                         IF Out_pointer > End THEN Out_pointer := Start END_IF
                         END
     END_IF
End Output_character
```

The program design language has now done its job and the routines can be translated into the appropriate assembly language.

```
CIRC      EQU *         This module implements a circular buffer
          MOVEM.L   A0–A1,–(SP)          Save working registers
          BCLR.L    #31,D0               Clear bit 31 of D0 (no error)
          CMPI.B    #0,D1                Test for initialize request
          BNE.S     CIRC1                IF not 0 THEN next test
          BSR.S     INITIAL              IF 0 THEN perform initialize
          BRA.S     CIRC3                and exit
CIRC1     CMPI.B    #1,D1                Test for input request
          BNE.S     CIRC2                IF not input THEN output
          BSR.S     INPUT                IF 1 THEN INPUT
          BRA.S     CIRC3                and exit
CIRC2     BSR.S     OUTPUT               By default OUTPUT
CIRC3     MOVEM.L   (SP)+,A0–A1          Restore working registers
          RTS                            End CIRCULAR
*
INITIAL   EQU *         This module sets up the circular buffer
          CLR.W     COUNT                Initialize pointers
          MOVE.L    #START,IN_POINTER    Set up In_pointer
          MOVE.L    #START,OUT_POINTER   Set up Out_pointer
          RTS
*
INPUT     EQU *         This module stores a character in the buffer
          MOVEA.L   IN_POINTER,A0        Get pointer to input
          MOVE.B    D0,(A0)+             Store character in buffer,
                                         update pointer
          CMPA.L    #END+1,A0            Test for wrap-round
          BNE.S     INPUT1               IF not end THEN skip reposition
          MOVEA.L   #START,A0            Reposition input pointer
INPUT1    MOVE.L    A0,IN_POINTER        Save updated pointer
          CMPI.W    #MAX,COUNT           Is buffer full?
          BEQ.S     INPUT2               IF full THEN deal with overflow
          ADDQ.W    #1,COUNT             ELSE increment character count
          RTS                            and return
INPUT2    BSET.L    #31,D0               Set overflow flag
          MOVEA.L   OUT_POINTER,A0       Get output pointer
          LEA.L     1(A0),A0             Increment Out_pointer
          CMPA.L    #END+1,A0            Test for wrap-round
          BNE.S     INPUT3               IF not wrap-round THEN skip fix
          MOVEA.L   #START,A0            ELSE wrap-round Out_pointer
INPUT3    MOVE.L    A0,OUT_POINTER       Update Out_pointer in memory
          RTS                            and return
*
```

```
OUTPUT     TST.W      COUNT              Examine state of buffer
           BNE.S      OUTPUT1            IF buffer not empty output
                                           character
           CLR.B      D0                 ELSE return null output
           BSET.L     #31,D0                 set underflow flag
           RTS                               and exit
OUTPUT1    SUBQ.W     #1,COUNT           Decrement COUNT for removal
           MOVEA.L    OUT_POINTER,A0     Point to next character to be
                                           output
           MOVE.B     (A0)+,D0           Get character and update pointer
           CMPA.L     #END+1,A0          Test for wrap-round
           BNE.S      OUTPUT2            IF not wrap-round THEN exit
           MOVEA.L    #START,A0          ELSE wrap-round Out_pointer
OUTPUT2    MOVE.L     A0,OUT_POINTER     Restore Out_pointer in memory
           RTS
```

The greatest flaw in the operational characteristics of our circular buffer is the way in which it deals with overflow. We designed the program to overwrite the oldest unread character in the buffer with the newest character. A more usual and simple approach is to reject any new characters once the buffer is full. In order to provide the host program with sufficient warning that the buffer is becoming dangerously full, a circular buffer sometimes returns a two-bit code that indicates its state; for example, $0,0$ = less than one-quarter full, $0,1$ = less than half full, $1,0$ = less than three-quarters full, and $1,1$ = full.

Using PDL to Design a
Command Line Interpreter (CLI)

The design of a command line interpreter (CLI) provides a somewhat more extended example of the application of a PDL to the construction of assembly language programs. A CLI is a program that collects a line of text from a processor's keyboard, parses it to extract a command, and then executes the command. Clearly, the CLI is often found in many text editors, word processors, monitors, and even interpreted languages.

The particular CLI to be designed in this case is intended to form part of a microprocessor system's monitor. Such a monitor is part of many low-cost, single board, educational computers and permits students to enter an assembly language program (sometimes in hexadecimal form only), preset memory locations, and then to execute the program. Frequently, a monitor provides debugging aids, allowing the students to follow the execution of their programs by displaying intermediate results on a display terminal. Chapter 11 considers further the development of a very basic monitor for a 68000 system.

The specifications of the CLI are given as follows:

1. Text is entered into a 64-character (i.e., byte) buffer and is terminated by a carriage return. The longest possible string that may be input is 63 characters plus a carriage return. Note that the carriage return is to be stored in the buffer.

2. In addition to the carriage return terminator, the CLI is to recognize the back space and the abort (ASCII control_A) characters. A back space deletes the last character received. If the line buffer is empty, inputting one or more back spaces has no effect. An abort character forces an immediate exit from the CLI routine with the carry bit of the CCR set to a logical one. Otherwise a return from the CLI is made only after a carriage return has been received. In this case, the state of the carry bit of the CCR is determined by the interpreter part of the routine.

3. Should more than 63 alphanumeric characters be received, representing a buffer overflow condition, the message "Buffer full—reenter command" is displayed on a new line, a further newline command issued, and the input procedure initiated as if the routine were being invoked for the first time.

4. Once a command line has been successfully input, it is interpreted. The first word in the input buffer is matched against the entries in a command table. If a successful match is found, the appropriate jump (transfer) address of the command is loaded into address register A0, the carry bit of the CCR cleared, and a return from the CLI made. If a match cannot be found, a return from the CLI is executed with the carry bit of the CCR set. In this case the contents of address register A0 are undefined.

5. The CLI may assume the existence of a subroutine GETCHAR that, when called, returns with an 8-bit ASCII character in the lower byte of data register D0. We assume that GETCHAR takes care of any character echo. The subroutine NEWLINE moves the cursor to the left-hand column of the next line on the display. The subroutine PSTRING displays the text string composed of ASCII characters occupying consecutive byte locations and terminated by a null (zero byte) pointed at by address register A4. These three subroutines have no effect on any register not mentioned previously.

6. No register other than A0 and the CCR must be affected by the CLI following a return from the CLI.

7. The structure of the command table is defined as follows:

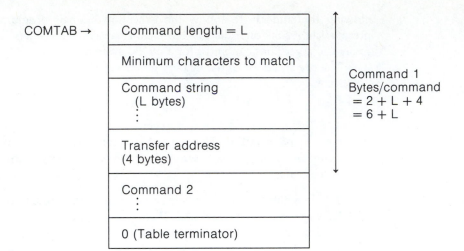

Each entry has four fields: (a) a byte that indicates the length of the command name in the table, (b) a byte that indicates the minimum number of characters that must be matched (e.g., MEM, MEMO, MEMOR, or MEMORY may be typed to invoke the MEMORY command), (c) the command string itself, whose length is given by entry (a), and (d) the 4-byte transfer address.

For example, the first two entries in the command table may be:

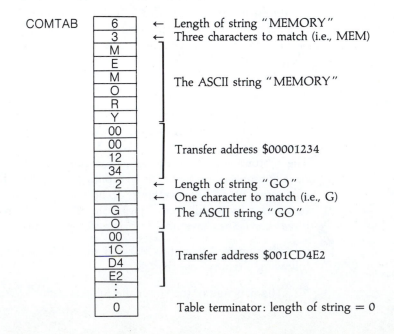

Having specified the problem, the next step is to translate it into a sufficiently elaborated PDL that its ultimate translation into 68000 assembly language involves no complex steps; that is, no single PDL statement should require translating into a stream of assembly language requiring embedded branch instructions of any kind.

PDL Level 1

The lowest level of PDL is rather trivial and is included here for the sake of completeness and to illustrate the process of top-down design.

```
Module: CLI

        Initialize variables

        Assemble the input line

        Interpret the line of text

        Exit

End CLI
```

PDL Level 2

At level 2 we cannot fully elaborate any part of the level 1 design as we do not, for example, yet know what variables must be initialized. We do know that registers must not be corrupted by this program, so we can make a note of this condition. Similarly, we can begin to consider the type of actions to be carried out by the major steps in level 1 above.

```
Module: CLI
        Initialize
                    Save working registers
                    Initialize any variables
                    Clear buffer
        Assemble
                    REPEAT
                            Get character
                            Deal with special cases
                            Store character
                    UNTIL   character = carriage return
        Interpret
                    Match command with command table
                    IF successful THEN Extract transfer address
                                  ELSE Set error indicator
                    END_IF
        Exit
                    Restore working registers
End CLI
```

PDL Level 3

At this stage, we can begin to consider the details of the actions defined at level 2. If we are lucky, this is the highest level of PDL necessary; otherwise another iteration (i.e., a higher PDL level) will be necessary. A little common sense tells us that this routine requires few variables other than pointers for the line buffer and for the table with which the match is made. However, there are enough variables to require some form of type declaration block as an aid to understanding the program.

Initialize

```
                Array of bytes: Comtab
                Array of bytes: Buffer
                Longword: Buffer_pointer
                Longword: Table_pointer
                Longword: Next_entry
                Longword: Transfer_address
                Byte:     String_length
                Byte:     Chars_to_match
                Byte:     Buffer_length = 64
                Equate:   Buffer_start = Buffer
                Equate:   Buffer_end := Buffer_start + Buffer_length − 1
                Equate:   Buffer_pointer := Buffer_start
                Equate:   Table_address = Comtab
                Equate:   Back_space = $08
                Equate:   Abort = $01
                Equate:   Carriage_return = $0D


                Save working registers on system stack
```

                Clear_buffer
End initialize

Clear_buffer

```
                FOR I := 0 TO Buffer_length − 1
                        Buffer[I] := 0
                END_FOR
```

End Clear_buffer

Assemble

```
                REPEAT
                IF Buffer_pointer = Buffer_end − 1
                    THEN  BEGIN
                            Newline
                            Display error message
                            Newline
                            Buffer_pointer := Buffer_start
```
                            Clear_buffer
```
                            END
                END_IF
```

```
                    Get character
                    IF character = Abort THEN Set Error_flag
                                              Exit
                    END_IF
                    IF character = Back_space
                       THEN  BEGIN
                             IF Buffer_pointer > Buffer_start
                                THEN Buffer_pointer := Buffer_pointer − 1
                             END_IF
                             END
                       ELSE  BEGIN
                             Store character
                             Buffer_pointer := Buffer_pointer + 1
                             END
                    END_IF
                 UNTIL character = carriage_return
          End Assemble
```

Interpret

```
                    Table_pointer := Table_address
                    REPEAT
                       Buffer_pointer := Buffer_start
                       String_length := Comtab[Table_pointer]
                       IF String_length = 0 THEN
                                              Set Fail
                                              Exit
                       END_IF
                       Chars_to_match := Comtab[Table_pointer + 1]
                       Next_entry := Table_pointer + String_length + 6
                       Table_pointer := Table_pointer + 2
                       Match
                       IF Success THEN
                               BEGIN
                               Transfer_address := Comtab[Next_entry − 4]
                               Exit
                               END
                               ELSE Table_pointer := Next_entry
                       END_IF
                    END_REPEAT
          End Interpret
```

Match

```
                    Set Fail
                    REPEAT
                       IF Buffer[Buffer_pointer] ≠ Comtab[Table_pointer]
                          THEN  BEGIN
                                Set Fail
                                Exit Match
                                END
```

```
                          ELSE  BEGIN
                                  Table_pointer := Table_pointer + 1
                                  Buffer_pointer := Buffer_pointer + 1
                                  END
                          END_IF
                    Chars_to_match := Chars_to_match − 1
                    UNTIL Chars_to_match = 0
                    Set Success
            End Match

        Exit
                    Restore registers from system stack
                    Return
            End Exit
```

Having reached this level of detail, we can readily translate the PDL into 68000 assembly language. As no fixed storage is necessary, apart from the line buffer, it is possible to use the 68000's registers as the pointers and temporary storage.

```
BUFFER_LENGTH           EQU  64
BACK_PACE               EQU  $08
ABORT                   EQU  $01
CARRIAGE_RETURN         EQU  $0D
BUFFER_START            EQU  $008000
BUFFER_END              EQU  BUFFER_START + BUFFER_LENGTH − 1
COMTAB                  EQU  $009000
*
* Registers              A0 = Pointer to transfer address
*                        A1 = Buffer_pointer
*                        A2 = Table_pointer
*                        A3 = Next_entry
*                        A4 = Pointer to error message
*                        D0 = Contains character from console
*                        D1 = String_length
*                        D2 = Chars_to_match
*
*********************************************************************
*
* INITIALIZE saves the working registers and clears the line buffer.
* Note that EXIT restores the registers
*
            ORG         $001000              Program origin
INITIALIZE  MOVEM.L     A1–A4/D0–D2, − (SP)  Save registers
            BSR.S       CLEAR                Clear the buffer
*                                            Fall through to ASSEMBLE
*
*
*********************************************************************
```

```
*
*  ASSEMBLE reads a line of text and stores it in the line buffer.
*  A back space deletes the previous character and an abort forces
*  an exit from the CLI with the C flag set
*
ASSEMBLE    CMPA.L   #BUFFER_END + 1,A1      Test for end of line buffer
            BNE.S    ASSEMBLE1               IF not full THEN continue
            BSR      NEWLINE                 ELSE display error
            LEA.L    MESSAGE,A4              Point to message
            BSR      PSTRING                 Print it
            BSR      NEWLINE
            BSR.S    CLEAR                   Clear buffer
ASSEMBLE1   BSR      GETCHAR                 Input an ASCII character
            CMPI.B   #ABORT,D0               Test for abort
            BNE.S    ASSEMBLE2               IF not abort THEN skip exit
            ORI.W    #$01,CCR                ELSE set error flag
            BRA.S    EXIT                    and leave CLI
ASSEMBLE2   CMPI.B   #BACK_SPACE,D0          Test for back space
            BNE.S    ASSEMBLE3               IF not back space THEN skip
            CMPA.L   #BUFFER_START,A1        Test for buffer empty
            BEQ      ASSEMBLE1               IF empty THEN get new character
            LEA.L    -1(A1),A1               ELSE move back pointer
            BRA      ASSEMBLE1               and get new character
ASSEMBLE3   MOVE.B   D0,(A1)+                Store the input
            CMPI.B   #CARRIAGE_RETURN,D0     Test for terminator
            BNE      ASSEMBLE                IF not terminator repeat
*                                            ELSE fall through to interpret

*************************************************************************
*
*  INTERPRET takes the first word in the line buffer and tries
*  to match it with an entry in COMTAB
*
INTERPRET   LEA.L    COMTAB,A2               A2 points to command table
INTERPRET1  LEA.L    BUFFER_START,A1         A1 points to line buffer
            CLR.L    D1                      Clear all 32 bits of D1
            MOVE.B   (A2),D1                 Get string length
            BNE.S    INTERPRET2              IF not zero THEN continue
            ORI.W    #$01,CCR                ELSE set error flag
            BRA.S    EXIT                    and return from CLI
INTERPRET2  MOVE.B   1(A2),D2                Get character to match from table
            LEA.L    6(A2,D1),A3             Get address of next entry
            LEA.L    2(A2),A2                Point to string in COMTAB
            BSR.S    MATCH                   Match it with line buffer
            BCC.S    INTERPRET3              IF C clear THEN success
            LEA.L    (A3),A2                 ELSE point to next entry
            BRA      INTERPRET1              Try again
INTERPRET3  LEA.L    -4(A3),A0               Get transfer address pointer
            MOVEA.L  (A0),A0                 Get transfer address from COMTAB
*                                            Fall through to exit
```

```
*
*******************************************************************
* EXIT is the only way out of CLI. Restore registers and exit with
* C clear for success and C set for failure. If C = 0, the
* transfer address is in A0
*
EXIT      MOVEM.L   (SP)+,A1–A4/D0–D2           Restore registers
          RTS                                   Return
*
CLEAR     MOVE.W    #BUFFER_LENGTH−1,D0  Clear the input buffer
          LEA.L     BUFFER_START,A1
CLEAR1    CLR.B     (A1)+
          DBF       CLEAR1,D0
          LEA.L     BUFFER_START,A1            Reset A1 to start of buffer
          RTS
*
*******************************************************************
*
* MATCH compares two strings for equality. The number of characters
* to match is in D2
* A1 = Buffer_pointer, A2 = Table_pointer
*
MATCH     CMPM.B    (A1)+,(A2)+    Compare two characters
          BNE.S     MATCH1         IF not equal THEN return
          SUBQ.B    #1,D2          ELSE decrement match count
          BNE       MATCH          IF not zero test next pair
          ANDI.W    #$FE,CCR       ELSE success, clear C flag
          RTS                      and return
MATCH1    ORI.W     #$01,CCR       Set fail flag
          RTS                      and return
```

Summary

In this chapter we have looked at some of the issues raised by the design of assembly language programs. Now that the semiconductor manufacturers have given us such powerful microprocessors that support high level constructs and modularity, creating assembly language programs in an undisciplined way becomes unreasonable. If programmers are still forced to resort to assembly language programming for reasons of speed or efficiency, they should use every tool available to them to produce reliable programs. Indeed, only by making use of the five components of program design identified in this chapter can we construct large and reliable assembly language programs that can be maintained by other people.

Unlike assembly language itself, program design techniques are not handed down from the manufacturer of the microprocessor. To a certain extent they are an art to be learned by the student. In a text of this length, it is possible to provide only guidelines. Programmers learn their trade only by writing programs.

However, as M. L. Shooman says in his book, *Software Engineering*, "The lessons in this chapter (i.e., program design tools and techniques) are not difficult to grasp, but many have found them hard to implement. The difficulty lies in the necessity of changing work habits and approaches which are intuitive and comfortable, and replacing them with a different set of disciplined principles." Note the emphasis Shooman places on discipline. The temptation to start coding straight from the problem is sometimes almost irresistible. Only by adopting a top-down approach and by making use of structured programming techniques can the programmer hope to achieve effective results. The program design language introduced in this chapter provides a method of designing assembly language programs while making use of top-down design and structured programming.

Problems

As this chapter has dealt with the topic of program design, the problems here are longer than those appearing elsewhere in the text. These problems should be regarded as "projects."

1. The IEEE format for a 32-bit floating-point number, N, is defined as:

S	E	F

where
S = sign bit (0 = positive, 1 = negative mantissa)
E = 8-bit exponent biased by 127
F = 23-bit fractional mantissa, together with an implicit leading 1 (the integer is not stored)
$N = (-1)^S \times 2^{(E-127)} \times (1 \cdot F)$

   a. Write a program to add two 32-bit floating-point numbers.
   b. Write a program to multiply two floating-point numbers.
   c. Write a program to convert a floating-point number to decimal form.
   d. Write a program to convert a decimal number to floating-point form.

2. Text is normally stored in character form with a byte holding each ASCII value. This is relatively inefficient for the storage of plain text in English; for example, the word "the" requires 24 bits of storage. Encoding it as a single symbol reduces the storage needed. Design a program to input text and compress it (using your own algorithm), and a program to reconstitute the compressed text and to print it out.

3. A keyboard encoder detects the closure of a switch at one of 64 cross-points in an 8 by 8 matrix. The output port initially places the value 11111110 on D_{00}–D_{07} and the input port reads D_{00}–D_{07}. If no key is pressed, the input reads 11111111. If, say, the leftmost key on row 0 is pressed, 01111111 is read.

The output port then puts 11111101 on the 8 rows and the input is read. This interrogates switches in the second row. The process is repeated sequentially, with the output going from 11111011 to 01111111 and back to 11111110. In this way, all 8 rows are continually scanned.

Write a program to control such a keyboard and produce a 6-bit code for each keystroke. The code returned by the program is 0, 0, R2, R1, R0, C2, C1, C0, where R stands for row and C for column. Assume that a procedure OUT_BYTE places the lower byte of D0 on lines D_{00} through D_{07} and that IN_BYTE reads the contents of D_{00} through D_{07} and places the result in the lower-order byte of D0.

Chapter 4

The 68000 CPU

Hardware Model

A microprocessor cannot function on its own and must be connected to external components to create a microcomputer. We will now examine the nature of the interface between the 68000 and the components needed to turn it into a viable system. We are not concerned with the internal operation of the 68000, but rather with the conditions that must be satisfied if it is to be incorporated in a system. In this chapter, we concentrate on the aspects of the 68000 that are common to all systems using this device. The more sophisticated facilities of the 68000 are glossed over and are dealt with in a later chapter.

All computers spend much of their time reading data from memory or writing it to memory. Consequently, this chapter places great emphasis on the 68000's interface to memory and its read and write cycles. This topic introduces the timing diagram and the protocols required to ensure a reliable exchange of data between the CPU and memory.

4.1 The 68000 Interface

The 68000 has 64 pins that may be arranged in nine groups as shown in figure 4.1. Each group of pins is labeled by the specific function performed by that group. For the purposes of this chapter, the functions of these nine groups are divided into three categories. These are the system support pins, the memory and peripheral interface pins, and the special-purpose pins not needed in a minimal application of the processor. Table 4.1 shows how the pins may also be classified by the direction of information flow. A pin can act as an input, an output, or a dual-function input/output pin.

The system support pins are those essential to the operation of the

FIGURE 4.1 Pinout of the 68000 and logical grouping of pins

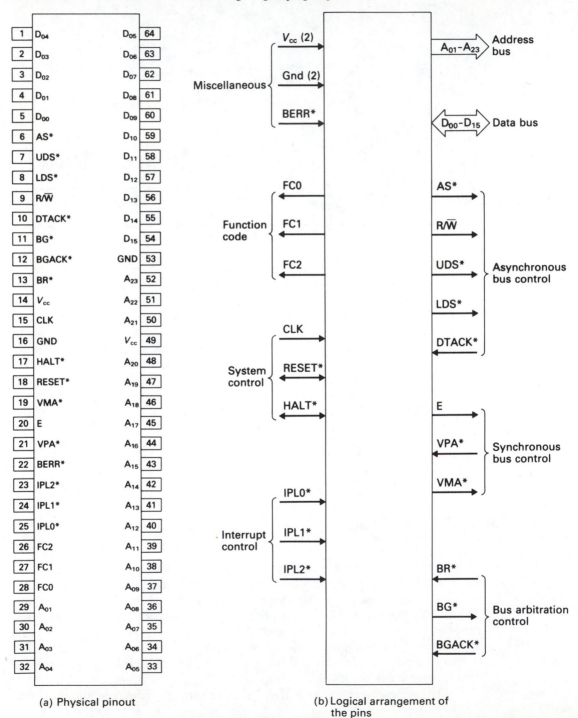

(a) Physical pinout

(b) Logical arrangement of the pins

TABLE 4.1   Input/output characteristics of the 68000's pins

SIGNAL NAME	MNEMONIC	TYPE	OUTPUT CIRCUIT
Power supply	V_{cc}	—	—
Ground	GND	—	—
Clock	CLK	Input	—
Reset	RESET*	I/O	OD
Halt	HALT*	I/O	OD
Address bus	A_{01}–A_{23}	Output	TS
Data bus	D_{00}–D_{15}	I/O	TS
Address strobe	AS*	Output	TS
Read/write	R/$\overline{W}$	Output	TS
Upper data strobe	UDS*	Output	TS
Lower data strobe	LDS*	Output	TS
Data transfer acknowledge	DTACK*	Input	—
Bus error	BERR*	Input	—
Enable	E	Output	TP
Valid memory address	VMA*	Output	TS
Valid peripheral address	VPA*	Input	—
Bus request	BR*	Input	—
Bus grant	BG*	Output	TP
Bus grant acknowledge	BGACK*	Input	—
Function code output	FC0, FC1, FC2	Output	TS
Interrupt priority level	IPL0*, IPL1*, IPL2*	Input	—

TS = tristate output	Input = input to the 68000
TP = totem-pole output	Output = output from the 68000
OD = open-drain output	I/O = input or output

processor in every system. These include the power supply, the clock input, the reset input, and similar functions. The memory and peripheral interface group of pins are those that connect the processor to an external memory subsystem. Special-purpose pins provide functions not needed in a basic system. These include interrupt management and bus arbitration facilities. Usually, special-purpose pins can be strapped to ground or V_{cc} (if they are inputs) and forgotten and left open circuits (if they are outputs).

System Support Pins

The first group of pins to be described consists of the system support pins, comprising the power supply, clock, reset, and halt functions. Throughout the chapter, and elsewhere, I have adopted the convention that an asterisk following a name indicates that the signal is active-low. The term *asserted*, when applied to a signal, means that it is placed in its active state. *Negated* means that it is placed in its inactive state.

Power Supply   In common with most other digital logic elements found in microprocessor systems, the 68000 requires a single $+5$ V power supply. Two V_{cc} (i.e., $+5$ V) pins and two ground (i.e., 0 V) pins are provided, thereby reducing the voltage drop between the V_{cc} terminals of the chip and the V_{cc} conductors within the chip itself.

Clock   The clock input is a single-phase TTL-compatible signal from which the 68000 derives all its internal timing. As the 68000 uses dynamic storage techniques internally, the clock input must never be stopped or its minimum or maximum pulse widths violated. Current versions of the 68000 have maximum clock rates of between 8 and 12.5 MHz. A memory access is called a *bus cycle* and consists of a minimum of four clock cycles. An instruction consists of one or more bus cycles.

RESET*   The active-low reset input of the 68000 forces it into a known state on the initial application of power. When a reset input is recognized by the 68000, it loads the supervisor stack pointer, A7, from memory location zero ($00 0000) and then loads the program counter from address $00 0004. The detailed sequence of actions taking place during a reset operation is dealt with in the section on exception handling. For correct operation during the power-up sequence, RESET* must be asserted together with the HALT* input for at least 100 ms—an incredibly long time by most microprocessor standards. This delay provides time for the chip's internal back-bias generator to generate the bias voltage required by its MOSFET transistors. At all other times, RESET* and HALT* must be asserted for a minimum of ten clock periods.

RESET* also acts as an output from the 68000 under certain circumstances. Whenever the processor executes the software instruction RESET, it asserts the RESET* pin for 124 clock cycles, which resets all external devices (i.e., peripherals) wired to the system RESET* line, but does not affect the internal operation of the 68000; that is, it allows peripherals to be reset without resetting the 68000 itself.

HALT*   Like the RESET* input, the active-low HALT* input is bidirectional and serves two distinct functions (in addition to that described previously). In normal operation, HALT* is an active-low input to the 68000. When asserted by an external device, HALT* causes the 68000 to stop processing at the end of the current bus cycle and to negate all control signals. Tristate outputs (data and address buses) are floated. However, the function code outputs are not floated when the 68000 is in the halt state.

One application of the HALT* input is to enable the 68000 to execute a single bus cycle at a time. By asserting HALT* just long enough to permit the processor to execute a single bus cycle, the 68000 can be stepped through a program cycle by cycle, which may be used to debug a system. The HALT* input has other applications that are not relevant in simple systems. In most basic 68000 systems, the HALT* pin is, effectively, connected to the RESET* pin.

Sometimes HALT* can act as an output. Whenever the 68000 finds itself in a situation from which it cannot recover (the so-called double bus error which is dealt with in chap. 6), it halts and asserts HALT* to indicate what has happened.

Figure 4.2 indicates how the system support pins are connected in a basic 68000 circuit. This diagram is intended to give the reader an idea of the "overhead" required to support the 68000; its operational details are considered later.

Memory and Peripheral Interface

This group of pins takes up 44 of the 68000's 64 pins and is used to read data from memory and to write data to it. As the 68000 treats peripherals exactly like memory components, the same pins are also used by all input/output transactions.

Address Bus   The address bus is provided by A_{01} to A_{23}, permitting 2^{23} 16-bit words to be uniquely addressed. The processor uses the address bus to specify the location of the word it is writing data into or reading data from. From table 4.1 it can be seen that the address bus is driven by tristate outputs, allowing the address bus to be controlled by a device other than the CPU under certain conditions.

The address bus has an auxiliary function and supports vectored interrupts (see chap. 6). Whenever the 68000 is interrupted, address lines A_{01}, A_{02}, and A_{03} indicate the level of the interrupt being serviced. During this so-called interrupt acknowledge phase, address lines A_{04} to A_{23} are set to a logical one level.

Data Bus   The data bus is 16 bits wide and transfers data between the CPU and its memory or peripherals. It is bidirectional, acting as an input during a CPU read cycle and as an output during a CPU write cycle. The data bus has tristate outputs which can be floated to permit other devices to access the bus. When the CPU executes an operation on a word, all 16 data bus lines are active. When it executes an operation on a byte, only D_{00} to D_{07} or D_{08} to D_{15} are active. During an interrupt acknowledge cycle, the interrupting device identifies itself to the CPU by placing an "interrupt vector number" on D_{00} to D_{07}.

The address and data buses operate in conjunction with five control signals: AS*, UDS*, LDS*, R/$\overline{W}$, and DTACK*. These signals are used to sequence the flow of information between the CPU and external memory.

AS*   The address strobe is active-low and, when asserted, indicates that the contents of the address bus are valid.

R/$\overline{W}$ The R/$\overline{W}$ (read/$\overline{write}$) signal provided by the 68000 determines the nature of a memory access cycle. Whenever the CPU is reading from memory R/$\overline{W}$ = 1, and whenever it is writing to memory R/$\overline{W}$ = 0. If the CPU is

FIGURE 4.2   Example of circuit required by the 68000's system support pins

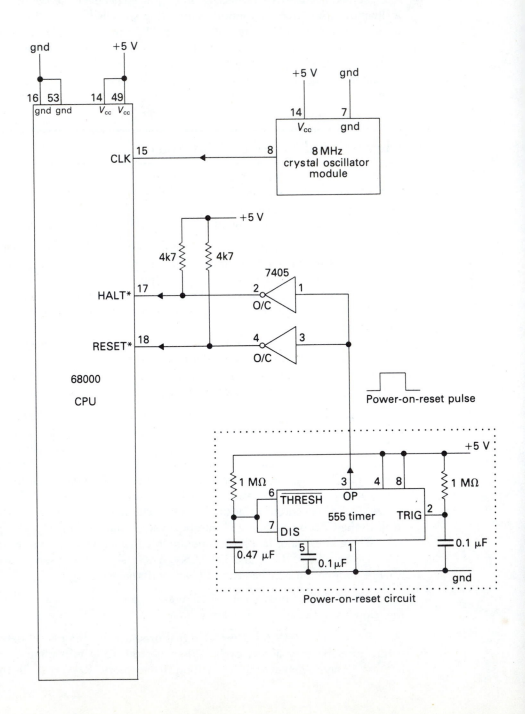

Power-on-reset circuit

performing an internal operation, R/$\overline{\text{W}}$ is always 1; that is, R/$\overline{\text{W}}$ is never in a logical zero state unless the CPU is executing a write to a memory location or a peripheral. However, the state of the R/$\overline{\text{W}}$ pin is undefined when the 68000 floats its control bus whenever it relinquishes control of the memory bus. Therefore, the designer must arrange for the R/$\overline{\text{W}}$ line to be pulled up to V_{cc} when the CPU is not controlling it. One of the most important aspects of microprocessor systems design is the avoidance of an unintentional write to a memory component.

UDS* and LDS*   The 68000 accesses memory via a 16-bit wide data bus. However, special provisions have to be made to enable it to access a byte of data instead of a word. When the 68000 accesses a word, both UDS* and LDS* are asserted simultaneously. When it wishes to access a single byte, UDS* is asserted if it is the upper byte (D_{08} to D_{15}) or LDS* if it is the lower byte (D_{00} to D_{07}). Table 4.2 defines the relationship between UDS*, LDS*, R/$\overline{\text{W}}$, and the data bus. Note that the expression DS* is sometimes used to indicate "UDS* and/or LDS*."

DTACK*   The active-low data transfer acknowledge input to the 68000 is a handshake signal generated by the device being accessed, and indicates that the contents of the data bus are valid and that the 68000 may proceed. When the processor recognizes that DTACK* has been asserted, it completes the current access and begins the next cycle. If DTACK* is not asserted, the processor generates wait-states (i.e., it idles) until it is or until an error state is declared. DTACK* may be generated by a timer that is triggered by the beginning of a valid memory access. When the timer counts up to a predefined value, it forces the DTACK* input to the 68000 low. This timer must be supplied by the system designer.

The way in which the asynchronous bus control group operates is dealt with

TABLE 4.2   Control of the data bus by UDS* and LDS*

R/$\overline{\text{W}}$	UDS*	LDS*	OPERATION	D_{08}–D_{15}	D_{00}–D_{07}
0	Negated	Negated	No operation	Invalid	Invalid
0	Negated	Asserted	Write lower byte	D_{00}–D_{07}	Data valid
0	Asserted	Negated	Write upper byte	Data valid	D_{08}–0_{15}
0	Asserted	Asserted	Write word	Data valid	Data valid
1	Negated	Negated	No operation	Invalid	Invalid
1	Negated	Asserted	Read lower byte	Invalid	Data valid
1	Asserted	Negated	Read upper byte	Data valid	Invalid
1	Asserted	Asserted	Read word	Data valid	Data valid

NOTE: In a byte write operation, the data on D_{00}–D_{07} is replicated on D_{08}–D_{15} for a lower-order byte access and the data on D_{08}–D_{15} is replicated on D_{00}–D_{07} for a higher-order byte access. This result is due to the current implementation of the 68000 and is not guaranteed in future versions of the 68000. However, this curious "anomaly" once caused me to spend several hours debugging a faulty 68000 system.

in some detail when the 68000 read and write cycles are described. The 68000 has three synchronous bus control pins (E, VPA∗, and VMA∗) that are not required in all systems and are described later.

Special Function Pins of the 68000

The 68000's pins in this group perform functions that are not necessarily needed in all applications of the processor. They are included here for the sake of completeness. Later chapters show how they are employed in sophisticated microprocessor systems. The special function pins of the 68000 fall into four groups: bus error control, which enables the 68000 to recover from certain types of error within the memory system; bus arbitration control, which allows more than one CPU to share the address and data buses; the function code outputs, which define the type of operation being executed by the 68000 and are used to control memory accesses in some systems; and the interrupt control interface, which allows a peripheral to signal its need for attention and permits the CPU to identify the source of the interrupt.

Bus Error Control

An active-low bus error input, BERR∗, is used by the microprocessor system to inform the 68000 that something has gone wrong with the bus cycle currently being executed. We may argue that this feature is one of the attributes distinguishing the 68000 from all 8-bit microprocessors and from some 16-bit microprocessors. The provision of a BERR∗ input permits the 68000 to recover gracefully from events that would spell disaster to other processors.

Sometimes an access is made to a memory location that is either faulty or nonexistent. The latter case may occur when a spurious address is generated due to a software error or it may be that the actual memory available in the system is less than the operating system "thinks." Whenever external logic detects such an anomaly, it asserts BERR∗. The precise nature of the action taken by the 68000 on recognizing that BERR∗ has been asserted is rather complex and is also dependent on the current state of the HALT∗ input. The behavior of the 68000 under these circumstances is dealt with later. For the moment we can state that the 68000 will either try to repeat (i.e., rerun) the faulty cycle or will generate an exception and inform the operating system of the bus error.

Bus Arbitration Control

When the 68000 has control of the system address and data buses, we call it the bus master. Many microprocessor systems include a mechanism whereby other microprocessors (or DMACs, direct memory access controllers) can also take control of the system bus. Consequently, some arrangement is necessary to inform the current bus master that the bus is needed by another device. The 68000 has three pins dedicated to bus arbitration control: bus request (BR∗), bus grant (BG∗), and bus grant acknowledge (BGACK∗). *Arbitration* is the term used to describe the sequence of events that takes place when a number of potential masters requests the bus simultaneously and one of them must be selected as the next bus master. The logic necessary to perform the arbitration is not part of the 68000 and must be designed to suit the user's own application. Some 68000 users employ the bus arbitration control logic to simplify the design of dynamic memory systems. We return to this topic in chapter 7. The three bus arbitration control pins of the 68000 are now briefly described.

BR∗   BR∗ is a bus request input and, when asserted, informs the CPU that another device wishes to take control of the system bus. All devices capable of being a bus master may drive the active-low bus request input with open-drain or open-collector outputs. Whenever a device wishes to take control of the bus, it first asserts BR∗, signaling its intent to the 68000.

BG∗   The 68000 asserts its active-low BG∗ (bus grant) output in response to the assertion of the BR∗ input, thereby indicating to the potential bus master that the current bus master is going to release control of the bus at the end of the current bus cycle. Once BG∗ has been asserted, the potential bus master can negate its BR∗ output.

BGACK∗   When the potential bus master detects that BG∗ has been asserted in response to its bus request, it asserts its bus grant acknowledge (BGACK∗) output, thereby informing the old bus master that the new bus master is now controlling the bus.

Function Code Outputs

In principle, a microprocessor simply reads instructions from memory, interprets them, and operates on data either within the processor itself or within the memory system. In practice, the operation of the processor is rather more complex because it may have to interact with external events through the interrupt mechanism. Moreover, the processor accesses different types of information in memory: instructions, data, the stack, and so on. Information about the nature of the operation being executed by the processor is often very important to the system designer; for example, such information can be employed to prevent one user from accessing a region of memory that may "belong" to another user or to the operating system.

This information is called function or status information and is provided by microprocessors (directly or indirectly) in varying amounts. The 68000 has three processor status outputs, FC0, FC1, and FC2, that indicate the type of cycle currently being executed. The function code becomes valid approximately half a state earlier than the contents of the address bus. Although the function code from the 68000 is not needed to build a working microcomputer, it can be used to enhance the operation of the system. One way of looking at the function code is to regard it as "an extension of the address bus." The significance of this statement will be made clear in chapter 7 when we discuss memory management.

Table 4.3 shows how FC0, FC1, and FC2 are interpreted. Of the eight states in table 4.3, three are marked "undefined, reserved," which tells us that these states may be reassigned in future versions of the 68000. Function code output FC2 distinguishes between two modes of operation of the 68000: supervisor and user. FC1 and FC0 divide memory space into data space and program space.

We can see from table 4.3 that, apart from interrupt acknowledge cycles, the 68000 is always in one of two states: user or supervisor. The concept of user and supervisor states does not exist for 8-bit microprocessors or for some 16-bit devices. User and supervisor states have a meaning only in the world of multi-tasking systems, where two or more programs (tasks) are running concurrently. The supervisor state is said to be the state of highest privilege, and certain instructions may be executed only in this state. In general, the supervisor state is closely associated with the operating system, while the less privileged user state is associated with user programs running under the operating system. By restricting the privileges available to the user state, individual programs are capable of causing less havoc if they crash.

The supervisor state is in force when the S bit of the processor status word is true. All exception processing (e.g., interrupt handling, bus error, and reset) is performed in the supervisor state, regardless of the state of the processor before the exception occurred. Consequently, the 68000 always powers-up in the supervisor state. A change from supervisor to user state can be carried out under program control, but it is impossible to move from the user to supervisor state by any sequence of instructions other than a TRAP. Only by the generation of an exception can a transfer from user to supervisor mode be made. Chapter 6 is devoted to the topic of exception handling by the 68000.

Table 4.3 also shows how it is possible to determine whether the processor is accessing program or data. The region of memory containing data is called *data*

TABLE 4.3   Interpreting the 68000's function code output

FUNCTION CODE OUTPUT			PROCESSOR CYCLE TYPE
FC2	FC1	FC0	
0	0	0	(Undefined, reserved)
0	0	1	User data
0	1	0	User program
0	1	1	(Undefined, reserved)
1	0	0	(Undefined, reserved)
1	0	1	Supervisor data
1	1	0	Supervisor program
1	1	1	Interrupt acknowledge

space, and the region containing instructions, *program space*. The meaning of the word "space" in this context is closer to the mathematician's use of the word (e.g., vector space) than to the everyday meaning.

One advantage of dividing memory space into program and data spaces is that it becomes possible to prevent a program from corrupting the data space of another program by detecting any access to program space that would corrupt the program. In chapter 2, we discovered that some of the 68000's instructions are privileged and that they can be executed only when the CPU is operating in the supervisor mode.

The function code denoted by FC0 = FC1 = FC2 = 1 is called *interrupt acknowledge* and indicates that the 68000 is currently acknowledging an interrupt.

Interrupt Control Interface

Three interrupt control inputs (IPL0*, IPL1*, IPL2*) are used by an external device to indicate to the 68000 that it requires service. These interrupts are encoded into eight levels (0 to 7). Level 0 has the lowest priority and indicates that no interrupt is requested. Level 7 is the highest priority interrupt. The interrupt mask bits, I_2, I_1, and I_0, of the status register determine the level of interrupt that will be serviced.

An interrupt request, indicated by a three-bit code on IPL0*, IPL1*, IPL2*, is serviced if it has a higher value than that currently indicated by the interrupt mask bits in the status register. A level-7 interrupt is handled rather differently because it is always serviced by the 68000.

Many peripherals capable of generating an interrupt have only a single interrupt request output. Consequently, most 68000-based microcomputer systems must use a priority encoder circuit to convert up to seven levels of interrupt request into a three-bit code that can then be fed into IPL0* to IPL2*.

Synchronous Bus Control

One important difference between the 68000 and many other microprocessors is that the 68000 is able to carry out asynchronous data transfers between itself and memory or peripherals. In order to understand the nature of asynchronous data transfers, synchronous transfers will be looked at first.

In a synchronous data transfer, the processor provides an address and some form of timing signal. Figure 4.3 demonstrates a simple synchronous data transfer—a CPU read from memory. At point A, a read cycle begins with the falling edge of the clock. At B, the CPU generates an address corresponding to the memory location being accessed. At C, the memory yields its data for the CPU to read. The current cycle ends at D with the falling edge of the clock. The time between C and D is called the data setup time of the CPU and is the time for which the CPU demands that the data be valid before the end of the cycle. In this arrangement the clock must allow enough time for the memory to access its data.

FIGURE 4.3   Synchronous data transfer

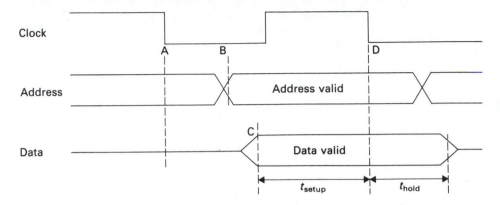

If sufficient time is not allowed and the setup time violated, the data obtained by the CPU may be invalid.

Strictly speaking, the 68000's synchronous bus control group of signals is not needed: all data transfers may take place asynchronously. The synchronous bus control group has been included entirely to simplify the interface between the 68000 and peripherals designed for use with the 6800, 6809 (or 6502) 8-bit synchronous bus microprocessors; that is, this group of signals makes the 68000 look like a 6800 to certain types of peripheral. Section 8.1 on interfacing techniques takes a more detailed look at the synchronous interface. Three control signals are included in this group: VPA∗ (valid peripheral address), VMA∗ (valid memory address), and E (enable).

VPA∗   The active-low valid peripheral address input is used by a device to indicate to the 68000 that a synchronous peripheral is being accessed. When the processor recognizes that VPA∗ has been asserted, it initiates a synchronous data transfer by means of VMA∗ and E.

VMA∗   VMA∗ is an active-low valid memory address output from the 68000 and indicates to the peripheral being addressed that there is a valid address on the address bus. The assertion of VMA∗ by the CPU is a response to the assertion of VPA∗ by an addressed peripheral.

E   The enable output from the 68000 is a timing signal required by all 6800 series peripherals and is derived from the 68000's own clock input. One E cycle is equal to ten 68000 clock cycles. The E clock is nonsymmetric: it is low for six clock cycles and high for four.

No defined phase relationship exists between the processor's own clock and the E clock. The E clock runs continuously, independently of the state of the 68000. Later we shall show how the synchronous bus group is used to interface the 68000 to typical 6800 series peripherals.

FIGURE 4.4   Asynchronous data transfer

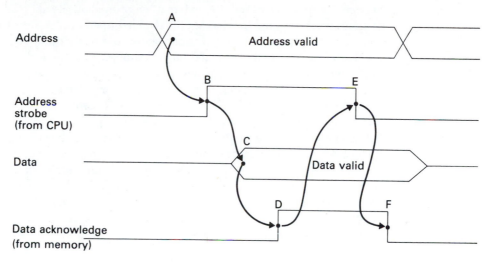

NOTE: Control signals shown are active-high.

Asynchronous Bus Control

An asynchronous data transfer is rather more complex, as can be seen from the simplified read cycle timing diagram in figure 4.4. The processor generates a valid address at point A and then asserts an address strobe at B. When the memory detects the address strobe, it places data on the data bus, which becomes valid at point C. The memory then informs the processor that it has valid data by asserting a data acknowledge signal at point D. The processor detects that the data is now ready, reads it, and negates its address strobe to indicate that it has read the data (point E). The memory then negates its data acknowledge signal at point F to complete the cycle.

The 68000 is not fully asynchronous because its actions are synchronized with its clock input. Although it may extend its memory access until an acknowledgment is received, the operation can be extended only in increments of one clock cycle.

4.2 Timing Diagram

Having explained the basic purpose of the pins of the 68000, we can now look at some of these functions in more depth. In this section we examine the read and write cycles of the 68000, which represent the most fundamental transactions between a processor and its external environment. Traditionally, the timing diagram has been used to illustrate the detailed operation of a microprocessor or a memory component. A timing diagram shows the relationship between the signals involved in a read/write cycle and time. Although the timing diagram is an educational aid, because it presents visually the relationship between a number of signals, it is principally a design tool. It enables an engineer to match components of different characteristics so that they will work together.

As we have not yet examined memory components and their characteristics, the timing diagrams presented here do not include fine detail. Chapter 5 examines the characteristics of memory components in more depth.

In recent years, the timing diagram has been supplemented by what may best be called a *protocol diagram* or *timing flowchart*. The protocol diagram is an abstraction of the timing diagram, which seeks to remove all detail in order to provide only the most essential information to the reader. The read and write cycles of the 68000 are explained here by means of both protocol flowcharts and timing diagrams.

The 68000 Read Cycle

This section considers the sequence of events taking place when the 68000 reads data from memory using its address and data buses in conjunction with the asynchronous group of bus control signals. The 68000 can read either a 16-bit word or an 8-bit byte in a single read cycle. As very little difference exists between these operations, only a word operation is described. The difference between a byte read and a word read is commented on later.

Figure 4.5 gives the protocol flowchart for a 68000 read cycle. Any read cycle involves two parties: the reader and the read. The reader is the 68000 and is represented by the bus master in figure 4.5. A bus master is the active device that is currently controlling the system bus; at any instant there can be only one bus master. A system can support several 68000s in a system, but only one may be the master at a time. Equally, a device other than a CPU may simulate a 68000 to gain control of the bus. The left-hand side of the diagram displays the actions carried out by the master (the 68000). Each block is labeled by the words in its top line. The numbered lines below the header describe the sequence of actions carried out by that block.

The right-hand side of the diagram displays the actions carried out by the slave during the transfer of information. The slave is, of course, the memory being accessed by the master. The protocol diagram is read from top to bottom so that the action "Address the slave" carried out by the master is followed by the slave with the action "Output the data." Note that actions within boxes may, or may not, take place simultaneously.

Figure 4.5 does not supply precise timing relationships or details of critical

FIGURE 4.5   Protocol flowchart for a 68000 read cycle

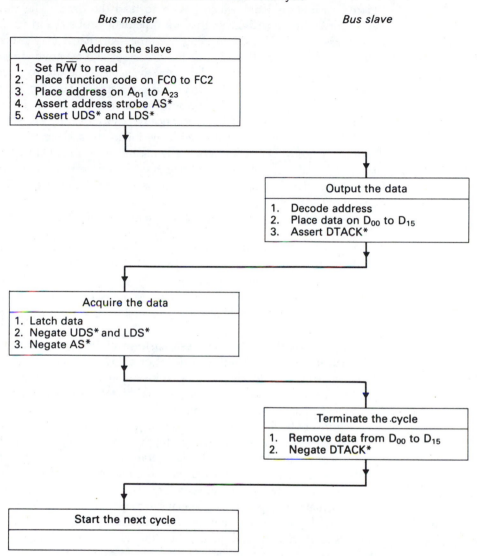

events; for example, in the block labeled "Output the data," it is the action of asserting DTACK* that allows the master to continue with the action "Acquire the data." This condition is not evident from figure 4.5, and therefore the diagram does not tell the whole story.

The essential feature of a 68000 asynchronous read cycle is the interlocked handshaking procedure taking place between the master and the slave. A read cycle starts with the master indicating its intentions by setting up an address and forcing R/$\overline{\text{W}}$ high. By asserting AS∗, UDS∗, and/or LDS∗, the CPU is saying, "Here's an address from which I wish to read the data." The slave detects the valid address strobe (AS∗) together with the data strobe(s) and starts to access the data. It asserts DTACK∗, informing the processor that it may proceed. DTACK∗ is the handshake from the slave to the processor and acknowledges that the slave has (or is about to have) valid data available. The microprocessor systems designer must provide suitable circuits to generate the appropriate delay between the start of a read (or write) cycle and the assertion of DTACK∗. If DTACK∗ is not asserted, the master will, theoretically, wait forever. As we shall see, the 68000 has provision for dealing with the failure of a slave to complete a handshake by asserting DTACK∗. When the master recognizes DTACK∗, it terminates the cycle by latching the data and negating the address and data strobes, thereby inviting the slave to terminate its actions by removing data from the bus and negating DTACK∗.

Before looking at the timing diagram of the 68000, some of the fundamental concepts it is designed to illustrate should be examined. Figure 4.6 shows four possible ways of displaying the timing diagram of a humble positive-edge triggered D flip-flop. This device has been chosen because it represents the basic memory element of which many memory systems are actually composed and because it latches data just as a microprocessor does. In other words, the microprocessor timing diagram is a scaled-up version of the timing diagram of the D flip-flop.

Figure 4.6a illustrates the idealized form of the timing diagram. All signals are either at a logical zero (lower) level or a logical one (upper) level. The transition between logic levels takes place instantaneously. At point A, the D input rises to a logical one level. At point B, the flip-flop is clocked, and the D input is latched and transferred to the Q output.

Figure 4.6b illustrates the actual behavior of a D flip-flop. All transitions between states are represented by sloping lines to show that they are never instantaneous. The sloping line is illustrative and does not indicate the actual rise- or fall-time of the signal. Timing diagrams are almost never drawn to scale.

The gradual transition between logic levels poses the question, "When does a signal actually change state?" The answer is, of course, that when a signal at the input of a logic element passes the device's switching threshold, the device responds to its new logical input. Unfortunately, the switching threshold for logic elements is not quoted in the specification. In any case, it varies from device to device. Many semiconductor manufacturers specify the switching characteristics of their devices by referring all timing to the point at which a signal passes a given level.

Thus, the reference level for output voltages is V_{OL} and V_{OH}, representing the guaranteed maximum output voltage in a logical zero state and the guaranteed minimum output in a logical one state, respectively. Similarly, the reference levels for inputs are V_{IL} (the maximum input guaranteed to be recognized as a low level) and V_{IH} (the minimum input guaranteed to be recognized as a high level). For Schottky TTL devices, the values of V_{OL}, V_{OH}, V_{IL}, V_{IL} are 0.4, 2.7, 0.8, 2.0 V, respectively. Some manufacturers specify the reference points as 10

FIGURE 4.6   Timing diagram of a D flip-flop

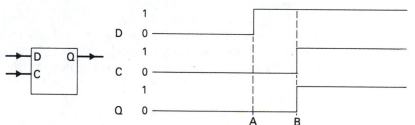

(a)   The idealized form of the timing diagram

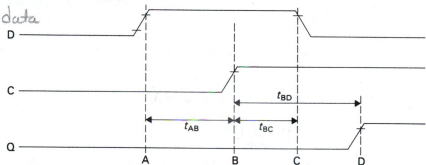

(b)   The actual behavior of a D flip-flop

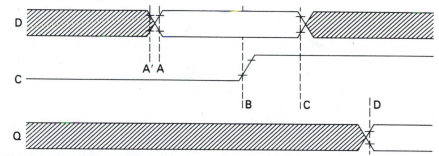

(c)   The general form of the timing diagram

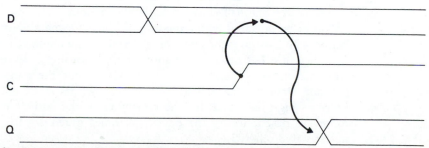

(d)   An alternative form of the timing diagram

and 90 percent of the high-level output of a gate; others choose the midpoint as the reference.

In figure 4.6b the time between the points A and B is labeled t_{AB}, and is measured from the point at which the D input has reached its logical one level (V_{IH}) and the point at which the clock has reached its logical one level. The value of t_{AB} is called the data setup time, and represents the minimum time for which data must be stable at the input of the flip-flop before it is clocked. At point C, the D input has left V_{IH} and is returning to a low level. The time between B and C (t_{BC}) is called the data hold-time, and is the minimum time for which the data must be held stable after the flip-flop has been clocked.

As a result of clocking the flip-flop, its Q output changes state at point D. The time t_{BD} is the maximum time taken for the output to become valid following a clock pulse.

So far, we have been concerned with specific changes of state (D changing from a low to a high level). Figure 4.6c gives the more general form of a timing diagram. The D input is represented by two parallel lines at logical zero and logical one levels. We are not interested in the actual value of the D input. Our concern rests with the points at which changes occur. At point A' the levels begin to change state, and at point A they have reached V_{IL} and V_{IH}. Point A is used as the reference point from which the setup time is measured. Prior to point A, the space between the parallel lines representing the D input is shaded and indicates that the data is invalid. Similarly, after the data hold-time has been exceeded (point C), the D input may change once more. Between points A and C the unshaded area represents the period for which the data must be stable.

An alternative way of showing timing diagrams is given in figure 4.6d. Sometimes it is wished to emphasize the relationship between signals on a cause and effect basis. The "cause" in figure 4.6d is the rising edge of the clock input. A line from this edge is drawn to the D input, showing that the rising edge of C causes D to be sampled. A line from the point at which D is sampled is drawn to the point at which Q changes state. This shows that the cause, D, results in the effect, Q.

A highly simplified version of a 68000 read cycle is presented in figure 4.7a. Each machine cycle consists of a minimum of four clock cycles and is divided into eight states labeled S0 to S7. All machine cycles start in state S0 with the clock high and end in state S7 with the clock low. As we shall see later, the machine read cycle may be extended indefinitely by the insertion of wait states (each with a duration of one half clock cycle) between clock states S4 and S5, allowing the 68000 to be operated with a mixture of both fast and slow memory components. Figure 4.7b illustrates the effect of wait states on a read cycle.

Figure 4.7 is designed to show the relationship between the 68000's asynchronous bus signals and between these signals and the states of the clock. During the first state, S0, all signals are negated with the exception of R/$\overline{\text{W}}$, which becomes high (i.e., read) for the remainder of the current machine cycle. In the following description of the 68000, all times given are for the 8-MHz version, unless stated otherwise.

In state S1, the address on A_{01} to A_{23} becomes valid and remains so until state S0 of the following cycle. In state S2 the address strobe, AS*, goes low, indicating that the contents of the address bus are valid. At this point we are tempted to say, "Why do we need AS*, as the falling edge of S2 can be used to indicate that the address is valid?" The answer to this question lies in the variations between different versions of the 68000. In the 12.5-MHz version, the possibility exists that AS* will not go low until state S3. The relationship between the clock and the 68000's signals is not what matters to the designer: it is the relationship between the signals themselves.

FIGURE 4.7   A 68000 read cycle

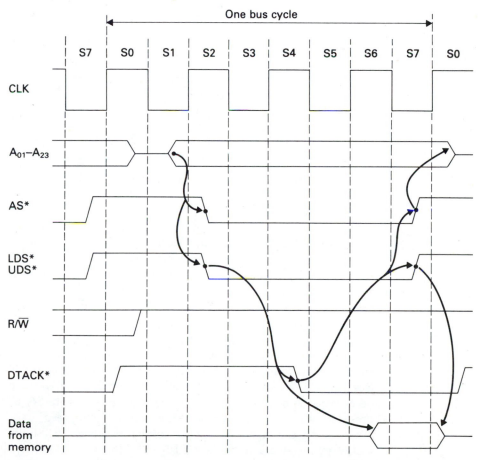

NOTE: The lines shown indicate indirect actions. For example, although the assertion of DTACK* in state S4 leads to the negation of AS* and UDS*/LDS* in state S7, the negation of these signals is actually triggered by the falling edge of the clock at the end of state S6.

(a)   Simplified timing diagram

FIGURE 4.7   (*Continued*)

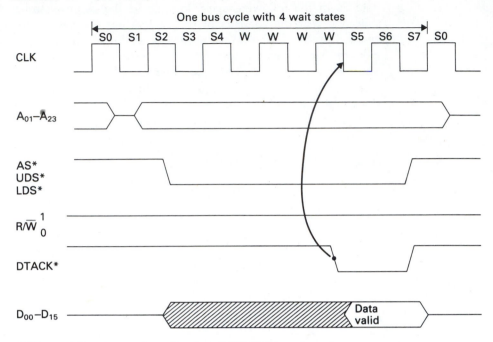

NOTE: Wait states are introduced until DTACK* is asserted.

(*b*) Simplified read cycle timing diagram with the insertion of wait states

In a read cycle, the timing specifications of the upper and lower data strobes (UDS* and LDS*) are the same as AS*. The falling edge of UDS* and/or LDS* initiates the memory access and, at the same time or after a suitable delay, triggers a data transfer acknowledge, DTACK*. Remember that the designer of the microprocessor system is responsible for providing suitable logic to control DTACK*. The delay between a data strobe going low and the falling edge of DTACK* must be sufficient to guarantee that enough time is allowed to access the memory currently being read. If DTACK* does not go low at least 20 ns before the end of state S4, wait states are introduced between S4 and S5 until DTACK* is asserted (see figure 4.7b). In figure 4.7 the assertion of the data strobe causes memory to be accessed and data to appear on the data bus in state S6, although the actual time depends on the access time of the memory being read.

During the final state of the current bus cycle, S7, both AS* and LDS*/UDS* are negated and the data is latched into the 68000 internally. The negation of these strobes causes the memory to stop putting data on the data bus and to return the bus to its high impedance (floating) state. DTACK* must be negated after the strobes have been negated. The address bus is floated (i.e., tristated) in the following S0 state and the read cycle is now complete.

The microcomputer designer needs to know the restrictions placed on his or

TABLE 4.4   Basic read cycle timing parameters of the 68000L8

PARAMETER NAME	SYMBOL	MINIMUM	MAXIMUM
Clock period	t_{cyc}	125	250
Clock width (low)	t_{CL}	55	125
Clock width (high)	t_{CH}	55	125
Clock high to address bus high impedance	t_{CHADZ}		80
Clock low to address valid	t_{CLAV}		70
Address valid to AS* low	t_{AVSL}	30	
Clock high to AS*, DS* low	t_{CHSL}	0	60
Clock low to AS*, DS* high	t_{CLSH}		70
AS*, DS* with low	t_{SL}	240	
Clock high to R/$\overline{W}$ high	t_{CHRH}	0	70
Clock high to FC valid	t_{CHFCV}		70
FC valid to AS* low	t_{FCVSL}	60	
Asynchronous input DTACK* setup time	t_{ASI}	20	
AS*, DS* high to DTACK* high	t_{SHDAH}	0	245
Data in to clock low setup-time	t_{DICL}	15	
DS* high to data invalid (data hold-time)	t_{SHDI}	0	
DTACK* low to data in setup-time	t_{DALDI}		90

her design by the timing diagram of a microprocessor. Figure 4.8 provides a more detailed read cycle timing diagram of the 68000. Table 4.4 gives the value of some of the read cycle timing parameters for the 68000L8.

The 68000 clock input is specified by three parameters. Its period, t_{cyc}, must not be less than 125 ns (for an 8-MHz clock) or more than 250 ns. The maximum limit is determined by the way in which the 68000 stores data internally as a charge on a capacitor. If the 68000 is not clocked regularly, internal data is lost, leading to unpredictable behavior of the processor.

Limits are also placed on the times for which the clock may be in either a high or a low state. A glance at table 4.4 reveals that the clock input should have an approximately symmetrical waveform with equal up- and down-times.

The address bus is floated within t_{CHADZ} seconds (80 ns maximum) of the start of S0. At no more than t_{CLAV} seconds (70 ns maximum) from the start of S1 the new address is placed on the address bus. The address strobe, AS*, is asserted no less than t_{AVSL} seconds (30 ns minimum) after the address has stabilized. AS* is a key parameter, because if the designer uses it to latch the address, he or she must choose a device with a setup-time less than t_{AVSL}.

FIGURE 4.8   Detailed read cycle timing diagram of the 68000

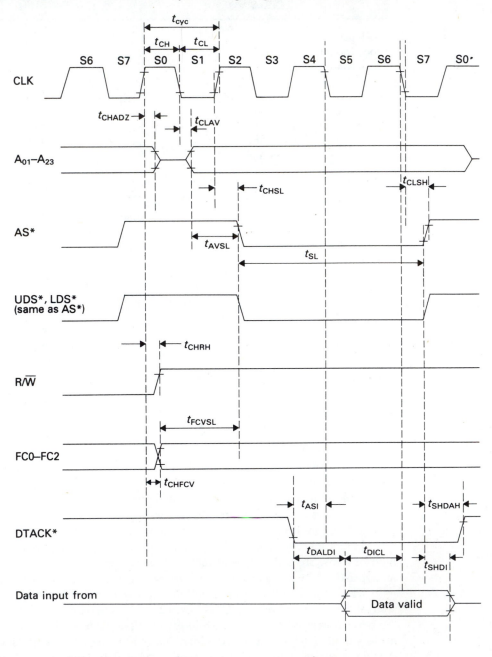

R/$\overline{\text{W}}$ is set high at the beginning of a read cycle no more than t_{CHRH} seconds (70 ns maximum) after the start of state S0, and stays high for the remainder of the current cycle. In practice, the designer can therefore forget about R/$\overline{\text{W}}$ during a read cycle, as it is high well before the other parameters are valid and remains high until well after they have changed.

The 68000 puts out its function code no more than t_{CHFCV} seconds (70 ns maximum) after the start of state S0 and no sooner than t_{FCVSL} seconds (60 ns minimum) before AS∗ is asserted. Consequently, the function code behaves like an address and can be latched by AS∗ at the same time as an address. The function code is available earlier than the address in order to give a memory management unit in a sophisticated system time to decode the type of memory being accessed. This topic is developed in chapter 7.

The key parameter governing the DTACK∗ handshake from the peripheral is its setup-time, t_{ASI} (20 ns minimum), before the falling edge of state S4. If DTACK∗ is asserted before its minimum setup-time, the next state will be S5. If DTACK∗ does not meet this setup-time, the processor introduces wait states after S4, until DTACK∗ is asserted at least t_{ASI} seconds before the falling edge of the next 68000 clock input.

The data from the memory being accessed is placed on the data bus and must satisfy setup- and hold-times similar to the input of the D flip-flop described earlier. The data must be valid at least t_{DICL} seconds (15 ns minimum) before the beginning of state S7.

During state S7, both address and data strobes are negated no more than t_{CLSH} seconds (70 ns maximum) after the falling edge of the clock. In order to meet the data hold-time of the 68000, the contents of the data bus must be stable for at least t_{SHDI} seconds (0 ns minimum) after the rising edge of the strobes. Here the minimum value of 0 ns means that the data may become invalid concurrently with the rising edge of AS∗ or LDS∗/UDS∗.

Memory Timing Diagram

Before we can perform any actual timing calculations on a 68000 read cycle, we have to look at some of the characteristics of memory. In this chapter we are concerned only with how the 68000 executes a memory access. The details of memory system design are left until chapter 5. For our present purposes, the memory device used to illustrate read/write cycles can be regarded as a "generic memory component." Figure 4.9 shows the timing diagram of an HM6116P-4 static random access memory component and figure 4.10 shows the pins through which it communicates with a microprocessor.

The HM6116P is byte orientated, and each read or write operation must involve an 8-bit byte. Two HM6116Ps must be configured in parallel to permit the 68000 to access one 16-bit word at a time. The HM6116P has eleven address inputs, labeled A_0 to A_{10}, allowing $2^{11} = 2,048$ locations to be uniquely accessed.

Three inputs, R/$\overline{\text{W}}$, OE∗, and CS∗, control the operation of the memory. Read/$\overline{\text{write}}$ (R/$\overline{\text{W}}$) determines the direction of data transfer during a memory

FIGURE 4.9   Timing diagram of an HM6116P-4 static RAM

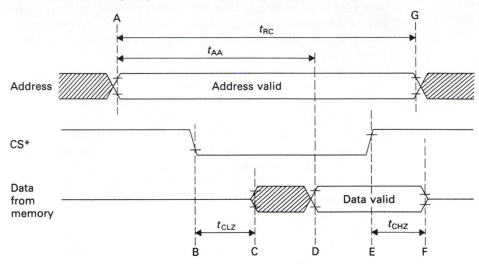

NOTE: R/W̄ is high for the duration of the read cycle and OE* is low. The read access is controlled entirely by CS*.

access. Output enable (OE∗) is an active-low control input that, when asserted, turns on the output circuits of the data drivers during a read access. Chip select (CS∗) is an active-low input that enables the chip during a read or write access.

The HM6116P is a static memory component that does not latch its address input. This means that the current memory cell is accessed as soon as an address is

FIGURE 4.10   Pinout of the HM6116P-4 static RAM

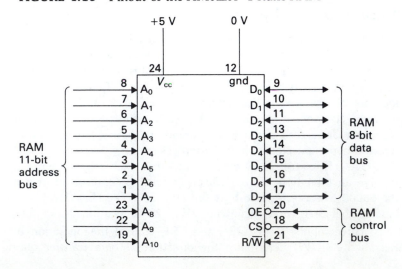

TABLE 4.5   Read cycle timing parameters of the HM6116P-4

PARAMETER	MNEMONIC	MINIMUM	MAXIMUM
Read cycle time	t_{RC}	200 ns	
Address access time	t_{AA}		200 ns
Chip select to output not floating	t_{CLZ}		15 ns
Chip deselect to output floating	t_{CHZ}	0 ns	50 ns

stable at the chip's address terminals. In figure 4.9 the address is stable between points A and G. This time is denoted by t_{RC}, the read cycle time, and has the minimum value of 200 ns (see table 4.5). Consequently, successive accesses to the HM6116P must be separated by at least 200 ns.

Neither the R/$\overline{W}$ line nor OE∗ appear in figure 4.9. We assume that R/$\overline{W}$ is high for the entire cycle and that OE∗ is permanently low. Unless OE∗ is used as a method of turning on and off the data bus drivers independently of the CS∗ input, it may be permanently asserted.

At point B, CS∗ is asserted to execute the read operation. In a 68000-based system, it is normally derived from one of the data strobes (UDS∗ or LDS∗). The action of CS∗ in a read cycle is to turn on the chip's data bus drivers. Consequently, the data bus comes out of its high impedance state, and data appears on the bus at point C, t_{CLZ} seconds after CS∗ is asserted. The maximum value of t_{CLZ} is 15 ns, which means that if CS∗ is asserted shortly after the current address has become valid, the data appearing on the data bus will not be valid. This condition is shown by the shaded region in figure 4.9. Not until point D, t_{AA} seconds after point A, do the contents of the data bus become valid and capable of being read by the computer. The duration between points A and D (i.e., t_{AA}) is the access time of the memory and is quoted as not more than 200 ns.

Chip select is negated at point E, which causes the data bus to be floated at point F. The maximum duration between points E and F is t_{CHZ} and is quoted as 50 ns.

Connecting the HM6116P RAM to a 68000 CPU

As an example of how the 68000 read cycle parameters affect its operation, consider the interface between the 68000 and a typical memory component. Figure 4.11 shows how two HM6116P 2K × 8 RAMs can be connected to a 68000 CPU. This circuit will work, although microprocessor systems sometimes isolate memory components from the 68000's address and data buses by means of buffers or data bus drivers. This subject is dealt with in chapter 10, when buses are treated in more depth.

The data bus of the 68000 is connected directly to the data buses of the HM6116Ps. RAM1 is connected to D_{00} to D_{07} and RAM2 to D_{08} to D_{15}. Note that this diagram raises an interesting practical problem. The data bus of all

FIGURE 4.11 Connecting the HM6116P-6 static RAM to a 68000 CPU

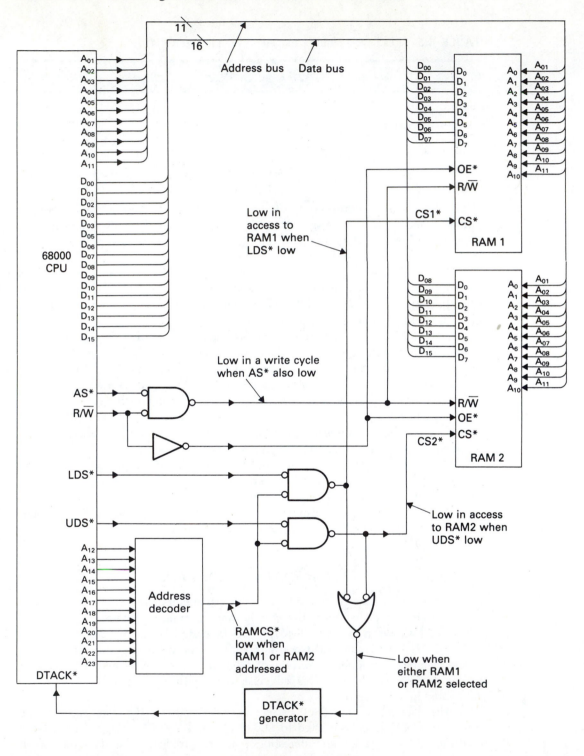

HM6116Ps has its pins labeled D_0 to D_7. As RAM1 has its D_0 connected to the 68000's D_{00}, etc., no problem exists. However, RAM2 has its D_0 connected to the 68000's D_{08}, etc., generating a problem of terminology. What do we (the writer, engineer, draftsperson) do when a line called X from component A is connected to a line called Y from component B? Clearly, we have a situation in which the same line has two different names.

The way out of this dilemma is to label lines by their system function, and the inputs and outputs of integrated circuits by the names used by the chip manufacturers. Whenever the name used by a chip manufacturer to define a pin differs from the name of a line connected to that pin, the manufacturer's name will appear only within the box representing the chip.

Address lines A_{01} to A_{11} from the 68000 are connected to the address inputs of the two HM6116P RAMs. The address inputs of the RAMs are wired in parallel, so that the same location is accessed in each chip simultaneously. Note also that A_{01} of the 68000 is connected to A_0 of the two HM6116Ps—illustrating the problem of terminology above.

The R/$\overline{W}$ input of each RAM is connected to the logical OR of AS* and R/$\overline{W}$ from the 68000. Therefore, the RAM can take part in a write cycle only when AS* is asserted. Each OE* is connected to the complement of R/$\overline{W}$ from the 68000 so that the RAM drives the data bus only in a CPU read cycle. Only the active-low chip select, CS*, inputs of the two RAMs are treated differently. Before dealing with CS*, a little needs to be said about address decoding.

Address lines A_{01} to A_{11} of the 68000 select one of 2K unique locations within the RAMs. Address lines A_{12} to A_{23} define 2^{12} or 4K possible blocks of 2K (note that 4K blocks of 2K words = 8M words). In order to uniquely assign the 2K words of RAM to one of these 4K possible blocks, address lines A_{12} to A_{23} must take part in a decoding process whereby only one of the 4K possible values spanned by these address lines is used to generate CS*.

The simplest possible address decoder is formed from a 74LS133 thirteen-input NAND gate whose output is active-low only when all address inputs are true. Thus, the RAMCS* output of the NAND is asserted whenever an address in the 2K word (i.e., 4K byte) range $FF F000 to $FF FFFF appears on the address bus.

Table 4.6 shows how the three signals, AS*, UDS*, and LDS*, from the CPU are combined with the RAMCS* signal from the address decoder to generate CS1* and CS2*. From table 4.6, it can be seen that CS2* is asserted (i.e., low) whenever AS*, RAMCS*, and UDS* are all asserted. Therefore, a simple OR gate can be used to derive CS2* from these signals. Similarly, CS1* can be generated in the same way, using LDS* instead of UDS*. Figure 4.11 demonstrates how little logic is needed to perform these functions.

Read Cycle Calculations

Having described the 68000's read cycle, the read cycle of a typical memory component, and a possible connection between the CPU and memory, the next

TABLE 4.6   Generating CS1* and CS2* from the 68000's strobes

INPUTS				OUTPUTS		
AS*	RAMCS*	UDS*	LDS*	CS2*	CS1*	Operation
1	X	X	X	1	1	No operation
X	1	X	X	1	1	No operation
0	0	0	0	0	0	Word read
0	0	0	1	0	1	Upper byte read
0	0	1	0	1	0	Lower byte read
0	0	1	1	1	1	No operation

NOTE: X = don't care (may be 1 or 0)
1 = true   (positive logic)
0 = false   (positive logic)

step is to determine whether the CPU-RAM combination violates any timing restrictions.

The principal timing parameter of the RAM is its access time t_{AA}, which must be sufficient to meet the data setup-time of the CPU (i.e., t_{DICL}). Figure 4.12 relates the essential features of the 68000's timing diagram to those of the HM6116P RAM. From the falling edge of S0 to the falling edge of S6, three full clock cycles take place, a total time of $3 \times t_{cyc}$. During this time, the contents of the address bus become valid (t_{CLAV}), the memory is accessed (t_{AA}), and the data setup-time met (t_{DICL}). Thus, the total time for this action is given by $t_{CLAV} + t_{AA} + t_{DICL}$. Putting the two equations together we get

$$3 \times t_{cyc} > t_{CLAV} + t_{AA} + t_{DICL}$$

or

$$t_{AA} < 3 \times t_{cyc} - t_{CLAV} - t_{DICL}$$

or

$$t_{AA} < 3 \times 125 - 70 - 15 \quad \text{(all values in ns)}$$

$$< 290 \text{ ns.}$$

The RAM must have an access time of less than 290 ns to work with the 68000L8 at 8 MHz. As the quoted value of t_{AA} for the HM6116P is 200 ns, the access time criterion is satisfied by a reasonable margin. An interesting consideration is what the demands on t_{AA} would have been if a 12.5-MHz version of the 68000 had been used. The value of t_{AA} is now given by

$$t_{AA} < 3 \times 80 - 55 - 10$$

$$< 175 \text{ ns.}$$

FIGURE 4.12   Read cycle timing diagram of a 68000 and HM6116P-4 combination

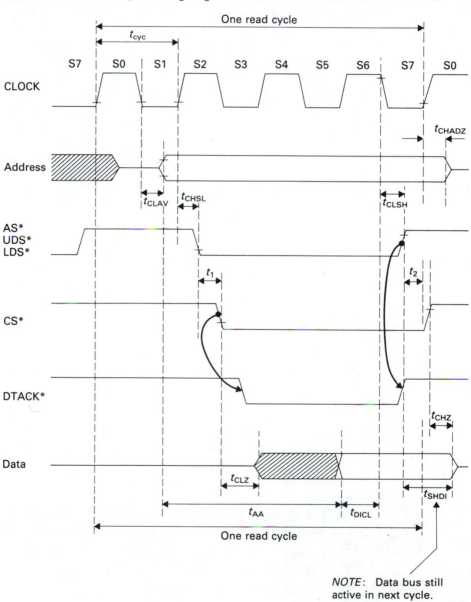

NOTE: Data bus still
active in next cycle.

Therefore, the HM6116P RAM cannot be used at 12.5 MHz without the addition of any wait states.

The next criterion to be considered is the value of the data hold-time (t_{SHDI} = 0 ns minimum) required by the CPU following the rising edge of AS*. No problem arises here because we can see from figure 4.12 that the address does not change until the start of state S0 in the next cycle, which means that the data from the RAM is valid (nominally) throughout state S7. Following the rising edge of AS*/UDS*/LDS*, the data bus drivers are turned off in the RAM. However, the data bus driver will not be floated instantly and the data hold-time of 0 ns will be met.

The control of CS* presents no problem. As CS* is derived from AS*, RAMCS*, and LDS*, it is asserted very early in a read cycle, approximately 10 ns (t_1) after the falling edge of AS*. This process turns on the data bus drivers in the RAM early in the cycle, although the data is invalid until after the RAM's access time has been met. At the end of a read cycle, CS* is negated when AS* rises no more than t_{CLSH} (70 ns) after the falling edge of state S6. The data bus is floated no more than $t_{CLSH} + t_2 + t_{CHZ}$ seconds after the start of S7. For a 68000L8 and 6116P-4 combination with $t_2 = 10$ ns, the guaranteed turn-off time is $70 + 10 + 60 = 140$ ns.

As the duration of S7 is nominally 62.5 ns, the data bus may not be floated until up to 77.5 ns into the following S0. Fortunately, the next access does not begin until S2, and so no chance of bus contention occurs; that is, the next access must not try to put data on the data bus until all the data bus drivers have been turned off following the current cycle. Chapter 10, which examines buses, looks at the read/write cycle timing diagram from the point of view of bus contention, the conflict arising when two devices try to drive the same bus simultaneously.

The 68000 Write Cycle

During a write cycle, the 68000 transmits a byte or word of data to either a memory component or a memory-mapped peripheral. When a byte is written, only 8 bits of data are transferred and the appropriate data strobe asserted. When a word is written, D_{00} to D_{15} transfer the word and both UDS* and LDS* are asserted simultaneously.

Figure 4.13 gives the protocol flowchart for a write cycle, which is very similar to the corresponding read cycle flowchart of figure 4.5. The essential differences are:

1.   The CPU provides data at the start of a write cycle.
2.   The bus slave reads this data.

A simplified timing diagram for a 68000 write cycle is given in figure 4.14. At the start of the cycle, an address is placed on A_{01} to A_{23}, and AS* asserted followed

FIGURE 4.13   Protocol flowchart for a word write cycle

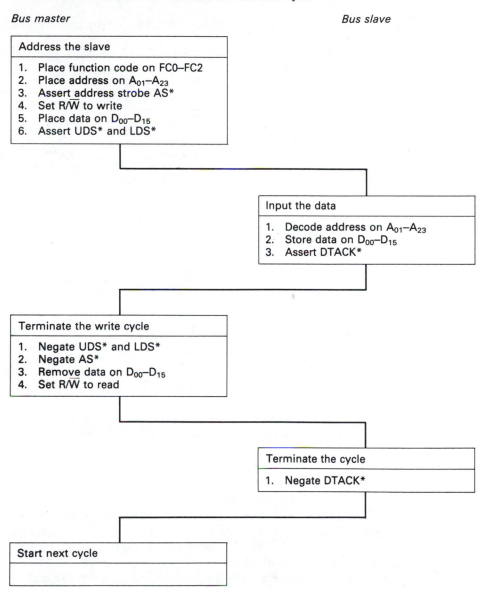

Bus master   *Bus slave*

Address the slave

1. Place function code on FC0–FC2
2. Place address on A_{01}–A_{23}
3. Assert address strobe AS*
4. Set R/$\overline{W}$ to write
5. Place data on D_{00}–D_{15}
6. Assert UDS* and LDS*

Input the data

1. Decode address on A_{01}–A_{23}
2. Store data on D_{00}–D_{15}
3. Assert DTACK*

Terminate the write cycle

1. Negate UDS* and LDS*
2. Negate AS*
3. Remove data on D_{00}–D_{15}
4. Set R/$\overline{W}$ to read

Terminate the cycle

1. Negate DTACK*

Start next cycle

by R/$\overline{W}$. Unlike the corresponding read cycle, the data strobes UDS* and LDS* are *not* asserted concurrently with the address strobe. The 68000 does not assert UDS* or LDS* until after the contents of the data bus have stabilized. Consequently, the data strobe can be used by memory to latch data from the CPU. After R/$\overline{W}$ has been asserted, the CPU places data on the data bus. Following this

FIGURE 4.14   Simplified write cycle timing diagram for the 68000

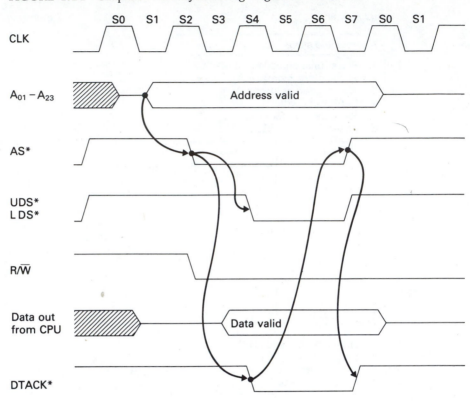

NOTE: The data strobe (UDS*/LDS*) is not asserted in a write cycle until one clock cycle after AS*. This allows the memory to use UDS*/LDS* to latch from the CPU.

procedure, one or both data strobes are asserted; that is, DS∗ is asserted approximately one clock period after AS∗ has gone low.

If DTACK∗ is asserted before the falling edge of the S4 clock, the write cycle is terminated without the addition of wait states. Otherwise wait states are introduced until DTACK∗ is asserted (and meets its setup-time) before the falling edge of the processor's clock.

At the end of a write cycle, AS∗ and DS∗ are negated simultaneously in response to the earlier assertion of DTACK∗.

A more detailed write cycle timing diagram is given in figure 4.15. Table 4.7 defines the parameters in figure 4.15 and gives their values for 8- and 12.5-MHz versions of the 68000. From figure 4.15 it can be seen that the sequence of events at the beginning of a write cycle is:

1. Address stable.

2. AS∗ asserted.

FIGURE 4.15   The 68000 write cycle timing diagram

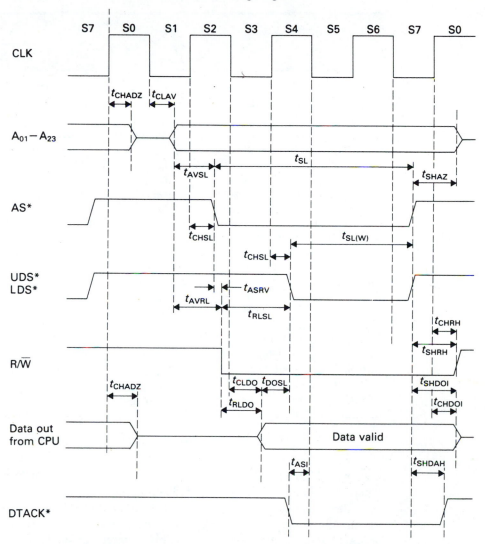

3.   R/$\overline{W}$ brought low.

4.   Data valid.

5.   Data strobe asserted.

Each of these events is separated by a nonzero period of time except for the 12.5-MHz 68000, whose address stable to AS* low (t_{AVSL}) is 0 ns minimum. This sequence is well suited to most memory systems, as they require the address to be stable before R/$\overline{W}$ makes its active transition.

At the end of the write cycle, the address and data strobes are negated;

TABLE 4.7   Write cycle timing parameters of the 68000

PARAMETER NAME	SYMBOL	8 MHz		12.5 MHz	
		MIN.	MAX.	MIN.	MAX.
Clock period	t_{cyc}	125	250	80	250
Clock high to data and address bus high impedance	t_{CHADZ}		80		60
Clock low to address valid	t_{CLAV}		70		55
Clock high to AS∗, DS∗ low	t_{CHSL}	0	60	0	55
Address valid to AS∗ low	t_{AVSL}	30		0	
Clock low to AS∗, DS∗ high	t_{CLSH}		70		50
AS∗, DS∗ high, to address invalid	t_{SHAZ}	30		10	
R/$\overline{W}$ low to DS∗ low (write)	t_{RLSL}	80		30	
AS∗ width low	t_{SL}	240		160	
DS∗ width low (write cycle)	$t_{SL(w)}$	115		80	
Address valid to R/$\overline{W}$ low	t_{AVRL}	20		0	
AS∗ low to R/$\overline{W}$ valid	t_{ASRV}		20		20
Clock high to R/$\overline{W}$ high	t_{CHRH}	0	70	0	60
AS∗, DS∗ high to R/$\overline{W}$ high	t_{SHRH}	40		10	
Clock low to data out valid	t_{CLDO}		70		55
R/$\overline{W}$ low to data bus low impedance	t_{RLDO}	30		10	
Data out valid to DS∗ low (write)	t_{DOSL}	30		15	
Data hold from clock high	t_{CHDOI}	0		0	
DS∗ high to data out invalid	t_{SHDOI}	30		15	
DTACK∗ setup-time	t_{ASI}	20		20	
AS∗, DS∗ high to DTACK∗	t_{SHDAH}	0	245	0	150

R/$\overline{W}$ is set high and the data bus is floated. However, some memory components require that their W∗ input be negated before their CS∗ inputs go inactive-high.

Before we consider the interface between a 68000 CPU and a memory component, the timing diagram of a memory component needs to be examined. Figure 4.16 gives the write cycle timing diagram of an HM6116 static RAM. Table 4.8 defines the parameters given in figure 4.16. Note that in figure 4.16 the chip's output enable, OE∗, is high throughout the write cycle.

The operation of the write cycle is entirely straightforward and no difficult conditions to be complied with exist. An address is presented to the chip and CS∗ and WE∗ asserted. A write cycle ends by either CS∗ or WE∗ being negated. Data from the processor must be valid t_{DW} seconds before the rising edge of CS∗ (or WE∗) and remain valid t_{DH} seconds afterward. Note that an address must be valid at least t_{AS} seconds before WE∗ is asserted and remain valid t_{WR} seconds after WE∗ has been negated.

FIGURE 4.16   Write cycle timing diagram of an HM6116 static RAM

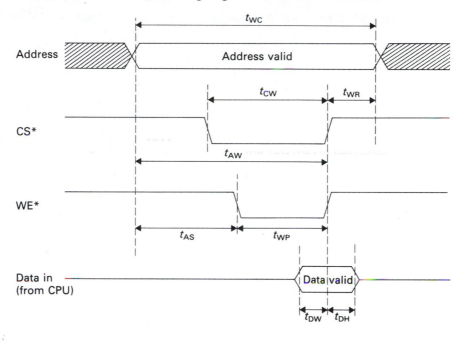

Write Cycle Calculations

The final step in considering the 68000's write cycle is to relate it to the write cycle of a typical memory component. For this exercise we use the circuit of figure 4.11. Figure 4.17 gives the write cycle timing diagram for the circuit of figure 4.11 with the appropriate timing parameters for both the 68000 and the HM6116P-4 static RAM.

TABLE 4.8   Write cycle parameters for figure 4.16

PARAMETER NAME	SYMBOL	MIMIMUM	MAXIMUM
Write cycle time	t_{WC}	150	~~150~~
Chip select low to end of write	t_{CW}	90	
Write recovering time	t_{WR}	10	
Address valid to end of write	t_{AW}	120	
Address setup-time	t_{AS}	20	
Write pulse width	t_{WP}	90	
Data setup-time	t_{DW}	40	
Data hold-time	t_{DH}	10	

FIGURE 4.17   Write cycle timing diagram of a 6116–68000 combination

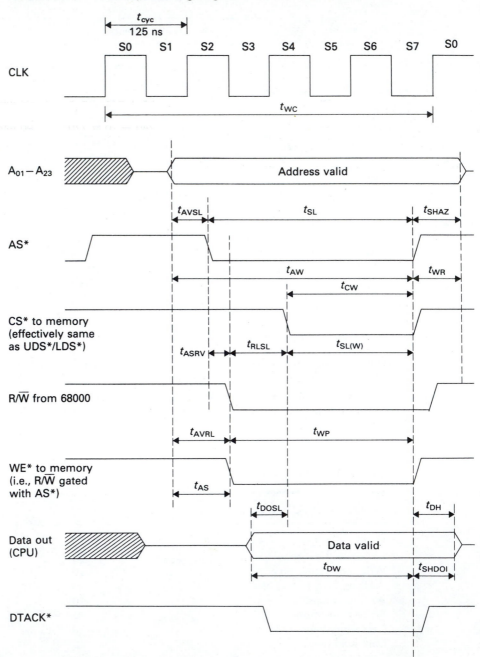

TABLE 4.9   Write cycle parameters of the HM6116-20 in terms of the 68000's parameters at 8 MHz

MEMORY PARAMETER	PARAMETER EXPRESSED IN 68000 TERMS	VALUE	REQUIRED	EXCESS
t_{wc}	$t_{AVSL} + t_{SL} + t_{SHAZ}$	$30 + 240 + 30 = 300$	150 min	150
t_{cw}	$t_{SL(w)}$	115	90 min	25
t_{WR}	t_{SHAZ}	30	10 min	20
t_{AW}	$t_{AVSL} + t_{SL}$	$30 + 240 = 270$	120 min	150
t_{AS}	t_{AVRL}	20	20 min	0
t_{WP}	$t_{SL} - t_{ASRV}$	$240 - 20 = 220$	90 min	130
t_{DW}	$t_{DOSL} + t_{SL(w)}$	$30 + 115 = 145$	40 min	105
t_{DH}	t_{SHDOI}	30	10 min	20

As in the case of the read cycle, the constraints on the memory component can all be written in terms of the 68000's parameters. These calculations are given in table 4.9. The final column in table 4.9 reports the excess time between the parameter required by the HM6116 and that provided by the 68000 at 8 MHz. In all cases, the excess value is positive, which indicates that the appropriate requirement is satisfied. In almost all cases the excess is quite large. The one exception is the address setup-time of the 6116, t_{AS}, which has a zero margin.

4.3 Minimal Configuration Using the 68000

People occasionally say to me, "How few chips does it take to build a microcomputer with a 68000 CPU?" In some ways this is an unfair question, because it tries to pin down the 68000 to a largely spurious figure of merit (i.e., a minimum chip-count design). This question takes no account of performance and is based on a rather dubious assumption that low chip count is related to low cost or ease of construction. Having given this warning, I am now going to look at a low chip-count 68000 microcomputer. My motives are twofold. I want to show which pins of the 68000 are essential to a simple microcomputer and which pins can be "forgotten" in a minimal design. Secondly, sometimes we need to produce a really small system, either as a teaching aid to illustrate the microprocessor or as a stand-alone controller. At this point in the text, the design of a 68000-based system is intended only to demonstrate the preceding points. Many of the details of the design cannot fully be appreciated until other sections of this text have been read.

While possible to design a 68000 microcomputer subject to the constraint of a minimum chip count, this is a rather pointless exercise, as the addition of one or two extra chips results in a vastly increased level of performance. Instead, I intend to design a system subject to the following constraints:

1. The microcomputer is to be used in a stand-alone mode and requires only a power supply and an external terminal.

2. It is intended to be used as a classroom teaching aid to demonstrate the characteristics of the 68000.

3. It must have a 16K-byte EPROM-based monitor.

4. Its speed (i.e., clock cycle time) is of little or no importance.

5. It must have at least 4K bytes of read/write memory.

6. It must have at least one RS232C serial I/O port and one parallel port.

7. It must be possible to expand the memory and peripheral space of the microcomputer later.

8. Interrupts and multiprocessor capabilities are not needed, but again the possibility of adding them later should exist.

The first step in designing our minimal system is to consider the major components, the ROM, RAM, and peripherals. The ROM is provided by two 8K × 8 components, the RAM by two 2K × 8 devices, and the peripherals by a 6821 peripheral interface adaptor (PIA) and a 6850 asynchronous communications interface adaptor (ACIA). Static RAM is used because it does not require the complex support circuitry needed by dynamic RAM (described in chap. 7). Figure 4.18 shows how the memory components are arranged in the microcomputer module.

The next step is to consider the memory and peripheral support circuitry. Clearly, the 16K bytes of ROM and the 4K bytes of RAM have to be selected out of the 68000's 16M bytes of memory space. The actual location of these devices within this space is largely unimportant, as long as the reset vectors are located at $00 0000. Consequently, the 16K bytes of ROM are situated at $00 0000 to $00 3FFF.

The circuit diagram of the control circuitry of the minimal single board computer is given in figure 4.19. Address decoding is carried out by three integrated circuits: IC1a, IC1b, IC2a, and IC3. These circuits divide the memory space in the region $00 0000 to $01 FFFF into eight blocks of 16K bytes. The first three consecutive blocks at the upper end of the memory space are devoted to ROM, RAM, and peripherals, respectively.

Whenever the Y0∗ or Y1∗ outputs of IC3 go active-low, signifying the selection of ROM or RAM, the output of NAND gate IC2b goes high. This output is complemented by open-collector inverter IC5a to become the processor's DTACK∗ input. Note that no delay is applied to DTACK∗, so we must match the processor's speed to its memory carefully.

The Y2∗ output of IC3 goes active-low whenever a peripheral is addressed in the 16K-byte memory space $00 8000 to $00 BFFF. Y2∗ is buffered by IC 5b

FIGURE 4.18   Block diagram of a minimal 68000-based microcomputer

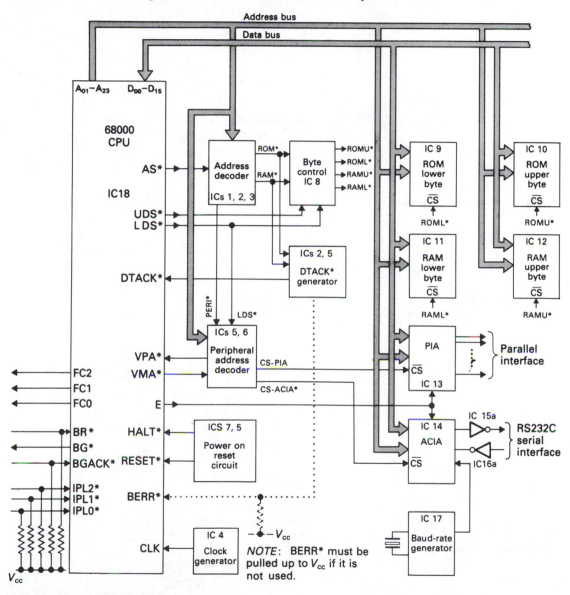

NOTE: BERR* must be pulled up to V_{cc} if it is not used.

NOTE: Function control, bus arbitration and interrupt request lines are either pulled up to V_{cc} or left open-circuit.

FIGURE 4.19   Circuit diagram of a minimal 68000-based microcomputer

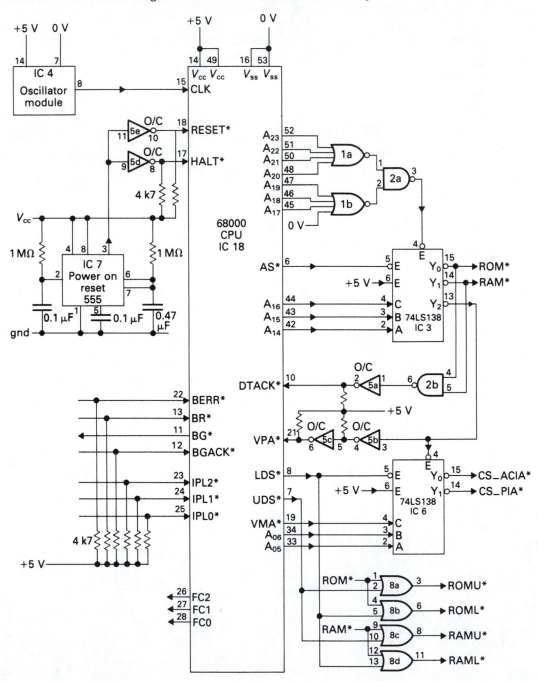

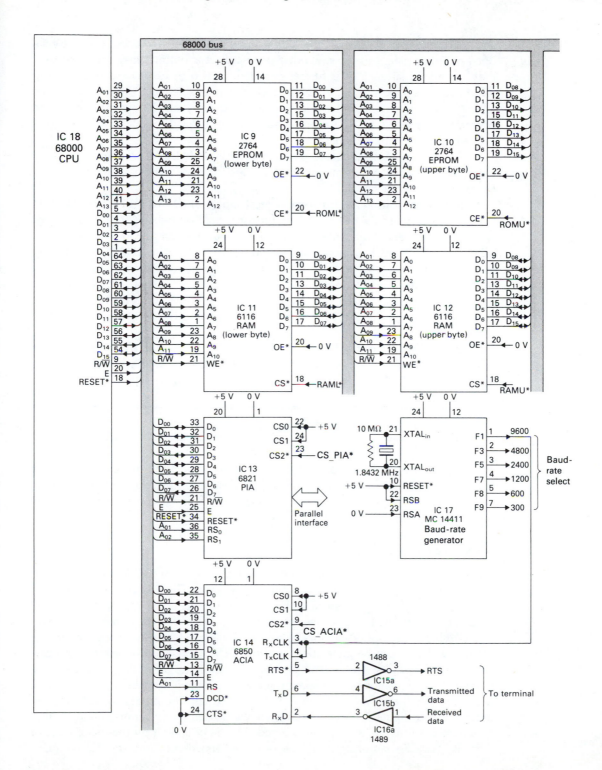

and IC5c in order to permit the VPA* input of the CPU to be driven by an open-collector gate. In this way, other open-collector outputs may drive VPA* if they are added latter. Y2* is further decoded by IC6 to generate peripheral chip selects for the PIA and ACIA. Note that IC6 is enabled by VMA* and LDS*, which means that a peripheral is synchronized to a 68000 synchronous cycle operation (triggered by VPA* being asserted) and that the CPU must address a lower byte to select a peripheral.

The power-on-reset circuit forces RESET* and HALT* low when the system is initially switched on. A monolithic DIL clock generator chip supplied the processor with its clock signal.

In this application the interrupt request inputs, IPL0* to IPL2*, are pulled up by resistors to their inactive state. The function code outputs, FC0 to FC2, are not required and are left unconnected. Both the bus request (BR*) and bus grant acknowledge (BGACK*) inputs are pulled up into their inactive-high states by resistors. The bus error input (BERR*) is not used and is also pulled up by a resistor. The 6850 ACIA requires its own clock, which is supplied by baud-rate generator IC17. Its serial inputs are buffered by a line receiver, IC16, and its outputs by a line transmitter, IC15. Chapter 9 describes the 6850 ACIA in greater detail.

In all, this minimal 68000 system contains eighteen integrated circuits. It works as it stands and can be expanded to become a more sophisticated system.

Critique of the Minimal Computer

The minimal computer of figures 4.18 and 4.19 is practical, but only just so. It lacks various features whose inclusion would cost little in terms of the chip count, but which would considerably enhance the system. Some of the areas in which the minimal computer could be improved are as follows.

*Control of DTACK**

The circuit of figure 4.19 exhibits a poor implementation of the DTACK* input to the 68000. Two problems have not been considered. The first concerns the operational speed of the processor. If the CPU is to run at its maximum rate and moderately fast RAM is used, we need to delay DTACK* only when the slower EPROM-based read-only memory is accessed. Figure 4.20 shows how individual DTACK* delays can be generated, one for RAM accesses (if necessary) and one for EPROM accesses. The second problem concerns the possibility of accesses to unimplemented memory. If a read or write access is made to memory not decoded in figure 4.19, the DTACK* input is not asserted and the processor will hang up indefinitely. In figure 4.20 a watchdog circuit is used to overcome this difficulty. When AS* is asserted, a timer is triggered. The timer is reset by the rising edge of AS*. If DTACK* is not asserted, the timer is "timed-out" and the BERR* input

FIGURE 4.20 Turning the minimal microcomputer into a general-purpose single board computer

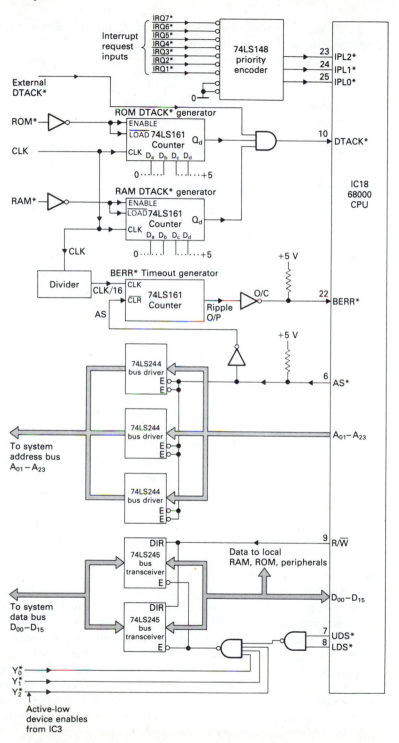

to the 68000 is asserted to indicate a bus error, thereby allowing the processor to detect and to recover from this error.

Control of Interrupts

While operation of the 68000 or any other processor in an interrupt-driven mode is not necessary, it is worthwhile to provide some form of interrupt facility in a general-purpose digital computer. Figure 4.20 shows how seven levels of interrupt request input can be provided by a 74LS148 priority encoder.

External Bus Interface

If a microprocessor system is to be expanded, it must be able to communicate with external systems via a bus. In a large system with many memory components or peripherals, connecting the 68000's pins directly to a system bus is impossible because the CPU cannot supply the current necessary to drive the distributed capacitance of the bus and all the inputs connected to it. Therefore, special-purpose circuits called bus drivers or buffers are interposed between the processor and the system bus. In addition to the bus drivers themselves, provision of control circuitry to avoid data bus contention is necessary, which could occur when the CPU reads from memory local to the processor module.

Summary

In this chapter we have introduced the hardware of the 68000 microprocessor from the point of view of the engineer who is going to design a microcomputer around the 68000. Our main focus of attention has been the 68000's data transfer bus, which the microprocessor uses to communicate with its memories and peripherals. An understanding of this bus and of the way in which information flows across the bus is essential to the designer of all microprocessor systems. Consequently, we have also examined the timing diagram of both the 68000 and a typical memory component because the art of microcomputer design consists largely of reconciling the timing diagram of a microprocessor with those of its memory and peripheral devices. We expand on the themes of timing diagrams and buses in chapters 5 and 10, respectively.

Some of the 68000's more esoteric pins such as its interrupt control pins and its bus arbitration control pins have been described. Later chapters show how these pins are used in 68000-based microprocessor systems.

The relationship between the 68000, its pins, and a microcomputer is highlighted by the design of a simple single board microcomputer at the end of this chapter. We do not intend that the reader should be in a position to understand fully the design of this microcomputer at this stage. The microcomputer has been introduced to provide an example of a complete system and to give an idea of the overall complexity of a basic microcomputer based on the 68000. Later chapters examine the various aspects of a microcomputer in greater detail and show how more complex systems can be built.

Problems

1. What is the difference between an asynchronous memory access and a synchronous memory access? How do these differences affect the designer of microprocessor systems? If a microprocessor could have only one type of interface, what would be the most suitable overall choice?

2. Can the 68000 be operated in a synchronous mode by strapping its DTACK* input to AS*? If the possibility exists to do this, what advantages and disadvantages would this mode of operation have?

3. Why cannot the 68000 be single-stepped through instructions simply by halting its clock after AS* has been negated at the end of a memory access?

4. What are the advantages and disadvantages of the protocol diagram as a design tool? In other words, what does each diagram reveal and what does it hide?

5. What is the meaning of data setup-time and data hold-time? Can either of these values be zero? Can they be negative? If the answer is yes to either of the last two questions, what does it imply?

6. Why does the 68000 require only one address strobe, AS*, but two data strobes, UDS* and LDS*?

7. In a 68000 read cycle, AS* and UDS*/LDS* are asserted simultaneously. In a write cycle, UDS*/LDS* is asserted approximately one clock cycle after AS*. What is the reason for this?

8. If a memory access cannot be completed by the slave asserting DTACK*, a watchdog timer on the CPU card asserts BERR* to force the processor out of its memory access. Suppose an engineer wished to know the value of FC0 to FC3, A_{01} to A_{23}, and D_{00} to D_{15} at the time BERR* was asserted? What logic would be necessary for this?

9. What is the maximum read cycle access time that a memory component may have if it is to be employed in an 8-MHz system with no wait states (use the parameters of table 4.4)? If a single wait state is permitted, what is the new maximum access time?

10. For the 60000–HM6116 combination, the following expressions relate 60000 parameters to HM6116 parameters during a write cycle. Show, by means of a timing diagram, that these expressions are valid.

a. $t_{WC} = t_{AVSL} + t_{SL} + t_{SHAZ}$
b. $t_{CW} = t_{SL(w)}$
c. $t_{WR} = t_{SHAZ}$
d. $t_{AW} = t_{AVSL} + t_{SL}$
e. $t_{AS} = t_{AVRL}$
f. $t_{WP} = t_{SL} - t_{ASRV}$
g. $t_{DW} = t_{DOSL} + t_{SL(w)}$
h. $t_{DH} = t_{SHDOI}$

11. Using the equations of question 10, the parameters of the 68000 (table 4.7), and the parameters of the HM6116 (table 4.8), investigate the write cycle for a 200-ns HM6116 and a 12.5-MHz 68000.

12. Figure 4.21a and b gives the circuit diagram of two typical DTACK* generators. Analyze their operation by providing a suitable timing diagram. The data on the shift register and the counter is given in figure 4.22a and b, respectively.

13. Design a circuit to permit a single bus cycle at a time to be executed. The HALT* line must normally be held in its active-low state and be negated long enough for the 68000 to execute a single bus cycle.

FIGURE 4.21   DTACK* generator

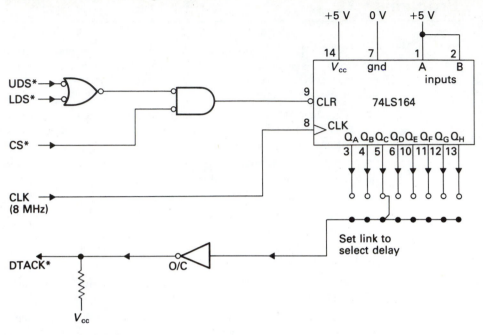

(a) Using a shift register

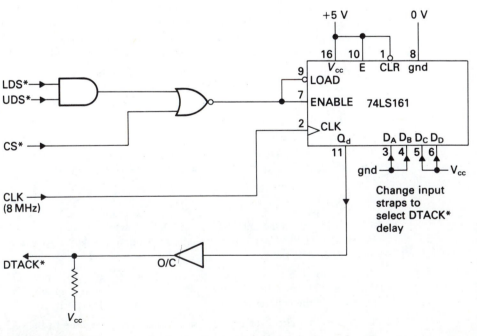

(b) Using a counter

FIGURE 4.22 The 74LS164 shift register and the 74LS161 binary counter

These 8-bit shift registers feature gated serial inputs and an asynchronous clear. The gated serial inputs (A and B) permit complete control over incoming data as a low at either (or both) input(s) inhibits entry of the new data and resets the first flip-flop to the low level at the next clock pulse. A high-level input enables the other input which will then determine the state of the first flip-flop. Data at the serial inputs may be changed while the clock is high or low, but only information meeting the setup requirements will be entered. Clocking occurs on the low-to-high-level transition of the clock input. All inputs are diode-clamped to minimize transmission-line effects.

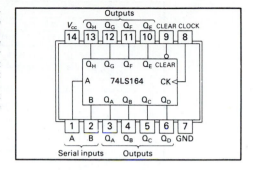

Function table

Inputs				Outputs			
CLEAR	CLOCK	A	B	Q_A	Q_B	$\cdots$	Q_H
L	X	X	X	L	L		L
H	L	X	X	Q_{AO}	Q_{BO}		Q_{HO}
H	↑	H	H	H	Q_{An}		Q_{Gn}
H	↑	L	X	L	Q_{An}		Q_{Gn}
H	↑	X	L	L	Q_{An}		Q_{Gn}

H = high level (steady state), L = low level (steady state)
X = irrelevant (any input, including transitions)
↑ = transition from low to high level
Q_{AO}, Q_{BO}, Q_{HO} = the level of Q_A, O_B, or Q_H, respectively, before the indicated steady-state input conditions were established
Q_{An}, Q_{Gn} = the level of Q_A or Q_G before the most recent ↑ transition of the clock, indicates a one-bit shift

Typical clear, shift, and clear sequences

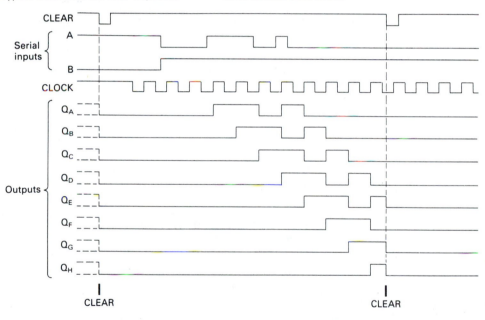

Functional block diagram

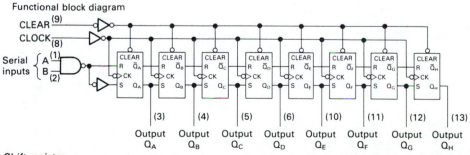

(a) Shift register

FIGURE 4.22 (*Continued*)

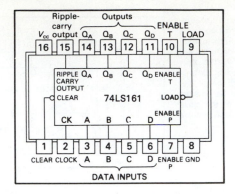

Typical clear, preset, count, and inhibit sequences

  Illustrated below is the following sequence:
1. Clear outputs to zero
2. Preset to binary twelve
3. Count to thirteeen, fourteen, fifteen, zero, one, and two

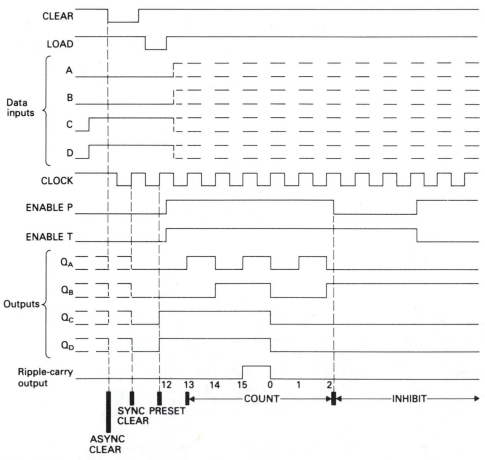

(b) Binary counter

Figure 4.22 Reprinted by permission of Texas Instruments

150

Chapter 5

Memories in

Microcomputer Systems

In this chapter we look at the "immediate access" or "random access" memory subsystem that holds programs and data required by the CPU. As memory systems design involves so many different concepts, the chapter is divided into three sections. The first deals with address decoding strategies and the second looks at circuits needed to interface a block of memory to a microprocessor's address bus. The third section examines the actual memory components themselves and considers their timing diagrams and their interface to the microprocessor's data bus. In order to keep the size of this chapter within reasonable bounds, more advanced memory topics are dealt with in chapter 7.

5.1 Address Decoding Strategies

We begin by examining the way in which memory components are interfaced to the 68000's address bus. A circuit is first designed to map the address space of a memory component on to the processor's address space. As we shall see, a number of different methods of designing the address decoding circuits are needed to implement such interfaces. All designers of microcomputers are confronted with the problem of synthesizing the most cost-effective address decoder subject to constraints of economics, reliability, testability, versatility, board area, chip count, power dissipation, and speed. The way in which these factors determine the design of address decoders is discussed in this chapter.

Memory Space

Before we introduce address decoding, a problem of notation must be dealt with. Strictly speaking, the 68000 is a machine that can address one of 8M words of memory with its twenty-three address lines, designated A_{01} through A_{23}. However, the 68000 permits the access of individual bytes of memory. Two data strobes, UDS* and LDS*, select one or both halves (i.e., bytes) of the memory word addressed by A_{01} through A_{23}. Because it permits byte accesses, the 68000 numbers its memory locations from \$00 0000 to \$FF FFFF, each pair of locations corresponding to a single word. The problem here is whether to treat the 68000 as having 16M addressable locations of 8 bits or 8M addressable locations of 16 bits.

For the purpose of this chapter, both conventions are used. We need to consider the 68000 as being byte addressable (i.e., 16M bytes) because it operates as a byte-addressable machine from the programmer's point of view. Equally, it appears as a word-addressable machine to the designer of address decoders, because the data control strobes, UDS* and LDS*, take no part in the address decoding process.

Figure 5.1 represents the 16M bytes of uniquely addressable locations accessible by the 68000 as a column, or linear list, from \$00 0000 to \$FF FFFF. An even address refers to the upper byte of a word, accessed when UDS* is asserted, and an odd address refers to the lower byte, accessed when LDS* is asserted.

The 16M bytes in figure 5.1 constitute an address space that is said to be spanned by the 68000's twenty-three address lines. The term "spanned" is used because any location in the address space is "reached" or specified by a unique value on A_{01} through A_{23}. The address space of figure 5.1 can be partitioned into blocks, each block containing a number of consecutive memory locations. Figure 5.2 shows the arrangement of three of these blocks and is called a *memory map*. Blocks may correspond to logical entities such as programs, subroutines, or

FIGURE 5.1   The 68000's address space

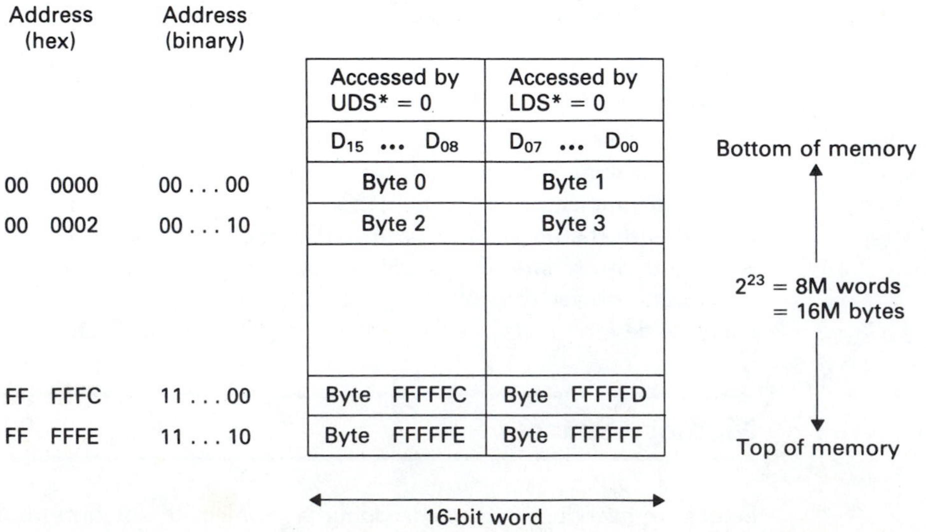

Address (hex)	Address (binary)	Accessed by UDS* = 0 $D_{15} \ldots D_{08}$	Accessed by LDS* = 0 $D_{07} \ldots D_{00}$	
00 0000	00 . . . 00	Byte 0	Byte 1	Bottom of memory
00 0002	00 . . . 10	Byte 2	Byte 3	
				2^{23} = 8M words = 16M bytes
FF FFFC	11 . . . 00	Byte FFFFFC	Byte FFFFFD	
FF FFFE	11 . . . 10	Byte FFFFFE	Byte FFFFFF	Top of memory

← 16-bit word →

FIGURE 5.2   Memory map

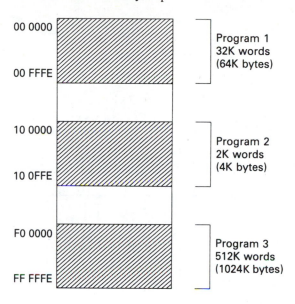

data structures, or to actual hardware devices such as ROM, read/write memory, or peripherals.

If a single memory component spanning the entire memory space of the 68000 existed, the problem of address decoding would not arise. Each of the 68000's twenty-three address lines would be connected to the corresponding address input of this 16M byte device. However, not only do microcomputers have memory components with fewer than 16M bytes of internal storage but they also invariably employ a wide range of devices whose internal storage may vary from 1M locations to just one location. It is this broad range of storage capacities that makes the life of the microcomputer designer so difficult.

Suppose the designer of a 68000-based microcomputer decides that 2K words of ROM and 2K words of RAM are needed for a certain application. Eleven address lines from the system address bus, A_{01} through A_{11}, are connected to the corresponding address inputs of the two memory components, M1 and M2, as shown in figure 5.3. Whenever a location spanned by A_{01} through A_{11} (i.e., $2^{11} = 2K$ words or 4K bytes) is addressed in M1, the corresponding location is also addressed in M2. The data buses of both memory components are connected to the data bus from the CPU. Because the data lines of M1 and M2 are connected together with D_i from M1 wired to D_i from M2, the data bus drivers in both memory components need to have tristate outputs, thereby avoiding the situation in which both outputs attempt to drive the bus to different logic levels simultaneously. Chapter 10 deals with this topic in more detail. Each memory component has an active-low chip-select input with which it controls its data bus drivers. Whenever the memory component is enabled by asserting its chip-select

FIGURE 5.3   Connecting two 2K memory components to an address bus

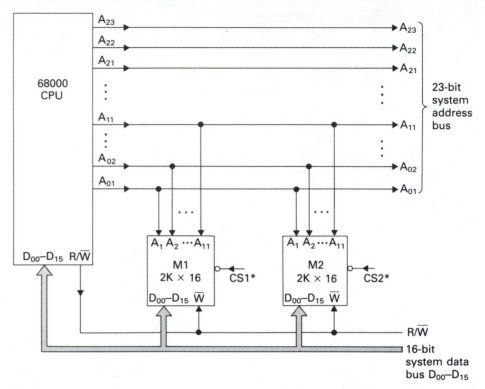

NOTE: The 2K × 16-bit memory components are hypothetical examples. A real system would use two 2K × 8-bit devices. Sixteen-bit wide memory components have been "invented" to simplify the system.

input, it is able to take part in a read or a write cycle. Negating the chip-select input of a memory component by putting it in an inactive-high state causes its data bus drivers to be turned off and its data bus outputs to be floated.

Let the chip-select input to M1, CS1*, be made a function of address lines A_{12} to A_{23}, where CS1* = $F1(A_{12}, A_{13}, \ldots, A_{23})$. Similarly, let CS2* be made a different function of A_{12} to A_{23}, where CS2* = $F2(A_{12}, A_{13}, \ldots, A_{23})$. The art of address decoding is to select functions F1 and F2 so that there is at least one combination of A_{12} to A_{23} that makes CS1* low and CS2* high and at least one combination that makes CS2* low and CS1* high. Under these circumstances, the conflict between M1 and M2 is resolved and the memory map of the system now consists of two disjoint blocks of memory, M1 and M2. This chapter considers three strategies for decoding A_{12} to A_{15} (i.e., choosing F1 and F2). These strategies are full address decoding, partial address decoding, and block address decoding.

Full Address Decoding

A microprocessor is said to have full address decoding when each addressable location within a memory component responds only to a single, unique address on the system address bus. In other words, all the microprocessor's address lines must be used to access each physical memory location, either by specifying a given device or by specifying an address within it.

Full address decoding can be applied to the problem of distinguishing between two memory components, M1 and M2, by constructing a logic network that uses address lines A_{12} to A_{23} to select either M1 or M2 but not M1 and M2. One of the many possible solutions is:

1. M1 is selected whenever
$$A_{12}\, A_{13}\, A_{14}\, A_{15}\, A_{16}\, A_{17}\, A_{18}\, A_{19}\, A_{20}\, A_{21}\, A_{22}\, A_{23} = 0\,0\,0\,0\,0\,0\,0\,0\,0\,0\,0\,0.$$

2. M2 is selected whenever
$$A_{12}\, A_{13}\, A_{14}\, A_{15}\, A_{16}\, A_{17},\, A_{18}\, A_{19}\, A_{20}\, A_{21}\, A_{22}\, A_{23} = 1\,0\,0\,0\,0\,0\,0\,0\,0\,0\,0\,0.$$

Figure 5.4 shows the memory map and the address decoder circuit for this solution.

Now let us look at a more practical example of full address decoding. The designer of a 68000 microcomputer has an application requiring 10K words of ROM arranged as a block of 2K words plus a block of 8K words, 2K words of random access read/write memory, two words for peripheral 1, and two words for peripheral 2. Five memory devices are therefore to be decoded and these will be called ROM1 (2K), RAM (2K), ROM2 (8K), PERI1 (2), and PERI2 (2), respectively. These devices each have an active-low chip-select input and may be located anywhere within the system's memory map, with the sole exception of ROM1, which must respond to addresses in the range $00 0000 to $00 0FFF. Note that we can write the range as $00 0000 to $00 0FFF or $00 0000 to $00 0FFE depending on whether we choose the last byte or the last word of the address block.

The first step in solving this problem is to construct an address table. Such a table is given in table 5.1, where the vertical columns represent the twenty-three address lines A_{01} to A_{23} and the rows represent the five memory components to be decoded. A cross, $\times$, in an address column means that that address line takes part in the selection of a location within the specified component. A 1 or 0 in an address column means that that address line must be 1 or 0 to select that component.

The address lines to be decoded for each memory component must be selected as either zero or one. How we perform this procedure is, to a certain extent, unimportant. In table 5.1, I selected the lowest possible address for each device subject to the constraint that an n-word block starts at an n-word bound-

FIGURE 5.4   Resolving the conflict between the memory components by full address decoding

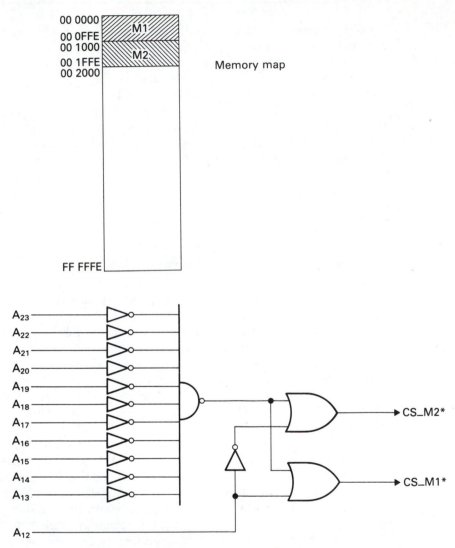

A possible address decoder for the above memory map

ary; for example, the 8K ROM starts on an 8K boundary. To achieve full address decoding we need only to decode *every* address line that does not select a location within a device and to ensure that no two devices can be accessed simultaneously.

We can see that when full address decoding is applied to the example in table 5.1, the two peripherals each require twenty-two address lines to be

TABLE 5.1   Address decoding table illustrating full address decoding

DEVICE	ADDRESS LINE																				
	23	22	21	20	...	15	14	13	12	11	10	09	08	07	06	05	04	03	02	01
ROM1	0	0	0	0	...	0	0	0	0	×	×	×	×	×	×	×	×	×	×	×
RAM	0	0	0	0	...	0	0	0	1	×	×	×	×	×	×	×	×	×	×	×
ROM2	0	0	0	0	...	0	1	×	×	×	×	×	×	×	×	×	×	×	×	×
PERI1	0	0	0	0	...	1	0	0	0	0	0	0	0	0	0	0	0	0	0	×
PERI2	0	0	0	0	...	1	0	0	0	0	0	0	0	0	0	0	0	0	1	×

decoded, as only one address line, A_{01}, selects a location (one of two) within the peripheral. A suitable address decoding arrangement is given in figure 5.5. Note that PERI1 is selected whenever A_{16}–A_{23} and A_{02}–A_{14} are all zero and A_{15} is a logical one. Twenty-two address lines need to be decoded and two 74LS133 thirteen-input NAND gates are pressed into service for this purpose. Whenever the outputs of both NAND gates are simultaneously low, the CS* output of the OR gate goes low, selecting PERI1. This circuit highlights one of the paradoxes of microcomputer design. The microcomputer and peripheral are available as two single chips and yet the address decoding circuit of figure 5.5 requires a total of seven chips (assuming that three hex invertors are used).

Partial Address Decoding

Partial address decoding is so called because all the address lines available for address decoding do not take part in the decoding process. Partial address decoding is the simplest, and consequently the most inexpensive, form of address decoding to implement. Figure 5.6 shows how the two 4K-byte blocks of memory depicted in figure 5.3 can be connected to a system address bus in such a way that both blocks of memory are never accessed simultaneously. The potential conflict between M1 and M2 is resolved by connecting CS1* directly to the highest-order address line, A_{23}, and by connecting CS2* to A_{23} via an invertor. In this way, M1 is selected whenever $A_{23} = 0$ and M2 is selected whenever $A_{23} = 1$.

We have now succeeded in distinguishing between M1 and M2 for the cost of a single invertor, but a heavy price has been paid. As M1 is selected by $A_{23} = 0$ and M2 by $A_{23} = 1$, obviously either M1 or M2 must always be selected. Thus, although the address bus can specify 16M different byte addresses, this decoding arrangement allows only 4K different locations to be accessed. Address lines A_{12} to A_{22} take no part whatsoever in the address decoding process and therefore have no effect on the selection of M1 or M2. Figure 5.7 shows the

FIGURE 5.5   Full address decoding network corresponding to table 5.1

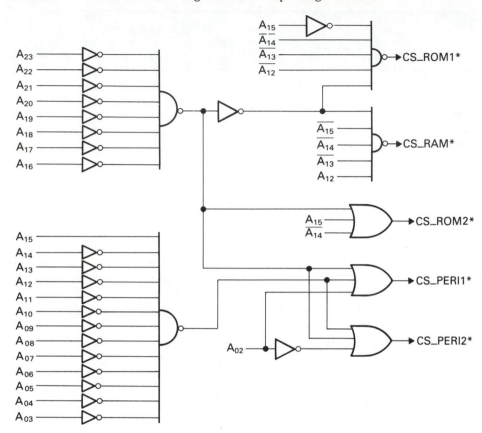

memory map corresponding to this arrangement. We can see that the memory space M1 appears 2,048 (i.e., 2^{11}) times in the lower half of the memory map and M2 is repeated 2,048 times in the upper half.

Partial address decoding was popular in the early days of the 8-bit microprocessor and is still found in small, dedicated systems where low cost is of paramount importance. The penalty paid for employing partial address decoding is that it prevents full use of the microprocessor's available memory space and produces difficulties when expanding the memory system at a later date.

Example of Partial Address Decoding

Consider now a more reasonable example of partial address decoding. We will take the same problem used in the preceding section on full address decoding. An address decoding table for this problem is given in table 5.2.

The first step is to fill the five rows with ×s for each address line used to select a location within the appropriate memory component; for example, address

FIGURE 5.6   Using partial address decoding to distinguish between two memory components

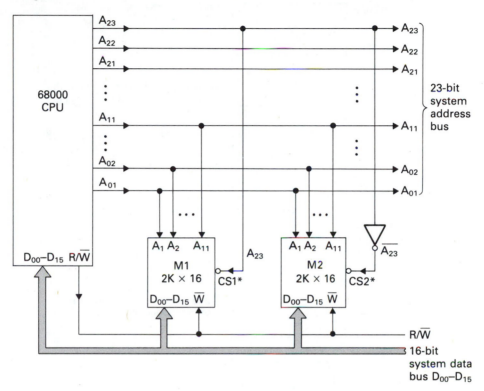

lines A_{01} through A_{11} select a location within ROM1 (2^{11} = 2K), while address lines A_{01} through A_{13} select a location within ROM2 (2^{13} = 8K). The next step is to select conditions for the higher-order address lines, which distinguish between the five memory components. One of the many possible ways of doing this is illustrated in table 5.2. From this table we can see that no combination of A_{21}, A_{22}, and A_{23} can be used to select two or more devices simultaneously. The reader may wonder why I have chosen A_{21}, A_{22}, and A_{23} to distinguish among these five components. The answer concerns the matter of style. We could have perfectly easily been able to decode, say, A_{14}, A_{15}, and A_{16} to perform the same function. In that case, address lines A_{17} to A_{23} would remain undecoded.

Having drawn the address decoding table, the primary addressing range of each component can be determined. The primary addressing range is calculated by setting all don't care conditions to zero and then reading the minimum and maximum address range taken by the component when the ×s are all 0s and all 1s, respectively. A slight complication arises because the 68000 uses byte addressing, so that an imaginary × representing A_{00} must be placed to the right of A_{01} in each row of table 5.2.

FIGURE 5.7   Memory map corresponding to figure 5.6

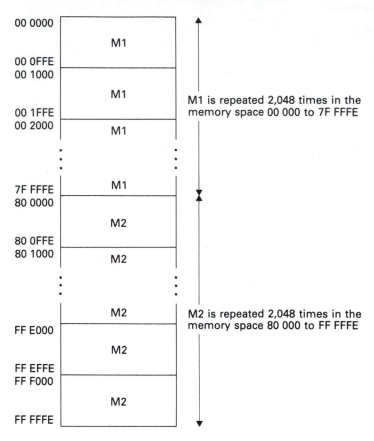

TABLE 5.2   Address table illustrating partial address decoding

DEVICE	ADDRESS LINE																			
	23	22	21	20	...	15	14	13	12	11	10	09	08	07	06	05	04	03	02	01
ROM1	0	0	0							×	×	×	×	×	×	×	×	×	×	×
RAM	0	0	1							×	×	×	×	×	×	×	×	×	×	×
ROM2	0	1						×	×	×	×	×	×	×	×	×	×	×	×	×
PERI1	1	0																		×
PERI2	1	1																		×

NOTE: An address entry that is neither a one nor a zero is a don't care condition; that is, that address line does not take part in the selection of the device.

FIGURE 5.8   Implementing the partial address decoding scheme of table 5.2

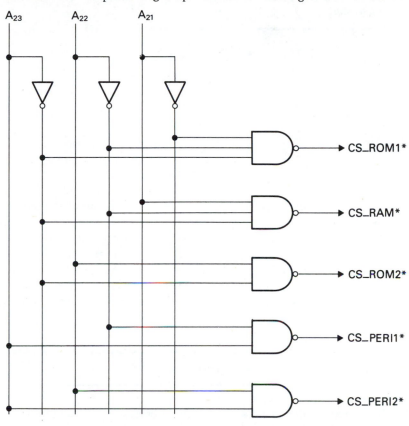

Consider first ROM1. Its primary address range is given by 000(000000000)00000000000[0] to 000(000000000)11111111111[1]. The don't care conditions have been placed in round brackets and A_{00} in square brackets. This condition corresponds to an address range of $00 0000 to $00 0FFF (i.e., 4K bytes). Similarly, PERI2 occupies the primary address range 11(000000000000000000000)0[0] to 11(000000000000000000000)1[1], or from $C0 0000 to $C0 0003.

A diagram of one possible implementation of the partial address decoding arrangement is given in figure 5.8. It is highly improbable that any designer would choose the address decoding scheme of table 5.2 or figure 5.8 because the memory map cannot be expanded. No further memory devices can be added as the existing memory devices fill the entire 8M words of memory space. Table 5.3 demonstrates a simple way of building some flexibility into the system.

In this case, the condition $A_{23} = 0$ is made a necessary condition to select all five memory components, which now take up the lower half of the memory space from $00 0000 to $7F FFFE. The 4M word memory space for which $A_{23} = 1$ is now available for future use and is labeled "SPACE" in table 5.3.

TABLE 5.3 Improved partial address decoding scheme

DEVICE	A_{23}	A_{22}	A_{21}	A_{20}	...
ROM1	0	0	0	0	
RAM	0	0	0	1	
ROM2	0	0	1		
PERI1	0	1	0		
PERI2	0	1	1		
SPACE	1				

In spite of its simplicity, partial address decoding is often shunned because the memory space allocated to a single memory device is repeated many times; for example, PERI1 in table 5.2 occupies one word of memory that is repeated 1M (2^{20}) times. Therefore, if a spurious memory access is made because of an error in a program, harm can possibly be caused by corrupting the memory location that responded to the spurious access. Equally, a limited form of partial address decoding is sometimes found in systems with large numbers of address lines because so many address lines are expensive to decode.

Block Address Decoding

Block address decoding is a compromise between partial address decoding and full address decoding. It avoids the inefficient use of memory space associated with partial address decoding by dividing the memory space into a number of blocks. The blocks are fully address decoded. If necessary, these blocks may be subdivided into smaller blocks.

In a typical application of block address decoding, a microprocessor's memory space may be divided into sixteen blocks of equal size by a single low-cost component. In the days of the 8-bit microprocessor, its 64K-byte memory space could easily be split into sixteen manageable blocks, each of 4K bytes. Today, dividing the 68000's 8M words of memory space into sixteen blocks yields a relatively massive block size of 512K words. Each of these blocks is four times larger than the entire memory space of a typical 8-bit microprocessor. Even so, splitting the 68000's memory space into sixteen blocks of 512K words would enable the system of table 5.2 and figure 5.8 to be built with a single address decoding component and would allow expansion from five memory devices to sixteen without the addition of extra logic.

In any real microcomputer, a mixture of partial address decoding, full address decoding, and block address decoding may be used to cater for the system's particular needs; for example, a system may apply full address decoding to address lines A_{23} to A_{17}, to select a block of 64K words from the 68000's memory space of 8M words. This 64K is then divided into sixteen blocks of 4K by a block address decoder. Some of these 4K blocks can be used to select 4K ROMs. Finally, partial address decoding may be used to locate two peripherals, each of four words, within one of these 4K pages. An example of this type of arrangement is provided later.

5.2 Designing Address Decoders

A number of ways exist of implementing the address decoding techniques described in section 5.1. In general, address decoding techniques can be divided into four groups: address decoding using random logic, address decoding using m-line to n-line decoders, address decoding using PROMs, and address decoding using programmable logic arrays, programmable gate arrays, or programmable array logic. Each of these techniques has its own advantages and disadvantages, the nature of which depends on the type of system being designed, the scale of its production, and whether or not it needs to be expandable.

Address Decoding with Random Logic

Random logic is the term describing a system constructed from small-scale logic such as AND, OR, NAND, and NOR gates and invertors. When address decoding with random logic is implemented, the chip-select input of a memory component is derived from the appropriate address lines by means of a number of SSI gates as required. The address decoding circuits of figures 5.5 and 5.8 both use random logic.

Address decoding entirely with random logic is found in relatively few systems, because it is rather costly in terms of the number of chips required. Moreover, it is always tailor-made for a specific application and therefore lacks the flexibility inherent in some other forms of address decoding circuit.

The only advantage of random logic address decoding is its speed. As it is tailor-made for any given system, it can use the fastest logic available and can therefore achieve the minimum propagation delay from address valid to chip-select valid. Sometimes, the very low cost of SSI gates also aids the case in favor of random logic address decoding. However, we should appreciate the fact that a rather large number of chips may be required, which increases the cost of designing and testing the microcomputer and reduces the board area available for memory and peripheral components.

Address Decoding with *m*-Line to *n*-Line Decoders

The problem of address decoding can be greatly diminished by means of data decoders that decode an *m*-bit binary code into one of *n* outputs, where $n = 2^m$.

FIGURE 5.9   The 74LS154 four-line to sixteen-line decoder

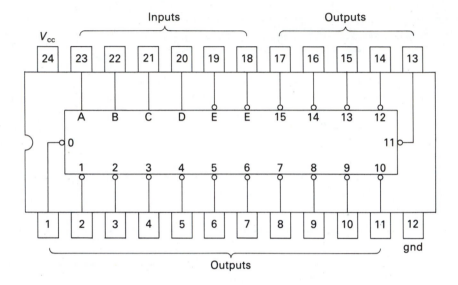

74LS154 truth table

E1	E2	D	C	B	A	0	1	2	3	4	5	6	7	8	9	10	11	12	13	14	15
0	0	0	0	0	0	0	1	1	1	1	1	1	1	1	1	1	1	1	1	1	1
0	0	0	0	0	1	1	0	1	1	1	1	1	1	1	1	1	1	1	1	1	1
0	0	0	0	1	0	1	1	0	1	1	1	1	1	1	1	1	1	1	1	1	1
0	0	0	0	1	1	1	1	1	0	1	1	1	1	1	1	1	1	1	1	1	1
0	0	0	1	0	0	1	1	1	1	0	1	1	1	1	1	1	1	1	1	1	1
0	0	0	1	0	1	1	1	1	1	1	0	1	1	1	1	1	1	1	1	1	1
0	0	0	1	1	0	1	1	1	1	1	1	0	1	1	1	1	1	1	1	1	1
0	0	0	1	1	1	1	1	1	1	1	1	1	0	1	1	1	1	1	1	1	1
0	0	1	0	0	0	1	1	1	1	1	1	1	1	0	1	1	1	1	1	1	1
0	0	1	0	0	1	1	1	1	1	1	1	1	1	1	0	1	1	1	1	1	1
0	0	1	0	1	0	1	1	1	1	1	1	1	1	1	1	0	1	1	1	1	1
0	0	1	0	1	1	1	1	1	1	1	1	1	1	1	1	1	0	1	1	1	1
0	0	1	1	0	0	1	1	1	1	1	1	1	1	1	1	1	1	0	1	1	1
0	0	1	1	0	1	1	1	1	1	1	1	1	1	1	1	1	1	1	0	1	1
0	0	1	1	1	0	1	1	1	1	1	1	1	1	1	1	1	1	1	1	0	1
0	0	1	1	1	1	1	1	1	1	1	1	1	1	1	1	1	1	1	1	1	0
0	1	×	×	×	×	1	1	1	1	1	1	1	1	1	1	1	1	1	1	1	1
1	0	×	×	×	×	1	1	1	1	1	1	1	1	1	1	1	1	1	1	1	1
1	1	×	×	×	×	1	1	1	1	1	1	1	1	1	1	1	1	1	1	1	1

FIGURE 5.10   The 74LS138 three-line to eight-line decoder

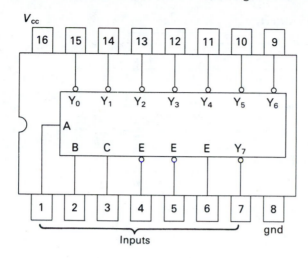

74LS138 truth table

E1	E2	E3	C	B	A	Y0	Y1	Y2	Y3	Y4	Y5	Y6	Y7
1	1	0	×	×	×	1	1	1	1	1	1	1	1
1	1	1	×	×	×	1	1	1	1	1	1	1	1
1	0	0	×	×	×	1	1	1	1	1	1	1	1
1	0	1	×	×	×	1	1	1	1	1	1	1	1
0	1	0	×	×	×	1	1	1	1	1	1	1	1
0	1	1	×	×	×	1	1	1	1	1	1	1	1
0	0	0	×	×	×	1	1	1	1	1	1	1	1
0	0	1	0	0	0	0	1	1	1	1	1	1	1
0	0	1	0	0	1	1	0	1	1	1	1	1	1
0	0	1	0	1	0	1	1	0	1	1	1	1	1
0	0	1	0	1	1	1	1	1	0	1	1	1	1
0	0	1	1	0	0	1	1	1	1	0	1	1	1
0	0	1	1	0	1	1	1	1	1	1	0	1	1
0	0	1	1	1	0	1	1	1	1	1	1	0	1
0	0	1	1	1	1	1	1	1	1	1	1	1	0

These devices effectively carry out the block address decoding described earlier in this chapter. The three most popular decoders in the range of MSI TTL circuits are the 74LS154 four-line to sixteen-line decoder, the 74LS138 three-line to eight-line decoder, and the 74LS139 dual two-line to four-line decoder. Figures 5.9 to 5.11 give the pinouts and truth tables for the 74LS154, 74LS138, and 74LS139, respectively. All three decoders have active-low outputs, making them particularly suitable for address decoding applications, because almost all memory components have active-low chip-select inputs. Here we will discuss only the 74LS138 decoder, as the other two are identical in principal and differ only in detail.

FIGURE 5.11   The 74LS139 dual two-line to four-line decoder

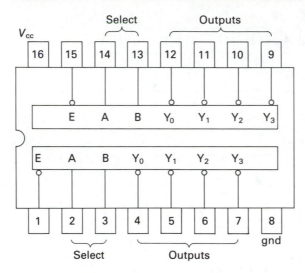

74LS139 truth table

Inputs				Outputs			
$\bar{E}$	B	A		Y0	Y1	Y2	Y3
1	×	×		1	1	1	1
0	0	0		0	1	1	1
0	0	1		1	0	1	1
0	1	0		1	1	0	1
0	1	1		1	1	1	0

The 74LS138 Three-Line to Eight-Line Decoder

The most popular of the m-line to n-line decoders is the 74LS138, which decodes a three-line input into one of eight active-low outputs, as indicated by figure 5.10. In addition to its three-line input, the 74LS138 has three enable inputs, of which two are active-low and one active-high. Therefore the 74LS138 is very easy to apply to address decoding circuits. Figure 5.12 demonstrates the versatility of the 74LS138 in five configurations. In each case we can assume that the decoders are being used in conjunction with a 68000 processor and that they are to be strobed by the processor's AS* output. Note that the address decoding ranges chosen in this example are entirely arbitrary and have been selected to illustrate the principles involved, rather than to represent any real system.

The difference between the examples in figure 5.12c and d is that the latter employs all the decoder's enable inputs to reduce the size of the eight decoded address blocks as far as possible, thereby yielding a block size of 8K words using only two chips. In figure 6.12c, where the enable inputs are not used to decode

FIGURE 5.12   Some applications of the three-line to eight-line decoder

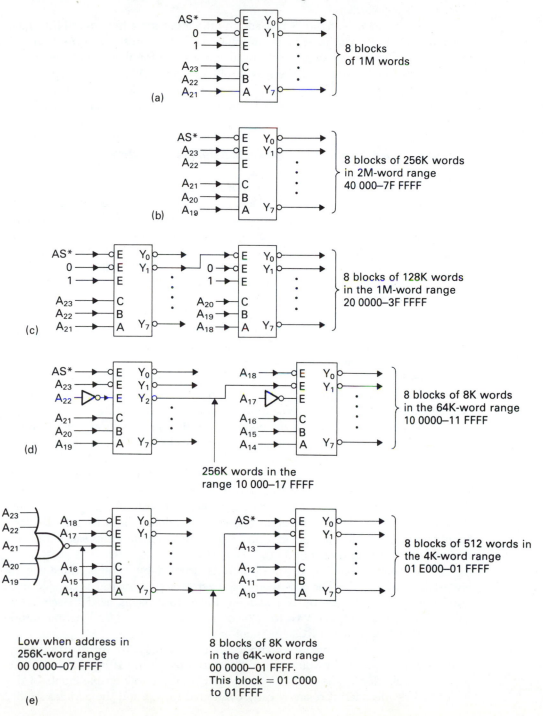

address lines, the minimum block size is 128K words. In figure 5.12d the minimum block size is 8K words.

The final example, figure 5.12e, adds a little logic and a five-input NOR gate to a two-74LS138 circuit to achieve a resolution of 512 words. This type of circuit might be used to decode eight blocks of memory space for allocation to memory-mapped peripherals. Note that the AS* strobe in figure 5.12e has been applied to the ENABLE* input of the second (i.e., lower-order) decoder, rather than to the first decoder. In this way the delay in the decoding circuit has been minimized.

Example of the Application of Block Address Decoders

Consider the following example of an address decoder for a 68000-based system using 74LS138 decoders. The bottom end of memory is populated by 16K words of ROM arranged as four blocks of 4K words. Each block is implemented by two $4K \times 8$ EPROMs. Up to eight memory-mapped peripherals in the 64-word (128-byte) range $01 0000 to $01 007F are needed and each peripheral occupies 8 words. The 8K words of read/write memory are provided by eight blocks of 1K words in the range $02 0000 to $02 3FFF. Each block is implemented by four $1K \times 4$ static memory components.

The memory map corresponding to the above arrangement is given in figure 5.13 and the address decoding scheme in table 5.4. In this example full address decoding is employed, so that all address lines must be used in either the selection of a device or of a location within a device.

From table 5.4 we can see that a necessary condition for the selection of all devices is that A_{18} through A_{23} are all logical zeros. This condition strongly suggests that the active-low enable inputs of a decoder or a NOR gate should be used to decode these six high-order address lines. Figure 5.14 shows one possible way of implementing the device-mapping scheme of table 5.4. Preliminary address decoding is performed by ICs 1a and 2. Together, these divide the 256K-word memory space in the region $00 0000 to $07 FFFF into eight 32K-word pages. Note that the devices in the memory map of figure 5.13 are arranged so that ROM is on page zero, peripherals on page one, and RAM on page two. Thus, IC1a and IC2 both decode the eight higher-order address lines to provide first-stage decoding for all other devices, and also provide for future expansion of the system by employing outputs Y3* to Y7* of IC2.

The address decoding of the ROMs is handled by another three-line to eight-line decoder, IC3. The 32K-word page zero selected by IC2 is divided into eight pages of 4K words by IC3 and the lower four pages used to select the ROMs. Note that outputs Y4* to Y7* of IC3 are not used and permit future expansion to 32K words of ROM without any additional logic.

As the read/write memory components occupy only 1K words of memory space, a further two address lines, in addition to those decoded by IC2, must take part in the selection of the RAM. Because the two active-low enable inputs of the RAM address decoder, IC6, are already connected to IC2 and the address strobe,

FIGURE 5.13   Memory map of a microcomputer

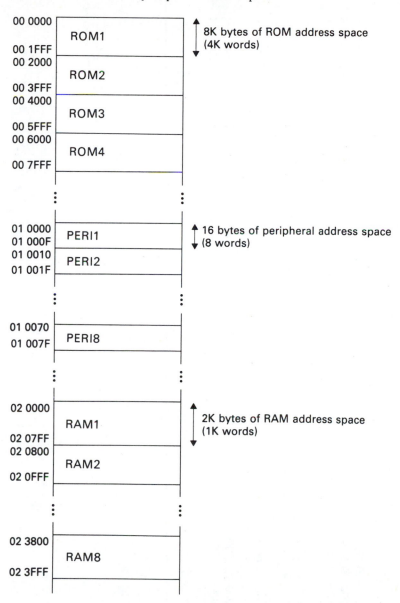

a two-input NOR gate, IC7a, is used to decode A_{15} and A_{14}. Address lines A_{11} to A_{13} select one of eight 1K-word blocks of RAM whenever IC6 is enabled.

The selection of the peripherals is a little more complicated, as a further nine address lines take part in the selection of the peripheral address space (i.e., A_{07} through A_{15}). This procedure would normally indicate that three 74LS138s are

TABLE 5.4 Address decoding table for figure 5.13

DEVICE	ADDRESS RANGE	ADDRESS LINES																			
		23	...	17	16	15	14	13	12	11	10	09	08	07	06	05	04	03	02	01	(00)
ROM1	00 0000–00 1FFF	0	...	0	0	0	0	0	X	X	X	X	X	X	X	X	X	X	X	X	X
ROM2	00 2000–00 3FFF	0	...	0	0	0	0	1	X	X	X	X	X	X	X	X	X	X	X	X	X
ROM3	00 4000–00 5FFF	0	...	0	0	0	1	0	X	X	X	X	X	X	X	X	X	X	X	X	X
ROM4	00 6000–00 7FFF	0	...	0	0	0	1	1	X	X	X	X	X	X	X	X	X	X	X	X	X
PERI1	01 0000–01 000F	0	...	0	1	0	0	0	0	0	0	0	0	0	0	0	0	X	X	X	X
PERI2	01 0010–01 001F	0	...	0	1	0	0	0	0	0	0	0	0	0	0	0	1	X	X	X	X
PERI8	01 0070–01 007F	0	...	0	1	0	0	0	0	0	0	0	0	0	1	1	1	X	X	X	X
RAM1	02 0000–02 07FF	0	...	1	0	0	0	0	0	0	X	X	X	X	X	X	X	X	X	X	X
RAM2	02 0800–02 0FFF	0	...	1	0	0	0	0	0	1	X	X	X	X	X	X	X	X	X	X	X
RAM8	02 3800–02 3FFF	0	...	1	0	0	0	1	1	1	X	X	X	X	X	X	X	X	X	X	X

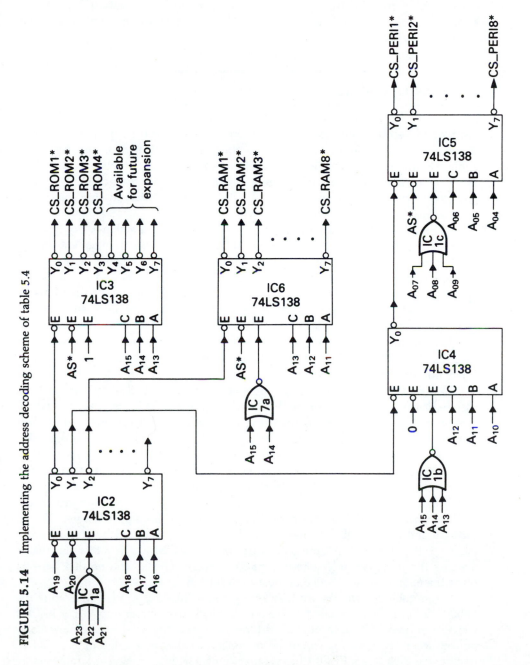

FIGURE 5.14 Implementing the address decoding scheme of table 5.4

necessary to fully decode the peripherals. However, as the peripherals are selected when address lines A_{07} through A_{15} are all zero, two NOR gates, IC1b and IC1c, may possibly be used to reduce the number of 74LS138s to two. Figure 5.14 shows how to do this. The process could have been carried further and IC4 eliminated by random logic.

Address Decoding with PROM

As address decoding involves nothing more complex than the generation of one or more chip-select outputs from a number of address inputs, any technique applied to the synthesis of Boolean functions can also perform address decoding. We have used m-line to n-line decoders to do this because they naturally exploit the block structure of memory. Another device most suited to this role is the programmable read only memory, PROM.

The PROM has m address inputs, p data outputs, and a chip-select input, as illustrated in figure 5.15. This diagram shows the logical arrangement of the PROM and an example of its use as an address decoder. Whenever it is enabled, the m-bit address at its input selects one out of 2^m possible p-bit words and applies it to the p data terminals. Thus, the PROM is nothing more than a look-up table. Instead of designing an address decoder by solving the Boolean equations relating the various device-select signals to the appropriate address lines, or by dividing memory into blocks with an m-line to n-line decoder, it is possible to program the PROM with the truth table directly relating addresses to device-select outputs.

When a PROM is disabled (i.e., deselected), its outputs float (assuming it has tristate drivers). Therefore, the outputs of the PROM need to be pulled up whenever it is disabled in order to force the active-low chip-select inputs into their inactive-high states. Alternatively, the PROM address decoder can be permanently enabled, with its enable (chip-select) input hard-wired to ground.

Unfortunately, one snag arises when PROMs are used as address decoders. As stated previously, a PROM with m address inputs stores 2^m words, each of p bits. The total capacity of this device is therefore $p \times 2^m$. Clearly, as m grows, the total number of bits increases exponentially. The relationship between PROM capacity and the size of the smallest block of memory decoded by it is given in table 5.5. It is assumed that the data width of the PROM is $p = 8$ bits and that it decodes the m higher-order bits in a 68000 system. The column headed $24 - m$ gives the number of undecoded address lines (including A_{00}).

From table 5.5 we can see that a very large PROM is needed to decode the 68000's address lines to select a reasonable block size; for example, if a PROM were to entirely decode a 68000's address bus and the smallest memory component were 2K words, it would be necessary to choose a value of m equal to twelve. An 8-bit $\times$ 4K PROM has a capacity of 32K bits, making it a rather large device to program, especially during development work.

FIGURE 5.15   PROM as an address decoder

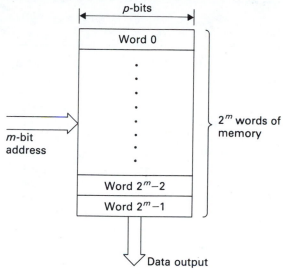

(a) Logical arrangement of PROM

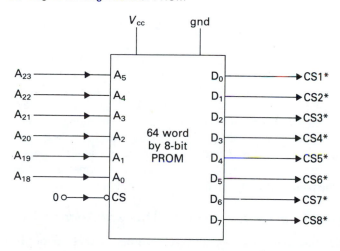

(b) PROM decodes high-order 6 address bits from CPU

Because microprocessors like the 68000 have enormous address spaces, compared to their 64K-byte ancestors, some of the basic (i.e., first-stage) address decoding is left to random logic devices and the fine address decoding is carried out by PROMs or m-line to n-line decoders. In the early days of the 8-bit microprocessor, when memories were generally very small, quite a few address lines were decoded. As time passed, memories with much larger capacities appeared

TABLE 5.5   Relationship between decoded block size and capacity of a PROM

m	2^m (words)	$p \times 2^m$ (bits)	$24 - m$	DECODED BLOCK SIZE $2^{(24-m)}$ (bytes)
3	8	64	21	2M bytes (1M words)
4	16	128	20	1M bytes (512K words)
5	32	256	19	512K bytes (256K words)
6	64	512	18	256K bytes (128K words)
7	128	1,024	17	128K bytes (64K words)
8	256	2,048	16	64K bytes (32K words)
9	512	4,096	15	32K bytes (16K words)
10	1,024	8,192	14	16K bytes (8K words)
11	2,048	16,384	13	8K bytes (4K words)
12	4,096	32,768	12	4K bytes (2K words)
13	8,192	65,536	11	2K bytes (1K words)

m = number of address inputs to the PROM
$p = 8$ = width of PROM's data output bus

and we were able to decode, say, 2K-byte components with a single three-line to eight-line decoder.

The situation with modern microprocessors is similar to the early days of the 8-bit processor, as far as address decoding is concerned. Even the 64K-bit (i.e., 8K-byte) static read/write RAM requires ten address lines to be decoded (i.e., A_{14} to A_{23}) when it is used with a 68000. Consequently, most 68000 systems have been forced to resort to multilevel address decoding. Where several types of memory component share the same module (e.g., the single board microcomputer), we often find it convenient to select a page of the processor's memory space by the simplest random logic decoder available and then to subdivide the page into the memory space of individual components by other means.

Example of the Design of a PROM-Based Address Decoder

Consider the following example. A designer wishes to produce a single board 68000 system with memory space containing ROM, RAM, and peripherals. The design criteria stress two points: the decoder must be cheap and it must be versatile. As memory components decline in price, the designer hopes to improve the system later, when high-density memories become even cheaper. Initially, the design calls for a minimum address space per ROM/RAM to be 1K words (2K bytes). A further criterion is that all ROM/RAM must be fully address decoded and the total peripheral I/O space limited to 1K words divided between eight peripherals. The basic system is to have the memory map defined by table 5.6.

At first sight, the allocation of memory may seem strange or arbitrary. The three ROMs occupy $00 0000 to $00 2FFF, the RAM from $00 C000 to

TABLE 5.6   Memory space allocation for an SBC

| DEVICE | ORGANIZATION | MEMORY SPACE | | ADDRESS RANGE (bytes) |
		WORDS	BYTES	
ROM1	2K × 8	2K	4K	00 0000–00 0FFF
ROM2	2K × 8	2K	4K	00 1000–00 1FFF
ROM3	2K × 8	2K	4K	00 2000–00 2FFF
RAM1	1K × 4	1K	2K	00 C000–00 C7FF
PERI1	2 × 8	128	256	00 E000–00 E0FF
PERI2	2 × 8	128	256	00 E100–00 E1FF
PERI3	4 × 8	128	256	00 E200–00 E2FF

$00 C7FF, and the peripherals from $00 E000 to $00 E2FF. I have chosen these ranges to permit later expansion without the problem of read-only memory overflowing into read/write memory space. When the system is fully expanded, the 2K × 8 ROMs can be replaced by 8K × 8 ROMs and then the ROM address space will extend from $00 0000 to $00 BFFF. The next step is to prepare an address table (table 5.7) to help us to determine the best way of arranging the address decoding circuitry.

From table 5.7 we can see that address lines A_{16} through A_{23} perform a page selection, as they are constant and independent of the device selected. These lines can therefore be decoded by a single logic element with eight inputs and a single output. If the peripherals are regarded as a single entity occupying 1K words of memory space, the additional address lines to be decoded in the selection of this block are A_{11} through A_{15}. The discrimination between peripherals is best done by decoding A_{08} to A_{10} with a three-line to eight-line decoder.

The decoding of A_{11} through A_{17} is performed by a 32-word × 8-bit PROM. Figure 5.16 provides the basic details of a possible implementation of table 5.7. Address lines A_{16} through A_{23} must all be active-low to enable the 32-word PROM. As is usual in 68000-based systems, the address decoder is enabled by AS*. When the PROM is disabled by the negation of AS*, its data outputs are all pulled up by resistors to their inactive-high levels. Whenever the PROM is enabled, address lines A_{11} to A_{15} interrogate one of its thirty-two locations and yield an 8-bit data value that directly controls the chip-select inputs of the memory devices to be decoded. When the peripheral group is selected by D_3 from the PROM going active-low, address lines A_{08} to A_{10} are further decoded by the three-line to eight-line decoder, to select one of the three peripherals.

This circuit displays some of the considerable advantages PROM address decoders have over random logic or *m*-line to *n*-line decoders. PROM-based decoders are able to select components having different memory sizes. Here, both 2K-word ROM memory spaces and 1K-word RAM memory spaces are selected

TABLE 5.7 Address decoding scheme for table 5.6

DEVICE	ADDRESS SPACE	ADDRESS LINE																	
		23	22	21	20	19	18	17	16	15	14	13	12	11	10	09	08	07	06
ROM1	00 0000–00 0FFF	0	0	0	0	0	0	0	0	0	0	0	0	X	X	X	X	X	X
ROM2	00 1000–00 1FFF	0	0	0	0	0	0	0	0	0	0	0	1	X	X	X	X	X	X
ROM3	00 2000–00 2FFF	0	0	0	0	0	0	0	0	0	0	1	0	X	X	X	X	X	X
RAM1	00 C000–00 C7FF	0	0	0	0	0	0	0	0	1	1	0	0	0	X	X	X	X	X
PERI1	00 E000–00 E0FF	0	0	0	0	0	0	0	0	1	1	1	0	0	0	0	0	X	X
PERI2	00 E100–00 E1FF	0	0	0	0	0	0	0	0	1	1	1	0	0	0	0	1	X	X
PERI3	00 E200–00 E2FF	0	0	0	0	0	0	0	0	1	1	1	0	0	0	1	0	X	X

FIGURE 5.16   PROM-based address decoder to implement table 5.8

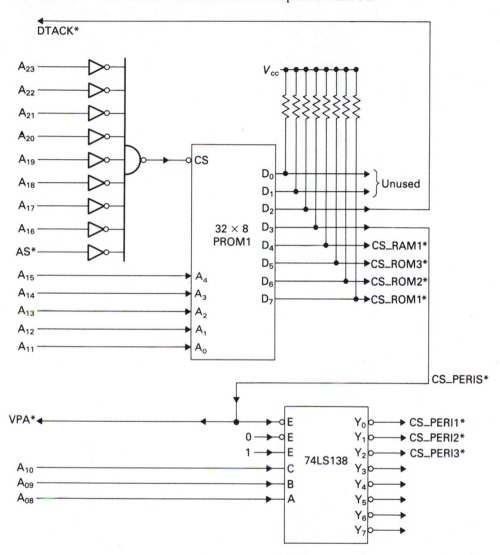

with the same PROM. To see how to do this, consider table 5.8, which is both a partial address decoding table (i.e., it shows only address lines A_{11} to A_{15}) and a listing of the contents of the PROM.

   The leftmost column of table 5.8 displays the address range decoded by that row (i.e., one of 32) of the table. The second column gives the five address inputs of the PROM, labeled A_0 to A_4, and relates them to the corresponding five address lines of the 68000, labeled A_{11} to A_{15}. The rightmost column provides the data appearing on the PROM's output lines corresponding to the address in

TABLE 5.8   Programming the address decoder PROM

ADDRESS RANGE OF THE 68000	SYSTEM ADDRESS LINES					SYSTEM DEVICE ENABLES					
	A_{15}	A_{14}	A_{13}	A_{12}	A_{11}	ROM1	ROM2	ROM3	RAM1	PERIs	DTACK*
	PROM ADDRESS INPUTS					PROM DATA OUTPUTS					
	A_4	A_3	A_2	A_1	A_0	D_7	D_6	D_5	D_4	D_3	D_2
00 0000–00 07FF	0	0	0	0	0	0	1	1	1	1	0
00 0800–00 0FFF	0	0	0	0	1	0	1	1	1	1	0
00 1000–00 17FF	0	0	0	1	0	1	0	1	1	1	0
00 1800–00 1FFF	0	0	0	1	1	1	0	1	1	1	0
00 2000–00 27FF	0	0	1	0	0	1	1	0	1	1	0
00 2800–00 2FFF	0	0	1	0	1	1	1	0	1	1	0
00 3000–00 37FF	0	0	1	1	0	1	1	1	1	1	1
00 3800–00 3FFF	0	0	1	1	1	1	1	1	1	1	1
00 4000–00 47FF	0	1	0	0	0	1	1	1	1	1	1
00 4800–00 4FFF	0	1	0	0	1	1	1	1	1	1	1
00 5000–00 57FF	0	1	0	1	0	1	1	1	1	1	1

Address
00 5800–00 5FFF
00 6000–00 67FF
00 6800–00 6FFF
00 7000–00 77FF
00 7800–00 7FFF
00 8000–00 87FF
00 8800–00 8FFF
00 9000–00 97FF
00 9800–00 9FFF
00 A000–00 A7FF
00 A800–00 AFFF
00 B000–00 B7FF
00 B800–00 BFFF
00 C000–00 C7FF
00 C800–00 CFFF
00 D000–00 D7FF
00 D800–00 DFFF
00 E000–00 E7FF
00 E800–00 EFFF
00 F000–00 F7FF
00 F800–00 FFFF

the middle column. These data outputs form the four device selects (D_4 to D_7), the peripheral group enable (D_3), and DTACK* (D_2).

Consider the selection of ROM1. This device is selected whenever a valid address in the range $00 0000 to $00 0FFF is put out by the processor. Note that this is a 4K-byte (2K-word) range and that the addressing range corresponding to any row of table 5.8 is only 2K bytes (1K words). Therefore, two rows in the table must be dedicated to RAM1. Thus, whenever $A_{15} = 0$, $A_{14} = 0$, $A_{13} = 0$, $A_{12} = 0$, and $A_{11} = 0$, or $A_{15} = 0$, $A_{14} = 0$, $A_{13} = 0$, $A_{12} = 0$, and $A_{11} = 1$, ROM1 is selected. Because ROM1 is selecting whenever $A_{11} = 0$ or $A_{11} = 1$, this address line is a don't care value in the selection of ROM1. If ROM1 occupied 4K words of memory space in the range $00 0000 to $00 1FFF, the first four entries in the D_7 column of table 5.8 would all be zero.

The memory space dedicated to RAM1 in the range $00 C000 to $00 C7FF is 1K words, so only a single zero appears in the corresponding row of table 5.8. Similarly, the block of peripherals is enabled by D_3 whenever an address in the range $00 E000 to $00 E7FF is placed on the address bus. We can see from figure 5.16 that a 74LS138 provides a third level of address decoding to give eight blocks of 128 words. Only three peripherals are currently implemented, allowing for expansion to eight without any additions or changes to the existing address decoding logic.

A more detailed and slightly modified version of this address decoder is given in figure 5.17. In this case, the primary address decoding is performed by the 9-bit comparator IC1, an Am29809. Here, only 8 of the 9 bits to be matched are used. When input $A_i = B_i$ for i = 1 through 9 and the device is enabled by $G* = 0$, its $E_{out}*$ pin goes active-low, enabling the secondary decoder, a 32 × 8-bit PROM, IC2. Outputs D_3 to D_7 of the PROM select the memory devices as above. The function of output D_2 requires further explanation. A glance at table 5.8 reveals that D_2 is active-low whenever a zero appears in columns D_4 to D_7. Thus, D_2 is the logical OR of D_4 to D_7 (negative logic). This allows D_2 to be connected to the CPU's DTACK* input after passing through a suitable delay generator, if necessary.

The decoding of memory-mapped peripherals is almost exactly the same as any other memory component. However, as the reader will discover in chapter 8, the 68000 has a special provision for dealing with certain peripherals originally designed for 6800-based systems. These devices are interfaced to the 68000 by means of its synchronous bus and are enabled by the 68000's VMA* output. The peripheral group output, D_3, does not take part in the generation of DTACK* as, for the purposes of this example, we assume that the peripherals are 6800-series devices and operated synchronously.

The peripheral select output of IC2, D_3, enables the peripheral decoder IC3, a three-line to eight-line decoder. D_3 is also connected to the 68000's VPA* input, so that a synchronous bus cycle is started whenever a peripheral is addressed. The three-line to eight-line decoder is enabled by UDS*, restricting all peripherals to the upper byte of a word, and by VMA*, which synchronizes a peripheral access to the 68000's E clock.

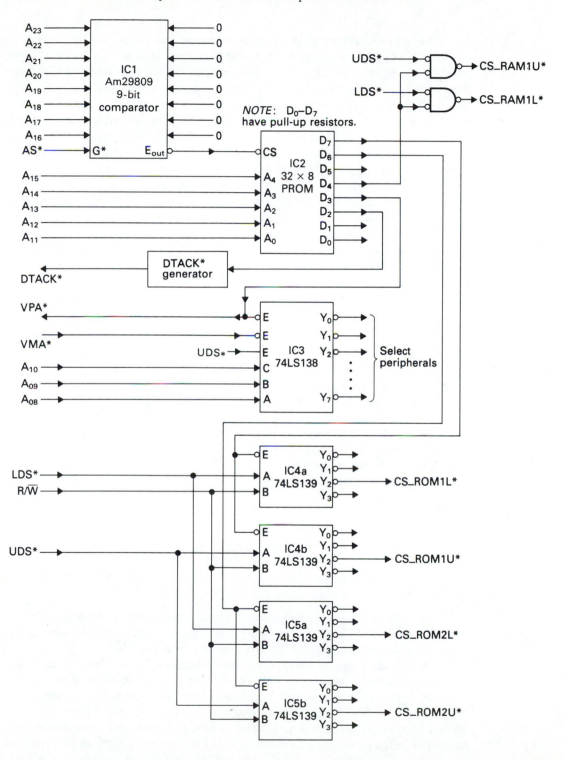

FIGURE 5.17   More complete address decoder to implement table 5.8

181

The actual selection of the ROMs themselves is performed by three dual two-line to four-line decoders, ICs 4, 5, and 6. For convenience, only two of these are shown in figure 5.17. The lower byte of a ROM is selected when its CS* from the PROM and LDS* from the CPU are low during a read cycle, which corresponds to output Y2* from the two-line to four-line decoder. The upper byte of a ROM is selected in the same way, but in this case UDS* is used instead of LDS*. Note that ROMs can be selected only in a read cycle. This measure is a wise precaution and avoids the data bus contention that would occur if the processor attempted to write to a ROM enabled during a memory write access. Indeed, the circuit could be made more sophisticated by using the Y0* outputs of the two-line to four-line decoders to detect a write access to a ROM and then forcing BERR* low to indicate a faulty bus cycle.

Selecting the RAM is somewhat easier, as the select signal from the PROM need only be strobed by UDS* or LDS* to select the upper and lower bytes of a word, respectively.

Advantages and Disadvantages of PROM Address Decoders

There are two great advantages of using a PROM as an address decoder: its ability to select blocks of differing size and its remarkable versatility. A PROM which decodes m address lines divides the memory space into 2^m equal blocks. In the preceding example, a 32K-word page was divided into 2^5 blocks of 1K words. Larger blocks than the minimum size can be decoded simply by increasing the number of active entries (in our case, zeros) in the appropriate data column of the PROM's address/data table. The size of the block of memory decoded by a data output is equal to the minimum block size multiplied by the number of active entries in the appropriate data column. A general expression for the decoded block size of a device is given by:

$$B = p \times 2^{(m-s-q)},$$

where
 B = decoded block size
 p = number of active entries in the appropriate data column
 m = number of address lines from the CPU
 s = number of address lines in primary (i.e., first-level) address decoding
 q = number of address lines decoded by the PROM.

As an example of the application of this formula, consider the address decoding of ROM1 in table 5.8. The values for p, m, s, and q are 2, 23, 8, and 5, respectively, giving a value for B of $2 \times 2^{(23-8-5)} = 2 \times 2^{10}$, or 2K words.

Address decoding by PROM is versatile because the selection of devices is determined by the programming of a PROM and not by the physical wiring of a decoder. This procedure makes it possible to configure a new system simply by programming a new PROM. In the example of table 5.8, we may replace, say, ROM1 by a larger version (e.g., a pair of 8K × 8 ROMs) just by increasing the number of zeros in the D_7 column of the PROM decoder. Therefore 8K words of

ROM would require eight zeros, occupying memory space from $00 0000 to $00 3FFF.

The major disadvantage of the PROM has already been stated; that is, an excessively large look-up table is needed to decode more than about eight address lines. A large PROM is not only more expensive than a small PROM but takes longer to program and is much more difficult to test.

Address Decoding with FPGA, PLA, and PAL

Up to the late 1970s, the systems designer had two basic elements with which to construct digital subsystems: the random logic element and the read-only memory. We have already seen how both of these are applied to address decoding circuits. The random logic element gives an optimum design from the point of view of speed, and the ROM-based decoder provides flexibility and compactness at the cost of a slightly slower speed and a restriction on the number of variables that can be handled economically. Today, new families of logic elements have appeared, giving the designer the best of both the random logic world and of the ROM world. These new devices have several names, but they all share one property—they are general-purpose logic elements and are configured by programming.

The simplest and most primitive of the new breed of programmable logic elements is the field programmable gate array, FPGA. The expression *field programmable* means that the array can be programmed or configured by the user in "the field" as opposed to the factory. Once an FPGA has been programmed, it cannot be reprogrammed. Figure 5.18 shows the internal arrangement of the 82S103 FPGA. Sixteen inputs, labeled A_0 to A_{15}, are converted into their true and complementary forms (i.e., A_i and A_i*) within the chip. Each of the resulting 32 terms is fed to the inputs of nine 32-input NAND gates. These inputs are passed through fusible links, which may be made open-circuit (i.e., "blown") or closed-circuit (i.e., left intact) during the FPGA's programming. Consequently, the output of the NAND gate can be made a function of between one and sixteen inputs in either their true or inverted forms. Alternatively, we may say that the output of the NAND gate is a function of all sixteen variables in either their true, complemented, or don't care form. The outputs of the NAND gates are fed via programmable EOR gates to nine output pins. Therefore, the outputs can be programmed to be active-high or active-low and the gates made to appear as AND or NAND gates, respectively. Finally, the outputs may be floated by disabling the chip by means of its active-low CE* input. The 82S102 is identical to the 82S103 but has open-collector rather than tristate outputs.

The 82S103 FPGA is a delight to use. In this one package, nine outputs can be synthesized from the products of sixteen input terms, with each term appearing in a true, false, or don't care form. In a 68000-based microcomputer, the 82S103 decodes up to sixteen address lines (i.e., A_{08} to A_{23}), giving a minimum block size

FIGURE 5.18   The 82S103 FPGA

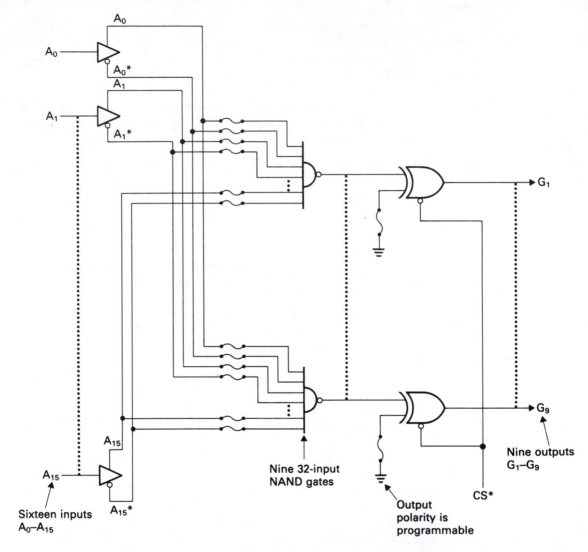

of 128 words or 256 bytes. As the 82S103 can decode so many inputs, the possibility often exists of dedicating some of these inputs to 68000 control functions, such as AS*, UDS*, and VMA*, while leaving plenty of inputs for address decoding. The following simple example shows its advantages.

Example of the Application of an FPGA

In the following example one thing should be appreciated. The example has been chosen to illustrate features of the FPGA. The reader should realize that this

FIGURE 5.19 Memory map of a 68000-based microcomputer

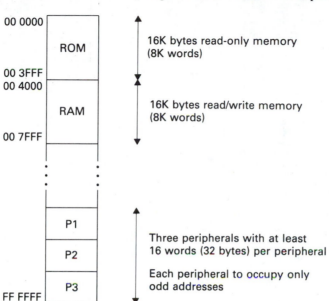

situation is generally true of any example in any book. However, in a real situation the FPGA will probably not be such a perfect device for the job. Life is never as neat as textbook examples suggest. Figure 5.19 gives the memory space of a 68000-based microcomputer with 8K words of ROM, 8K words of RAM, and three memory-mapped peripherals. The aim of the address decoder designer is to minimize the chip count in the decoder.

We can see from figure 5.19 that the memory components are located consecutively at the bottom of the memory space and the peripherals at the top end of the memory space. Furthermore, the peripherals are allocated a fixed quantity of memory space, subject to the provision of at least 16 words per peripheral. The peripherals are to occupy only odd addresses for which LDS* is active-low.

The first thing to consider in this application is the allocation of control lines to the FPGA. Both UDS* and LDS* take part in the selection of the upper and lower bytes of memory space, and VMA* is necessary to select the peripherals. Furthermore, we can use $R/\overline{W}$ to make certain that the ROM is selected only during a read cycle. The number of devices to be selected is seven, assuming that 8K × 8 chips are used to implement the ROM and RAM. This process leaves two out of the FPGA's nine outputs free. These outputs can be used to provide a DTACK* and a VPA* input to the 68000. Table 5.9 shows how the 82S103 is programmed to implement the addressing scheme of figure 5.19. A dash (—) in a column indicates that the input is a don't care condition.

Consider first the selection of the two 8K × 8 ROM components, occupying from $00 0000 to $00 3FFF. The same address lines select both ROMs, as

TABLE 5.9 Implementing figure 5.19 with an 82S103 FPGA

CONNECTIONS TO THE FPGA INPUTS FROM A 68000 SYSTEM

| DEVICE | $R/\overline{W}$ | UDS* | LDS* | VMA* | A_{23} | A_{22} | A_{21} | A_{20} | A_{19} | A_{18} | A_{17} | A_{16} | A_{15} | A_{14} | A_{13} | A_{12} |
| | A_{15} | A_{14} | A_{13} | A_{12} | A_{11} | A_{10} | A_{9} | A_{8} | A_{7} | A_{6} | A_{5} | A_{4} | A_{3} | A_{2} | A_{1} | A_{0} |
									FPGA INPUTS							
ROMU	1	0	—	—	0	0	0	0	0	0	0	0	0	0	—	—
ROML	1	—	0	—	0	0	0	0	0	0	0	0	0	0	—	—
RAMU	—	0	—	—	0	0	0	0	0	0	0	0	0	1	—	—
RAML	—	—	0	—	0	0	0	0	0	0	0	0	0	1	—	—
DTACK*	—	—	—	—	0	0	0	0	0	0	0	0	0	—	—	—
PERI1	—	—	0	0	1	1	1	1	1	1	1	1	1	1	0	1
PERI2	—	—	0	0	1	1	1	1	1	1	1	1	1	1	1	0
PERI3	—	—	0	0	1	1	1	1	1	1	1	1	1	1	1	1
VPA*	—	—	0	—	1	1	1	1	1	1	1	1	1	1	—	—

186

they share identical word address spaces. However, the upper ROM is selected only when UDS* is asserted and the lower ROM when LDS* is asserted. Note that R/$\overline{W}$ must be high to select the ROMs.

The RAMs are selected by an address in the range \$00 4000 to \$00 7FFF. As in the case of the ROMs, one is enabled by UDS* and one by LDS*. The state of the R/$\overline{W}$ line then represents a don't care condition, as the RAM may be written to or read from.

DTACK* is asserted whenever an address in the range \$00 0000 to \$00 7FFF appears on the address bus. Unfortunately, DTACK* is not synchronized with UDS* or LDS* as the FPGA cannot provide a logical OR capability. In a real system this procedure may have to be done externally.

The peripherals each occupy 2K words of memory because address lines A_{12} to A_{23} are left to be decoded by the FPGA after four of its inputs have been dedicated to control functions. Had fewer control lines been decoded by the FPGA, more address lines could have been decoded and the peripheral block sizes reduced. All peripherals are selected only when LDS* is asserted. Whenever an odd address in the 8K-word range \$FF C000 to \$FF FFFF appears on the address bus, the VPA* output of the FPGA is asserted, causing the processor to assert VMA* in turn. The assertion of VMA* is a necessary condition for the selection of the peripherals. Note that VPA* is also asserted by an address in the range \$FF C000 to \$FF C7FF, which is not used in this application. This situation is an irritation, but is not particularly dangerous!

Figure 5.20 shows how the FPGA, programmed according to table 5.9, is connected to a 68000 CPU. Of all the address decoders described so far, the FPGA requires least in the way of support circuitry.

Unlike the PROM, the FPGA can decode sixteen address lines without requiring an excessive amount of programming. Unfortunately, the FPGA's outputs do not have a logical OR capability with, say, one output being the logical OR of three other outputs. Other types of programmable logic element now exist that can remedy this situation.

PLA

One of the first of the field programmable logic elements to become widely available was the field programmable logic array, FPLA. Before we look at this device, examination of its near neighbor, the PROM, proves instructive.

Figure 5.21 illustrates the logical structure of a PROM. An n-bit address input is decoded into one of 2^n outputs, and that output is then used to look up an m-bit word in a table of 2^n words. The contents of each word in the table are programmable by the user. It is essential to note that for each of the 2^n possible inputs a corresponding word in the storage matrix always exists.

Figure 5.22 illustrates the way in which a PROM is arranged in terms of its internal gate structure. The n-bit input is decoded into one of 2^n product terms by a fixed array of AND gates. This array is said to be fixed, because it is not programmable by the user. The outputs from the AND gates are fed to OR gates

FIGURE 5.20   FPGA operated as an address decoder

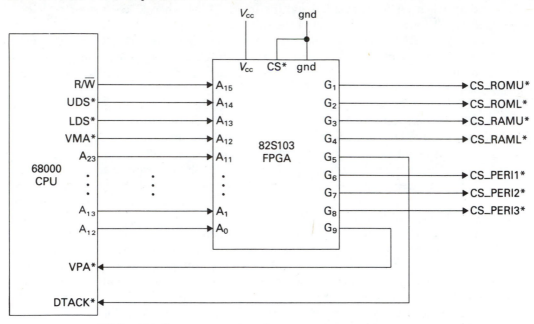

NOTE: This figure assumes that all memory components have access time sufficiently low that the 68000 can operate without wait states and that DTACK* from the FPGA can be connected directly to the 68000's DTACK* input.

(the storage matrix); for example, in figure 5.22 an input A_2, A_1, $A_0 = 0, 0, 1$ causes the $\overline{A}_2 \cdot \overline{A}_1 \cdot A_0$ product term to be asserted, with the result that any connections between this product line and an OR gate force the output of that gate to be true. In other words, the OR matrix is programmed by the user.

The great disadvantage of the PROM, from the point of view of the systems designer, is its exhaustive storage array. Limited storage is often a hindrance simply because every possible product term must have its own storage location, whether or not that product term represents a don't care condition. The FPLA is a development of the PROM, which remedies this situation.

Figure 5.23 shows the arrangement of an FPLA in terms of gate arrays. This situation is almost identical to the PROM, except that the n-line to 2^n-line decoder has been replaced by a programmable array of AND gates. Now instead of having 2^n AND gates, each with all of the product terms in their true or complement forms, a vastly reduced number of AND gates exists whose inputs may be variables, their complements, or don't care states. A typical FPLA has forty-eight AND gates for sixteen input variables, compared with the 65,536 required by a sixteen-input PROM. The 82S100 is a typical $16 \times 48 \times 8$ FPLA. The description, $16 \times 48 \times 8$, means that it has sixteen inputs, forty-eight storage locations (i.e., forty-eight product terms), and eight outputs.

FIGURE 5.21   Logical structure of a PROM

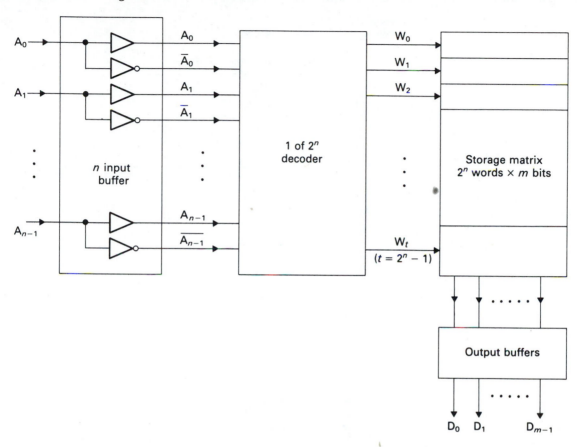

Because the FPLA has a programmable address decoder implemented by the AND gates, product terms can be created that contain between one and n variables in exactly the same way as the FPGA described earlier. Indeed, except for the OR matrix, the FPLA would be equivalent to the FPGA.

The principle application of the FPLA is in the synthesis of relatively complex logic systems (often state machines) that would otherwise require many random logic components. Generally speaking, the FPLA is not really appropriate as an address decoder, as simpler devices are often adequate. However, its programmable OR matrix can be helpful in ORing product terms, as the following example demonstrates.

Suppose a $16 \times 48 \times 8$ FPLA is to be applied to the example introduced in figure 5.19 and table 5.9. We can generate product terms for the selection of the devices as follows:

FIGURE 5.22   Structure of a PROM in terms of gate arrays

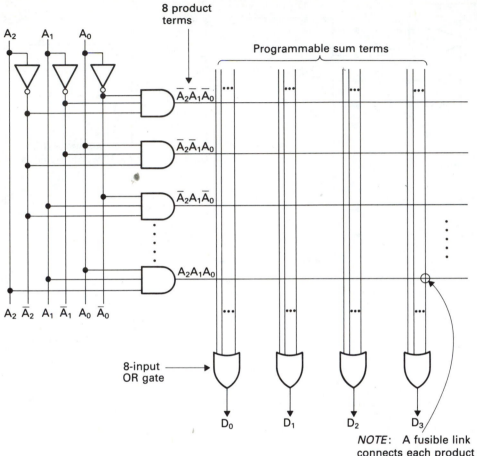

ROMU: $P0 = R/\overline{W}.UDS*.\overline{A_{14}.A_{15}.A_{16}.A_{17}.A_{18}.A_{19}.A_{20}.A_{21}.A_{22}.A_{23}}$

ROML: $P1 = R/W.LDS*.\overline{A_{14}.A_{15}.A_{16}.A_{17}.A_{18}.A_{19}.A_{20}.A_{21}.A_{22}.A_{23}}$

RAMU: $P2 = UDS*.A_{14}.\overline{A_{15}.A_{16}.A_{17}.A_{18}.A_{19}.A_{20}.A_{21}.A_{22}.A_{23}}$

RAML: $P3 = LDS*.A_{14}.\overline{A_{15}.A_{16}.A_{17}.A_{18}.A'_{19}.A_{20}.A_{21}.A_{22}.A_{23}}$

PERI2: $P4 = LDS*.VMA*.\overline{A_{12}}.A_{13}.A_{14}.A_{15}.A_{16}.A_{17}.A_{18}.A_{19}.A_{20}.A_{21}.A_{22}.A_{23}$

PERI3: $P5 = LDS*.VMA*.A_{12}.A_{13}.A_{14}.A_{15}.A_{16}.A_{17}.A_{18}.A_{19}.A_{20}.A_{21}.A_{22}.A_{23}$

VPA*: $P6 = LDS*.A_{14}.A_{15}.A_{16}.A_{17}.A_{18}.A_{19}.A_{20}.A_{21}.A_{22}.A_{23}$

These are the seven product terms to be programmed into the AND gate array. The eight outputs of the FPLA, D_0 to D_7, are formed from the logical ORs of the product terms. Note that this arrangement supports only two peripherals, as the FPLA has eight outputs as opposed to the FPGA's nine. In this example the sum terms are defined as:

CSROMU: $D_0 = \overline{P0}$
CSROML: $D_1 = \overline{P1}$
CSRAMU: $D_2 = \overline{P2}$
CSRAML: $D_3 = \overline{P3}$
CSPERI2: $D_4 = \overline{P4}$
CSPERI3: $D_5 = \overline{P5}$
DTACK*: $D_6 = \overline{P0 + P1 + P2 + P3}$
VPA*: $D_7 = \overline{P6}$

The only advantage exhibited by the FPLA over the FPGA here is that DTACK* is the logical OR of the chip-select outputs of the ROM and RAM. Thus, the FPLA does not generate a DTACK* if a write access is made to a ROM, while the FPGA implementation does.

FIGURE 5.23   Structure of the FPLA in terms of gate arrays

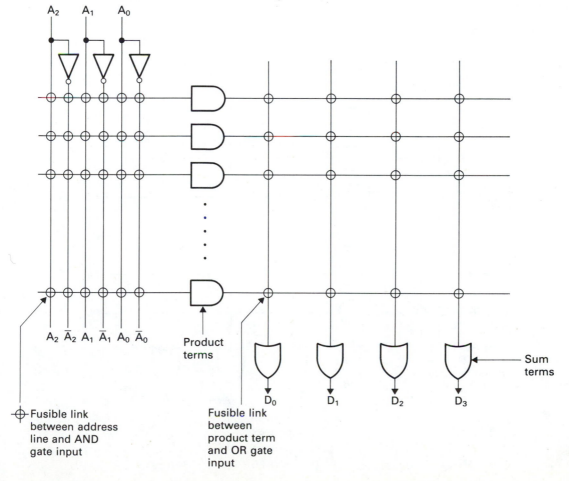

PAL

The most recent family of programmable logic elements is the programmable array logic, PAL. The PAL is not to be confused with its more complex neighbor, the PLA, discussed previously. The PAL is an intermediate device falling between the simple gate array and the more complex programmed logic array (PLA). The PLA has both programmable AND and OR arrays, while the PAL has a programmable AND array but a fixed OR array. In short, the PAL is an AND gate array whose outputs are ORed together in a way determined by the manufacturer of the device.

Figure 5.24 illustrates the principle of the PAL with a hypothetical three-input PAL with three outputs. The inputs, A_0 to A_2, generate six product terms, P0 to P5. These product terms are, of course, user programmable and may include

FIGURE 5.24   Principle of the PAL

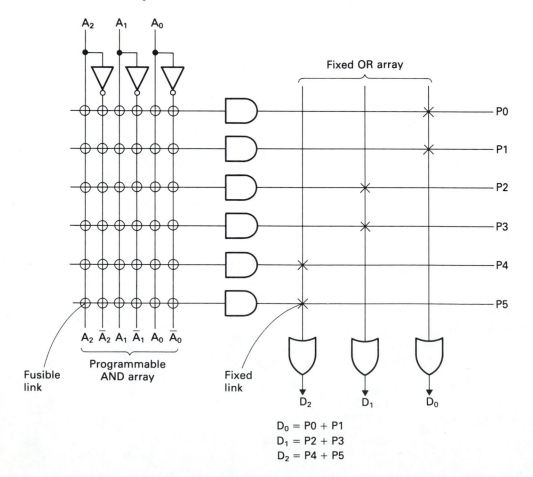

$$D_0 = P0 + P1$$
$$D_1 = P2 + P3$$
$$D_2 = P4 + P5$$

an input variable in a true, complement, or don't care form. The product terms are applied to three 2-input OR gates to generate the outputs D_0 to D_2. Each output is the logical OR of two product terms. Thus, $D_0 = P0 + P1$, $D_1 = P2 + P3$, and $D_2 = P4 + P5$. Note that I have chosen three pairs of products. I could have chosen three triplets so that $D_0 = P1 + P2 + P3$, $D_1 = P4 + P5 + P6$, etc. In other words, the way in which the product terms are ORed together is an arbitrary function of the device and is not programmable by the user.

The structure of the PAL springs from the observation that most designers do not require large numbers of sum terms and the absence of a programmable OR array is of little importance. In fact, throughout this section on address decoders the reader will have observed that few OR expressions have been necessary. As far as address decoding is concerned, OR expressions arise almost exclusively from groups of decoded devices; for example, DTACK* is asserted when

FIGURE 5.25   Some typical PALs

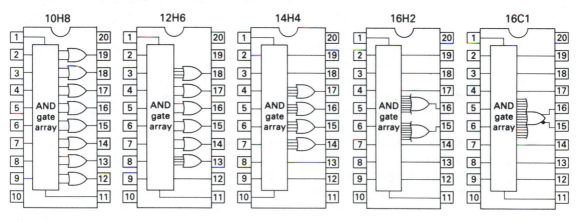

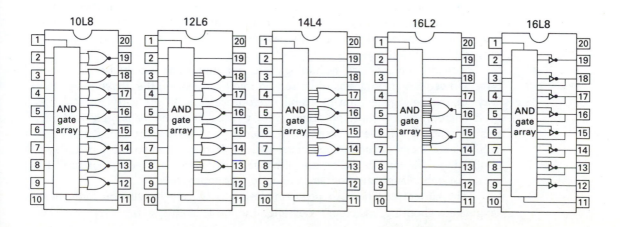

any of the memory components decoded by the PAL is accessed. Similarly, VPA*
is asserted whenever a peripheral is accessed.

Figure 5.25 (see p. 193) gives the details of just some of the PALs now
available with active-low outputs. They are designated by the number of inputs,
output polarity, and the number of outputs; for example, the 14L4 has fourteen
inputs and four active-low outputs.

5.3 Designing Static Memory Systems

In this section we are going to look at the semiconductor components used to
store programs and data in a microcomputer. Here the word *semiconductor* is
needed to distinguish between the fast semiconductor memories that can store or
retrieve information in a time comparable with the cycle time of a processor and
the much slower electromechanical memories such as disks or tapes operating at
speeds many orders of magnitude lower than semiconductor memories.

Although today's memory components play a passive role in the organization of a computer, as they perform no arithmetic or logical operations on the
data they store, they have played a most active role in the development of microprocessor systems. The relationship between the microprocessor and its memory
is analogous to that between an automobile and the highways. The active element
(processor or automobile) is useless without its resources (memory or highways).
In the last decade the greatest progress has been made in the realm of memory
technology rather than in microprocessor design. The truth is that microprocessors are much more powerful than they were, but once 1,024-bit memories
were the state of the art, while today 256K-bit memories are rolling off the
production line. Less than a decade has seen an improvement of two orders of
magnitude in the density of memory components. I doubt whether Intel would
call their 8086 microprocessor 256 times more powerful than their 8080A, or
Motorola their 68000 microprocessor 256 times more powerful than their 6809.
Not only has the capacity of memory components increased dramatically in the
last decade; significant improvements have been made in their speed, their ease of
use, and their power consumption.

Advances in memory technology are not important merely because they
have allowed larger programs to be run on microprocessors; they have paved the
way for the new generation of 16-bit microprocessors. In the early days of the
8-bit microprocessor, most programs were written in assembly language. While
this approach is suitable for very small programs, or for tightly coded programs
with limited memory, or for optimized code, it is not suited to most of today's
applications. Modern programs are often very large and the techniques used to
create assembly language programs are no longer appropriate.

The current approach to program design is to rely heavily on high level
languages, choosing, wherever possible, the best language for the job. This

method requires large memories to hold the source program, compiler, operating system, and other software tools. As interpreters are generally cheaper to produce and are less memory intensive, most of the personal computer manufacturers have opted for an interpreted high level language rather than a compiled language. By the same type of historical accident that put San Francisco on the San Andreas fault, BASIC has been adopted as the language (or, rather, family of languages) of the personal computer. As memory technology gives us cheaper memory components, compiler and interpreter writers produce more sophisticated software, and microprocessor manufacturers move to the next generation of processors to support the software.

Although low-cost memory has made large microprocessor systems possible, it is still feasible to design more modest systems with relatively little memory. By developing software on a large system and transferring the resulting object code (i.e., machine code) to a small system, we are able to produce dedicated computers with the minimum memory needed to carry out their intended functions. Small memory makes economic sense in embedded systems.

Static Random Access Memory Characteristics

In cases where a microprocessor system operates as a general-purpose digital computer, the bulk of the immediate access memory is likely to be read/write random access memory, because a wide range of different programs are run on the computer. When a microprocessor is dedicated to a specific application such as a chemical process controller, the majority of the immediate access memory is more likely to be implemented as read-only memory, because the application-oriented program is never altered. The designer of any microcomputer must decide how the read/write RAM is to be implemented. Should it be implemented with static or with dynamic RAM?

Static read/write RAM is often the designer's first choice, because it is so much easier to use than dynamic read/write RAM. Unlike dynamic memories, static memories do not require any action to be taken to periodically refresh their contents; nor do they require the address multiplexing circuitry peculiar to dynamic memory.

The basic circuit diagram of a typical NMOS static-storage cell is given in figure 5.26. The most significant feature of this cell is that six transistors are required to store a single bit of information. As we shall see later, dynamic memory cells store their data as an electrical charge on the internal capacitance of a single transistor, and therefore require fewer transistors per cell than static memories. Because more components per cell exist in a static memory, a dynamic memory of a given chip (i.e., silicon die) size can always store more data (approximately four times as much) than a corresponding static memory chip of the same size.

From the preceding remarks, we should observe that the designer of a

FIGURE 5.26   Static RAM memory cell

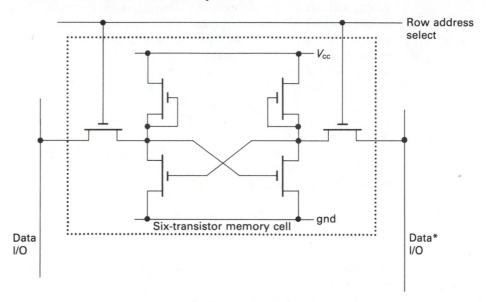

memory system has the choice between low-cost, high-density dynamic RAM with its more complex control circuitry and the more expensive static RAM that is easier to use. In any given situation the designer must weigh up all the relative merits of both systems.

Memory Configuration

Over the years the density of memory chips has increased and the price per bit declined. As each new memory chip appears, it has the effect of depressing the price of its more humble antecedents. Table 5.10 gives the details of some of the static memory components currently available. Some represent the next generation of chips and are currently designed only for very high performance

TABLE 5.10   Characteristics of some static RAM chips

STATIC RAM	TOTAL CAPACITY	ORGANIZATION	POWER (mW)	ACCESS TIME (ns)	PINS
TMS 4044–45	4,096	4,096 × 1	495	450	18
MK4118	8,192	1,024 × 8	400	250	24
TMS 4016–25	16,384	2,048 × 8	495	250	24
HM 6167H	16,384	16,384 × 1	400	45	20
HM 6264P–15	65,536	8,192 × 8	200	100	28
MB84256–10	262,144	32,768 × 8	350	100	28

FIGURE 5.27   2K × 16-bit memory organization with 2K × 8 chips

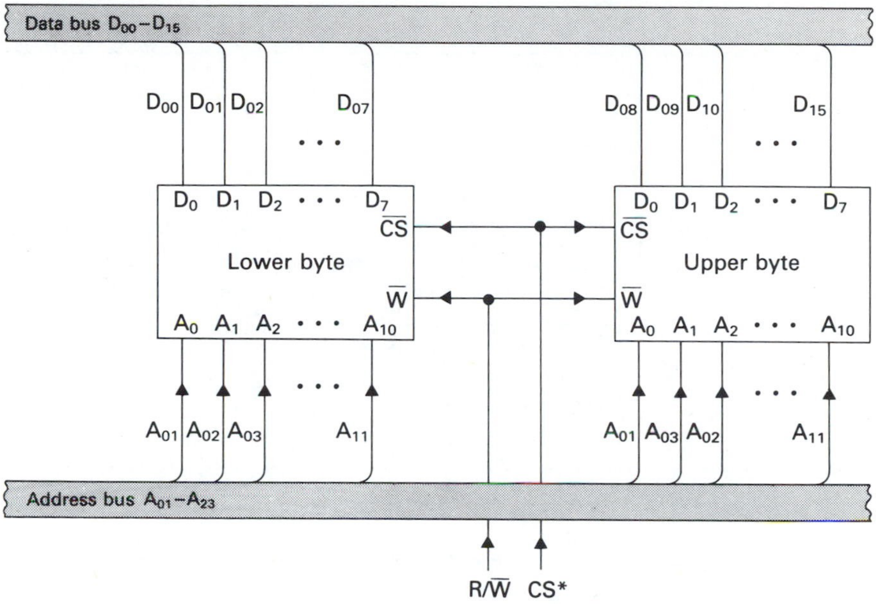

equipment. These chips are tomorrow's mainstream devices.

The trend in memory component design is to create either 1-bit wide memories or 8-bit ("bytewide") memories (some 4-bit and 16-bit wide devices are also available). People who design memory modules do not lose much sleep when deciding whether to choose 1- or 8-bit wide chips for their product. A simple rule-of-thumb is: if it is possible to use 1-bit wide components then do so. For example, suppose that a microcomputer is equipped with 2K words by 16 bits of RAM and that 16K-bit chips are to be used for economic reasons. The designer has no reasonable choice other than the arrangement of figure 5.27. The system address bus is connected to the eleven address inputs of both chips in parallel, so that when an 8-bit location is addressed in one chip, the corresponding location is addressed in the other. Bits D_0 to D_7 from the low-order chip are connected to bits D_{00} to D_{07} of the data bus, and bits D_0 to D_7 of the high-order chip are connected to bits D_{08} to D_{15}. The chip-select and read/write inputs of both memories are connected together. In the following examples we will forget about byte addressing for convenience.

Now consider the design of a 16K word by 16-bit memory. A designer is able to use either sixteen 16K by 1 chips, or sixteen 2K by 8 chips. Although the outcome is nominally the same, figures 5.28 and 5.29 show the results of using 16K × 1 and 2K × 8 chips, respectively. In figure 5.28 all the memory components' address lines are connected in common to the system address bus. Each memory component contributes one data line, which is connected to the appropriate line of the system data bus.

FIGURE 5.28   Memory organization 1—16K words × 16 with 16K × 1 chips

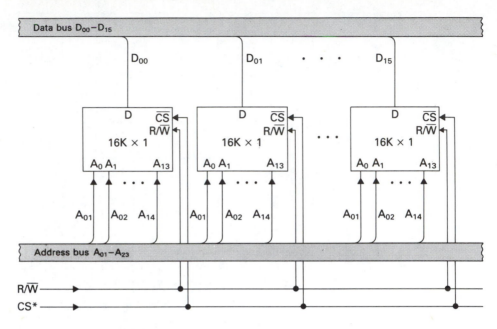

Things are rather different in figure 5.29. The chips are arranged as eight pairs, one member of the pair being connected to data lines D_{00} to D_{07} of the system data bus and the other connected to data lines D_{08} to D_{15}. All eleven address lines from each of the RAMs are connected to the system address bus. The fact must immediately be obvious that only eleven address lines are taking part in the selection of a memory location instead of the fourteen required by a 16K word array. The additional address lines A_{12}, A_{13}, and A_{14} are decoded into one of eight lines, each of which selects one of the eight pairs of RAMs; that is, the 16K memory space has been partitioned into eight blocks of 2K and a decoder is needed to distinguish between the blocks.

Clearly, the arrangement of figure 5.29 is inferior to that of figure 5.28 because extra logic is required without providing any added benefit whatsoever. Another two reasons indicate why 16K × 1 chips beat 2K × 8 chips. The 2K × 8 chip is available in a 24-pin DIL package with a nominal area (or footprint) of $1.2 × 0.6 = 0.72$ in². As the 16K × 1 chip has three more address lines but seven less data lines, it can be packaged in a 20-pin DIL chip with a footprint of only $1.0 × 0.3 = 0.3$ in². Finally, the arrangement of figure 5.28 means that each data line from the system bus is loaded by just one data input/output connection to a RAM chip. However, in figure 5.29 each data line from the system bus is connected in parallel to the corresponding data line of each of the eight pairs of 2K × 8 RAM. This condition represents an eightfold increase in data bus loading, reducing the noise immunity of the data bus.

FIGURE 5.29   Memory organization 2—16K words × 16 with 2K × 8 chips

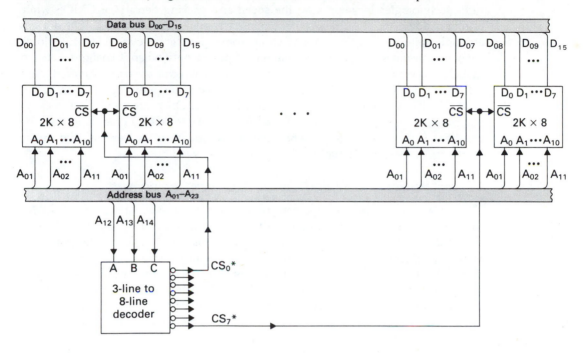

CMOS RAM

Just as houses can be built of straw, wood, or brick, semiconductor devices can be manufactured by a number of different technologies. The three most important processes are bipolar, NMOS, and CMOS. Bipolar technology has been around longest, and is seen most frequently in TTL (transistor-transistor logic) devices. The advantage of bipolar logic is its great speed. Unfortunately, bipolar devices cannot yet be constructed with the same density as NMOS and CMOS components. In any case, bipolar logic is power-hungry and consumes large quantities of energy, making the cooling of equipment a limiting factor in systems design.

NMOS technology has replaced the earlier PMOS technology and is used to fabricate the majority of microprocessors and memory devices. Although NMOS is not as fast as bipolar logic, it consumes much less power. A close relative of NMOS is CMOS logic, which has the highly desirable property of consuming very little power. Not long ago the engineer was faced with a nasty dilemma: choose bipolar logic for high speed but at the expense of being forced to implement everything in small- or medium-scale integration; choose CMOS logic for low-power operation but suffer very slow switching speeds, a density less than NMOS, and a hefty price tag; or choose NMOS as a compromise.

Semiconductor manufacturers have tried to combine the best features of all three technologies by improving the speed and packing density of CMOS while bringing down its price. Before continuing I should explain that CMOS devices are not quite as frugal with power as some people believe. A CMOS logic element consumes an appreciable amount of power only when it changes state, so that the power consumption rises with the rate at which a system is clocked. At a sufficiently high clock rate, CMOS systems can consume more power than equivalent NMOS systems. However, when idle, a CMOS component consumes an amazingly tiny amount of power. Because of this factor CMOS memories may be operated from small batteries when the prime source of power (i.e., the public electricity supply) is interrupted.

Characteristics of a Typical CMOS Memory Component

The pinout and internal arrangement of a typical 8K × 8-bit static CMOS RAM, the HM6264LP, is given in figure 5.30. In a world plagued by a general lack of standards, a reasonable measure of agreement has been made on the pinout of memory components. Not only are similar memory components from different manufacturers plug compatible, but read-only memory and read/write memory can be interchanged. Thus, the HM6264LP read/write memory is pinout compatible with 8K × 8 EPROMs such as the 2764. This fact is important because the same PCB can be used for read-only or read/write memories. Moreover, engineers can write programs, test them in read/write memory, and then, only when they are working correctly, commit them to read-only memory and replace the RAM with ROM.

The principal features of the HM6264LP and similar static CMOS read/write memories are their low power consumption when active (typically 200 mW) and their tiny power consumption when in a standby mode (typically 0.1 mW). The standby mode comes into operation when the V_{cc} supply voltage is reduced from its normal 5 V to no less than 2.0 V. This allows computers to be designed with nonvolatile memory by powering CMOS chips from small batteries when the system is not connected to the line supply.

The 6264 Read Cycle

A slightly simplified version of the HM6264LP-10 timing diagram is given in figure 5.31. The suffix 10 denotes that this device has a 100 ns access time. In order to read data from the chip, the appropriate address must be applied to the memory, CS1∗ brought low, CS2 high, and OE∗ low. Data becomes valid after the shortest of t_{AA}, t_{CO_1}, or t_{CO_2} has been satisfied. To the designer this situation means that the address, CS1∗, and CS2 must be asserted as close together as possible if the minimum access time of the HM6264LP-10 is to be achieved. If, for example, the address becomes valid but CS1∗ and CS2 are asserted 70 ns later, then the data does not become valid until 70 ns + t_{CO_1} = 170 ns later.

The output enable line, OE∗, causes the data bus lines to assume a low impedance state no sooner than 5 ns (t_{OLZ}) after OE∗ is asserted and no later than

■ FEATURES
- Fast access time   100 ns/120 ns/150 ns (max.)
- Low-power standby   Standby: 0.1 mW (typ.)
  Low-power operation   Operating: 200 mW (typ.)
- Single +5 V supply
- Completely static memory . . . no clock or timing strobe required
- Equal access and cycle time
- Common data input and output, three-state output
- Directly TTL compatible: all input and output
- Standard 28-pin package configuration
- Pinout compatible with 64K EPROM HM482764

■ BLOCK DIAGRAM

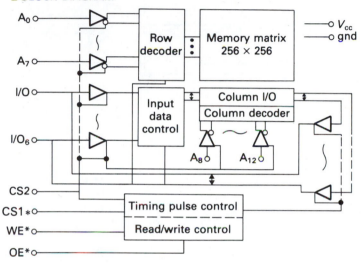

■ PIN APPRANGEMENT

NC	1	28	V_{cc}
A_{12}	2	27	WE*
A_7	3	26	CS2
A_6	4	25	A_8
A_5	5	24	A_9
A_4	6	23	A_{11}
A_3	7	22	OE*
A_2	8	21	A_{10}
A_1	9	20	CS1*
A_0	10	19	I/O_8
I/O_1	11	18	I/O_7
I/O_2	12	17	I/O_6
I/O_3	13	16	I/O_5
gnd	14	15	I/O_4

(Top view)

■ ABSOLUTE MAXIMUM RATINGS

Item	Symbol	Rating	Unit
Terminal voltage*	V_T	−0.5† to +7.0	V
Power dissipation	P_T	1.0	W
Operating temperature	T_{opr}	0 to +70	°C
Storage temperature	T_{stg}	−55 to +125	°C
Storage temperature (under bias)	T_{bias}	−10 to +85	°C

* With respect to gnd
† Pulse width 50 ns

■ TRUTH TABLE

WE*	CS1*	CS2	OE*	Mode	I/O pin
X	1	X	X	Not selected (power down)	High Z
X	X	0	X		High Z
1	0	1	1	Output disabled	High Z
1	0	1	0	Read	Dout
0	0	1	1	Write	Din
0	0	1	0		Din

FIGURE 5.31   Simplified read cycle timing diagram of an HM6264LP-10 RAM

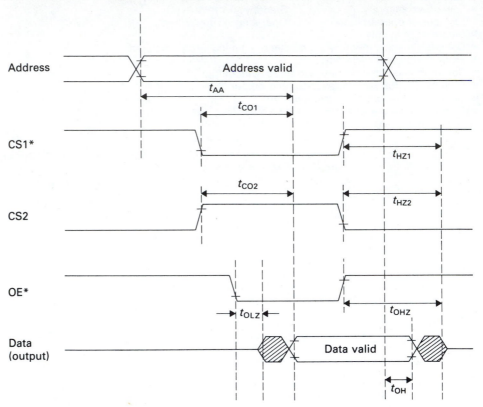

Symbol	Parameter	Value for HM6264P–10
t_{AA}	Address access time	100 ns max.
t_{CO1}	Chip select to output	100 ns max.
t_{CO2}	Chip select to output	100 ns max.
t_{HZ1}	Chip select to output float	35 ns max.
t_{HZ2}	Chip select to output float	35 ns max.
t_{OLZ}	Output enable to output low Z	5–50 ns
t_{OHZ}	Output disable to output float	35 ns max.
t_{OH}	Output data hold	10 ns min.

50 ns. These figures are of interest to the systems designer who is going to use OE* to control data bus contention. The HM6264LP-10 may be operated with OE* permanently grounded, in which case the chip is controlled solely by CS1*, CS2, and WE*. If OE* can be grounded and forgotten, why have the manufacturers provided it? The short answer is that the HM6264LP-10 comes in a 28-pin package and only 25 pins are strictly necessary to implement an 8K × 8 read/write RAM. Of the other three pins, one is NC (not connected = not used), one is

a second chip-select input, and the remaining pin has been given the function of turning the data bus drivers on and off during a read cycle. The long answer concerns bus contention in microprocessor systems. Figure 5.32 illustrates a hypothetical but realistic situation. Two memory components, M1 and M2, are connected to a system's address and data bus. During memory read cycle 1, memory M1 is selected, and during memory read cycle 2, memory M2 is selected.

FIGURE 5.32   Relationship between output enable and bus contention in a read cycle

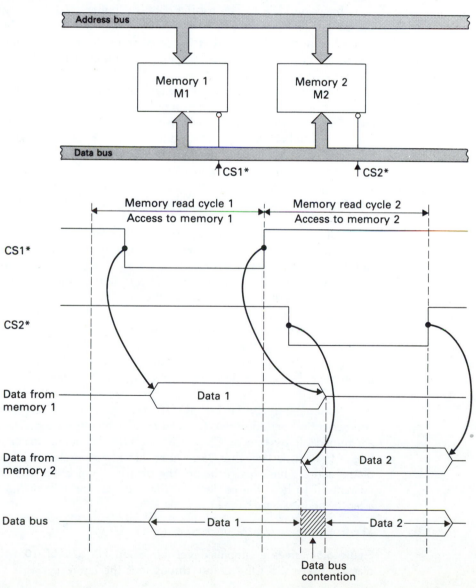

The timing diagram shows the behavior of the data outputs from M1 and M2, which are labeled data 1 and data 2, respectively. Suppose that M1 has data bus drivers with relatively long turn-off times. Therefore the data bus from M1 is in a low impedance state well into cycle 2. Now suppose that M2 has data bus drivers with relatively fast turn-on times, so that the data bus from M2 goes into a low impedance state very early in cycle 2. As the data buses from both memories are connected to the same system data bus, a period follows when two devices are simultaneously trying to drive it. This situation is shown by the shaded portion in figure 5.32 and is potentially harmful to the system.

By using OE* to control the data bus buffers of the memory components, the danger of bus contention may be avoided. Almost invariably, chip select is derived from the CPU's read/write signal and data strobes. In general, bus drivers are turned off more rapidly by negating an output enable than by negating write enable or chip select.

Another form of data bus contention solved by the output enable pin is related to a memory write cycle. Suppose a microprocessor begins a write cycle and puts out a valid address early in the cycle, as illustrated in figure 5.33. If the address is valid at time t_{AV}, the memory will be selected t_{CS} seconds later, where t_{CS} is the delay involved in decoding the address. The time at which the data bus from the memory assumes a low impedance state is given by $t_{AV} + t_{CS} + t_{OE}$, where t_{OE} is the time delay between chip select going low and the data bus low impedance state. In other words, the memory is behaving as if the current cycle were a read cycle.

All read/write memory components automatically disable their data bus drivers when its WE* input is forced low. Consequently, any data bus contention cannot take place later than $t_{AV} + t_{WD} + t_{WE}$, where t_{WD} is the delay between address valid and WE* going low and t_{WE} is the time required to turn off the memory's data output drivers when WE* goes high.

Data bus contention occurs in the period between the times when the data bus buffers of the memory are turned on by chip select (CS*) going low and then off by WE* going low. This situation is given by: $(t_{AV} + t_{WD} + t_{WE}) - (t_{AV} + t_{CS} + t_{OE}) = t_{WD} + t_{WE} - t_{CS} - t_{OE}$. If this value is zero or negative there is no problem, but if it is positive some action must be taken to avoid this type of contention.

Returning to the HM6264LP-10 read cycle timing diagram of figure 5.31, another critical period during the read cycle comes at its end. The data bus buffers are turned off by one of CS1*, CS2, or OE* becoming inactive. The data bus begins to float no later than 35 ns after the chip is deselected. Should the contents of the address bus change before the data bus is floating, the HM6264LP-10 is guaranteed to hold the contents of the data bus for at least t_{OH} seconds (10 ns) after the address has changed.

Write Cycle

Figure 5.34 gives a simplified version of an HM6264LP-10 write cycle timing diagram for which OE* is low throughout the entire cycle. A valid write cycle

FIGURE 5.33   Relationship between output enable and bus contention in a write cycle

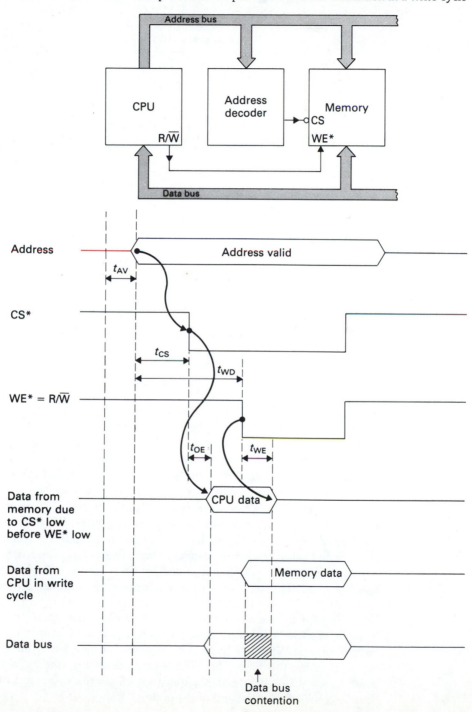

FIGURE 5.34   Simplified version of the HM6264LP-10 write timing diagram

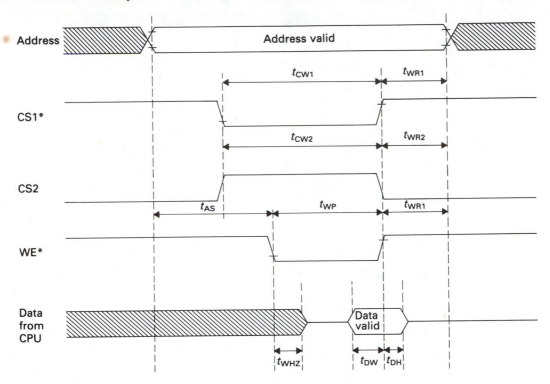

takes place when CS1∗ is low, CS2 high, and WE∗ low. The write cycle begins when the last of these three signals is asserted and ends when the first of them is negated. The only setup requirement for these three control signals is that the contents of the address bus be valid for at least t_{AS} (i.e., 0 ns) before they are asserted. Clearly, letting the address settle after CS1∗, CS2, or WE∗ are asserted may result in an erroneous write to a random address location.

In order to sustain a write cycle, both CS1∗ and CS2 must be asserted for $t_{CW} = 80$ ns (t_{CW} is the smaller of t_{CW1} and t_{CW2}) and WE∗ for at least $t_{WP} = 60$ ns. After the end of a write cycle, the contents of the address bus must not change for a period called the write recovery time. This is t_{WR1}, and is 5 ns minimum in the case of a write cycle being ended by CS1∗ or by WE∗ being negated, or is $t_{WR2} = 15$ ns minimum in the case of a write cycle terminated by the negation of CS2.

As OE∗ is asserted for the duration of the write cycle, the data bus driver may be in a low impedance state for up to $t_{WHZ} = 35$ ns maximum following the falling edge of WE∗. We have already seen that data bus contention must not be allowed during this time. The CPU must place data on the memory's data lines at least $t_{DW} = 40$ ns before the termination of a write cycle and maintain it for at least $t_{DH} = 0$ ns after the end of the cycle.

CMOS Memory and Battery Back-up

Like many other CMOS memory components, the HM6264LP-10 is able to operate in a special power-down or data-retention mode, in which the supply voltage, V_{cc}, is reduced to no less than 2.0 V. Under these conditions the memory must be deselected with either CS1* at no less than 0.2 V below V_{cc} or CS2 at no more than 0.2 V above ground. When powered down, the HM6264LP-10 consumes less than 50 μA through its V_{cc} pin. Such a low current can readily be supplied by a small on-board battery. Figure 5.35 gives the low V_{cc} data-retention waveform for the case where the memory is deselected by CS1* going high. We must conform with this sequence if data is not to be lost.

In order to bring the HM6264LP-10 into a power-down mode safely, CS1* must first rise to at least 2.2 V while V_{cc} is at its nominal 5.0 V level. This situation has the effect of deselecting the chip. The V_{cc} supply may then be reduced to its data-retention value of 2.0 V minimum. Note that in figure 5.35, as V_{cc} falls, CS1* tracks it, and that CS1* must not drop below $V_{cc} - 0.2$ V during this process. When $V_{cc} = 2.0$ V, the memory is in its power-down mode, consuming no more than 250 μW. To bring the memory out of its power-down mode, V_{cc} must be returned to its normal value of 5 V. During this transition, CS1* must track V_{cc} up to at least 2.2 V. Once V_{cc} has settled, the chip can be accessed after a period equal to the read cycle time (100 ns).

In theory, the power-down mode of this and other CMOS memories is quite unremarkable. In practice, the procedure can be a bit of a nightmare, because three very practical problems arise in the design of battery backed-up or "nonvolatile" CMOS read/write memories: the switchover from normal V_{cc} to its standby

FIGURE 5.35   Low V_{cc} data-retention waveform controlled by CS1*

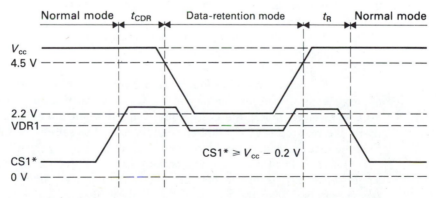

t_{CDR} = 0 ns min.

t_R = 100 ns min.

value, the control of chip select or write enable during this time, and the control of the memory's other inputs (i.e., address lines) while the system is in standby mode. These problems will be dealt with later in this section. First we must look at the power supply requirements of CMOS memories.

The designer of battery backed-up CMOS memory is faced with the choice of the battery that will actually supply the standby power. This choice can be difficult as several types of battery are available and many considerations are involved in the design of a standby power supply. Apart from cost and physical size, the four most important parameters affecting the selection of a battery are its type, its capacity (measured in ampere-hours), its temperature range, and its self-discharge current.

There are two basic types of battery: primary and secondary. A primary battery delivers its current, becomes exhausted, and is thrown away. A secondary battery is rechargeable and can be topped up whenever necessary. Popular primary cells are carbon-zinc, alkaline, silver oxide, mercury, or lithium-iodine. Secondary cells are typically lead-acid or nickel-cadmium (Ni-cad). Most battery back-up systems employ secondary cells rather than nonrechargeable primary cells. One reason for this is due to a characteristic of all cells, and is called self-discharge, which means that cells gradually discharge even though no current is being drawn from their terminals. Therefore, these cells have a finite shelf-life, beyond which they cannot be relied upon. If battery backed-up memory is to be very reliable and to operate without a frequent change of batteries, secondary cells must be used. However, the lithium-iodine primary cell is an exception to this rule and has a negligible self-discharge current, remaining active for at least ten years. Moreover, the lithium-iodine battery is less affected by temperature than other types and can operate over the range from -54 to $74°C$.

Storage cells are normally the designer's first choice for battery backed-up memory arrays, as they can be recharged from the line power supply while the system is running. Of the various types of storage cell, the nickel-cadmium cell is generally preferred as it is of moderately low cost, it does not contain a spillable liquid like some lead-acid cells, it is available in small sizes suitable for direct mounting on printed circuit boards, and its output voltage is constant as it is discharged. As a single nickel-cadmium cell has an output of 1.2 V, two or three in series need to be connected to obtain the 2.4 or 3.6 V needed to furnish the standby voltage.

Unfortunately, nickel-cadmium cells have a high self-discharge current of approximately 1 percent per day at $15°C$ to as much as 8 percent per day at $50°C$. Therefore, unless the cell is fully charged when a power failure occurs, its useful life may be severely limited. Furthermore, the self-discharge current limits the time that the system can be operated before the battery must be recharged.

This simplest type of battery back-up circuit is given in figure 5.36, where a single diode, D1, is placed between the system power supply and the CMOS power supply. When the anode of the diode is at 5 V, it conducts, providing a CMOS V_{cc} and a charging current to the nickel-cadmium battery. The resistor R_c, in series with the battery, limits the charging current. A recommendation is given

FIGURE 5.36   Single-diode battery isolation

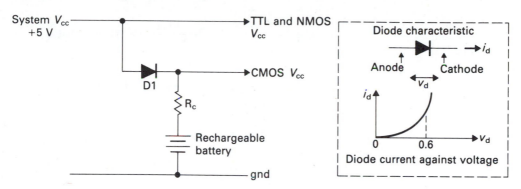

that nickel-cadmium batteries be charged at a current of $C/10$, where C is the capacity of the cell in ampere-hours. If a typical battery has a capacity of 100 mA-h, the charging current should ideally be 10 mA. The charging resistor is given by $10(V_{cc} - V_{bat})/C$. Two 1.2-V cells in series with 100 mA-h capacity require a current-limiting resistor of $10(5 - 2.4)0.1 = 260\ \Omega$.

If the main supply in figure 5.36 falls, diode D1 becomes reverse biased and ceases to conduct. Now the CMOS V_{cc} is supplied by the battery. Unfortunately, the simple scheme of figure 5.36 presents a potential difficulty. In normal operation the TTL and NMOS V_{cc} supply is 5 V. The CMOS supply is 5 V less the voltage drop across the diode, which is approximately 0.6 V for a silicon diode. Therefore, the CMOS V_{cc} supply sits at 4.4 V. As the CMOS memories are driven by NMOS or TTL signals, it is possible for an input to exceed the CMOS V_{cc} value (i.e., 4.4 V). This condition may harm the CMOS device, because bipolar junctions within the chip can be forward biased, causing very high values of I_{cc} to be drawn.

Figure 5.37 provides a possible solution to this problem. A second diode is placed in series with the V_{cc} supply to TTL and NMOS devices. Now the TTL V_{cc} and CMOS V_{cc} track each other, stopping the TTL V_{cc} from rising appreciably above the CMOS V_{cc}. This circuit requires a main voltage supply of 5.6 V to allow for the 0.6-V drop across D2. Unfortunately, many microprocessor systems provide only a 5-V supply to the individual modules of the system. The circuit of figure 5.37 could be used if the diodes were germanium types rather than silicon. A germanium diode has a forward voltage drop of only 0.2 V, so that a system supply of 5 V would be suitable. Alas, a germanium diode also has an appreciable leakage current when it is reverse biased. The period for which a battery can back up the main supply is therefore reduced, as some current will flow from the battery through the diode to ground.

An alternative arrangement is given in figure 5.38, where a PNP transistor, T2, supplies the CMOS V_{cc} in normal operation. When T2 is conducting, the voltage across it is 0.2 V, which means that the CMOS V_{cc} closely matches the

FIGURE 5.37   Dual-diode battery isolation

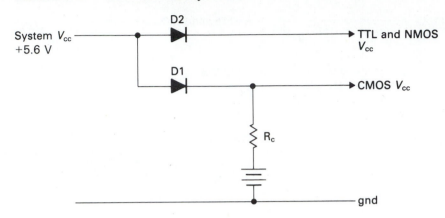

TTL V_{cc}. If the main supply falls, transistor T1 is turned off, turning off T2 and permitting the battery to supply the CMOS V_{cc}. All the circuits described in figures 5.36 to 5.38 automatically solve the CS1*: V_{cc} tracking problem if CS1* is pulled up to V_{cc} (standby) during the power-down/standby/power-up modes.

Another area to which the designer of battery backed-up CMOS memories must pay careful attention is the state of the inputs to the CMOS device when it is powered down. Figure 5.39 shows a typical CMOS input stage. Components D1, D2, and R form a protective network designed to eliminate the CMOS circuit's susceptibility to static electricity, and do not affect the circuit under normal operation. The key to CMOS's low power consumption can be found in the P-type and N-type metal oxide transistors in series (T1 and T2, respectively, in figure 5.39). As only one transistor in the pair is in the on-state (i.e., conducting) at a time, no direct current path exists between V_{cc} and ground, apart from a tiny leakage current through the off-transistor.

FIGURE 5.38   Isolation of the battery by a transistor circuit

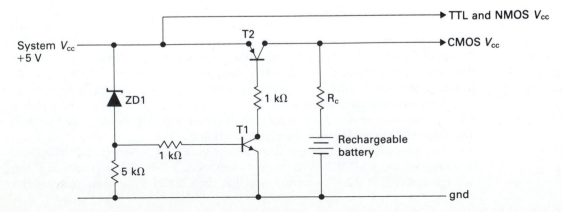

FIGURE 5.39   Input circuit of a CMOS gate

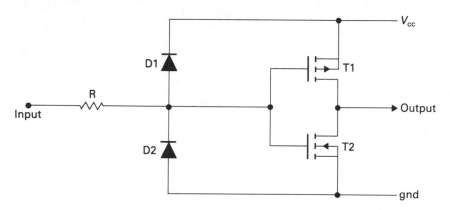

If the input to a CMOS gate is ever allowed to float, a possibility exists that it may settle at a level midway between V_{cc} and ground, which has the effect of turning on both the P-channel transistor and the N-channel transistor simultaneously. Under these circumstances a direct path goes between V_{cc} and ground and an appreciable current can flow through both output transistors in series. Although this current is not large by the standards of microcomputer systems, it can be a magnitude or two greater than the V_{cc} power-down current taken by the memory component.

Floating inputs to CMOS devices can be eliminated by careful attention to the interface between the memory chip and the rest of the system. The inputs to the CMOS device must either be pulled up to the CMOS V_{cc} or down to ground. Some authorities suggest that CMOS inputs should have pull-up resistors to V_{cc} or pull-down resistors to ground, to stop any inputs floating while the system is powered down. However, many low-power Schottky devices used to drive CMOS memories have low impedance outputs (unlike that of standard TTL) when their V_{cc} is grounded, as it is during the power-down mode. Consequently, if LSTTL gates drive CMOS inputs, pull-up resistors must not be used, as current will flow through them and the LSTTL driver from V_{cc} to ground. Equally, pull-down resistors are not needed, as the LSTTL outputs automatically pull the CMOS input down to ground level.

If a guarantee can be made that the low-power Schottky logic driving the CMOS chip has a low impedance output when its $V_{cc} = 0$ V, then it is an excellent driver for all the CMOS inputs that may safely be in a low state during the power-down mode. Of course, the active-low chip-select input cannot be driven by LSTTL. A recommendation is also made that the write enable input to the CMOS memory be pulled up during the power-down mode. This condition is not essential if the active-low chip-select input is in a logical one state, but it is a wise precaution.

The possible circuit diagram of an 8K × 16-bit memory using two HM6264LP-10s is given figure 5.40. Address and data lines are buffered by four

FIGURE 5.40   Example of a CMOS memory module backed up by battery

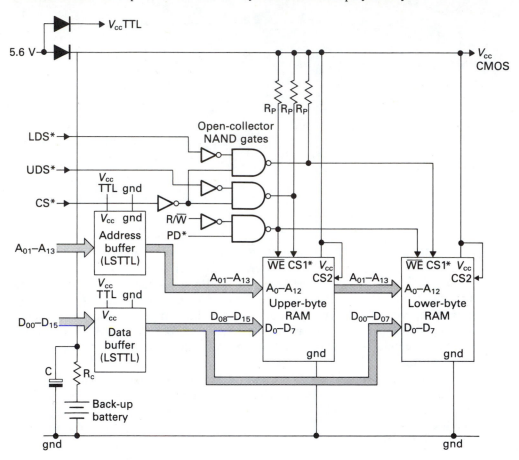

NOTE: PD* = power_down*
        (low when V_{cc} below nominal value)

LSTTL buffers operating from the TTL V_{cc} supply. The CS1* input of the two memories is derived from (CS* + UDS*) and (CS* + LDS*), as in any other 68000-based system. Normally, OR gates would be used to generate these functions, but as no OR gate with open-collector outputs is available, NAND gates with inverted inputs are used to achieve the same effect. Similarly, the write enable inputs of the memories are driven by a NAND gate with an open-collector output. All TTL gates are driven from the TTL V_{cc} supply.

When the system is powered down, address and data inputs are clamped at a low level by the LSTTL bus drivers. The outputs of the open-collector gates are pulled up to V_{cc} CMOS by the resistors labeled R_p, thereby becoming an impossibility for data within the memory to be corrupted. When power is reapplied to the system, the write enable and CS1* inputs automatically track V_{cc} CMOS as it rises toward V_{cc} TTL.

During the power-down mode, the current supplied by the battery drives the memory components together with leakage currents flowing through the decoupling capacitor C, the reverse-biased diode, and the outputs of the open-collector gates. The current taken by the memories is typically 1 to 50 μA maximum. By using a tantalum low-leakage capacitor and a low-leakage silicon diode, these components should cause little drain from the battery.

The leakage current into the open-collector gates is somewhat higher: a maximum value of 100 μA is quoted for LSTTL gates. Therefore, the current supplied by the battery can be up to 3×100 μA $+ 2 \times 50$ μA, or 400 μA maximum. A PCB-mounting Ni-cad with a capacity of 100 mA-h should be able to supply this current for 250 hours, or over 10 days.

Figure 5.40 shows the active-high CS2 input of the memories connected to V_{cc} CMOS. This input can also be used to force a power-down mode when V_{cc} TTL falls. In figure 5.41 a CMOS operational amplifier controls CS2. The operational amplifier is a CMOS type and is powered from V_{cc} CMOS. The noninverting input of the op-amp is given by V_{cc} TTL[R2/(R1 + R2)] and the inverting input by V_{cc} CMOS[R4/(R3 + R4)]. The resistors are selected to make the noninverting input more positive than the inverting input. In normal operation V_{cc} TTL is equal to V_{cc} CMOS, and the op-amp's output is driven high to enable CS2. When V_{cc} TTL falls, the output of the op-amp drops to ground—0.1 V—and

FIGURE 5.41   Controlling the 6264LP-10's CS2 input by a CMOS op-amp

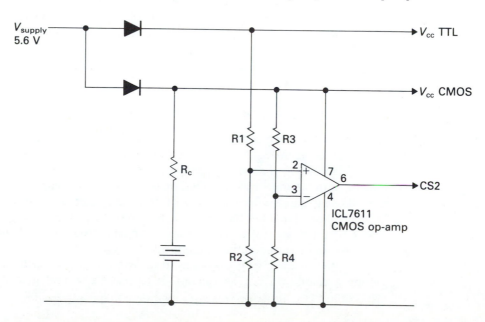

disables the memory components. It should be noted that the ICL7611 CMOS op-amp has an output slew rate of only 0.016 V/μs when operated at 10 μA. This means that the output will take approximately 300 μs before CS2 drops to its lower level.

EPROM

The Erasable and Programmable Read-Only Memory, EPROM, is a nonvolatile memory component that can be programmed and reprogrammed by the user with relatively low-cost equipment. Unlike most static and dynamic memory components, EPROM is largely available in byte-wide form. Some word-wide EPROMs are now in use. Typical EPROMs vary from 2K $\times$ 8 to 64K $\times$ 8 bits.

The function of an EPROM is to store programs and data that are never, or only infrequently, modified. An alternative to the EPROM is the mask programmed ROM. These are cheaper than EPROMs in large-volume production, but cannot be reprogrammed and are not used unless the scale of production is sufficient to absorb the initial cost of setting up the mask.

EPROMs are found mainly in four applications: in embedded systems where they hold firmware, in personal computers where they hold the operating system and/or interpretors for HLLs, in bootstrap loaders in general-purpose digital systems, and in the development of microprocessor systems. In an embedded system, programs are held in EPROM, as backing store is not appropriate in most cases. General-purpose systems must have at least sufficient EPROM to hold the bootstrap loader that reads the operating system from disk. Some manufacturers put much of the operating system in EPROM to increase the speed of the system and to reduce the demands on the system read/write memory.

The EPROM is useful in developing microprocessor systems because a program can be developed on one computer, stored in EPROM, and then plugged into the system under development.

Characteristics of EPROM

An EPROM memory cell consists of a single NMOS field-effect transistor and is illustrated in figure 5.42. A current flows between the V_{ss} and V_{dd} terminals through a positive channel. By applying a charge to a gate electrode, the current flowing in the channel can be turned on or off. A special feature of the EPROM is the "floating gate," which is insulated from any conductor by means of a thin layer of silicon dioxide—an almost perfect insulator. By placing or not placing a charge on the floating gate, the transistor can be turned on or off and hence a one or a zero can be stored in the memory cell.

As the floating gate is entirely insulated, we are left with the problem of getting a charge on it. The solution is to place a second gate close to it but

FIGURE 5.42   Structure of an EPROM memory cell

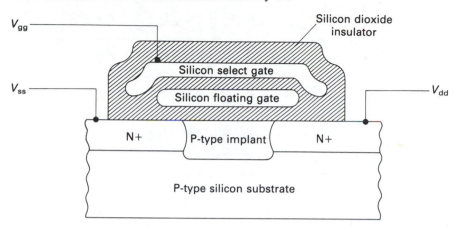

insulated from it. By applying a charge to this second and noninsulated gate, some electrons flow between the noninsulated and the floating gates. The voltage necessary to achieve this condition is typically 21–25 V. In general, EPROMs are not programmed while they are in their "normal" environment. They are plugged into a special-purpose EPROM programmer because they require a non-TTL voltage during programming and a write cycle is very much longer than a typical read cycle. Although circuits can be designed that program EPROMs in the equipment where they are used, such an approach is most rare.

Another reason why EPROMs are programmed in special-purpose equipment is due to their method of erasure. Once an EPROM has been programmed its stored data can be erased only by removing the charge trapped on the floating gates. The charge is removed by exposing the surface of the chip to ultraviolet (UV) light. Consequently, the EPROM chip must be mounted behind a transparent window, removed from inside its equipment, and placed under a UV lamp. The window above the EPROM chip is made of quartz, because glass is opaque to UV. As the chip must be removed to erase it, the need to place it in a special programmer creates no further hardship.

Although microprocessor systems have been plagued by a lack of standardization, one area of limited success is in EPROM pinout. Two widely used series of EPROMs exist, the 25-series and the 27-series. The 27-series is frequently preferred because its EPROMs are "compatible" with the pinout of typical byte-wide static RAMs; that is, equipment can be designed so that RAM and EPROM chips are interchangeable with little effort.

Figure 5.43 gives the pinout of some of the 27-series EPROMs. Note that the pinouts are arranged so that equipment can be designed to accommodate several different sizes of EPROM by simply modifying jumpers on a PCB; for example, a 24-pin 2732 (4K × 8) EPROM will fit in a 28-pin socket wired for a 2764 (8K × 8) EPROM with minimal effort. The 2732 is plugged in so that its

FIGURE 5.43 Pinout of some EPROMs. (Reprinted by permission of Elektor Electronics Magazine)

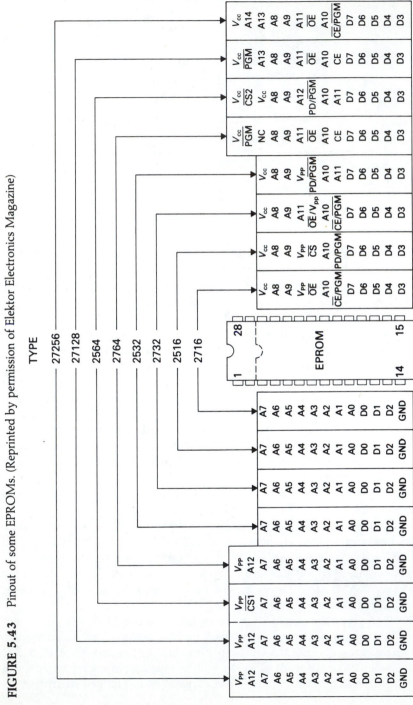

216

FIGURE 5.44   Read cycle timing diagram of an EPROM

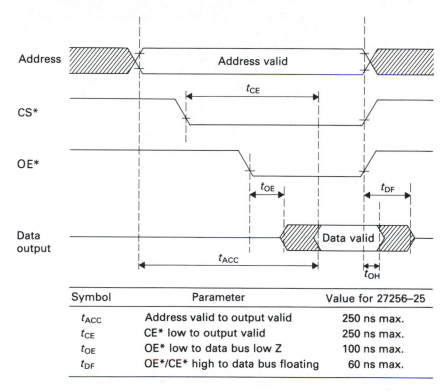

Symbol	Parameter	Value for 27256–25
t_{ACC}	Address valid to output valid	250 ns max.
t_{CE}	CE* low to output valid	250 ns max.
t_{OE}	OE* low to data bus low Z	100 ns max.
t_{DF}	OE*/CE* high to data bus floating	60 ns max.

pin 12 (ground) is in the pin 14 position in the 28-pin socket. Pin 26 on a 2764 is marked NC (not connected) in figure 5.43 and is connected to +5 V to become the 2732's V_{cc} supply.

Using an EPROM is simplicity itself. Figure 5.44 gives the timing diagram of a 27256 EPROM and figure 5.45 shows how two 27256s are connected to a 68000 CPU. An address is applied to the 256's fifteen address inputs, CS* is asserted, and OE* is forced active-low when R/$\overline{W}$ is high. We could strap OE* to ground, as the data output buffers are also enabled by CS*. Some CPUs use OE* to avoid data bus contention. The only two considerations in the design of EPROM memories are the access time calculation and the danger of data bus contention.

In a 68000 system, access time is taken care of by providing the appropriate DTACK* delay. Most EPROMs are slower than static RAM and have access times of 200–450 ns from address valid. Unfortunately, EPROMs have relatively long values of OE* high (or CS* high) to data bus floating. A typical value is 80–150 ns, which means that the EPROM is driving the data bus well into the next cycle. Care should be taken to avoid any other device driving the data bus until this time has elapsed.

FIGURE 5.45   Connecting a 27256 EPROM to a 68000 CPU

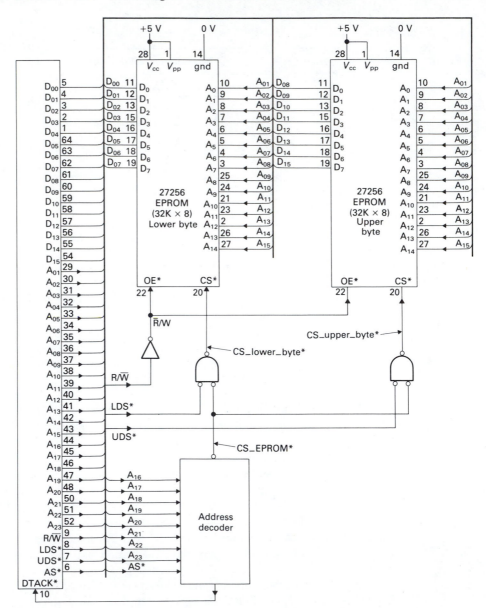

Summary

A situation where a memory component could simply be bolted onto a microprocessor to create a microcomputer (apart from I/O devices) would be very convenient. We have demonstrated that interfacing memory components of a microprocessor is, in fact, no trivial task. The designer has to construct an address decoder to map the memory space of address components onto the address space of the microprocessor. An address decoder can be designed using the address decoding techniques and devices introduced at the start of this chapter. The actual circuit employed must take account of the type of memory map required by the processor and whether or not flexibility has to be built into the system.

We have described the characteristics of the static memory component and in chapter 7 look at its more complex counterpart, the dynamic RAM. Anyone wishing to connect memory components to a microprocessor must be aware of the two important design considerations discussed here. The first is the relationship between the timing characteristics of the memory component and the timing requirements of the microprocessor. The second is the danger of data bus contention that arises when the memory and the microprocessor both attempt to drive the data bus at the same time.

A memory component of particular interest described in this chapter is the CMOS static RAM, which is able to enter a power-down mode in which it retains data while consuming virtually no power. This ability to store data when the microcomputer is powered down can be used to hold system data when the microcomputer is switched off.

Problems

1. Design address decoding networks to satisfy the following memory maps:
   a. RAM1   00 0000–00 FFFF
      RAM2   01 0000–01 FFFF
      I/O_1   E0 0000–E0 001F
      I/O_2   E0 0020–E0 003F
   b. ROM1   00 0000–00 3FFF
      ROM2   00 4000–00 7FFF
      ROM3   00 8000–00 BFFF
      RAM   04 0000–07 FFFF
      I/O   08 0000–08 00FF

Compare and contrast the various ways of implementing these address decoders.

   2. A manufacturer designs a single-board computer with eight pairs of byte-wide EPROMs to hold system firmware. The designer decides to cater for three EPROM sizes: $4K \times 8$, $8K \times 8$, and $16K \times 8$. Design an address decoder that will allow the size of each EPROM to be user selectable by means of jumpers on the PCB.

   3. A 68000 systems is to have up to eight 256K word pages of read/write memory, up to eight 8K word pages of EPROM, and up to eight 128 word pages of I/O space. The designer wishes to make the 68000 memory map *user definable* under software control. Therefore, the address from the CPU must be compared with addresses set up by the user in order to generate the necessary device-select signals. Design an arrangement that will do this. Note that the address decoding network itself is to be permanently mapped at the address $FF FFE0 and that, following a reset, the first page of ROM is mapped at $00 0000–$00 3FFF.

Chapter 6

Exception Handling

and the 68000

In this chapter, we examine two closely related topics, interrupts and exceptions. Most readers will already be familiar with the "interrupt," which is a specific example of the more general "exception." As their name suggests, exceptions correspond to events that alter the normal execution of a program. An interrupt is a message to the CPU from an external device seeking attention. Such devices are normally I/O peripherals of the type to be described in chapters 7 and 8. Other exceptions described in this chapter include bus errors that arise from faulty bus cycles and software errors that are caused by certain "events" arising out of the software. We first look at the interrupt that is implemented by all microcomputers. A general introduction to exceptions then follows. The middle section of this chapter shows how the 68000 implements exception handling. Finally, we briefly look at how exceptions are used to implement real-time systems.

6.1 Interrupts

A computer executes the instructions of a program sequentially unless a jump or conditional branch modifies their order or unless a subroutine is called. In such cases, any deviation from the sequential execution of instructions is determined by the programmer. Deviations caused by conditional branches or subroutines are said to be synchronous, because they occur at predetermined points in the program. Under certain circumstances this arrangement is very inefficient. Suppose a microprocessor is reading data from a keyboard at an average rate of 250 characters per minute, corresponding to approximately 4 characters per second. In a 68000 system, the processor reads the status of a memory-mapped peripheral to determine whether or not a key has been pressed. If no key has been pressed, a branch is made back to the instruction that reads the status of the peripheral and the cycle continues until a key is pressed. The following program shows how this is done:

```
KEY_STATUS   EQU       $F00000            Location of input status word
KEY_VALUE    EQU       KEY_STATUS + 2     Location of input data word
             LEA. L    KEY_STATUS, A0     A0 points to key_status
             LEA. L    KEY_VALUE, A1      A1 points to key_value
TEST_LOOP    BTST      #0, (A0)           Test status (i.e., LSB)
             BEQ       TEST_LOOP          Repeat while LSB clear
             MOVE. B   (A1), D1           Read the data
```

The two instructions, BTST #0,(A0) and BEQ TEST_LOOP, constitute a "polling loop," which is executed until the least-significant bit of the status word is true, signifying that the data from the keyboard is valid.

These two instructions take 20 clock cycles to execute, requiring 2 μs with a 10-MHz clock. Thus, for each key pressed, the polling loop is executed approximately 100,000 times! Quite clearly, this use of the computer is grossly inefficient. In some applications of the microprocessor, the time wasted in executing a polling loop is of little significance, as the computer has nothing better to do with its time. If I am sitting at the keyboard of my personal computer thinking about the next word to enter, it is of no consequence that the CPU is patiently asking the keyboard if it has a new character every 2 μs or so.

More sophisticated applications of computers cannot afford to let the CPU while away its time executing a polling loop. These computers have many tasks to perform and can always find something useful to do. A queue of programs may be waiting to be run, or some peripheral may need continual attention while another program is being run, or a background task and a foreground task may exist. A technique for dealing more effectively with input/output transactions has been implemented on all microprocessors and is called an interrupt-handling mechanism. An interrupt request line, IRQ, is connected between the peripheral and the CPU. Whenever the peripheral is ready to take part in an input/output operation, it asserts the IRQ line and invites the CPU to deal with the transaction. The CPU is free to carry out background tasks between interrupt requests from the peripheral.

An interrupt is clearly an asynchronous event, because the processor cannot know at which instant a peripheral such as a keyboard will generate an interrupt. In other words, the interrupt-generating activity (i.e., the keyboard) bears no particular timing relationship to the activity the computer is carrying out between interrupts. When an interrupt occurs, the computer first decides whether to deal with it (i.e., to service it) or whether to ignore it for the time being. If the computer is doing something that must be completed, it ignores interrupts. Should the computer decide to respond to the interrupt, it must carry out the following sequence of actions:

1. Complete its current instruction. All instructions are indivisible, which means they must be executed to completion. A more sophisticated architecture might allow the temporary suspension of an instruction.

2. The contents of the program counter must be saved in a safe place, in order to enable the program to continue from the point at which it was interrupted, after the interrupt has been serviced. The program counter is invariably saved on the stack so that interrupts can, themselves, be interrupted without losing their return addresses.

3. The state of the processor is saved on the stack. Clearly, we would be unwise to allow the interrupt service routine to modify, say, the value of the carry flag, so that an interrupt occurring before a BCC instruction would affect the operation of the BCC after the interrupt had been serviced. In general, the servicing of an interrupt should have no effect whatsoever on the execution of the interrupted program. This statement will be qualified later when we deal with a special type of synchronous event called a software interrupt.

4. A jump is then made to the location of the interrupt-handling routine, which is executed like any other program. After this routine has been executed, a return from interrupt is made, the program counter restored, and the system status word returned to its preinterrupt value.

Before we examine the way in which the 68000 deals with interrupts, we should consider some of the key concepts emerging from any discussion of interrupts.

Nonmaskable Interrupts

An interrupt request is so called because it is a request, and therefore carries the implication that it may be denied or deferred. Whenever an interrupt request is deferred, we say that it is masked. Sometimes the computer needs to respond to an interrupt no matter what it is doing. Most microprocessors have a special interrupt request input, called a nonmaskable interrupt input, NMI. This interrupt cannot be deferred and must always be serviced. A nonmaskable interrupt is normally reserved for events such as loss of power. In this case, a low-voltage detector generates a nonmaskable interrupt as soon as the power begins to decay. This situation forces the processor to deal with the interrupt and to perform an orderly shutdown of the system, before the power drops below a critical level and the computer fails completely. The 68000 has a single, level 7, nonmaskable interrupt request.

Prioritized Interrupts

In an environment where more than one device is able to issue an interrupt request, we need to provide a mechanism to distinguish between an important interrupt and a less important one. For example, if a disk drive controller generates an interrupt because it has some data ready to be read by the processor, the interrupt must be serviced before the data is lost and replaced by new data from the disk drive. On the other hand, an interrupt generated by a keyboard interface probably has from 250 ms to several seconds before it must be serviced. Therefore, an interrupt from a keyboard can be forced to wait if interrupts from devices requiring immediate attention are pending.

For these reasons, microprocessors are often provided with prioritized interrupts. Each interrupt has a predefined priority, and a new interrupt with a priority lower than or equal to the current one cannot interrupt the processor until the current interrupt has been dealt with. Equally, an interrupt with a higher priority can interrupt the current interrupt. The 68000 provides seven levels of interrupt priority.

Vectored Interrupts

A vectored interrupt is one in which the device requesting the interrupt automatically identifies itself to the processor. Some 8-bit microprocessors lack a vectored interrupt facility and have only a single active-low interrupt request input (IRQ∗). When IRQ∗ is asserted, the processor recognizes an interrupt but not its source. The processor must now examine, in turn, each of the peripherals that may have initiated the interrupt. To do this, the interrupt-handling routine interrogates a status bit associated with each of the peripherals.

More sophisticated processors have an interrupt acknowledge output line (IACK) that is connected to all peripherals. Whenever the CPU has accepted an interrupt and is about to service it, the CPU asserts its interrupt acknowledge output. An interrupt acknowledge from the CPU informs the peripheral that its interrupt is about to be serviced. The peripheral then generates an "identification number" that it puts on the data bus, allowing the processor to calculate the address of the interrupt-handling routine appropriate to the peripheral. This is called a vectored interrupt. The 68000 provides the designer with both vectored and nonvectored interrupt facilities.

Now that we have introduced the hardware interrupt, the next step is to examine the more general form of interrupt, the exception.

6.2 Exceptions

"Exception" is a word that has trickled down from the world of the mainframe computer. Like an interrupt, an exception is a deviation from the normal sequence of actions carried out by a computer. Interrupts are asynchronous exceptions, initiated by hardware. Some processors, like the 68000, support other types of exception originating from errors detected by the system hardware; for example, an exception can be generated when the processor tries to read data from memory and something goes wrong, such as an attempt to read from nonexistent memory or the detection of a memory error.

As well as exceptions raised by external hardware, exceptions are also initiated by software. Some are related to errors such as an attempt to execute an illegal or nonexistent operation code. Others are actually generated by the programmer; for example, the TRAP instruction acts like a hardware interrupt in the sense that an interrupt-handling procedure is invoked by it. We will see later that a TRAP can be used to implement special instructions not normally part of the processor's instruction set.

The 68000 deals with both hardware and software exceptions in a consistent and logical fashion. The exception-handling facilities of the 68000 are one of the main factors lifting it out of the world of the 8-bit processor.

6.3 Exceptions and the 68000

Exception handling in the 68000 is intimately bound up with the notion of privileged states associated with that processor. At any instant, the 68000 is in one of two states: user or supervisor. By forcing the individual user programs to operate only in the user state and by dedicating the supervisor state to the operating system, we are able to provide users with a degree of protection against one program corrupting another. The relationship between privileged states and exception processing is simple. An exception always forces the 68000 to assume the supervisor state. Therefore, individual user programs have no direct control over exception processing and interrupt handling.

Privileged States

The supervisor state is the higher state of privilege and is in force whenever the S bit of the status register (i.e., bit 13) is true. All of the 68000's instructions can be executed while the processor is in this state. The user state is the lower state of privilege and certain instructions cannot be executed in this state. Each of the two states has its own stack pointer, so that the 68000 has two A7 registers. The user mode A7 is called the user stack pointer, USP, and the supervisor mode A7 is called the supervisor stack pointer, SSP. Note that the SSP cannot be accessed from the user state, whereas the USP can be accessed in the supervisor state by means of the MOVE USP, An and MOVE An, USP instructions.

All exception processing is carried out in the *supervisor* state, because an exception forces a change from the user to the supervisor state. Indeed, the only

FIGURE 6.1   State diagram of user and supervisor state transitions

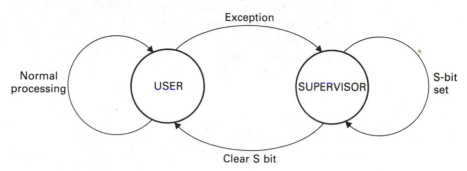

way of entering the supervisor state is by means of an exception. Figure 6.1 shows how a transfer is made between the 68000's two states. Note that an exception causes the S bit in the 68000's status register to be set and the super-visor stack pointer to be selected at the start of the exception, with the result that the return address is saved on the supervisor stack and not on the user stack. While the processor is in the supervisor state, the function code output from the processor (FC2, FC1, FC0) is 1, 0, 1 if the supervisor is executing a memory access involving data or 1, 1, 0 if it is accessing an instruction from memory.

The change from the supervisor to the user state is made by clearing the S bit of the status register. This change is carried out by the operating system when it wishes to run a user program. Four instructions are available for this operation: RTE, MOVE.W ⟨ea⟩,SR, ANDI.W #$XXXX,SR, and EORI.W #$XXXX,SR. The #$XXXX represents a 16-bit literal value in hexadecimal form. The RTE (return from exception) instruction terminates an exception-handling routine and restores the value of the program counter and the old status register stored on the stack before the current exception was processed. Consequently, if the 68000 were in the user state before the current exception forced it into the supervisor state, an RTE restores the processor to its old (i.e., user) state.

A MOVE.W ⟨ea⟩,SR loads the status register with a new value that will force the system into the user state if the S bit is clear. Similarly, the Boolean operations, AND immediate and EOR immediate, both may affect the state of the S bit; for example, to clear the S bit, the instruction ANDI.W #$DFFF,SR is executed.

In the user state, the programmer must not attempt to execute certain in-structions; for example, the STOP and RESET instructions are not available to the programmer. Why? The answer is because the RESET instruction forces the RESET* output of the 68000 low and resets any peripherals connected to this pin. Some of these peripherals may be in use by another program. The whole philos-ophy behind user/supervisor states is to prevent this type of thing from happen-ing. Similarly, a STOP instruction has the effect of halting the processor until certain conditions are met; it is not allowed in the user state because a user program should not be allowed to bring the entire system to a standstill.

Any instructions affecting the S bit in the upper byte of the status register (i.e., RTE, MOVE.W ⟨ea⟩,SR, ANDI.W #$XXXX,SR, ORI.W #$XXXX,SR, EORI.W #$XXXX,SR) are also not permitted in the user mode. Note that no instruction that performs useful computation is barred from the user mode. Only certain system operations are privileged. Suppose the programmer is either wilful or ignorant and tries to set the S bit by executing an ORI.W #$2000,SR. Obviously, nothing can prevent him or her from writing the instruction and running the program containing it.

When the program is run, the illegal operation, ORI.W #$2000,SR, violates the user privilege by trying to enter the supervisor mode and forces an exception to be generated. This situation causes a change of state from user to supervisor. "Ah!" you may say, "this seems rather like punishing a shoplifter by giving him a reward!" After all, the "punishment" for trying to enter the supervisor state is to be forced into it. The effect of attempting to execute an ORI.W #$2000,SR is to raise a software exception called a privilege violation, forcing a jump to the specific routine dealing with this type of exception. The way in which exception states are entered and processed is dealt with later.

Once the exception-handling routine dealing with the privilege violation has been entered, the user no longer controls the processor. The operating system has now taken over. In other words, in attempting to enter the supervisor state through the front door, the user has fallen through a hole in the floor and is now trapped. It is highly probable that the exception-handling routine will deal with the privilege violation by terminating the user's program.

Exception Types

A number of different exception types are supported by the 68000, some of which are associated with external hardware events such as interrupts and some of which are associated with internally generated events such as privilege violations. Provision has been included for new types of exception in future versions of the 68000. A list follows of the exception types currently implemented. The way in which these exceptions are implemented is described later.

Reset   An externally generated reset is caused by bringing the RESET* and HALT* pins low for at least ten clock pulses (or > 100 ms on power-up) and is used to place the 68000 in a known state at start-up or following a totally irrecoverable system collapse. The reset is a unique exception because there is no "return from exception" following a reset.

Bus error   A bus error is an externally generated exception, initiated by hardware driving the 68000's BERR* pin active-low. It is a "catch-all" exception because the systems designer may use it in many different ways and is provided to enable the processor to deal with hardware faults in the system. A typical use of the BERR* input is to indicate either a faulty memory access or an access to a nonexistent memory.

Interrupt The 68000 has three interrupt request inputs, IPL0* to IPL2*, that are encoded and indicate one of seven levels of interrupt. To obtain maximum benefit from the interrupt request inputs, we need to apply an eight-line to three-line priority encoder to convert one of seven interrupt request inputs from peripherals into a 3-bit code. The eighth code represents no interrupt request. A section of this chapter is devoted to the way in which the 68000 handles interrupt requests, because the designers of the 68000 have made the interrupt request facility unusually flexible.

Address error An address error exception occurs when the processor attempts to read a 16-bit word or a 32-bit longword at an odd address. If we think about this concept, attempting to read a word at an odd address would require two accesses to memory—one to access the odd byte of an operand and the other to access the even byte at the next address. Address error exceptions are generated when the programmer does something silly. Consider the following fragment of code:

```
MOVEA.L   #$7000,A0   Load A0 with $00 7000
MOVE.B    (A0)+,D0    Load D0 with the byte pointed at by A0, and
                      increment A0 by 1
MOVE.W    (A0)+,D0    Load D0 with the word pointed at by A0, and
                      increment A0 by 2
```

The third instruction results in an address error, because the previous operation, MOVE.B (A0)+,D0, causes the value in A0 to be incremented from $7000 to $7001. Therefore, when the processor attempts to execute MOVE.W (A0)+,D0, it finds it is trying to access a word at an odd address. In many ways, an address error is closer to an exception generated by an event originating in the hardware than by one originating in the software. The bus cycle that leads to the address error is aborted as the processor cannot complete the operation.

Illegal instruction In the good old days of the 8-bit microprocessor, we had fun finding out what effect "unimplemented" op-codes had on the processor; for example, if the value $A5 did not correspond to a valid op-code, an enthusiast could try and execute it and then see what happened. This situation was possible because the control unit (i.e., instruction interpreter) of most 8-bit microprocessors was implemented by random logic.

To reduce the number of gates in the control unit of the CPU, some semiconductor manufacturers have not attempted to deal with illegal op-codes. After all, if users try to execute unimplemented op-codes, they deserve everything they get. In keeping with the 68000's approach to programming, an exception is generated whenever an operation code is read that does not correspond to the bit pattern of the first word of one of the 68000's legal instructions.

Divide by zero If a number is divided by zero, the result is meaningless and often indicates that something has gone seriously wrong with the program attempting to carry out the division. For this reason, the 68000's designers decided to make any attempt to divide a number by zero an exception-generating event. Good programmers should write their programs so that they never try to divide a number by zero, and therefore the divide-by-zero exception should not arise. It is intended as a fail-safe device to avoid the meaningless result that would occur if a number was divided by zero.

CHK instruction   The check register against bounds instruction, CHK, has the assembly language form CHK ⟨ea⟩,Dn and has the effect of comparing the contents of the specified data register with the operand at the effective address. If the lower-order word in the register, Dn, is negative or is greater than the upper bound at the effective address, an exception is generated; for example, when the instruction CHK D1, D0 is executed, an exception is generated if

$$[D0(0:15)] < 0 \qquad \text{or} \qquad [D0(0:15)] > [D1(0:15)].$$

Oddly enough, the CHK instruction works only with 16-unit words, and therefore cannot be used with an address register as an effective address. The CHK exception has been included to help compiler writers for languages such as Pascal that have facilities for the automatic checking of array indexes against their bounds.

TRAPV instruction   When the trap on overflow instruction, TRAPV, is executed, an exception occurs if the overflow bit, V, of the condition code register is set. Note that an exception caused by dividing a number by zero occurs automatically, while TRAPV is an instruction equivalent to: "IF V = 1 THEN exception ELSE continue."

Privilege violation   If the processor is in the user state (i.e., the S bit of the status register is clear) and attempts to execute a privileged instruction, a privilege violation exception occurs. As well as any logical instruction that attempts to modify the state of the status register, the following three instructions cannot be executed in the user state: STOP, RESET, MOVE ⟨ea⟩,SR.

Trace   A popular method of debugging a program is to operate in a trace mode, in which the contents of all registers are printed out after each instruction has been executed. The 68000 has a built-in trace facility. If the T bit of the status register (bit 15) is set (under software control), a trace exception is generated after each instruction has been executed. The exception-handling routine called by the trace exception can be constructed to offer programmers any facilities they need.

Line 1010 emulator   Operation codes, whose four most-significant bits (bits 12 to 15) are 1010 or 1111, are unimplemented in the 68000, and therefore represent illegal instructions. However, the 68000 generates a special exception for op-codes whose most-significant nibble is 1010 (also called line ten). The purpose of this exception is to emulate instructions on future versions of the 68000. Suppose a version of the 68000 is designed that includes floating-point operations as well as the normal 68000 instruction set. Clearly, it is impossible to run code intended for the floating-point processor on a normal 68000. However, by using 1010 as the four most-significant bits of the new floating-point instructions, an exception is generated each time the 68000 encounters one of these instructions. The line 1010 exception can then be used to allow the 68000 to emulate its more sophisticated brother.

Line 1111 emulator   The line 1111 (or line F) emulator behaves in almost exactly the same way as the line 1010 emulator, except that it has a different exception-handling routine.

Uninitialized interrupt vector   The 68000 supports vectored interrupts, so that an interrupting device can identify itself and allow the 68000 to execute the appropriate interrupt-handling routine without having to poll each device in turn. Before a device can identify itself, it must first be correctly configured by the programmer. If a 68000-series peripheral is unconfigured and yet generates an interrupt, the 68000 responds by raising an "uninitialized interrupt vector" exception. The 68000-series peripherals are designed to supply the initialized interrupt vector number, $0F, during an IACK cycle if they have not been initialized by software. Their interrupt vector registers are loaded with $0F following a reset operation.

Spurious interrupt   If the 68000 receives an interrupt request and sends an interrupt acknowledge but no device responds, the CPU generates a spurious interrupt exception. To implement the spurious interrupt exception, external hardware is required to assert BERR* following the nonappearance of either DTACK* or VPA* a reasonable time after an interrupt acknowledge has been detected.

TRAP (software interrupt)   The 68000 provides sixteen instructions of the form TRAP #I, where I = 0, 1, ..., 15. When this instruction is executed, an exception is generated and one of sixteen exception-handling routines called. Thus, TRAP #0 causes TRAP exception-handling routine 0 to be called, and so on. The TRAP instruction is very useful indeed. Suppose we wish to write a program that is to run on all 68000 systems. The greatest problem comes in dealing with input or output transactions. One 68000 system may deal with input in a very different way to every other 68000 system. However, if everybody agrees that, say, TRAP #0 means input a byte and TRAP #1 means output a byte, then the software becomes truly portable. All that remains to be done is for an exception handler to be written for each 68000 system to actually implement the input or output as necessary. The TRAP exception is dealt with in section 6.5.

Exception Vectors

Having described the various types of exception supported by the 68000, the next step is to explain how the processor is able to determine the location of the corresponding exception-handling routine. Every exception has a vector associated with it and that vector is the 32-bit absolute address of the appropriate exception-handling routine. All exception vectors are stored in a table of 512 words, extending from address $00 0000 to $00 03FF.

A list of all the exception vectors is given in table 6.1, while figure 6.2 shows the physical location of the 255 vectors in memory. The left-hand column of table 6.1 gives the vector number of each entry in the table. The vector number is a value that, when multiplied by four, gives the address, or offset, of an exception vector; for example, the vector number corresponding to a privilege violation is 8 and the appropriate exception vector is to be found at memory location $8 \times 4 = 32 = \$20$. Therefore, whenever a privilege violation occurs, the CPU reads the longword at location $20 and loads that word into its program counter.

Although we have said that two words of memory space are devoted to each 32-bit exception vector, the reset exception (vector number zero) is a special case. The 32-bit longword at address $00 0000 is not the address of the reset-handling routine, but the initial value of the supervisor stack pointer. The actual reset exception vector is at address $00 0004. Thus, the reset exception takes four words of memory instead of the usual two. The 68000's designers have been very clever here. The first operation performed by the 68000 following a reset is to load the system stack pointer. This operation is important because, until a stack is defined, the 68000 cannot deal with any other type of exception. Once the stack pointer has been set up, the reset exception vector is loaded into the program counter and processing continues normally. The reset exception vector is, of course, the initial (or cold-start) entry point into the operating system.

Yet another difference exists between the reset vector and all other exception vectors. The reset exception vector and supervisor stack pointer initial value both lie in the supervisor program space, denoted by SP in table 6.1. Thus, when

FIGURE 6.2   Memory map of the 68000's vector table

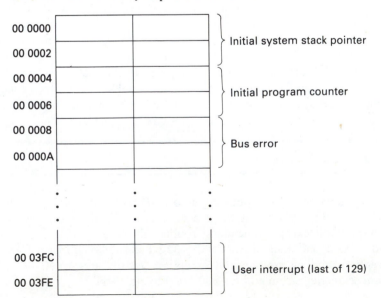

TABLE 6.1   Exception vectors and the 68000

VECTOR NUMBER	VECTOR (hex)	ADDRESS SPACE	EXCEPTION TYPE
0	000	SP	Reset—initial supervisor stack pointer
–	004	SP	Reset—initial program counter value
2	008	SD	Bus error
3	00C	SD	Address error
4	010	SD	Illegal instruction
5	014	SD	Divide by zero
6	018	SD	CHK instruction
7	01C	SD	TRAPV instruction
8	020	SD	Privilege violation
9	024	SD	Trace
10	028	SD	Line 1010 emulator
11	02C	SD	Line 1111 emulator
12	030	SD	(Unassigned—reserved)
13	034	SD	(Unassigned—reserved)
14	038	SD	(Unassigned—reserved)
15	03C	SD	Uninitialized interrupt vector
16	040	SD	(Unassigned—reserved)
⋮	⋮	⋮	⋮
23	05C	SD	(Unassigned—reserved)
24	060	SD	Spurious interrupt
25	064	SD	Level 1 interrupt autovector
26	068	SD	Level 2 interrupt autovector
27	06C	SD	Level 3 interrupt autovector
28	070	SD	Level 4 interrupt autovector
29	074	SD	Level 5 interrupt autovector
30	078	SD	Level 6 interrupt autovector
31	07C	SD	Level 7 interrupt autovector
32	080	SD	TRAP #0 vector
33	084	SD	TRAP #1 vector
⋮	⋮	⋮	⋮
47	0BC	SD	TRAP #15 vector
48	0C0	SD	(Unassigned—reserved)
⋮	⋮	⋮	⋮
63	0FC	SD	(Unassigned—reserved)
64	100	SD	User interrupt vector
⋮	⋮	⋮	⋮
255	3FC	SD	User interrupt vector

NOTE: SP = supervisor program space
          SD = supervisor data space

the 68000 accesses these vectors, it puts out a function code of 1, 1, 0 on FC2, FC1, FC0, respectively. All other exception vectors lie in supervisor data space (SD) and the function code 1, 0, 1 is put out on FC2, FC1, FC0 when one of these is accessed.

Certain vectors, numbers 12 to 14, 16 to 23, and 48 to 63, have been reserved for possible future enhancements of the 68000. Indeed, vector number 14 has already been assigned as a "format error exception" on the 68010 CPU. The 68020 has implemented several other exceptions not assigned by the 68000.

Using the Exception Table

In any 68000 system, an exception vector table must be maintained in memory. Although the complete table is 512 words (1,024 bytes) long, we do not strictly need to fill it entirely with exception vectors; for example, if the system does not implement vectored interrupts, the memory space from $00 0100 to $00 03FF does not need to be populated with user interrupt vectors. Personally, unless forced to do otherwise, I would always reserve the memory space $00 0000 to $00 03FF for the exception vector table, even if I were not using the whole of the table. I would preset all unused vectors to the spurious exception-handling routine vector, which would be wholly in line with the philosophy of always providing a recovery mechanism for events that may possibly happen and that cause the system to crash if not adequately catered for.

The humble 8-bit microprocessor also has its own vector table, containing relatively few vectors, corresponding to the very limited exception-handling facilities of most 8-bit devices. This table is invariably maintained in the same read-only memory holding the processor's operating system or monitor. The act of putting exception vectors in a read-only memory is blessed by the fact that the table is always there immediately after power-up, but is cursed by its inflexibility. Once a table is in ROM, the vectors cannot be modified to suit changing conditions. In practice, whenever a vector has to be variable, the 8-bit processors use a vector pointing to another table in read/write memory containing the actual exception-handling vector.

As the 68000 is so much more sophisticated than 8-bit devices and a dynamic or flexible response is sometimes required for the treatment of exception-handling routines, the exception vector table is frequently held in read/write rather than in read-only memory. The operating system, held either in ROM or loaded from disk, sets up the exception vector table early in the initialization process following a reset. Unfortunately, a big blot looms on the horizon in the shape of the reset vector. The two things that *must* be in read-only memory are the reset vector and the system monitor or bootstrap loader. Clearly, when the system is powered-up and the RESET* input asserted, the reset exception vector and supervisor stack pointer, loaded from $00 0004 and $00 00000, respectively, must be in read-only memory.

At first sight, it might be thought that it is necessary to place the whole exception vector table in ROM, as it is not possible to get a four-word ROM just for the reset vector and a (512 — 4)-word read/write memory for the rest of the

FIGURE 6.3   Overlaying the read/write exception vector table ROM. A read access to addresses in the range $00 0000 to $00 0007 automatically retrieves the corresponding data in the range $00 1000 to $00 1007

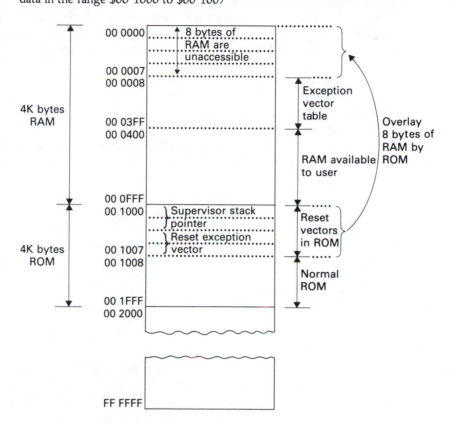

table. Hardware designers have solved the problem by locating the exception vector table in read/write memory and overlaying this with ROM whenever an access in the range $00 0000 to $00 0007 is made.

Figure 6.3 gives a possible memory map corresponding to this situation. The 4K bytes of memory in the range $00 0000 to $00 0FFF are provided by read/write memory. As we shall see, the region of RAM at $00 0000 to $00 0007 is not accessible by the processor. Read/write memory extending from $00 0008 to $00 03FF holds the exception vector table, which is loaded with vectors as dictated by the operating system. The remaining read/write memory from $00 0400 to $00 0FFF is not restricted in use and is freely available to the user or the operating system.

The 4K bytes of memory space from $00 1000 to $00 1FFF are populated by read-only memory. The first 8 bytes of this ROM, from $00 1000 to $00 1007, contain the reset vectors. We now need to arrange the hardware of the 68000 system so that a read access to the reset vectors automatically fetches them from the ROM rather than the read/write memory. One possible way of achieving this situation is demonstrated by the circuit of figure 6.4. The read/write and read-only memory elements are supplied by conventional 2K × 8 chips and their circuitry is entirely straightforward. Read/write memory is selected when CSRAM∗ is active-low and read-only memory when CSROM∗ is active-low. The part of the circuit of interest to us here is that part concerned with the generation of CSRAM∗ and CSROM∗.

As address lines A_{01} to A_{11} take part in selecting locations within the memory components, the twelve remaining address lines, A_{12} to A_{23}, must take part in the address decoding process, if the memory is to be fully decoded. Gates IC1, IC2, and IC3 generate an active-low output (labeled BLOCK∗) when A_{14} to A_{23} are all low. The five-input NOR gate, IC8, produces an active-high output, SELRAM, whenever BLOCK∗ is low, both A_{12} and A_{13} are low, and AS∗ is active-low. If we were not concerned with remapping the reset vectors, the complement of SELRAM could be used to select the RAM components.

Similarly, the output, SELROM, of the five-input NOR gate, IC13, is active-high when the memory space $00 1000 to $00 1FFF is addressed while R/$\overline{\text{W}}$ is high, denoting a read access to ROM. Our aim is to detect a read to the reset exception space and then disable the read/write memory and enable the ROM.

ICs 4, 5, 6, 7, and 15 (in conjunction with BLOCK∗) generate an active-low signal, RESVEC∗, whenever the 68000 reads from address $00 0000 to $00 0007. The SELRAM signal is NANDed with RESVEC∗ in IC10 to give the active-low signal, CSRAM∗, that enables the read/write memory. During a normal access to RAM, RESVEC∗ is high. If SELRAM goes high, CSRAM∗ goes low, selecting the read/write memory. Should an access be made to the reset vectors, RESVEC∗ goes low, forcing CSRAM∗ high and deselecting the read/write memory.

The read-only memory is selected by ICs 13, 9, and 14. SELROM is inverted by IC9 and ANDed with RESVEC∗ to give the active-low ROM-enable signal, CSROM∗. During a normal access to ROM in the region $00 1000 to $00 1FFF, SELROM goes high, forcing CSROM∗ low.

If a read-access to the reset vectors is made, RESVEC∗ goes active-low, forcing CSROM∗ low and enabling the read-only memory. Note that the first 8 bytes of the ROM can be accessed either from addresses $00 0000 to $00 0007 or from $00 1000 to $00 1007.

Exception Processing

The 68000 responds to an exception in four identifiable phases. In phase one, the processor makes a temporary internal copy of the status register and modifies the current status register ready for exception processing. This process involves setting the S bit and clearing the T bit (i.e., TRACE bit). The S bit is set, as all exception processing takes place in the supervisor mode. The T bit is cleared because having the processor in the trace mode during exception processing is

FIGURE 6.4   Implementing an overlaid reset vector

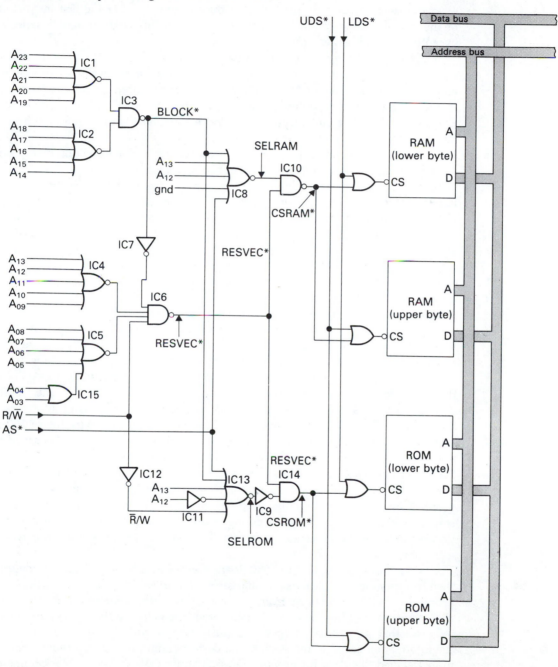

undesirable. Remember that the trace mode forces an exception after the execution of each instruction. If the T bit were set, an instruction would trigger a trace exception which would, in turn, cause a trace exception after the first instruction of the trace-handling routine had been executed. In this way, an infinite series of exceptions would be generated.

Two specific types of exception have a further effect on the contents of the status word. After a reset, the interrupt mask bits are automatically set to indicate an interrupt priority of level 7. An interrupt causes the interrupt priority to be set to the same value as the interrupt currently being processed. As we shall see, the CPU responds only to interrupts with a priority greater than that reflected by the interrupt mask bits.

In phase two, the vector number corresponding to the exception being processed is determined. Apart from interrupts, the vector number is generated internally by the 68000 according to the exception type. If the exception is an interrupt, the interrupting device places the vector number on data lines D_{00} to D_{07} of the processor data bus during the interrupt acknowledge cycle, signified by a function code (FC2, FC1, FC0) of 1, 1, 1. Under certain circumstances, described when dealing with interrupts at the end of the next section, an external interrupt can generate a vector number internally in the 68000, in which case the interrupting device does not supply a vector number. Once the processor has determined the vector number, it multiplies it by four to extract the location of the exception-processing routine within the exception vector table.

In phase three, the current "CPU context" is saved on the system stack. The CPU context is all the information required by the CPU to return to normal processing after an exception. A reset does not, of course, cause anything to be saved on the stack, as the state of the system is undefined prior to a reset. Phase three of the exception processing is complicated by the fact that the 68000 divides exceptions into two categories and saves different amounts of information according to the nature of the exception. The information saved by the 68000 is called the "most volatile portion of the current processor context" and is saved in a data structure called the exception stack frame. Figure 6.5 shows the structure of the exception stack frame. Note that exceptions are classified into three groups. We will return to this point shortly. The information saved during group 1 or group 2 exceptions is only the program counter (two words) and the system status register, temporarily saved during phase one, and is the minimum information required by the processor to restore itself to the state it was in prior to the exception.

Exceptions handled by the 68000 are divided into three groups according to their priority and characteristics, and are categorized in table 6.2. Basically, a group 0 exception originates from hardware errors (the address error has all the characteristics of a bus error but is generated internally by the 68000) and often indicates that something has gone seriously wrong with the system. Therefore, the information saved in the stack frame corresponding to a group 0 exception is more detailed than that for groups 1 and 2. Figure 6.5b shows the stack frame of group 0 exceptions—except for a reset, which does not save information on the stack.

FIGURE 6.5   Stack frame for: *a*, group 1 and group 2 and *b*, group 0 exceptions

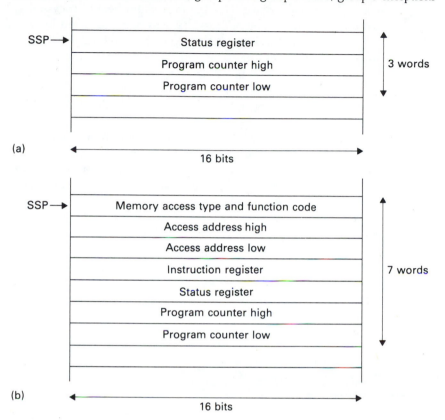

(a)

(b)

TABLE 6.2   Exception grouping according to type and priority

GROUP	EXCEPTION TYPE	TIME AT WHICH PROCESSING BEGINS
0	Reset Bus error Address error	Exception processing begins within two clock cycles
1	Trace Interrupt Illegal op-code Privilege	Exception processing begins before the next instruction
2	TRAP TRAPV CHK Divide by zero	Exception processing is started by normal instruction execution

The additional information saved in the stack frame by a group 0 exception is a copy of the first word of the instruction being processed at the time of the exception and the 32-bit address that was being accessed by the aborted memory access cycle. The third new item saved is a 5-bit value giving the function code displayed on FC2, FC1, FC0 when the exception occurred, together with an indication of whether the processor was executing a read or a write cycle and whether it was processing an instruction or not. This information is diagnostic and may be used by the operating system when dealing with the cause of the exception.

The fourth, and final, phase of the exception-processing sequence consists of a single operation—the loading of the program counter with the 32-bit address pointed at by the exception vector. Once this operation has been performed the processor continues to execute instructions normally. These instructions are, of course, the exception-handling routine.

When an exception-handling routine has been run to completion, the instruction "return from exception," RTE, is executed to restore the processor to the state it was in prior to the exception. RTE is a privileged instruction and has the effect of restoring the status register and program counter from the values saved on the system stack. The contents of the program counter and status register just prior to the execution of the RTE are lost. RTE cannot be used after a group 0 exception to execute a return.

6.4 Hardware-Initiated Exceptions

Three types of exception are initiated by events taking place outside the 68000 and are communicated to the CPU via its input pins: the reset, the bus error, and the interrupt. Each of these three exceptions has a direct effect on the hardware design of a 68000-based microcomputer. We now examine each of these subroutines in more detail.

Reset

A reset is a special type of exception because it takes place only under two circumstances: a power-up or a total and irrecoverable system collapse. Following the detection of a reset by the RESET* pin being asserted for the appropriate duration, the 68000 loads the supervisor stack pointer with the longword at memory location $00 0000 and then loads the program counter with the longword at memory location $00 0004. Once this has been done, the 68000 begins to execute its start-up routine.

In section 6.3 we stated that the exception vector table is frequently located in read/write memory and that the circuit of figure 6.4 can be used to overlay the first 8 bytes of the read/write memory with ROM containing the reset vectors. The only other circuitry associated with the 68000's reset mechanism is that connected to the RESET* pin itself.

The designers of the 68000, in an attempt to minimize the number of pins, have made RESET* a bidirectional input/output, which complicates the design of the reset circuitry. In normal operation, the RESET* pin is an input. Almost all microprocessor systems connect every device that can be reset to the RESET* pin, which means that all devices are reset along with the 68000 at power-up or following a manual reset. The 68000 is also capable of executing a software RESET instruction, which forces its RESET* pin active-low, resetting all devices connected to it. This facility has been provided to permit a system reset under software control that does not affect the processor itself. Consequently, the RESET* pin of the 68000 cannot be driven by gates with active pull-up circuits. RESET* must be driven by open-collector or open-drain outputs.

Another aspect of a hardware-initiated reset to be noted is that both RESET* and HALT* must be asserted simultaneously. We should remember that the HALT* pin is also bidirectional and must also be driven by an open-collector or open-drain output. If RESET* and HALT* are asserted together following a system crash, they must be held low for at least ten clock cycles to ensure satisfactory operation. However, at power-up they must be held low for at least 100 ms after the V_{cc} supply to the 68000 has become established.

A possible arrangement of a reset circuit for the 68000 is given in figure 6.6. IC1, a 555 timer, generates an active-high pulse at its output terminal shortly after the initial application of power. The timer is configured to operate in an astable mode, generating a single pulse whenever it is triggered. The time constant of the output pulse (i.e., the duration of the reset pulse) is determined by resistor R2 and capacitor C2. R1 and C1 trigger the circuit on the application of power. The output is buffered and inverted by IC2a to become the system active-low, power-on-reset pulse (POR*), which can be used by the rest of the system as appropriate.

The output of the timer is also connected to one terminal of a two-input OR gate, IC3. If either input goes high, the output goes high, forcing both HALT* and RESET* low via inverting buffers IC2b and IC2c, respectively. Both buffers have open-collector outputs that are pulled up toward V_{cc} by 4.7 kΩ resistors.

A manual reset facility is provided by an RS bistable constructed from two cross-coupled NAND gates, IC4a and IC4b. The RS bistable de-bounces the switch to avoid multiple reset pulses. In normal operation, the push button is in the NC (normally closed) position and the output of IC4b is low. When the button is pushed into its NO (normally open) position, the output of IC4b rises, generating a reset pulse. The duration of this pulse is determined by the time for which the button is depressed, and is likely to be many orders of magnitude longer than the ten clock pulse minimum required by the 68000. Once more, we should stress that a manual reset should not be used until all other forms of recovery have failed.

FIGURE 6.6   Control of RESET∗ in a 68000-based system

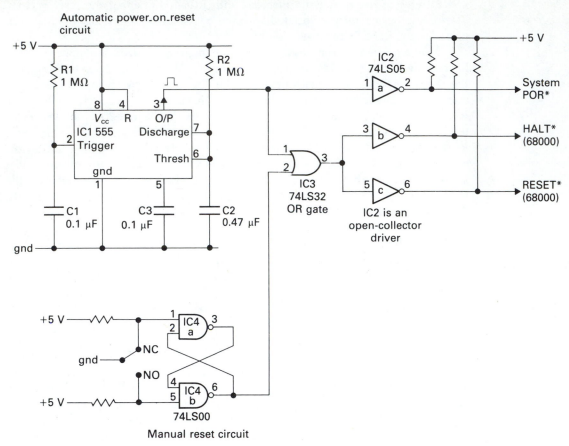

Bus Error

A bus error is an exception raised in response to a failure by the system to complete a bus cycle. There are many possible failure modes, and the details of each depend on the type of hardware used to implement the system. Therefore, the detection of a bus error has been left to the systems designer, rather than to the 68000 chip itself. All the 68000 provides is an active-low input, BERR∗, that, when asserted, generates a bus error exception.

Figure 6.7 gives the timing requirements that the BERR∗ input must satisfy. In order to be recognized during the current bus cycle, BERR∗ must fulfil one of two conditions. BERR∗ must be asserted at least t_{ASI} seconds (the asynchronous input setup time) before the falling edge of state S4 or it must be asserted at least t_{BELDAL} (BERR* low to DTACK* low) seconds before the falling edge of DTACK*. BERR* must be maintained active-low until t_{SHBEH} (AS* high to BERR* high) seconds after the address and data strobes have become inactive. The minimum value of t_{SHBEH} is 0 ns, implying that BERR* may be negated concurrently with AS* or DS*. It is important to realize that, if BERR* meets the timing requirement t_{ASI}, it will be processed in the current bus cycle irrespective of the state of DTACK*.

A number of reasons exist why BERR* may be asserted in a system. Typical applications of BERR* are given as follows:

1. Illegal memory access. If the processor tries to access memory at an address not populated by memory, BERR* may be asserted. Equally, BERR* may be asserted if an attempt is made to write to a memory address that is read-only. A decision as to whether to assert BERR* in these cases is a design decision; it is not mandatory. All 8-bit microprocessors are quite happy to access nonexistent memory or to write to ROM! The philosophy of 68000 systems design is to trap events that may lead to unforeseen

FIGURE 6.7   Bus error input (BERR*) timing diagram

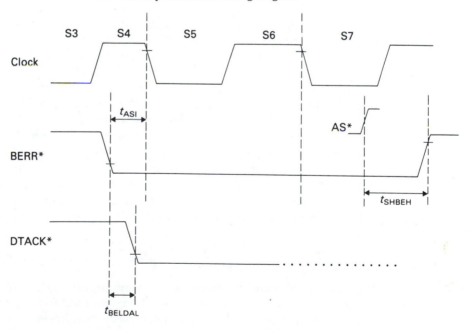

t_{ASI} = 20 ns minimum
t_{BELDAL} = 20 ns minimum
t_{SHBEH} = 0 ns minimum

circumstances. If the processor tries to write to ROM, the operating system can intervene because of the exception raised by BERR*.

2.   Faulty memory access. If error-detecting memory is employed, a read access to a memory location where an error is detected can be used to assert BERR*. In this way the processor will never try to process data that is in error due to a fault in the memory.

3.   Failure to assert VPA*. If the processor accesses a synchronous bus device and VPA* is not asserted after some time-out period, BERR* must be asserted to stop the system from hanging up and waiting for VPA* forever.

4.   Memory privilege violation. When the 68000 is used in a system with some form of memory management, BERR* may be asserted to indicate that the current memory access is violating a privilege. This access may be by one user to another user's program. In a system with virtual memory, it may result from a page fault, indicating that the data being accessed is not currently in read/write memory. Chapter 7 deals with memory management.

Bus Error Sequence

When BERR* is asserted by external logic and satisfies its setup timing requirements, the processor negates AS* in state S7. As long as BERR* remains asserted, the data and address buses are both floated. When the external logic negates BERR*, the processor begins a normal exception-processing sequence for a group 0 exception. Figure 6.5b shows that additional information is pushed on the system stack to facilitate recovery from the bus error. Once all phases of the exception-processing sequence have been completed, the 68000 begins to deal with the problem of the bus error in the BERR* exception-handling routine. It must be emphasized that the treatment of the hardware problem which led to the bus error takes place at a software level within the operating system. For example, if a user program generates a bus error, the exception-processing routine may abort the user's program and provide him or her with diagnostic information to help deal with the problem. The information stored on the stack by a bus error exception (or an address error) is to be regarded as diagnostic information only, and should not be used to institute a return from exception. In other words, the 68000 does not support a direct return from a group 0 exception. The 68010 does!

Rerunning the Bus Cycle

It is possible to deal with a bus error in a way that does not involve an exception. If, during a memory access, the external hardware detects a memory error and asserts both BERR* and HALT* simultaneously, the processor attempts to rerun the current bus cycle.

Figure 6.8 demonstrates a rerun cycle. A bus fault is detected in the read cycle and both BERR* and HALT* are asserted simultaneously. As long as the HALT* signal remains asserted, the address and data buses are floated and no

FIGURE 6.8   Rerunning the bus cycle

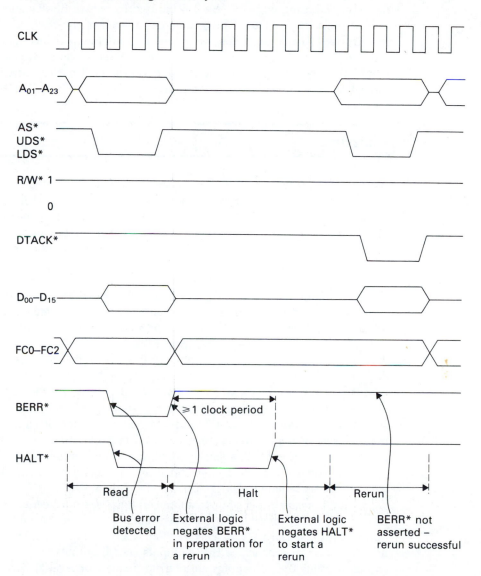

external activity takes place. When HALT∗ is negated by the external logic, the processor will rerun the previous bus cycle using the same address, the same function codes, the same data (for a write operation), and the same control signals. For correct operation, the BERR∗ signal must be negated at least one clock cycle before HALT∗ is negated.

A possible implementation of bus error control in a sophisticated 68000-

based system might detect a bus error and assert BERR* and HALT* simultaneously. The rising edge of AS* can be used to release BERR* and then HALT* at least a clock cycle later. This guarantees a rerun of the bus cycle. Of course, if the error is a "hard" error (i.e., is persistent), rerunning the bus cycle will achieve little and external logic will once again detect the error. A reasonable strategy would be to permit, say, three reruns and, on the next cycle, assert BERR* alone, forcing a conventional bus error exception.

Interrupt

As we have seen, an interrupt is a request for service generated by some external peripheral that the 68000 implements within the framework of its overall exception-handling procedures. In keeping with the 68000's general versatility, it offers two schemes for dealing with interrupts. One is intended for modern peripherals specially designed for 16-bit processors, while the other is more suited to earlier 8-bit 6800-series peripherals.

An external device signals its need for attention by placing a 3-bit code on the 68000's interrupt request inputs, IPL0*, IPL1*, IPL2*. The code corresponds to the priority of the interrupt and is numbered 0 to 7. A level 7 code indicates the highest priority, level 1 the lowest priority, and level 0 indicates the default state of no interrupt request. While peripherals with three interrupt request output lines that generated a 3-bit interrupt priority code would be perfectly possible to design, it is easier to have a single interrupt request output and to design external hardware to convert its priority into a suitable 3-bit code for the 68000.

Figure 6.9 shows a typical scheme for handling interrupt requests in a 68000 system. A 74LS148 eight-line to three-line priority encoder is all that is needed to translate one of the seven levels of interrupt request into a 3-bit code. Table 6.3 gives the truth table for this device. Input, EI*, is an active-low enable input, used in conjunction with outputs GS* and EO* to expand the 74LS148 in systems with more than seven levels of priority.

As the enable input and expanding outputs are not needed in this application of the 74LS148, table 6.3 has been redrawn in table 6.4 with inputs 1 to 7 renamed IRQ1* to IRQ7*, respectively, and outputs A0 to A2 renamed IPL0* to IPL2*. It must be appreciated that all inputs and all outputs are active-low, so that an output value 0, 0, 0 denotes an interrupt request of level 7, while an output 1, 1, 1 denotes a level 0 interrupt request (i.e., no interrupt). However, note that the interrupt mask bits of the status register are active-high, so that a level 5 interrupt mask is represented by 101, while a level 5 interrupt request on IPL0* to IPL2* is represented by 010.

Inspection of table 6.4 reveals that a logical zero on interrupt request input i forces interrupt request inputs 1 to i − 1 into don't care states; that is, if interrupt IRQi* is asserted, the state of interrupt request inputs IRQ1* to IRQ(i − 1)* has no effect on the output code IL0* to IPL2*. This property is the one that the

FIGURE 6.9   Interrupt request encoding

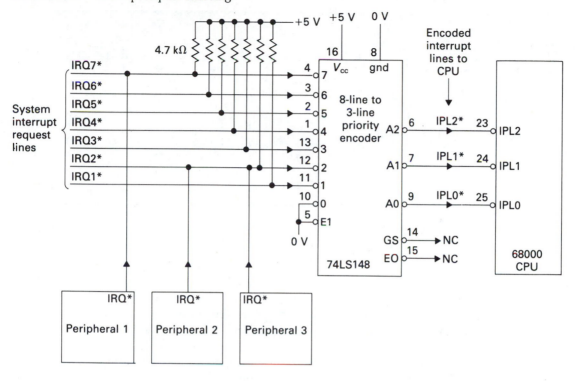

TABLE 6.3   Truth table for the 74LS148 eight-line to three-line priority encoder

	INPUTS								OUTPUTS				
EI*	0	1	2	3	4	5	6	7	A2	A1	A0	GS*	EO*
1	×	×	×	×	×	×	×	×	1	1	1	1	1
0	1	1	1	1	1	1	1	1	1	1	1	1	0
0	×	×	×	×	×	×	×	0	0	0	0	0	1
0	×	×	×	×	×	×	0	1	0	0	1	0	1
0	×	×	×	×	×	0	1	1	0	1	0	0	1
0	×	×	×	×	0	1	1	1	0	1	1	0	1
0	×	×	×	0	1	1	1	1	1	0	0	0	1
0	×	×	0	1	1	1	1	1	1	0	1	0	1
0	×	0	1	1	1	1	1	1	1	1	0	0	1
0	0	1	1	1	1	1	1	1	1	1	1	0	1

TABLE 6.4   Truth table for a 74LS148 configured as in figure 6.9

	INPUTS							OUTPUTS		
LEVEL	IRQ1*	IRQ2*	IRQ3*	IRQ4*	IRQ5*	IRQ6*	IRQ7*	IPL2*	IPL1*	IPL0*
7	×	×	×	×	×	×	0	0	0	0
6	×	×	×	×	×	0	1	0	0	1
5	×	×	×	×	0	1	1	0	1	0
4	×	×	×	0	1	1	1	0	1	1
3	×	×	0	1	1	1	1	1	0	0
2	×	0	1	1	1	1	1	1	0	1
1	0	1	1	1	1	1	1	1	1	0
0	1	1	1	1	1	1	1	1	1	1

NOTE: $0 = low\ level\ signal\ (< V_{IL})$
$1 = high\ level\ signal\ (> V_{IH})$
$× = don't\ care$

microprocessor systems designer relies on. Devices with high-priority interrupts are connected to the higher-order inputs. Should two or more levels of interrupt occur simultaneously, only the higher value is reflected in the output code to the 68000's IPL pins.

Figure 6.9 demonstrates that the 74LS148 does not restrict the system to only seven devices capable of generating interrupt requests. More than one device can be wired to a given level of interrupt request, as illustrated by peripherals 2 and 3. If either peripheral 2 or 3 (or both) asserts its interrupt request output (IRQ*), a level 2 interrupt is signaled to the 68000, provided that levels 3 to 7 are all inactive. The mechanism to distinguish between an interrupt from peripheral 2 and one from peripheral 3 will be discussed later. Chapter 10 on computer buses introduces a mechanism called *daisy-chaining* that enables several devices to share the same level of interrupt priority and yet permits only one of them to respond to an IACK cycle.

Processing the Interrupt

All interrupts to the 68000 are latched internally and made pending. Group 0 exceptions (reset, bus error, address error) take precedence over an interrupt in group 1. Therefore, if a group 0 exception occurs, it is serviced before the interrupt. A trace exception in group 1 takes precedence over the interrupt, so that if an interrupt request occurs during the execution of an instruction while the T bit is asserted, the trace exception has priority and is serviced first. Assuming that none of the above exceptions has been raised, the 68000 compares the level of the interrupt request with the value recorded in the interrupt mask bits of the processor status word.

If the priority of the pending interrupt is lower than, or equal to, the current processor priority denoted by the interrupt mask, the interrupt request remains pending and the next instruction in sequence is executed. Interrupt level 7 is treated slightly differently, as it is always processed regardless of the value of the interrupt mask bits. In other words, a level 7 interrupt always interrupts a level 7 interrupt, if one is currently being processed. Any other level of interrupt can be interrupted only by a higher level of priority. Note that a level 7 interrupt is edge sensitive and is interrupted only by a high-to-low transition on IRQ7*.

Once the processor has made a decision to process an interrupt, it begins an exception-processing sequence as described earlier. The only deviation from the normal sequence of events dictated by a group 1 or group 2 exception is that the interrupt mask bits of the processor status word are updated before the exception-processing continues. The level of the interrupt request being serviced is copied into the current processor status. Therefore, the interrupt cannot be interrupted unless the new interrupt has a higher priority. An example should make the effect and implications clearer.

Suppose that the current (i.e., preinterrupt) interrupt mask is level 3. If a level 5 interrupt occurs, it is processed and the interrupt mask set to level 5. If, during the processing of this interrupt, a level 4 interrupt is requested, it is made pending, even though it has a higher priority than the original interrupt mask. When the level 5 interrupt has been processed, a return from exception is made and the former processor status word restored. As the old interrupt mask was 3, the pending interrupt of level 4 is then serviced.

Unlike other exceptions, an interrupt may obtain its vector number externally from the device that made the interrupt request. As stated earlier, two ways of identifying the source of the interrupt exist, one vectored and one autovectored. A vectored interrupt is dealt with first.

Vectored Interrupt

After the processor has completed the last instruction before recognizing the interrupt and stacked the low-order word of the program counter, it executes an interrupt acknowledge cycle (IACK cycle). During an IACK cycle, the 68000 obtains the vector number from the interrupting device, with which it will later determine the appropriate exception vector. Figure 6.10 shows the sequence of events taking place during an IACK cycle. From figure 6.10 we can easily see that an IACK cycle is nothing special—it is just a modified read cycle. Because the 68000 puts out the special function code 1, 1, 1 on FC2, FC1, and FC0 during an IACK cycle, the interrupting device is able to detect the interrupt acknowledge cycle. At the same time, the level of the interrupt is put out on address lines A_{01} to A_{03}. The IACK cycle should not decode memory addresses A_{04} to A_{23} and memory components should be disabled when FC2 through FC0 = 1, 1, 1. The device that generated the interrupt at the specified level then provides a vector number on D_{00} through D_{07} and asserts DTACK*, as in any normal read cycle. The remainder of the IACK cycle is identical to a read cycle. Figure 6.11 provides the timing diagram of an IACK cycle. However, if the IACK cycle is *not*

FIGURE 6.10   Interrupt acknowledge sequence

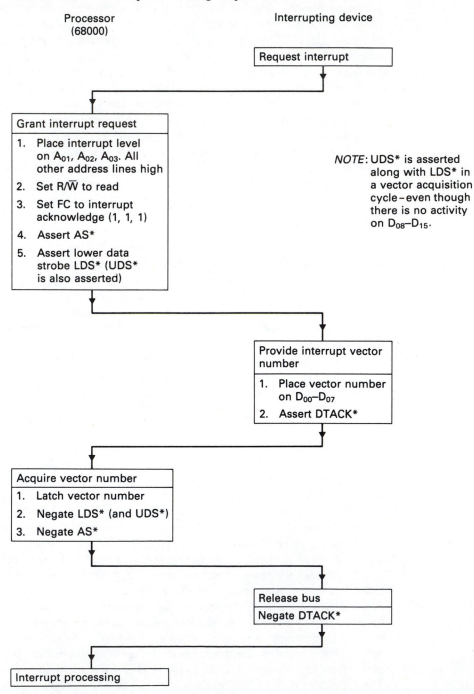

FIGURE 6.11   Interrupt acknowledge and the IACK cycle. (Reprinted by permission of
Motorola Limited)

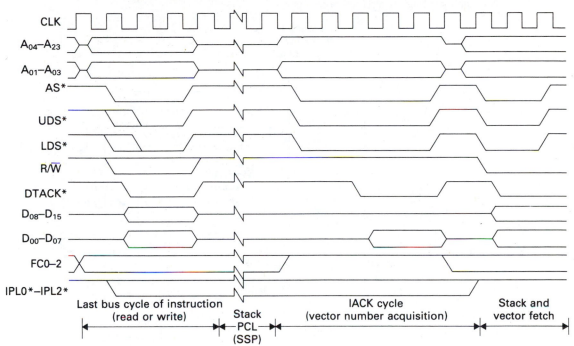

terminated by the assertion of DTACK*, BERR* must be asserted by external
hardware to force a spurious interrupt exception. Note that the IACK cycle falls
between the stacking of the low-order word of the program counter and the
stacking of the high-order word.

After the peripheral has provided a vector number on D_{00} to D_{07}, the processor multiplies it by four to obtain the address of the entry point to the
exception-processing routine from the exception vector table. Although a device
can provide an 8-bit vector number giving 256 possible values, a space is reserved
in the exception vector table for only 192 unique vectors. This space is more than
adequate for the vast majority of applications. However, note that a peripheral can
put out vector numbers 0 to 63 as nothing exists to stop these numbers being
programmed into the peripheral, and the processor does not guard against this
situation. In other words, if a peripheral is programmed to respond to an IACK
cycle with, say, a vector number 5, then an interrupt from this device would cause
an exception corresponding to vector number 5—the value also appropriate to a
divide-by-zero exception. While I can see times that this procedure might be
useful, allowing interrupt vector numbers to overlap with other types of exceptions seems an oversight.

A possible arrangement of hardware needed to implement a vectored interrupt scheme is given in figure 6.12. A peripheral asserts its interrupt request
output, IRQ5*, that is encoded by IC3 to provide the 68000 with a level 5

FIGURE 6.12   Implementing the vectored interrupt

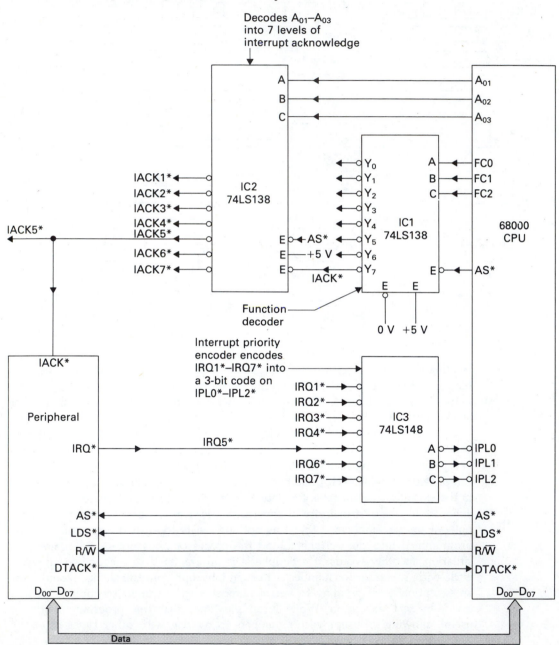

interrupt request. When the processor acknowledges this request, it places 1, 1, 1 on the function code output that is decoded by the three-line to eight-line decoder IC1. The interrupt acknowledge output (IACK*) from IC1 enables a second three-line to eight-line decoder, IC2, that decodes address lines A_{01} to A_{03} into seven levels of interrupt acknowledge. In this case, IACK5* from IC2 is fed back to the peripheral, which then responds by placing its vector number onto the low-order byte of the system data bus. If the peripheral has not been programmed to supply an interrupt vector number, it should place $0F on the data bus, corresponding to an uninitialized interrupt vector exception.

Autovectored Interrupt

As we have just seen, a device that generates an interrupt request must be capable of identifying itself when the 68000 carries out an interrupt acknowledge sequence. This situation presents no problem for modern 68000-based peripherals such as the 68230 PI/T.

Unfortunately, older peripherals originally designed for 8-bit processors do not have interrupt acknowledge facilities and are unable to respond with the appropriate vector number on D_{00} to D_{07} during an IACK cycle. The systems designer could overcome this problem by designing a subsystem that supplied the appropriate vector as if it came from the interrupting peripheral. Such an approach is valid but a little messy. Who wants a single-chip peripheral that needs a handful of components just to provide a vector number in an IACK cycle?

An alternative scheme is available for peripherals that cannot provide their own vector number. An IACK cycle, like any other memory access, is allowed to continue past state S4 by the assertion of DTACK*. If, however, DTACK* is not asserted but VPA* is asserted, the 68000 carries out an autovectored interrupt.

Valid peripheral address, VPA*, belongs to the 68000's synchronous data bus control group and has already been introduced briefly in chapter 4; it will be mentioned again in chapter 8 on input/output techniques. When asserted, VPA* informs the 68000 that the present memory access cycle is to be synchronous and to "look like" a 6800-series memory access cycle. If the current bus cycle is an IACK cycle, the 68000 executes a "spurious read cycle;" that is, an IACK cycle is executed, but the interrupting device does not place a vector number on D_{00} to D_{07}. Nor does the 68000 read the contents of the data bus. Instead, the 68000 generates the appropriate vector number internally.

The 68000 reserves vector numbers 25 to 31 (decimal) for its autovector operation (see table 6.1). Each of these autovectors is associated with an interrupt on IRQ1* to IRQ7*; for example, if IRQ2* is asserted followed by VPA* during the IACK cycle, vector number 26 is generated by the 68000 and the interrupt-handling routine address is read from memory location $00 0068.

Should several interrupt requesters assert the same interrupt request line, the 68000 will not be able to distinguish between them. Autovectored interrupts can be used and the appropriate interrupt-handling routine may poll each of the pos-

FIGURE 6.13   Timing diagram of an autovectored interrupt. (Reprinted by permission of Motorola Limited)

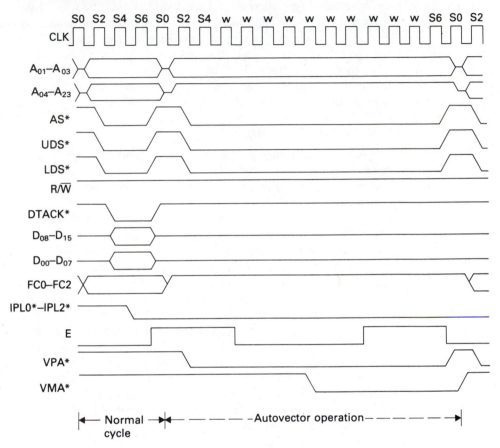

sible requesters in turn; that is, the status register of each peripheral must be read to determine the source of the interrupt.

The timing diagram of an autovector sequence is given in figure 6.13 and is almost identical to the vectored IACK sequence of figure 6.11, except that VPA* is asserted shortly after the interrupter has detected an IACK cycle from FC0 to FC2. Because VPA* has been asserted, wait states are introduced into the current read cycle in order to synchronize the cycle with VMA*. Note that this is a dummy read cycle, as nothing is read (the autovector is generated internally and no device places data on D_{00} to D_{07} during the cycle). An IACK cycle differs from a read cycle in two ways: FC0 to FC2 = 1, 1, 1 and VMA* is asserted.

The hardware necessary to implement an autovectored interrupt is minimal. Figure 6.14 shows a possible arrangement involving a typical 6800-series peripheral that requests an interrupt in the normal way by asserting its IRQ* output. This arrangement is prioritized by IC3, and an acknowledge signal is generated by ICs 1 and 2 exactly as in figure 6.12, which deals with the vectored interrupt.

FIGURE 6.14   Hardware needed to implement an autovectored interrupt

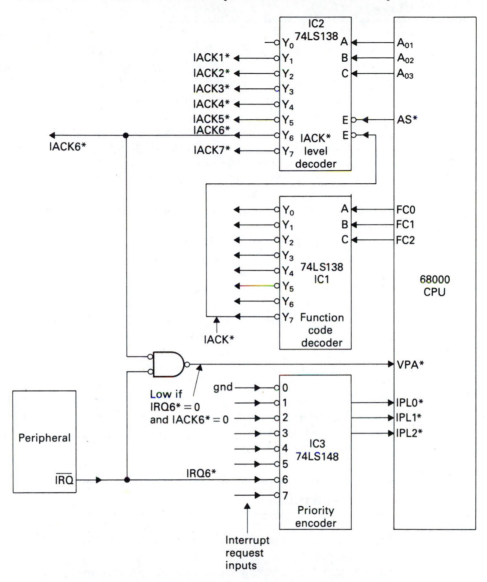

The interrupting device cannot, of course, respond to an IACK* signal. Instead, the appropriate interrupt acknowledge signal from the 68000 is combined with the interrupt request output from the peripheral in an OR gate. Only when the peripheral has asserted its IRQ* and the correct level of IACK* has been generated does the output of the OR gate go low to assert VPA* and force an autovectored interrupt.

6.5 *Software-Initiated Exceptions*

A software-initiated exception is one that occurs as the result of an attempt to execute certain types of instruction—excepting the address error, which is really classified as a hardware-initiated interrupt. Software-initiated interrupts fall into two categories: those executed deliberately by the programmer and those representing a "cry for help."

The "cry for help" group comprises the illegal op-code, privilege violation, TRAPV, and divide-by-zero exceptions, which are all exceptions that are normally generated by something going wrong. Therefore, the operating system needs to intervene and sort things out. The nature of this intervention is very much dependent on the structure of the operating system. Often, in a multiprogramming environment, the individual task creating the exception will be aborted, leaving all other tasks unaffected.

Consider the illegal op-code exception. This exception is raised when the 68000 attempts to execute an operation code that does not form part of the 68000's instruction set. The only way that this can happen is when something has gone seriously wrong—an op-code has been corrupted in memory or a jump has been made to a region containing nonvalid 68000 code. The latter event frequently results from wrongly computed GOTOs. Clearly, once such an event has occurred, to continue trying to execute further instructions is futile as they have no real meaning. By generating an illegal op-code exception, the operating system can inform users of the problem and invite them to do something about it.

Software exceptions deliberately initiated by the programmer are the trace, the trap, and the emulator. The trace exception mode is in force whenever the T bit of the status word is set. After each instruction has been executed, a trace exception is automatically generated. This procedure allows the user to monitor the execution of a program.

Trace Exceptions

The 68000 enters the trace mode by executing, typically, an OR.W #$8000,SR when the processor is in the supervisor mode. The simplest trace facility would allow the user to dump the contents of all registers on the CRT terminal after the execution of each instruction. Unfortunately, this situation leads to the production of vast amounts of utterly useless information; for example, if the 68000 were executing an operation to clear an array by executing a CLR.L (A4)+ instruction 64K times, the human operator would not wish to see the contents of all registers displayed after each CLR.

A better approach is to display only the information needed. Before the trace mode is invoked, the user informs the operating system of the conditions under which the results of a trace exception are to be displayed. Some of the events that can be used to trigger the display of registers during a trace exception are:

1. The execution of a predefined number of instructions; for example, the contents of registers may be displayed after, say fifty instructions have been executed.

2. The execution of an instruction at a given address, which is equivalent to a break point.

3. The execution of an instruction falling within a given range of addresses or the access of an operand falling within the same range.

4. As event 3 above, but the contents of the register are displayed only when an address generated by the 68000 falls *outside* the predetermined range.

5. The execution of a particular instruction; for example, the contents of the registers may be displayed following the execution of a TAS instruction.

6. Any memory access that modifies the contents of a memory location, that is, any write access.

Several of the above conditions may be combined to create a composite event; for example, the contents of registers may be displayed whenever the 68000 executes write accesses to the region of memory space between $3A 0000 and $3A 00FF.

Emulator Mode Exceptions

The emulator mode exceptions provide the systems designer with tools to develop software for new hardware, before that hardware has been fully realized. Suppose a company is working on a coprocessor to generate the sine of a 16-bit fractional operand. For commercial reasons, it may be necessary to develop software for this hardware long before the coprocessor is in actual production.

By inserting an emulator op-code at the point in a program at which the sine is to be calculated by the hardware, the software can be tested as if the coprocessor were actually present. When the emulator op-code is encountered, a jump is made to the appropriate emulator-handling routine. In this routine, the sine is calculated by conventional techniques.

TRAP Exception

The trap is the most useful software user-initiated exception available to the programmer. Indeed, it is one of the more powerful functions provided by the 68000.

To be honest, no real differences exist between traps and emulator exceptions: they differ only in their applications. Sixteen traps, TRAP #0 to TRAP #15, are associated with exception vector numbers 32 to 47 decimal ($80 to $BF), respectively.

Just as emulator exceptions are used to provide functions in software that will later be implemented in hardware, the trap exceptions create new operations or "extra codes" not provided directly by the 68000 itself. However, the purpose of the trap is to separate the details of certain "housekeeping" functions from the user or applications level program.

Consider input/output transactions. These transactions involve real hardware devices and the precise nature of an input operation on system A may be very different from that on system B, even though both systems put the input to the same use. System A may operate a 6850 ACIA in an interrupt-driven mode to obtain data, while system B may use an Intel 8055 parallel port in a polled mode to carry out the same function. Clearly, the device drivers (i.e., the software that controls the ports) in these systems differ greatly in their structures.

Applications programmers do not wish to consider the fine details of I/O transactions when writing their programs. One solution is to use a jump table and to thread all I/O through this table. Figure 6.15 illustrates this approach. We can see from figure 6.15 that the applications programmer deals with all device-dependent transactions by indirect jumps through a jump table; for example, all console input at the applications level is carried out by BSR GETCHAR. At the address GETCHAR in the jump table, the programmers insert a link (i.e., JMP INPUT) to the *actual* routine used in their own system.

This approach to the problem of device dependency is perfectly respectable. Unfortunately, it suffers from the limitation that the applications program must be

FIGURE 6.15 Jump table

```
            •
            ORG      $001000           ] Jump table
GETCHAR     JMP      INPUT             ]
OUTCHAR     JMP      OUTPUT            ] INPUT, OUTPUT,
GETSECTOR   JMP      DISK_IN           ]   DISK_IN, DISK_OUT
PUTSECTOR   JMP      DISK_OUT          ]   provided by user

            •
            •
            BSR      GETCHAR     input char
            •
            •
            •                                  Application program
            BSR      PUTSECTOR   write sector   (address of subroutines not
            •                                   system dependent)
            •
```

tailored to fit on to the target system, which is done by tagging on the jump table. An alternative approach, requiring no modification whatsover to the applications software, is provided by the TRAP exception. This approach leads to truly system-independent software.

When a trap is encountered, the appropriate vector number is generated and the exception vector table interrogated to obtain the address of the trap-handling routine. Note that the exception vector table fulfils the same role as the jump table in figure 6.15. The difference is that the jump table forms part of the applications program, while the exception vector table is part of the 68000's operating system.

An example of a trap handler is found on the Motorola ECB computer, which is known as the "TRAP #14 handler" and provides the user with a method of accessing functions within the ECB's monitor software without the user having to know their addresses. The versatility of a trap exception can be increased by passing parameters from the user program to the trap handler. The TRAP #14 handler of TUTOR (the monitor on the Motorola ECB) provides for up to 255 *different* functions to be associated with TRAP #14. Before the trap is invoked, the programmer must load the required function code into the least-significant byte of D7; for example, to transmit a single ASCII character to port 1, the following calling sequence is used:

```
OUTCH  EQU     248            Equate the trap function to name of activity
       MOVE. B  # OUTCH, D7   Load trap function in D7
       TRAP     # 14          Invoke TRAP # 14 handler
```

Table 6.5 gives a list of the functions provided by the TRAP #14 exception handler of the TUTOR monitor on the ECB.

6.6 Interrupts and Real-Time Processing

There are those who believe that hardware is hardware, software is software and never the twain shall meet. While this maxim may be applied to certain areas of my book (e.g., address decoding), it cannot be applied to hardware-initiated interrupts. An interrupt is a request for service from some device requiring attention. The request has its origin in hardware, but the response (the servicing of the interrupt) is at the software level. Therefore, to deal with one aspect without at least some consideration of the other is difficult. We have already examined how a device physically signals an interrupt request and how the 68000 begins executing an interrupt-handling routine. Now we shall briefly look at the impact of the interrupt mechanism on a processor's software.

One of the reasons that interrupt handling sometimes appears a little remote to the student of computer technology is the almost total absence of interrupt-

TABLE 6.5   Functions provided by the TRAP 14 handler on the EBC. (Reprinted by permission of Motorola Limited)

FUNCTION VALUE	FUNCTION NAME	FUNCTION DESCRIPTION
255	—	Reserved functions—end of table indicator
254	—	Reserved function—used to link tables
253	LINKIT	Append user table to TRAP 14 table
252	FIXDAOD	Append string to buffer
251	FIXBUF	Initialize A5 and A6 to BUFFER
250	FIXDATA	Initialize A6 to BUFFER and append string to BUFFER
249	FIXDCRLF	Move CR, LF, string to buffer
248	OUTCH	Output single character to port 1
247	INCHE	Input single character from port 1
246	—	Reserved function
245	—	Reserved function
244	CHRPRNT	Output single character to port 3
243	OUTPUT	Output string to port 1
242	OUTPUT21	Output string to port 2
241	PORTIN1	Input string from port 1
240	PORTIN20	Input string from port 2
239	TAPEOUT	Output string to port 4
238	TAPEIN	Input string from port 4
237	PRCRLF	Output string to port 3
236	HEX2DEC	Convert hex values to ASCII encoded decimal
235	GETHEX	Convert ASCII character to hex
234	PUTHEX	Convert 1 hex digit to ASCII
233	PNT2HX	Convert 2 hex digits to ASCII
232	PNT4HX	Convert 4 hex digits to ASCII
231	PNT6HX	Convert 6 hex digits to ASCII
230	PNT8HX	Convert 8 hex digits to ASCII
229	START	Restart TUTOR; perform initialization
228	TUTOR	Go to TUTOR; print prompt
227	OUT1CR	Output string plus CR, LF, to port 1
226	GETNUMA	Convert ASCII encoded hex to hex
225	GETNUMD	Convert ASCII encoded decimal to hex
224	PORTIN1N	Input string from port 1; no automatic line feed
223–128	—	Reserved
127–0	—	User-defined functions

handling facilities on some personal computers. In other words, interrupts are a "luxury" rather than a "necessity."

At the start of this chapter, we said that interrupts were closely associated with input/output transactions. Without an interrupt mechanism, an input or output device must be polled in order to determine whether or not it is busy. During the polling, the CPU is performing no useful calculations. By permitting a peripheral to indicate its readiness for input or output by asserting an interrupt request line, the possibility exists to free the processor to do other work while the peripheral is busy. Implicit in this statement is the assumption that the processor has something else to do while the peripheral is busy. This situation leads us to the concept of multitasking (the execution of a number of programs or "tasks" apparently simultaneously) and the operating system (the mechanism that controls the execution of the tasks).

Multitasking

Multitasking (or multiprogramming) is a method of squeezing greater performance out of a processor (i.e., a CPU) by chopping the programs up into tiny slices and executing slices of different programs one after the other, rather than by executing each program to completion before starting the next. This concept should not be confused with multiprocessing, which is concerned with the subdivision of a task between several processors.

Figure 6.16 illustrates two tasks (or "processes"), A and B. Each of these tasks requires several different resources (i.e., input/output via a VDT, disk access, CPU time) during its execution. One way of executing the tasks would be "end to end," with task A running to completion before the beginning of task B. This situation is clearly inefficient as, for much of the time, the processor is not actively involved with either task. Figure 6.17 shows how the system can be made more efficient by scheduling the activities carried out by tasks A and B in such a way as to make the best use of the resources; for example, in time-slot 3, task A is accessing the disk while task B is using the CPU.

If we examine the idealized picture presented by figure 6.17, it is immediately apparent that two components are needed to implement a multitasking

FIGURE 6.16 Example of the application of multitasking. Two tasks in terms of the resources they require during their execution

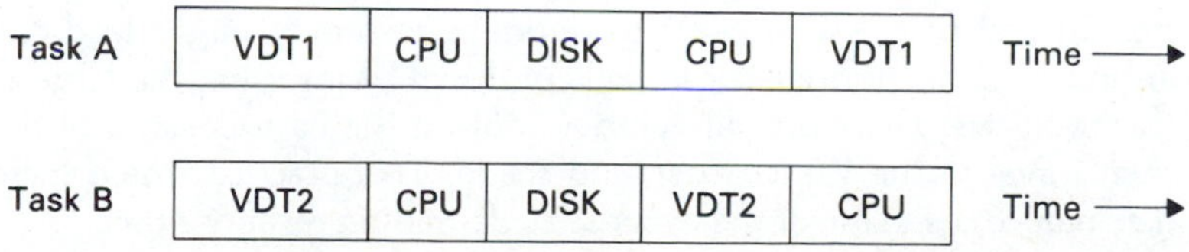

| Task A | VDT1 | CPU | DISK | CPU | VDT1 | Time ⟶ |

| Task B | VDT2 | CPU | DISK | VDT2 | CPU | Time ⟶ |

FIGURE 6.17   Scheduling the two tasks of figure 6.16

Resource	Activity					
	Slot 1	Slot 2	Slot 3	Slot 4	Slot 5	Slot 6
VDT1	Task A				Task A	
VDT2	Task B				Task B	
Disk			Task A	Task B		
CPU		Task A	Task B	Task A		Task B

⟶ Time

system: a scheduler that allocates activities to tasks and a mechanism that switches between tasks. The first is called the operating system and the second the interrupt mechanism.

Real-Time Operating System

We find difficulty in defining a "real-time" system precisely as "real-time" means all things to all people. Possibly the simplest definition is that a real-time system responds to a change in its circumstances within a meaningful period; for example, if a number of users are connected to a multitasking computer, its operation can be called real-time if it responds to the users almost as if each of them had sole access to the machine. Therefore, a maximum response time of no more than 10 seconds must be guaranteed. Similarly, a real-time system controlling a chemical plant must respond to changes in the chemical reactions fast enough to control them. In this instance the maximum guaranteed response time may be of the order of milliseconds.

Real-time and multitasking systems are closely related but are not identical. The former optimizes the response time to events while trying to use resources efficiently. The latter optimizes resource utilization while trying to provide a reasonable response time. If this situation is confusing, consider the postal system. Here we have an example of a real-time process that offers a (nominally) guaranteed response time (i.e., speed of delivery) and attempts to use its resources well (i.e., pick-up, sorting, and delivery take place simultaneously). Suppose the postal service were made purely multitasking at the expense of its real-time facilities. In that case, the attempt to optimize resources might lead to the following argument. Transport costs can be kept down by carrying the largest load with the least vehicles. Therefore, all vehicles wait on the East Coast until they are full and then travel to the West Coast, and so on. This practice would increase efficiency (i.e., reduce costs) but at the expense of degrading response time.

Real-Time Kernel

Operating systems, real-time or otherwise, can be very complex pieces of software extending to 1M bytes or so in size. We are concerned here only with the heart (kernel or nucleus) of a real-time operating system, its scheduler.

The kernel of a real-time operating system has three functions:

1.   The kernel deals with interrupt requests. More precisely, a first-level interrupt handler determines how a request should be treated. These requests include timed interrupts that switch between tasks after their allocated time has been exhausted, interrupts from peripherals seeking attention, and software interrupts or exceptions originating from the task currently running.

2.   The dispatcher or scheduler that determines the sequence in which tasks are executed.

3.   The interprocess (intertask) communication mechanism. Tasks often need to exchange information or to access the same data structures. The kernel provides a mechanism to do this. We will not discuss this topic further, other than to say that a message is often left in a "mailbox" by the originator and is then "collected" by the task to which it was addressed.

A task to be executed by a processor may be in one of three states: running, ready, or blocked. A task is running when its instructions are currently being executed by the processor. A task is ready if it is able to enter a "running state" when its turn comes. A task is blocked or dormant if it cannot enter the running state when its turn comes. Such a task is waiting for some event to occur (such as a peripheral becoming free) before it can continue. Figure 6.18 gives the state diagram for a task in a real-time system.

FIGURE 6.18   State diagram of a real-time system

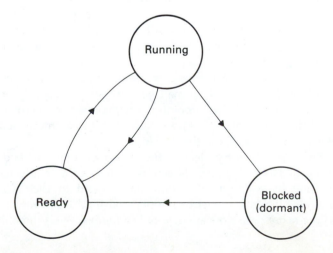

FIGURE 6.19   Task control block

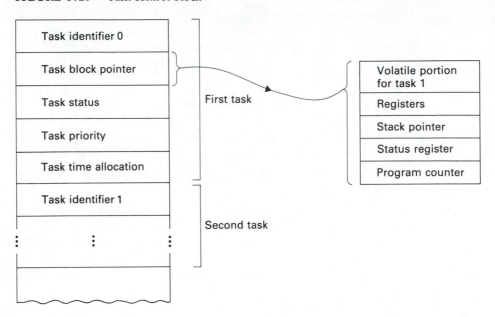

The difference between a running task and a waiting or blocked task lies in the task's *volatile portion*. The volatile portion of a task is the information needed to execute the instructions of that task. This portion includes the identity of the next instruction to be executed, the processor status word, and the contents of any registers being used by the task.

When a task is actually running, the CPU's registers, PC, PSW, data, and address registers, define the task's volatile environment, but when a task is waiting or dormant, this information must be stored elsewhere. All real-time kernels maintain a data structure called a task control block (TCB), which stores a pointer to the volatile portion of each task. The TCB is also called: a run queue, task table, task list, and task status table.

Figure 6.19 gives a hypothetical example of a task control block. Each task is associated with an identifier, which may be a name or simply its number in the task control block. The task block pointer, TBP, contains a vector that points to the location of the task's volatile portion. Note that it is not necessary to store the actual volatile portion of a task in the TCB itself.

The "task status" entry defines the status of the task and marks it as running, ready, or blocked. A task is activated (marked as ready to run) or suspended (blocked) by modifying its task status word in the TCB. The "task priority" indicates the task's level of priority and the "task time allocation" is a measure of how many time slots are devoted to the task every time it runs.

Interrupt Handling and Tasks

The mechanism by which tasks are switched is called a real-time clock, RTC. This generates periodic interrupts that use the kernel to locate the next runnable task and to run it. How do we deal with interrupts originating from sources other than the RTC?

Two ways of dealing with general interrupts and exceptions exist. One is to regard them as being outside the scope of the real-time task scheduling system and to service them as and when they occur (subject to any constraints of priority). An alternative and much more flexible approach is to integrate them into the real-time task structure and to regard them as tasks just like any user task. We will adopt this latter approach in our examination of a real-time kernel.

Figure 6.20 describes a possible arrangement of an interrupt handler in a real-time system. When either an interrupt or an exception occurs, the appropriate interrupt-handling routine is executed by means of the 68000's exception vector table. However, this interrupt-handling routine does not service the interrupt request itself, but simply locates the appropriate interrupt-handling routine in the TCB and changes its status from blocked to runnable. The next time that this task is encountered by the scheduler, it may be run. I say "may be" because, for example, a TRAPV (trap on overflow) exception may have a very low priority and will not be dealt with until all the more urgent tasks have been run. Such an arrangement is called a "first-level" interrupt handler. The strategy of figure 6.20 can be modified by permitting the first-level interrupt handler to take "pre-emptive" action; that is, the interrupt handler not only marks its own task as

FIGURE 6.20   Interrupt handling in a real-time kernel

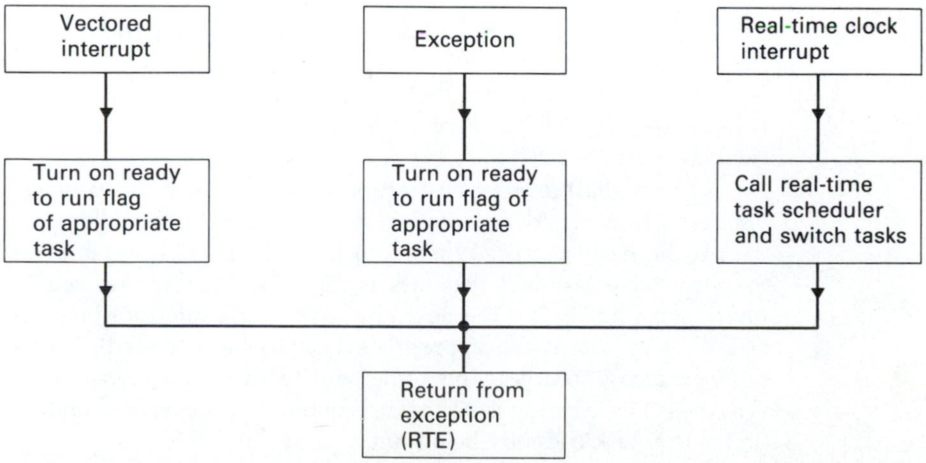

runnable but suspends the currently running task as if there had been a real-time clock interrupt.

The real-time interrupt is physically implemented by connecting the output of a pulse generator to one of the 68000's IRQ* inputs. Generally speaking, a relatively high priority interrupt (e.g., IRQ5* or IRQ6*) is reserved for this function. The highest priority interrupt, IRQ7*, is frequently dedicated to the abort (i.e., panic) button and is used by the engineer to restart a system when it has crashed. Whenever an RTC interrupt is detected, its first-level handler (i.e., the vector table in the 68000) invokes the scheduler part of the real-time kernel.

There are two major approaches to task scheduling, a fixed priority (or round-robin scheme) and a priority scheme. The round-robin scheme runs tasks in order of their appearance in the TCB. When the task with the highest number (i.e., bottom of the TCB) has been run (or found to be blocked) the next task to be run is the task with the lowest number. In a prioritized scheme, entries in the TCB are examined sequentially, but only a task whose priority is equal to the current highest priority may be run.

All interrupts and exceptions from sources other than the real-time clock simply mark the associated task as runnable. This process changes the task's status from *blocked* to *runnable* and takes only a few microseconds.

Designing a Real-Time Kernel for the 68000

To conclude this chapter on exception handling, we look at the skeleton design of a simple real-time kernel for a 68000-based microcomputer. Tasks running in the user mode have eight levels of priority from 0 to 7. Priority seven is the highest, and no task with a priority P_j may run if a task with a priority P_i (where $i > j$) is runnable. Each task has a time-slice allocation and may run for that period before a new task is run.

We can assume that the timed interrupt is generated by a hardware timer that pulses IRQ5* low every 10 ms. All other interrupts and exceptions are dealt with as in figure 6.20.

The highest level of abstraction in dealing with this problem is illustrated in figure 6.21. A timed interrupt causes the time_to_run allocation of the current task to be decremented. When zero is reached, the task table is searched for the next runnable task and that task is run. The time_to_run counter is reset to its maximum value before the next task is run. Any interrupt or exception other than TRAP #15 causes the appropriate task to be activated. A TRAP #15 allows user programs to access the kernel and to carry out certain actions. Note that a TRAP #15 exception is not asynchronous—it is executed under program control in the user task currently being run.

FIGURE 6.21   Real-time kernel. This diagram is an elaboration of that of figure 6.20. Here, TRAP #15 has been reserved to provide user access to the real-time system

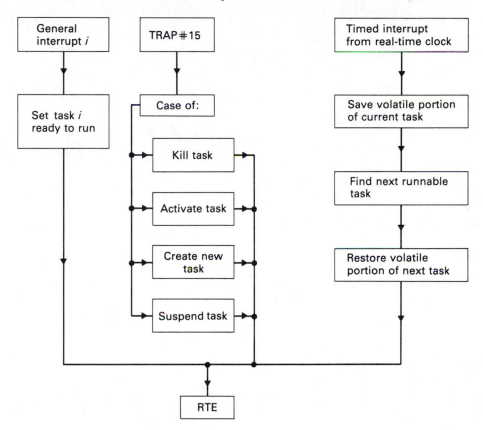

A suitable task control block structure for this problem is defined in figure 6.22. A separate task control block is dedicated to each task; these are arranged as a circular linked list with each individual TCB pointing to the next one in the chain. The last entry points to the first. Each TCB description occupies 88 bytes: a longword pointing to the next TCB, a 2-byte task number, an 8-byte name, a 2-byte task status word (TSW), a 70-byte task volatile portion, and two reserved bytes. Note that in this arrangement, a task's volatile environment is part of the TCB itself. The task volatile portion is a copy of all the working registers belonging to the task at the moment it was interrupted (A0 to A7 and D0 to D7), plus its program counter and status register. The stored value of A7 is, of course, the user stack pointer (USP) and not the supervisor stack pointer. The format of the TSW is also given in figure 6.22, which contains a time_to_run field, a priority field (0 to 7), plus a 2-bit activity field.

FIGURE 6.22   Task control block arranged as a linked list

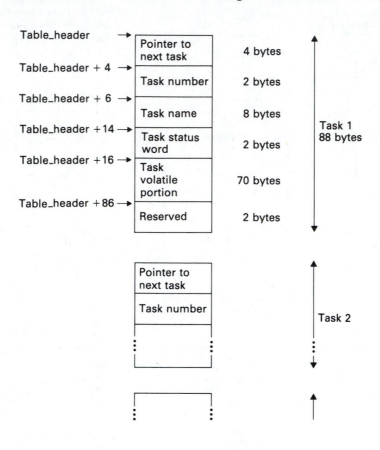

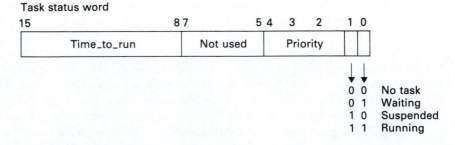

The first-level pseudocode program to implement the real-time kernal of figure 6.21 is as follows:

```
Module: Interrupt_i
        Activate interrupt_i
        RTE
End module

Module: TRAP_15
        CASE I OF
                1: Kill_task
                2: Activate_task
                3: Create_new_task
                4: Suspend_task

        RTE
End module

Module: Timed_interrupt
        Decrement time_to_run
        IF time_to_run = 0 THEN
                        BEGIN
                        Move working registers to TCB
                        Save USP in TCB
                        Transfer PSW from stack to TCB
                        Transfer PC from stack to TCB
                        Find next active task
                        Load new USP from TCB
                        Restore working registers from TCB
                        Transfer new PSW, PC from TCB to stack
                        Reset time_to_run
                        END

        END_IF
        RTE
END module.
```

I do not intend to deal with multitasking in great detail and therefore the level 1 PDL is only partially elaborated to produce the following level 2 PDL:

```
Module Interrupt_i:
                Calculate address of associated task
                Get TSW_address for this task
                Clear bit 1 of TSW at TSW_address
                Set bit 0 of TSW at TSW_address
                RTE
End module

Suspend_task:
                Calculate address of associated task
                Get TSW_address for this task
                Clear bit 0 of TSW at TSW_address
                Set bit 1 of TSW at TSW_address
                RTE
End suspend_task
```

```
Module Timed_interrupt:
                            Global variable: Current_pointer
                                          : Current_priority
                                          : Time_to_run
                       Time_to_run := Time_to_run − 1
                       IF Time_to_run = 0 THEN
                                          BEGIN
                                          Time_to_run := Max_time
                                          Newtask
                                          END
                       END_IF
                       RTE
End module

Newtask: {This swaps "task volatile environments"}
          Push A0–A6, D0–D7 on system stack
          Task_volatile_pointer := Current_pointer + 16
          Copy A0–A6, D0–D7 from stack to [Task_volatile_pointer]
          Copy PC, SR from stack to [Task_volatile_pointer + 64]
          Copy USP to [Task_volatile_pointer + 60]
          Mark current task as waiting
          Next_task {Find the next runnable task}
          Task_volatile_pointer := Current_pointer + 16
          Transfer A0–A6, D0–D7 from TCB to stack
          Transfer USP from TCB to USP
          Transfer PC, SR from TCB to supervisor stack
          Transfer A0–A6, D0–D7 from stack to registers
End Newtask

Next_task: {This locates the next runnable task in the TCB}
          Temp_pointer := Current_pointer
          Temp_priority := Current_priority
          Next_pointer := Current_pointer
          Next_priority := Current_priority
          REPEAT
                IF Next_priority > =
                    Temp_priority AND Next_TSW(0: 1) = waiting
                    THEN
                    BEGIN
                       Temp_priority := Next_priority
                       Temp_pointer := Next_pointer
                    END
                END_IF
                Next_pointer := [Next_pointer]
                Next_TSW    := [Next_pointer + 14]
                Next_priority := Next_TSW(2: 4)
          UNTIL Next_pointer = Current_pointer
          Current_pointer    := Temp_pointer
          Current_priority    := Temp_priority
          Mark new task as running
END Next_task
```

Having outlined the PDL required to implement part of the RTL task-switching kernel, the next step is to convert the PDL to 68000 assembly language form (assuming the absence of a suitable high level language). The only fragments of code provided here are NEWTASK, which switches tasks, and NEXT_TASK, which locates the next runnable task in the list of TCBs. These subroutines are for illustrative purposes only and are too basic for use in a real multitasking system.

```
****************************************************************
*
*     Newtask switches tasks by saving the volatile portion of the current task in its
*     TCB, transferring the volatile portion of the next task to run to the supervisor
*     stack and then copying all registers on the stack to the 68000's registers. The
*     new task is run by copying the new PC and SR from the TCB to the stack and
*     then executing an RTE. Newtask runs in the supervisor mode and the
*     supervisor stack is active. Note that all tasks are assumed runnable—bits 1,0 of
*     the TSW not used
*
*     A2 = Current_ptr    (points to the TCB of the current task)
*     A1 = Temp_ptr       (temporary pointer to a TCB during the search)
*     A0 = Next_ptr       (pointer to TCB of next task in chain of TCBs)
*     D2 = Current_prty   (the priority of the current task)
*     D1 = Temp_prty      (priority of a task during the search)
*     D0 = Next_prty      (priority of the next task in the chain of TCBs)
*
NEWTASK   MOVEM.L   A0–A6/D0–D7,–(A7)   Save all registers on the stack
          MOVEA.L   CURRENT_P, A2       Pick up the pointer to this (the
          LEA.L     16(A2), A2          current task) and point at its
*                                       volatile portion.
          MOVE.W    #34, D0             Transfer all registers on the stack
NEW_1     MOVE.W    (A7)+,(A2)+         to the current TCB. This saves the
          DBRA      D0, NEW_1           task (D0–D7, A0–A6, PC, SR).
          MOVE.L    USP, A1             Get the current user stack pointer
          MOVE.L    A1,–10(A2)          and store it in A7 position in TCB.
*
          MOVEA.L   CURRENT_P, A2       Restore A2 to top of current TCB
          BSR.S     NEXT_TASK           before finding the next task.
          MOVE.L    A2, CURRENT_P       Save pointer to new current task
          LEA.L     86(A2), A2          A2 points at the bottom of the
*                                       volatile portion in the new TCB.
          MOVE.W    #34, D0             Copy all the registers in the new
NEW_2     MOVE.W    –(A2),–(A7)         volatile portion to the supervisor
          DBRA      D0, NEW_2           stack.
          LEA.L     60(A2), A2          Move the USP from the new TCB to
          MOVE.L    A2, USP             the user stack pointer.
*
          MOVEM.L   (A7)+, A0–A6/D0–D7  Move registers on stack to 68000's
*                                       actual registers (except A7, SR, PC)
          LEA.L     4(A7), A7           Skip past the A7 position on stack
          RTE                           Run the new task by loading PC, SR
*                                       from the stack into the PC and SR.
*
```

```
NEXT_TASK   EQU  *            Locate the next runnable task in the linked list
*                             of TCBs. The next task must have a priority greater
*                             than or equal to that of the current task.
*
            MOVEM.L  A0–A1/D0–D2, − (A7)   Save all working registers
            LEA.L    (A2), A1              Preset ptrs : Tmp_ptr := Current_ptr
            LEA.L    (A2), A0                          Next_ptr := Current_ptr
            MOVE.W   14(A2), D2                        D2 := Current TSW
            AND.W    #$001C, D2            Mask D2 (TSW) to priority bits
            MOVE.W   D2, D1               D1 := Temp_prty
            MOVE.W   D2, D0               D0 := Next_prty
*
NEXT_1      CMP.W    D1, D0               REPEAT IF Next_prty < Temp_prty
            BMI.S    NEXT_2                       THEN locate next TCB in list
            MOVE.W   D0, D1                       ELSE Temp_prty := Next_prty
            LEA.L    (A0), A1                          Temp_ptr := Next_ptr
NEXT_2      MOVE.L   (A0), A0                 Locate next TCB in list
            MOVE.W   14(A0), D0               Get TSW of next task in list
            AND.W    #$001C, D0               Mask D0 (new TSW) to priority bits
            CMPA.L   A2, A0               UNTIL Current_ptr = Temp_ptr
            BNE      NEXT_1
            LEA.L    (A1), A2             A2 = new current task = temp task
            MOVEM.L  (A7) + , A0–A1/D0–D2   Restore working registers
            RTS                          Return with A2 pointing at new TCB
```

Summary

In this chapter we have discovered that the 68000 supports one of the most comprehensive exception-handling mechanisms found on any microprocessor. Although it is, of course, perfectly possible to design and to program a microprocessor system without recourse to either software exceptions or to hardware exceptions (i.e., interrupts), the exception-handling capability of the 68000 greatly facilitates the design of real-time systems.

The 68000 provides prioritized and vectored interrupts enabling many peripherals to interact with the CPU in real-time with a much greater efficiency than that of earlier 8-bit microprocessors. Just as importantly, the 68000 implements its prioritized and vectored interrupt structure with a minimum of additional components.

A special feature of the 68000's exception-handling mechanism is its ability to recovery from system faults that would probably spell disaster in other microprocessor systems. By careful control of the 68000's BERR* input, the designer can create a microcomputer that is able to recover from a wide range of faulty bus cycles.

The 68000's software exceptions provide both protection against certain classes of software error (e.g., the illegal op-code) and a means of accessing the operating system via the TRAP. The importance of the TRAP, which links user programs to operating system ultilities, cannot be stressed enough. Programs that use TRAPs to perform input/output operations can be made portable and largely system independent.

The 68000's dual operating modes is a feature that appeals most to the designer of secure real-time and multitasking systems. All user tasks are carried out in the user mode, while all exception handling takes place in the more privileged supervisor mode. Consequently, user tasks are forced to access system resources in a highly controlled and therefore highly reliable fashion.

Problems

1. I know of one large corporation that makes computer systems to control sections of rail track. The designers of these systems are not permitted to use interrupts in their designs. All I/O must be polled. Why do you think that this decision has been taken? HINT: Railway control is a high-security application of computers.

2. Suppose you have to use a non-68000-series peripheral that signals an interrupt by asserting a single active-low IRQ* output. Due to timing considerations, the peripheral must make use of the 68000's vectored interrupt facilities. Design the necessary logic interface to make this peripheral look like a 68000-series component. The logic must respond to an interrupt acknowledge from the 68000 "in the usual way." Attention must also be paid to the way in which the interrupt vector number is initially loaded into the interface. Also, don't forget the response to uninitialized interrupts!

3. Consider a 68000 system with n peripherals capable of generating a vectored interrupt. Suppose the ith peripheral generates a level I_i interrupt request which requires t_i seconds to service and the mean time between interrupts is f_i seconds. How would you investigate the likely behavior of such a system?

4. A print spooler prints one or more files as background jobs while the processor is busy executing a foreground job. Design a basic print spooler that will print a file. Assume the existence of GETCHAR, which reads a character from the disk drive, and PUTCHAR, which sends a character to the printer. The spooler operates in conjunction with a real-time clock that periodically generates a level 5 interrupt. Clearly state any other assumptions you use in solving this problem.

5. Most 68000 interrupt mechanisms are prioritized as described earlier in this chapter. Design an interrupt handler with seven inputs (IRQ1* to IRQ7*) and three outputs (IPL0* to IPL2*) that implements a round-robin scheme. In this arrangement, the most recently serviced interrupt level becomes the lowest level of priority and the highest level of priority is the next level in numeric sequence.

6. The 68000 interrupt structure requires several external packages if its full facilities are to be used. Suppose that only four interrupt levels are needed (IRQ4* to IRQ7*). Design a minimum component circuit that is able to support four levels of vectored interrupt. HINT: Think PROM.

7. A 68000-based microcomputer has the requirement that an interrupt be generated at least every T seconds. Design a circuit to generate an interrupt on IRQ1* every T seconds *provided that* interrupts IRQ2* to IRQ7* have not been asserted during the previous T seconds.

8. Design a circuit that would assert both BERR* and HALT* for a rerun bus cycle, whenever a signal, MEMORY_ERROR*, is asserted. The circuit should provide for three successive reruns and then, if not successful, generate a BERR* alone.

9. Investigate the rate at which tasks should be switched in a multitasking system. HINT: What is the overhead required to switch tasks? The answer to this question will require you to state any assumptions you have made concerning task switching.

Chapter 7

The 68000

in Larger Systems

In this chapter we look at some of the topics that concern the designer of *larger systems*. By larger systems, we mean microcomputers that have relatively large memories and employ components or techniques that are not necessary in some of the more basic microcomputers. The three topics to be discussed here are the application of the 68000's BR*, BG*, and BGACK* lines, the principles of dynamic memory systems design, and memory management techniques.

7.1 Bus Arbitration Control and Multimaster Systems

Up to now we have considered systems with a single bus master, that is, microcomputers in which only one device is capable of initiating the transfer of information between itself and a memory component or peripheral. In less basic systems two or more devices may act as bus masters. Some of these bus masters may be intelligent peripherals and some may be CPUs.

An intelligent peripheral can be designed to move data directly to or from memory without the active intervention of a CPU. Such action is called direct memory access and is described further in chapter 8.

In a multiprocessor system, two or more CPUs operate simultaneously on different parts of a problem; for example, one CPU might be reading data from an interface and processing the results, while a second processor is digesting the data previously read by the interface. In general, these multiprocessor systems are arranged so that each processor has some, but not all, of the resources it needs; for example, a module may contain a 68000 CPU, I/O devices, and read/write memory. Figure 7.1 illustrates such an arrangement.

FIGURE 7.1   Multiprocessor system

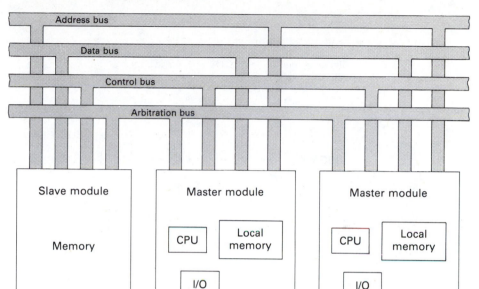

Three modules are shown in figure 7.1: a slave module and two bus masters, each containing a 68000 CPU. If only one bus master existed, the communication between it and the memory module would be exactly as described in chapter 4. The 68000 generates an address, asserts AS∗, sets R/W to indicate the data direction, and then reads from or writes to the data bus. The data transfer is acknowledged by the memory module that asserts DTACK∗ to complete the bus cycle.

In a multimaster system, more than one processor may wish to use the system bus at any time. Therefore, a mechanism called bus arbitration is required to decide which processor is entitled to access the bus if a conflict arises. Chapter 10 on buses looks at the way the VMEbus solves this problem. Here, we are going to examine the facilities provided by the 68000 to enable it to operate in a multimaster environment.

The 68000 is provided with three signals enabling it to give up the bus in an orderly fashion. Figure 7.2 illustrates the bus arbitration signals, two of which are inputs and one of which is an output. If a multimaster system is not required, both inputs (BR∗ and BGACK∗) can be pulled up to V_{cc} and all three pins "forgotten."

Assume that a certain 68000 is currently a bus master and is using the system bus. When another device wishes to become a bus master, it asserts the 68000's BR∗ (bus request) input. The 68000 *must* respond to this request. A bus request cannot be masked or prioritized like an interrupt. In chapter 10 we will see that *external* logic is necessary if we wish to implement a prioritized bus request.

FIGURE 7.2   Bus arbitration control signals and the 68000

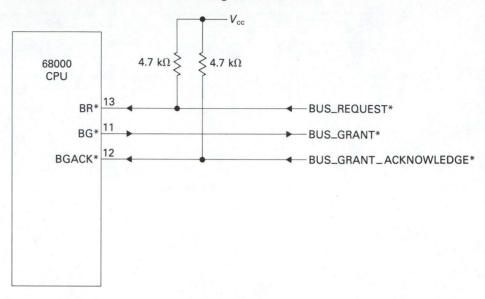

After BR* has been asserted and internally latched by the 68000, the CPU asserts its BG* (bus grant) output, which indicates to the requesting device that the current bus master will give up the bus at the end of the present bus cycle.

When the requesting device detects the assertion of BG*, it waits until AS*, DTACK*, and BGACK* (bus grant acknowledge) have all been negated before asserting its own BGACK* output. This situation indicates that the current bus master is not accessing the bus (AS* negated), the current bus slave is not accessing the bus (DTACK* negated), and no other potential master is about to use the bus (BGACK* negated). The requesting device may release (i.e., negate) BR* after the BG* handshake from the current bus master has been detected.

Once BGACK* has been asserted by the new bus master, the old bus master cannot access the bus as long as BGACK* is asserted. The old bus master then negates its BG* output. Note that, at this stage, only BGACK* is being asserted by the new bus master. Therefore, BR* can be asserted by another potential bus master. The timing diagram of a bus arbitration sequence is given in figure 7.3.

If the 68000 is used in a simple arrangement where only one other potential bus master exists, little or no extra logic is required. Later in this chapter, we will demonstrate how bus arbitration can be used to refresh dynamic memory. However, when several potential bus masters exist, some arbitration logic is required to deal with the near simultaneous requests for bus mastership from several devices. As indicated earlier, chapter 10 shows how the VMEbus deals with this situation.

It is important to note that the system designer must provide suitable logic to control BR*, BG*, and BGACK*; for example, in a system with many potential bus masters, an arbitration network is required to select one of the competing

FIGURE 7.3   Timing diagram of a bus arbitration sequence. (Reprinted by permission of Motorola Limited)

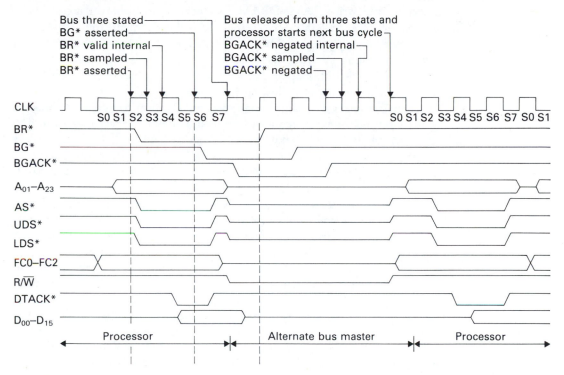

BR∗s and to pass control to the successful bus master. We indicate one possible example of the control of a 68000's bus arbitration lines in the following section on dynamic memory.

7.2 Designing Dynamic Read/Write RAM Systems

Dynamic memory is a form of low-cost, random access, semiconductor memory that is usually associated with memory arrays larger than about 128K bytes. Smaller arrays are frequently implemented as static RAM. My favorite apocryphal comment on dynamic memory is found in an article by L. T. Hauck in *Byte* (July 1978): "What's the difference between static RAM and dynamic RAM? Static RAM works and dynamic RAM doesn't!" Perhaps the answer should have been, "Static memory works on its own—dynamic memory has to be made to work for you." In this section we are going to look at how dynamic memory operates, the problems inherent in the design of a dynamic memory system, and the way in which it can be interfaced to a 68000-based microcomputer.

Dynamic read/write RAM (DRAM for short) is available in a number of different formats like its static counterpart. At the moment the "preferred" dynamic memory is organized as 256K × 1 bits. The older 16K part is still being sold to support existing systems, and the 1M × 1 part is finding its way into the newer and more sophisticated applications of microprocessors. Here we shall consider the 64K device because of its low cost and popularity.

A dynamic memory stores information as an electrical charge on a capacitor forming the interelectrode capacitance of a metal oxide field-effect transistor. This capacitor is not perfect, it is "leaky," and the charge held on it is gradually lost. Consequently, some mechanism is needed to periodically restore the charge on the capacitor before it leaks away. This process is called "refreshing" and has to be performed at least once every 2 ms.

Semiconductor manufacturers have argued, quite rightly, that putting very high density memory chips in physically large packages is irrational because the object of producing compact memory modules is thus defeated. As a 64K × 1 RAM requires 16 address lines ($2^{16} = 64$K), a dynamic RAM component might be expected to have at least 16 address, 2 power, 1 chip select, 1 R/$\overline{W}$ and 1 data pin, or at least 21 pins in all. Such an arrangement would require a 24-pin package taking up a nominal $1.2 \times 0.6 = 0.72$ in^2 of board space.

The majority of dynamic memories have multiplexed address buses, so that a 16-bit address (for a 64K chip) is fed in as two separate 8-bit values. The address bus requirement is thus reduced to 8 pins, but two strobes are needed to latch the address. The RAS* (row address strobe) latches the 8-bit row address and then the CAS* (column address strobe) latches the 8-bit column address. The address multiplexing and the control of RAS* and CAS* strobes are performed off-chip with logic supplied by the user. Therefore, a 64K dynamic RAM can now fit into a 16-pin DIL package, taking up a board space of $0.8 \times 0.3 = 0.24$ in^2.

Figure 7.4 gives the internal arrangement of a typical 64K dynamic memory and figure 7.5 its pinout. The data is stored in one of eight arrays, each of 8,192 bits. Not enough space exists here to delve into the internal operation of the dynamic memory, as its circuitry is so complex. Early dynamic RAMs required three power supplies of $+12$, $+5$, and -5 V. The $+12$ V was necessary to achieve clock pulses of adequate amplitude within the chip and the -5 V provided the substrate bias. Fortunately for the systems designer, current 16K and larger chips operate from the system $+5$ V V_{cc} supply alone. Dynamic memories still need a negative V_{bb} supply, but they now derive it on-chip from an internal V_{bb} generator.

Yet another difficulty associated with dynamic memory is called the alpha-particle problem. The capacitance on which each bit of data is stored is exceedingly tiny (both electrically and physically). An alpha-particle (i.e., helium ion) passing through a memory cell can cause sufficient ionization to corrupt the stored data. This condition creates a so-called *soft error*, as the cell has not been permanently damaged but has lost its stored data. The alpha-particle contami-

FIGURE 7.4   Internal arrangement of a typical 64K dynamic RAM

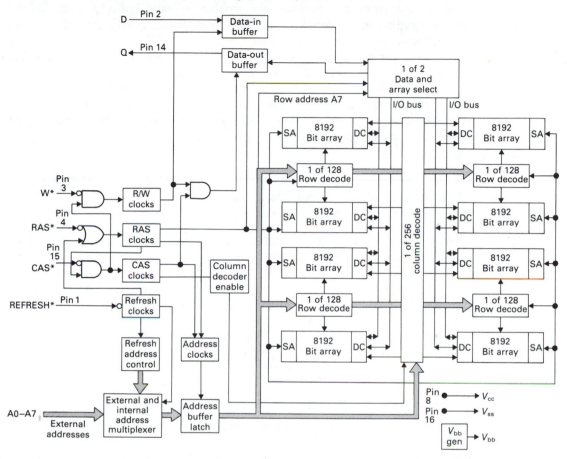

FIGURE 7.5   Pinout of a typical 64K dynamic RAM

PIN ASSIGNMENT

†REFRESH*	1●	16	V_{ss}
D	2	15	CAS*
W*	3	14	Q
RAS*	4	13	A_6
A_0	5	12	A_3
A_2	6	11	A_4
A_1	7	10	A_5
V_{cc}	8	9	A_7

†If pin is not used, it should be connected to V_{cc} through a 10K resistor

PIN NAMES	
REFRESH*	Refresh
A_0–A_7	Address input
D	Data in
Q	Data out
W*	Read/write input
RAS*	Row address strobe
CAS*	Column address strobe
V_{cc}	Power (+ 5 V)
V_{ss}	Ground

nation comes largely from the encapsulating material. Semiconductor manufac-turers have attempted to minimize the problem by careful quality control of the material used to encapsulate the chip. Even with careful quality control, reducing the soft-error rate to zero is impossible.

One approach to soft-error control is to build special memory arrays that can detect, and even correct, soft errors. As long as soft errors are relatively infrequent, this approach yields a very large mean time between undetected soft errors. Error detection and correction is not yet done inside the memory com-ponents: it must be provided by the memory systems designer. Section 7.3 returns to this problem.

Dynamic RAM Timing Diagram

Now we are going to examine the timing diagram of the DRAM and its specifi-cation sheets. The purpose of this exercise is to enable engineers to design memory modules using DRAM chips.

Few things in the known universe are more terrifying than the timing diagram of a dynamic RAM. Not only does this diagram (in fact there are several diagrams) look hopelessly complex but thirty-five or more parameters are associ-ated with it. The best way of approaching the dynamic RAM timing diagram is to strip it of all but its basic features. Once this simplified model has been digested, fine details can be added later.

Dynamic Memory Read Cycle

Figure 7.6 gives an outline of the basic dynamic memory timing diagram during a read cycle. In order to put this diagram into context, figure 7.7 shows the arrange-ment of a 64K-word $\times$ 16-bit memory based on the 64K $\times$ 1 chip. Each memory component has its eight address inputs (labeled A_0 to A_7) connected to the eight outputs of the address multiplexer, MPLX. The inputs to the address multiplexer are A_{01} to A_{08} (the row address) and A_{09} to A_{16} (the column address) from the 68000. Assume that when MPLX is low the row address is selected and when high the column address is selected.

The data-in (D_i) and data-out (D_o) pins of each memory component in figure 7.7 are strapped together in this application and are connected to the system data bus after suitable buffering. Four signals, MPLX, RAS*, CAS*, and W*, control the operation of the memory system. The timing control module must furnish these signals from the available system control signals. In other words, the design of the timing control module will vary from one microprocessor system to another, as each processor has its own unique timing signals. Note that figure 7.7 is simplified in two ways. We have not provided the byte/word control required by the 68000 and no facilities for refreshing the dynamic memory are yet available. A read cycle in figure 7.6 lasts from A to E and has a minimum duration

FIGURE 7.6   Basic read cycle timing diagram of a dynamic RAM

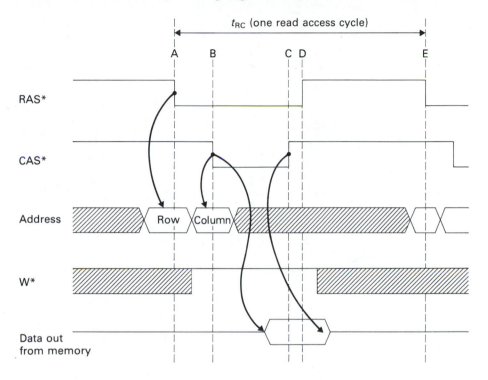

of t_{RC}, the read cycle time. For convenience, this section illustrates the dynamic memory timing diagram with the HM4864-2, a 150-ns component. The minimum value for t_{RC} is given as 270 ns. Note that the dynamic memory, unlike the static memory that has equal access and cycle times, has a cycle time much greater (270 ns) than its access time (150 ns). The designer of a dynamic memory system cannot, therefore, begin the next access as soon as the current one has been completed because the dynamic memory performs an internal operation, known as a precharging, between accesses.

The first step in a read cycle is to provide the chip with the lower-order bits of the address on its eight address inputs, A_0 to A_7. Then, at point A, the row address strobe, RAS*, is brought active-low to strobe the row address into the chip's internal latches. Note that once this process has been done, the low-order address is redundant and is not needed for the rest of the cycle. Contrast this with the static RAM, in which the address must be stable for the entire read or write cycle.

The eight higher-order address bits are then applied to the address inputs of the memory, and the column address strobe (CAS*) brought active-low at point B to latch the column address. Now the entire 16-bit address has been acquired by the memory, and the contents of the system address bus can change.

FIGURE 7.7 Arrangement of a 64K-word × 8-bit dynamic RAM module (byte/word control not included here)

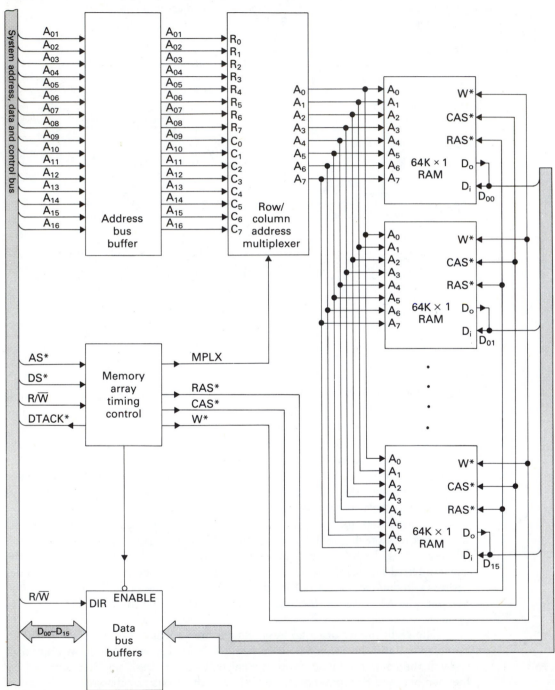

Once CAS∗ has gone low, the addressed memory cell responds by placing data on its data-output terminal, allowing the CPU to read it. At the end of a read cycle, CAS∗ returns inactive-high and the data bus drivers are turned off, floating the data bus. RAS∗ and CAS∗ may both go high together, or in any order. The order does not matter as long as all other timing requirements are satisfied. To make an explanation of the DRAM more tractable, we will break it up into its component parts, beginning with a discussion of the role of the address pins.

Address Timing

The details of the address timing requirements are given in figure 7.8. This diagram is just an enlargement of the address bus timing in figure 7.6. In fact, the timing requirements are effectively the same as those of a typical latch. The row address must be stable for a minimum of t_{ASR} seconds before the falling edge of the RAS∗ strobe. As the minimum value of t_{ASR} is quoted as 0 ns, the address has a zero setup time and does not have to be valid prior to the falling edge of RAS∗. In the worst case, the address must be valid coincident with the falling edge of RAS∗. Once RAS∗ is low, the row address must be stable for t_{RAH}, the row address hold-time, before it can change. The hold-time is 20 ns minimum, which

FIGURE 7.8   Details of the address timing of a dynamic RAM

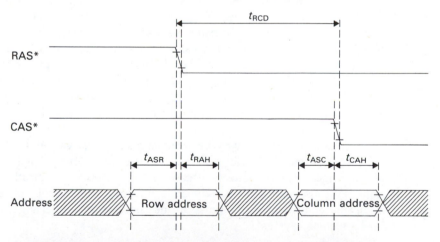

MNEMONIC	SIGNAL NAME	VALUE (ns)
t_{RCD}	Row-to-column strobe lead-time	20–50
t_{ASR}	Row address setup-time	0 min.
t_{RAH}	Row address hold-time	20 min.
t_{ASC}	Column address setup-time	−10 min.
t_{CAH}	Column address hold-time	45 min.

TABLE 7.1   Address timing parameters of three 150-ns 64K × 1 DRAMs

PARAMETER		MCM6665A–15		TMS4164–15		MB 8264–15	
Row address setup-time	t_{ASR}	0 ns min.	$t_{su(RA)}$	0 ns	t_{ASR}	0 ns min.
Row address hold-time	t_{RAH}	20 ns min.	$t_{h(RA)}$	20 ns	t_{RAH}	15 ns min.
Column address setup-time	t_{ASC}	0 ns min.	$t_{su(CA)}$	−5 ns	t_{ASC}	0 ns min.
Column address hold-time	t_{CAH}	35 ns min.	$t_{h(CLCA)}$	45 ns	t_{CAH}	45 ns min.
RAS* to CAS* delay	t_{RCD}	30–75 ns	t_{RLCL}	20–50 ns	t_{RCD}	25–50 ns

restricts the time before which the column address may be multiplexed onto the chip's address pins.

Once the row address hold-time has been satisfied and the column address multiplexed onto the memory's address pins, CAS* may go low. The column address setup-time, t_{ASC}, is quoted as −10 ns minimum, so that CAS* may go low up to 10 ns *before* the column address has stabilized. After CAS* has gone low, the column address must be stable for a further t_{CAH} seconds, the column address hold-time, before it may change. Once t_{CAH} (45 ns minimum) has been satisfied, the address bus plays no further role in the current access.

An important parameter in Figure 7.8 is t_{RCD}, the row-to-column strobe lead-time. For the HM4864-2 the *minimum* value of t_{RCD} is quoted as 20 ns and the *maximum* value as 50 ns. We must appreciate the fact that the limiting values of t_{RCD} are not fundamental parameters of the memory—they are derived from other parameters. The minimum value of t_{RCD} is determined by the row address hold-time plus the time taken for the address from the multiplexer to settle.

The maximum value of t_{RCD} is a pseudo maximum. This value is not a maximum determined by the device, but a maximum that, if exceeded operationally, extends the access time of the memory. We will return to this point later.

Timing parameters vary between nominally equivalent devices from different manufacturers. This variation is sometimes larger than that in the parameters of static memory components. Table 7.1 provides some indication of the variations. A consequence is that dynamic memory components of equal size and nominally equivalent access times are not necessarily interchangeable in any particular memory system.

Data Timing

Having latched an address in the chip, the data appears at the data-out pin, as depicted in figure 7.9. Only RAS*, CAS*, and the data-out signals have been included for clarity. We assume that the address setup- and hold-times, and all other relevant parameters, have been satisfied.

The data at the data-out pin is valid no later than t_{RAC}, the access time from the row address strobe, following the falling edge of RAS*. This time is, of

FIGURE 7.9   Data access timing of a DRAM in a read cycle

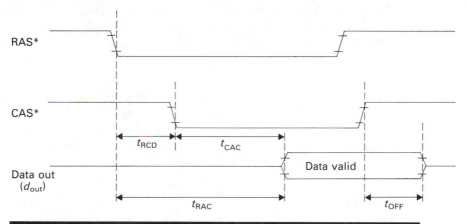

MNEMONIC	SIGNAL NAME	VALUE (ns)
t_{RCD}	Row-to-column strobe lead-time	20–50
t_{CAC}	Access time from column address strobe	100 max.
t_{RAC}	Access time from row address strobe	150 max.
t_{OFF}	Output buffer turn-off time	0–40

course, the quoted access time of the chip and is 150 ns for an HM4864-2. However, in the world of the dynamic RAM, all is not so simple. The row access time is achieved only if other conditions are met, as we shall see.

The column address strobe has two functions: it latches the column address, which interrogates the appropriate column of the memory array, and it turns on the data-output buffers. For these reasons, data is not available for at least t_{CAC}, the access time from CAS* low, after the falling edge of CAS*. The maximum value of t_{CAC} is 100 ns. In other words, reading the data is a two-part process: accessing the memory cell and placing the data on the chip's data-out pin. The following two examples should make this distinction clear.

Suppose that CAS* goes low at the minimum time after the falling edge of RAS* (i.e., $t_{RCD} = 20$ ns); data will appear at the data-out pin no later than $t_{RCD} + t_{CAC} = 20$ ns $+ 100$ ns $= 120$ ns later. At this time, the data is not guaranteed to be valid, as the minimum value of t_{RAC} (i.e., 150 ns) has not been met. However, once t_{RAC} has been satisfied, the data will be valid.

Now suppose that the falling edge of CAS* is delayed beyond the maximum quoted value of t_{RCD}. Say that CAS* is asserted 100 ns after RAS*. The data will not be valid until $t_{RCD} + t_{CAC} = 100$ ns $+ 100$ ns $= 200$ ns later. This value exceeds t_{RAC} by 50 ns.

We should now be able to see why the maximum value of t_{RCD} given in the data sheets of dynamic RAMs is a pseudo maximum. This value is not a maximum determined by the memory, but a limit that, if exceeded operationally, throws away access time. There is little point in buying an expensive 150-ns chip and then limiting its access time to 250 ns by a careless design that exceeds a maximum of t_{RCD}. The relationship between $t_{RCD}(max)$, t_{RAC}, and t_{CAC} is

$$t_{RCD}(max) = t_{RAC} - t_{CAC}.$$

At the end of a read cycle when CAS* goes high, the data bus drivers are turned off and the bus floats t_{OFF} (t_{OFF} = output buffer turn-off delay) seconds later. The maximum value of t_{OFF} is 40 ns. Note that RAS* does not play any part in the ending of a read (or write) cycle. RAS* may be negated before or after CAS*, as long as its timing requirements are met.

W* Timing

The timing diagram of the W* input to the dynamic memory is given in figure 7.10, which is a very simple diagram demonstrating that W* must be high at least t_{RCS} seconds before the falling edge of CAS* and remain high until at least t_{RCH} seconds after the rising edge of CAS*. Both t_{RCS} and t_{RCH} are quoted as 0 ns minimum, which means that W* must be high for a read cycle the entire time that CAS* is low.

FIGURE 7.10   Read cycle timing diagram of the W* input of a dynamic RAM

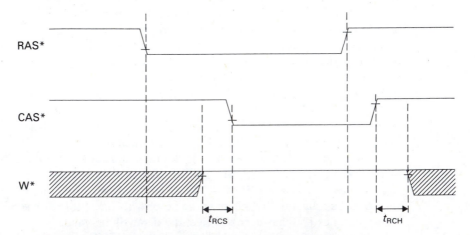

MNEMONIC	NAME	VALUE (ns)
t_{RCS}	Read command setup-time	0 min.
t_{RCH}	Read command hold-time	0 min.

RAS* and CAS* Timing

The final part of the read cycle timing diagram is given in figure 7.11 and concerns the timing requirements of the row and column address strobes, RAS* and CAS*. We should appreciate that the RAS* and CAS* clocks are responsible for controlling several internal operations within the chip, as well as the more mundane tasks of latching addresses and controlling tristate buffers. Although figure 7.11 looks relatively complex with its eight timing parameters, it is entirely straightfoward, and no critical parameters leading to engineering difficulties exist as in the case of the RAS*, CAS*, and address multiplex timing in figure 7.8. Basically, figure 7.11 illustrates the maximum and minimum times for which RAS* and CAS* must be high and low, and the relationship between RAS* and CAS*.

A fundamental parameter of figure 7.11 is t_{RC}, the read cycle time—the minimum time that must elapse between successive memory cycles. This time is quoted as 270 ns for the HM4864-2, which has a 150-ns read access time. The corollary of these figures is that the cycle time must be taken into account when designing memory systems; for example, if a microprocessor had a 250-ns cycle time, this dynamic RAM could not be relied upon, even if its 150-ns read access

FIGURE 7.11   Timing diagram of the RAS* and CAS* strobes

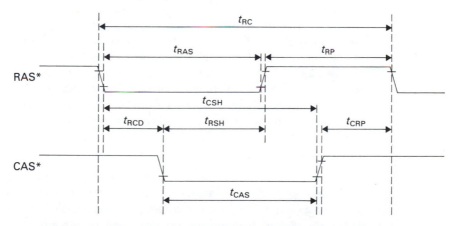

MNEMONIC	NAME	VALUE (ns)
t_{RC}	Random access cycle time	270 min.
t_{RAS}	Row address strobe pulse width	150–10,000
t_{RP}	Row address strobe precharge time	100 min.
t_{CSH}	CAS* hold-time	150 min.
t_{RCD}	Row-to-column strobe lead-time	20–50
t_{RSH}	RAS* hold-time	100 min.
t_{CAS}	Column address strobe pulse width	100–10,000
t_{CRP}	Column-to-row strobe precharge time	−20 min.

time were more than adequate. Interestingly, the value of 270 ns for t_{RC} is the minimum value necessary for reliable operation over the device's full temperature range of 0 to 70°C. If the ambient temperature were guaranteed to be always lower than 70°C, the value of t_{RC} would be improved as the device slows with increasing temperature.

The RAS* clock must be asserted for at least t_{RAS} seconds (the row address strobe pulse width) during each read access, which has a minimum value of 150 ns and a maximum value of 10,000 ns. The maximum value is related to the need to refresh the device and creates no problems, as it is many times longer than a processor's read cycle. The only danger in a 68000 system would arise if DTACK* were not asserted in a read cycle and the processor hung up with RAS* held low. This situation is normally avoided by asserting BERR* after a suitable time-out.

After RAS* has been negated, it must remain high for at least t_{RP} seconds, the row address strobe precharge time. The precharge time is a characteristic of dynamic memories and relates to an operation internal to the chip. The minimum value of t_{RP} is 100 ns and no maximum value is specified, subject to the constraint that the memory needs to be refreshed periodically. The final constraint on the timing of RAS* is its hold-time with respect to CAS*, t_{RSH}. RAS* must remain low for at least t_{RSH} seconds after CAS* has been asserted. The RAS* hold-time is quoted as a minimum of 100 ns.

The column address strobe timing requirements are analogous to those of the row address strobe. CAS* must be asserted for no less than t_{CAS} seconds (100 ns), it must be negated for at least t_{CRP} seconds (-20 ns) before the falling edge of the next RAS* clock, and it must be asserted for at least t_{CSH} seconds (150 ns) measured from the falling edge of the current RAS* clock.

The full timing diagram of a HM4864-2 dynamic memory is given in figure 7.12 so that all the points discussed so far may be related to each other.

Dynamic Memory Write Cycle

The write cycle timing diagram of a dynamic RAM is rather more complex than the corresponding read cycle diagram, because more stringent requirements are placed on the W* input and on the data input. Having already worked through the read cycle timing diagram, we do not need to plough through the same material again. Figure 7.13 gives the full timing diagram of an HM4864-2 64K × 1 dynamic RAM during a write cycle. Figure 7.14 is a copy of figure 7.13, but includes only parameters that differ between the read and write cycles. We can immediately see that all the timing requirements of the RAS*, CAS*, and address inputs are identical in both read and write cycles.

Write Timing

Consider first the requirements of the W* input. This signal has to satisfy six conditions. It is latched by the falling edge of the CAS* clock and has a setup-time of t_{WCS} seconds. The minimum value of t_{WCS} is -20 ns, implying that W*

FIGURE 7.12   Full timing diagram of a DRAM in a read cycle

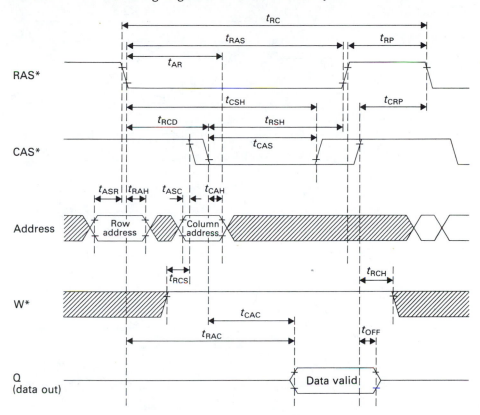

can be asserted as late as 20 ns *after* the falling edge of CAS∗. Once asserted, it has a minimum down-time of t_{WP} seconds (write pulse width = 45 ns) and must not be negated until at least t_{WCH} seconds (write pulse hold-time = 45 ns) after the falling edge of CAS∗.

In addition to these parameters, W∗ must be asserted at least t_{RWL} seconds (write command to row strobe lead-time) before the rising edge of RAS∗ and at least t_{CWL} seconds (write command to column strobe lead-time) before the rising edge of CAS∗. These values are both quoted as 45 ns. Finally, W∗ must not be negated until at least t_{WCR} seconds (the write command pulse hold-time referenced to RAS∗) after the falling edge of RAS∗. This has a minimum value of 95 ns. At this point we can be forgiven for thinking that the dynamic RAM is a hideously complex device and that we would rather stick to static RAM. An old saying exists: "Look after the pennies and the pounds take care of themselves." The same thing is true of dynamic RAM. Look after the RAS∗ and CAS∗ clocks and the W∗ input will take care of itself. Well almost. To illustrate this point consider a simple example in which the write pulse is made equal to the CAS∗ clock.

FIGURE 7.13   Full timing diagram of a DRAM in a write cycle

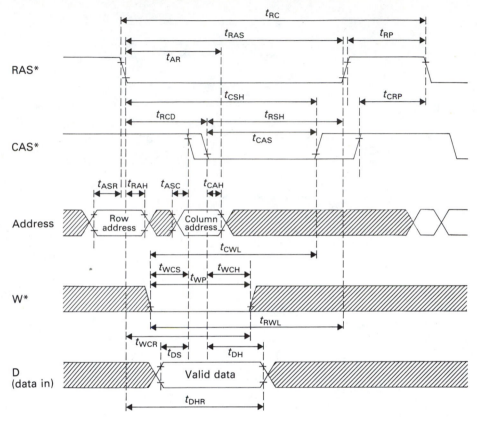

Figure 7.15 illustrates this situation. The RAS* pulse is given the minimum possible value of $t_{RAS} = 150$ ns. CAS* is derived from RAS* by delaying its falling edge by 50 ns from RAS, to yield a value for t_{RCD} of 50 ns and for t_{CAS} of 100 ns (its minimum permissible down-time). As stated previously, the W* signal is obtained by gating the R/$\overline{W}$ output of the processor with CAS*. Below the timing diagram of figure 7.15 are the six parameters associated with W* during a write cycle. Also given are their minimum requirements together with the actual values achieved by this circuit. In each case the right-hand column gives the margin by which the requirement is satisfied. A negative value would indicate a failure to meet a requirement. As no entry in this column is negative, it can be concluded that this circuit satisfies all constraints on W*. Note that the margin on the write command setup-time is only 20 ns, of the order of the propagation delay through two gates. A margin as low as this would require careful attention to fine detail in a real circuit.

Data Timing in a Write Cycle

Data is written into the memory on the falling edge of the CAS* clock. The requirements for data-input timing are entirely straightforward and involve only

FIGURE 7.14   Details of the write cycle timing diagram of a DRAM

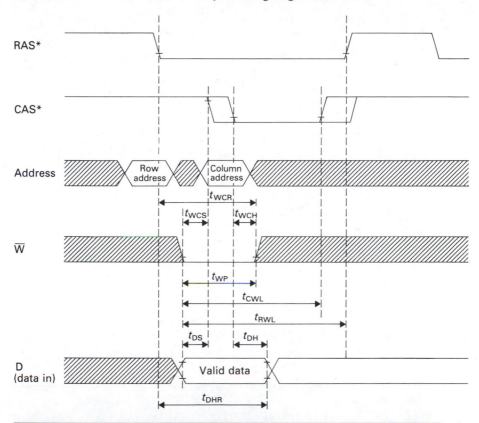

MNEMONIC	NAME	VALUE (ns)
t_{WCR}	Write command time referenced to RAS*	95 min.
t_{WCS}	Write command setup-time	-20 min.
t_{WCH}	Write command hold-time	45 min.
t_{WP}	Write command pulse width	45 min.
t_{CWL}	Write command to column strobe lead-time	45 min.
t_{RWL}	Write command to row strobe lead-time	45 min.
t_{DS}	Data setup-time	0 min.
t_{DH}	Data hold-time	45 min.
t_{DHR}	Data hold-time referenced to RAS*	95 min.

three parameters (see figure 7.14). The data to be written into the memory must be valid for t_{DS} seconds (the data setup-time) before the falling edge of CAS* and must be maintained for t_{DH} seconds (the data hold-time) following the falling edge of CAS*. The data setup-time is 0 ns (minimum) and the data hold-time is 45 ns (minimum). Data must also meet a data hold-time criterion with respect to the

FIGURE 7.15   Dealing with the W* timing in a dynamic RAM

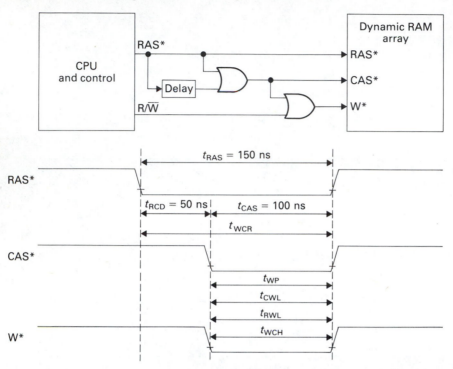

PARAMETER	NAME	MINIMUM VALUE (ns)	ACTUAL VALUE (ns)	MARGIN (ns)
t_{WCS}	Write command setup-time	−20	0	+20
t_{CWL}	Write command to column strobe lead-time	45	100	+55
t_{WP}	Write command pulse width	45	100	+55
t_{RWL}	Write command to row strobe lead-time	45	100	+55
t_{WCR}	Write command hold-time referenced to RAS*	95	150	+55
t_{WCH}	Write command hold-time	45	100	+55

falling edge of RAS*. Once RAS* has been asserted, the data must not change for at least t_{DHR} seconds (95 ns minimum). In general, the data timing requirements are not critical during a write cycle. However, as the data from the processor is latched into the memory by the falling edge of the CAS* clock, which often occurs early in a write cycle, it is necessary for the processor to supply its data output very early in a write cycle. Otherwise CAS* must be delayed until data from the processor is available.

Besides the normal read and write cycles, dynamic memories can be operated in other modes: a page mode and a read-modify-write cycle. Page mode operations involve sequential reads or writes to different column addresses, while the row address remains fixed and RAS* low. This condition speeds up the cycle time of the device and has applications in CRT display circuits in which memory is always accessed sequentially. The read-modify-write cycle is a memory access in which a write immediately follows a read and therefore avoids the need to latch the row and column addresses twice. These variations on the normal memory access cycles will not be considered further here.

Dynamic Memory Refresh Timing

Having dealt with the read and write cycles, the next step is to look at the refresh process for a dynamic RAM. Because of the way in which a dynamic memory cell operates, with an automatic write-back of information following a destructive readout, all that is needed to refresh a memory cell is to periodically read its contents (at least once every 2 ms). Even better news is that when a particular row is accessed, all columns in that row are refreshed. Therefore, only 128 refresh operations need be carried out every 2 ms. Note that the number of rows in a 64K chip is 128 rather than 256, because of the way in which the memory is internally partitioned.

Refreshing can be carried out either by hardware or by software. If the software can be guaranteed to perform at least 128 read or write cycles to the row addresses specified by the chip's A_0 to A_6 address inputs, then no additional hardware is required. Of course, guaranteeing 128 refresh cycles every 2 ms can be rather difficult. What happens if the reset button is pushed, or if. . .?

The vast majority of dynamic memories rely on hardware refreshing techniques. These are divided into two classes: RAS*-only refresh and pin 1 refresh on certain types of dynamic memory. Figure 7.16 presents a timing diagram of the RAS*-only refresh. For the duration of the refresh cycle, CAS* is inactive-high and the data-in and W* inputs are don't care conditions. A glance at figure 7.16 reveals that there are no new timing parameters. RAS* behaves as it does in any normal memory access and the row address for the refresh is latched exactly in the same way as any other access. Thus, in order to execute a refresh, the row address is applied to A_0 through A_6 and RAS* brought low for one cycle, while CAS* is held high. This procedure could not be simpler, but every silver lining delineates a nasty black cloud. In this case, the simple refresh operation is, indeed, the silver lining, while fitting the refresh cycle into the processor's normal sequence of operations is the black cloud. Somehow a logic subsystem has to take a decision to perform one or more memory refresh cycles and then to interleave them with normal processor memory accesses. How this is done depends on the nature of the system. We will shortly look at the design of a possible refresh controller for a 68000 system.

An alternative form of refreshing is called "pin 1" refreshing, because it uses pin 1 on 64K dynamic RAMs. Other 64K RAMs without this mode of refreshing

FIGURE 7.16   RAS*-only refresh timing of a dynamic memory

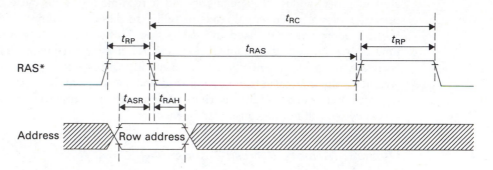

MNEMONIC	NAME	VALUE (ns)
t_{RP}	Row address strobe precharge time	100 min.
t_{RC}	Random access read cycle time	270 min.
t_{RAS}	Row address strobe pulse width	150–10,000
t_{ASR}	Row address setup-time	0 min.
t_{RAH}	Row address hold-time	20 min.

FIGURE 7.17   Pin 1 refresh mode—single cycle

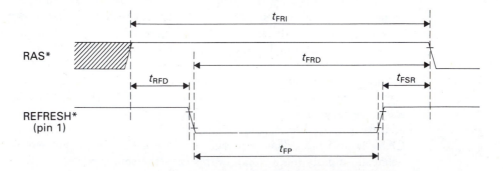

MNEMONIC	NAME	VALUE (ns)
t_{FRI}	RAS* inactive time during refresh	370 min.
t_{RFD}	RAS* to REFRESH* delay	− 10 min.
t_{FRD}	REFRESH* to RAS* delay-time	320 min.
t_{FSR}	REFRESH* to RAS* setup-time	− 30 min.
t_{FP}	REFRESH* pulse period	60–2,000

FIGURE 7.18   Pin 1 refresh mode—multiple cycles

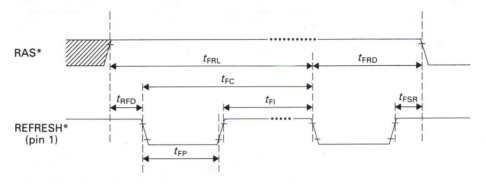

MNEMONIC	NAME	VALUE (ns)
t_{FRL}	RAS* to REFRESH* lead-time	370 min.
t_{FRD}	REFRESH* to RAS* delay-time	320 min.
t_{FC}	Refresh cycle time	270 min.
t_{RFD}	RAS* to REFRESH* delay	−10 min.
t_{FI}	REFRESH* inactive time	60 min.
t_{FSR}	REFRESH* to RAS* setup-time	−30 min.
t_{FP}	REFRESH* pulse period	60–2,000

leave pin 1 unconnected. Figure 7.17 illustrates the operation of the pin 1 refresh mode available on the 6664A-15 dynamic RAM. RAS* is held high while the REFRESH* input on pin 1 is forced active-low. The timing requirements are self-explanatory. The only noteworthy points are t_{FRI} (the RAS* inactive time during a refresh cycle) and t_{FRD} (REFRESH* to RAS* delay time). These times are relatively long, 370 and 320 ns, respectively, and might cause timing problems in some systems if a pin 1 refresh cycle is to be interleaved with normal processor cycles.

As t_{FRI} and t_{FRD} are relatively long compared to the refresh pulse period, t_{FP}, with its 60 ns minimum, operation of the 6664A in a pulsed pin 1 refresh mode in which REFRESH* is pulsed while RAS* is high is advantageous. A timing diagram for this situation is given in figure 7.18. A single-row refresh cycle has a minimum duration of $t_{FC} = 270$ ns, which is equal to the chip's normal cycle time. In a pulsed refresh mode, a batch of rows are refreshed in one burst rather than by executing 128 separate pin 1 refresh cycles.

Dynamic RAM Controller

Now that we have examined the operation of the DRAM, the next step is to show how it is actually used in microcomputers. A block diagram of the functional

FIGURE 7.19   Structure of a dynamic memory module

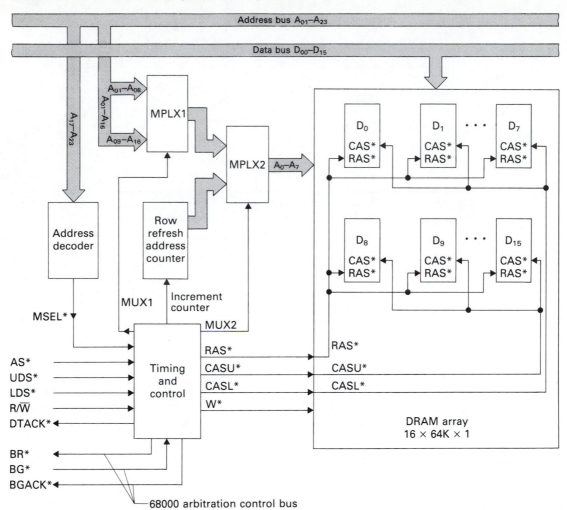

parts of a dynamic memory system is given in figure 7.19, and is intended to be used in a 68000-based system without pin 1 refresh mode DRAMs. The memory is organized as 64K 16-bit words, with independent byte control. During normal (i.e., nonrefresh) operation, the address decoder provides an active-low output, MSEL*, whenever a valid address within the array is generated by the computer. This action triggers the timing generator, which synthesizes all the control signals required for the RAM array and the address multiplexers. MUX1 selects the row or column address from the system address bus, while MUX2 selects the row/column address from MUX1 or from the row counter during a refresh. MUX1 and MUX2 together form a three-way multiplexer and the DRAM address input is given by table 7.2.

TABLE 7.2   Multiplexing the DRAM's address inputs between row and column and refresh addresses

MUX1	MUX2	DRAM ADDRESS
0	0	Refresh
0	1	System row address
1	0	Refresh
1	1	System column address

One difficulty associated with 16-bit systems is the need to carry out byte operations on only half a word. While two completely independent memory systems could be designed, one for the lower and one for the upper byte, such an approach would be hopelessly inefficient. In order to access data in a dynamic memory, both RAS* and CAS* are involved in a cycle. Therefore, by negating either RAS* or CAS* to one half of a word, that byte is disabled and takes no part in the memory access. However, as refresh operations are applied to all bits of a word, RAS* should not be gated with UDS* or LDS*. In any case, RAS* should not be gated with UDS*/LDS* because the data strobe is asserted late in a 68000 write cycle. In figure 7.19, the CAS* inputs to the sixteen DRAMs are divided into two groups of eight, CASL* and CASU*. CASL* is formed by gating CAS* with LDS* and CASU* by gating CAS* with UDS*.

The complex part of the dynamic memory system is the timing and control circuit, which must perform both normal read/write memory cycles and memory refreshes. The way in which memory refreshes are slotted into the operation of the processor is a difficult design decision and many factors have to be taken into account; for example, should the refreshing be interleaved with normal memory accessing or should it be done separately by stopping the processor and then carrying out a burst of refresh cycles? The decision is difficult because many factors have to be considered, some of which are economic and some technical. In general, interleaving refresh cycles, a process called hidden or transparent refresh, has the advantage that the processor is not slowed down, but it requires faster memory because a refresh and a normal memory access have to be completed within the same processor cycle. Equally, burst mode refresh does not call for faster memory, but the processor is halted during the refresh process.

DRAM Control and the ECB

An example of a 68000 dynamic memory system is provided by the Motorola 68000 single-board educational computer. This computer uses 16K × 1 components, but the principles are valid for components of any size. Figure 7.20 gives the basic circuit of the timing generator for the read and write cycles. The actual arrangement of the dynamic memories and the row/column/refresh address multi-

FIGURE 7.20   Dynamic memory control on the ECB

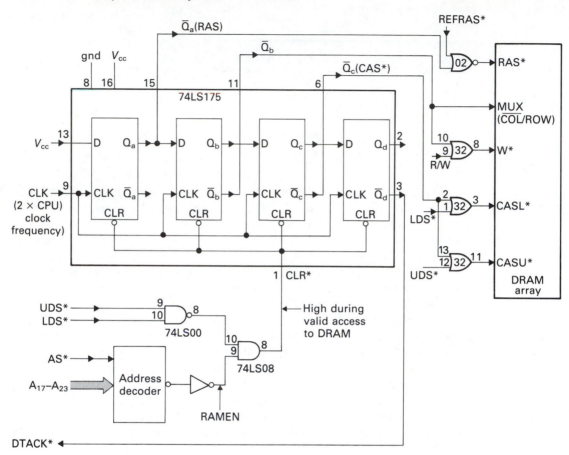

plexers is not included here as it is entirely straightforward. The read cycle timing diagram for this circuit is provided in figure 7.21.

The component at the heart of the controller is a 74LS175 4-bit shift register, clocked at twice the rate of the CPU clock. As long as the dynamic memory block is not being accessed (i.e., both LDS* and UDS* high or RAMEN low), the output (CLR*) of the two-input AND gate is low and the shift register is cleared with $Q_a = Q_b = Q_c = Q_d = 0$.

Whenever the processor addresses the array, RAMEN goes active-high, enabling one input to the AND gate. As soon as LDS* or UDS* is asserted, the second input to the AND gate rises and its output, CLR*, becomes high. The shift register is now enabled and a logical one is shifted along on each rising edge of the 8-MHz clock. Note that the ECB has a 4-MHz version of the 68000.

On the first clock pulse, the Q_a output rises to a high level because the serial input to the shifter is tied to V_{cc}. The Q_a output from the shift register is

FIGURE 7.21   Read cycle timing diagram for figure 7.20

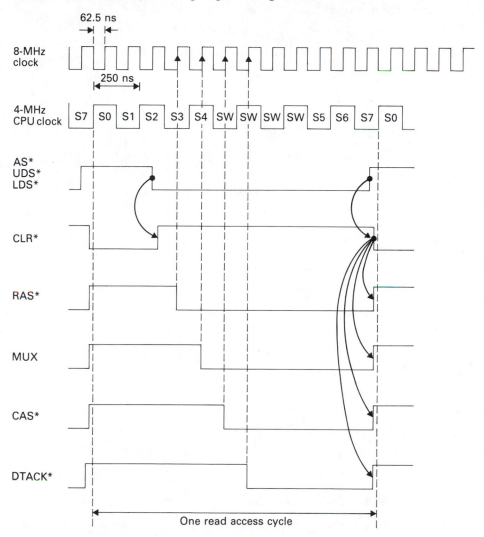

NORed with REFRAS* from the refresh circuitry (to generate RAS* pulses during refresh cycles) and inverted by the NOR gate to provide the system RAS*. On the next rising edge of the 8-MHz clock, Q_b goes high and Q_b* low. Q_b* acts as the row/column multiplex control signal and also gates the R/$\overline{W}$ signal from the 68000. The next rising edge of the 8-MHz clock sets Q_c and resets Q_c* to generate CAS*. This procedure is followed one clock pulse later by DTACK* (Q_d*). The falling edge of DTACK* is recognized by the 68000 and the memory access continues with state S5. During S7, AS* is negated (together with UDS* and LDS*) and the shift register cleared, forcing RAS*, CAS*, MUX, W*, and DTACK* high, simultaneously.

FIGURE 7.22   Dynamic memory refresh and the ECB—simplified version. (Reprinted by permission of Motorola Limited)

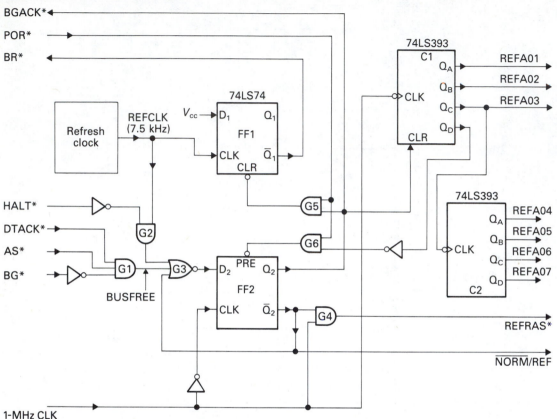

NOTE: C1 and C2 are counters that provide the DRAM array with a 7-bit refresh address REFA01 to REFA07.

DRAM Refresh on the ECB

The simplified circuit diagram of the dynamic refresh generator on the 68000 ECB is given in figure 7.22 and its timing diagram in figure 7.23. A refresh clock operating at 7.54 kHz signals the need for a burst of refresh cycles every $1/(7.54 \times 10^3) = 0.133$ ms. This design does not carry out all refreshes in one burst—it performs eight cycles every 0.133 ms, completing all 128 row refreshes in $0.133 \times 16 = 2.128$ ms. By distributing the refresh operation over sixteen bursts of eight cycles, the processor is not held up for any appreciable length of time.

The refresh control circuitry on the ECB employs the 68000's bus arbitration signals described earlier in this chapter. Further details on bus arbitration are provided in chapter 10.

At power-up, POR∗ (power-on-reset from the processor control circuitry) goes low, clearing FF1 and setting FF2. Any well-designed circuit should

FIGURE 7.23   Timing diagram for memory refresh on the ECB

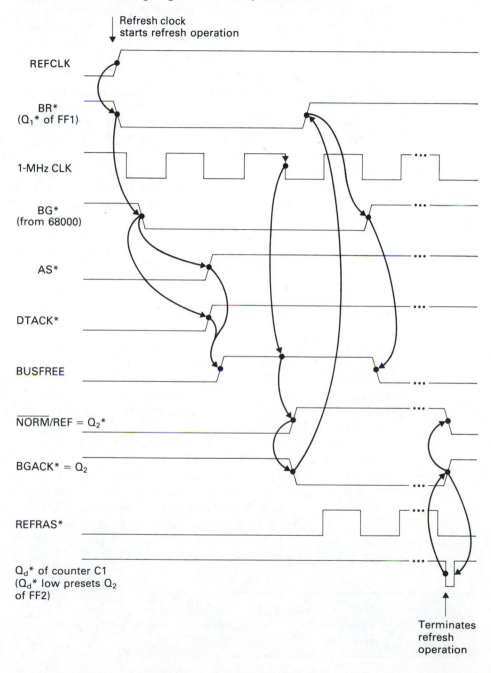

be similarly initialized and placed in a "safe state." In this state, Q_1* (i.e., BR*) is negated (i.e., high) and Q_2* (i.e., $\overline{\text{NORM/REF}}$) is low, signifying normal operation. When the refresh clock, a simple RC oscillator, generates a rising edge, FF1 is set and BR* asserted. The 68000 detects the bus request and asserts its bus grant output, BG*. AND gate G1 detects the condition BG* = 0, AS* = 1, DTACK* = 1, which occurs when the 68000 has relinquished the bus and forces input D_2 of FF2 low. Note that the other two inputs to NOR gate G3 (at this time) are both low—one because we will assume HALT* is negated and the other because Q_2* $(\overline{\text{NORM/REF}})$ is low after FF2 has been preset.

When D_2 is low, FF2 is cleared on the falling edge of the 1-MHz clock. Q_2 is connected to the 68000's bus grant acknowledge input (BGACK*) and, while low, stops the processor from regaining control of the bus. At the same time, the output of AND gate G5 is forced low, clearing FF1 and negating BR*. Thus, FF1 has done its job in this burst of refresh cycles and is once more in its initial state.

When FF2 is cleared, its Q_2* output goes high. Q_2* is also the $\overline{\text{NORM/REF}}$ line controlling the address multiplexer to the RAM array. When high, $\overline{\text{NORM/REF}}$ selects the address from the refresh column counter (ICs C1 and C2). Q_2* is also fed back to the D_2 input of FF2 via OR gate G3, so that once Q_2* is high, the flip-flop is held in this state and no longer depends on the state of BG* from the CPU, as BG* is automatically cleared following the negation of BR*. FF2 is now "locked up" with Q_2* high and can only be released by the assertion of its PRE* (preset) input.

The final role played by Q_2* is to gate the 1-MHz clock in AND gate G4, the output of which is the pulsed RAS* needed in the refresh cycle. Because Q_2, when low, allows counter C1 to operate, three bits of the refresh address appear on REFA01 through REFA03, which form part of the dynamic RAM's row refresh address. This counter is clocked at the refresh rate—1 MHz. A second stage counter, C2, is clocked by C1 after eight cycles and provides the remaining four row refresh addresses—REFA04 through REFA07.

After the 3-bit counter C1 has produced eight pulses, its Q_D output rises and disables AND gate G6, which presets FF2, causing Q_2 (i.e., BGACK*) to be negated, freeing the processor by releasing BGACK*. At the same time, Q_2* (i.e., $\overline{\text{NORM/REF}}$) goes low, disabling AND gate G4 and removing the refresh clock (REFRAS*). The system is now in its normal state, with BR*, BG*, and BGACK* all negated. The only change since the start of the cycle is that counter C2 has been advanced by one, so that the next time the refresh clock generates a pulse, the following eight row addresses will be refreshed.

7.3 Error Detection and Correction in Memories

In this section we examine one of the major problems associated with computer memory systems, that of read errors. A read error is said to occur when the data read back from a memory cell differs from that originally written to the cell. There are two classes of error: the hard error and the soft error. A hard error is one that is repeatable and that always happens under the same circumstances. Typically, one bit of a particular word may be permanently stuck at a logical one (or zero) level. Hard errors are due to faults in the memory system and are removed by repairing the damage, that is, by replacing the faulty chip.

A soft error is a form of transient error and is not normally repeatable. In this case a memory cell may corrupt its data contents, say, once in one hundred years. Such an error is not caused by a fault in the ordinary sense of the word, but can cause as much trouble as any hard error. It is almost impossible to prevent occasional soft errors occurring in a large memory array, particularly if dynamic memory components are employed. However, their effects can be greatly reduced by the following techniques.

The advent of low-cost, large dynamic memory systems has led to renewed interest in codes for the detection, or detection and correction, of errors in memory arrays. Error detection and correction is not a new subject; its growth can be traced to 1948 when Shannon proved that it is theoretically possible to transmit information over a noisy channel without error, as long as the channel capacity is not exceeded. Shannon's work was important because of the growing need for reliable data communication over long distances.

Dynamic memory cells are not as reliable as their static counterparts, in which positive feedback is used to hold a transistor in an on- or off-state. A dynamic memory cell suffers from soft errors due to both ionizing background radiation and pattern sensitivity. The latter problem occurs when a cell is sensitive to particular data patterns stored in adjacent cells. These errors are not frequent, but, if the probability of error in a single cell is finite, the mean time between failure (MTBF) in a memory system declines as the size of the array is increased; for example, the MTBF of a memory array composed of 1,000 chips with a failure rate of 0.001 percent per thousand hours is approximately one year. Of course, a single soft error in such a large memory array once a year on average is not always of any importance. Occasionally, however, even such a low error rate cannot be tolerated. Medical, aviation, and nuclear power applications are areas where soft errors may prove to have hard consequences.

To apply error detection and correction technology to memory arrays in order to reduce the probability of undetected soft errors is now possible (economically speaking). Hard errors can be detected by test software and the faulty chip replaced. The coding of messages for error detection/correction has become an area of great sophistication, requiring the engineer to have a very deep mathematical background. Fortunately for the computer engineer, the basic principle behind error detection/correction is rather elementary and the most popular form of error correction used with memory arrays is also one of the oldest and simplest.

Before continuing, three definitions must be made. An error-detecting code is able to determine that a message has been corrupted and is not valid. Further details about the nature of the error cannot be provided. An error-correcting code both detects and corrects certain types of error in a message; for example, a typical error-correcting code can correct a single error in an *m*-bit message and detect, but not correct, a 2-bit error. Note that I have used the word *message* because the language and terminology of error-detecting/correcting codes comes largely from the world of telecommunications. In what follows, I use *word* to correspond to *message* in the preceding text. A *source word* applies to the information to be encoded and a *code word* applies to the information after encoding. At the moment, the source word is not associated with a particular bit length; that is, it does not imply a 16-bit word as used throughout the rest of this text.

Forward error correction (FEC) is a technique whereby the source word is encoded to give the code word, and an error in the code word can be corrected automatically. This situation contrasts with *automatic retransmission request* (ARQ), which is an error-correction technique associated with data links. Under the ARQ mode, the receiver requests the retransmission of any message it determines to be in error. Error-correcting memories use forward error-correction techniques, as they cannot request the restorage of faulty data!

The basis of all forms of error correction and detection is redundancy. For example, a human reader detects a spelling error in a book, because English is a highly redundant language. Although there are $26 \times 26 = 676$ possible combinations of two letters, from AA to ZZ, only about thirty legal combinations of two letters exist. By knowing the valid combinations, an error can be detected if a given code differs from all possible valid codes.

The simplest possible binary error-detecting code is the single-bit parity code. A single bit is appended to the source word to create the code word. This additional bit, the parity bit, is chosen to force the total number of ones in the code word (including the parity bit itself) to be even, if the code is even parity, or odd if it is odd parity. Consider the example of table 7.3, where a 2-bit source word is encoded into a 3-bit code word with even parity.

Note that the code word has 3 bits, allowing $2^3 = 8$ combinations, but only four of these combinations are legal. A full list of possible code words is given in table 7.4, together with an indication of their validity.

On the left-hand side of table 7.4 the sequence of code words is presented in natural binary order, while on the right-hand side it is presented in the Gray code

TABLE 7.3   Single-bit even-parity code

SOURCE WORD	CODE WORD
0 0	0 0 0
0 1	0 1 1
1 0	1 0 1
1 1	1 1 0

$$\uparrow$$
Parity bit

TABLE 7.4   Three-bit even-parity code

NATURAL BINARY SEQUENCE		GRAY CODE SEQUENCE	
CODE WORD	VALIDITY	CODE WORD	VALIDITY
0 0 0	Valid	0 0 0	Valid
0 0 1	Invalid	0 0 1	Invalid
0 1 0	Invalid	0 1 1	Valid
0 1 1	Valid	0 1 0	Invalid
1 0 0	Invalid	1 1 0	Valid
1 0 1	Valid	1 1 1	Invalid
1 1 0	Valid	1 0 1	Valid
1 1 1	Invalid	1 0 0	Invalid

order. In a Gray code sequence only one bit changes between successive code words. When the Gray code is examined, we can clearly see that no two adjacent *valid* code words exist. Thus, if one of the bits of a valid code word is changed by an error, the resulting code word is invalid and the error can be detected. Unfortunately, if two bits are changed the resulting code word is valid and the error cannot be detected.

Figure 7.24 illustrates the 3-bit even parity code in three-dimensional space. Note, once again, that no two valid code words are adjacent.

By adding sufficient redundancy to a code word, construction of an error-detecting and -correcting code becomes possible. Figure 7.25 shows how this situation can be achieved with a trivial source word of one bit and a code word of three bits. Although there are $2^3 = 8$ possible code words, only two valid codes exist: 000 and 111. Each valid code is separated by a minimum of three bit changes. Suppose a single error occurs and one bit of the code word is changed. From figure 7.25 we can see that a single error yields a code word one unit from the correct value and two units from the other possible values. Thus, if 100, 010,

FIGURE 7.24   Eight 3-bit even-parity code words

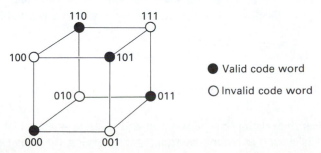

FIGURE 7.25   Three-bit error-correcting code word

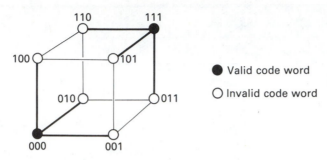

- ● Valid code word
- ○ Invalid code word

or 001 is received, the correct code word is assumed to be 000 and the corresponding source word 1. The philosophy behind this code is that single bit errors are infrequent and, therefore, double bit errors are very rare, so that when an invalid code word is received, the closest valid code word can be taken as the corrected data value. These results can be generalized to any number of bits. In what follows, the number of bits in the source word is m and the number of bits in the code word n. The redundant bits are given by r, where $r = n - m$.

The total number of possible code words is 2^n and the total number of valid code words is 2^m. Consequently, there are $2^n - 2^m$ error states:

$$\text{Error states} = 2^n - 2^m$$

$$= 2^{(m+r)} - 2^m \qquad \text{because } r = n - m$$

$$= 2^m(2^r - 1).$$

In other words, $2^r - 1$ error states per valid state exist. In the previous example of a 3-bit code with $n = 3$ and $m = 1$, there are $2^2 - 1 = 3$ error states per valid code word. Figure 7.25 demonstrates the validity of this result.

An m-bit source word yields 2^m valid code words, providing $n2^m$ possible single-error code words. The factor n appears because each n-bit valid code word can have n single bit errors, as an error is possible in any one of the n bit positions. In order to correct a single error, there must be at least as many possible error states as words with single bit errors. If this situation were not true, two or more single bit errors would share the same error state and we would not find it possible to work backward from the error state to the valid code word. Therefore:

$$2^m(2^r - 1) \geq n2^m$$

$$(2^r - 1) \quad \geq n$$

$$2^r - 1 \quad \geq m + r.$$

Table 7.5 gives the relationship between m and n for $m = 4$ to 119. In each case, the value of r is chosen as the minimum integer satisfying the above equation.

TABLE 7.5   Relationship between source and code wordlength

SOURCE WORD BITS m	CODE WORD BITS n	REDUNDANT BITS r
4	7	3
8	12	4
12	17	5
16	21	5
20	25	5
24	29	5
28	34	6
32	38	6
⋮	⋮	⋮
57	63	6
⋮	⋮	⋮
119	126	7

Table 7.5 shows that very few additional bits are required to provide a single bit error-correction capability to relatively large source wordlengths. Unfortunately, single bit error-correcting codes become less attractive as the source wordlength drops below about 16 bits.

Hamming Codes

One of the earliest and still the most popular type of single bit error-correcting code is the Hamming code. An n, m Hamming code has an n-bit code wordlength and an m-bit source wordlength. This class of codes is popular because it is relatively easy to implement with standard MSI TTL gates. The Hamming code adds parity bits to a source word in such a way that the recalculation of the parity bits, after the word has been stored, not only indicates the presence of an error (if any) but also points to its location. In order to appreciate the operation of a Hamming code, consider the 7,4 Hamming code. The information bits in this code are written I_i and the redundant, or check, bits, C_i. The code word can therefore be represented by:

7	6	5	4	3	2	1
I_4	I_3	I_2	C_3	I_1	C_2	C_1

Note that the bit positions are numbered 1 through 7 (rather than 0 through 6) and that the check bits, C_1, C_2, C_3, are placed in binary sequence (i.e., 1, 2, 4, 8,

TABLE 7.6   Parity equations for a 7,3 Hamming code

CODE BIT NUMBER	7	6	5	4	3	2	1	
CODE BIT	I_4	I_3	I_2	C_3	I_1	C_2	C_1	
	1	1	1	1	0	0	0	← MSB of 3-bit number
	1	1	0	0	1	1	0	
	1	0	1	0	1	0	1	← LSB of 3-bit number

...) in positions 1, 2, and 4. The parity equations for the check bits are derived from table 7.6.

Below each of the bit positions of the code word in table 7.6 is the binary value of the position; for example, bit position 6, representing I_3, is located above binary code $110_2 = 6$. The parity equations are derived by reading across the columns of the binary code lines, and including each bit position with a logical one in the parity equation; that is:

MSB bit $C_3 \oplus I_2 \oplus I_3 \oplus I_4 = 0$

Middle bit $C_2 \oplus I_1 \oplus I_3 \oplus I_4 = 0$

LSB bit $C_1 \oplus I_1 \oplus I_2 \oplus I_4 = 0.$

An example should make things clearer. Suppose the source word is I_4, I_3, I_2, $I_1 = 1, 0, 1, 1$. We can substitute the values of I_1 to I_4 in the above equations to obtain the check bits:

$C_3 \oplus 1 \oplus 0 \oplus 1 = 0;$ therefore, $C_3 = 0;$

$C_2 \oplus 1 \oplus 0 \oplus 1 = 0;$ therefore, $C_2 = 0;$

$C_1 \oplus 1 \oplus 1 \oplus 1 = 1;$ therefore, $C_1 = 1.$

The 7-bit code word, I_4, I_3, I_2, C_3, I_1, C_2, C_1, is given by 1, 0, 1, 0, 1, 0, 1. Suppose this code word is stored in memory and then read back as 1, 1, 1, 0, 1, 0, 1 with an error in bit position 6. The next step is to recalculate the parity equations:

MSB bit $C_3 \oplus I_2 \oplus I_3 \oplus I_4 = 0 \oplus 1 \oplus 1 \oplus 1 = 1$

Middle bit $C_2 \oplus I_1 \oplus I_3 \oplus I_4 = 0 \oplus 1 \oplus 1 \oplus 1 = 1$

LSB bit $C_1 \oplus I_1 \oplus I_2 \oplus I_4 = 1 \oplus 1 \oplus 1 \oplus 1 = 0.$

The parity equations are no longer all equal to zero. Their value is 110_2, which is the binary value 6. The position of the bit in error is indicated, namely the bit 6 position.

Figure 7.26 illustrates the arrangement needed to implement an error-correcting memory (ECM). The *m*-bit data input is used to calculate an *r*-bit check

FIGURE 7.26   Conceptual arrangement of an error-correcting memory

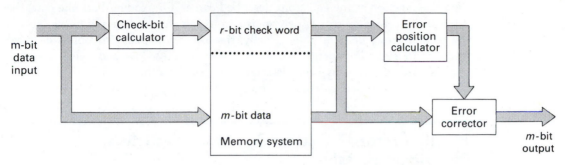

word, which is stored along with the data. When the memory is read, the n-bit code word determines the position of any error. This information can then be used to correct a faulty bit.

A detailed implementation of a 7,4 Hamming code single bit error-correcting memory is given in figure 7.27. A parity tree formed by three pairs of

FIGURE 7.27   Possible arrangement of a 7,4 Hamming code ECM

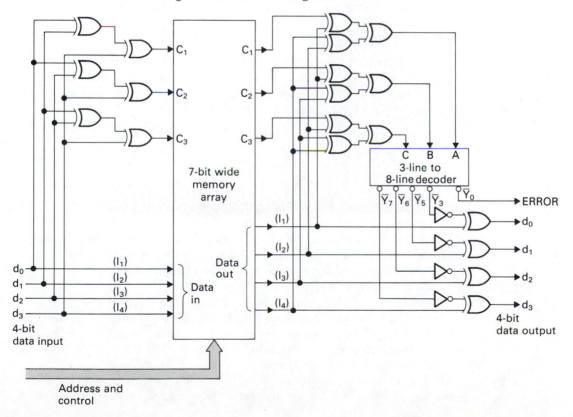

cascaded EOR gates generates the check bits. Note that the parity circuits perform the same function as the equations described earlier. On reading back the data, the 3-bit position of the error is determined from the stored data and check bits by the second group of EOR gates. Finally, the 3-bit error position code is decoded into one of eight lines. The first output, Y0∗, is active-low and, when asserted, implies that no error has been detected. Four of the other lines feed EOR gates that invert the erroneous data bit to correct it.

Practical Error-Detection/Correction Systems for Microprocessors

Table 7.5 tells us that only five check bits are required to implement a 16-bit, single bit error-correcting memory for a microprocessor. Unfortunately, table 7.5 does not tell the whole story. Two particular issues are raised by practical arrangements of error-correcting memories. The first is that the basic Hamming code is not normally used, as its performance can be considerably improved by the addition of another check bit. The second is the problem arising when a 16-bit microprocessor attempts to carry out operations on 8-bit bytes.

Modified Hamming Code

The standard Hamming code described earlier provides single bit error detection and correction. If a word is corrupted by a double bit error, the code fails either to correct or, more importantly, to detect it. The reason for this can be seen from the parity equations for a 7,4 Hamming code repeated below:

$$C_3 = I_2 \oplus I_3 \oplus I_4$$
$$C_2 = I_1 \oplus I_3 \oplus I_4$$
$$C_1 = I_1 \oplus I_2 \oplus I_4 .$$

Suppose I_3 is corrupted in storage. This information bit affects the value of check bits C_2 and C_3, because it appears only in the equations for these check bits. If both I_1 and I_2 are corrupted, only check bits C_2 and C_3 are affected, because the double bit error in the calculation of C_1 does not affect the result. However, C_2 and C_3 are also affected by an error in I_3. Therefore, a double error in I_1 and I_2 appears as a single error in I_3!

In order to implement a single bit error-correcting, double bit error-detecting code, we need to employ five check bits, arranged so that each bit of the source word is protected by three of the check bits. Table 7.7 gives the modified Hamming code adopted by Texas Instruments in their 74LS637 8-bit parallel error-detection and -correction circuit.

An × in table 7.7 indicates that the bit of the source word takes place in the generation of the check bit on the same row; e.g., $C_0 = d_7 \oplus d_6 \oplus d_4 \oplus d_3$.

TABLE 7.7 Modified Hamming code for $m = 8$, $r = 5$

CHECK BIT	EIGHT-BIT SOURCE WORD							
	d_7	d_6	d_5	d_4	d_3	d_2	d_1	d_0
C_0	×	×		×	×			
C_1	×		×	×		×	×	
C_2		×	×		×	×		×
C_3	×	×	×				×	×
C_4				×	×	×	×	×

Note that each data bit is involved in the calculation of exactly three check bits (i.e., there are three ×s in each of the columns).

During a write cycle to memory, the 8-bit data word is used to generate a 5-bit check word, which is stored along with the data. On reading back the data and check word, the five check bits are recalculated and, if they are the same as the retrieved check bits, the data is assumed to be error free.

If a single error occurs in the stored data bits, d_0 to d_7, exactly three of the recalculated bits differ from the retrieved check bits. If one of the check bits is corrupted, only one error is detected when the check bits are read back.

Any 2-bit error alters an even number of check bits. This fact can be used to interrupt the processor and inform it that an uncorrectable error has been detected. In 68000-based systems, the detection of a multiple error may either be used to assert BERR* in order to abort the current memory access or to rerun the bus cycle. Three or more simultaneous errors cannot be handled by this code and the error-detection circuitry will "see" the three errors as: a single correctable error, an uncorrectable error, or no error at all.

As in the case of the basic Hamming code, error correction is achieved by determining the location of the bit in error and then inverting it. Table 7.8 gives the error location table corresponding to a single bit error. The syndrome error code is the EXCLUSIVE OR of the regenerated check word and the retrieved check word.

Problem of Byte Operations on a 16-Bit Word

The most irritating problem associated with codes for error detection/correction is due to the modern 16-bit processor's ability to operate on a whole 16-bit word or just one byte of it. Suppose a 16-bit data word is used with a 22,16 modified Hamming code. Whenever a new word is written to memory, the appropriate six check bits are calculated and stored. On reading back the 22-bit code word, automatic single bit error correction can be performed by the memory array or a multiple error signaled should the need arise.

TABLE 7.8   Locating a single error with a modified Hamming code

ERROR LOCATION	SYNDROME ERROR CODE				
	C_0	C_1	C_2	C_3	C_4
Data bit D_7	0	0	1	0	1
Data bit D_6	0	1	0	0	1
Data bit D_5	1	0	0	0	1
Data bit D_4	0	0	1	1	0
Data bit D_3	0	1	0	1	0
Data bit D_2	1	0	0	1	0
Data bit D_1	1	0	1	0	0
Data bit D_0	1	1	0	0	0
Check bit C_0	0	1	1	1	1
Check bit C_1	1	0	1	1	1
Check bit C_2	1	1	0	1	1
Check bit C_3	1	1	1	0	1
Check bit C_4	1	1	1	1	0
No error	1	1	1	1	1

Imagine that the processor wishes to read one byte of a word. Clearly, the whole word must be read to carry out the error-correction process, as check bits are distributed throughout the word. The situation is much worse if we wish to write to one byte of a word; that is, one byte of a 16-bit word is to be updated while the other byte remains unaffected. This action is simply not possible. We first need to read the 22-bit code word, perform an error check on it, and then extract the byte to be retained. Then the new byte from the processor is appended to the retrieved byte and the appropriate six check bits generated for the whole 16-bit word. Therefore, although the error-correction circuitry itself is relatively simple, the error-correcting memory system becomes quite complex. Even worse, system throughput is reduced as two memory accesses are necessary for each CPU access: one to read the old word from memory and another to restore half the old word plus the "new" byte.

An alternative, but hardly elegant, arrangement is to design the 16-bit error-correcting memory as two entirely independent 8-bit memories. Not only does this duplicate the error-correcting hardware, but a total of twelve check bits per 16-bit word is required if two 6-bit modified Hamming codes are used. Although this procedure almost doubles the cost of the main memory, it is still cheaper than relying on the better error performance of static read/write memory, if the memory array is sufficiently large.

Figure 7.28 gives the block diagram of an 8-bit ECM using a modified 13,8 Hamming code and figure 7.29 its detailed implementation. To construct a 16-bit version, two identical 8-bit ECMs must be used, with one enabled by LDS* and one by UDS*, as shown in figure 7.30. The detailed implementation of figure 7.29

FIGURE 7.28 Eight-bit error-correcting memory

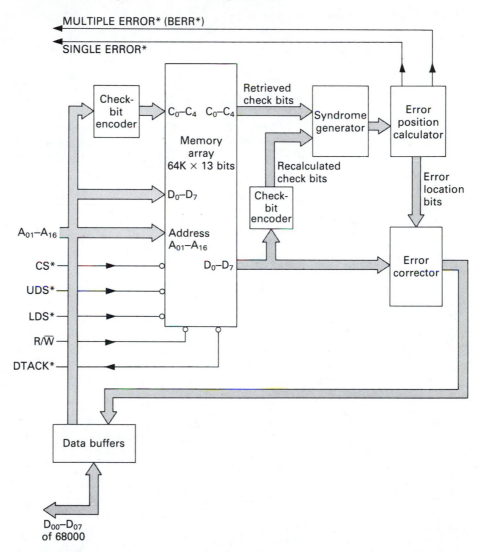

reduces the parts count by replacing EOR parity tree generators with PROM look-up tables. In a read cycle, the five check bits, C_0 through C_4, are generated by applying the eight data inputs to the address inputs of a 256 × 8 PROM. The data outputs of the PROM directly provide the check bits.

On read-back a second, and identical, 256 × 8 PROM recalculates the check bits from the retrieved data. The recalculated and stored check bits are fed to five EOR gates to compute the syndrome for the word currently being accessed. This syndrome is applied to another 32 word × 8-bit PROM, which looks up the

FIGURE 7.29   Implementing the 8-bit ECM

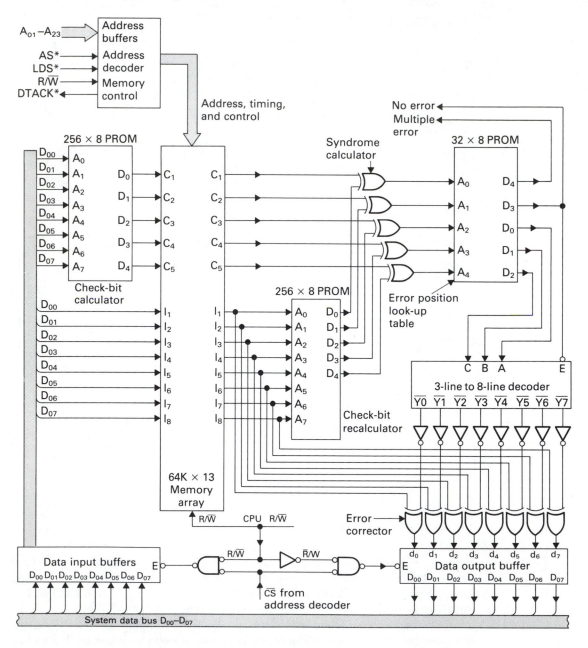

FIGURE 7.30   Sixteen-bit byte-accessible ECM

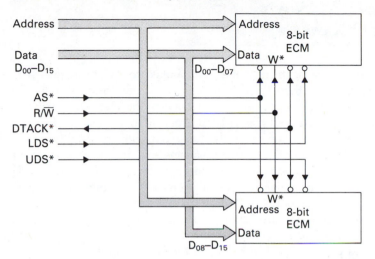

position of any single bit error and applies it to the *error location* output. This information is fed to a three-line to eight-line decoder that controls the 8-bit programmable inverter. If no error exists, the three-line to eight-line decoder is disabled and no data bit is inverted. If the syndrome detects more than one error (i.e., an even number of check bits corrupted), the multiple error flag from the 32×8 PROM is asserted.

In any practical implementation of 68000-based ECM, the designer is faced with the problem of what to do when one or more errors are detected. You may think that a single error can be forgotten as it is automatically corrected. In principle, this statement is true. Each time the faulty byte is read, its error is corrected. However, no margin is left for a second and therefore uncorrectable error. A better strategy is to detect each single bit error, inform the processor, and let it write back the word in error, which will ensure that the error is removed, as both the data and check bits will then be error free.

If two or more errors occur, the processor must be informed. This action can be taken by any conventional technique. The processor may be interrupted, RESET*, or BERR* asserted to abort the cycle. The latter action seems most reasonable, as a reset is too drastic and an interrupt will not be serviced until the faulty data has been read and possible harm done.

A useful addition to the ECM described previously is some form of error-logging circuitry, which may be implemented in software by the processor itself keeping track of each error or can be realized by an auxiliary circuit on the ECM module that records the address and data associated with each error. Such an approach enables a possible determination of the state of the memory module's health. If the frequency of soft errors rises above its expected level, an operator can be informed and memory chips replaced after the processor has determined their location from the error log.

7.4 Memory Management and Microprocessors

Memory management is the term applied to any technique that takes an address generated by the CPU and employs it to calculate the address in memory being accessed by the processor. The concept of memory management often seems obscure, because no reason is apparent as to why the address at the address pins of a microprocessor should be tampered with in order to access the appropriate memory location. This section explains why memory management is necessary on some microprocessor systems and how this operation is achieved.

Another reason for the air of mystery surrounding memory management is its application only to sophisticated microprocessor systems. Almost all introductory texts ignore memory management because it is entirely unnecessary in many small- to medium-scale microcomputers. In such machines the address generated by the processor is indeed the same address as the location of the data in memory.

The key to understanding the role of memory management is an appreciation of the meaning of logical address space (LAS) and physical address space (PAS). In the simplest terms, the logical address space of a microprocessor is the address space made up by all the addresses it can place on its address bus; that is, the logical address space is the address space made up of all the addresses that can be generated by the CPU. Thus, the logical address space of an 8-bit microprocessor with a 16-bit address bus is $2^{16} = 64K$ bytes. The 68000 has a massive 16M-byte logical address space.

We should appreciate that the size of the logical address space does not depend on the addressing mode used to specify an operand; nor does it depend on whether a program is written in a high level language, assembly language, or machine code. The instruction MOVE. B D4,TEMPERATURE permits the program to specify the logical address of TEMPERATURE as any one of 16M bytes. No matter what technique is used, the 68000 cannot specify a logical address greater than $2^{24} - 1$ simply because the number of bits in its program counter is limited to 24 (by the address pins of the 68000 in this case). Of course, in a real system, programmers may not be able to choose *any* logical address for their programs and data, because no actual memory components may be located at that address. *Strictly speaking*, the 68000 has a logical address space of 2^{32} bytes because the program counter is a 32-bit register, even though the 68000 has only a 24-bit external address bus.

Physical address space is the address space spanned by all the actual address locations in the processor's memory system. This space is the physical memory, the memory that is in no sense abstract and costs real dollars and cents to implement. In other words, the system's main memory makes up the physical address space. While the logical address space of a computer is limited by the number of bits used to specify an address, the physical address space is frequently limited only by its cost.

The four fundamental objectives of memory management systems are:

1.   The organization of systems in which the amount of physical address space exceeds that of the logical address space.

2.   The organization of systems in which the logical address space exceeds the physical address space.

3.   Memory protection, which includes schemes that prevent one user from accessing the memory space of another user.

4.   The freeing of the programmer from any considerations of where his or her programs and data are to be located in memory.

Any real memory management unit may not attempt to achieve all these goals (the first two are mutually exclusive). Note that the second goal (i.e., logical address space greater than physical address space) is especially important to designers of 68000-based systems. In fact, when memory management is applied to this problem, it is frequently referred to as *virtual memory technology*. Virtual memory is almost synonymous with *logical* memory.

Let us first take the case where the physical memory space is greater than the logical memory space. Not very long ago, 8-bit microprocessors had small physical memories due to the relatively high cost of memory components. In those days the programs executed on such microprocessor systems were rather small. Once a time existed when integer BASIC was regarded as something special. By the early 1980s, many general-purpose 8-bit microcomputers had a full complement of 64K bytes of RAM because of the introduction of low-cost 16K and 64K DRAMs. Such a large memory made bigger programs possible and speeded up operations like text processing by permitting a larger chunk of the text to reside in immediate access memory at any given instant. Unfortunately, the new low-cost memory chips could not be used to create 128K or larger memories without some sleight of hand. Obviously, a CPU with a 16-bit address bus can access a maximum of 64K bytes of logical address space, but cannot specify a unique location in 128K bytes (2^{17} bytes) of physical memory without ambiguity.

Memory management techniques solved this problem by bank switching. The physical memory is arranged as a number of separate banks of 64K bytes and the processor is allowed access only to one bank of 64K bytes of physical memory space at any time. In other words, the 64K-byte logical address space of the processor is mapped onto a 64K region of the physical address space. Figure 7.31 illustrates this technique of memory mapping and figure 7.32 shows how it is implemented at the conceptual level, by passing the logical address from the processor through an address translation unit (ATU). How this process is done is dealt with later.

Now consider the more interesting problem from the point of view of the designer of systems with 20-bit or more address buses. Under these circumstances, the processor will probably have a larger logical address space than its physical address space. After all, not many 68000 systems are in existence with a full complement of 16M bytes of random access memory, but many 68000 systems

FIGURE 7.31   Mapping logical address space onto physical address space

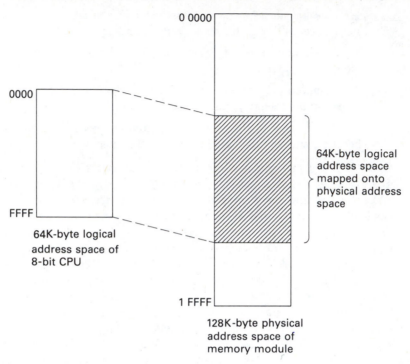

have 256K bytes of RAM and need to run programs with a logical address space of more than 256K bytes.

This problem is caused by economics and has always plagued the mainframe industry. In the late 1950s, mainframes were available with large logical address spaces but tiny 2K or so blocks of RAM. A group of computer scientists at Manchester University in the United Kingdom proposed a memory management technique, now known as virtual memory, to deal with this situation. The logical (or virtual) address space is mapped onto the available physical address space as shown in figure 7.33. As long as the processor accesses data in the logical space that is mapped onto the existing physical address space, all is well. We have been performing this process all the way through this text, because we have assumed

FIGURE 7.32   Using address translation to achieve memory mapping

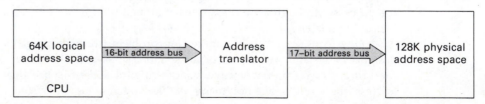

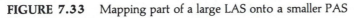

FIGURE 7.33   Mapping part of a large LAS onto a smaller PAS

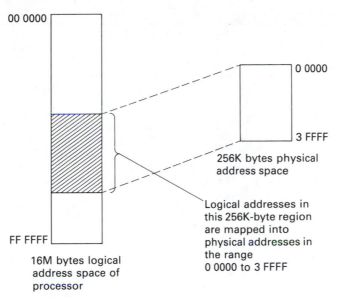

that an address from the 68000 is passed directly (i.e., unchanged) to the system's address bus. However, when the processor generates the logical address of an operand that cannot be mapped on to the available physical address space, we have a problem.

The solution adopted at Manchester is delightfully simple. Whenever the processor generates a logical address for which no corresponding physical address exists, the operating system stops the current program, fetches a block of data containing the desired operand from its disk store, places this block in physical memory (overwriting old data), and tells the memory management unit that a new relationship exists between logical and physical address space. In other words, the program or data is held on disk and only the parts of the program currently needed are transferred to the physical RAM. The memory management unit keeps track of the relationship between the logical address generated by the processor and that of the data currently in physical memory. This process is very complex in its details and requires *harmonization* of the processor architecture, the memory management unit, and the operating system. People dream of simple virtual memory systems and have nightmares about real ones.

Memory Mapping

Although this text is concerned mainly with 16-bit microprocessor systems with their large logical memory spaces, this section looks at the problems of micro-

FIGURE 7.34   Memory mapping by bank switching

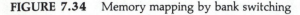
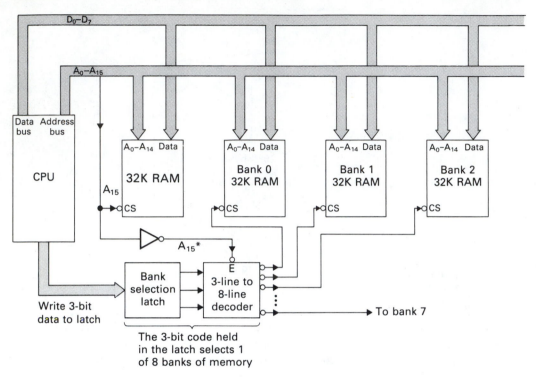

processors with smaller logical memory spaces than physical memory spaces. Such microprocessors are normally 8-bit devices. I have included this section for the sake of completeness, as memory mapping and virtual memory are really inverse operations. In any case, 8-bit microprocessor systems will still be around for some time. Moreover, a time may come when even the 68000 has more than 16M bytes of RAM and the designer may have to resort to memory mapping.

The most primitive form of memory-mapping system is illustrated in figure 7.34, in which the physical address space is provided by a fixed bank of 32K bytes of memory plus two to eight switchable banks of 32K bytes of memory. The fixed block of physical memory is arranged so that it is selected whenever A_{15} from the processor is a logical zero. Therefore, this region of physical memory is permanently mapped onto the 32K bytes of logical memory in the range $0000 to $7FFF; that is, logical addresses from $0000 to $7FFF have identical physical addresses.

Whenever A_{15} from the processor is high, the three-line to eight-line decoder is enabled and one of its outputs goes low to select a bank of 32K bytes of memory. The actual bank of memory selected depends on the state of the 3-bit code stored in the latch. Figure 7.35 shows the memory map corresponding to figure 7.34. The 32K bytes of logical memory space can be translated to the

FIGURE 7.35   Memory map corresponding to figure 7.34

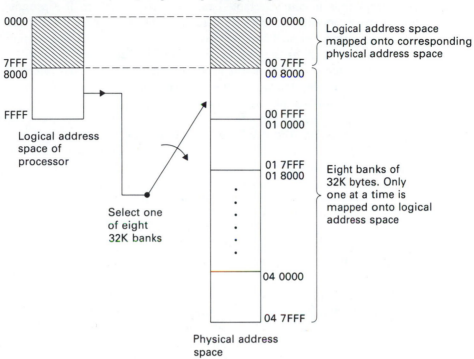

memory space of any of the eight 32K banks of physical address space. Note that the processor can always access 64K bytes of both logical and physical memory space at any instant. The process of bank switching provides the CPU with a window through which it can see one of the eight possible banks of switched memory.

However, bank switching or any other form of memory management is useless without the software necessary to control it. Consider a program running in the lower half of the address space ($0000 to $7FFF) in figures 7.34 and 7.35. As both logical and physical addresses are equivalent and the physical memory space is never switched out (i.e., made inaccessible to the processor), no special programming problems exist. Now suppose a program in one of the eight switchable banks is to be executed.

A jump to the desired program cannot be executed unless that bank is currently selected. Therefore, before the jump is executed, the calling program in the fixed memory must select the appropriate block by loading its value in the bank-selection latch. Note that once the new bank is selected, the old bank is switched out and cannot be accessed without reloading the bank-selection latch. Thus, if a program running in the fixed memory is accessing a data table in one bank and calls a subroutine in another bank, then the data table cannot be accessed from the subroutine.

A particular disadvantage of bank switching is the impossibility of jumping from code in one selectable bank to code in another. If a program is running in bank A and a jump is to be made to bank B, we need to first select bank B and then carry out the jump. However, if the code in bank A modifies the bank-selection latch, bank B will be selected immediately and the JUMP instruction to B will not be executed, as it is in the locked-out bank A. Therefore, the next instruction to be executed will be the instruction in bank B with the same logical address as the JUMP instruction in bank A.

The only way to effect a jump from one bank to another is to jump first to a location within the fixed memory (where LAS = PAS), switch banks, and then jump to the desired location in the new bank. Therefore, programmers must write their programs with this object always in mind. Consequently, bank switching places a considerable burden on the programmer. We shall soon see that other types of memory management lessen this burden, some to a point where memory management becomes totally invisible to the systems programmer.

Bank switching is not difficult to implement and is very cheap. It is useful for systems requiring large data tables that can be switched in as required. Equally, it can be used to implement systems where the operating system software and other utilities (interpreters, editors, word processors) are held in read-only memory. This facility speeds up the system, as the utilities are switched-in rather than loaded from disk. The disadvantage of bank switching is the "granularity" of the blocks switched in and out. Clearly, switching tiny blocks of memory would be hopelessly inefficient, as memory cards populated with large numbers of low-density memory components would be required.

Indexed Mapping

A much better approach to bank switching is called indexed mapping. Instead of performing the bank switching by loading a special latch, the identity of the bank to be selected forms part of the logical address itself; for example, a CPU with a 16-bit address bus may specify a logical address as $XYYY, where X is the 4-bit bank-selection address and $YYY the 12-bit address within a bank. Therefore, the banks can be switched rapidly and a jump from one bank to another becomes possible, as the address part of the JUMP automatically selects the new bank. In what follows, the term *page* will be employed rather than *bank*. I have done this to be consistent with other authors writing on this topic. The words *block, bank, page,* and *chunk* are variously interchangeable and all describe the same thing—a unit of memory space.

Figure 7.36 shows how the p most-significant bits from the CPU's logical address interrogate a table of 2^p locations to determine the current physical memory block. Each of these locations contains a q-bit value ($q > p$), giving the higher-order q bits of the physical address. For example, an 8-bit microprocessor with $p = 4$ provides sixteen pages of 4K bytes. If $q = 8$, the physical memory size is $2^q \times 4K = 256 \times 4K = 1M$ bytes. Once again, we must stress that,

FIGURE 7.36   Address translation by indexed mapping

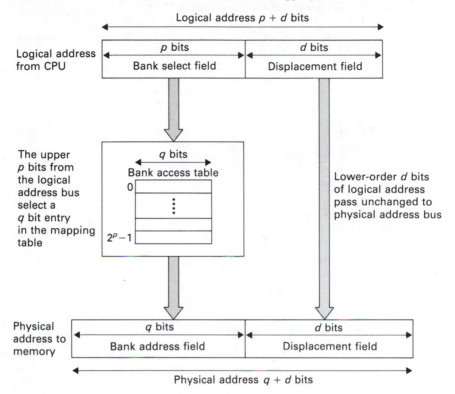

although there are 256 pages of physical memory, only sixteen of these can be accessed at any time, as there are only sixteen entries in the mapping table.

The contents of the mapping table permit sixteen windows to be opened onto the physical memory space. This table is loaded and controlled by the operating system, so that the processor is always *viewing* the 64K bytes of physical memory currently of most interest. Figure 7.37 shows how the logical address space is mapped onto the physical address space. In this example, $p = 4$ and $q = 8$ to give 4K pages with an 8-bit processor. For each of the sixteen 4K pages of logical address space, the page table or mapping registers (the left-hand side of figure 7.37) contain the corresponding page of the physical address space; for example, a logical address $0XXX is mapped onto the physical address $0 0XXX. Similarly, the logical address $4XXX is mapped onto the physical address $1 1XXX.

We must stress that, although the translation of logical addresses into physical addresses is automatically carried out by hardware, the management of the index registers (i.e., translation table) is performed by software—frequently the operating system itself. However, one exception to this rule does exist. At switch-on or following a system reset, part of the processor's logical address space is

FIGURE 7.37   Logical-to-physical address translation; for example, the logical address $A123 is mapped into the physical address $0 2123

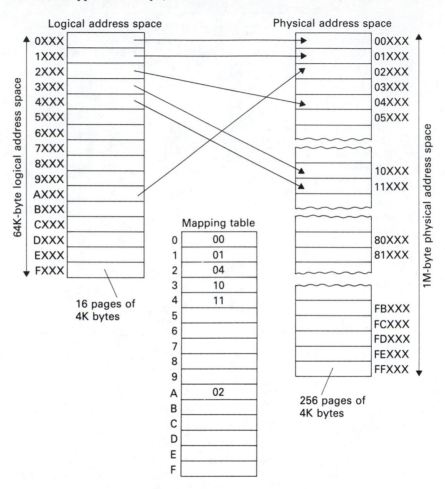

mapped onto a fixed region of the physical address space. We must do this mapping because the state of the address translation table is undefined at switch-on; for example, the logical address range $F000 to $FFFF in a 6809-based microprocessor system may be mapped onto, say, the physical address range $0 0000 through $0 0FFF following the initial application of power. The 6809 stores its reset vector at $FFFE and $FFFF, and the physical address block should contain the initialization routine in ROM to load the operating system from disk and to set up the address mapping table.

The way in which the mapping table is used is relatively simple. If the physical memory is considered to be a treasure house of resources (programs, data structures, text, etc.), the operating system opens windows onto these resources as they are required by any program currently being executed. The only limitation is

FIGURE 7.38   The TI 74LS610 memory mapper. Note that MA_0 to MA_3 (A_{12} to A_{15}) are the four higher-order logical address bits to be mapped into eight (or twelve) higher-order physical address bits. RS_0 to RS_3 (A_0 to A_3) are used to access the mapping table when it is set up to the operating system

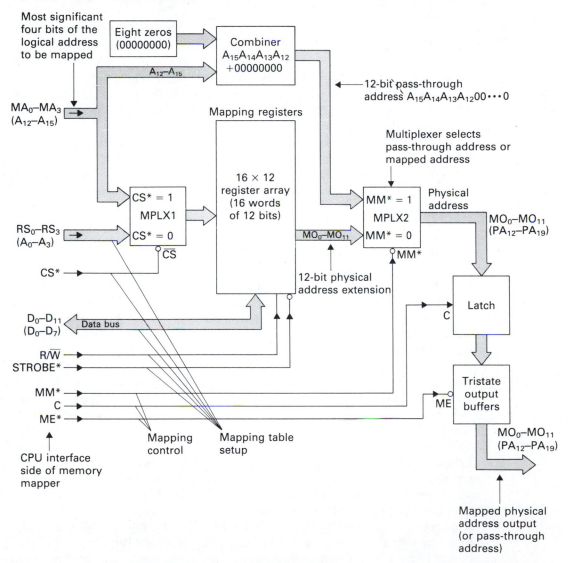

that the processor cannot directly address more than 64K bytes without the operating system switching in new pages (and of course switching out old pages).

An excellent implementation of memory mapping is provided by the TI 74LS610 memory mapper, which is available in a 40-pin DIL package and which translates a 4-bit map address from a processor into a 12-bit address for use by the physical memory. Figure 7.38 provides a block diagram of this device. Two notations have been used in figure 7.38: TI's own terminology and the notation appropriate to an 8-bit microprocessor. The latter notation appears in parentheses; for example, the mapping address input is called MA_0 to MA_3 by TI, but is also labeled (A_{12} to A_{15}), as the mapping is invariably applied to the highest-order four bits of the processor's address bus.

During normal operation of the 74LS610, its CS* input is inactive-high and its MM* (map mode) input is active-low. In this state, the four map address inputs (MA_0 to MA_3) interrogate the 16-word × 12-bit register file to produce a 12-bit map output (MO_0 to MO_{11}). These bits form the twelve higher-order bits of the physical address. Whenever the map mode input, MM*, is high, the four map address inputs are passed through unchanged to the four high-order bits of the map outputs; that is, when MM* = 1 the output is given by MA_3, MA_2, MA_1, MA_0, 0, 0, 0, ..., 0. The pass-through mode is necessary to provide the processor access to its reset vectors, independently of the state of the mapping table.

When CS* is active-low, the 74LS610 becomes a peripheral device and the processor can read or write to its mapping table. To write new data into the table, CS* = 0, $R/\overline{W}$ = 0, and STROBE* = 0. To examine the contents of the table, CS* = 0, $R/\overline{W}$ = 1. The location being examined (one of sixteen) is determined by the state of the four select inputs, RS_0 to RS_3, which are normally wired to the least-significant bits of the processor's address bus.

Finally, the mapped address on MO_0 to MO_{11} can be latched by bringing the C (clock) input low, and the output of the latch is placed on the system physical address bus by asserting the active-low map enable (ME*) input. In many implementations of the 74LS610, C is connected to V_{cc} to transparently pass addresses through the latch, and ME* is connected to ground to permanently enable the tristate outputs.

Figure 7.39 shows how the 74LS610 is employed in a 6809-based microcomputer. A problem arising when the 74LS610 is to be connected to an 8-bit processor is the arrangement of the mapper's 12-bit data bus. There are two solutions. One is to execute two write cycles, the first to an external 4-bit latch to hold, say, D_8 to D_{11}, and the second to the mapper to transfer D_0 to D_7 from the CPU together with D_8 to D_{11} from the latch. Such an approach requires a handful of chips to interface the mapper's data bus to the 6809's data bus. Alternatively, if only eight bits of physical address extension are required, the extra four bits of the mapper's data bus can be forgotten. The latter approach is taken in figure 7.39, where D_0 to D_3 of the mapper's input are not used and D_4 to D_{11} of the mapper are connected to D_0 to D_7 from the CPU. Similarly, bits MO_0 to MO_3 of the map output are not used and MO_4 to MO_{11} form bits PA_{12} to PA_{19} of the physical address bus. The reason for this mode of connection will become clear later.

In normal operation, CS* = 1 and MM* = 0, with the result that address bits A_{12} to A_{15} from the 6809 are transformed directly by the mapper into physical address bits PA_{12} to PA_{19} to give a 1M-byte physical address space and logical/physical page sizes of 4K bytes. Logical address lines A_0 to A_{11} from the CPU become physical address lines PA_0 to PA_{11}.

FIGURE 7.39   Using the 74LS610 with a 6809 8-bit CPU

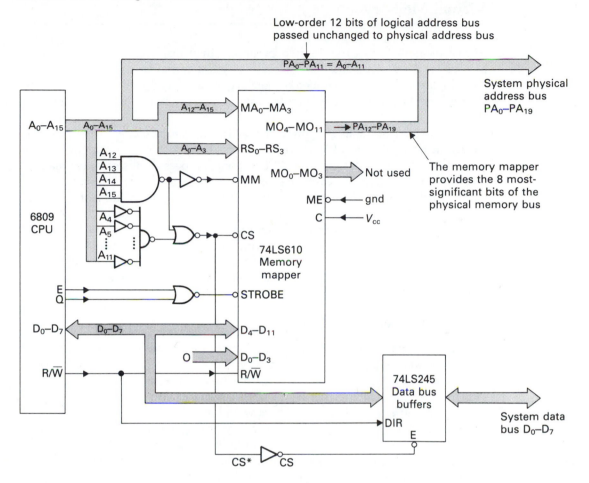

Whenever the processor generates a logical address in the range $F000 to $FFFF, the output of the NAND gate goes low, forcing MM* high. Now the mapper goes into its pass-through mode and MA_0 to MA_3 are passed on to MO_8 to MO_{11} while MO_0 to MO_7 are set to a logical zero. In the arrangement of figure 7.39, a logical address in the range $F000 to $FFFF is mapped into a physical address in the range $F 0000 to $F 0FFF.

The 74LS610 itself is memory mapped in the 16-byte logical address range $F000 to $F00F. Any CPU read/write accesses in this range accesses the mapping table. Note that this range also overlaps 16 bytes of the pass-through address range. Consequently, the pass-through memory must either be disabled when the mapper is accessed or the system's data bus buffers disabled as shown in figure 7.39.

Virtual Memory

Virtual memory systems serve two purposes: they map logical addresses onto physical address space and they allocate physical memory to tasks running in logical address space. Virtual memory techniques are found in systems where the physical memory space is less than the logical memory space and in multitasking systems.

We would be foolish to pretend that justice can be done to the topic of virtual memory in a text of this size and at this level. While reasonable to expect readers to be able to design a 68000-based microprocessor system after reading this book, it would be unreasonable to expect them to design a 68000 system with virtual memory. Quite simply, virtual memory systems are not one-man efforts. They are designed by teams and require many man-hours to produce, because the management of virtual memory is not only rather complex but is also found almost exclusively in systems with multiuser or multitasking operating systems. Therefore, only an overview of virtual memory and microprocessors is given here, together with a brief description of the MC68451 memory management unit (MMU).

Memory Management and Tasks

In chapter 6 we introduced the idea of multitasking systems that execute a number of *tasks* or *processes* concurrently by periodically switching between tasks. Clearly, multitasking is viable only if several tasks reside in main memory at the same time. If this condition were not so, the time required to transfer an "old" task to disk and to swap in a "new" task would be prohibitive.

Figure 7.40 demonstrates how memory management is applied to multitasking. Two tasks, A and B, are in physical memory at the same time. The left-hand side of figure 7.40 shows how the tasks are arranged in logical address space. Each task has its *own* logical memory space (e.g., program and stack) but accesses *shared* resources lying in physical memory space. Programmers are entirely free to choose their own addresses for the various components of their tasks; that is, task A and task B can each access the same data structure in physical memory, even though they use different logical addresses.

A memory management unit maps the logical addresses chosen by the programmer onto the physical memory space. As we shall see, any logical address generated by the CPU is automatically mapped to the appropriate physical address by the MMU. Note that the operating system is responsible for setting up the logical-to-physical mapping tables, which is a very complex process and is well beyond the scope of this text. Basically, whenever a new task is created, the operating system is informed of the task's memory requirements. The operating system then searches the available physical memory space for free memory blocks and allocates these to the task. Therefore, after a time, the physical memory space may become very fragmented, with the segments belonging to each task interwoven in a complex pattern. A good operating system attempts to perform

FIGURE 7.40 Mapping logical address space onto physical address space in a multitasking environment

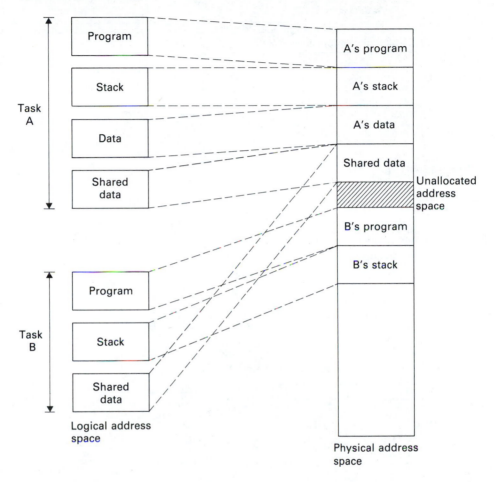

memory allocation efficiently and should leave the minimum number of unused blocks of physical memory.

A powerful feature of memory mapping is that each logical memory segment can be associated with various "permissions;" for example, memory can be made read-only, write-only, accessible only by the operating system or by a given task, or shared between a group of tasks. Without this facility, nothing would be available to stop one task from corrupting the memory space belonging to another task.

Address Translation

In a virtual memory system, where the logical address space is greater than the available physical address space, the processor may possibly generate a logical

FIGURE 7.41 Page table and virtual memory

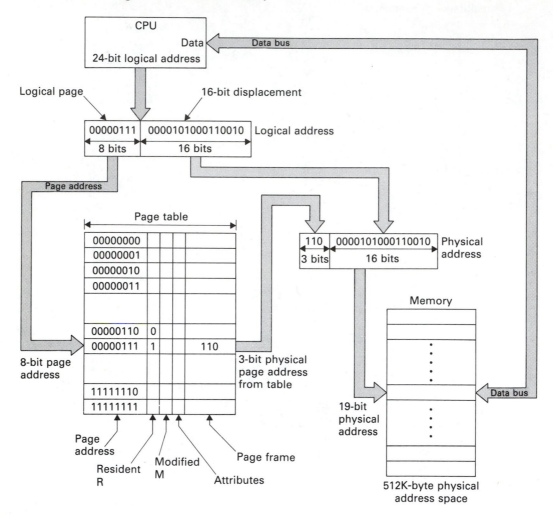

address for which no actual physical memory exists. Therefore, the virtual memory management unit must perform two distinct functions. The first is to map logical addresses onto the available physical memory and the second is to deal with the situation arising when the physical address space "runs out." Figure 7.41 shows how the first objective is achieved.

Although memory mapping and virtual memory are inverse operations, the diagram of figure 7.41 is remarkably similar to the memory mapping arrangement of figure 7.36. The 24-bit logical address from the processor is split into a 16-bit displacement, which is passed directly to the physical memory, and an 8-bit page address. The page address specifies the page (one of $2^8 = 256$) currently accessed by the processor.

The page table (compare it with the index mapping table) contains 256 entries, one for each logical page; for example, in figure 7.41 the 8-bit logical page address is 00000111. In each entry of the table is a 3-bit page frame address that provides the three most-significant bits of the physical address. In this case, the page frame is 110. Notice how the logical address has been condensed from $8 + 16$ bits to $3 + 16$ bits. Therefore, the logical address 0000011100001010000110010 is mapped onto the physical address 1100000101000110010.

Although 256 entries are in the page frame table, the page frame address is only 3 bits, limiting the number of physical pages to eight. Consequently, a unique page frame cannot be associated with each logical page number. Each page address has a single-bit R-field labeled *resident* associated with it. If the R bit is set, that page frame is currently in physical memory. If the R bit is clear, the corresponding page frame is not in the physical memory and the contents of the page frame field are meaningless.

Whenever a logical address is generated and the R bit found to be clear, an event called a *page fault* occurs. At this point the fun begins. Once a memory access is started that attempts to access a logical address whose page is not in memory (the R bit is found to be clear), the operating system suspends the current instruction as it cannot be completed. Typically, the BERR* input of a 68000 or a 68010 is asserted to indicate a bus fault.

Now the operating system must intervene to deal with the situation. Although the information accessed was not in the random access physical memory, it will be located in the disk store, which is normally a hard disk drive. The operating system retrieves the page containing the desired memory location from disk, loads it in the physical memory, and updates the page table accordingly. The suspended instruction can then be executed.

This procedure is simple, isn't it? Well, it is not entirely simple. When the operating system fetches a new page, it must overwrite a page of physical memory. Remember that one of the purposes of virtual memory is to permit relatively small physical memories to simulate large memories. A strategy is required to deal with the replacement of "old" pages by "new" ones. The classic paging policy is called the least recently used (LRU) algorithm. The page that has not been accessed for the longest period of time is overwritten by the new page. The LRU algorithm has been found to work well in practice. However, notice that the operating system must know when each page is accessed if this algorithm is to work. Another problem that the operating system has to deal with is the divergence between the data stored in RAM and the data held on disk. If the page fetched from disk contains only program information, it will not be modified in RAM and therefore overwriting it causes no problems. If, however, the page is a data table or some other data structure, it may be written to while it is in RAM. In this case, the page cannot just be overwritten by the new page.

In figure 7.41 we can see that each entry in the table has an M (modified) bit. Whenever that page is accessed by a write operation, the M bit is set. When this page is to be overwritten the operating system checks the M bit and, if set, it first rewrites this page to the disk store before fetching the new page.

Finally, when the new page has been loaded, the address translation table updated, the M bit cleared, and the R bit set, the processor can rerun the instruction that was suspended. Unfortunately, the 68000 does not store enough information following the assertion of BERR* (caused by a page fault) to rerun the suspended instruction. However, the 68010 has been introduced to deal with this situation. The 68010 is nominally identical to the 68000 but has features to allow it to fully recover from a bus error. Therefore, the stack frame saved after a bus error exception must be increased from 7 words (68000) to 26 words.

From the preceding description, we can see that the amount of effort involved every time a page fault occurs is rather large. As long as page faults are relatively infrequent, the system works well because of a phenomenon called *locality of reference*. Most data is clustered so that once a page (or even a group of pages) is brought from disk, the majority of memory accesses will be found within these pages. When the data is not well ordered or when there are many unrelated tasks, the processor ends up by spending nearly all its time swapping pages in and out and the system effectively grinds to a halt. This situation is called *thrashing*.

The MC68451 Memory Management Unit

The MC68451 MMU (referred to in this section as the MMU) is primarily intended to manage memory resources in multitasking systems. It also provides virtual memory support. Any virtual memory system using the MMU should also have a 68010 CPU, as the 68000 is not really capable of resuming processing after a bus error.

Like many of today's special-purpose peripherals, the MC68451 is an exceedingly complex beast and the space devoted to it here can do little other than to give an insight into its operation. Having digested this section, the reader should then be in a position to tackle its data sheet.

The MMU has 32 address translation registers, permitting up to 32 pages of logical memory to be mapped onto physical memory. Unlike the schemes described so far in this chapter, these pages are of a user-definable size and extend from a minimum of 256 bytes to a maximum of 16M bytes, in powers of two. Note that page sizes may be mixed, so that a single MMU can support pages of 256 bytes and of, say, 2M bytes simultaneously. Page sizes varying by powers of two are required to implement *the binary buddy algorithm*, which is used to allocate memory space to tasks. The MC68451 data sheet employs the term *segment* to describe pages, and this term is used throughout this section on the MMU. The MMU operates in a stand-alone mode, or up to eight MMUs can be operated in parallel to provide a maximum of $8 \times 32 = 256$ segments. Some people feel that this number is too low for today's sophisticated multitasking systems. Here, only single-MMU systems are described.

Address Mapping and the 68451 MMU

A highly simplified block diagram of the heart of the 68451 MMU is given in figure 7.42. The MMU maintains a table of 32 descriptor registers, each made up of 72 bits. Descriptor registers provide all the information needed to map a logical address within a segment onto its physical address. Each descriptor is composed of the six fields shown in figure 7.42. Three fields are 16 bits wide and perform the actual logical-to-physical address translation and three are 8 bits wide and are devoted to the control of the mapping process.

The first major difference between the 68451 MMU and the type of memory-mapping scheme described earlier (see figure 7.41) lies in the selection of the segment descriptors. In figure 7.41, the page table contains an entry for each possible logical address segment; that is, the higher-order bits of the logical address interrogate the appropriate entry in the mapping table, look up the corresponding page frame, and access the required information (i.e., the segment descriptor). The MMU employs an associative addressing technique to interrogate the table of 32 descriptors. The higher-order logical address bits from the processor and the function code are fed to each of the 32 descriptors *simultaneously*. Any descriptor that matches (i.e., is associated with) the current logical address takes part in the address translation process. If no descriptor indicates a match, the

FIGURE 7.42   Simplified view of part of the 68451 MMU address translation mechanism

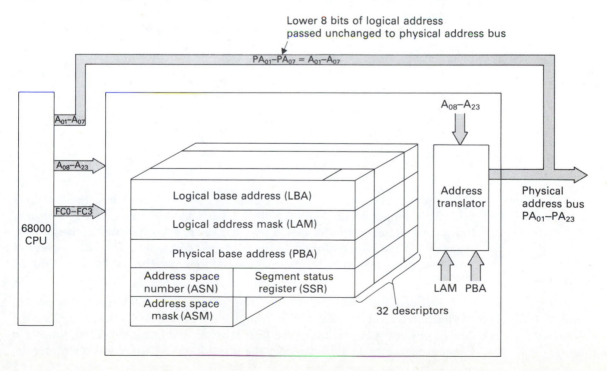

MMU signals a page fault. The MMU does this by asserting its FAULT* output, which is connected to the 68000's BERR* input.

An associative memory technique is necessary to match the logical page (segment) address with available descriptors, because the MMU's segments (page frames) can be as small as 256 bytes. If an MMU had a descriptor for each of the possible segments, the mapping table would contain not 32 but 65,536 entries!

In order to understand how the address translation process operates, we need to define the function of the three 16-bit descriptor registers. These registers are the logical base address (LBA), the logical address mask (LAM), and the physical base address (PBA).

Logical base address (LBA)   The contents of the LBA provide the most-significant bits of the logical segment address, which corresponds to the logical page number. In order to provide a variable segment size, we can mask out some of the bits in the LBA and reduce the effective size of the LBA register from 16 bits to between 1 and 15 bits. This action is carried out by the logical address mask.

Logical address mask (LAM)   The LAM is a 16-bit mask that defines the bit positions in the LBA to be used in the definition of the size of a logical segment. A logical one in the LAM defines the corresponding bit position in the LBA as taking part in the segment logical address. A logical zero in the LAM means that the corresponding bit position in the LBA does not take part in the segment logical address. An example should make the relationship between LBA and LAM clear. Suppose that the size of a logical segment starting at address \$04 0000 is 4K bytes and the LAM contains the value \$FFF0. The contents of the LBA and LAM are:

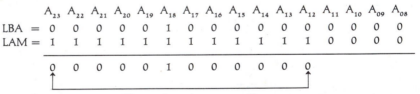

Effective logical segment address

Thus, the LAM converts the 16-bit logical base address field into a 12-bit address field. Only logical address bits A_{12} to A_{23} from the CPU take part in matching this logical address segment. Bits A_{01} to A_{11} select a location within the 4K-byte segment and are passed directly to the physical address bus. The LBA register of this descriptor responds to any logical address in the range \$04 0000 to \$04 0FFF.

Physical base address (PBA)   The PBA is a 16-bit address that is used in conjunction with the logical address from the 68000 and the LAM to calculate the desired physical address. Just as the LBA provides the first address (i.e., lowest) in a logical segment, the PBA provides the first address in a physical segment—the desired physical address. The logical address bits corrresponding to zeros in the LAM are passed directly through the MMU to become physical address bits (together with A_{01} to A_{07}). Where a bit of the LAM is a logical one, the corresponding bit of the PBA register is passed to the physical address bus. In other words, the PBA of a descriptor supplies the higher-order bits of its physical address.

Continuing the example above, suppose that the contents of the PBA register in the segment descriptor are 0001 1000 0011 0000 (i.e., $1830). If a logical address $04 0123 is generated by the processor, what is the corresponding physical address?

As this logical address falls in the range determined by the LBA and LAM, the descriptor responds by calculating the physical address. The LAM register also masks the PBA so that the twelve most-significant bits of the PBA form the corresponding physical address bits (i.e., 0001 1000 0011). The remaining 4 bits of the 16-bit higher-order logical address (i.e., 0001) are passed unchanged to the physical address bus. Finally, logical address bits A_{00} to A_{07} do not take part in the mapping process and are transferred directly to the physical address bus. Therefore, the final physical address is

$$0001 \quad 1000 \quad 0011 \quad 0001 \quad 0010 \quad 0011 \quad \text{or} \quad \$18\ 3123.$$

At this point the reader may feel a little unhappy because the logical address range and the physical address range of the MMU are *both* 16M bytes! What happened to the problem of the physical address space being less than the logical address space? The answer is that the 68451 MMU is a very general purpose device and can perform memory management, if called upon, over a physical memory space of 16M bytes. However, the user of the MMU may populate this physical address space with, say, only 256K bytes of memory. The programmer (in practice, the operating system) is then responsible for making sure that the segment descriptors map the logical address space of the programs and their data onto this 256K bytes of physical address space.

Address Space Matching

Up to now we have implied that the 68451 MMU automatically carries out its logical-to-physical address translation process using nothing more than the logical address from the CPU and information stored in the descriptor registers. In fact, an important step in the translation process has been omitted.

Basically speaking, each logical address segment is associated with an address space *type*. If the processor is not currently addressing the correct type of address space, the MMU does not permit an address translation even though the current logical segment is defined by one of the 32 descriptors.

Whenever the 68000 CPU accesses memory, it puts out a function code on FC0 to FC2 to indicate the type of access that is being carried out. Table 4.3 in chapter 4 illustrates the relationship between the function code and type of bus cycle in progress. These function codes can easily be viewed as pointing to different types of address space; for example, when FC2, FC1, FC0 = 0, 0, 1 the processor is accessing *user data space* and when FC1, FC1, FC0 = 1, 1, 0 it is accessing *supervisor program space*. We can regard the function code as an extension of the address bus. Just as A_{23} divides memory space into an upper and a lower 8M-byte page, the function code divides memory space into a 16M-byte supervisor data space, a 16M-byte supervisor instruction space, etc. The 68000 can therefore be said to have an effective address space of $4 \times 16 = 64M$ bytes, because the MMU recognizes sixteen types of address space (not eight!).

The MMU has four function code inputs, FC0 to FC3. Three of these inputs are derived directly from the 68000 CPU and the fourth (FC3) is normally derived from BGACK* via an inverter. By using BGACK* as a pseudo function code input to the MMU, we are able to define a set of eight address spaces associated with DMA operations or with other processors. The MMU maintains an address space table (AST), as illustrated in figure 7.43. For each of the sixteen possible combinations of FC0 to FC3, there is an 8-bit entry in the AST that is assigned a cycle address space number (CASN) by the programmer (or operating system). The CASN corresponds to a task number; for example, when the processor accesses user data space, the task number (i.e., CASN) may be 0000 0011 ($03), and when the processor accesses user program space, the task number may be

FIGURE 7.43   Address space matching

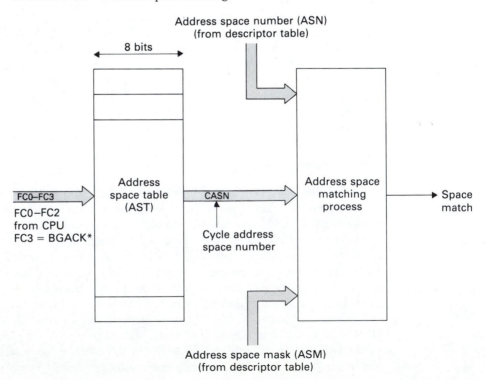

0000 0010 ($02). Remember that the sixteen entries (CASNs) in the AST are loaded into the MMU by the programmer and are not determined by the MMU itself. Thus, for every memory access, a cycle address space number is calculated by the MMU, depending on the type of address space being accessed.

The function code is used to obtain a cycle address space number (CASN) from the address space table (AST). The CASN is used together with the address space number (ASN) and the address space mask (ASM) from the descriptor table to generate a space match signal. If space match is not asserted then no logical segment matching the current cycle address space number has been found.

Having calculated a CASN, the next step is to use it in the address translation process. Each of the 32 segment descriptors in figure 7.42 contains an 8-bit address space number (ASN) field, which associates that segment with a particular ASN and therefore with a particular task. A task is said to comprise all the logical segments with the same ASN. In other words, at any instant the value of FC0 to FC3 from the CPU looks up the current cycle address space number in the address space table. This value of CASN is then matched with the descriptor selected by the logical address being put out by the CPU. If the ASN in the descriptor does not correspond to the CASN from the AST, no match occurs and the MMU asserts its FAULT* output.

Note that each segment descriptor also has an address space mask (ASM) field. The ASM is used to determine which bits of the segment's ASN should be masked with the value from the address space table produced during the current cycle. The purpose is to permit address spaces to be shared between several tasks.

To clarify the purpose of the address space table and the ASN, we must consider the multitasking environment. Suppose task A is being executed. Let task A be a user task and let the entries in the AST corresponding to user data and user program space both be $01. Assume that all segment descriptors have their ASMs equal to 11111111 ($FF), so that all bits of the ASN from the descriptor must match those from the AST. A descriptor whose ASN is $01 will be used in the address translation process, assuming the processor is currently addressing its logical address range. If the segment has the correct logical address range but its ASN does not match the CASN from the AST, no address translation takes place and the MMU asserts its FAULT* output.

At any time, only one task number can be associated with each of the sixteen different types of address space. Therefore, the MMU may, theoretically, support up to sixteen tasks simultaneously. However, as the various combinations of FC0 to FC2 from the CPU define only five address spaces implemented by the 68000 (and one is only for interrupt acknowledgment), the address spaces of greatest interest to the systems designer are user and supervisor address space and program and data address space. Consequently, in a practical system, an MMU may support two tasks: the supervisor task (i.e., operating system) and the user task. The operating system is able to rapidly switch between several user tasks simply by modifying the values in the user address spaces of the AST; for example, if user task A has an ASN of $01 and user task B an ASN of $02, just loading $01 or $02 in the FC3, FC2, FC1, FC0 = 0, 0, 0, 1 and 0, 0, 1, 0 entries of the AST selects the appropriate task. Moreover, because only those segment descriptors whose own address space numbers (masked by the ASM) match CASN from the AST in the current bus cycle, several user tasks sharing the *same* logical address space are possible.

Segment Status Register (SSR)

Each descriptor has an eight-bit segment status register that provides additional information about the nature of the segment. Currently, six bits of the SSR have defined meanings. Brief descriptions of these bits follow. In all but one case, the term *reset* means a reset to segment 0 of the master MMU. The meaning of this term will be made clear when we discuss initializing the MMU.

U (used)   The U bit is set if the segment has been accessed since it was defined. It is cleared by a reset or by writing a zero into this bit. The operating system may read the U bit to determine whether the segment is currently active.

I (interrupt)   The I bit is set (or cleared) under program control and, when set, forces an interrupt whenever the segment is accessed. This bit can be used as an aid to debugging. It is also cleared by a reset.

IP (interrupt pending)   The IP bit is set if the I bit is set when the segment is accessed. This bit indicates that the associated segment was the source of the MMU's interrupt request. It is cleared under software control, by a reset, or when the segment's E bit is clear.

M (modified)   The M bit is set by the MMU if the segment has been written to since it was defined. If a segment is to be swapped out of physical memory, the old segment must be saved if the M bit is set. If the M bit is clear, the segment can be overwritten. The M bit is cleared under software control or by a reset.

WP (write protect)   The WP bit is set by the operating system to write-protect the segment. Once the WP bit has been set, any attempt to write to the logical address space spanned by the segment will cause a write violation and the assertion of the MMU's FAULT* output. The WP bit is cleared under software control or by a reset.

E (enable)   The E bit, when set under software control, enables the segment to take part in the address translation process. In other words, setting E = 1 activates the segment and setting E = 0 turns off the segment. The function of the E bit is to remove any segment descriptors from the pool of 32, until they are actively engaged in the address translation process. The E bit is cleared by software or by an unsuccessful load descriptor register operation. The bit is *not* cleared by a reset.

In addition to the 32 descriptors and the 16-entry address space table, the MMU has a set of six 8-bit registers and a temporary descriptor. The registers perform various functions from providing interrupt vectors to storing global status information. The temporary descriptor has the same structure as other descriptors and can be loaded with data from the system bus. This data is then transferred to any of the 32 descriptors selected by the programmer.

Operating the 68451 MMU

As stated earlier, the precise operational details of the MMU are rather complex and readers must refer to its data sheet if they want to use this component. Here only the details of most interest are given. In particular, the application of the 68451 in multiple-MMU systems is not considered.

Figure 7.44 shows how the MMU is connected between a 68000 processor and the system's physical address bus. Note that the MMU itself is address mapped onto the PAB (physical address bus) and not the logical address bus, because its active-low chip-select input is derived from PA_{01} to PA_{23}. Due to the limitations of chip packaging, the MMU cannot support a separate data bus (it already has 64 pins) and therefore its data input, D_{00} to D_{15}, from the CPU is

FIGURE 7.44   Connecting the 68451 MMU to a 68000 CPU

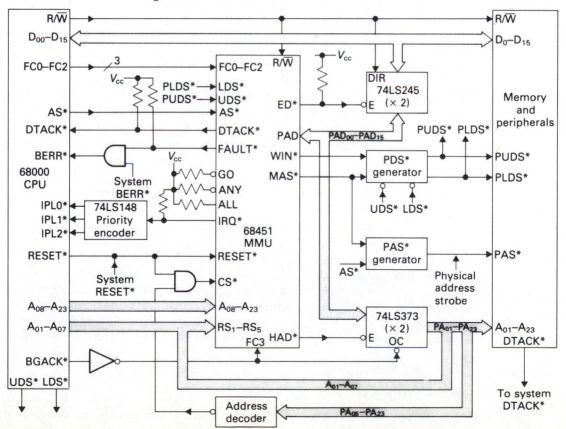

multiplexed onto its address outputs, PAD_0 to PAD_{15}. Support circuitry is therefore required to multiplex the address and to latch the data from D_{00} to D_{15}. Two outputs from the MMU, ED*, and HAD*, control the data and address buses.

The hold address (HAD*) output controls the external latches on the address bus. HAD* is asserted by the MMU to hold the physical address stable in the latches. The enable data (ED*) output controls the data transceivers between the 68000 data bus and the MMU. When ED* is asserted, the data transceivers are enabled and drive the data bus. The MMU asserts ED* only during a read/write access to it or during an IACK* cycle.

The MMU communicates with a 68000 CPU using the conventional AS*, UDS*, LDS*, and DTACK* signals. The mapped address strobe (MAS*) output from the MMU is used to generate mapped data strobes for the system memory. Although AS* is asserted early in a read cycle by the CPU, MAS* cannot be asserted by the MMU until the address translation process has taken place. Adding an MMU to a system creates a rather severe penalty in terms of the memory cycle time. A memory cycle is extended from 8 to 12 cycles.

The MMU has three control signals that enable it to communicate with other MMUs; these are global operation (GO*), any (ANY*), and all (ALL). In single-MMU applications, these signals should be pulled up to V_{cc} by a resistor. One MMU must always be designated the master MMU by arranging its CPU interface so that *both* RESET* and CS* are asserted *simultaneously*. Nonmaster MMUs are reset in the normal way by asserting their RESET* inputs alone. Even in single-MMU systems, RESET* and CS* must be asserted simultaneously.

When a master MMU is reset, segment zero has zero loaded into its logical address mask (LAM), its ASN is loaded with zero, its ASM is loaded with $FF, and its E bit is enabled. The sixteen entries in the AST are cleared to zero and all segments other than zero are disabled by clearing their E bits. Because of these actions, all logical addresses from the 68000 are passed unchanged to the physical address bus following a reset, which gives the operating system an opportunity to set up the MMU by loading the descriptors. Each descriptor is loaded by copying the information into the temporary descriptor and then transferring the information to the appropriate descriptor.

Switching from one task to another is called context switching and is performed by the operating system running in the supervisor state. The operating system changes the first two entries in the AST (AST1 = user data space, AST2 = user program space) to the ASN of the new task to be run. The new values of the program counter and status register (obtained from the new task's TCB) are pushed onto the supervisor stack. When an RTE is executed, the new task runs. Context switching is the same as *task switching* described in chapter 6, except that the task number in the AST is also changed each time a new task is run.

Summary

In this chapter we have looked at some topics of interest to the designer of sophisticated microprocessor systems. Bus arbitration control is necessary in systems with two or more bus masters. The 68000 is well suited to multimaster systems because of its three bus arbitration control signals which make it possible for a potential bus master to request the bus and for the 68000 to relinquish the bus in an orderly manner.

One of the most significant features of today's general-purpose microcomputers is their very large memories. We have examined the characteristics of the dynamic RAM and demonstrated that it is not as difficult to use as its data sheets sometimes suggest. Because DRAM must be refreshed periodically, the designer of DRAM memory arrays must decide whether to interleave refresh cycles with normal memory accesses or whether to use the 68000's bus arbitration control signals to request the bus and then perform a burst of refresh cycles.

Powerful microcomputers with large memories often use memory management techniques to map logical addresses onto physical addresses. We have briefly examined the 68451 memory management unit which carries out the logical-to-physical address translation and which allows the operating system to associate blocks of memory with particular tasks.

Problems

1. The minimum number of bus arbitration lines required to implement a multiprocessor system is two (BR* and BG*). Why does the 68000 have an additional BGACK* line and what are the advantages of a three-line bus control protocol over a two-line protocol?

2. Design an error-logging system for an error-detecting and -correcting memory. Whenever an error is detected, a low priority interrupt is generated by the error-detection circuit and the operating system then makes a note of the location of the word in error and of the bit in error. Running statistics of error locations are recorded so that systematic errors can be located and the faulty chip replaced. Design the hardware and software needed to carry out this function.

3. The following 7,3 Hamming-coded words are read from memory. Each code word is constructed according to table 7.6 and the standard Hamming code. Which codes are in error and what should the correct data word be? The words are written in the order: I_4, I_3, I_2, I_1, C_3, C_2, C_1.

a.	0	0	0	0	0	0	0
b.	1	1	1	1	1	1	1
c.	1	0	1	1	1	1	1
d.	1	0	1	0	0	1	0
e.	1	0	1	0	0	1	1

4. A 68451 MMU has three descriptors in use. The contents of these descriptors (LBA, LAM, PBA) are now given. Using the information presented, draw an address map that illustrates the logical-to-physical address translation process.

LBA_1 = $00 0000	LAM_1 = $FF F000	PBA_1 = $00 0000
LBA_2 = $00 1000	LAM_2 = $FF FF00	PBA_2 = $FF F000
LBA_3 = $30 0000	LAM_3 = $F0 0000	PBA_3 = $10 0000
LBA_4 = $70 0000	LAM_4 = $FF F000	PBA_4 = $F0 0000

5.   Design a simple memory management system for a 68000 system without using a 68541 MMU. The logical memory space is to be divided up into 8,192 (i.e., 2^{13}) pages of 1K words by mapping the high-order logical address bits A_{11} to A_{23} into physical address bits PA_{11} to PA_{23}. Address bits A_{01} to A_{10} from the 68000 are passed unchanged to become PA_{01} to PA_{10}. All segments are of fixed size.

The mapping is to be performed by two 8K × 8-bit static RAMs operated as a look-up table. These RAMs are connected in parallel so that an 8-bit logical address yields 16 bits from memory. Eight bits form the desired physical address. The other 8 bits can be used to provide the M bit, E bit, etc.

Design the circuitry required to support this arrangement, paying attention to the way in which the mapping RAM is loaded and to the reset function. (Following a reset the operating system must be able to set up the table.) Calculate the overhead in terms of access time if the mapping RAM has an access time of 100 ns, the main memory has an access time of 200 ns, and the 68000 runs at 8 MHz.

Chapter 8

The Microprocessor

Interface

All microcomputers must be able to transfer information between themselves and an external system. The external system can vary from a CRT terminal to the valves and temperature or pressure sensors in an oil refinery. The three topics of greatest interest in this chapter are the microprocessor interface, the direct memory access interface controller (DMAC), which is able to control data transfers between a memory and a peripheral automatically, and the 68230 parallel interface and timer, which is a very versatile 8- or 16-bit parallel port. The term *parallel* indicates that the interface is able to input or output a byte or a word in one single operation. Chapter 9 examines interfaces that transfer information between computers and peripherals serially, one bit at a time.

8.1 Introduction to Microprocessor Interfaces

One of the greatest design limitations placed on the microprocessor, or on any other chip of similar complexity, is the number of connections between the chip and an external system. The 68000 requires 43 of its 64 pins just to communicate with memory. If the 68000 were to have a dedicated I/O interface, either a larger package would be required or some of the CPU's other features would have to be abandoned.

Fortunately, microprocessors do not require a dedicated I/O interface. The existing address, data, and control buses can handle I/O transactions as if they were normal memory accesses. This approach is called *memory-mapped input/output* and requires no overhead in the way of hardware or software (i.e., special I/O instructions).

Modest penalties have to be paid for the use of memory-mapped I/O. All data transfers must be of the same width as a normal memory access. More importantly, some of the address space must be dedicated to I/O space. This fact may be important where 8-bit microprocessors with their limited 64K-byte address spaces are concerned. Locating I/O space within memory space also runs the risk of errors due to spurious accesses to peripheral space. Imagine the effect of accidentally writing to the control register of a memory-mapped disk controller. Yet another disadvantage of memory-mapped I/O is the lack of the special-purpose I/O signals needed to control the operation of an external peripheral.

The 68000 has such a large memory space that the loss of a few bytes to I/O space is unimportant. The lack of special I/O control lines has been dealt with by locating I/O control functions within the I/O ports, rather than in the CPU itself. We shall soon see how a typical parallel I/O port, the 68230 PI/T, implements these control functions.

Figure 8.1 illustrates the essential components of a typical memory-mapped I/O system. The I/O port is the interface between the CPU and the actual peripheral hardware. Really sophisticated ports, like disk controllers, are microcomputers in their own right. The host CPU communicates with such a port by transmitting commands along with I/O data.

Electrical Interface

Within the microcomputer, all well-behaved digital signals fall either below V_{OL} or above V_{OH}. When signals venture out of the CPU, they may be forced to abandon TTL levels and to conform with the signal levels in the peripheral equipment. Figure 8.2 illustrates the electrical interface between the interface port connected to the CPU and the external system proper.

One of the simplest input circuits is the switch of figure 8.3a. A switch connects a signal line to V_{cc} (through a pull-up resistor) or to ground. The switch may be a conventional device, a reed relay, a pressure switch, or a limit sensor. Mechanical switches suffer from bounce—the contacts do not make a clean connection, but bounce for a few milliseconds. To avoid spurious signals from a switch, a simple debounce circuit can be constructed from two cross-coupled NAND gates.

Sometimes the input is already in a binary form but is not TTL compatible. An example of this situation is given in Chapter 9 where the two-level signals found on serial interfaces are described. These signals are typically -12 V or $+12$ V. In such circumstances, a level translator (figure 8.3b) is needed to convert the input signal to a TTL-level signal.

Often the signals in the equipment to be connected to the computer are in analog form and have an infinite number of values within a specified range; for example, a pressure transducer produces an output of from 9 to 12 V as the air pressure varies from 0 to 16 lb/in². In this case an analog-to-digital converter,

FIGURE 8.1   Essential components of a memory-mapped I/O port

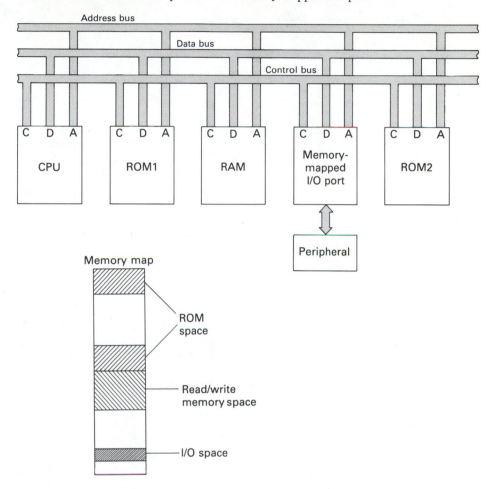

FIGURE 8.2   Microprocessor interfaces

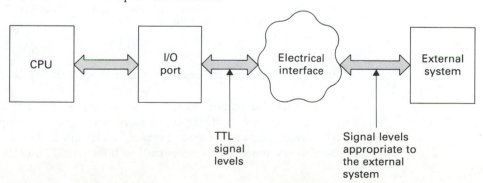

FIGURE 8.3   Examples of electrical interfaces—the input circuit

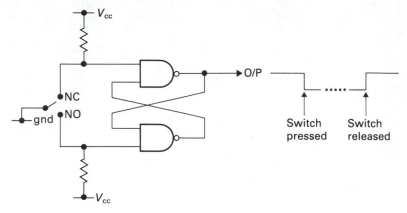

(a) Electrical interface to switch (debounced by RS flip-flop)

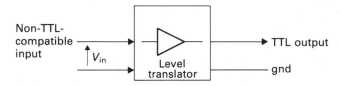

(b) Electrical interface between two-level non-TTL-compatible signal input and CPU input port

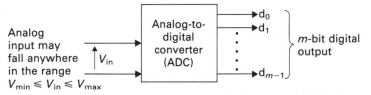

(c) Electrical interface between an infinitely variable input and a quantized 2^m-level output represented as an m-bit value (normally at TTL levels)

ADC, is needed to transform the analog signal into an m-bit digital representation (figure 8.3c).

Consider now the output from a port. A TTL-level signal may control a relay as shown in figure 8.4a. This permits low-level signals in a digital system to switch high power loads in external systems. Although a TTL-level signal can operate some relays directly, it is more usual to buffer the TTL output from a port

FIGURE 8.4 Examples of electrical interfaces—the output circuit

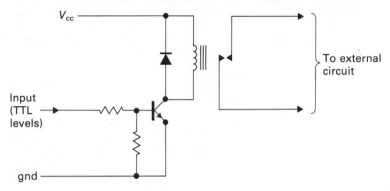

(a) The TTL input energizes a relay and closes a switch

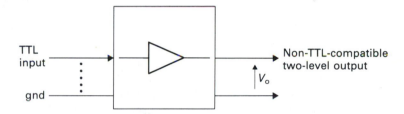

(b) A two-level TTL input is converted into a two-level non-TTL-compatible output

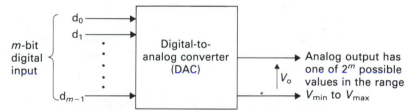

(c) An m-bit TTL-compatible input is converted to a 2^m-level analog signal

as shown. When the output is a logical zero, the transistor is in the off-state and the relay is not energized. When the output is in a logical one state, the transistor is turned on, the relay energized, and the switch closed. The switch may control an external system.

If the external circuit requires a two-level non-TTL signal, a level translator can be used as in figure 8.4b. Similarly, analog signals can be created by a digital-to-analog converter (figure 8.4c). The treatment of input/output circuits is beyond the scope of this text and is generally found in texts on "instrumentation and control." Here, we are more interested in the digital interface between the 68000 and the external system.

The 68000 Synchronous Interface

In chapter 4 we introduced the 68000's asynchronous bus, by which the CPU communicates with memory. It is perfectly possible to use this bus to communicate with memory-mapped peripherals. All we need is a peripheral that "looks like" a memory component, as far as the 68000 is concerned.

In the dark ages before the dawn of the 68000, we had the 6800 8-bit microprocessor and its 6800-series peripherals, such as the 6850 ACIA, the 6821 PIA, and the 68488 IEEE bus interface. All these peripherals interface easily to a 6800 bus through its synchronous interface. Unfortunately, they cannot be interfaced to the 68000's asynchronous bus directly. To permit designers to use the low-cost, tried, and tested 6800-series peripherals, the 68000 has been provided with three synchronous bus control signals—VPA*, VMA*, and E.

In order to understand why 6800-series peripherals cannot be used with the asynchronous bus, we must look at the timing diagram of one of these devices. Figure 8.5 gives the read and write cycle timing diagrams of the 6850 ACIA. Note that the timing parameters of its address inputs (i.e., RS = register select), its chip select, and its R/$\overline{W}$ input are all specified with respect to an enable clock input.

Microcomputers based on the 6800, 6809, or 6502 CPU all have some form of clock output, which is synchronized with their memory accesses and provides the enable input to the 6850 and similar peripherals. If these peripherals are interfaced to the 68000, an enable (or E) clock with the appropriate relationship between the 68000's address and data strobes needs to be provided. Although a suitable interface between the 68000 and a 6800-series peripheral is not difficult to design, it is messy. A handful of TTL devices would be required to satisfy the timing requirements of a 6800-series peripheral. Fortunately, the problem has been solved by putting the necessary synchronization circuitry on-chip.

The 68000 produces an E (enable) clock output, suitable for use with 6800-series peripherals. The E clock has a frequency of one tenth of the system clock and a low-to-high mark-space ratio of 6 : 4; that is, it is low for six CLK cycles and high for four CLK cycles. Equally importantly, the E clock is free running and bears no fixed relationship with any internal activity within the 68000.

Figure 8.6 gives the recommended interface between a 6800-series peripheral and a 68000. As these peripherals have byte-wide data buses, they are interfaced either to D_{00} to D_{07} or to D_{08} to D_{15} from the CPU. An address decoder detects an access to the peripheral's memory space and SELECT* goes active-low, following the assertion of AS* and LDS*/UDS*. A *conventional* peripheral would, of course, have its CS* input connected directly to SELECT*. However, in this case, SELECT* is connected to the 68000's valid peripheral address (VPA*) input via an open-collector buffer. Therefore, when the peripheral is selected, VPA* is asserted and the 68000 informed that the current bus cycle is to be a *synchronous* cycle. The cycle is not terminated by the assertion of DTACK*, and DTACK* must remain negated throughout the cycle.

FIGURE 8.5   Timing diagram of a 6800-series I/O port

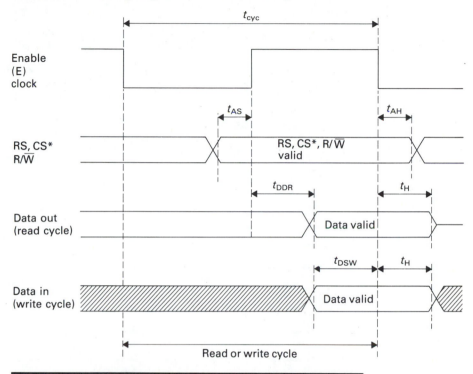

MNEMONIC	NAME	VALUE (ns)
t_{AS}	Address setup-time	160 min.
t_{AH}	Address hold-time	10 min.
t_{DDR}	Data delay-time (access time)	320 max.
t_H	Data hold-time (read)	10 max.
t_{DSW}	Data setup-time (write)	195 min.
t_H	Data hold-time (write)	10 min.

On detecting the assertion of VPA∗, the 68000 monitors its E clock and then asserts its valid memory address (VMA∗) output at the appropriate point in the E cycle. VMA∗ is combined with the output of the address decoder to provide the necessary CS∗ input to the peripheral. Note that CS∗ should *not* be strobed with AS∗ or with UDS∗/LDS∗, as these signals are negated before the end of a synchronous access. Because the cycle is synchronous, it is terminated automatically on the falling edge of the E clock. Figure 8.7 gives the protocol flow diagram of a synchronous bus cycle. This protocol flow diagram is equally valid for read and write cycles.

Now let us examine the timing diagram of a synchronous bus cycle.

FIGURE 8.6   Interface between a 68000 CPU and a 6800-series port

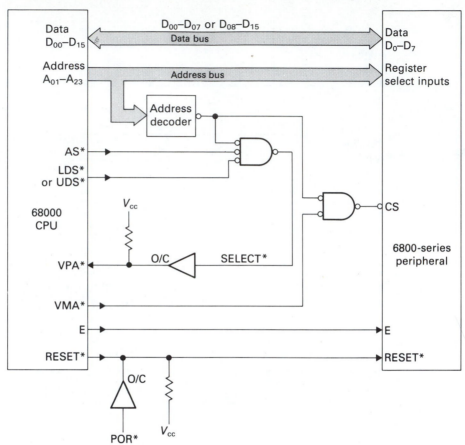

Figure 8.8 gives two timing diagrams: one relates to the best case and one to the worst case. In any synchronous cycle, the external decoder asserts VPA* within typically 100 ns of the assertion of AS*, which is recognized by the 68000 on the falling edge of S4 (just like DTACK*). No wait states are introduced (at this point) if VPA* meets its setup-time, t_{ASI}, before the falling edge of S4.

In the best case (figure 8.8a), VPA* is recognized as being asserted three clock cycles before the rising edge of E. VMA* is synchronized with E and is asserted after the introduction of one wait cycle following S4. A clock state after the next falling edge of E, VMA*, is negated to end the bus cycle. Note that even in the best case, six wait cycles are introduced and the minimum cycle time is twenty states or ten clock cycles.

In the worst case (figure 8.8b), VPA* is asserted less than three clock cycles before the rising edge of E, and an entire E cycle elapses before internal synchronization is achieved. We can see from figure 8.8b that a worst-case synchronous cycle requires thirty-eight clock states.

FIGURE 8.7   Protocol flow diagram for the 68000 synchronous cycle

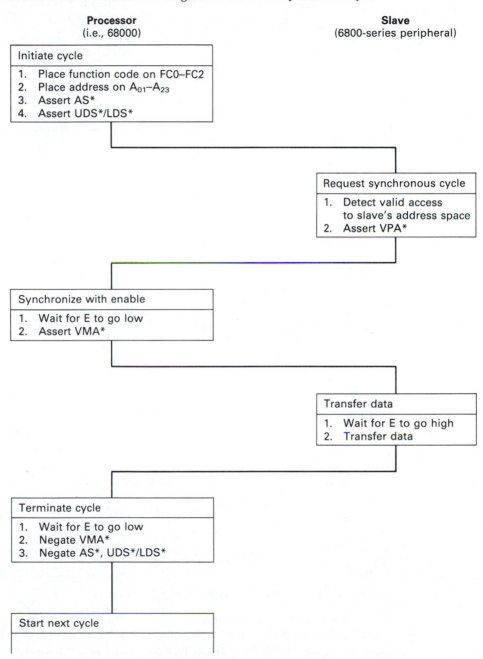

FIGURE 8.8   Timing diagram of a synchronous access cycle. (Reprinted by permission of Motorola Limited)

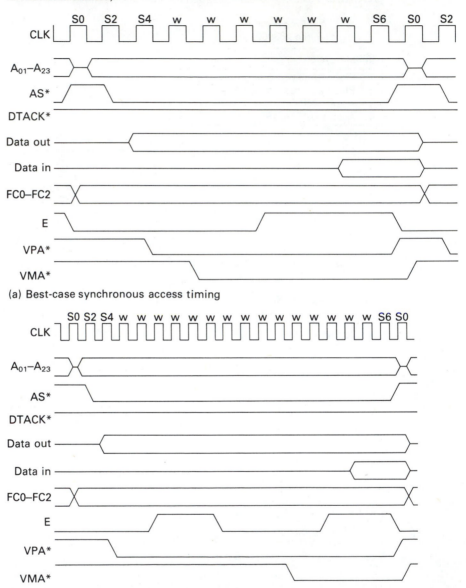

(a) Best-case synchronous access timing

(b) Worst-case synchronous access timing

The advantage of the 68000's synchronous cycle is the ease with which it permits interfacing with 6800-series peripherals. Its disadvantage is its excessively long bus cycle. A 68000 with an 8-MHz clock has worst-case synchronous bus cycles of 38×62.5 ns $= 2375$ ns $= 2.375$ μs. In many applications, this situation is perfectly acceptable. However, some 6800-series peripherals (like the 68B54 advanced data-link controller) operate with an enable clock frequency of 2 MHz.

FIGURE 8.9   Circuit diagram of an interface between a 6800-series peripheral and the 68000's asynchronous bus. (Reprinted by permission of Motorola Limited)

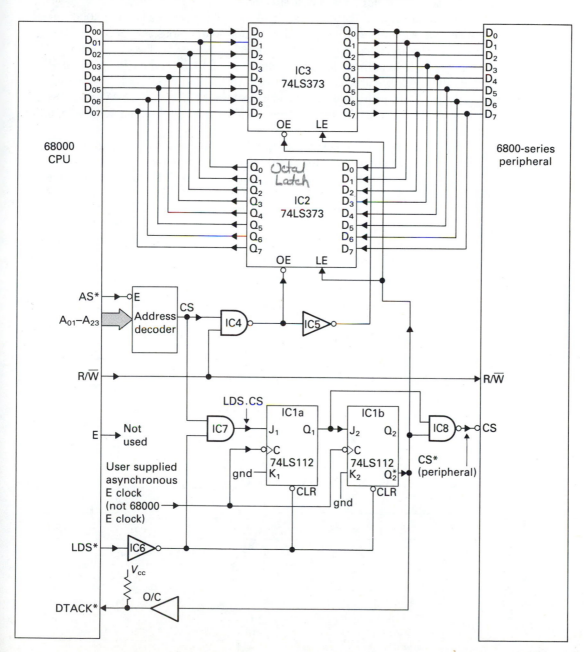

These peripherals cannot be interfaced to the 68000's synchronous bus and still operate at their full rates. One solution is to abandon 6800-series peripherals and use the newer 68000-series peripherals that interface to the CPU's asynchronous bus. This solution is not always cost effective.

A second solution is to interface 6800-series peripherals to the 68000's *asynchronous* bus as outlined in Motorola's Application Note AN-808. The circuit diagram of this interface is given in figure 8.9 (see p. 351). Two JK flip-flops, ICs 1a and 1b, are held in their clear state whenever LDS* from the CPU is negated.

If the CPU executes a memory access to the peripheral's address space, the active-high CS from the address decoder enables AND gate IC7. When LDS* is asserted in the same cycle, the J_1 input to IC1a goes high along with its CLR* input.

Both flip-flops are clocked by E, which is generated by a user-supplied circuit and is not obtained from the 68000. This circuit allows E clocks of a much greater frequency than the 68000's E clock operating at CLK/10. When E makes a negative transition, the Q_1 output of IC1a is asserted. Q_1 is NANDed with CS in IC8 to generate an active-low chip select for the peripheral. Figure 8.10 gives the timing diagram for figure 8.9.

The next falling edge of E clocks Q_1 into flip-flop 1b, forcing Q_2 high and Q_2* low. Q_2* is returned to the 68000 as DTACK*, and therefore terminates the

FIGURE 8.10   Timing diagram for the interface of figure 8.9

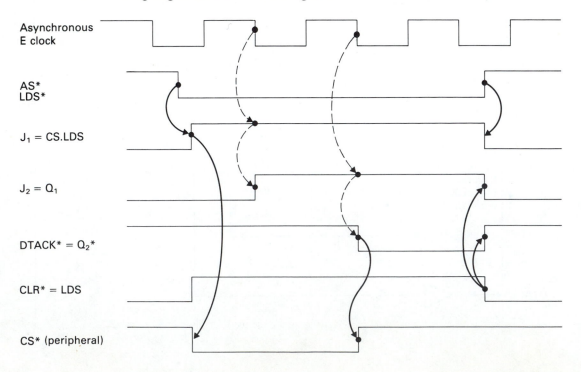

current bus cycle by negating AS* and LDS*, thereby, in turn, clearing flip-flops 1a and 1b to complete the access. This circuit reduces the bus cycle times by an average of 32 percent over the 68000's synchronous cycle and permits the E clock to operate at the maximum rate supported by the peripheral. Octal latches IC2 and IC3 synchronize the data bus with the peripheral access and provide the appropriate data setup- and hold-times.

8.2 Direct Memory Access

Both programmed I/O and interrupt-driven I/O require the CPU to take an active part in the input/output process. When a peripheral transfers data to a port, the CPU must read it and then store it in memory (if it is required later). Similarly, when a peripheral is ready for data, the CPU must read data from memory and transfer it to the output port. These actions both reduce the data transfer rate between the microcomputer and the peripheral, and occupy the CPU with house-keeping duties.

Direct memory access (DMA) bypasses the CPU-peripheral bottleneck and permits the transfer of data between a peripheral and the microcomputer's random access memory without the active intervention of the CPU. This process allows exceedingly high data transfer rates—often of the order of 2M bytes/s.

Figure 8.11 gives an idea of the hardware needed to support DMA. At the heart of the system is a direct memory access controller (DMAC), which can be obtained as a single LSI chip. In a sense, the DMAC is a coprocessor that shares similar privileges with the CPU—that is, it is able to take control of the system bus.

Most DMACs are connected to the processor's address, data, and control buses exactly like any other peripheral. The CPU can read from and write to their internal registers. A minimum DMAC register set includes an address register that points to the source/destination of data to be transferred from/to memory, a count register that contains the number of bytes to transfer, and status and control registers.

The CPU sets up a DMA operation by writing the appropriate parameters into the DMAC's registers. The DMAC then requests access to the system bus. When granted access by the CPU, the DMAC opens bus_switch_1 and closes bus_switch_2 and bus_switch_3 (figure 8.11). The DMAC puts out an address on the address bus and generates all the control signals necessary to move data between the peripheral and memory. Two signals, busy and done, synchronize data transfers between the DMAC and an external peripheral. When all the data has been transferred, the DMAC may interrupt the CPU, if it is programmed to do so.

The operating details of any DMAC vary from device to device and are closely related to the CPU with which it works. The DMAC must be able both to emulate CPU bus cycles and to request the bus from the CPU. Some DMACs

FIGURE 8.11   Hardware needed to support DMA mode I/O

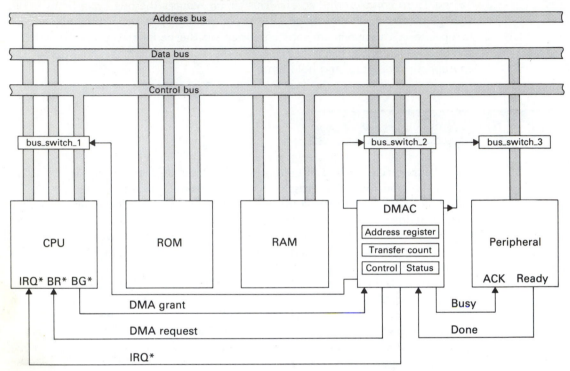

interleave DMA operations with normal CPU memory accesses while others operate in a burst mode, carrying out a number of DMA cycles at a time (i.e., without intervening CPU cycles).

The SCB68430 DMAC

The 68450 is the *standard* DMAC intended for application in 68000-based systems. Because the 68450 is a rather complex and expensive device, the Signetics SCB68430 DMAC has been designed to provide a basic DMA facility in 68000 systems. The 68430 provides a *compatible* subset of the 68450's functions. Figure 8.12 gives a block diagram of the SCB68430 and its interface pins. Here, we provide only an outline of the operation of a DMAC and indicate the principles involved in designing a DMA interface.

The left-hand side of figure 8.12 shows the interface to the 68000 system bus. Note that many lines such as AS* and R/$\overline{\text{W}}$ are bidirectional. These lines act as inputs when the 68000 is accessing the DMAC and as outputs when the DMAC is accessing memory through the bus. Because the DMAC has a limited

FIGURE 8.12   Structure of the SCB68430 DMAC

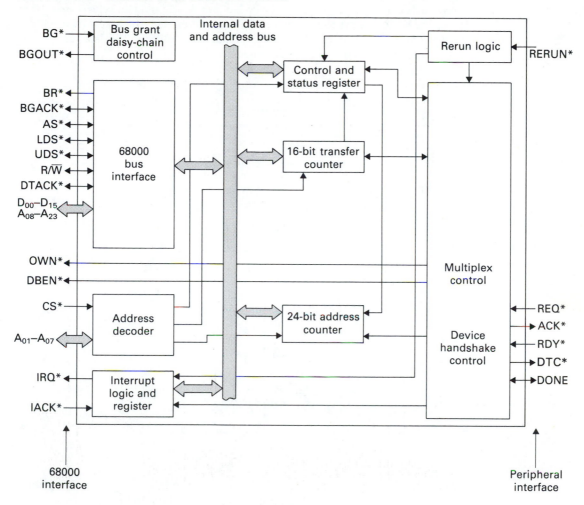

number of pins (48), its address and data buses are multiplexed. Figure 8.13 illustrates the additional hardware needed to interface the DMAC to a 68000 bus. OWN* is an active-low open-collector output from the DMAC that is asserted whenever the DMAC is a bus master. DBEN* (data bus enable) is also an active-low open-collector output that is asserted by the DMAC whenever it is being accessed by the CPU, that is, whenever CS* is asserted or when IACK* is asserted and the DMAC has an interrupt pending.

The 68430 communicates with a peripheral by means of five control lines. These lines allow the peripheral to request data transfers and the DMA controller to manage the data transfer between the peripheral and the memory. Some of the more sophisticated peripheral chips have pins that can directly be connected to a DMA controller. However, the systems designer often has to provide an interface

FIGURE 8.13   Interfacing the SCB68430 DMAC to a 68000 system. Note that as the SCB6840 uses a multiplexed address and data bus, bus drivers and transceivers are used to interface the DMAC to the 68000's nonmultiplexed address and data buses. The DMAC generates two signals to control these buffers: DBEN* and OWN*. The data bus between the peripheral and the system bus is not shown here

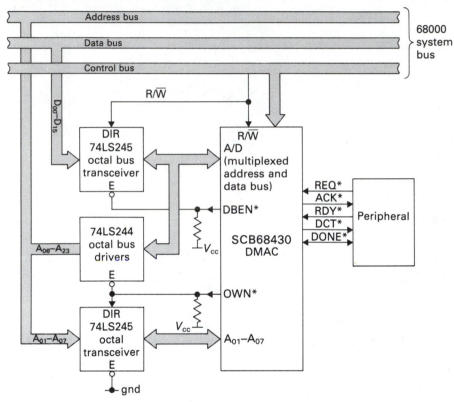

between the *peripheral-side* pins of the DMAC and the interface pins of the peripheral. The five pins of the 68430 dedicated to peripheral control are as follows:

REQ* (request)   This input to the DMAC from the peripheral requests service and causes the DMAC to request control of the bus from the current bus master (i.e., the 68000 CPU).

ACK* (request acknowledge)   ACK* is asserted by the DMAC to indicate that it has control of the bus and the cycle is now beginning. ACK* is asserted at the beginning of every bus cycle after AS* has been asserted and negated at the end of every bus cycle.

RDY* (device ready)   RDY* is asserted by the requesting device (i.e., peripheral) to indicate to the DMAC that valid data has either been stored or put on the bus. If negated, RDY* indicates that data has not been stored or presented, causing the DMAC to enter wait states.

DTC∗ (device transfer complete)   DTC∗ is asserted by the DMAC to indicate to the peripheral that the requested data transfer is complete. On a write to memory, DTC∗ indicates that the data from the peripheral has been successfully stored. On a read from memory, it indicates to the peripheral that the data from memory is present on the data bus and should be latched. Note that DTC∗ is asserted after *each* data bus transfer. DONE∗ is asserted at the end of a batch of data transfers.

DONE∗ (done)   DONE∗ is a dual-function, active-low input or output pin. As an open-collector output, DONE∗ is asserted by the DMAC concurrently with the ACK∗ output to indicate that the transfer count is exhausted and that the DMAC's operation is complete. As an input, if DONE∗ is asserted by the peripheral before the transfer count reaches zero, it forces the DMAC to abort the operation and (if enabled) generate an interrupt request.

DMAC Operation

A DMA transfer takes place in a number of stages. The CPU first sets up the DMAC's registers (see the next section) to define the quantity of data to be moved, the type of DMA operation, and the direction of data transfer (to or from memory). During this phase, the DMAC behaves exactly like any other memory-mapped peripheral.

The DMAC is activated by a request for service from its associated peripheral. When the peripheral asserts REQ∗, the DMAC requests control of the bus by asserting its BR∗ output, waiting for BG∗ from the bus master, and then asserting BGACK∗.

Once the DMAC has control of the bus, it generates all the timing signals needed to transfer data between the peripheral and memory. DMA transfers take place in either the burst mode or in the cycle-stealing mode. In the burst mode several operands are transferred in consecutive bus cycles. In the cycle-stealing mode, the system bus may be relinquished between successive data transfers, allowing DMA and normal processing to be interleaved.

DMAC's Registers

The SCB68430 has seven register select inputs, A_{01} to A_{07}, permitting up to 128 internal registers to be uniquely specified. However, this device has only twelve registers, as it is a single-channel DMAC and supports only one peripheral at a time. The more complex 68450 DMAC supports up to four independent DMA channels. Table 8.1 gives the names and address offsets of the SCB68430's internal registers. The registers do not have sequential addresses because this device is software compatible with the 68450 and its register set is, therefore, a subset of the 68450's.

A DMA operation is set up by loading the 24-bit memory address counter

TABLE 8.1   The registers of the SCB68430

ADDRESS (A_{07}–A_{01})	OFFSET (hex)	MNEMONIC	NAME
0000000 (0)	00	CSR	Channel status register
0000000 (1)	01	CER	Channel error register
0000010 (0)	04	DCR	Device control register
0000010 (1)	05	OCR	Operation control register
0000011 (1)	07	CCR	Channel control register
0000101 (0)	0A	MTCH	Memory transfer counter high
0000101 (1)	0B	MTCL	Memory transfer counter low
0000110 (1)	0D	MACH	Memory address counter high
0000111 (0)	0E	MACM	Memory address counter middle
0000111 (1)	0F	MACL	Memory address counter low
0010010 (1)	25	IVR	Interrupt vector register

NOTE: The number in parentheses in the address column represents A_{00}. If $A_{00} = 0$, UDS$*$ is asserted. If $A_{00} = 1$, LDS$*$ is asserted. The SCB68430 data sheet treats registers as either the upper or lower half of a 16-bit word; for example, CSR and CER together form a word, with CSR having bits 8–15 and CER bits 0–7.

(MAC) with the location of the source/destination of the first operand. Once initialized, the MAC automatically increments after each data transfer. The increment is 1, 2, or 4, depending on whether the DMAC is programmed to transfer bytes, words, or longwords, respectively. The 16-bit memory transfer counter (MTC) is initialized by loading it with the number of transfers to be made during the current operation. The MTC is decremented after each transfer.

The interrupt vector register (IVR) is loaded with the vector to be placed on the data bus during an IACK cycle initiated by the CPU. Only the seven most-significant bits of the IVR are gated onto the data bus during an IACK cycle. The least-significant bit of the vector is set to zero by the DMAC if a normal termination occurred or to a one if the operation was terminated by an error condition. A reset to the DMAC presets the IVR to $0F, corresponding to the uninitialized vector exception.

The operating mode of the SCB68430 is determined by the device control register (DCR), the operation control register (OCR), and the channel control register (CCR). Bit 15 of the DCR determines whether the DMAC operates in a burst mode (DCR_15 = 0) or in a cycle steal mode (DCR_15 = 1). The burst mode allows a peripheral to request the transfer of multiple operands using consecutive bus cycles. In the cycle steal mode, the peripheral requests a single operand transfer at a time. Each request for service by the peripheral results in a request for bus arbitration by the DMAC.

The operation control register uses three bits, OCR_7, OCR_5, and OCR_4, to determine the direction and size of the data transfer. If OCR_7 is a logical zero,

TABLE 8.2   Bits OCR_4 and OCR_5 of the operation control register

OCR_5	OCR_4	OPERAND SIZE
0	0	Byte transfer. If the LSB of the MAC is 0, UDS* is asserted during the transfer. If the LSB of the MAC is 1, LDS* is asserted. The MAC is incremented by 1 after each transfer. The transfer count is decremented by 1 before each byte is transferred.
0	1	Word transfer. The transfer counter decrements by 1 before each word is transferred and the MAC increments by 2 after each transfer.
1	0	Longword transfer. The 32-bit operand is transferred as two 16-bit words. The transfer counter is decremented by 1 before the entire longword is transferred and the MAC is incremented by 2 after each transfer.
1	1	Double-word transfer. The operand size is 32 bits and is transferred as a *single* 32-bit word. The MAC is incremented by 4 after each operand transfer and the transfer counter is decremented by 1 before it. This mode is included for compatibility with the VME bus.

data is transferred from memory to the peripheral. If OCR_7 is a logical one, data is transferred from the peripheral to memory. OCR_5 and OCR_4 determine the size of each operand as illustrated in table 8.2.

Three bits of the channel control register, CCR_7, CCR_4, and CCR_3, are used by the DMAC. When CCR_7 makes a zero to one transition (under software control), the DMA operation is initiated. This should, of course, be done only when all the other registers have previously been initialized. Bit CCR_4 is a software abort and may be set to terminate the current data transfer and to place the DMAC in an idle state. Setting CCR_4 causes the channel_operation_complete and error bits in the CSR to be set, the channel_active_bit in the CSR to be reset, and the pending bit (CCR_7) to be reset. Bit CCR_3 is an interrupt enable bit. When clear, it disables DMAC interrupts. When set, it enables an interrupt request on the completion of a data transfer.

The channel status register (CSR), together with the channel error register (CER), provide the host CPU with an indication of the status of the DMAC. The status and error bits are defined as follows:

CSR_15 (channel operation complete)   CSR_15 is set following the termination of an operation—whether that operation was successful or not. This bit must be cleared to start another operation.

CSR_13 (normal device termination)   CSR_13 is set when the peripheral terminates the DMAC operation by asserting the DONE* line while the peripheral was being acknowledged. CSR_13 must be cleared to start another operation.

FIGURE 8.14   Transfer protocol flowchart for a DMAC memory-to-peripheral data transfer

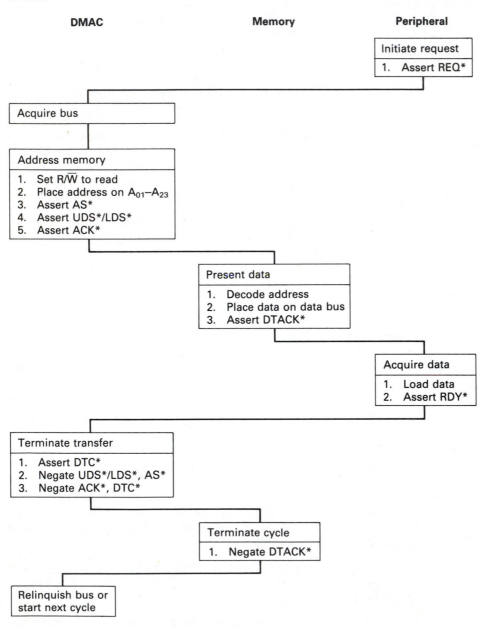

CSR_12 (error)   When set, CSR_12 indicates the termination of a DMA operation by an error. Its cause can be determined by reading the channel error register. CSR_12 must be cleared to start another channel operation. When cleared, the channel error register is also cleared.

CSR_11 (channel active)   CSR_11 is set (by the DMAC) after the channel has been started and remains set until the channel operation terminates. It is automatically cleared by the DMAC.

CSR_8 (ready input state)   CSR_8 reflects the state of the RDY* input at the time the CSR is read. CSR_8 = 0 if RDY* = 0 and CSR_8 = 1 if RDY* = 1.

CER_4 to CER_0 (error code)   These five bits of the channel error register indicate the source of an error when CER_12 is set. Only three values are defined by the SCB68430:

00000   No error.

01001   Bus error. A bus error occurred during the last bus cycle generated by the DMAC.

10001   Software abort. The channel operation was terminated by a software abort.

Using the SCB68430 DMAC is relatively straightforward. All that is required is a peripheral conforming to the DMAC's data transfer control signals. The DMAC is programmed according to its control registers as described previously and, once CCR_7 has been set, it executes the DMA operation as programmed and sets CSR_15 when the operation is complete. Figure 8.14 provides the protocol flowchart for a memory-to-peripheral operation. Further details of the SCB68430 are found in its data sheet.

8.3 The 68230 Parallel Interface/Timer

We are now going to look at the way in which a parallel I/O port can be constructed between a microcomputer and an external system. In particular, we will show how a sophisticated parallel interface can be implemented by the 68230. The 68230 parallel interface/timer (PI/T) is a general-purpose peripheral, with the primary function of an 8- or a 16-bit parallel interface between a computer and an external system, and a secondary function as a programmable timer. In this section, we examine the characteristics of the 68230 PI/T. The novice may be forgiven for wondering why a special parallel interface is necessary. After all, what is wrong with an octal D latch? In principle, the PI/T is little more than a set of latches which store I/O information. In practice, the PI/T has had many powerful attributes linked to its basic function, and all of these facilities are programmable.

Figure 8.15 provides an example of the simplest possible parallel output port

FIGURE 8.15   Basic output port using octal latches

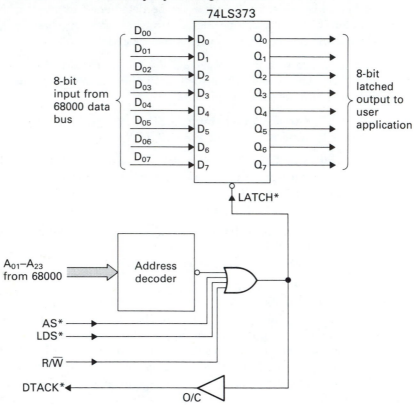

based on the 74LS373 octal D latch. A small quantity of TTL is needed to trap a valid write access to the latch, clock it, and return DTACK* to the 68000. The poverty of this design lies in the absence of any two-way communication between the CPU and the peripheral to which the port is connected. This situation leads to *open-loop* operation, in which the CPU transfers data to the latch by means of a write operation, but lacks any feedback from the peripheral; for example, the peripheral cannot tell the CPU either that it has received the data or that it is ready for new data. These functions could be included in the arrangement of figure 8.15, but would require a large number of SSI and MSI chips. The 68230 PI/T provides all these functions in one 48-pin chip. Before we look at the 68230 itself, we need to define some important concepts related to input/output techniques.

I/O Fundamentals

The 68230 PI/T furnishes the systems designer with two things fundamental to all but the most primitive I/O ports. These facilities are handshaking and buffering.

Handshaking permits data transfers to be interlocked with an external activity (e.g., a disk drive), so that data is moved at a rate in keeping with the peripheral's capacity. *Interlocked* means that the next action cannot go ahead until the current action has been completed. Buffering is a facility that permits an overlap in the transfer of data between the CPU and the PI/T, and between the PI/T and its associated peripheral; for example, the PI/T may be obtaining the next byte of data from a disk controller while the CPU is reading the last byte from the PI/T. Buffering requires some temporary storage.

Input Handshaking

Figure 8.16 illustrates the sequence of events taking place when the PI/T operates in its interlocked handshake input mode, and is similar to the asynchronous memory access discussed in chapter 4. For the time being, we are assuming that the PI/T has two data transfer control lines: an edge-sensitive input H1 and an output H2. These control lines are additional to the PI/T's parallel I/O bus. The PI/T also has internal status flags, readable by the CPU, that indicate the status of the handshake inputs; for example, H1S is set by an active transition on H1. The status flags can be read by the CPU at any time. The following description describes a single-buffered input operation. Note that the 68230 can operate in several different modes, which will be described shortly.

At state (a) in figure 8.16, control output H2 from the PI/T is in its asserted state, indicating to the peripheral that the PI/T is ready to receive data. The 68230 permits the sense of H1 and H2 to be programmed by the user. At state (b), the peripheral forces an active transition on the PI/T's H1 input, informing it that data is available on the PI/T's data input bus. Asserting H1 sets a status bit within the PI/T and generates an interrupt request if it is programmed to do so. At state (c), H2 is negated by the PI/T, informing the peripheral that the data has been accepted. Equally, the PI/T is no longer in a position to receive further data. At state (d), H1 is negated by the peripheral, informing the PI/T that the peripheral has acknowledged the data transfer. At state (e), the PI/T asserts H2 to indicate that it is once more ready to receive data from the peripheral. At this stage, the system is in the same condition as state (a), and a new cycle may commence.

The timing diagram of two successive interlocked handshake input transfers is given in figure 8.17. Two cycles are shown because the PI/T is double-buffered. Double-buffering means that the PI/T can be receiving a new input while storing the previous input. In the first cycle, H2 is negated after H1 has been asserted and H2 is reasserted automatically after approximately four clock cycles because the input has been transferred from PI/T's *initial input latches* to its *final input latches* and the initial input latches are once more free to accept data. However, on the second input cycle, H2 remains inactive-high (i.e., it is not self-clearing) because both input buffers are full. Only when the CPU reads from the storage buffer does the H2 output reassert itself.

Double-buffering means that data can be transferred at almost the maximum rate at which the CPU can read the PI/T, without information being lost. Had the

FIGURE 8.16   Closed-loop data transfer and the input handshake

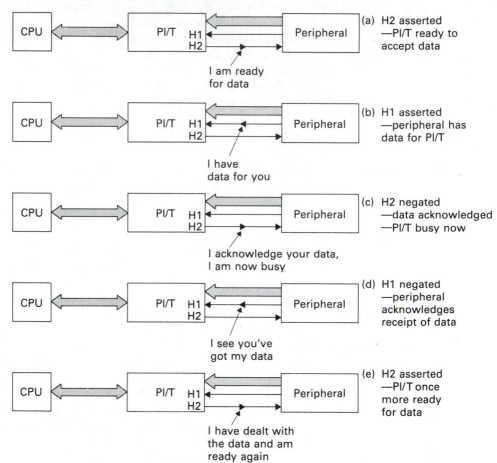

(a) H2 asserted
—PI/T ready to
accept data

I am ready
for data

(b) H1 asserted
—peripheral has
data for PI/T

I have
data for you

(c) H2 negated
—data acknowledged
—PI/T busy now

I acknowledge your data,
I am now busy

(d) H1 negated
—peripheral
acknowledges
receipt of data

I see you've
got my data

(e) H2 asserted
—PI/T once
more ready
for data

I have dealt with
the data and am
ready again

PI/T been supplied with many more buffers (making it a FIFO), instantaneous data rates of several times the host processor's transfer rate could have been supported.

Output Handshaking

The PI/T implements double-buffered output transfers in very much the same fashion as the corresponding input transfers. Figure 8.18 shows the sequence of events taking place during an output transfer and figure 8.19 provides the corresponding timing diagram for two cycles of double-buffered output.

An output transfer starts at state (a) in figure 8.18, with the CPU loading data into the PI/T's output register, which causes H2 to be asserted after a delay of two clock cycles. This condition indicates to the peripheral that the data is available. At state (b), the peripheral asserts the PI/T's H1 input to indicate that it has read the data. The assertion of H1 causes the PI/T to negate H2 at state (c),

FIGURE 8.17   Two consecutive input cycles using interlocked handshaking with double-buffered input

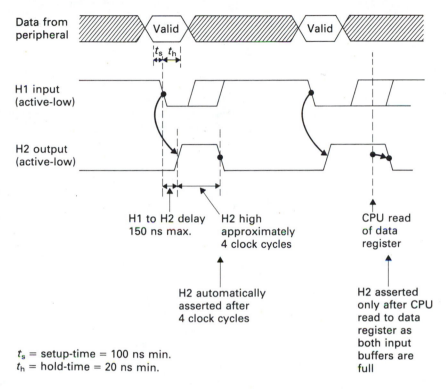

t_s = setup-time = 100 ns min.
t_h = hold-time = 20 ns min.

indicating that the PI/T has acknowledged the peripheral's receipt of data. In turn, the peripheral negates H1 at state (d) to indicate that it is once more ready for data. Finally, the processor loads new data into the PI/T and H2 is asserted again to indicate a data-ready state at point (e).

The timing diagram of figure 8.19 also illustrates the effect of double-buffering on an output data transfer. Initially, both the PI/T's output buffers are empty. When data is first loaded into the PI/T by the CPU, the data is transferred to the chip's output terminals and H2 asserted. At this point, one of the two output buffers is full. The buffer connected to the CPU is called the *initial O/P buffer* and that connected to the output pins is called the *final output buffer*.

When the next write to the PI/T's data register is made, the data is not immediately transferred to the output buffer and therefore the PI/T is in a busy state and cannot accept new data. Only when H1 is asserted by the peripheral does the PI/T transfer its latest data to the output register. Now the PI/T may once more accept data from the CPU. As in the case of input transfers, the CPU knows when the PI/T is ready for data by examining the state of the H1 flag bit, H1S.

FIGURE 8.18   Closed-loop data transfer and the output handshake

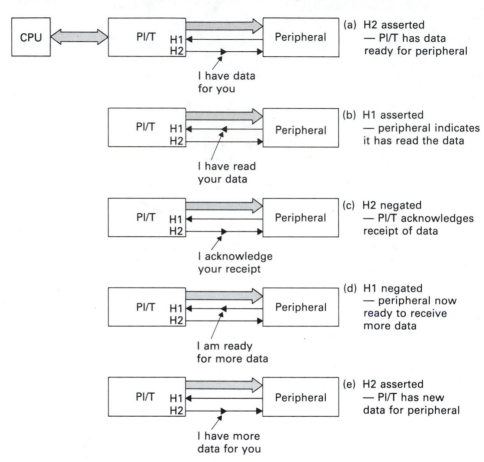

(a) H2 asserted
— PI/T has data
ready for peripheral

(b) H1 asserted
— peripheral indicates
it has read the data

(c) H2 negated
— PI/T acknowledges
receipt of data

(d) H1 negated
— peripheral now
ready to receive
more data

(e) H2 asserted
— PI/T has new
data for peripheral

Structure of the 68230 PI/T

The 68230 parallel interface and timer is available in a 48-pin package that interfaces to the 68000's asynchronous data bus via its eight data pins and fully supports DTACK* and vectored interrupts. The key feature of the PI/T is its two
independent 8-bit, programmable I/O ports and its third dual-function C port. The
C port can be programmed to operate as a simple I/O port without handshaking
and double-buffering. However, the C port can also be programmed to act as a
timer. In the latter mode, some of the port C pins perform other system functions.
The PI/T also supports DMA operation in conjunction with a suitable DMA
controller.

Figure 8.20 provides a block diagram of the internal structure of the PI/T

FIGURE 8.19   Two consecutive cycles of output using interlocked handshaking and double-buffering

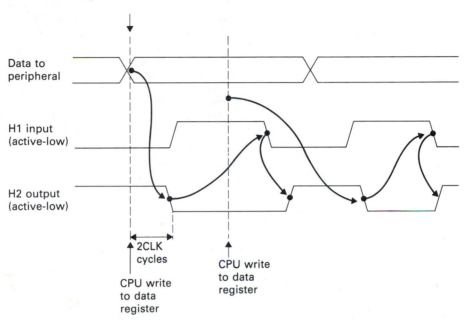

and its pinout. The possible interface between a 68000 and a PI/T is presented in figure 8.21. The two 8-bit ports A and B and their handshake lines (H1, H2 for port A and H3, H4 for port B) are entirely application dependent and are unconnected in figure 8.21.

The interface between the 68230 PI/T and a 68000 CPU is simplicity itself. D_0 to D_7 from the PI/T is connected to D_{00} to D_{07} from the CPU (or alternatively to D_{08} to D_{15}, if the upper byte is to be used). Address lines A_{01} to A_{05} from the CPU are connected to the PI/T's five register select pins (RS_1 to RS_5) to enable the CPU to access any of the 32 addressable registers. The PI/T is accessed whenever its CS* input is active-low. CS* is derived from A_{06} to A_{23}, LDS*, and AS*. The active-low, open-drain DTACK* output from the PI/T is connected directly to the 68000's DTACK* input or to any suitable DTACK* point that is also driven by open-collector (or open-drain) outputs. The R/$\overline{W}$, RESET*, and CLK inputs to the PI/T are supplied by the 68000. Note that the CLK input does not have to be synchronized with the 68000's own clock.

Port C is a dual-function port and may be used as a simple 8-bit I/O port "without frills" or it may be used to support the chip's timer, interrupt, or DMA functions. The timer takes up three pins of port C (PC2 = T_{IN}, PC3 = T_{OUT}, PC7 = TIACK*). The PI/T supports a fairly simple 24-bit timer that has an optional (i.e., programmable) 5-bit input prescaler. The counter counts either clock pulses at the CLK input or pulses at the PC2/T_{IN} pin. The timer output, PC3/T_{OUT}, generates the single or periodic pulses required by external equipment

FIGURE 8.20   Internal arrangement of the 68230 PI/T. (Reprinted by permission of Motorola Limited)

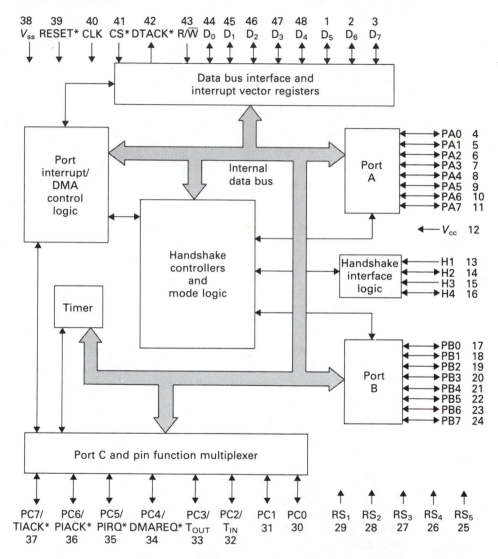

or it can be connected to one of the CPU's interrupt request inputs to generate timed interrupts. The PC7/TIACK∗ input must be derived from the 68000's interrupt acknowledge circuitry and acknowledges an interrupt generated by an active transition on PC3/T_{OUT}. Of course, these three pins may be used as simple port C I/O pins if the timer function is not required.

Three other system functions are provided by port C. PC5/PIRQ∗ is a composite interrupt request output for parallel ports A and B. PC6/PIACK∗ is the corresponding interrupt acknowledge input to the PI/T. PC4/DMAREQ∗ is a

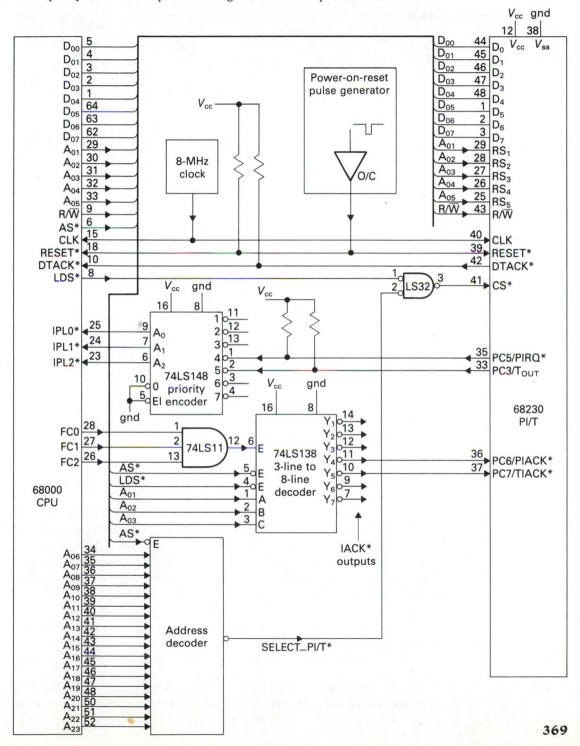

FIGURE 8.21 Interface between a 68000 CPU and a 68230 PI/T. Note that PC5/PIRQ* is used to generate a level 4 interrupt request and PC6/PIACK* is used to receive a level 4 IACK* from the 68000. PC3/T$_{OUT}$ and PC7/TIACK* provide a level 5 interrupt request and interrupt acknowledge from the timer part of the 68230

369

TABLE 8.3   The 68230's internal register set

REGISTER SELECT BITS					REGISTER MNEMONIC	REGISTER DESCRIPTION	TYPE
RS_5	RS_4	RS_3	RS_2	RS_1			
0	0	0	0	0	PGCR	Port general control register	R/W
0	0	0	0	1	PSRR	Port service request resister	R/W
0	0	0	1	0	PADDR	Port A data direction register	R/W
0	0	0	1	1	PBDDR	Port B data direction register	R/W
0	0	1	0	0	PCDDR	Port C data direction register	R/W
0	0	1	0	1	PIVR	Port interrupt vector register	R/W
0	0	1	1	0	PACR	Port A control register	R/W
0	0	1	1	1	PBCR	Port B control register	R/W
0	1	0	0	0	PADR	Port A data register	R/W
0	1	0	0	1	PBDR	Port B data register	R/W
0	1	0	1	0	PAAR	Port A alternate register	R only
0	1	0	1	1	PBAR	Port B alternate register	R only
0	1	1	0	0	PCDR	Port C data register	R/W
0	1	1	0	1	PSR	Port status register	R/W
1	0	0	0	0	TCR	Timer control register	R/W
1	0	0	0	1	TIVR	Timer interrupt vector register	R/W
1	0	0	1	1	CPRH	Counter preload register high	R/W
1	0	1	0	0	CPRM	Counter preload register middle	R/W
1	0	1	0	1	CPRL	Counter preload register low	R/W
1	0	1	1	1	CNTRH	Counter register high	R only
1	1	0	0	0	CNTRM	Counter register middle	R only
1	1	0	0	1	CNTRL	Counter register low	R only
1	1	0	1	0	TSR	Timer status register	R/W

DMA request output from the PI/T and may be used in conjunction with an external DMA controller to request a DMA operation between the peripheral connected to port A or port B and the system memory.

Table 8.3 defines the addresses and the names of the PI/T's 23 internal registers. Out of the 32 possible addresses on RS_1 to RS_5, nine values are not used and, when accessed, these null registers return the value $00. Although table 8.3 appears complex, the registers can be divided into functional groups: PI/T control and status, port A/B data and data direction registers, and counter registers. The functions of these registers are dealt with later.

Operating Modes of the PI/T

At first sight, the PI/T appears to be an exceedingly complex chip because it is a general-purpose device and supports so many different modes of operation. Each of the PI/T's operating modes are really very straightforward. The A and B ports of the PI/T can be configured to operate in seven ways. The ports are divided into four modes together with their submodes. The modes select the type of buffering (none/single/double) and whether the ports operate as independent 8-bit ports or as a combined 16-bit port. The operating modes of the PI/T are determined by bits 6 and 7 of its global control register (PGCR); that is, both port A and port B must operate in the same mode. However, the individual port control registers may be programmed to permit independent submodes of ports A and B.

Mode 0 Operation

Figure 8.22 illustrates the PI/T's mode 0 operation and its three submodes 00, 01, and 1X. These submodes are so called because they are chosen by setting bits 7 and 6 of the relevant port control register (PACR or PBCR). In figure 8.22, only port A is shown. Port B behaves in exactly the same way as port A, except that H3 acts like H1 and H4 acts like H2.

In modes 0 and 1, a data direction register (DDR) is associated with each port. PADDR controls port A and PBDDR independently controls port B. Each bit of the data direction register determines whether the corresponding bit of the port is an input or an output. A logical zero in bit i of a DDR defines the corresponding bit of a port as an input. A logical one defines the bit as an output. The contents of both DDRs are set to zero after a reset; for example, if PADDR is loaded with 00011111, PA5 to PA7 are inputs and PA0 to PA4 are outputs. This operating mode is called *undirectional* because it is changed only by resetting the PI/T or by reconfiguring the DDRs.

We can see from figure 8.22 that the submodes differ in terms of the buffering they permit on their inputs and outputs. The direction of data transfer that permits *double-buffering* is known as the primary data direction of the port. Data transfers in the primary direction are controlled by handshake pins H1, H2 for port A and H3, H4 for port B.

Mode 0, Submode 00

In submode 00, double-buffered input is provided in the primary direction. Output from the PI/T is single-buffered. Data is latched into the input register by the asserted edge of H1 and H2 behaves according to its programmed function defined in table 8.4. Up to now, we have discussed only the interlocked handshake mode offered by H1 and H2. It can be seen from table 8.4 that PACR_3 to PACR_5 may be used to define H2 as a simple output (i.e., an output at a logical 0 or logical 1 level), an interlocked handshake output, or a pulsed handshake output. In the latter case, the H2 output is asserted as in the interlocked mode of figures 8.17 and 8.19, but is negated *automatically* after approximately four clock cycles. In what follows, H1S and H2S are the status bits associated with H1 and H2, respectively, which are bits PSR_0 and PSR_1.

FIGURE 8.22   The PI/T in mode 0 (unidirectional 8-bit mode). Note that a dot in any register implies that that bit does not take part in the selection of either the mode or the submode. Only port A is shown here

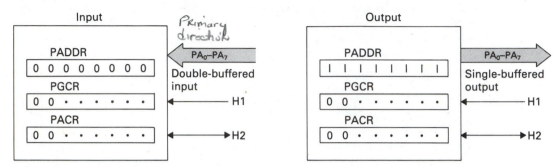

Submode 00   Pin-definable double-buffered input or single-buffered output

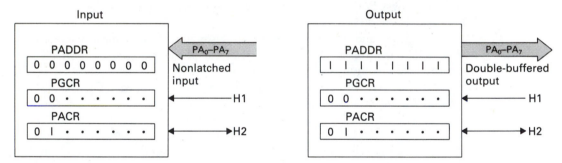

Submode 01   Pin-definable double-buffered output or single-buffered input

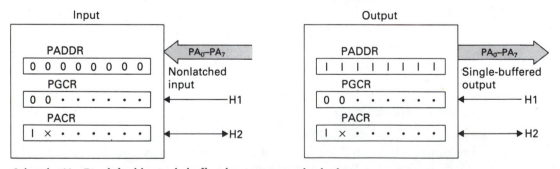

Submode 1X   Pin-definable single-buffered output or nonlatched input

Mode 0, Submode 01

In submode 01, the primary data direction is from the PI/T and double-buffered output is provided. Input in this mode is nonlatched; that is, the input read by the CPU reflects the state of the input pin at the moment it is read. The programming of the port A control register in submode 01 is given in table 8.5 and is almost exactly the same as that of table 8.4, with the exception of the submode control

TABLE 8.4   Port A control register (PACR) in mode 0, submode 00

Bit	PACR7 PACR6	PACR5 PACR4 PACR3	PACR2	PACR1 PACR0
Function	0 0	H2 control	H2 interrupt enable	H1 control

←——Submode 00——→

PACR5	PACR4	PACR3	H2 CONTROL	
0	×	×	H2 edge-sensitive input	H2S set on asserted edge
1	0	0	H2 output—negated	H2S always clear
1	0	1	H2 output—asserted	H2S always clear
1	1	0	H2 output—interlocked handshake	H2S always clear
1	1	1	H2 output—pulsed handshake	H2S always clear

H1 is the input strobe, double buffer

PACR2	H2 INTERRUPT ENABLE
0	H2 interrupt disabled
1	H2 interrupt enabled

PACR1	PACR0	H1 CONTROL
0	×	H1 interrupt and DMA request disabled
1	×	H1 interrupt and DMA request enabled
×	×	H1S status bit set if input data available

NOTE: H1S = H1 status bit of the port status register
         H2S = H2 status bit of the port status register

field and the H1 status control bit, PACR_0. When PACR_0 = 0, the H1 status bit is set if *either* port A initial or final output latches can accept data and is clear otherwise. When PACR_0 = 1, the H1 status bit is set if *both* port A output latches are empty and is clear otherwise. In other words, we can program H1S to indicate the state *fully empty* or the state *half empty*.

Mode 0, Submode 1X

In mode 0, submode 1X (see figure 8.22), simple bit I/O is available in both directions. Double-buffered I/O cannot be used in either direction. Data read from

TABLE 8.5   Port A control register (PACR) in mode 0, submode 01

Bit	PACR7	PACR6	PACR5	PACR4	PACR3	PACR2	PACR1	PACR0
Function	0	1		H2 control		H2 interrupt enable		H1 control

←——— Submode 01 ———→

PACR1	PACR0	
0	×	H2 interrupt and DMA request disabled
1	×	H2 interrupt and DMA request enabled
×	0	H1S indicates initial or final O/P latches empty
×	1	H1S indicates both O/P latches empty

a pin programmed as an input is the instantaneous (i.e., nonlatched) signal at that pin. Data written to an output is single-buffered. H1 is an edge-sensitive input only and plays no part in any handshaking procedure related to the PI/T.

H2 may be programmed as an edge-sensitive input that sets status bit H2S when asserted. As in the case of the other submodes described previously, H2 can be programmed as an output and set or cleared under program control. Table 8.6 defines the options available in this submode.

Mode 1 Operation

In mode 1, the two 8-bit ports are combined to act as a single 16-bit port. This port is still *unidirectional* in the sense that the primary direction of data transfer is associated with double-buffering and handshake control, and ports A and B data direction registers define whether the individual bits of the 16-bit port are to act as inputs or outputs. Figure 8.23 illustrates the possible configurations of the PI/T in mode 1 operation.

A combined port raises two problems—what do we do about the two pairs of handshake signals (H1, H2 and H3, H4) and what about the two port control registers (PACR and PBCR)? In this mode, port B supplies the handshake signals and the control register (PBCR). The port A control register is used in conjunction with H1 and H2 to provide the 16-bit port with additional facilities. Table 8.7 defines the effect of the PACR on the mode 1 operation of the PI/T.

In mode 1, the port A control register simply treats H1 as an edge-sensitive input and H2 as an edge-sensitive input or an output that may be set or cleared.

Mode 1, Submode X0

In mode 1, submode X0, double-buffered inputs or single-buffered outputs of up to 16 bits are possible. Note that the PI/T has only an 8-bit interface to the 68000

TABLE 8.6   Port A control register (PACR) in mode 0, submode 1 ×

Bit	PACR7	PACR6	PACR5	PACR4	PACR3	PACR2	PACR1	PACR0
Function	1	×	H2 control			H2 interrupt enable	H1 control	

← ——— Submode 1 × ——— →

PACR5	PACR4	PACR3	H2 FUNCTION	
0	×	×	Edge-sensitive input	H2S set on asserted edge
1	×	0	H2 output—negated	H2S always clear
1	×	1	H2 output—asserted	H2S always clear

PACR1	FUNCTION
0	H1 interrupt disabled
1	H1 interrupt enabled

PACR0	FUNCTION
×	H1 is an edge-sensitive input and H1S is set by an asserted edge of H1

so that a 16-bit word must be transferred to the CPU as 2 bytes. Port A should be read before port B. For compatibility with the MOVEP instruction, port A should contain the most-significant byte of data. The operation of the 16-bit port is determined by the port B control register, the structure of which is given in table 8.8. The signal at each input is latched asynchronously with the asserted edge of H3 and placed in either the initial input latch or the final input latch. As in mode 0 operation, H4 may be programmed to act as an input, a fixed output, or a pulsed/interlocked handshake signal.

For pins programmed as outputs, the data path consists of a single latch driving the output buffer. Data written to this port's data register does not affect the operation of any handshake pin, status bit, or any other aspect of the PI/T.

Mode 1, Submode X1

In mode 1, submode X1, double-buffered outputs or nonlatched inputs of up to 16 bits are possible. Data is written to the PI/T as two bytes. The first byte (most significant) is written to the port A data register and the second byte to the port

FIGURE 8.23   PI/T in mode 1 (unidirectional 16-bit mode)

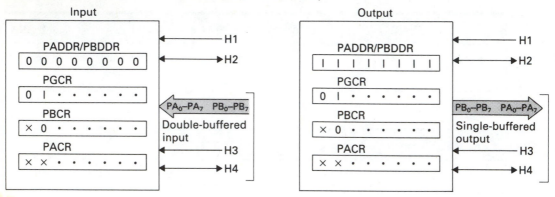

Submode X0   Pin-definable double-buffered input or single-buffered output

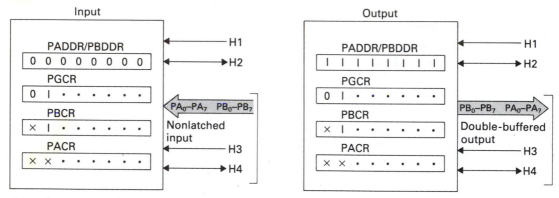

Submode X1   Pin-definable double-buffered output or nonlatched input

B data register (in that order). The PI/T then automatically transfers the 16-bit data to one of the output latches.

The port A control register and associated handshake signals (H1 and H2) behave exactly as in mode 1, submode X0, defined by tables 8.7 and 8.6. In a similar fashion, the port B control register behaves rather like the same register in

TABLE 8.7   The format of port A control register during a mode 1 operation

Bit	PACR7 PACR6	PACR5 PACR4 PACR3	PACR2	PACR1 PACR0
Function	0 0	H2 control	H2 interrupt enable	H1 control

Port A submode ←———————→ PACR_0–PACR_5 behave exactly as in mode 0
submode 1 × —see table 8.6.

TABLE 8.8   Format of the port B control register during a mode 1, submode X0 operation

Bit	PBCR7 PBCR6	PBCR5 PBCR4 PBCR3	PBCR2	PBCR1 PBCR0
Function	× 0	H4 control	H4 interrupt enable	H3 control

Submode ×0

PBCR5	PBCR4	PBCR3	H4 FUNCTION	
0	×	×	Edge-sensitive input	H4S set on asserted edge
1	0	0	Output—negated	H4S always cleared
1	0	1	Output—asserted	H4S always cleared
1	1	0	Output—interlocked handshake	H4S clear
1	1	1	Output—pulsed handshake	H4S clear

PBCR2	H4 INTERRUPT ENABLE
0	The H4 interrupt is disabled
1	The H4 interrupt is enabled

PBCR1	H3 SERVICE REQUEST ENABLE
0	The H3 interrupt and DMA request are disabled
1	The H3 interrupt and DMA request are enabled

PBCR0	H3 STATUS CONTROL
×	The H3S status bit is set any time input data is present

mode 1, submode X0. The only differences are in bits PBCR_7 and PBCR_6, which are set to 0, 1 to select this mode, and in bit PBCR_0. When PBCR_0 is zero, the H3S status bit is set when either the initial or final output latch of ports A and B can accept new data. Otherwise it is clear. When PBCR_0 is one, the H2S status bit is set when both the initial and final output latches of ports A and B are empty, and is clear otherwise.

Mode 2

Mode 2 offers bidirectional I/O and is illustrated in figure 8.24. Port A is used for bit I/O transfers with no associated handshake pins and provides unlatched input or single-buffered output. Individual pins can be programmed as inputs or outputs by the setting or clearing bits in the port A data direction register. Port B is the "workhorse" and acts as a bidirectional, 8-bit, double-buffered I/O port. The handshake pins are all associated with port B and operate in two pairs. H1, H2 control output transfers and H3, H4 control input transfers. The instantaneous direction of the data is determined by the H1 handshake pin; that is, the *external device* determines the direction of data transfer. The port B data direction register has no effect in this mode because only byte I/O is permitted in mode 2. Similarly, ports A and B submode fields do not affect PI/T operation in mode 2.

The output buffers of port B are controlled by the level on the H1 input. When H1 is negated, the port B output buffers are enabled and its pins drive the output bus. Note that all eight buffers are enabled because individual pins cannot be programmed as inputs or outputs in modes 2 and 3. Generally, H1 is negated by a peripheral in response to the assertion of H2, which indicates that new output data is present in the double-buffered latches. Following acceptance of the data, the peripheral asserts H1, disabling the port B output buffers. H1 acts as an edge-sensitive input.

Double-buffered input transfers   Data at the port B input pins is latched on the asserted edge of H3 and deposited in one of the input latches. The corresponding H3 status bit, H3S, is set whenever input data, which has not been read by the host computer, is present in the input latches. As in all other modes, H4 is programmable. In modes 2 and 3, H4 can be programmed to perform two functions:

1.   H4 may be an output pin in the interlocked handshake mode. H4 is asserted when the port is ready to accept new data and is negated asynchro-

FIGURE 8.24   PI/T configured for mode 2 (bidirectional 8-bit mode)

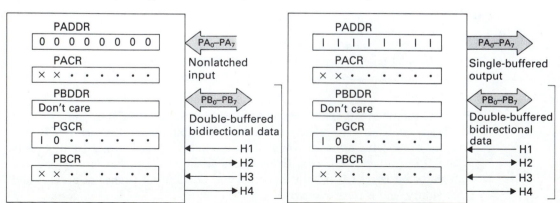

nously following the asserted edge of the H3 input. As soon as one of the input latches becomes ready to receive data, H4 is reasserted. Once both input latches are full, H4 remains negated until data is read by the host processor.

2. H4 may be an output pin in the pulsed input handshake mode. H4 is asserted when the input port is ready to receive new data exactly as in function 1 and is automatically cleared (negated) approximately four clock cycles later. Should a subsequent active transition on H3 take place while H4 is asserted, H4 is negated asynchronously; that is, once the active edge of H4 has been detected by the peripheral, new data may be loaded into the double-buffered input latches.

Double-buffered output transfers   Data is written into one of the PI/T's output latches by the host processor. The peripheral connected to port B accepts data by asserting H1. The H1 status bit may be programmed to be set when either one or both output buffers are empty or only when both output buffers are empty. H2 may be programmed to act in one of two modes:

1. H2 may be an output pin in the interlocked output handshake mode and is asserted whenever the output latches are ready to accept new data from the host processor. H2 is negated asynchronously following the asserted edge of H1. As soon as one or both output latches become available, H2 is reasserted. When both output latches are full, H2 remains asserted until at least one latch is emptied.

2. H2 may be an output pin in the pulsed output handshake protocol. H2 is asserted whenever the output latches are ready to accept new data, but is automatically negated approximately four clock cycles later. Should the asserted edge of H1 be detected while H2 is asserted, H2 is negated asynchronously.

The programming of port control registers A and B in mode 2 is illustrated in tables 8.9 and 8.10. Note that, in this mode, many bits are don't care functions.

Mode 3

Mode 3 operation is an extension of mode 2 and is illustrated in figure 8.25. In mode 3, both ports A and B are dedicated to 16-bit double-buffered input/output transfers. As in mode 2, H1 and H2 control output transfers and H3 and H4 control input transfers. The function of the port control registers (PACR, PBCR) in mode 3 is exactly the same as in mode 2 and therefore tables 8.9 and 8.10 also apply to mode 3.

Mode 3 provides a relatively convenient way of transferring data between the PI/T and 16-bit peripherals at high speed. The word "relatively" has been included because the PI/T interfaces to its host processor by an 8-bit data bus, allowing 16-bit peripheral-side data transfers but denying 16-bit CPU-side data

FIGURE 8.25   PI/T configured for mode 3 (bidirectional 16-bit mode)

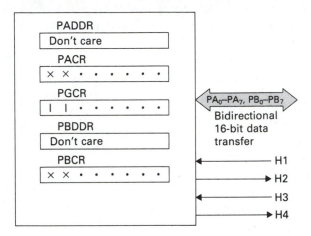

transfers. However, by using the 68000's MOVEP (move peripheral instruction), 16-bit data transfers can be performed with only one instruction.

Registers of the PI/T

So far, we have looked at the PI/T from the point of view of its operational modes and discussed its internal registers only when the need arose. Here we provide further details on the PI/T's internal registers. Table 8.3 gives the names and mnemonics of the 68230's registers together with the register select lines (RS_1 to RS_5) needed to access them. In the following discussion, registers are also specified in terms of their offset addresses. The offset address is given with

TABLE 8.9   Format of the port A control register during a mode 2 operation

Bit	PACR7	PACR6	PACR5	PACR4	PACR3	PACR2	PACR1	PACR0
Function	×	×	×	×	H2 mode	H2 interrupt enable	H1 control	

Submode × × (don't care) ← (PACR7, PACR6, PACR5, PACR4)

PACR3: 0 Interlocked handshake / 1 Pulsed handshake

PACR1, PACR0: PACR_1, PACR_0 exactly as in table 8.5

TABLE 8.10   Format of the port B control register during a mode 2 operation

Bit	PBCR7	PBCR6	PBCR5	PBCR4	PBCR3	PBCR2	PBCR1	PBCR0
Function	×	×	×	×	H4 mode	H4 interrupt enable	H3 control	

Submode × × (don't care)

0 Interlocked handshake
1 Pulsed handshake

PBCR_1, PBCR_0 exactly as in table 8.4

respect to the device's base address, assuming that RS_1 to RS_5 are connected to A_{01} to A_{05}, respectively; for example, the address offset of PGCR is 0 and of TSR it is \$34. Note that the offset is a *byte* value.

Port General Control Register (PGCR, offset = \$00)

The PGCR is a global register that determines the operating mode of the PI/T. Bits 6 and 7 of the PGCR select the PI/T's operating mode (see table 8.11), bits 4 and 5 enable the handshake pairs H1, H2 and H3, H4, and bits 0 to 3 determine the sense of the four handshake lines; for example, setting PGCR_1 = 1 defines the active transition on H2 as a zero to one.

Port Service Request Register (PSRR, offset = \$02)

The port service request register is also a global register and determines the circumstances under which the PI/T may request service. Table 8.12 gives the

TABLE 8.11   Format of the port general control register (PGCR)

Bit	PGCR7	PGCR6	PGCR5	PGCR4	PGCR3	PGCR2	PGCR1	PGCR0
Function	Port mode control		H34 enable	H12 enable	H4 sense	H3 sense	H2 sense	H1 sense

00 Mode 0
01 Mode 1
10 Mode 2
11 Mode 3

0 = disable
1 = enable

Sense = 0 assertion level low
Sense = 1 assertion level high

NOTE: The H12 and H34 enable/disable fields enable or disable the operation of the H1, H2 or H3, H4 handshake lines. All bits of the PGCR are cleared after a reset operation. The handshake lines are enabled only when PGCR_5 and PGCR_4 are set under program control to avoid spurious operation of the handshake lines until the PI/T has been fully configured.

TABLE 8.12 Format of the port service request register (PSRR)

Bit	PSRR7	PSRR6 PSRR5	PSRR4 PSRR3	PSRR2 PSRR1 PSRR0
Function	×	SVCRQ	Operation select	Port interrupt priority

0× PC4/DMAREQ* = PC4 (DMA not used)

10 P4C/DMAREQ* = DMAREQ* and is associated with double-buffered transfers controlled by H1. H1 does not cause interrupts in this mode.

11 P4C/DMAREQ* = DMAREQ* and is associated with double-buffered transfers controlled by H3. H3 does not cause interrupts in this mode.

OPERATION SELECT		INTERRUPT PIN FUNCTION SELECT	
PSRR4	PSRR3		
0	0	PC5/PIRQ* = PC5	No interrupt support
		PC6/PIACK* = PC6	No interrupt support
0	1	PC5/PIRQ* = PIRQ*	Autovectored interrupts supported
		PC6/PIACK* = PC6	Autovectored interrupts supported
1	0	PC5/PIRQ* = PC5	
		PC6/PIACK* = PIACK*	
1	1	PC5/PIRQ* = PIRQ*	Vectored interrupts supported
		PC6/PIACK* = PIACK*	Vectored interrupts supported

PORT INTERRUPT PRIORITY			ORDER OF INTERRUPT PRIORITY			
PSRR2	PSRR1	PSRR0	HIGHEST ⟵⟶ LOWEST			
0	0	0	H1S	H2S	H3S	H4S
0	0	1	H2S	H1S	H3S	H4S
0	1	0	H1S	H2S	H4S	H3S
0	1	1	H2S	H1S	H4S	H3S
1	0	0	H3S	H4S	H1S	H2S
1	0	1	H3S	H4S	H2S	H1S
1	1	0	H4S	H3S	H1S	H2S
1	1	1	H4S	H3S	H2S	H1S

format of the PSRR, which is split into three logical fields: a service request field (SVCRQ) that determines whether the PI/T generates an interrupt or a DMA request when H1 or H3 are asserted, an operation select field that determines whether two of the dual-function pins belong to port C or perform special-purpose functions, and an interrupt priority control field. A DMA request is signified by an active-low pulse on the DMAREQ* (direct memory access request) pin for three clock cycles.

Port Data Direction Registers (PDDRA, offset = $04; PDDRB, offset = $06; PDDRC, offset = $08)

The port data direction registers determine the direction and buffering characteristics of each of the appropriate port pins. A logical one in a PDDR bit makes the corresponding port I/O pin act as an output, while a logical zero makes the pin an output. All DDRs are cleared to zero after a reset.

The port C PDDR behaves in the same way as the other two PDDRs and determines whether each dual-function pin chosen for port C operation is an input or an output pin.

Port Interrupt Vector Register (PIVR, offset = $0A)

The port interrupt vector register contains the upper-order 6 bits of the four port interrupt vectors. The contents of this register may be read in one of two ways: by an ordinary read cycle to the PIVR at offset address $0A or by a port interrupt acknowledge bus cycle.

During a normal read cycle, no "consequence" following the reading of this register exists. However, when the PIVR is read during an interrupt acknowledge cycle, the least two significant bits are determined by the source of the interrupt, as illustrated in table 8.13.

As an example, if the PIVR is loaded with 01101100 ($6C) during the PI/T's initialization phase, an interrupt initiated by H2 will yield an interrupt vector number of 01101101 ($6D). Similarly, an interrupt initiated by H4 will yield an interrupt vector number of 01101111 ($6F). This procedure is followed to avoid having four separate vector number registers. After the RESET* input to the PI/T

TABLE 8.13   Relationship between PIVR0, PIVR1, and interrupt source

INTERRUPT SOURCE	PIVR1	PIVR0
H1	0	0
H2	0	1
H3	1	0
H4	1	1

has been asserted, the contents of the PIVR are initialized to $0F, which is, of course, the *uninitialized vector* number.

Port Control Registers (PCRA, offset = $0C; PCRB, offset = $0E)

These registers determine the submode operation of ports A and B and control the operation of the handshake lines. The programming of these two registers has already been dealt with when the operating modes of the PI/T were described.

Port Data Registers (PADR, offset = $10; PBDR, offset = $12; PCDR, offset = $18)

Port A and port B data registers are holding registers between the CPU-side bus of the PI/T and its port pins and internal buffer registers. These registers may be written to or read from at any time and are not affected by a reset on the PI/T.

The port C data register, PCDR (offset = $18), is a holding register for moving data to and from port C or its alternate-function pins. The exact nature of an information transfer depends on the type of cycle (read or write) and on the way in which port C is configured. Table 8.14 shows how the PCDR is affected by read/write accesses. Pins configured as port C functions offer single-buffered output or nonlatched input.

Note that we are able to directly read the state of a dual-function pin even when it is used for non-port-C functions. We are also able, of course, to generate non-port-C functions "manually" by switching back to port C mode and writing to the PCDR. The port C data register is readable and writable at all times and is not affected by the state of the RESET* pin.

Port Alternate Registers (PAAR, offset = $14; PBAR, offset = $16)

Port A and port B alternate registers provide a way of reading the state of port A and port B pins, respectively. Both PAAR and PBAR are read-only and their contents reflect the actual instantaneous logic levels at the I/O pins. Writing to PAAR or PBAR results in a DTACK* handshake, but no data is latched by the

TABLE 8.14   Accessing the port C data register

OPERATION	PORT C FUNCTION		ALTERNATE FUNCTION	
	PCDDR = 0	PCDDR = 1	PCDDR = 0	PCDDR = 1
Read PCDR	Read pin	Read output register	Read pin	Read output register
Write PCDR	Output register, buffer disabled	Output register, buffer enabled	Output register	Output register

TABLE 8.15   Format of the port status register

Bit	PSR7	PSR6	PSR5	PSR4	PSR3	PSR2	PSR1	PSR0
Function	H4 level	H3 level	H2 level	H1 level	H4S	H3S	H2S	H1S

Bits set or cleared by instantaneous level on handshake pin.

Bits set by assertion of handshake pin as programmed.

PI/T and the bus cycle has no other effect on the PI/T. These registers are not affected by the operating modes of the PI/T.

Port Status Register (PSR, offset = $1A)

The port status register is the global register that reflects the activity of the handshake pins. The format of the PSR is given in table 8.15. Bits PSR_4 through PSR_7 reflect the instantaneous level at the respective handshake pin and are independent of handshake pin sense bits in the PGCR. Bits PSR_0 through PSR_3 are the handshake status bits and are set or cleared as specified by the appropriate operating mode. Each of these bits is active-high and is set when the appropriate handshake line is asserted.

Timer Part of the PI/T

The 68230 contains a single timer that interfaces to the host processor through the same CPU-side pins as the parallel interface and interfaces to external systems (or to the 68000 interrupt structure) through the alternate function pins of port C. Typical functions performed by the 68230 (or any other timer) are: the generation of square waves of programmable frequencies, the generation of single pulses of programmable duration, the production of single or periodic interrupts, and the measurement of frequency or elapsed time. A timer is, essentially, a simple device consisting of a counter that is clocked, typically, downward toward zero. By selecting the clock rate and the initial contents of the counter, a specific delay between starting the counter and the moment it reaches zero can be generated. If the counter is reloaded every time it reaches zero, we have a method of generating repetitive action.

Figure 8.26 shows the three peripheral-side interface lines of the timer together with its associated registers. The timer contains a 24-bit synchronous down-counter (CNTR) that is loaded from three 8-bit counter preload registers (CPR). The synchronous counter is clocked either by the system clock (CLK) or by an external input applied to T_{IN}. The clock may, optionally, be prescaled by 32.

FIGURE 8.26   Timer function of the 68230 PI/T

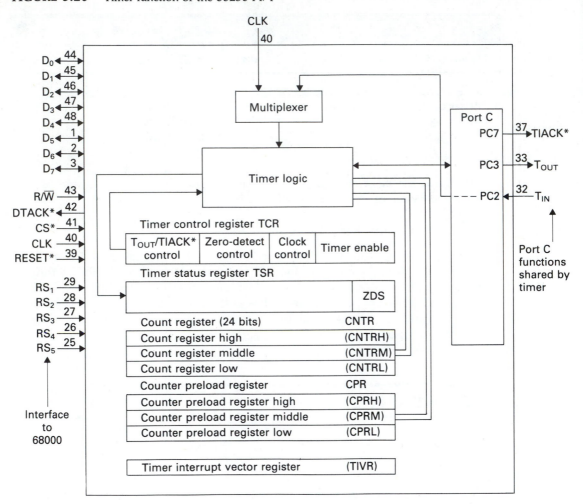

As the counter clocks downward, it eventually reaches zero and sets the zero-detect status bit (ZDS) of the timer status register (TSR). This event can be used to assert the T_{OUT} output from the timer. If T_{OUT} is connected to IRQ1* to IRQ7*, an interrupt may be generated.

The operating mode of the timer is determined by the timer control register, whose format is given in table 8.16. This table is rather complex but, in principle, it controls: (1) the choice between the port C option and the timer option on three dual-function pins; (2) whether the counter is loaded from the counter preload register or rolls over when zero detect is reached; (3) the source of the clock input; (4) whether the clock source is prescaled (i.e., divided by 32); and (5) whether the timer is enabled or disabled.

TABLE 8.16   Format of the timer control register

Bit	TCR7 TCR6 TCR5	TCR4	TCR3	TCR2 TCR1	TCR0
Function	T_{OUT}/TIACK* control	ZD control	×	Clock control	Timer enable

TCR7	TCR6	TCR5	T_{OUT}/TIACK* CONTROL
0	0	×	PC3/T_{OUT}, PC7/TIACK* are port C functions
0	1	×	PC3/T_{OUT} is a timer function. In the run state T_{OUT} provides a square wave that is toggled on each zero-detect. The T_{OUT} pin is high in the halt state. PC7/TIACK* is a port C function.
1	0	0	PC3/T_{OUT} is a timer function. In the run or halt state it is used as a timer interrupt request output. The timer interrupt is disabled—the pin is always three-stated. PC7/TIACK* is a timer function. Since interrupt request is negated, the PI/T produces no response to an asserted TIACK*.
1	0	1	PC3/T_{OUT} is a timer function and is used as a timer interrupt request output. The timer interrupt is enabled and T_{OUT} is low whenever the ZDS bit is set. PC7/TIACK* is a timer function and acknowledges interrupts generated by the timer. This combination supports vectored interrupts.
1	1	0	PC3/T_{OUT} is a timer function. In the run or halt state, it is used as a timer interrupt request output. The timer interrupt is disabled. PC7/TIACK* is a port C function.
1	1	1	TC3/T_{OUT} is a timer function and is used as a timer interrupt request output. The timer interrupt is enabled and T_{OUT} is low when the ZDS status bit is set. PC7/TIACK* is a port C function. Autovectored interrupts are supported.

TCR4	ZERO-DETECT CONTROL
0	The counter is loaded from the counter preload register on the first clock to the 24-bit counter after zero-detect; counting is then resumed.
1	The counter rolls over on zero-detect and then continues counting.

TABLE 8.16—*Continued*

TCR2	TCR1	CLOCK CONTROL
0	0	PC2/T_{IN} is a port C function. Counter clock is from CLK prescaled by 32. The timer enable bit determines whether the timer is in the run or halt state.
0	1	PC2/T_{IN} is a timer input. The prescaler is decremented on the falling edge of the CLK input and the 24-bit counter is decremented when the prescaler rolls over from \$00 to \$1F. The timer is in the run state when the enable bit is one and the T_{IN} pin is high. Otherwise the timer is in the halt state.
1	0	PC2/T_{IN} is a timer input and is prescaled by 32. The prescaler is decremented following the rising transition of T_{IN} after being synchronized with the internal clock. The 24-bit counter is decremented when the prescaler rolls over from \$00 to \$1F. The timer enable bit determines whether the timer is in the run or halt state.
1	1	PC2/T_{IN} is a timer input and prescaling is not used. The 24-bit counter is decremented following the rising edge of the signal at the T_{IN} pin after being synchronized with the internal clock. The timer enable bit determines whether the timer is in the run or halt state.

TCR0	TIMER ENABLE BIT
0	Timer disabled
1	Timer enabled

The 68230 has an independent timer interrupt vector register (TIVR) that supplies an 8-bit vector whenever the timer interrupt acknowledge pin, TIACK*, is asserted. The TIVR is automatically loaded with the unitialized interrupt vector, \$0F, following a reset.

Timer States

The timer is always in one of two states: running or halted. The control of the timer's state is effected by loading the appropriate value into the timer control register (table 8.16). The characteristics of the two states are given below:

1. *Halt state*
   a. The contents of the counter are stable (do not change) and can be reliably and repeatedly read from the count registers.

b. The prescaler is forced to $1F whether or not it is in use.

c. The ZDS bit is forced to zero, regardless of the contents of the 24-bit counter.

2. *Run state*

a. The counter is clocked by the source programmed in the timer control register.

b. The counter is not *reliably* readable.

c. The prescaler is allowed to decrement if it is so programmed.

d. The ZDS status bit is set when the counter makes a $00 0001 to $00 0000 transition.

Timer Applications

The timer section of the PI/T is not as complex as a first reading of table 8.16 would suggest. In order to illustrate the operation of the timer, some of its possible applications are now presented.

Real-time clock A real-time clock, RTC, generates an interrupt at periodic intervals and may be used by the operating system to switch between several tasks (see chapter 6) or to update a record of the time-of-day. In this configuration, the T_{OUT} pin is connected to one of the host processor's interrupt request inputs and the TIACK* input used as an interrupt request input to the timer. The T_{IN} pin may be used as a clock input or the system clock selected. The format of the TCR needed to select the real-time clock mode is given in table 8.17.

The host processor first loads the counter preload registers with a 24-bit value and then configures the TCR as described previously. The timer enable bit of the TCR may be set at any time counting is to begin—it need not be set during the timer initialization phase.

When the counter counts down from $00 0001 to $00 0000, the ZDS status bit is set and the T_{OUT} pin asserted to generate an interrupt request. At the next clock input to the 24-bit counter, the counter is loaded with the contents of the counter preload register. The host processor should clear the ZDS status bit to

TABLE 8.17 Format of the TCR in the real-time mode

Bit	TCR7	TCR6	TCR5	TCR4	TCR3	TCR2	TCR1	TCR0
Value	1	×	1	0	0	0	0	1
Function	T_{OUT}/TIACK* control			ZD control		Clock control		Timer enable
	PC3/T_{OUT} = T_{OUT} timer interrupt enabled; T_{OUT} low when ZDS set			Counter reload on zero detect		Counter clock = CLK/32		

FIGURE 8.27   Timing diagram of the PI/T as a real-time clock

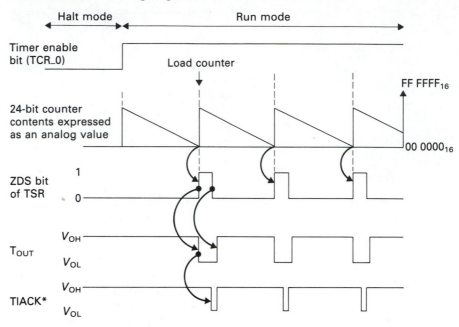

remove the source of the interrupt. The operation of the timer in this mode can be illustrated in PDL and by the timing diagram of figure 8.27:

```
REPEAT WHILE Timer_enable_bit = 1
        FOR I = Counter_preload_value DOWN_TO 0
                Clear ZDS_bit
                Negate T_OUT
        END_FOR
        Set ZDS_bit
        Assert T_OUT
END_REPEAT
```

Square wave generator   In this mode, the timer produces a square wave at its T_{OUT} terminal and interrupts are not generated. The format of the TCR in the square wave mode is almost identical to that of the real-time mode—the only major difference is that bit 7 of the TCR is clear. A glance at table 8.16 reveals that TCR7 controls T_{OUT}. When TCR7 is clear, the signal at the T_{OUT} pin is toggled every time the counter counts down to zero and the ZDS bit is set.

Figure 8.28 provides a timing diagram for the timer in the square wave mode. Note that, as above, the timer counting source may be obtained from CLK or from T_{IN} and may be prescaled by 32.

Interrupt after timeout   In this mode, the timer generates an interrupt after a programmed period of time has elapsed. As in the case of the real-time clock, T_{OUT} is connected to the appropriate interrupt request line of the host

FIGURE 8.28   Timing diagram of the PI/T as a square wave generator

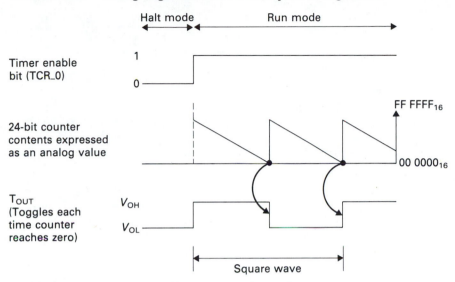

processor and TIACK∗ may be used as an interrupt acknowledge input. The source of timing may be derived from the system clock or from T_{IN}.

Table 8.18 gives the format of the TCR appropriate to this mode and the other operating modes discussed here. This configuration is similar to the real-time clock mode, except that the zero detect bit of the TCR is set. Consequently, when the counter reaches zero it rolls over to its maximum value rather than being loaded from the counter load registers. Figure 8.29 illustrates this process.

TABLE 8.18   Format of the TCR in various operating modes of the PI/T

Bit	TCR7	TCR6	TCR5	TCR4	TCR3	TCR2	TCR1	TCR0	MODE
	1	×	1	0	0	00 or	1×	1	1
	0	1	×	0	0	00 or	1×	1	2
	1	×	1	1	0	00 or	1×	1	3
	0	0	×	1	0	0	0	1	4
	0	0	×	1	0	1	×	1	5
	1	×	1	1	0	0	1	1	6
Function	T_{OUT}/TIACK∗ control			ZD control		Clock control		Timer enable	

Mode 1 = real-time clock   Mode 4 = elapsed time measurement
Mode 2 = square wave generator   Mode 5 = pulse counter
Mode 3 = interrupt after timeout   Mode 6 = period measurement

FIGURE 8.29   Timing diagram of the PI/T as a timeout interrupt generator

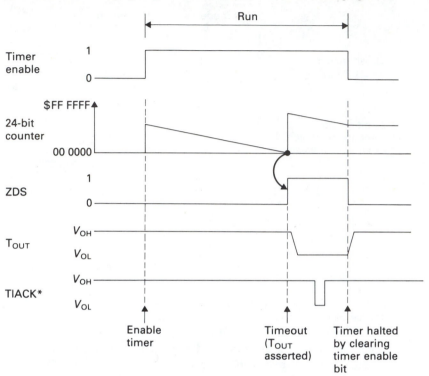

Once the interrupt has been serviced, the host processor can halt the timer and, if necessary, read the contents of the counter. At this point, the number in the counter gives an indication of the time elapsed between the interrupt request and its servicing.

Elapsed time measurement   This configuration allows the host processor to determine the time that elapses between the triggering of the 68230 timer and its halting by clearing its enable bit. Table 8.18 (mode 4) gives the format of the TCR in this mode. The processor initializes the timer by loading its counter preload register with $FF FFFF (all ones) and setting its TCR and then enables it by setting TCR_0. The value $FF FFFF is selected because it provides the longest possible counting period.

Once TCR_0 has been set, the prescaler counts down toward zero and decrements the counter each time it rolls over from $00 to $1F. When the event, whose action signals the end of the timing period, takes place, the processor clears the enable bit (TCR_0) and halts the countdown. The processor determines the timing period by reading the contents of the counter registers. Note that we are able to program the TCR to permit an external clock to be connected to T_{IN}. When an external clock or pulse generator is connected to the T_{IN} input and the TCR initialized, as in table 8.18, mode 5, the timer can be used to count the number of pulses at the T_{IN} pin between the points at which TCR_0 is set and cleared.

By setting bits TCR_2, TCR_1 to 0, 1, respectively, the timer can be started and stopped by T_{IN} (table 8.18, mode 6). In this case, the timer requires that both TCR_0 *and* T_{IN} be high before counting may begin. Therefore, once TCR_0 has been set under software control, counting begins only when T_{IN} goes high and stops when T_{IN} returns low. If T_{IN} is controlled by external circuitry, the processor can determine the period between the positive and negative transition of T_{IN}.

Summary

This chapter has introduced the interface between a microprocessor and an external device. We have looked at two aspects of interfaces in some detail—the DMA controller and the parallel interface/timer. Such peripherals are exceedingly complex because of their highly programmable modes of operation and their dependence on the system to which they are connected. However, the peripheral chip has done as much as any other component to make today's low-cost microcomputer a reality. Without serial and parallel interfaces, CRT controllers, and floppy disk controllers, the microcomputer would require large numbers of MSI chips to implement these interfaces.

Most of this chapter is devoted to the 68230 PI/T, one of the most sophisticated parallel ports available. The great advantage of the 68230 is its ability to operate as a 16-bit port or as two independent 8-bit ports. Each of these two modes has a wide range of handshaking procedures and can provide either single or double buffering of data. All these variations mean that the PI/T can easily interface with a very wide range of parallel ports with a minimum amount of user-supplied hardware or software.

Problems

1. Explain the meaning of the following terms:
   a. Nonbuffered input (or output)
   b. Single-buffered input (or output)
   c. Double-buffered input (or output)
   d. Open-loop data transfer
   e. Closed-loop data transfer
   f. Handshaking

2. Design a simple, single-channel DMA controller for the 68000 using SSI and MSI logic. The DMAC has a two-wire interface to the peripheral, consisting of REQ* and ACK*. When REQ* is asserted by a peripheral, the DMAC requests the bus by using its bus arbitration control lines, BR*, BG*, and BGACK*. The DMAC executes a single cycle of DMA at a time. When the transfer is complete, the DMAC asserts ACK* to indicate that it is ready for the next transfer.

3. A printer has an 8-bit parallel Centronics interface that consists of an 8-bit parallel data bus and three control lines. DSTB∗ is an active-low pulsed data strobe that indicates to the printer that the data on the data bus is valid. BUSY∗ is an output from the printer that, when high, indicates to the computer that the printer cannot accept data. ACKNGL∗ is an active-low response from the printer to DSTB∗ and indicates that the printer has captured the data. Design a suitable interface between a computer and the printer using a 68230 PI/T and write a program to control the PI/T.

4. Why does the 68230 PI/T have both port A and B data registers *and* port A and B alternate registers?

5. What is the effect of loading the following data values into the stated registers of a 68230 PI/T?

    a. $00 into PADDR (assume mode 0)
    b. $F0 into PADDR (assume mode 0)
    c. $FA into PADDR (assume mode 0)
    d. $5A into PADDR (assume mode 3)
    e. $00 into PGCR
    f. $F0 into PGCR
    g. $18 into PSRR
    h. $6E into PACR (assume $1F in PGCR)

6. Write an initialization routine to set up a 68230 PI/T with port A as an 8-bit double-buffered input port and port B as an 8-bit double-buffered output port. The PI/T is to operate in an interrupt-driven mode and all control signals are active-low. Port A uses H2 in a fully interlocked handshake mode and port B uses H4 in a pulsed handshake mode.

7. Initializing a 68230 PI/T is no fun because of its complexity. We would be better advised to use a menu-driven initialization program that displays options on the screen and asks the user to select the desired option(s). Write a program in any suitable language that will provide a menu-driven initialization program for the 68230 PI/T. The user must be invited to supply the options in plain English; for example, "Do you require 8-bit on 16-bit data transfers?"

Chapter 9

The Serial Input/
Output Interface

The vast majority of general-purpose microcomputers, except some entirely self-contained portable models, use a serial interface to communicate with remote peripherals such as CRT terminals. The serial interface, which moves information from point to point one bit at a time, is generally preferred to the parallel interface, which is able to move a group of bits simultaneously. This preference is not due to the high performance of a serial data link but to its low cost, simplicity, and ease of use. In this chapter we first describe how information is transmitted serially and then examine a typical parallel-to-serial and serial-to-parallel chip that forms the interface between a microprocessor and a serial data link. Because serial data link can operate in one of two modes, asynchronous or synchronous, a separate section is devoted to each mode. We also take a brief look at some of the standards for the transmission of serial data. The chapter ends with the description of a suitable serial interface for a 68000-based system. Throughout this chapter, the word *character* refers to the basic unit of information transmitted over a data link. The term character has been chosen because many data links transmit information in the form of text, so that the unit of transmitted information corresponds to a printed character.

Figure 9.1 illustrates the basic serial data link between a computer and a CRT terminal. A CRT terminal requires a two-way data link because information from the keyboard is transmitted to the computer and information from the computer is transmitted to the screen. Note that the *transmitted* data from the computer becomes the *received* data at the CRT terminal. Although this statement is an elementary and self-evident observation, confusion between transmitted and received data is a common source of error in the linking of computers and terminals.

A more detailed arrangement of a serial data link in terms of its functional components is given in figure 9.2. The heart of the data link is the box labeled "serial interface," which translates data between the form in which it is stored

FIGURE 9.1   Serial data link

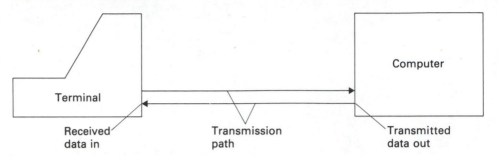

within the computer and the form in which it is transmitted over the data link. The conversion of data between parallel and serial form is often performed by a single LSI device called an asynchronous communications interface adaptor (ACIA).

The line drivers in figure 9.2 have the function of translating the TTL level signals processed by the ACIA into a suitable form for sending over the transmission path. The transmission path itself is normally a twisted pair of conductors, which accounts for its very low cost. Some systems employ more esoteric transmission paths such as fiber optics or infrared (IR) links. The connection between the line drivers and transmission path is labeled *plug and socket* in figure 9.2 to emphasize that such mundane things as plugs become very important if interchangeability is required. International specifications exist for this situation and for other aspects of the data link.

The two items at the computer end of the data link enclosed in "clouds" in figure 9.2 represent the software components of the data link. The lower cloud

FIGURE 9.2   Functional units of a serial data link

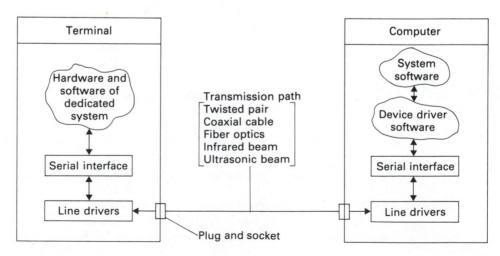

contains the software that directly controls the serial interface itself by performing operations such as transmitting a single character or receiving a character and checking it for certain types of error. On top of this software sits the application-level software, which uses the primitive operations executed by the lower-level software to carry out actions such as listing a file on the screen.

9.1 Asynchronous Serial Data Transmission

By far the most popular serial interface between a computer and its CRT terminal is the asynchronous serial interface. This interface is so called because the transmitted data and the received data are not synchronized over any extended period and therefore no special means of synchronizing the clocks at the transmitter and receiver is necessary. In fact, the asynchronous serial data link is a very old form of data transmission system and has its origin in the era of the teleprinter.

Serial data transmission systems have been around for a long time and are found in the telephone (human speech), Morse code, semaphore, and even the smoke signals used by American Indians. The fundamental problem encountered by all serial data transmission systems is how to split the incoming data stream into individual units (i.e., bits) and how to group these units into characters. For example, in Morse code the dots and dashes of a character are separated by an intersymbol space, while the individual characters are separated by an inter-character space, which is three times the duration of an intersymbol space.

First we examine how the data stream is divided into individual bits and the bits grouped into characters in an asynchronous serial data link. The key to the operation of this type of link is both simple and ingenious. Figure 9.3 gives the format of data transmitted over such a link.

An asynchronous serial data link is said to be character oriented, as information is transmitted in the form of groups of bits called characters. These characters are invariably units comprising seven or eight bits of "information" plus two to four control bits, and frequently correspond to ASCII-encoded characters. Initially, when no information is being transmitted, the line is in an idle state. Traditionally, the idle state is referred to as the *mark level*. By convention this corresponds to a logical one level.

When the transmitter wishes to send data, it first places the line in a *space* level (i.e., the complement of a mark) for one element period. This element is called the start bit and has a duration of T seconds. The transmitter then sends the character, one bit at a time, by placing each successive bit on the line for a duration of T seconds, until all bits have been transmitted. Then a single parity bit is calculated by the transmitter and sent after the data bits. Finally, the transmitter sends a stop bit at a mark level (i.e., the same level as the idle state) for one or two bit periods. Now the transmitter may send another character whenever it

FIGURE 9.3   Format of asynchronous serial data

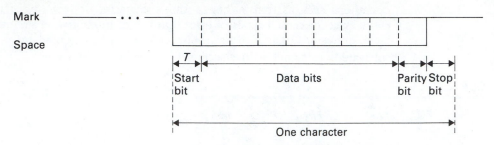

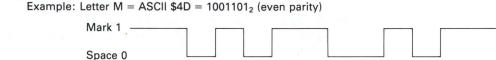

Example: Letter M = ASCII \$4D = 1001101_2 (even parity)

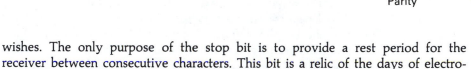

wishes. The only purpose of the stop bit is to provide a rest period for the receiver between consecutive characters. This bit is a relic of the days of electro-mechanical receivers and is not now strictly required for technical reasons, existing only for the purpose of compatibility with older equipment.

As the data wordlength may be 7 or 8 bits with odd, even, or no parity bits, plus either one or two stop bits, a total of twelve different possible formats can be used for serial data transmission—and this is before we consider that there are about seven commonly used values of T, the element duration. Connecting one serial link with another may therefore be difficult because so many options are available.

At the receiving end of an asynchronous serial data link, the receiver continually monitors the line looking for a start bit. Once the start bit has been detected, the receiver waits until the end of the start bit and then samples the next N bits at their centers, using a clock generated locally by the receiver. As each incoming bit is sampled, it is used to construct a new character. When the received character has been assembled, its parity is calculated and compared with the received parity bit following the character. If they are not equal, a parity error flag is set to indicate a transmission error.

The most critical aspect of the system is the receiver timing. The falling edge of the start bit triggers the receiver's local clock, which samples each incoming bit at its nominal center. Suppose the receiver clock waits $T/2$ seconds from the falling edge of a start bit and samples the incoming data every T seconds thereafter until the stop bit has been sampled. Figure 9.4 shows this situation. As the receiver's clock is not synchronized with the transmitter clock, the sampling is not exact.

FIGURE 9.4 Effect of unsynchronized transmitter and receiver clocks. Note that vertical lines with arrows indicate the points at which the received data is sampled

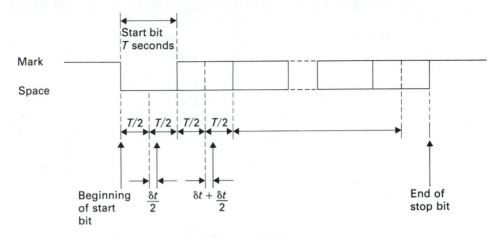

Let us assume that the receiver clock is running slow, so that a sample is taken every $T + \delta t$ seconds. The first bit of the data is sampled at $(T + \delta t)/2 + (T + \delta t)$ seconds after the falling edge of the start bit. The stop bit is sampled at time $(T + \delta t)/2 + N(T + \delta t)$, where N is the number of bits in the character following the start bit. The total accumulated error in sampling the stop bit is therefore $(T + \delta t)/2 + N(T + \delta t) - (T/2 + NT)$ or $(2N + 1)\delta t/2$ seconds. For correct operation, the stop bit must be sampled within $T/2$ seconds of its center so that:

$$\frac{T}{2} > \frac{(2N + 1)\delta t}{2}$$

or

$$\frac{\delta t}{T} < \frac{1}{2N + 1}$$

or

$$\frac{\delta t}{T} < \frac{100}{2N + 1} \quad \text{as a percentage.}$$

If $N = 9$ for a 7-bit character + parity bit + one stop bit, the maximum permissible error is $100/19 = 5$ percent. Fortunately, almost all clocks are now crystal controlled, and the error between transmitter and receiver clocks is likely to be a tiny fraction of 1 percent.

The most obvious disadvantage of asynchronous data transmission is the need for a start, parity, and stop bit for each transmitted character. If 7-bit characters are used, the overall efficiency is only $7/(7 + 3) \times 100 = 70$ percent. A less obvious disadvantage is due to the character-oriented nature of the data link. Whenever the data link connects a CRT terminal to a computer few problems arise, as the terminal is itself character oriented. However, if the data link is being used to, say, dump binary data to a magnetic tape, problems arise. If the data is arranged as 8-bit bytes with all 256 possible values corresponding to valid data elements, it is difficult (but not impossible) to embed control characters (e.g., tape start or stop) within the data stream because the same character must be used both as pure data (i.e., part of the message) and for control purposes.

If 7-bit characters are used, pure binary data cannot be transmitted in the form of one character per byte. Two characters are needed to record each byte and this condition is clearly inefficient. We will see later how synchronous serial data links overcome this problem.

We have now described how information can be transmitted serially in the form of 7- or 8-bit characters. The next step is to show how these characters are encoded.

ASCII Code

Although computing generally suffers from a lack of standardization, the ASCII code is one of the few exceptions. Many microcomputers employ the ASCII code to represent information in character form internally, and for the exchange of information between themselves and CRT terminals. The ASCII code, or American Standard Code for Information Interchange, is one of several codes used to represent alphanumeric characters. As long ago as the 1920s, the Baudot or Murray code was designed for the teleprinter. This code, still used by the international telex service, represents characters by five bits. As this system provides only 2^5 unique values, one of the 32 possible values acts as a shift, affecting the meaning of the following characters. The effective number of characters available is thereby increased.

The ASCII code employs seven bits to give a total of 128 unique values. These bits are sufficient to provide a full 96-character upper and lower case printing set, together with 32 characters to control the operation of the data link and the terminal itself. The ASCII code has now been adopted universally, and is almost identical to the International Standards Organization ISO-7 code.

Had the ASCII code been developed today, it would almost certainly be an 8-bit code. Unfortunately, the ASCII character set does not include "national" characters such as the German umlaut or the French accents. Moreover, a graphical character set similar to that used by Teletex would have been very helpful. However, microcomputer manufacturers have tended to design their own graphics codes, leading to incompatibility.

Table 9.1 presents the ASCII code. The binary value of a character is obtained by reading the three most-significant bits at the top of the column in which the character occurs and then taking the four least-significant bits from its

TABLE 9.1   ASCII code

$b_3b_2b_1b_0$		$b_6b_5b_4$ 0 — 000	1 — 001	2 — 010	3 — 011	4 — 100	5 — 101	6 — 110	7 — 111
0	0000	NUL	DLC	SP	0	@	P	'	p
1	0001	SOH	DC1	!	1	A	Q	a	q
2	0010	STX	DC2	"	2	B	R	b	r
3	0011	ETX	DC3	#	3	C	S	c	s
4	0100	EOT	DC4	$	4	D	T	d	t
5	0101	ENQ	NAK	%	5	E	U	e	u
6	0110	ACK	SYN	&	6	F	V	f	v
7	0111	BEL	ETB	'	7	G	W	g	w
8	1000	BS	CAN	(	8	H	X	h	x
9	1001	HT	EM	)	9	I	Y	i	y
A	1010	LT	SUB	*	:	J	Z	j	z
B	1011	VT	ESC	+	;	K	[	k	{
C	1100	FF	FS	,	<	L	\	l	|
D	1101	CR	GS	–	=	M	]	m	}
E	1110	SO	RS	.	>	N	Λ	n	~
F	1111	SI	VS	/	?	O	_	o	DEL

row. For example, the character "m " is in the column headed 110 and the row headed 1101; therefore, the binary code for "m" is 110 1101 (or \$6D in hexadecimal).

9.2 Asynchronous Communications Interface Adaptor (ACIA)

One of the first general-purpose interface devices produced by the semiconductor manufacturers was the asynchronous communications interface adaptor, or ACIA. The ACIA relieves the system software of all the basic tasks involved in converting data between serial and parallel forms; that is, the ACIA contains almost all the logic necessary to provide an asynchronous data link between a computer and an external system.

One of the earliest and still popular ACIAs is the 6850 illustrated in figure 9.5. This particular ACIA will be described because it is much easier to understand than some of the newer ACIAs and is still widely used in microcomputers. Once the reader understands how the 6850 ACIA operates, he or she can read the data sheet of any other ACIA. Like any other digital device, the 6850 has a hardware model, a software model, and a functional model. We look at the

FIGURE 9.5   The 6850 ACIA

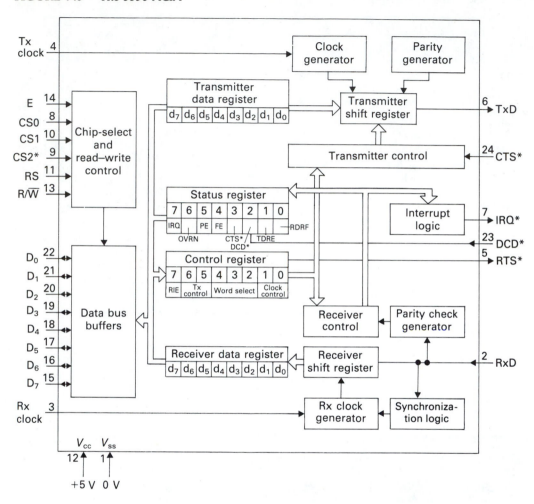

hardware model first. Figure 9.6 gives the hardware model of the 6850 together with its timing diagram. From the designer's point of view, the 6850's hardware can be subdivided into three sections: the CPU side, the transmitter side, and the receiver side.

CPU Side

As far as the CPU is concerned, the 6850 behaves almost exactly like a static read/write memory; figure 9.6 shows the read and write cycles on the same diagram. However, one important difference exists between the 6850 and conventional RAM. The 6850's memory accesses are synchronized to an external E or

FIGURE 9.6   Hardware model of the ACIA and its timing diagram

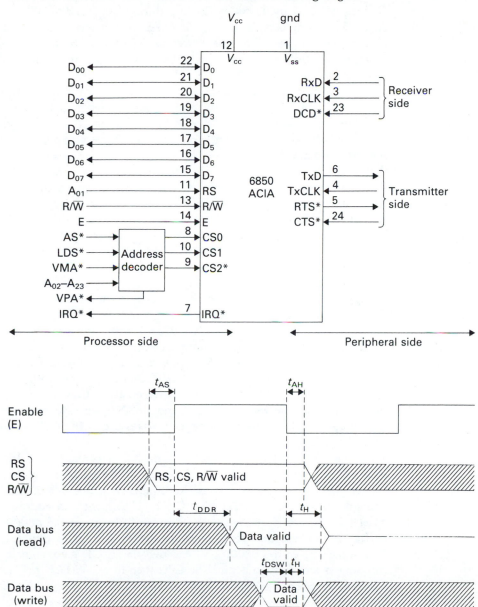

enable clock. In 6800- or 6809-based systems, this situation presents no problem as the processor itself is also synchronized to the E (or $\phi 2$ in 6800 terminology) clock that it provides. In the case of the 68000, the ACIA must be interfaced either by using VPA* and VMA* or asynchronously by means of additional logic.

The ACIA is a byte-oriented device and can be interfaced to D_{00} through D_{07} and strobed by LDS*, or to D_{08} through D_{15} and strobed by UDS*. The ACIA has a single register select line, RS, that determines the internal location (i.e., register) addressed by the processor. Typically, RS is connected to the processor's A_{01} address output, so that the lower location is selected by address X and the upper by address $X + 2$.

Three chip-select inputs are provided, two of which are active-high and one active-low. This spectacular display of overkill comes from the days when address decoders were relatively expensive and memories small. By using the chip selects alone, partial address decoding is possible to achieve without any additional components. In many modern systems just one of the chip-select inputs takes part in the address decoding process. The remaining two are permanently enabled. This situation is unfortunate, as the other two pins could have provided the ACIA with additional features—such as a RESET* input or an on-chip clock.

The 6850 has an interrupt request output, IRQ*, that can be connected to any of the 68000's seven levels of interrupt request input. As the 6850 does not support vectored interrupts, autovectored interrupts must be used in the way described in chapter 6.

Unusually, the 6850 does not have a RESET* input because there were not enough pins to provide the function and the manufacturer felt that RESET* was the most dispensable of functions. When power is first applied, some sections of the ACIA are reset automatically by an internal power-on-reset circuit. Afterwards, a secondary reset by software is performed, as we shall describe later.

The CPU side of the 6850 has a clock input labeled E (i.e., ENABLE). As with other 6800-series peripherals, the E input must be both free running and synchronized to read/write accesses between the ACIA and the processor. The simplest interface between the ACIA and a 68000 processor is given in figure 9.7. This circuit is entirely conventional and makes use of the CPU's synchronous bus control signals.

The lower byte of the 68000's data bus is connected to the ACIA's data input/output pins, D_0 to D_7, which locate all the ACIA's registers in the lower half of words at odd addresses. Remember that the 68000 address space is arranged so that lower-order bits (D_{00} to D_{07}) have odd addresses and higher-order bits (D_{08} to D_{15}) have even addresses. Whenever the 68000 addresses the ACIA, the address decoder detects the access and forces SELECT_ACIA* low. This signal drives the 68000's VPA* low via an OR gate, signaling that a synchronous bus cycle is to begin. The CPU then forces VMA* low and the ACIA is selected by SELECT_ACIA*, VMA*, and LDS* all being low simultaneously. During this access, R/$\overline{\text{W}}$ from the CPU determines the direction of data transfer and A_{01} the location of the internal register selected in the ACIA.

The lower portion of figure 9.7 is intended to show how the ACIA is operated in the autovectored interrupt mode. When the ACIA forces its IRQ* line low, a level 5 interrupt is signaled to the CPU. Assuming this level is enabled, IACK5* from the decoder goes low and is then ANDed with IRQ* from the ACIA and connected to VPA* via an OR gate. The purpose of ANDed IACK5*

FIGURE 9.7   Interface between a 6850 ACIA and a 68000 CPU

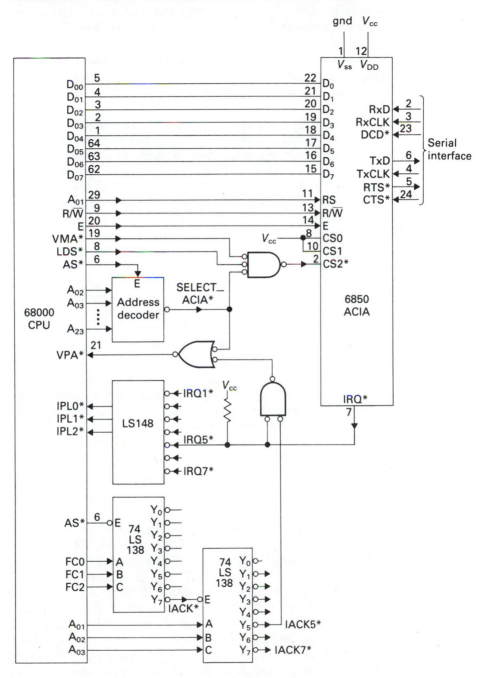

with IRQ* is to permit an interrupt acknowledge to the 68000 (via VPA*) only when the ACIA is putting out an interrupt request while an interrupt acknowledge at the appropriate level is being indicated by the CPU.

Receiver and Transmitter Sides of the ACIA

One of the great advantages of peripherals like the 6850 ACIA is that they isolate the CPU from the outside world both physically and logically. The *physical isolation* means that the engineer who is connecting a peripheral device to a microprocessor system does not have to worry about the electrical and timing requirements of the CPU itself. In other words, all the engineer needs to understand about the ACIA is the nature of its transmitter-side and receiver-side interfaces. Similarly, the peripheral performs a *logical isolation* by hiding the details of information transfer across it; for example, the operation of transmitting a character from an ACIA is carried out by the instruction MOVE. B D0,ACIA_DATA, where register D0 contains the character to be transmitted and ACIA_DATA is the address of the data register in the ACIA. All the actions necessary to actually serialize the data and append start, parity, and stop bits is carried out automatically (i.e., invisibly) by the ACIA.

Here, only the essential details of the ACIA's transmitter and receiver sides are presented, because the way in which they function is described more fully when we come to the logical organization of the 6850. The peripheral-side interface of the 6850 is divided into two entirely separate groups—the receiver group, which forms the interface between the ACIA and a source of incoming data, and the transmitter group, which forms the interface between the ACIA and the destination for outgoing data. *Incoming* and *outgoing* are used with respect to the ACIA. The nature of these signals is strongly affected by one particular role of the ACIA—its role as an interface between a computer and the public switched telephone network via a modem.

Receiver Side

Incoming data to the ACIA is handled by three pins: RxD, RxCLK, DCD*. Like all other inputs and outputs to the ACIA, these are TTL-level compatible signals. The RxD (receiver data input) pin receives serial data from the transmission path to which the ACIA is connected. The idle (mark) state at this pin is a TTL logical one level. A receiver clock is provided at the RxCLK (receiver clock) input pin by the systems designer. The RxCLK clock must be either the same, 16, or 64 times the rate at which bits are received at the data input terminal. Many modern ACIAs include on-chip receiver and transmitter clocks, relieving the system designer of the necessity of providing an additional external oscillator.

The third and last component of the receiver group is an active-low DCD* (data carrier detect) input. DCD* is intended for use in conjunction with a modem and, when low, indicates to the ACIA that the incoming data is valid. When inactive-high, DCD* indicates that the incoming data might be erroneous. This situation may arise if the level (i.e., signal strength) of the data received at the end of a telephone line drops below a predetermined value or the connection itself is broken.

Transmitter Side

The transmitter side of the ACIA comprises four pins: TxCLK, TxD, RTS*, and CTS*. The transmitter clock input (TxCLK) provides a timing signal from which the ACIA derives the timing of the transmitted signal elements. In most applications of the ACIA, the transmitter and receiver clocks are connected together and a common oscillator used for both transmitter and receiver sides of the ACIA. Serial data is transmitted from the TxD (transmit data) pin of the ACIA, with a logical one level representing the idle (mark) state.

An active-low request to send (RTS*) output indicates that the ACIA is ready to transmit information. This output is set or cleared under software control and can be used to switch on any equipment needed to transmit the serial data over some data link. Some use it to switch on a cassette recorder when the ACIA is interfaced to a magnetic tape recording system.

An active-low clear to send (CTS*) input indicates to the transmitter side of the ACIA that the external equipment used to transmit the serial data is ready. When negated, this input inhibits the transmission of data. CTS* is a modem signal that indicates that the transmitter carrier is present and that transmission may go ahead.

Operation of the 6850 ACIA

The software model of the 6850 has four user-accessible registers as defined in table 9.2. These registers are: a transmit data register (TDR), a receive data register (RDR), a system control register (CR), and a system status register (SR). As there are four registers and yet the ACIA has only a single register select input, RS, a way must be found to distinguish between registers. The ACIA uses the

TABLE 9.2   Register selection scheme of the 6850 ACIA

ADDRESS	RS	R/$\overline{\text{W}}$	REGISTER TYPE	REGISTER FUNCTION	
00 E001	0	0	Write only	Control register	(CR)
00 E001	0	1	Read only	Status register	(SR)
00 E003	1	0	Write only	Transmit data register	(TDR)
00 E003	1	1	Read only	Receive data register	(RDR)

NOTE: *Base address of ACIA = $00 E001.*

R/$\overline{\text{W}}$ input to make this distinction. Two registers are read-only (i.e., RDR, SR) and two are write-only (TDR, CR). Although a perfectly logical, indeed an elegant, thing to do, I do not like it. I am perfectly happy to accept read-only registers, but I am suspicious of the write-only variety because the contents of a write-only register are impossible to verify. Suppose I have a program with a bug that executed an unintended write to a write-only register. I cannot detect the change by reading back the contents of the register.

Table 9.2 also gives the address of each register, assuming that the base address of the ACIA is $00 E001 and that it is selected by LDS*. The purpose of this exercise is twofold: it shows that the address of the lower-order byte is odd and that the pairs of read-only and write-only registers are separated by two (i.e., $00 E001 and $00 E003).

Control Register

Because the ACIA is a versatile device and can be operated in any of several different modes, the control register permits the programmer to define its operational characteristics. This job can even be done dynamically if the need ever arises. Table 9.3 shows how the eight bits of the control register are grouped into four logical fields.

Bits CR0 and CR1 determine the ratio between the transmitted or received bit rates and the transmitter and receiver clocks, respectively. The clocks operate at the same, 16, or 64 times the data rate. Most applications of the 6850 employ a receiver/transmitter clock at 16 times the data rate with CR1 = 0 and CR0 = 1. Setting CR1 = CR2 = 1 is a special case and serves as a software reset of the ACIA. A software reset clears all internal status bits, with the exception of CTS* and DCD*. A software reset to the 6850 is invariably carried out during the initialization phase of the host processor's reset procedures.

The *word select* field, bits CR2, CR3, and CR4, determines the format of the received or transmitted characters. The eight possible data formats are given in table 9.3. Note that these bits also enable the type of parity (if any) and the number of stop bits to be defined under software control, which is one of the nice features of a programmable peripheral. Possibly the most common data format for the transmission of information between a processor and a CRT terminal is: start bit + 7 data bits + even parity + 1 stop bit. The corresponding value of CR4, CR3, CR2 is 0, 1, 0.

The *transmitter control* field, CR5 and CR6, selects the state of the active-low request to send (RTS*) output and determines whether or not the transmitter section of the ACIA may generate an interrupt by asserting its IRQ* output. In most systems, RTS* is active-low whenever the ACIA is transmitting, because RTS* is used to activate equipment connected to the ACIA. The programming of the transmitter interrupt enable, and for that matter the receiver interrupt enable, is very much a function of the operating mode of the ACIA. If the ACIA is operated in a polled-data mode, interrupts are not necessary.

If the transmitter interrupt is enabled, an interrupt is generated by the transmitter whenever the transmit data register (TDR) is empty, signifying the need for

TABLE 9.3   Structure of the ACIA's control register

BIT	CR7	CR6 CR5	CR4 CR3 CR2	CR1 CR0
Function	Receiver interrupt enable	Transmitter control	Word select	Counter division

CR1	CR0	DIVISION RATIO
0	0	1
0	1	16
1	0	64
1	1	Master reset

CR4	CR3	CR2	WORD SELECT			
			DATA WORD LENGTH	PARITY	STOP BITS	TOTAL BITS
0	0	0	7	Even	2	11
0	0	1	7	Odd	2	11
0	1	0	7	Even	1	10
0	1	1	7	Odd	1	10
1	0	0	8	None	2	11
1	0	1	8	None	1	10
1	1	0	8	Even	1	11
1	1	1	8	Odd	1	11

CR6	CR5	TRANSMITTER CONTROL	
		RTS*	TRANSMITTER INTERRUPT
0	0	Low (0)	Disabled
0	1	Low (0)	Enabled
1	0	High (1)	Disabled
1	1	Low (0)	Disabled and break

CR7	RECEIVER INTERRUPT ENABLE
0	Receiver may not interrupt
1	Receiver may interrupt

new data from the CPU. When the ACIA's clear to send (CTS*) input is inactive-high, the TDR empty flag of the status register is held low, inhibiting any transmitter interrupt.

Setting both CR6 and CR5 to a logical one simultaneously creates a special case. When both these bits are high, a *break* is transmitted by the transmitter data output pin. A break is a condition in which the transmitter output is held at the active level (i.e., space or TTL logical zero) continuously. This condition may be employed to force an interrupt at a distant receiver, because the asynchronous serial format precludes the existence of a space level for longer than about ten bit periods. The term *break* originates from the old current-loop data transmission system when a break was affected by disrupting (i.e., breaking) the flow of current round a loop.

The *receiver interrupt enable* field consists of one bit, CR7, that enables the generation of interrupts by the receiver when it is set (CR7 = 1) and disables receiver interrupts when it is clear (CR7 = 0). The receiver asserts its IRQ* output, assuming CR7 = 1, when the receiver data register full (RDRF) bit of the status register is set, indicating the presence of a new data character ready for the CPU to read. Two other circumstances also force a receiver interrupt. An overrun (see later) sets the RDRF bit and generates an interrupt. Finally, a receiver interrupt can also be generated by a high-to-low transition at the active-low data carrier detect (DCD*) input, signifying a loss of the carrier from a modem. Note that CR7 is a composite interrupt enable bit and enables all the three forms of receiver interrupt described previously. To enable either an interrupt caused by the RDR being empty or an interrupt caused by a positive transition at the DCD* pin alone is impossible.

Status Register

The eight bits of the read-only status register are depicted in table 9.4 and serve to indicate the status of both the transmitter and receiver portions of the ACIA at any instant.

SR0—receiver data register full (RDRF)   When set, the RDRF bit indicates that the receiver data register (RDR) is full and a new word has been received. If the receiver interrupt is enabled by CR7 = 1, a logical one in SR0 also sets the interrupt status bit SR7 (i.e., IRQ). The RDRF bit is cleared either by reading the data in the receiver data register or by carrying out a software reset on the control register. Whenever the data carrier detect (DCD*) input is inactive-

TABLE 9.4   Format of the status register

BIT	SR7	SR6	SR5	SR4	SR3	SR2	SR1	SR0
Function	IRQ	PE	OVRN	FE	CTS	DCD	TDRE	RDRF

high, the RDRF bit remains clamped at a logical zero, indicating the absence of any valid input.

SR1—transmitter data register empty (TDRE)   The TDRE bit is the transmitter counterpart of the RDRF bit, SR0. A logical one in SR1 indicates that the contents of the transmit data register (TDR) have been sent to the transmitter and that the register is now ready to transmit new data. TDRE is cleared either by loading the transmit data register or by performing a software reset. If the transmitter interrupt is enabled, a logical one in bit SR1 (i.e., TDRE) also sets bit SR7 of the status word. Note again that SR7 is a composite interrupt bit because it is also set by an interrupt originating from the receiver side of the ACIA. If the clear to send (CTS*) input is inactive-high, the TDRE bit is held low, indicating that the terminal equipment is not ready for data.

SR2—data carrier detect (DCD*)   This status bit, associated with the receiver side of the ACIA, is normally employed when the ACIA is connected to the telephone network via a modem. Whenever the DCD* input to the ACIA is inactive-high, SR2 is set. A logical one on the DCD* line generally signifies that the incoming serial data is faulty, which also has the effect of clearing the SR0 (i.e., RDRF) bit, as possible erroneous input should not be interpreted as valid data.

When the DCD* input makes a low-to-high transition, not only is SR2 set but the composite interrupt request bit, SR7, is also set if the receiver interrupt is enabled. Note that SR2 remains set even if the DCD* input later returns active-low. This action traps any occurrence of DCD* high, even if it goes high only briefly. To clear SR2, the CPU must read the contents of the status register and then the contents of the data register.

SR3—clear to send (CTS*)   The CTS* bit directly reflects the status of the CTS* input on the ACIA's transmitter side. An active-low level on the CTS* input indicates that the transmitting device (modem, paper tape punch, teletype, cassette recorder, etc.) is ready to receive serial data from the ACIA. If the CTS* input and therefore the CTS* status bit are high, the transmit data register empty bit, SR1, is inhibited (clamped at a logical zero) and no data may be transmitted by the ACIA. Unlike the DCD* status bit, the logical value of the CTS* status bit is determined only by the CTS* input and is not affected by any software operation on the ACIA.

SR4—framing error (FE)   A framing error is detected by the absence of a stop bit and indicates a synchronization (i.e., timing) error, a faulty transmission, or a break condition. The framing error status bit, SR4, is set whenever the ACIA determines that a received character is incorrectly framed by a start bit and a stop bit. The framing error status bit is automatically cleared or set during the receiver data transfer time and is present throughout the time that the associated character is available. In other words, an FE bit is generated for each character received and a new character overwrites the old one's FE bit.

SR5—receiver overrun (OVRN)   The receiver overrun status bit is set when a character is received by the ACIA but is not read by the CPU before a subsequent character is received, overwriting the last character, which is now lost. Consequently, the receiver overrun bit indicates that one or more characters in the data stream have been lost. The OVRN status bit is set at the midpoint of the last bit of the second character received in succession without a read of the RDR having occurred. Synchronization of the incoming data is not affected by an overrun error—the error is due to the CPU not having read a character, rather than by any fault in the transmission and reception process. The overrun bit is cleared after reading data from the RDR or by a software reset.

SR6—parity error (PE)   The parity error status bit, SR6, is set whenever the received parity bit in the current character does not match the parity bit of the character generated locally in the ACIA from the received data bits. Odd or even parity may be selected by writing the appropriate code into bits CR2, CR3, and CR4 of the control register. If no parity is selected, then both the transmitter parity generator and receiver parity checker are disabled. Once a parity error has been detected and the parity error status bit set, it remains set as long as the erroneous data remains in the receiver register.

SR7—interrupt request (IRQ)   The interrupt request status bit, SR7, is a composite active-high (note!) interrupt request flag, and is set whenever the ACIA wishes to interrupt the CPU, for whatever reason. The IRQ bit is set active-high by any of the following events:

1.   Receiver data register full (SR0 set) and receiver interrupt enabled.

2.   Transmitter data register empty (SR1 set) and transmitter interrupt enabled.

3.   Data carrier detect status bit (SR2) set and receiver interrupt enabled.

Whenever SR7 is active-high, the active-low open-drain IRQ* output from the ACIA is pulled low. The IRQ bit is cleared by a read from the RDR, or by a write to the TDR, or by a software master reset.

Using the 6850 ACIA

The most daunting thing about many microprocessor interface chips is their sheer complexity. Often this complexity is more imaginary than real, because such peripherals are usually operated in only one of the many different modes that are software selectable. This fact is particularly true of the 6850 ACIA. Figure 9.8 shows how the 6850 is operated in a minimal mode. Only its serial data input (RxD) and output (TxD) are connected to an external system. The request to send (RTS*) output is left unconnected and clear to send (CTS*) and data carrier detect (DCD*) are both strapped to ground at the ACIA.

In a minimal (and noninterrupt) mode, bits 2 to 7 of the status register can be ignored. Of course, the error-detecting facilities of the ACIA are therefore

FIGURE 9.8   Minimal serial interface using the 6850 ACIA

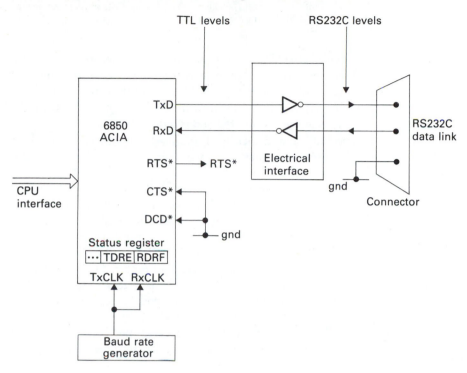

thrown away. The software necessary to drive the ACIA in this minimal mode consists of three subroutines: an initialization, an input, and an output routine:

```
ACIAC       EQU       $E0001              Address of control/status register
ACIAD       EQU       ACIAC+2             Address of data register
RDRF        EQU       0                   Receiver data register full
TDRE        EQU       1                   Transmitter data register empty

INITIALIZE  MOVE.B    #%00000011,ACIAC    Reset the ACIA
            MOVE.B    #%00011001,ACIAC    Set up control word—disable
            RTS                           interrupts, RTS* low, 8 data
                                          bits, even parity, 1 stop bit,
                                          16 × clock

INPUT       BTST.B    #RDRF,ACIAC         Test receiver status
            BEQ       INPUT               Poll until receiver has data
            MOVE.B    ACIAD,D0            Put data in D0
            RTS
```

```
OUTPUT    BTST. B   #TDRE, ACIAC          Test transmitter status
          BEQ       OUTPUT                Poll until transmitter ready for data
          MOVE. B   D0, ACIAD             Transmit the data
          RTS
```

The INITIALIZE routine is called once before either input or output is carried out and has the effect of executing a software reset on the ACIA followed by setting up its control register. The control word %00011001 (see table 9.3) defines an 8-bit word with even parity and a clock rate (TxCLK, RxCLK) 16 times the data rate of the transmitted and received data.

The INPUT and OUTPUT routines are both entirely straightforward. Each tests the appropriate status bit and then reads data from or writes data to the ACIA's data register.

It is also possible to operate the ACIA in a minimal interrupt-driven mode. The IRQ* output is connected to one of the 68000's seven levels of interrupt request input and arrangements are made to supply the CPU with VPA* during an interrupt acknowledge cycle. Both transmitter and receiver interrupts are enabled by writing 1, 0, 1 into bits CR7, CR6, CR5 of the status register.

When a transmitter or receiver interrupt is initiated, it is still necessary to examine the RDRE and TDRE bits of the status register to determine that the ACIA did indeed request the interrupt and to separate transmitter and receiver requests for service. The effect of interrupt-driven I/O is to eliminate the time-wasting polling routines required by programmed I/O.

Figure 9.9 shows how the ACIA can be operated in a more sophisticated

FIGURE 9.9   General-purpose serial interface using the 6850 ACIA

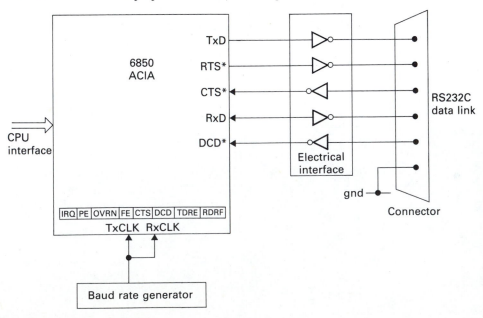

mode. The reader may be tempted to ask, "Why bother with a complex operating mode if the 6850 works quite happily in a basic mode?" The answer is that the operating mode in figure 9.9 provides more facilities than the basic mode of figure 9.8.

In Figure 9.9 the transmitter side of the ACIA sends an RTS* signal and receives a CTS* signal from the remote terminal equipment. Now the remote equipment is able to say, "I am ready to receive your data," by asserting CTS*. In the cut-down mode of figure 9.8, the ACIA simply sends data and hopes for the best!

Similarly, the receiver side of the ACIA uses the data carrier detect (DCD*) input to signal to the host computer that the receiver circuit us in a position to receive data. If DCD* is negated, the terminal equipment is unable to send data to the ACIA.

The software necessary to receive data when operating the 6850 in its more sophisticated mode is considerably more complex than that of the previous example. Provision for a full input routine is not possible here, as such a routine would include recovery procedures from the errors detected by the 6850 ACIA. These procedures are, of course, dependent on the nature of the system and the protocol used to move data between a transmitter and receiver. However, the following fragment of an input routine gives some idea of how the 6850's status register is used:

```
ACIA          EQU     $⟨ACIA address⟩
ACIAD         EQU     ACIA + 2
RDRF          EQU     0                      Receiver_data_register_full
TDRE          EQU     1                      Transmitter_data_register_empty
DCD           EQU     2                      Data_carrier_detect
CTS           EQU     3                      Clear_to_send
FE            EQU     4                      Framing_error
OVRN          EQU     5                      Over_run
PE            EQU     6                      Parity_error
*
INPUT         MOVE.B  ACIAC,D0               Get status from ACIA
              BTST    #RDRF,D0               Test for received character
              BNE.S   ERROR_CHECK            If character received, then test SR
              BTST    #DCD,D0                Else test for loss of signal
              BEQ     INPUT                  Repeat loop while CTS clear
              BRA.S   DCD_ERROR              Else deal with loss of signal
ERROR_CHECK   BTST    #FE,D0                 Test for framing error
              BNE.S   FE_ERROR               If framing error, deal with it
              BTST    #OVRN,D0               Test for overrun
              BNE.S   OVRN_ERROR             If overrun, deal with it
              BTST    #PE,D0                 Test for parity error
              BNE.S   PE_ERROR               If parity error, deal with it
              MOVE.B  ACIAD,D0               Load the input into D0
              BRA.S   EXIT                   Return
```

```
DCD_ERROR       Deal with loss of signal
                BRA.S    EXIT
FE_ERROR        Deal with framing error
                BRA.S    EXIT
OVRN_ERROR      Deal with overrun error
                BRA.S    EXIT
PE_ERROR        Deal with parity error
EXIT            RTS
```

9.3 Synchronous Serial Data Transmission

The type of asynchronous serial data link described in section 9.1 is widely employed to link relatively slow peripherals such as printers and VDTs with processors. Where information has to be transferred between the individual computers of a network, synchronous serial data transmission is a more popular choice. In a synchronous serial data transmission system, the information is transmitted continuously without gaps between adjacent groups of bits. I use the expression *groups of bits* because synchronous systems can transmit entire blocks of pure binary information at a time, rather than transmitting information as a sequence of ASCII-encoded characters. Before continuing, we need to point out that synchronous serial data links are often used in a much more sophisticated way than their asynchronous counterparts, which simply move data between a processor and its peripheral. This section covers only the basic details of a synchronous serial data link.

Two problems face the designer of a synchronous serial system. One is how to divide the incoming data stream into individual bits and the other is how to divide the data bits into meaningful units.

Bit Synchronization

As synchronous serial data transmission involves very long (effectively infinite) streams of data elements, the clocks at the transmitting and receiving ends of a data link must therefore be permanently synchronized. If a copy of the transmitter's clock were available at the receiver, no difficulty would be encountered in breaking up the data stream into individual bits. As this arrangement requires an extra transmission path between the transmitter and the receiver, it is not a popular solution to the problem of bit synchronization.

A better solution is found by encoding the data to be transmitted in such a way that a synchronizing signal is included with the data signal. Here, we do not

FIGURE 9.10   Phase-encoded synchronous serial bit stream

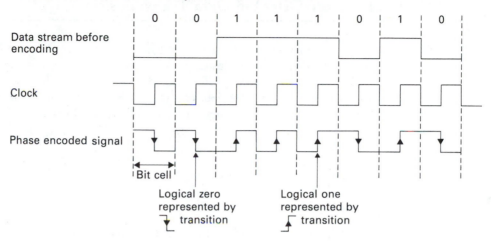

delve deeply into the ways in which this situation may be achieved but show one popular arrangement.

The basic method of extracting a timing signal from synchronous serial data is illustrated in figure 9.10. The serial data stream is combined with a clock signal to give the encoded signal, which is actually transmitted over the data link. The encoding algorithm is simple. A logical one is represented by a positive transition in the center of a bit cell and a logical zero by a negative transition. This form of encoding is called phase encoding (PE) or Manchester encoding and is widely used. At the receiver, the incoming data can readily be split into a clock signal and a data signal. Integrated circuits that modulate or demodulate Manchester-encoded signals are readily available.

Word Synchronization

Having divided the incoming stream into individual data elements (i.e., bits), the next step is to group the bits together into meaningful units. I have called these *words*, although they may vary from eight bits long to thousands of bits long. At first sight, dividing a continuous stream of bits into individual groups of bits might appear to be a most difficult task. Infactitisquiteaneasytasktoform-bitsintowords. Here I have deleted interword spacing in my plain text, making it harder, but not impossible, to read. The reader examines the string of letters and looks for recognizable groups corresponding to valid words in English. A similar technique can be applied to continuous streams of binary data. Two basic modes of operation of synchronous serial data links exist: character oriented and bit oriented. In the former, the data steam is divided into separate characters and in the latter it is divided into much longer blocks of pure binary data.

Character-Oriented Data Transmission

In character-oriented data transmission systems, the information to be transmitted is encoded in the form of (usually) ASCII characters. One of the most popular character-oriented systems is called BISYNC or binary synchronous data transmission. Take, for example, the four-character string "Alan;" it would be sent as the sequence of four seven-bit characters. The individual letters are ASCII encoded as:

$$A = \$41$$

$$l = \$6C$$

$$a = \$61$$

$$n = \$6E$$

Putting these together and reading the data stream from left to right with the first bit representing the least-significant bit of the "A," we get:

1000001001101110000110111011.

Some method is needed of identifying the beginning of a message. Once this has been done, the bits can be divided into characters by arranging them into groups of seven (or eight if a parity bit is used) for the duration of the message.

The ASCII code includes a number of characters specifically designed to control the flow of data over a synchronous serial data link. One such character is SYN (as in SYNchronization), whose code is $16 or 0010110. SYN is used to denote the beginning of a message. The receiver reads the incoming bits and looks for the string 0010110, representing a SYN and therefore the start of a message. Unfortunately, such a simple scheme is fatally flawed. The end of one character might be combined with the beginning of the following character to create a false SYN pattern. To avoid this situation, two SYN characters are transmitted sequentially. The receiver reads the first SYN and then looks for the second. If the receiver does not find another SYN, it assumes a false synchronization and continues looking for a valid SYN.

In addition to the synchronization character, the ASCII code provides other characters, such as STX (start of text), to help the user format data into meaningful units. However, character-oriented data transmission systems are not as popular as bit-oriented systems and are therefore not dealt with further here.

Bit-Oriented Data Transmission

While the ASCII code is excellent for representing text, it is ill-fitted to the representation of pure binary data. Pure binary data can be anything from a core dump (a block of memory) or a program in binary form to floating-point numbers. When data is represented in character form, choosing one particular character (e.g., SYN) as a special marker is easy. When the data is in a pure binary form, choosing any particular data word as a reserved marker or flag is apparently impossible. Bit-oriented protocols (BOPs) have been devised to handle pure binary data.

Fortunately, a remarkably simple and very elegant technique can be used to solve this problem. The beginning of each new block of data, called a frame, is denoted by the special (i.e., unique) binary sequence 01111110. Whenever the receiver detects this pattern, it knows that is has found the start (or end) of a block of data. The special sequence 01111110 is called an opening or closing flag. Of course, we still have the problem of what to do if we wish to send the pattern 01111110 as part of the data stream to be transmitted. Clearly, it cannot be sent in the form it occurs naturally, as the receiver would regard it as an opening or closing flag.

The transmitter avoids the preceding problem by a process called *bit-stuffing*. Whenever the pattern 011111 is detected at the transmitter (i.e., five ones in series), the transmitter says, "If the next two bits are a one followed by a zero, a spurious flag will be created." Therefore, the transmitter inserts (i.e., stuffs) a zero after the fifth logical one in succession, in order to avoid the generation of a flag pattern. In this way, a flag can never appear by accident in the transmitted data stream.

At the receiver, the incoming bit stream is examined and opening or closing flags deleted from the data stream. If the sequence 0111110 is found, the zero following the fifth logical one is deleted, as it *must* have been inserted at the transmitter. In this way, any bit pattern may be presented to the transmitter, as bit-stuffing prevents the accidental occurrence of the opening or closing flag. Figure 9.11 illustrates the process of bit-stuffing.

Modern bit-oriented synchronous serial data transmission systems have largely been standardized and use the HDLC data format. HDLC stands for *high-level data link control*. Information is transmitted in the form of packets or frames, with each packet separated by one or two flags as described previously. The format of a typical HDLC frame is given in figure 9.12. Following the opening flag is an address field of 8 bits, which defines the address of the secondary station (or slave) in situations where a master station may be in communication with several slaves. An address field allows the master to send a message to one of its slaves without ambiguity. Any slave receiving a message whose address does not match that in the address field of a frame ignores that frame. Figure 9.13 shows the arrangement of a typical master-slave system. Remember that we have already stated that synchronous serial transmission systems are frequently used in more sophisticated ways than their asynchronous counterparts.

Following the address field is an 8-bit control field that controls the operation of the data link. The purpose of this field is to permit an orderly exchange of messages and to help detect and deal with lost messages. All that need be said here is that the control field provides the HDLC scheme with some very powerful facilities that are almost entirely absent in simple synchronous serial data links described earlier. The control field is followed by an optional data field

FIGURE 9.11   Process of bit-stuffing

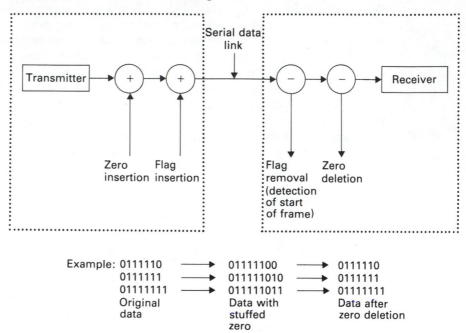

```
Example: 0111110  ⟶  01111100  ⟶  0111110
         0111111  ⟶  011111010 ⟶  0111111
         01111111 ⟶  011111011 ⟶  01111111
         Original      Data with      Data after
         data          stuffed        zero deletion
                       zero
```

(information field or I field) containing the data to be transmitted. The I field is optional because frames may be transmitted for purely control purposes without an I field. Immediately after the I field (or control field if the I field is absent) comes the frame check sequence, FCS, which is a very powerful error-detecting code of 16 bits' length that is able to detect the vast majority of errors (single or multiple bit) in the preceding fields. We are not able to go into detail about the theory of the FCS here, but the following notes should help.

The p bits in the packet, or frame, between the opening flag and the FCS itself are regarded as forming the coefficients of a polynomial of degree p. This polynomial is divided by a standard polynomial using modulo two arithmetic to yield a quotient and a 16-bit remainder. The quotient is discarded and the remainder forms the 16-bit FCS. At the receiver, the bits between the opening flag and received FCS are divided by the same generator polynomial to yield a local FCS.

FIGURE 9.12   High-level data link control format

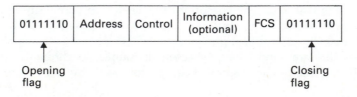

Opening flag

Closing flag

FIGURE 9.13   Master-slave data transmission

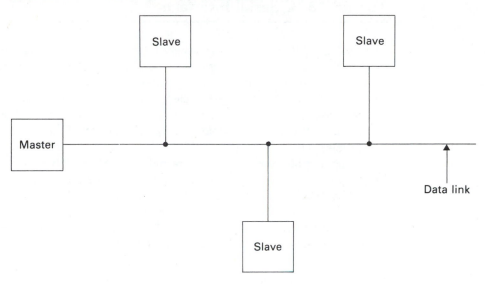

If the local FCS is the same as the received FCS, we can assume that the frame is free from all transmission errors. If they differ, the current frame is rejected.

Following the FCS is a closing flag, 01111110. Some arrangements require a closing flag for the current frame to be followed by an opening flag for the next frame. Other systems use one flag both to close the current frame and to open the next frame.

Clearly, a synchronous system is more efficient than an asynchronous system because of the absence of start, parity, and stop bits for each transmitted character. However, the real advantage of a synchronous system combined with the HDLC frame structure is its ability to control a data transmission system.

9.4 Serial Interface Standards (RS-232 and RS-422/RS-423)

Because of the low cost of a serial interface and transmission path, the serial data link is used to connect a very wide range of peripherals to computer equipment. Once only teletypes and modems were likely to be connected to a computer by serial data links. Today, almost any peripheral, from CRT terminals to graphics tablets to disk drives, may use serial data links. Therefore, the data link should be standardized so that a peripheral from one manufacturer can be plugged into the serial port of a computer from another manufacturer.

Such a serial interface standard has been created by the Electronic Industries Association (EIA) and is known as the RS-232C serial interface.

The RS-232C Serial Interface

The EIA RS-232C standard was largely intended to link data terminal equipment (DTE) with data communications equipment (DCE). The DCE corresponds to the computer or terminal and the DTE corresponds to the modem or similar line equipment. RS-232C specifies the electrical and mechanical aspects of the serial interface together with the functions of the signals forming the interface. In theory, any RS-232C compatible DCE can be connected directly to any RS-232C compatible DTE.

Alas, the life of the computer technician is filled with time-wasting requests by programmers to get their printer to work with their computer—both of which have "RS-232C" serial interfaces. I put "RS-232C" in quotation marks because many (the majority?) equipment suppliers implement their own subset of an RS-232C interface. The likelihood that the subset of the RS-232C interface in the printer is incompatible with the subset in the computer is highly probable.

Mechanical Interface

Fortunately, the vast majority of equipment suppliers adhere to the mechanical aspects of the RS-232C standard and use the D-type connectors illustrated in figure 9.14. This connector is available in 9-, 15-, 25-, 37-, and 50-pin versions, but only the 25-way D connector may be used with RS-232C standard serial data links. The pinout of this connector is given in table 9.5, although we must appreciate the fact that very few implementations of the RS-232C standard implement the full standard.

Electrical Interface

The RS-232C standard is intended to provide serial communication facilities over relatively short distances and its electrical specifications reflect this. Table 9.6 gives the basic electrical parameters of the standard and figure 9.15 shows how the electrical interface may be implemented.

The circuit of figure 9.15 uses a single-ended bipolar unterminated circuit; that is, the circuit is single-ended (i.e., unbalanced) because the signal level to be transmitted is referred to ground and one of the signal-carrying conductors is grounded at both ends of the data link. The circuit is unterminated because no requirement exists in the RS-232C standard to match the characteristic impedance of the receiver to that of the transmission path.

One of the key parameters in table 9.6 is the receiver maximum input threshold of -3 to $+3$ V. A space is guaranteed to be recognized if the input is more positive than $+3$ V and a mark is guaranteed to be recognized if the input is more negative than -3 V. The threshold separating mark and space levels is truly massive. Unless a transmitter can produce a voltage swing at the end of a transmission path of greater than 6 V, the received signal falls outside the

FIGURE 9.14   D-type connector

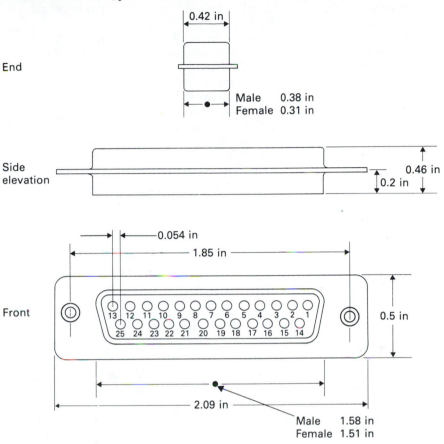

FIGURE 9.15   RS-232C interface

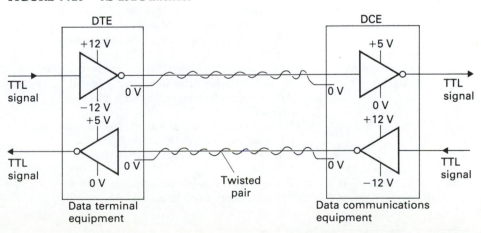

TABLE 9.5   Pinout of the RS-232C 25-way connector

PIN	NAME	FUNCTION
1	Protective ground	Electrical equipment frame and d.c. power ground
2	Transmitted data	Serial data generated by the DTE
3	Received data	Serial data generated by the DCE
4	Request to send	When asserted indicates that the DTE is ready to transmit primary data
5	Clear to send	When asserted indicates that the DCE is ready to transmit primary data
6	Data set ready	When asserted indicates that the DCE is not in a test, voice, or dial mode, that all initial handshake, answer tone, and timing delays have expired
7	Signal ground	Common ground reference for all circuits except protective ground
8	Received line signal detector	When asserted indicates that carrier signals are being received from the remote equipment
9	Reserved	
10	Reserved	
11	Unassigned	
12	Secondary received line signal detector	When asserted indicates that the secondary channel data carrier signals are being received from the remote equipment
13	Secondary clear to send	When asserted indicates that the DCE is ready to transmit secondary data
14	Secondary transmitted data	Low-speed secondary data channel generated by the DTE
15	Transmitted signal element timing	The signal on this line provides the DTE with signal element timing information
16	Secondary received data	Low-speed secondary channel data generated by the DCE
17	Receiver signal element timing	The signal on this line provides the DTE with signal element timing information
18	Unassigned	
19	Secondary request to send	When asserted indicates that the DTE is ready to transmit secondary channel data
20	Data terminal ready	When asserted indicates that the data terminal is ready
21	Signal quality detector	When asserted indicates that the received signal is probably error free; when negated indicates that the received signal is probably in error
22	Ring indicator	When asserted indicates that modem has detected a ringing tone on the telephone line
23	Data signal rate detector	Selects between two possible data rates
24	Transmit signal element timing	The signal on this line provides the DCE with signal element timing information
25	Unassigned	

TABLE 9.6   EIA RS-232C electrical interface characteristic

CHARACTERISTIC	VALUE
Operating mode	Single ended
Maximum cable length	15 m
Maximum data rate	20 kilobaud
Driver maximum output voltage (open-circuit)	$-25\ V < V < +25\ V$
Driver minimum output voltage (loaded output)	$-25\ V < V < -5\ V$ OR $+5\ V < V < +25\ V$
Driver minimum output resistance (power off)	300 Ω
Driver maximum output current (short-circuit)	500 mA
Maximum driver output slew rate	30 V/μs
Receiver input resistance	3–7 kΩ
Receiver input voltage	$-25\ V < V_i < +25\ V$
Receiver output state when input open-circuit	Mark (high)
Receiver maximum input threshold	-3 to $+3$ V

minimum requirements of RS-232C. However, most real receivers for RS-232C signals have *practical* input thresholds well below -3 to $+3$ V. Therefore, as most engineers have noticed, it is often possible to have much longer transmission paths than the standard stipulates.

Interfacing to RS-232C lines is now very easy, as the major semiconductor manufacturers have produced suitable line drivers and receivers. Figure 9.16 gives details of the 1488 quad RS-232C line driver and figure 9.17 gives details of the 1489 quad RS-232C line receiver. An example of the application of these chips is given in figure 9.18. Note that the 1489 receiver has an input control pin that can be used to define the amount of hysteresis at the input. We may leave this pin floating, in which case the input switching threshold is approximately 1 V.

RS-232C Interconnection Subset

So far we have seen three forms of RS-232C interconnection: the most basic arrangement of figure 9.8, the somewhat more complete circuit of figure 9.9, and the full RS-232C interface of table 9.5. A glance at table 9.5 makes it very clear that the RS-232C standard is aimed squarely at linking computer equipment with modems. Consequently, many of the facilities offered by the RS-232C standard are irrelevant to the engineer who wishes to connect a CRT terminal to a micro-computer.

Figure 9.19 shows a possible connection between two DTEs. As one DTE is

FIGURE 9.16   The 1448 quad line driver

FUNCTIONAL DESCRIPTION

The 1488 is a quad line driver that conforms to EIA specification RS–232C. Each driver accepts one or two TTL/DTL inputs and produces a high-level logic signal on its output. The HIGH and LOW logic levels on the output are defined by the positive and negative power supplies of plus and minus 9 volts, the output levels are guaranteed to meet the ±6-volt specification with a 3 kΩ load. There is an internal 300 Ω resistor in series with the output to provide current limiting in both the HIGH and LOW logic levels. The 1488 driver is intended for use with the 1489 or 1489A quad line receivers.

LOGIC SYMBOL

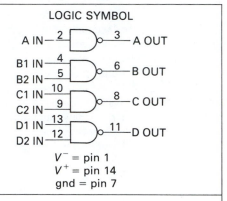

V^- = pin 1
V^+ = pin 14
gnd = pin 7

CIRCUIT DIAGRAM
(one driver shown)

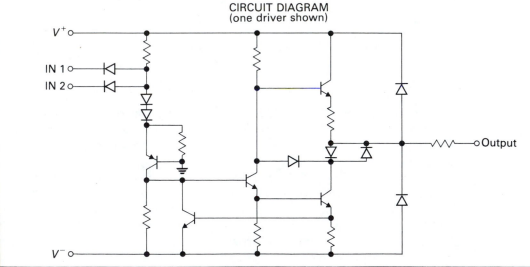

CONNECTION DIAGRAM
Top view

V^- ⟦1	14⟧ V^+
A IN ⟦2	13⟧ D1 IN
A OUT ⟦3	12⟧ D2 IN
B1 IN ⟦4	11⟧ D OUT
B2 IN ⟦5	10⟧ C1 IN
B OUT ⟦6	9⟧ C2 IN
gnd ⟦7	8⟧ C OUT

FIGURE 9.17   The 1449 quad line receiver

FUNCTIONAL DESCRIPTION

The 1489 and 1489A are quad line receivers whose electrical characteristics conform to EIA specification RS–232C. Each receiver has a single data input that can accept signal swings of up to ±30 V. The output of each receiver is TTL/DTL compatible, and includes a 2 kΩ resistor pull-up to V_{cc}. An internal feedback resistor causes the input to exhibit hysteresis so that a.c. noise immunity is maintained at a high level even near the switching threshold. For both devices, when a driver is in a LOW state on the output, the input may drop as LOW as 1.25 V without affecting the output. Both devices are guaranteed to switch to the HIGH state when the input voltage is below 0.75 V. Once the output has switched to the HIGH state, the input may rise to 1.0 V for the 1489 or 1.75 V for the 1489A without causing a change in the output. The 1489 is guaranteed to switch to a LOW output when its input reaches 1.6 V and the 1489A is guaranteed to switch to a LOW output when its input reaches 2.25 V. Because of the hysteresis in switching thresholds, the devices can receive signals with superimposed noise or with slow rise and fall times without generating oscillations on the output. The threshold levels may be offset by a constant voltage by applying a d.c. bias to the response control input. A capacitor added to the response control input will reduce the frequency response of the receiver for applications in the presence of high-frequency noise spikes. The companion line driver is the 1468.

LOGIC SYMBOL

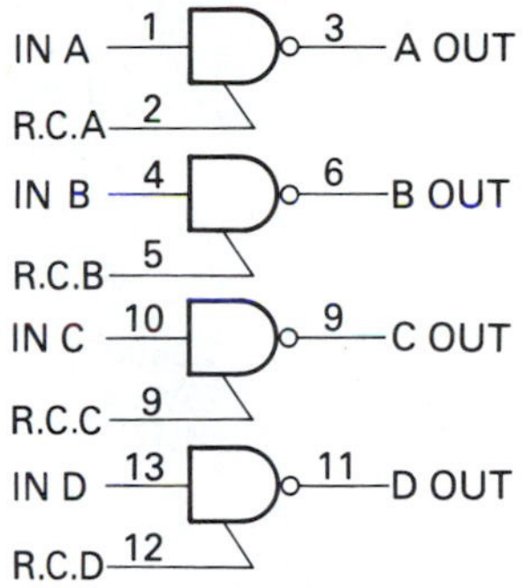

V_{cc} = pin 14
gnd = pin 7

CIRCUIT DIAGRAM
(one receiver)

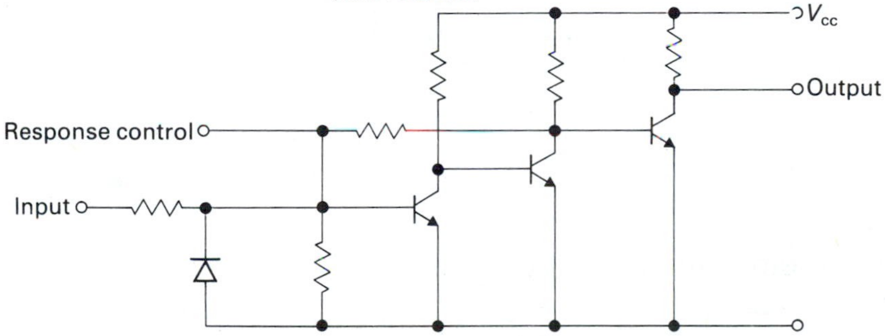

CONNECTION DIAGRAM
Top view

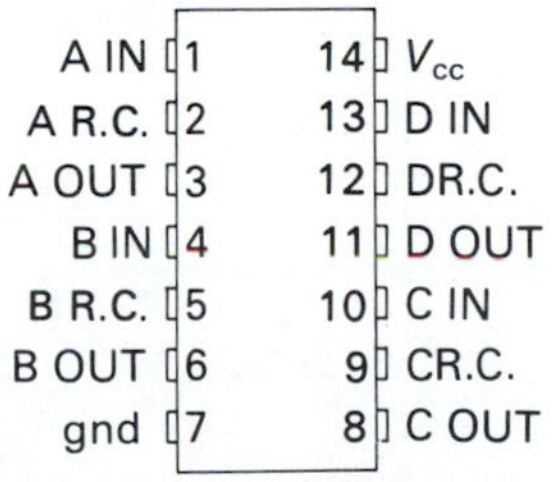

A IN	1	14	V_{cc}
A R.C.	2	13	D IN
A OUT	3	12	DR.C.
B IN	4	11	D OUT
B R.C.	5	10	C IN
B OUT	6	9	CR.C.
gnd	7	8	C OUT

the sink for the other's data, making the cross-connections shown in figure 9.19 is necessary. These cross-connections are frequently made at the junction of the cable and the connector. Such a cable linking a DTE to another DTE is called a *null modem* cable. When a DTE is connected to a modem (i.e., DCE) such a cross-over is not necessary.

FIGURE 9.18   Example of an RS-232C data link

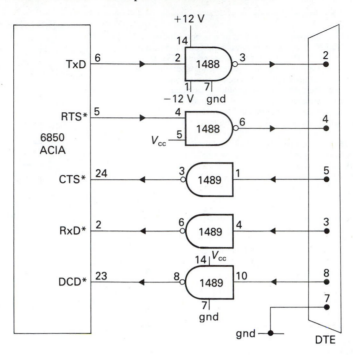

FIGURE 9.19   Connecting two DTEs together

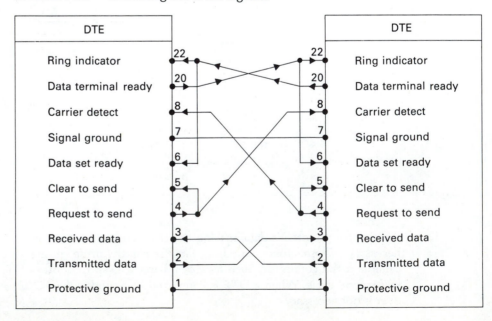

Many DTEs do not even use the subset of figure 9.19; for example, at the computer end of a computer-to-printer serial data link, no request to send (RTS) output may be provided. If the printer requires that its carrier detect input be driven by RTS, we need to strap the printer's carrier detect input to a logical one condition.

The RS-422 and RS-423 Serial Interfaces

The RS-232C interface is now thought to be rather limited because of its low bandwidth and its maximum transmission path of only 15 m. Two improved standards for serial data links have been approved by the EIA. These standards are the RS-422 and RS-423, which define the electrical characteristics of a data link. Unlike RS-232C, these standards refer only to the electrical aspects of a data link.

Table 9.7 gives the basic electrical parameters of the RS-423 and RS-422 standards and figure 9.20 shows how they are arranged. The RS-423 standard differs little from the RS-232C standard of table 9.6. Indeed, the only real difference is that the RS-423 standard specifies much smaller receiver thresholds, permitting both a longer cable length and a higher signaling rate.

The RS-422 standard offers a significant improvement over both the

TABLE 9.7   EIA RS-422 and RS-423 electrical interfaces

CHARACTERISTIC	RS-423 VALUE	RS-422 VALUE
Operating mode	Single ended	Differential
Maximum cable length	700 m (2,000 ft)	1,300 m (4,000 ft)
Maximum data rate	300 kilobaud	10 megabaud
Driver maximum output voltage (open-circuit)	$-6\text{ V} < V_o < +6\text{ V}$	6 V between outputs
Driver minimum output voltage (loaded output)	$-3.6\text{ V} < V_o < +3.6\text{ V}$	2 V between outputs
Driver minimum output resistance (power off)	100 mA between -6 and $+6$ V	100 μA between $+6$ and -0.25 V
Driver maximum output short-circuit current	150 mA	150 mA
Maximum driver output slew rate	Determined by cable length and modulation rate	No limit on slew rate necessary
Receiver input resistance	>4 kΩ	>4 kΩ
Receiver maximum input voltage	$-25\text{ V} < V_i < +25\text{ V}$	-12 to $+12$ V
Receiver maximum input threshold	-0.2 to 0.2 V	-0.2 to $+0.2$ V

FIGURE 9.20   RS-432 and RS-422 serial interfaces

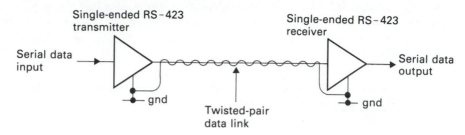

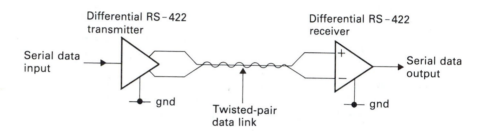

RS-232C and RS-423 standards by adopting a balanced transmission mode. Balanced transmission requires two transmission paths per signal, because information is transmitted as a differential voltage between the two conductors. Noise voltages due to ground currents are introduced as common mode voltages that affect *both* transmission paths equally and have little effect on the differential signal between the lines. RS-422 systems can operate over distances of 15 m at 10 megabaud or over distances of 1300 m at 100 kilobaud.

9.5 Serial Interface for the 68000

Instead of providing a relatively sterile textbook example of a 68000 serial interface based on the ACIA, examining the serial interface in Motorola's MEX68KECB single board microcomputer is most instructive. After all, this board is designed by real engineers to provide the maximum functionality while minimizing the board area taken up by the interface components and keeping their cost low.

Figure 9.21 shows how the ECB is arranged with respect to a terminal and a host computer. In a minimal mode, only the terminal interface on port 1 is necessary. This interface permits the user to interact with the ECB and to develop and debug software. The ECB has a parallel printer interface and an audio cassette interface, allowing programs and data to be printed and stored on tape, respec-

FIGURE 9.21   Relationship between the ECB, its console terminal, and a host computer

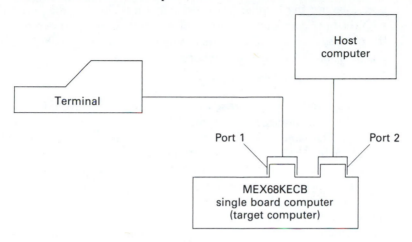

tively. Unfortunately, the serial interface is rather slow and does not have any file-handling capability.

By connecting the ECB to a host computer via the ECB's second serial interface, port 2, a moderately powerful 68000 development system can be created. During my own initial 68000 development work, I used a 6809-based system running under the Flex 09 operating system as a host computer. After a reset, the ECB communicates with the terminal through port 1. If the command TM ⟨exit character⟩ is entered, the ECB goes into its transparent mode. The expression ⟨exit character⟩ represents the character that must be entered from the terminal to leave the transparent mode. The default value is control A (ASCII $01).

Once the transparent mode has been entered, the terminal is effectively connected to port 2 and the 68000 on the ECB simply monitors the input from the terminal until it encounters the exit character. Therefore, the user can operate the host computer as if the ECB did not exist; for example, in the transparent mode I am able to edit a 68000 assembly language program on my 6809 system and then assemble it into 68000 machine code using a cross-assembler. Once this process has been done, the exit character is entered and the terminal is once more "connected" to the ECB.

The next step is to transfer the machine code file on disk in the 6809 system to the memory on the ECB. This step is performed by the load command, which moves object data in S-record format from an external device to the 68000's memory. S-record format is a way of representing machine code memory dumps. The syntax of the load command is

LO[port number] [;⟨options⟩][=text].

Square brackets enclose options. Port number 2 (the default port number) specifies the host computer. Other options are not of interest here. The "[=text]" field is available only with port 2 and causes the text following the " = " to be sent to port 2 before the loading is carried out, thus allowing the user to communicate with the host computer. Suppose, for example, that we have a program on disk in the 6809 system in S-record format whose file name is PROG23. BIN. To transfer this program to the 68000's memory space, we enter

    LO2;=LIST PROG23. BIN

from the terminal, which sends the message "LIST PROG23. BIN" to the host computer. The message is interpreted by the Flex 09 operating system as meaning "list the file named PROG23. BIN." This file is then transmitted to port 2 and stored in the 68000's memory by its monitor software. When the loading is complete, the program can be executed and debugged using any of the ECB's facilities. Finally, the transparent mode may be entered and the source file, PROG23. TXT, reedited on the 6809 system. This process is repeated until the software has been debugged.

Figure 9.22 gives the circuit diagram of the serial interface of port 1 and port 2 on the ECB. This diagram has been slightly simplified and redrawn from that appearing in the ECB user manual. Figure 9.22 includes both the serial interface between the ACIAs and the ports, and the interface between the ACIAs and the 68000.

Interface between the ACIAs and the 68000 on the ECB

The CPU side of the ACIAs is fairly conventional as they are both connected directly to the 68000's data bus without additional buffering. Port 1 is connected to D_{08} to D_{15} and strobed by UDS∗, while port 2 is connected to D_{00} to D_{07} and strobed by LDS∗. Address line A_{01} is connected to the register select input, RS, of each ACIA and is used to distinguish between the control/status and data register.

To simplify address decoding, each of the three ACIA's chip-select inputs are pressed into service: CS2∗ is connected to UDS∗ or LDS∗ to select between ACIAs, CS1 is connected to the output of the primary address decoding network, ACIA_CS1, and CS0 is connected to A_{06} from the CPU. Primary address decoding is performed by IC29a, a five-input NOR gate, and IC30, a three-line to eight-line decoder. These two chips decode A_{16} to A_{23} to produce an active-low signal, Y1∗, from IC30. Y1∗ is combined with VMA∗ from the 68000 in a NOR gate, IC33a, to give the active-high ACIA_CS1 signal. Note that the ACIAs are not fully address decoded and take up the half of the 64K-byte page of memory space from $01 0000 to $01 FFFF for which A6 = 1.

Because the ACIA is interfaced to the 68000's synchronous bus, VPA∗ must be asserted whenever an ACIA is accessed. ICs 32a, 34b, and 45c perform this function. Note that VPA∗ is also asserted when the VPAIRQ∗ input to IC45c is asserted.

The final aspect of the interface between the ACIA and the CPU to be dealt

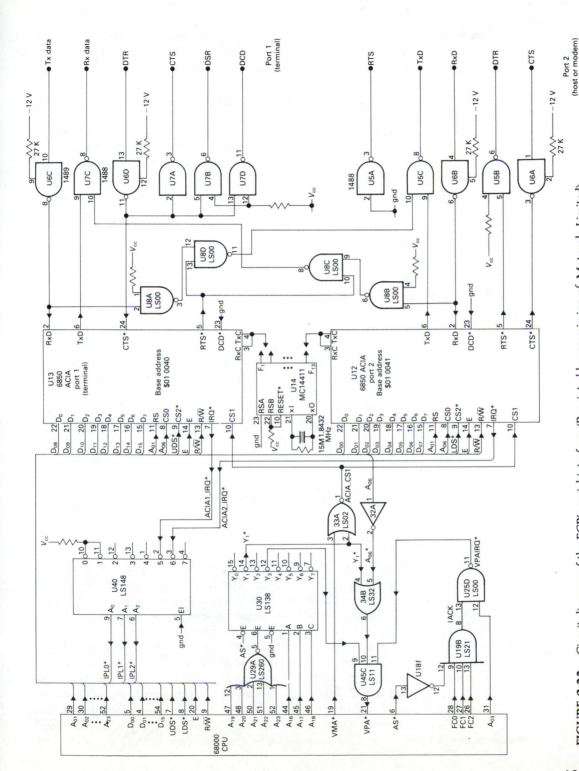

FIGURE 9.22 Circuit diagram of the ECB's serial interface. (Reprinted by permission of Motorola Limited)

433

with is the interrupt-handling hardware. Both ACIAs have independent interrupt request outputs. IRQ* from port 1 is wired to the level 5 input of a 74LS148 priority encoder (IC40) and IRQ* from port 2 is wired to the level 6 interrupt input.

During an interrupt acknowledge cycle, the output of the four-input AND gate IC19b goes active-high to generate an IACK signal. When a level 4 through 7 interrupt is acknowledged, A_{03} is high during the IACK cycle. Therefore, by combining A_{03} with IACK in IC25d, an active-low VPAIRQ* signal generated. VPAIRQ* is fed back to VPA* via IC45c, as indicated earlier. This arrangement converts interrupt levels 4 to 7 into autovectored interrupts, greatly simplifying the hardware design at the cost of reducing the number of possible interrupt vectors.

Serial Interface Side of the ACIAs

IC14, an MC14411 baudrate generator, provides the transmitter and receiver clocks of the two ACIAs with a source of element timing at 16 times the baudrate of the transmitted or received signal elements. Jumpers on the ECB must be positioned to select the appropriate clock output from the MC14411 for both ACIAs. We should note that if the terminal is to communicate with the host computer, both ACIAs must operate at the same baudrate.

Little comment need be made about the connection of the ACIA's RS-232C signals to their respective ports. However, one interesting feature has been added to the ECB. Whenever the RTS* output of the port 1 (i.e., terminal) ACIA is asserted active-low, both ports 1 and 2 operate independently. However, whenever RTS* from ACIA1 is negated, ICs 6c, 8a, 8d, and 5c route the incoming data from port 1 to the outgoing data on port 2. Incoming data on port 2 is routed to port 1 via ICs 6b, 8b, 8c, and 7c when RTS* is negated. Consequently, negating RTS* connects port 1 to port 2. This is, of course, exactly what happens when the ECB enters its transparent mode. The software required to operate this type of serial link is described in detail in the section dealing with a monitor in chapter 11.

Summary

In this chapter we have looked at the serial interface used to link digital systems to video display terminals and to modems. The simplest method of transmitting serial data is based on a character-oriented asynchronous protocol. If microprocessors had to perform the task of controlling serial links themselves, a considerable part of their power would be lost. We have examined the 6850 ACIA, which performs all serial to parallel and parallel to serial conversion itself. Once a 6850 ACIA is interfaced to a microprocessor, all the microprocessor has to do is to read data from or write data to the appropriate port. Moreover, the ACIA also checks the received data for both transmission and framing errors, further reducing the burden placed on the host microprocessor. Part of the power of the 6850 lies in its ability to cater for a wide variety of serial formats that are selectable under program control. The 6850 also provides three modem control signals, which further simplifies the design of a serial data link between a microprocessor system and a terminal or modem.

We have looked at the electrical interface between the serial transmission path and the microprocessor system. As the TTL-level voltages found in digital equipment are not best suited to transmission paths longer than a few meters, we have described the RS232C, the RS422, and the RS423 standards for the transmission of serial data over transmission paths that extend to 1000 meters or more.

Problems

1. What is the difference between asynchronous and synchronous transmission systems? What are the advantages and disadvantages of each mode of transmission?

2. What are the functions of the DCD*, CTS*, and RTS* pins of the 6850 ACIA?

3. The control register of a 6850 ACIA is loaded with the value $B5. Define the operating characteristics of the ACIA resulting from this value.

4. The status register of the 6850 is read and is found to contain $43. How is this value interpreted?

5. Write an exception-handling routine for a 6850 ACIA to deal with interrupt-driven input. Each new character received is placed in a 4K-byte circular buffer. Your answer must include schemes to (a) deal with buffer overflow and (b) deal with transmission errors.

6. Is connection of the output of an RS-423 transmitter to the input of an RS-232C receiver possible without violating the parameters of either standard? Is connection of an RS-232C output to an RS-423 input possible?

Chapter 10

Microcomputer Buses

In this chapter we look at the design of the system bus, which acts as the computer's skeleton, holding all its other "organs" (the functional modules) together. We would not consider it unreasonable to say that the microprocessor bus has done as much to promote the growth of the microcomputer industry as the CPU or the memory chips themselves. We begin by introducing the bus and then describe its electrical characteristics and its interface to microprocessors and to memories or peripherals. At the end of this chapter, we include an introduction to the VMEbus, which is a standard bus and is closely associated with professional 68000-based microcomputers.

The bus is nothing more than a number of parallel conductors designed to transfer information between separate modules or cards in a microprocessor system. Although not an exciting or glamorous component, the bus serves two vital purposes. Firstly, it makes the production of complex systems with large quantities of memory and peripherals possible. If components were wired together on a point-to-point basis, without a bus, the sheer number of interconnections would be uneconomic. Secondly, once a standard for a bus has been promulgated, independent manufacturers can produce their own cards to plug into another's bus. The S100 bus and the Apple bus are spectacular examples of this process.

Figure 10.1 illustrates some of the concepts that must be dealt with when microcomputer buses are discussed. While, strictly speaking, we have only one bus—the system bus—most engineers talk about the *data bus*, the *address bus*, and the *control bus*. These buses are really logically distinct subgroups of the system bus. We must also appreciate that the d.c. power fed to the various cards of a system is usually supplied by the system bus.

What is a bus? A bus is the electrical highway linking the modules of a computer system. This statement conceals far more than it reveals. Figure 10.2 shows why this is the case by illustrating the three factors influencing the design of a suitable bus, which are: its mechanical specification, its electrical specification, and its protocol. The mechanical specification governs the physical aspects of the bus (size, material, connectors), the electrical specification governs the requirements that must be met by the signals on the bus, and the protocol governs the

FIGURE 10.1   Microcomputer bus

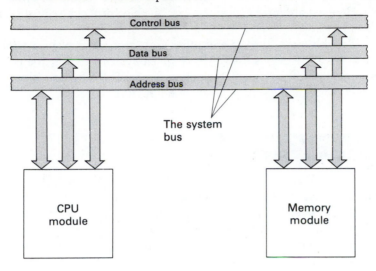

FIGURE 10.2   Components of a bus

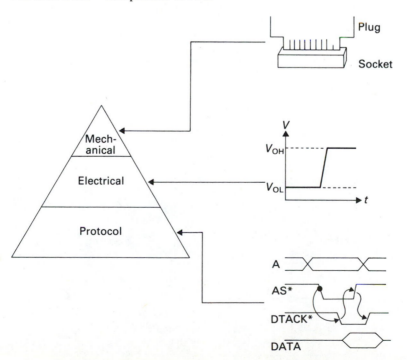

sequence of signals that must be complied with to ensure an orderly exchange of data. Here we are most concerned with the electrical characteristics and the protocols of buses.

Possibly more than in any other area, economics plays a vital role in determining the type of bus used by any given system; that is, the economics of bus design and construction are its limiting factor. This situation is particularly true at the mechanical and electrical levels of figure 10.2.

10.1 *Mechanical Layer*

The fact is sad but true that the mechanical nature of a bus largely determines its cost but has very little direct influence on its electrical performance. The mechanical aspects of a bus comprise those elements related to the physical structure of the bus, its mounting within the computer system, its physical dimensions and weight, its strength, and its reliability.

One of the simplest forms of bus is illustrated in figure 10.3 and consists of a motherboard, or backplane, into which a number of cards or daughterboards plug. Electrically, the bus is composed of parallel copper conductors running along the length of the motherboard. These conductors are generally arranged on a 0.1- or 0.15-inch pitch. At regular intervals along the motherboards are edge connectors into which the daughterboards are plugged.

We can see from figure 10.3 that the *fingers* on the daughterboard make

FIGURE 10.3   Motherboard and daughterboard

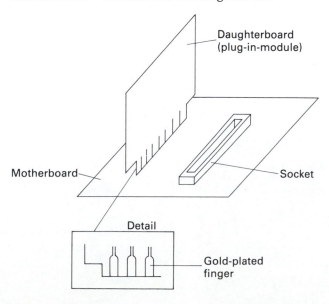

contact with spring-loaded connectors in the edge connector. Thus, the *i*th pin on one daughtercard is connected to the *i*th pin of all daughtercards. This arrangement is found in the Apple II, the IBM PC, and the popular S100 bus, because it offers the cheapest form of bus mechanics.

Unfortunately, the type of bus mechanics illustrated in figure 10.3 is relatively unreliable. Wear and tear due to repeated card insertion and removal, or the gradual ingress of dirt or corrosive agents, eventually lead to intermittent contact between the motherboard and daughterboards. Gold-plated connectors have a higher reliability than tin-plated connectors, but are considerably more expensive. More than anywhere else, the reliability of the hardware is very much related to its cost.

In addition to the reliability of the electrical contacts, the edge connectors and daughterboards must be manufactured to quite tight physical tolerances; for example, if, say, 50 fingers are on a daughterboard and the pitch of the fingers

FIGURE 10.4   Two-part connector

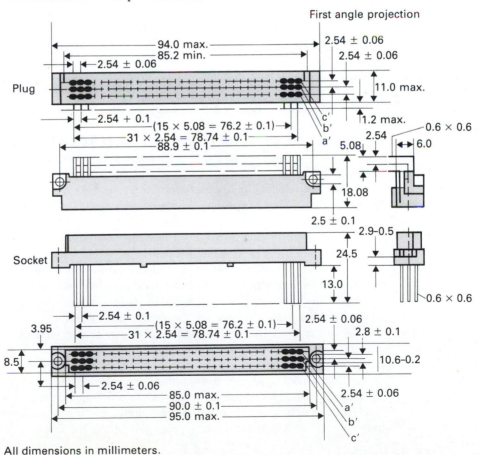

All dimensions in millimeters.

varies by *e* from its nominal value, the accumulated error may be up to 50*e*. Such a large error may make insertion of the daughterboard into an edge connector impossible.

The favored mechanical arrangement of the motherboard-daughterboard connection in many of today's professional and semiprofessional systems is the so-called two-piece connector. One part of the connector is attached to the motherboard and the other to the daughterboard. When a card is plugged into the motherboard, the physical connection takes place at the connector-connector level, rather than at the connector-card level in figure 10.3.

The arrangement of one of the most popular types of two-piece connector is given in figure 10.4 (see p. 439). The connectors are designed to be mechanically compatible with the Eurocard System as defined by IEC 297 and DIN 41494. The connectors themselves are compatible with the DIN 41612 standard. By making both the connectors and the cards on which they are located an international standard, the designers know that if they buy a connector or a module conforming to the relevant standard, they will achieve a guaranteed level of compatibility; that is, the designer is freed from the tyranny of the single supplier. A DIN 41612 connector has 32 pins in one to three rows, providing a 32-, 64-, or 96-way bus. This arrangement is sufficient for many of the new 32-bit microprocessor systems.

10.2 Electrical Characteristics of Buses

Each line of a bus distributes a digital signal from the card supplying it to all the other cards receiving it. Behind this seemingly trivial remark lie many complex design considerations. Even if we forget, for the time being, the problems of bus arbitration and signal timing protocols, three aspects are vital to the electrical characteristics of bus design: bus drivers, bus receivers, and bus transmission characteristics.

A bus driver is an active device that can change the logical level of the bus line it is driving. As each module capable of driving the bus has its own bus drivers, some mechanism must be provided to avoid bus contention. Bus contention is a situation in which two or more modules attempt to drive the bus simultaneously. Later we shall see that there are two solutions to the problem of bus contention: the tristate output and the open-collector output.

A bus receiver reads the logical level on the line to which it is connected. In principle, any TTL-compatible input may act as a bus receiver. In practice, special-purpose bus receivers have been designed whose characteristics have been optimized to provide high-speed, good noise immunity, and minimal bus loading.

Ideally, once a logic level is applied at one point on a bus, the same logic level should appear at all other points along the bus instantaneously. Unfortunately, real signals on real buses propagate along the bus at a finite speed and

suffer reflections at the end of the bus or at any change in bus impedance. More is
said about the flow of electrical energy down a conductor in the last part of this
section.

Bus Drivers

Although digital systems operate with logical zero and logical one levels, many
different logic elements that both generate and detect these levels are evident.
Figure 10.5 shows a bus line driven by an NMOS output stage (typical of a
microprocessor output). This bus is connected to receivers fabricated with NMOS,
TTL, low-power Schottky TTL, and CMOS technology. The purpose of
figure 10.5 is to demonstrate that many different types of receiver circuit exist. As
may be imagined, these different input circuits also have a spread of electrical
characteristics.

Figure 10.6 illustrates the connection between a driver and a single receiver.
Figure 10.6a represents the system in a logical zero state and figure 10.6b the
same system in a logical one state. To the right of the general diagrams are
examples of NMOS drivers connected to low-power Schottky TTL receivers.
When considering the interconnection of logic elements, two sets of characteristics must be satisfied—those relating to voltage levels and those relating to
current levels.

One figure of merit often quoted for a logic element is its d.c. noise immunity. The d.c. noise immunity of a logic element is the amount of noise that can be
tolerated at its input without exceeding V_{IL} (in a low state) or falling below V_{IH}
(in a high state). The d.c. noise immunity of a logic element is defined as

High-level noise immunity $= V_{OH} - V_{IH}$

Low-level noise immunity $= V_{IL} - V_{OL}$.

Obviously, the noise immunity of any device must be greater than zero, and the
higher the figure the better. Table 10.1 gives the basic parameters of four of the
most popular types of logic element found in today's microprocessor systems.
The noise immunity for each possible combination of logic family to logic family
is presented in table 10.2. For each combination, two values are given: the low-
level noise immunity and the high-level noise immunity; for example, when LS
TTL is connected to S TTL, the noise immunity (low level/high level) is 0.3/
0.7 V. As the worst value has to be taken, the quoted noise immunity for this
combination is 0.3 V.

Note that the high-level noise immunity for all logic families driving CMOS
inputs (except CMOS outputs) is negative; that is, these families are not able to
drive CMOS inputs because TTL V_{OH} values are too low. However, it is sometimes possible to drive CMOS inputs with TTL-compatible gates if the TTL
outputs are pulled up to V_{cc} by means of a 2–6-kΩ resistor.

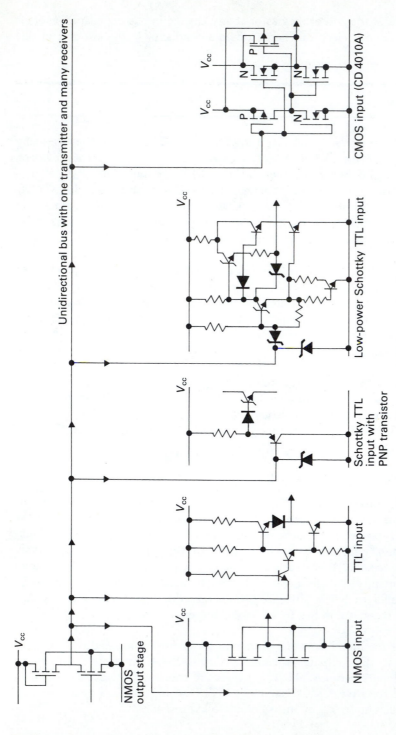

FIGURE 10.5 Bus driver. (Reprinted by permission of Prentice Hall International)

442

FIGURE 10.6   Connecting bus drivers to bus receivers

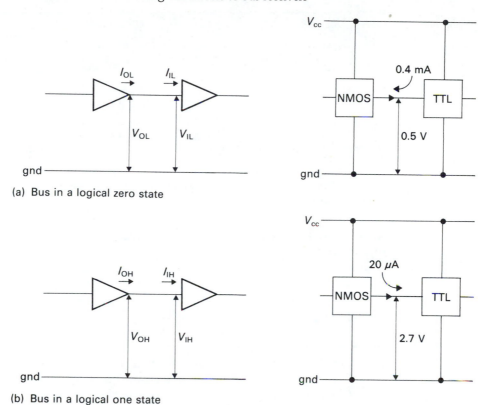

(a) Bus in a logical zero state

(b) Bus in a logical one state

TABLE 10.1   Characteristics of four types of logic element

CHARACTERISTIC	LOGIC FAMILY					UNITS
	LS TTL	S TTL	ALS TTL	NMOS	CMOS	
V_{OL}	0.5	0.5	0.4	0.4	0.01	volts
V_{OH}	2.7	2.7	2.7	2.4	4.99	volts
V_{IL}	0.8	0.8	0.8	0.8	1.5	volts
V_{IH}	2.0	2.0	2.0	2.0	3.5	volts
I_{OL}	8	20	4	1.6	0.4	mA
I_{OH}	−400	−1,000	−400	−200	−500	μA
I_{IL}	−0.4	−2.0	−0.4	2.5 μA	10 pA	mA
I_{IH}	20 μA	50 μA	20	2.5 μA	10 pA	mA
Propagation delay	9.5	3	4	25	35	ns
Input capacitance	3.5	—	—	10–160	5	pf

TABLE 10.2   Noise immunity of various gate combinations

OUTPUT LOGIC	INPUT LOGIC				
	LS TTL	S TTL	ALS TTL	NMOS	CMOS
LS TTL	0.3/0.7	0.3/0.7	0.3/0.7	0.3/0.7	1.0/−0.8
S TTL	0.3/0.7	0.3/0.7	0.3/0.7	0.3/0.7	1.0/−0.8
ALS TTL	0.4/0.7	0.4/0.7	0.4/0.7	0.4/0.7	1.1/−0.8
NMOS	0.4/0.4	0.4/0.4	0.4/0.4	0.4/0.4	1.1/−1.0
CMOS	0.79/2.99	0.79/2.99	0.79/2.99	0.79/2.99	1.45/1.45

NOTE: Each value is presented as "logical zero/logical one" noise immunity. The effective value is the lower of this pair.

Current Levels and Digital Circuits

Not only do the voltage characteristics of bus drivers and bus receivers have to be matched, but their current characteristics must also be considered. As figure 10.6 demonstrates, a device driving a single LS TTL input must be able to source 20 μA in a logical one state and to sink 0.4 mA in a logical zero state. To a first approximation, a bus driver must be able to source (or sink) sufficient current to hold all the receivers on the bus in a logical one (or zero) state.

When the output of, say, an NMOS gate changes state, it attempts to drive the load to which it is connected from a logical one state to a logical zero state, or vice versa. Figure 10.7 shows an NMOS output driving an NMOS input. Suppose the upper transistor changes state from off to on, as the output switches from a logical zero to a logical one. Current flows both into the NMOS input and into the distributed capacitance in the circuit.

This capacitance is made up of the output capacitance of the driver, of the bus itself, and of all receivers connected to the bus. Sometimes, the total capacitive loading on the bus may be rather large. When the upper transistor turns on, the distributed capacitance charges through the resistance of the transistor as illustrated in figure 10.8. If the switching threshold of the input is V_T, the input does not change state until the capacitance charges from V_{OL} to V_T. Consequently, one of the limiting factors in designing microcomputer buses is the rate at which drivers can supply current to charge the bus capacitance and the number of highly capacitive inputs connected to the bus.

Because the capacitive loading of CMOS and NMOS inputs is so great, a common practice is to isolate them from the bus by means of bus drivers and bus receivers. Figure 10.9 illustrates a bus line driven by a bus driver on one card. Other cards, which listen to this bus line, interface to it by means of receivers. As most buses are specified so that each card connected to them must not present

FIGURE 10.7   An NMOS output driving an NMOS input stage. (Reprinted by permission of Prentice Hall International)

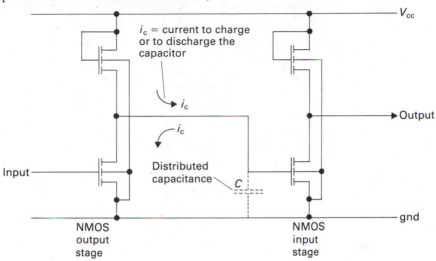

more than one LS TTL load, we sometimes need to employ a local bus within a card and then buffer this with further buffers as illustrated in figure 10.9.

The great advantage of bus drivers and receivers is that the characteristics or behavior of the bus are made independent of the electrical properties of the

FIGURE 10.8   Charging the distributed capacitance of an input circuit. (Reprinted by permission of Prentice Hall International)

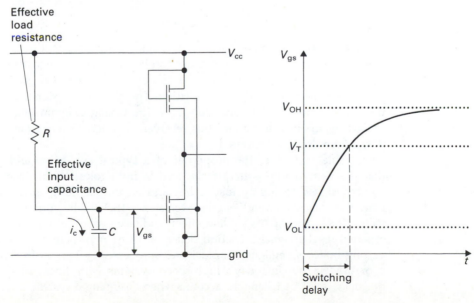

FIGURE 10.9   Bus drivers and receivers

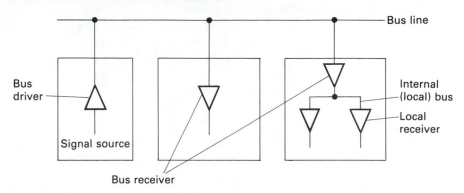

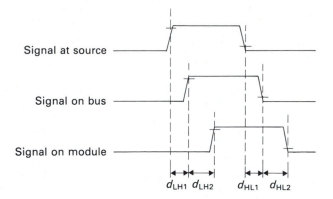

modules connected to the bus. As we shall see, the propagation of signals on the bus is also determined by its transmission-line behavior, rather than by the characteristics of the many NMOS or CMOS devices connected to it. Unfortunately, a price has to be paid for this bus isolation. This price is the signal delay incurred by the drivers and receivers. In figure 10.9, the timing diagram illustrates the delay caused by the bus driver and bus receiver in series. When a module has a local bus, a third delay is incurred.

Table 10.3 gives the properties of a typical bus driver and receiver. Note that the same device is frequently used in both roles; that is, the device has an input designed to lightly load a bus and an output designed to source or sink large bus currents. From this table we can see that the bus driver/receiver has low values for I_{IL} and I_{IH} (its loading effect) and large values of I_{OL} and I_{OH} (its driving capability). The signal transition delay of 18 ns maximum for a 74LS241 noninverting buffer is negligible in older microprocessor systems with clocks running at 1 or 2 MHz, but in today's high-speed systems with clocks of 8 MHz upward, this delay must be taken into account when designing a system.

TABLE 10.3 Characteristics of a bus driver/receiver

PARAMETER UNITS	74LS241
V_{IH} min. V	2.0
V_{IL} max. V	0.8
V_{OH} min. V	2.4
V_{OL} max. V	0.5
I_{IH} max. μA	2.0
I_{IL} max. μA	-200
I_{OH} max. mA	-15
I_{OL} max. mA	24
I_{OS} max. mA	-225
t_{PLH} max. ns	18
t_{PHL} max. ns	18

NOTES: I_{OS} = short-circuit output current
t_{PLH} = low-to-high signal propagation delay
t_{PHL} = high-to-low signal propagation delay

Passive Bus Drivers

Up to now, we have considered the situation depicted in figure 10.9, where a single bus driver is connected to the bus and communicates with many receivers. No provision has yet been added to permit several transmitters to share the bus. Simply connecting more than one TTL output stage to the bus is not a possible solution, as figure 10.10 demonstrates.

In figure 10.10 the outputs of two totem-pole stages are directly connected together via the bus. Suppose that output G1 is in a logical zero state. The lower transistor in its totem-pole, T2, conducts, pulling the bus down to ground level (i.e., V_{OL}). Suppose also that output G2 is in a logical one state with the upper transistor, T3, of its totem-pole conducting. Now G2 is trying to pull the bus upward to V_{OH}.

Clearly, this situation is contradictory. The bus cannot be at both V_{OL} and V_{OH} simultaneously. What actually happens is that a low-impedance path exists between V_{cc} and ground through T3 and T2 via the bus. The short-circuit current flowing along this path may burn out both gates. At best the state of the bus is undefined.

There are two basic approaches to allowing more than one output to control the bus. The first uses drivers with outputs that may only pull the bus down to V_{OL}, which avoids the situation where one driver pulls the bus down to V_{OL}

FIGURE 10.10   Effect of connecting two TTL output stages together

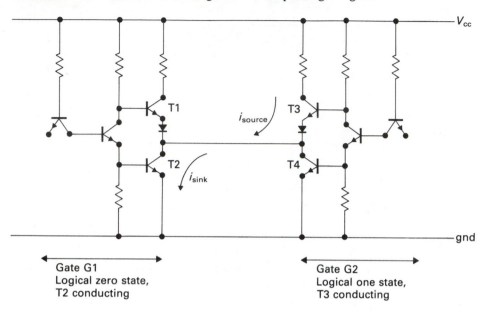

Gate G1
Logical zero state,
T2 conducting

Gate G2
Logical one state,
T3 conducting

while another attempts to pull it up to V_{OH}. The V_{OH} level on the bus is produced passively by means of a pull-up resistor between the bus and V_{cc}. The second solution involves the so-called tristate driver that can be electrically disconnected from the bus when it is not actively forcing the bus up to V_{OH} or down to V_{OL}. We will deal first with the passive pull-up solution.

The totem-pole output circuit of gate G1 in figure 10.10 is always pulled up to V_{cc} when T1 is turned on or down to ground when T2 is turned on. An open-collector output dispenses with the upper transistor (T1). The term *open-collector* is used because the collector of the lower transistor has no path to V_{cc} within the gate itself. Therefore, this arrangement can only actively pull the output down to ground. The gate still has a two-state output, but instead of V_{OL}/V_{OH} states it has V_{OL}/floating states. In the floating state, the voltage level at the output is determined by the level of the signal on the bus.

Figure 10.11 shows how two-open-collector outputs drive the same bus line. The key to understanding the open-collector bus driver is that, when a transmitter is not driving the bus, its output must be in a logical one state. Suppose that in figure 10.11 both transmitters are simultaneously in logical one states. Both output transistors will be turned off and the bus will be left to float. A pull-up resistor, R, defines the state of the bus whenever it is not actively pulled down to ground. This resistor pulls the bus up toward V_{cc}, so that an input connected to the bus sees a voltage not less than its required V_{IH}.

If transmitter 1 is currently controlling the bus, it will either be in a logical one state with R defining the level on the bus or it will be in a logical zero state.

FIGURE 10.11   Open-collector bus driver. (Reprinted by permission of Prentice Hall International)

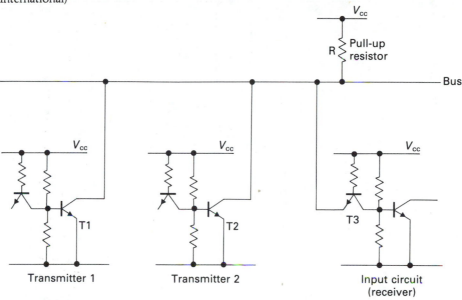

In the latter case, T1 is turned on and the bus pulled down toward ground. The voltage at the collector of T1 (i.e., its output) is its saturation voltage (V_{cs}), and current can now flow out of the transistor in the receiver circuit (i.e., T3) and into T1. If for any reason more than one bus driver is turned on, the current flowing through R and the receiver input is simply divided between the outputs in the logical zero state.

As any open-collector transmitter can pull down the bus to a logical zero state, the arrangement is called *wired OR logic*. Of course, if a transmitter puts out a constant logical zero, the bus cannot be used by any other device. When this condition occurs, at least no potentially harmful situation exists.

Calculating the Pull-up Resistor Value

The value of the pull-up resistor required by a bus driver with open-collector outputs is obtained by considering the two limiting conditions—the maximum resistance that will guarantee a logical one on the bus and the minimum resistance that will keep dissipation inside the bus drivers within limits:

1.   *Maximum value of R.* The maximum value of R is given by calculating the voltage drop across R when the bus is pulled up to V_{OH}, its minimum guaranteed high-level state. This state is shown by figure 10.12a. When the bus is at V_{OH}, the current flowing through R consists of two components: the input current flowing into any receiver connected to the bus and the leakage current flowing into each open-collector driving the bus.

FIGURE 10.12   Current flowing in open-collector circuits

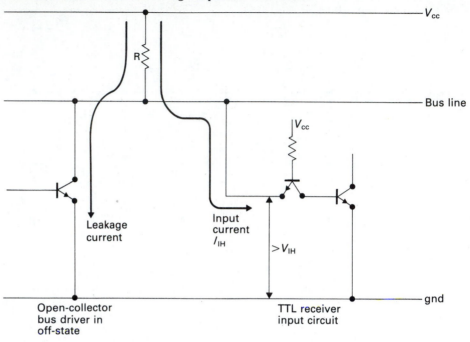

(a) Bus pulled up to V_{cc} passively

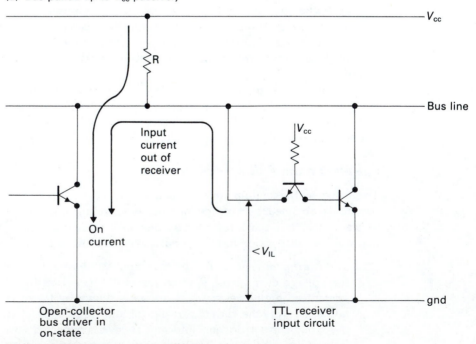

(b) Bus pulled down to ground actively

Suppose a system has m transmitters and n receivers. The total current flowing in R is $m \times I_{leakage} + n \times I_{IL}$. For LS TTL devices, $I_{leakage}$ is less than 250 μA and I_{IH} is 20 μA. Suppose we design the system to give a high-level d.c. noise margin of 0.4 V. The value of V_{IH} for TTL gates is 2.0 V, giving a required value of V_{OH} equal to 2.4 V.

The voltage across R in a logical one state is $V_{cc} - 2.4 = 2.6$. Therefore, the maximum value of R is given by

$$R_{max} = \frac{2.6}{m \times 0.00025 + n \times 0.00002}.$$

For ten receivers and ten transmitters, the maximum value of R is

$$R_{max} = \frac{2.6}{10 \times 0.00025 + 10 \times 0.00002} = \frac{2.6}{0.0025 + 0.0002}$$

$$= 1,000 \ \Omega.$$

2. *Minimum value of R.* To calculate the minimum value of R, we consider the case in which a single bus driver is turned on to pull the bus down to no more than V_{OL}. This situation is illustrated in figure 10.12b. The current sunk by the active output dissipates energy in the output transistor and too large a current flow will physically destroy the transistor. To make matters worse, the active output must not only sink the current through R but also the current out of any receiver circuits connected to the bus (i.e., I_{IL}).

The current flowing through R when the bus is in a logical zero state is given by $I_{OL} - n \times I_{IL}$. Therefore, the minimum value of R is given by

$$R_{min} = \frac{V_{cc} - V_{OL}}{I_{OL} - n \times I_{IL}}.$$

For one receiver with $I_{IL} = 0.4$ mA, $V_{OL} = 0.4$ V, and $I_{OL} = 16$ mA, we have

$$R_{min} = \frac{5 - 0.4}{0.016 - 0.0004} = \frac{4.6}{0.0156} = 300 \ \Omega.$$

Had ten receivers been connected to the bus, the minimum value of R would be increased to 4.6/0.012 mA = 380 Ω.

As the pull-up resistor may lie between 380 and 1,000 Ω, a compromise value of 470–680 Ω seems quite reasonable.

The NMOS technology equivalent of the open-collector output is the open-drain output circuit, whose output is the drain of an NMOS transistor without its usual active pull-up. In this case, the value of the pull-up resistor is normally recommended as typically 3 kΩ by the NMOS manufacturers.

Tristate Logic

Buses capable of being driven by more than one transmitter are almost invariably controlled by tristate (or three-state) buffers. We will now examine the characteristics of tristate bus drivers and show how they are used to implement microcomputer buses.

A tristate logic element is a device whose output circuit can assume one of three distinct states: a logical zero with the output actively pulled down to ground; a logical one with the output actively pulled up to V_{cc}; and a high-impedance state in which the output is floating and is electrically isolated from the buffer's circuitry. Figure 10.13a gives the logical representation of a tristate output

FIGURE 10.13 *a*, Logical representation and *b*, the circuit diagram of a tristate output stage. (Reprinted by permission of Prentice Hall International)

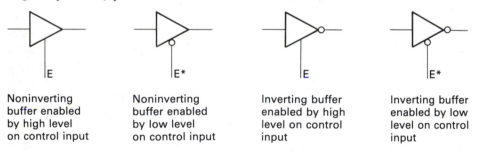

Noninverting
buffer enabled
by high level
on control input

Noninverting
buffer enabled
by low level
on control input

Inverting buffer
enabled by high
level on control
input

Inverting buffer
enabled by low
level on control
input

(a)

(b)

Control section

Tristate buffer

circuit and figure 10.13b the circuit diagram of a typical gate. All tristate outputs have a control input labeled invariably: E (enable), CS (chip select), or OE (output enable). When this control input is asserted, the tristate output behaves *exactly* like the corresponding TTL output and provides a low-impedance path to ground or V_{cc}, depending only on the state of the output. When the control input, E, is negated, the tristate output goes into its high-impedance state, irrespective of any other activity within the device or of the state of its other inputs. Most tristate gates are arranged so that their enable inputs are active-low.

Because of the popularity of tristate bus drivers, semiconductor manufacturers have produced a range of bus drivers and transceivers to suit today's microprocessors. These devices are 4, 6, or 8 bits wide and are available with inverting or noninverting outputs. A transceiver is a transmitter-receiver and is able to drive the bus or to receive data from it—but not both activities at the same time! One of the most popular families of tristate buffer/transceiver is the 74LS240 series. The basic features of this series are given in table 10.4.

The buffers in table 10.4 differ largely in terms of their control arrangements and in whether they are inverting or noninverting; for example, the 74LS240 is organized as two independent quad buffers, each with its own active-low enable. The groups are able to operate entirely independently, or with the two enables strapped together and the whole device treated as a single octal buffer. Figure 10.14 shows how each of the buffers in table 10.4 is arranged internally.

The 74LS241 is organized as two separate quad buffers, with one group of four enabled by an active-high signal and the other by an active-low signal. By connecting the enables together and wiring the two pairs back to back (i.e., output of one pair to input of the other), we can operate the device as a quad bidirectional transceiver. The 74LS241 is useful when a module has *separate* input and output data buses.

Tristate Bus Drivers in Microprocessor Systems

The next step in our consideration of bus drivers is to examine how tristate bus drivers can be applied to the design of microcomputer buses. Figure 10.15 shows

TABLE 10.4   Characteristics of the 74LS240 series tristate buffers

DEVICE	PINS	TYPE	POLARITY	FUNCTION	CONTROL
74LS240	20	2 × quad	Inverting	Driver	E∗ for each quad
74LS241	20	2 × quad	Noninverting	Driver	E∗, E
74LS242	14	Quad	Inverting	Transceiver	E∗ = read, E = write
74LS243	14	Quad	Noninverting	Transceiver	E∗ = read, E = write
74LS244	20	2 × quad	Noninverting	Driver	E∗ for each quad
74LS245	20	Octal	Noninverting	Transceiver	E∗, DIR = direction

FIGURE 10.14   Logical arrangement of the buffers in table 10.4

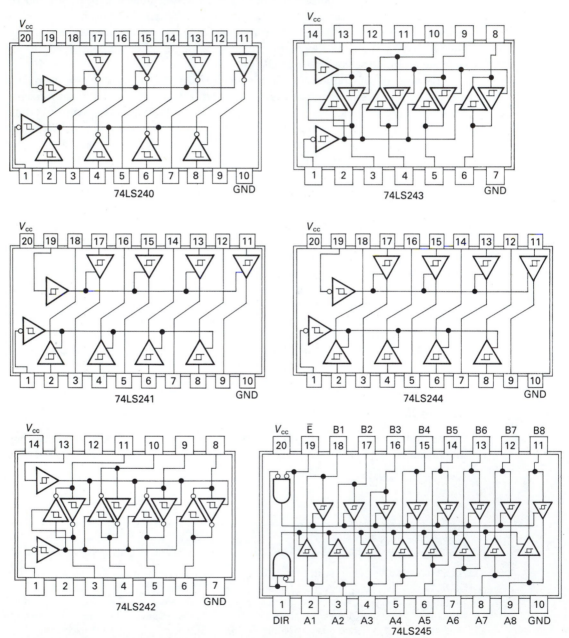

FIGURE 10.15   Tristate bus driver in a microcomputer

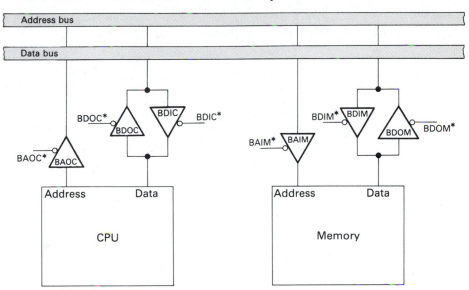

how tristate bus drivers are used in a microprocessor system. Each bus driver or receiver is denoted by a four-letter code as follows:

First letter   B   = buffer
Second letter A/D = address/data bus buffer
Third letter   I/O = data direction with respect to bus
                I   = in from the bus (i.e., receiver)
                O   = out to the bus (i.e., transmitter)
Fourth letter C/M = CPU/memory (location of buffer).

For example, an address from the CPU is buffered onto the bus by BAOC. Each buffer is enabled by an active-low signal, labeled by the same name at the buffer itself. Thus, BAOC is enabled by BAOC*.

The address buffers in figure 10.15, BAOC and BAIM, buffer an address from the CPU onto the bus and an address from the bus onto the memory module, respectively. A more detailed diagram of the address bus part of figure 10.15 is given in figure 10.16. Three 74LS244 noninverting bus drivers buffer the 23-bit address from the CPU, assumed to be a 68000, onto the system address bus.

The 74LS244 is arranged as two groups of four buffers with active-low enable inputs. In figure 10.16 all six enable inputs of the address bus buffers on the computer card are connected together and enabled by BAOC*. If no device other than the CPU is ever to take control of the address bus, strapping BAOC* permanently to a logical zero becomes perfectly reasonable.

Many real systems have provision either for direct memory access or for

FIGURE 10.16   Controlling the tristate address buffers

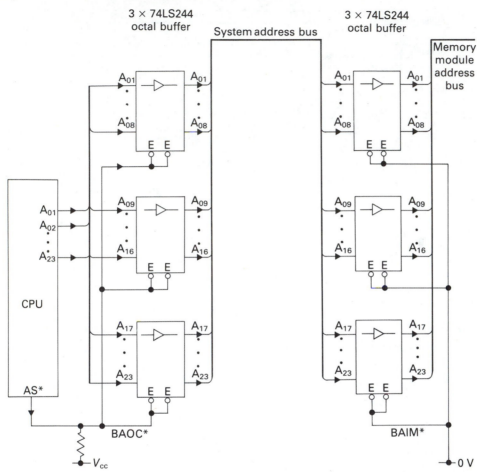

multiprocessing. Both these modes of system operation allow a device other than the CPU to take control of the system bus and to access memory or peripherals. In this case, the 68000's address bus buffers must be turned off while another *bus master* is controlling the bus. One simple way of achieving this end is to connect BAOC* to AS* from the CPU. The 68000 asserts AS* only when it is actively accessing memory. Therefore, if the 68000 is not accessing memory, AS* is inactive-high and the address buffers are turned off, leaving the bus for another controller.

On the memory card, another three 74LS244s buffer the address from the address bus and drive the address inputs of the memory components. As no device on this board will ever control either the system address bus or the address bus local to the card, enabling these buffers permanently becomes an entirely reasonable proposition.

The arrangement of the data buffers is rather more complex because the data bus is bidirectional. Figure 10.15 shows two pairs of buffers: BDOC and BDIC on the CPU card and BDOM and BDIM on the memory card. Unlike the address bus, the control of the data bus represents a reasonably difficult problem for the systems designer. Not least of the problems facing the designer is the restriction that no two data bus buffers must ever try to drive the data bus simultaneously.

A more detailed description of the data bus drivers and receivers is provided by figure 10.17. One of the most popular data bus driver-receivers is the 74LS245 octal transceiver, two of which are necessary to buffer the 68000's 16-bit data bus.

FIGURE 10.17   Controlling the data bus buffers

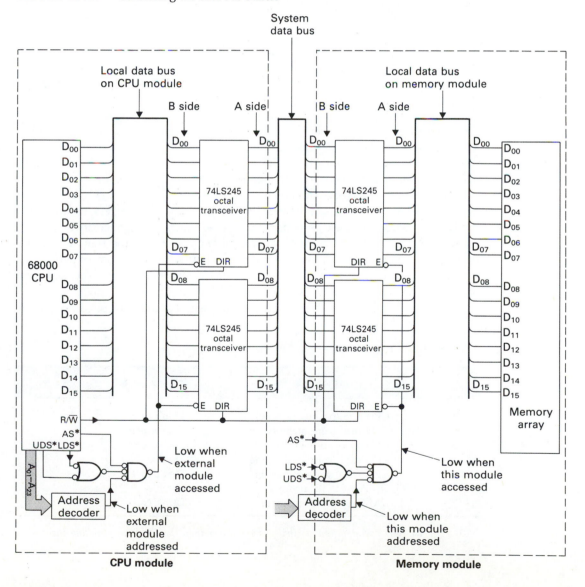

Each 74LS245 octal transceiver is controlled by two inputs: an active-low enable, E∗, and DIR. Whenever E∗ is inactive-high, both bus drivers and bus receivers are disabled and their outputs floated. Whenever E∗ is active-low, the transceiver either moves data from its A-side terminals to its B-side terminals, or vice versa. The actual direction of information flow is determined by the state of the transceiver's DIR (direction) input. A high level on DIR selects A-side to B-side transmission and a low level selects B-side to A-side transmission.

In figure 10.17, the buffers on the CPU card are connected with their B side to the 68000 data bus and their A side to the system data bus. DIR is connected directly to the 68000's R/$\overline{W}$ output. Whenever the 68000 sets R/$\overline{W}$ = 0, the transceivers move data from the CPU to the system bus (i.e., side B to side A), and when R/$\overline{W}$ = 1, they move data from the system data bus to the CPU data bus (i.e., side A to side B).

Similarly, the transceivers on the memory card are also controlled by the 68000's R/$\overline{W}$ output. In this case the transceivers are wired so that their B side is connected to the system bus and their A side to the local data bus on the memory card.

When designing a circuit to enable the data bus transceivers, all that need be remembered is that no two bus drivers may attempt to put data on the same bus at the same time. This restriction includes not only the system data bus but also the local data buses in both the CPU and memory cards. Local memory on the CPU card comprises memory components whose I/O data pins are connected to the CPU side of the system data bus buffers.

Let us consider first the control of the data bus transceivers on the CPU module. Seven states must be considered. These states are defined in table 10.5, where use can see that three possible control states exist for the transceivers: (1) enable, (2) disable, (3) don't care. When the 68000 is reading from or writing to external memory via the system bus, the transceivers must be enabled and their data direction controlled by R/$\overline{W}$ from the CPU.

When the CPU is reading from its local memory, the data bus transceivers

TABLE 10.5   Seven states of the CPU data bus transceivers

CASE	OPERATION	DATA BUS TRANSCEIVER
1	CPU idle (no bus activity)	Don't care
2	CPU read from memory card	Enable read
3	CPU write to memory card	Enable write
4	CPU read from local memory	Disable
5	CPU write to local memory	Don't care
6	DMA write to memory card	Disable
7	DMA read from memory card	Don't care

NOTE: A DMA operation implies that a device other than the CPU is controlling the system bus.

on the CPU card *must* be disabled. If this action is not taken, the local memory will place its data on the local data bus while the bus transceivers are still controlling the local bus. Consequently, whenever a read to local memory is detected, the transceivers must be disabled. Similarly, if a card other than the CPU module becomes a bus master (e.g., for a DMA operation), the bus transceivers on the CPU card must not attempt to put data on the system bus during a write by the alternate bus master.

Some states in table 10.5 are labeled "don't care," that is, actions of the data bus transceivers do not affect the operation of those don't care states. Therefore, during any period in which the CPU is idle, it does not matter whether the data bus transceivers are turned off, driving the system data bus, or driving the local data bus, as long as no other device is attempting to drive the same bus.

In the vast majority of well-designed systems, data bus transceivers have their outputs floated unless they are explicitly being used to drive data from one bus to another. Thus, all the *don't care* states in table 10.5 are replaced *disable* states.

As the 68000 asserts AS* and one or both data strobes during a memory access, these may be used to control the data bus transceivers on the CPU card. Unless AS* and UDS* or LDS* are asserted, the transceivers are turned off and their outputs floated.

When the 68000 performs a valid access to local memory on the CPU card, an address decoder must detect an address from the CPU falling in this range and employ it to turn off the data bus transceivers. Figure 10.17 shows how this action can be taken.

The control of the data bus transceivers on the memory card is almost identical to the control of the corresponding transceivers on the CPU card. The transceivers may be enabled only when the CPU card (or any other bus master) is generating the appropriate memory access signals (AS*, UDS*/LDS*) and when the memory being accessed falls within the memory card.

Bus Contention and Data Bus Transceivers

Having decided that the main criterion in designing data bus transceiver circuits is the avoidance of bus contention and having produced such a circuit, the reader may be forgiven for thinking that our problems are over. What we have avoided is static data bus contention; that is, for any given state, no two bus drivers attempt to drive the data bus at the same time.

Alas, another problem waits in the wings in the form of dynamic data bus contention. This contention is called dynamic because it is associated with changes of state on the bus and is due to overlap as the old bus driver switches off and the new one switches on; for example, when the processor is executing a write cycle to the memory card, buffer BDOC is placing data on the system bus and buffer BDIM is receiving this data. When the write cycle is followed by a read cycle, the transceivers must be turned around. Therefore, buffer BDOM must not turn on until BDOC has turned off.

In order to analyze the problems of dynamic data bus contention, we need a detailed diagram of the address and data bus buffering and control arrangements. Figure 10.18 provides us with this information. Note that the full analysis of such a system is rather complex because of the large number of buffers in the signal and control paths. The next step is to examine all possible modes of data bus contention in both the write-to-read and read-to-write changes of state. Here we provide two examples of possible bus contention.

FIGURE 10.18   Data bus contention and the bus transceiver

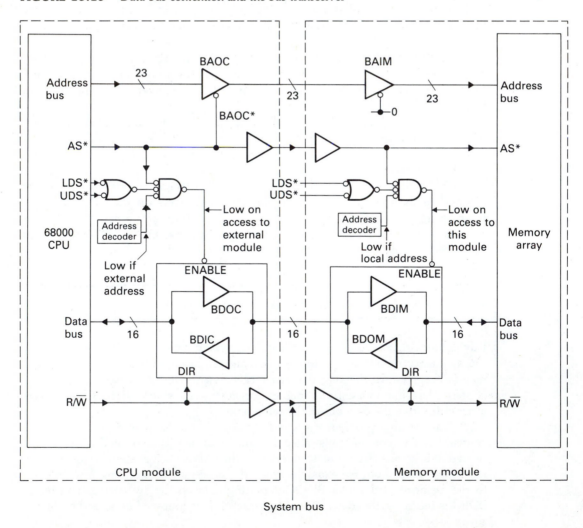

FIGURE 10.19 Write-to-read contention between BDOC and BDOM

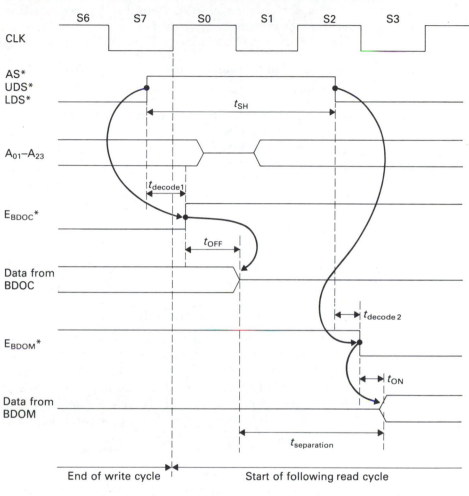

Write-to-Read Data Bus: Data Bus Contention

Suppose the 68000 is executing a write cycle to the memory card. Buffer BDOC on the CPU card is driving the data bus. At the end of the write cycle, BDOC is turned off by the negation of AS* and UDS*/LDS*. In the following read cycle, buffer BDOM on the memory card begins to drive the bus. We need to determine that BDOC-on does not overlap BDOM-on. Figure 10.19 gives the timing diagram for the switchover between a write and a read cycle.

At the end of the write cycle, AS* is negated and $E_{BDOC}*$ rises after a delay, $t_{decode1}$ seconds, due to the buffer control circuitry on the CPU card. After a further t_{OFF} seconds, the data bus buffer is turned off and the data bus floats. At the start of the read cycle, valid address and data strobes, AS* and UDS*/LDS*, cause $E_{BDOM}*$ on the CPU card to be asserted. This action takes place $t_{decode2}$ seconds after the assertion of AS*. A further t_{ON} seconds later, the data bus transmitter on the memory card is turned on.

The time between BDOC turning off and BDOM turning on, $t_{separation}$, is

$$t_{separation} = t_{SH} - t_{decode1} - t_{OFF} + t_{decode2} + t_{ON}.$$

Assume the following values:

$$
\begin{aligned}
t_{SH} &= 150 \text{ ns min. (8 MHz), 65 ns min. (12.5 MHz)}\\
t_{decode1} &= 30 \text{ ns max.}\\
t_{OFF} &= 25 \text{ ns max.}\\
t_{decode2} &= 10 \text{ ns min.}\\
t_{ON} &= 10 \text{ ns min.}
\end{aligned}
$$

Therefore,

$$
\begin{aligned}
t_{separation} &= 115 \text{ ns (8-MHz 68000)}\\
&= 30 \text{ ns (12.5-MHz 68000)}
\end{aligned}
$$

As the separation is positive, one buffer is turned off before the other is turned on and no problem arises.

Write-to-Read CPU: Data Bus Contention

A second form of contention can take place between the data bus driver in the 68000 itself and the data bus receivers (BDIC) on the CPU card. Figure 10.20 shows this situation. The data bus drivers in the 68000 may be active for up to t_{CHADZ} seconds following the rising edge of S0 in the next cycle. As the data bus receivers (BDIC) are not turned on until $t_{decode2} + t_{ON}$ following the falling edge of AS*, the separation between the on-times of the two buffers is given by

$$
\begin{aligned}
t_{separation} &= 2 \times t_c - t_{CHADZ} + t_{CHSL} + t_{decode2} + t_{ON}\\
&= 2 \times 62.5 - 80 + 0 + 10 + 10\\
&= 65 \text{ ns (8 MHz)}\\
t_{separation} &= 2 \times 40 - 60 + 0 + 10 + 10\\
&= 40 \text{ ns (12.5 MHz)}
\end{aligned}
$$

These values are positive for both the 8- and 12.5-MHz versions of the 68000. Of course, other forms of dynamic bus contention also exist, but these are left as an exercise for the student.

Buses as Transmission Lines

Now that we have struggled with bus drivers and crept through the minefield of bus contention, we have one last hurdle to overcome—the transmission line properties of the bus. In other words, having determined that only one output is

FIGURE 10.20   Write-to-read contention between the CPU and BDIC

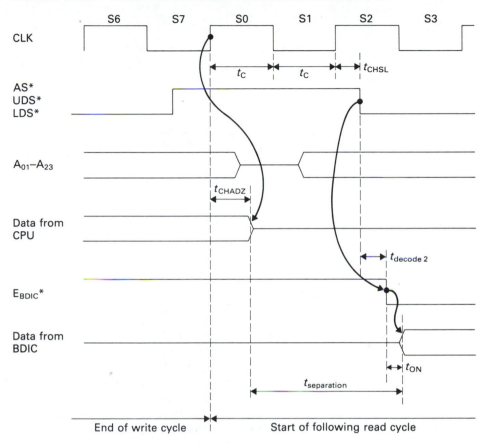

actively driving the bus and with enough current to clamp the bus at V_{OH} or V_{OL}, things can still go wrong! In short, a pulse propagated along the bus can be sufficiently distorted to produce misleading effects. Why this happens and what can be done about it is the subject of this section.

The term *transmission line* may be new to computer scientists with little background in electrical engineering. As a matter of fact, the origin of what is now called electronics evolved from a study of the effect of transmission lines on digital data! In the 1850s engineers had already observed that signals received at the ends of long submarine telegraph cables were noticeably distorted. A cleanly switched signal at the transmitting end was received as a slowly changing signal at the far end of the cable.

The sponsors of the project to lay the first transatlantic cable linking North America with Europe asked Professor Thomson (later Lord Kelvin) to investigate the problem. In May 1855 he presented a paper to the Royal Society that was to become the cornerstone of modern transmission line theory.

FIGURE 10.21   Idealized view of a transmission line

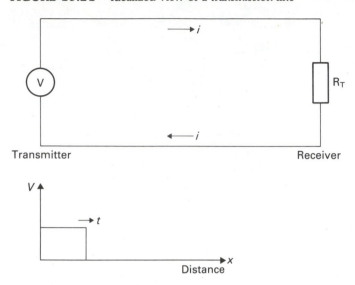

Figure 10.21 illustrates an idealized form of a transmission line. This transmission line is made up of a bus (conductor) and a ground return path. At one end a voltage source (the driver) can place a step voltage on the line and at the far end the line is terminated by a resistor, R_T.

Suppose the voltage between the ends of the line is initially everywhere zero and a step voltage of V is applied at the transmitter. This step corresponds to a zero-to-one transition of a bus driver in a digital system. Because of the fundamental electrical properties of matter, it is not possible for an electrical disturbance to travel down a circuit instantaneously. The resistance, inductance, and capacitance of the transmission line affect the way the pulse flows down it.

The propagation delay of a pulse on a transmission line is given by $\sqrt{LC}$ per unit length, where L is the inductance and C the capacitance of the bus (both per unit length). In free space (i.e., a vacuum), a signal propagates at the speed of light, 3×10^8 m/s (i.e., 30 cm/ns). Practical buses have values of $\sqrt{LC}$ greater than free space and signals propagate at about 15–20 cm/ns. The propagation delay may not seem much, but with buses of tens of centimeters, the signal delay may reach 10 ns or more. Such a value is of the order of a gate delay and cannot always be neglected in timing calculations.

It would be bad enough if the transmission line were only to introduce a pure delay into our model for the propagation of signals along a bus. We have not yet thought about the current flowing in the transmission line. When the transmitter in figure 10.21 creates a voltage step of V, what current flows in the bus? Ohm's law provides us with the formula $I = V/R$, where R is the resistance of the bus plus its load R_T. If we have learned one thing from this book, it is that nothing in microcomputer systems design is simple. At the time the pulse is

TABLE 10.6   Characteristic impedance of typical buses

BUS TYPE	CHARACTERISTIC IMPEDANCE (Ω)
Coaxial cable	50–75
Twisted pair	100–120
Two tracks separated by 1 inch	200–300
PCB tracks	50–150
Strip line	50
Free space	376

generated, the current does not "kno_w_" the value of R_T. How could it? A disturbance travels down the line at $1/\sqrt{LC}$ and cannot "see ahead" of itself!

Therefore, what current actually flows down the line? Because of the electrical nature of matter, the transmission line has a characteristic impedance, Z_o, whose value is determined by the geometry of the bus and the properties of the dielectric separating the signal path of the bus and its ground return. Table 10.6 gives the characteristic impedances of typical buses. From table 10.6 it can be seem that the characteristic impedance of typical backplanes is approximately 100 Ω. The characteristic impedance of a transmission line is given by $\sqrt{L/C}$, where L and C are the distributed inductance and capacitance per unit length.

We now have a step voltage of V moving down the line at $1/\sqrt{LC}$ meters per second with a current of V/Z_o amperes. All good things must come to an end, and the pulse eventually reaches the end of the line. If the bus is terminated by a load equal to its characteristic impedance, the pulse is dissipated in the load and the voltage at all points along the bus remains at V.

If the bus is not terminated by Z_o, the pulse is reflected from the termination back toward its source. To understand why this happens, consider the effect of the pulse arriving at the termination R_T. Immediately before the pulse reaches R_T, the relation between the pulse and current in the bus is given by $V = I/Z_o$. On reaching the termination, Ohm's law must be obeyed, and $I_T = V_T/R_T$, where I_T = the current in the termination and V_T = the voltage across the terminator.

The current flowing in the load can be defined as the sum of two components:

$$I_T = I_i + I_r$$

where I_i = incident current and I_r = reflected current. Therefore,

$$I_T = \frac{V_T}{R_T} = \frac{V_i + V_r}{R_T}.$$

However,

$$I_i = \frac{V_i}{Z_o} \quad \text{and} \quad I_r = -\frac{V_r}{Z_o}.$$

The minus sign indicates that the reflected voltage, V_r, is moving away from the terminator and back toward the generator. These equations can be rearranged to give

$$\frac{V_i}{Z_o} - \frac{V_r}{Z_o} = \frac{V_i + V_r}{R_T} = \frac{V_i}{R_T} + \frac{V_r}{R_T},$$

that is,

$$V_i\left(\frac{1}{Z_o} - \frac{1}{R_T}\right) = V_r\left(\frac{1}{Z_o} + \frac{1}{R_T}\right)$$

or

$$V_r = V_i \frac{R_T - Z_o}{R_T + Z_o} = V_i G$$

Thus, the reflected voltage can be calculated in terms of the load impedance R_T and the characteristic impedance of the line Z_o. Consider the three limiting cases: $R_T = Z_o$ (line terminated by characteristic impedance), $R_T = 0$ (short-circuit), and $R_T =$ infinity (open-circuit):

1. Matched line $\quad V_r = V_i \dfrac{R_T - R_T}{R_T + R_T} = 0$ (no reflected wave).

2. Short-circuit $\quad V_r = V_i \dfrac{0 - Z_o}{0 + Z_o} = -V_i$ (inverted pulse reflected).

3. Open-circuit $\quad V_r = V_i \dfrac{\infty - Z_o}{\infty + Z_o} = V_i$ (pulse reflected).

Note that when the termination is zero, the reflected wave has an equal amplitude but opposite polarity to the incident wave. These waves cancel to produce a zero voltage, which is reassuringly in line with common sense. When the incident wave reaches the short-circuit, the voltage across the lines must fall to zero, which travels back down the line to the generator.

Real transmission lines fall between the extremes. Suppose that $Z_o = 100 \ \Omega$ and the line is terminated by 150 Ω. The reflection coefficient is therefore

$$\frac{R_T - Z_o}{R_T + Z_o} = \frac{150 - 100}{150 + 100} = \frac{50}{250} = \frac{1}{5}.$$

In this case, the reflected voltage is $V_i/5$. When the reflected voltage has traveled back down the line, it reaches the generator and is reflected, exactly as it was at the terminator. In this case, the new reflected voltage is given by

$$V_r = V_i \frac{R_G - Z_o}{R_G + Z_o}$$

FIGURE 10.22   Effect of a mismatch on a pulse on a transmission line

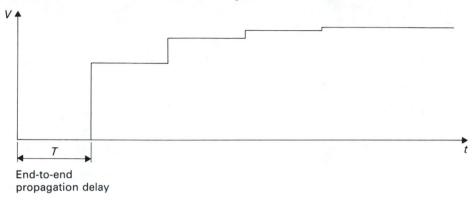

End-to-end
propagation delay

where R_G = resistance of generator. A pulse is therefore reflected to and fro between the generator and transmission line termination until, in the limit, the voltage on the bus reaches its steady-state value of $VR_T/(R_G + R_T)$.

Figure 10.22 illustrates the effect of applying a pulse to a transmission line with mismatches at both the generator and terminator. In any real system the waveform will be much more complex as the impedance of the transmission line is not uniform, the transmission line contains nonlinear elements (i.e., semiconductors), and reflections occur at discontinuities in the transmission line such as connectors and circuits connected to the line (so-called stubs).

These theories are very nice, but where are they getting us? The answer is that unless a bus is terminated by a reasonable approximation to its characteristic impedance, fast pulses will suffer from reflections that may play havoc with the system's operation. In the early days of the microcomputer (mid 1970s), little attention was paid to bus design. Fortunately, clock speeds were rather low and relatively long times were needed for signals to settle and reflections to die down. Today clock rates of 8 to 20 MHz or more make bus design critical.

Bus designers now attempt to define the characteristic impedance of a bus by controlling its geometry. They also provide ground return paths as close as possible to each signal line.

Terminating the Bus

To reduce reflections, the ends of a transmission line should be terminated by connecting a resistance, equal to Z_o, across the line. The value of Z_o is approximately 100 Ω for a typical PCB. Unfortunately, if a 100-Ω resistor is wired between a bus line and ground, the upper logic level will be pulled down and the noise immunity reduced. Equally, connecting a 100-Ω resister between the bus and V_{cc} will pull up the lower logic level and reduce the low-level noise immunity. Remember that the terminator can be connected between the bus and ground *or* V_{cc}, as a low impedance exists between ground and V_{cc} as far as transients are concerned.

FIGURE 10.23   Terminating the bus

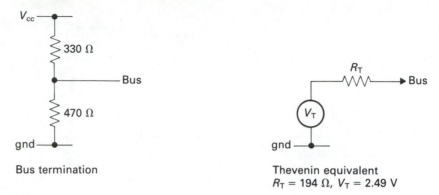

Bus termination

Thevenin equivalent
$R_T = 194\ \Omega,\ V_T = 2.49\ V$

The classic solution to bus termination is illustrated in figure 10.23. Two resistors are connected to the bus, one to ground and one to V_{cc}. A typical resistor pair is 330 Ω to V_{cc} and 470 Ω to ground. The bus termination circuit can be reduced to its Thevinin equivalent of a single resistance of 194 Ω connected to a voltage source of 2.94 V. Thus, the line is terminated without being pulled down to ground or up to V_{cc}.

A refinement of this circuit, illustrated in figure 10.24, is rather misleadingly called an *active termination* circuit. A voltage regulator produces the desired termination voltage and a single resistor of 120 Ω is connected between this voltage source and each of the bus lines to be terminated.

FIGURE 10.24   Active bus termination

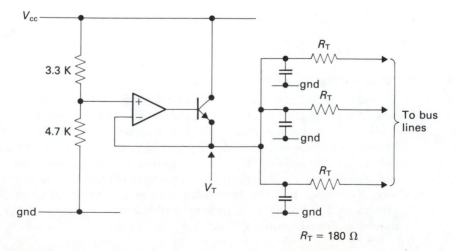

$R_T = 180\ \Omega$

Designing a Microcomputer Bus

It should be apparent by now that the design of a bus is no trivial matter. If a relatively low clock rate is anticipated, conventional wisdom may help the designer. The three pillars of conventional wisdom are:

1. Allow each signal time for all reflections to have died away to vanishingly small proportions; for example, the contents of address and data buses should not be sampled until, say, 100 ns after they are nominally valid.

2. Apply matched terminations to each end of the bus. As a perfect match is impossible to obtain, a termination of approximately 100 Ω should severely attenuate reflections.

3. Load the bus as little as possible and avoid long stubs. A stub is an extension to the bus rather like a T junction.

A better approach to bus design is to buy a bus off the shelf. This course may not be a particularly adventurous path I'll admit, but sometimes caution should be exercised in systems design. Few areas of microprocessor systems design are as complex as the design of reliable buses. Many manufacturers subcontract the analysis of their buses to noted academics, but this is not always helpful. Academics differ more on their attitude to bus design than on almost any other area. Today ready-made buses can be obtained that are constructed to international standards from reputable manufacturers. Such buses are produced by state-of-the-art technology to minimize reflections and cross-talk. I would not design a bus for a high-speed microcomputer without facilities to test and modify my design in the light of experience. Necessary equipment for such testing includes oscilloscopes with rise-times an order of magnitude better than the pulses I wish to observe.

10.3   VMEbus

Now that we have described the way in which a bus operates, we are going to look at a bus designed specifically for 68000 systems. The VMEbus is intended to support the 68000-series microcomputers and is a backplane bus. The VMEbus is asynchronous only in the sense that the 68000 is asynchronous; that is, memory accesses of a variable duration are possible by means of the 68000's DTACK* input. The VMEbus is really a synchronous bus, as the latching of addresses and data is controlled by a system clock.

Motorola developed its own bus, the VERSAbus, for use on its EXORmacs 68000 development system. The VERSAbus is a particularly large (physically) bus, and a version suited to the popular Eurocard was developed by Motorola in 1981. The Eurocard is available as a single card (160 × 100 mm) or as a double card (160 × 233.4 mm). The bus developed for these cards was called the *Versa Module Europe* bus and is now known as the VMEbus.

The VMEbus was rapidly adopted as a standard by industry and is now supported by Motorola, Signetics, Mostek, Philips, and Thomson-EFCIS. Although the Eurocard originated in Europe, it is also popular in the United States and is beginning to displace other, more conventional, formats. Today, many independent manufacturers produce a wide range of Eurocard modules for the VMEbus.

In September 1983 the IEEE Standards Board gave their approval to the VMEbus standards group and assigned project number P1014 as the IEEE reference number to this bus during its development phase. The VMEbus was approved by the IEEE in 1984 and is therefore known officially as the IEEE 1014 bus. Similarly, the International Electrotechnical Commission, IEC, started formal standardization of the VMEbus in 1982 and called it the IEC 821 bus.

A definitive treatment of the VMEbus is impossible to provide here. The VME system architecture manual that defines the bus is several hundred pages long. Only an overview of the bus and its characteristics can be given. The purpose of the VMEbus is to allow the systems designer to put together a microprocessor system by buying off-the-shelf hardware and software components. This approach can be very economical, particularly as it frees the designer to spend more time on those parts of the system that must be custom-made. The formal objectives of the VMEbus are:

1. To provide communication facilities between two devices (i.e., cards) on the VMEbus without disturbing the internal activities of other devices interfaced to it. In plain English, we can plug in a new card without "harming" the existing system.

2. To specify the electrical and mechanical system characteristics required to design devices that will reliably and unambiguously communicate with other devices interfaced to the VMEbus.

3. To specify protocols that precisely define the interaction between the VMEbus and devices interfaced to it.

4. To provide terminology and definitions that precisely describe system protocols.

5. To allow a broad range of design latitude so that the designer can optimize cost and/or performance without affecting system compatibility.

6. To provide a system where performance is primarily device limited, rather than system interface limited.

The VMEbus has been designed with flexibility in mind and can operate with data widths of 8, 16, or 32 bits, and with 24- or 32-bit address buses. The VMEbus complements all the powerful features of the 68000 (except for its synchronous bus) and has important facilities of its own.

VMEbus Mechanics

VMEbus cards are designed to slot into a 19-inch (482.6 mm) rack that may be either 3U (132.5 mm) or 6U (265.9 mm) high. Figure 10.25 shows a card frame that supports both the single Eurocard (3U height) and double Eurocard (6U height) formats. The cards themselves are either single-height boards 100 mm (3.937 inch) by 160 mm (6.299 inch) deep or double-height boards 233.35 mm (9.187 inches) high and 160 mm deep. Figure 10.26 illustrates a double-height board. A clever feature of the VMEbus is its two connectors, called P1 and P2. If the VMEbus had all the facilities it needed on one connector, it would be unwieldy. Moreover, the cut-down version (i.e., 3U size) of a Eurocard would be impossible to construct.

The approach adopted by the VMEbus is to define a primary connector P1 and a secondary connector P2. All the functions necessary to implement a basic VMEbus are provided by P1, which permits the construction of a system based entirely on standard Eurocards. Connector P2 provides expansion facilities, per-

FIGURE 10.25   Card frame. (Reprinted by permission of Motorola Limited)

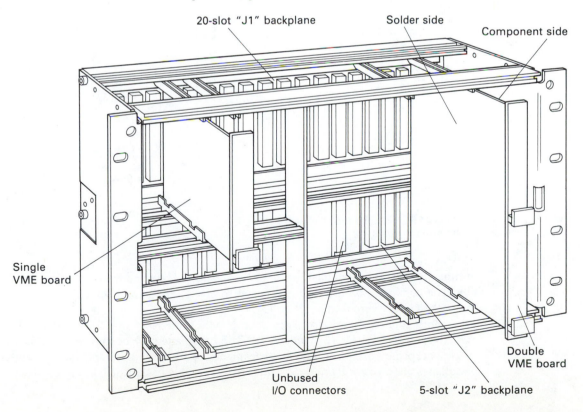

FIGURE 10.26 Dimensions of a double-height VME card. (Reprinted by permission of Motorola Limited)

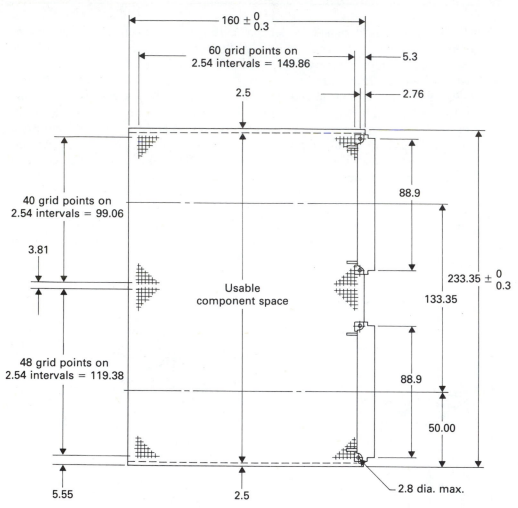

NOTES: Board thickness 1.6 ± 0.2 reference IEC 249–2.
All dimensions are shown in millimeters.

mitting the bus to be extended from 24 to 32 address bits and from 16 to 32 data bits. The connector on the card is referred to as P1 (or P2) and the connector on the backplane is referred to as J1 (or J2).

Both connectors are two-piece devices with three rows of 32 pins (96 in all) and conform to DIN 41612 standard. A VME backplane may be implemented as a single backplane (for P1) or a double backplane for P1 and P2. Invariably, separate backplanes are used for P1 and P2, rather than a double backplane.

Functions Provided by the VMEbus

Although the VMEbus is a single entity and is not physically subdivisible, its specification logically divides the bus into four distinct subbuses, as illustrated in figure 10.27. The positions along the VMEbus into which cards are plugged are called slots. In VMEbus terminology, a module is a collection of electronic components with a single functional purpose. More than one such module may exist on the same card.

From figure 10.27, we can see that the VMEbus system definition specifies a number of modules that form the interface between the VMEbus backplane and the various user modules making up the microcomputer. The functional modules forming part of the VMEbus specification are:

1. *DTB requester.* "DTB" stands for data transfer bus and includes the address and signal paths necessary to execute a data transfer (8, 16, or 32 bits) between a DTB master and a DTB slave. A DTB requester is a module on the same board as a master or interrupt handler and is capable of requesting control of the data transfer bus whenever its master or interrupt handler needs it.

2. *Interrupter.* An interrupter is a functional module capable of requesting service from a master subsystem by generating an interrupt request. The interrupter must also provide status information when the interrupt handler requests it.

3. *Interrupt handler.* An interrupt handler is a functional module capable of detecting interrupt requests and initiating appropriate responses.

4. *DTB arbiter.* A data transfer bus arbiter is a functional module that receives requests for the DTB from other modules, prioritizes them, and grants the bus to the appropriate requester.

5. *DTB slave.* A DTB slave, or simply slave, is a functional module capable of responding to a data transfer operation initiated by a master; for example, a memory module is a typical DTB slave.

6. *DTB master.* A DTB master, or simply master, is a functional module capable of initiating bus transfers. A 68000 is a prime example of a DTB master. Note that all 68000s are not necessarily DTB masters. A 68000 on a card may operate entirely locally and may not be able to access the VMEbus itself.

Now that we have defined the functions of some of the modules forming part of the VMEbus specification, we can look at the four groups of signals making up the VMEbus. These are:

1. *Data transfer bus.* The data transfer bus is the data and address pathways and their associated control signals, and is employed for the purpose of

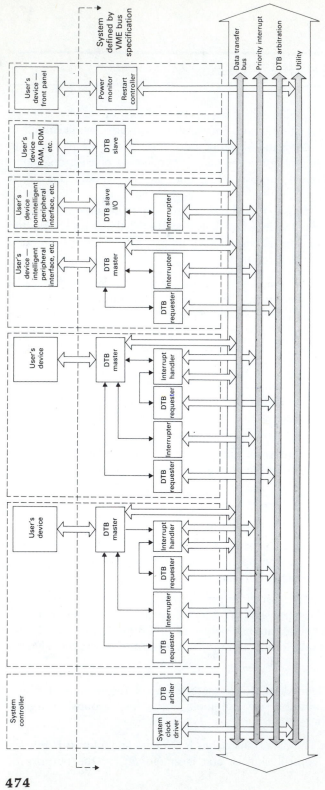

FIGURE 10.27 VMEbus. (Reprinted by permission of Motorola Limited)

transferring data from a DTB master to a DTB slave. Of all the buses, the DTB most closely matches the corresponding pin functions (i.e., the asynchronous bus) of the 68000.

2. *DTB arbitration bus.* At any instant a VMEbus can be configured with only one master that is capable of transferring data between itself and one or more slaves. The DTB arbitration bus and its associated DTB arbiter module provide a means of transferring control of the DTB between two or more masters in an orderly manner.

3. *Priority interrupt bus.* The priority interrupt bus and its associated modules extend the interrupt-handling capabilities of the 68000 microprocessor (see chap. 6). The priority interrupt capability of the VMEbus provides a means by which devices can request interruption of normal bus activity and can be serviced by an interrupt handler. These interrupt requests can be prioritized into a maximum of seven levels.

4. *Utilities bus.* The utilities bus is a "miscellaneous functions bus" by another name and includes the system clock, a system reset line, a system fail line, and an a.c. fail line.

The pin assignments of the P1 connector of the VMEbus are given in table 10.7. These pins provide all the functionality of the four subbuses. Table 10.8 gives the pin assignments of the P2 connector. We can see that the J2 bus is divided between user-defined I/O pins and an extension of the J1 address and data buses to 32 bits. The J2 bus is not considered further here.

Data Transfer Bus

As stated previously, the DTB is little more than an extension of the 68000's asynchronous bus. Moreover, the specification of the DTB is given in terms of the timing diagrams and protocol flow diagrams introduced in chapter 4. The signals of the DTB are defined in table 10.9.

Eight- or sixteen-bit data transfers are controlled exactly as in the 68000 itself, with DS1* replacing UDS* and DS0* replacing LDS*. A new function is provided by LWORD*, which, when asserted, permits a 32-bit longword data transfer on D_{00} to D_{31}. Note that longword transfers require that both P1 and P2 connectors be present. Longword data transfers can, of course, be implemented by the 68020 CPU, but not by a 68000 or a 68010. In systems that do not support 32-bit data transfers, the DTB master must put an inactive-high level on LWORD*.

A special feature of the DTB is the 6-bit address modifier, bits AM0 to AM5. The purpose of the address modifier bits is to allow the master to pass up to six bits of additional information to a slave during a data transfer. The modifier bits may provide the information present on FC0 to FC2 from the 68000. To a great extent, the way in which this information is encoded and actually employed is left up to the user. Some possible applications of the address modifier bits are now given:

TABLE 10.7   P1 pin assignments on the J1 VMEbus

PIN NUMBER	SIGNAL MNEMONIC		
	ROW A	ROW B	ROW C
1	D_{00}	BBSY*	D_{08}
2	D_{01}	BCLR*	D_{09}
3	D_{02}	ACFAIL*	D_{10}
4	D_{03}	BG0IN*	D_{11}
5	D_{04}	BG0OUT*	D_{12}
6	D_{05}	BG1IN*	D_{13}
7	D_{06}	BG1OUT*	D_{14}
8	D_{07}	BG2IN*	D_{15}
9	GND	BG2OUT*	GND
10	SYSCLK	BG3IN*	SYSFAIL*
11	GND	BG3OUT*	BERR*
12	DS1*	BR0*	SYSRESET*
13	DS0*	BR1*	LWORD*
14	WRITE*	BR2*	AM5
15	GND	BR3*	A_{23}
16	DTACK*	AM0	A_{22}
17	GND	AM1	A_{21}
18	AS*	AM2	A_{20}
19	GND	AM3	A_{19}
20	IACK*	GND	A_{18}
21	IACKIN*	SERCLK	A_{17}
22	IACKOUT*	SERDAT*	A_{16}
23	AM4	GND	A_{15}
24	A_{07}	IRQ7*	A_{14}
25	A_{06}	IRQ6*	A_{13}
26	A_{05}	IRQ5*	A_{12}
27	A_{04}	IRQ4*	A_{11}
28	A_{03}	IRQ3*	A_{10}
29	A_{02}	IRQ2*	A_{09}
30	A_{01}	IRQ1*	A_{08}
31	−12 V	+5 standby	+12 V
32	+5 V	+5 V	+5 V

1.   *System partitioning.* Slaves may be programmed with an address modifier value that must match the value on AM0 to AM5 if they are to take place in a valid data exchange with a master. In this way, a slave may be assigned to a given master even though other masters generate addresses falling within the slave's address range. Accesses by other masters will be ignored. The effect of this situation is to partition the slaves among the masters.

TABLE 10.8   P2 pin assignments on the J2 VMEbus

PIN NUMBER	SIGNAL MNEMONIC		
	ROW A	ROW B	ROW C
1	User I/O	+5 V	User I/O
2	User I/O	GND	User I/O
3	User I/O	Reserved	User I/O
4	User I/O	A_{24}	User I/O
5	User I/O	A_{25}	User I/O
6	User I/O	A_{26}	User I/O
7	User I/O	A_{27}	User I/O
8	User I/O	A_{28}	User I/O
9	User I/O	A_{29}	User I/O
10	User I/O	A_{30}	User I/O
11	User I/O	A_{31}	User I/O
12	User I/O	GND	User I/O
13	User I/O	+5 V	User I/O
14	User I/O	D_{16}	User I/O
15	User I/O	D_{17}	User I/O
16	User I/O	D_{18}	User I/O
17	User I/O	D_{19}	User I/O
18	User I/O	D_{20}	User I/O
19	User I/O	D_{21}	User I/O
20	User I/O	D_{22}	User I/O
21	User I/O	D_{23}	User I/O
22	User I/O	GND	User I/O
23	User I/O	D_{24}	User I/O
24	User I/O	D_{25}	User I/O
25	User I/O	D_{26}	User I/O
26	User I/O	D_{27}	User I/O
27	User I/O	D_{28}	User I/O
28	User I/O	D_{29}	User I/O
29	User I/O	D_{30}	User I/O
30	User I/O	D_{31}	User I/O
31	User I/O	GND	User I/O
32	User I/O	+5 V	User I/O

2.   *Memory map manipulation.* Slaves may be designed to respond to more than one range of addresses, the actual range depending on the current address modifier received from the master. Thus the master places the system resources in selected map locations by providing different address modifier codes.

3.   *Privileged access.* Because slaves may be designed to respond to some address modifier values and not to others, different levels of privilege may

TABLE 10.9   Signals of the data transfer bus (DTB)

VMEBUS MNEMONIC	68000 MNEMONIC	NAME
A_{01}–A_{31}	A_{01}–A_{23}	Address bus
D_{00}–D_{31}	D_{00}–D_{15}	Data bus
AS*	AS*	Address strobe
LWORD*	None	Longword
DS1*	UDS*	Data strobe 1
DS0*	LDS*	Data strobe 0
WRITE*	R/$\overline{W}$	Write
DTACK*	DTACK*	Data acknowledge
BERR*	BERR*	Bus error
AM0–AM5	None	Address modifier bus

be established. A master executing a data bus transfer (DBT) puts out a level of privilege on AM0 to AM5 and a slave responds only if it is able to operate at that level of privilege.

4.   *Address range determination.* As a full implementation of the VMEbus offers 32 address bits, each slave requires a rather large amount of address decoding circuitry (see chap. 5) to determine whether the current address in the 4G-byte range falls within its own range. By using address modifier bits to specify a short address on A_{01} to A_{15}, a standard address on A_{01} to A_{23}, or an extended address on A_{01} to A_{31}, slaves with rather simpler address decoding circuits may be built.

The revision C, October 1985 VMEbus specification defines three categories of address modifier code: short addressing (A_{01} to A_{15}) codes, standard addressing (A_{01} to A_{23}) codes, and extended addressing (A_{01} to A_{31}) codes. Some people have suggested that slaves with 23-bit addresses respond to the hex codes 39, 3A, 3D, and 3E on AM0 to AM5.

Data transfer on the VMEbus   When a module wishes to transfer data to or from a slave, it must first acquire control of the bus (if it is not already a bus master) via its bus requester module, to be described later. Once a module is a bus master, it executes a data transfer in very much the same way as a 68000. Of course, adaptation of a 68000 CPU to the VMEbus is very easy: only the appropriate buffering between the chip and the bus is needed. Other CPUs can be interfaced to the VMEbus but not necessarily as conveniently as the 68000.

Figure 10.28 defines the VMEbus protocol for a DTB byte read cycle. This diagram is essentially the same as the protocol diagram for a 68000 read cycle in chapter 4, apart from its greater detail and the inclusion of LWORD* and IACK*. The setting of IACK* high indicates that the master is not executing an interrupt acknowledge cycle.

The VMEbus specification also provides a number of timing diagrams to

FIGURE 10.28 Protocol flowchart for a DTB single-byte read cycle

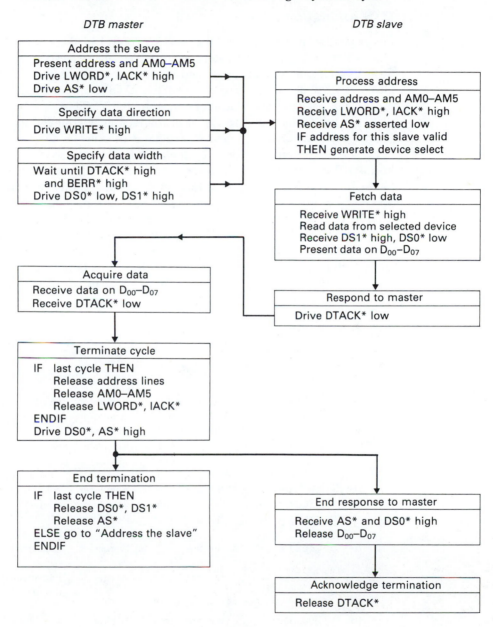

augment the protocol diagrams. Once more, these diagrams mirror the 68000's read and write cycle timing diagrams.

DTB Arbitration

Bus arbitration is a mechanism that enables control of the DTB to be passed to one master in a group of masters, all of which are requesting use of the DTB. Systems with only one processor and no other "processor-like" modules such as DMA devices do not require the VMEbus DTB arbitration facilities. Here we discuss only the arbitration facilities offered by the VMEbus.

The arbitration bus has a total of fourteen lines arranged into two groups. One is made up of lines driven by requester modules in DTB masters and the other is made up of lines driven by the arbiter, which must be physically located in slot 1. Table 10.10 gives the names and mnemonics of the arbitration bus lines. Note that the VMEbus supports four levels of arbitration (the 68000 itself supports only one level). Two types of module take part in an arbitration process: the DTB requesters forming part of a bus master and the DTB arbiter that belongs to the system controller and acts on the bus globally.

Whenever a situation arises where a number of entities are competing for limited resources (be they people or bus masters), an algorithm must be devised to deal with the distribution of the resources. In human terms, we can adopt "fair

TABLE 10.10   VMEbus arbitration bus

PIN/ROW	MNEMONIC	NAME	GROUP	FUNCTION
12b	BR0*	Bus request 0	Requester	Used by requester to
13b	BR1*	Bus request 1	Requester	gain access to the
14b	BR2*	Bus request 2	Requester	DTB
15b	BR3*	Bus request 3	Requester	
5b	BG0OUT*	Bus grant out 0	Requester	Used by requester to
7b	BG1OUT*	Bus grant out 1	Requester	pass on BGIN* from the
9b	BG2OUT*	Bus grant out 2	Requester	arbiter
11b	BG3OUT*	Bus grant out 3	Requester	
1b	BBSY*	Bus busy	Requester	Indicates bus busy
2b	BCLR*	Bus clear	Arbiter	Informs master that the DTB is needed
4b	BG0IN*	Bus grant in 0	Arbiter	Used by arbiter to
6b	BG1IN*	Bus grant in 1	Arbiter	indicate level of
8b	BG2IN*	Bus grant in 2	Arbiter	DTB access
10b	BG3IN*	Bus grant in 3	Arbiter	

shares for all" policies, "first-come first-served" policies, or "survival of the fittest" policies. Similar strategies have been applied to the VMEbus and are known as arbiter options. The three options available are:

1.   *Option RRS (round robin select)*. The RRS option assigns priority to the DTB masters on a rotating basis. The four levels of bus request (BR0* to BR3*) are treated as a cycle (i.e., BR0*—BR3*—BR2*—BR1*—BR0*—BR3*—BR2* ...), with BR3* following BR0*. At any instant, one of these four levels is made the highest level so that this level may gain control of the bus. If that level does not wish to use the bus, the next level downward is tested, and so on. Once a particular level is found to be requesting access, that level is granted access.

After the bus has been released, the next lower level is tested and the cycle continues. Consequently, all levels are tested in turn and no level is ever left out. Round robin select is a fair method of arbitration.

2.   *Option PRI (prioritized)*. The PRI option assigns a level of priority to each of the bus request lines from BR3* (highest) to BR0* (lowest). Whenever a master requests access to the DTB bus, the arbiter deals with the request by comparing the new level of priority with the old (i.e., current) level. A higher priority request always defeats a lower priority request. Option PRI is similar to the 68000's own interrupt request facilities. It is not a fair strategy, as a low-level request may, theoretically, never be serviced if higher priority devices are "greedy."

3.   *Single level (SGL)*. The SGL option provides a minimal bus arbitration facility using bus request line BR3* only. The priority of individual modules is determined by *daisy-chaining*, so that the module next to the arbiter module in slot 1 of the VMEbus rack has the highest priority. As the position of a module moves further away from the arbiter, its priority reduces.

Scheduling algorithms other than the above three types of arbitration may be used on the VMEbus. The arbitration algorithm selected is a choice exercised by the user.

Arbitration lines   The physical arrangement of the VMEbus arbitration lines is presented in figure 10.29 and the logical relationship of the lines and the arbiter and requester module is given in figure 10.30. Note that in figure 10.29, the bus_grant_in and the bus_grant_out lines are broken and run only from slot to slot rather than from end to end. A bus_grant_in from a left-hand module (i.e., higher priority requester module) is passed out on its right as a bus_grant_out signal. By convention, the level of a request is written as x (where $x = 0, 1, 2,$ or 3). Therefore, the BGxOUT* of one module is connected to the BGxIN* of its right-hand neighbor.

The arrangement of Figure 10.29 is called daisy-chaining because of its "head-to-tail" nature and adds a special feature to a bus line. A normal continuous bus line passes a signal in both directions to all devices connected to it. The

FIGURE 10.29   Arrangement of VMEbus arbitration lines on the J1 bus. The bus_grant_in lines of slot 1 are driven by the arbiter which is normally plugged into slot 1; that is, the BGxIN* pins of slot 1 are *not* driven from the VMEbus

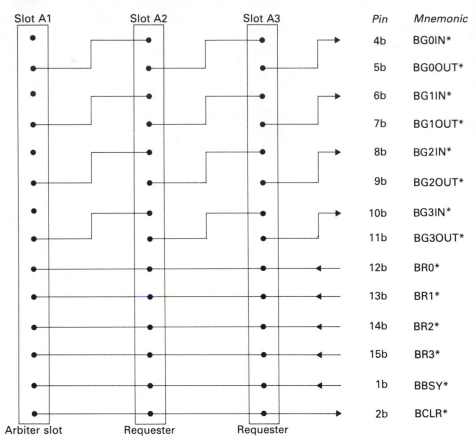

daisy-chained line is unidirectional, passing a signal from one specific end to another. Moreover, each module connected to (i.e., receiving from and transmitting to) a daisy-chained line may either pass a signal on down the line or inject a signal of its own onto the line.

A DTB requester module makes a bid for control of the system bus by asserting one of the bus request lines, BR0* to BR3*. Note that only one line is asserted and that that line is chosen by assigning a given priority to the requester. The priority may be assigned by on-board user-selectable jumpers or dynamically by software.

The arbiter, on receiving a request for the bus, may (depending on the option in force) assert one of its bus_grant_out lines (BG0OUT* to BG3OUT*). The bus_grant_out signal then propagates down the daisy-chain. Each BGxOUT* arrives at the BGxIN* of the next module. If that module does not require access to the bus, it passes on the request on its BGxOUT* line. If, however, the module does wish to request the bus, it does not assert its BGxOUT* signal. Daisy-chaining provides automatic prioritization, because bus requesters further down the line do not receive a bus grant if it has already been accepted by a higher-priority requester.

Once a bus requester has been granted control of the data transfer bus by an active level on its BGxIN* input, it asserts bus busy (BBSY*) active-low. By asserting BBSY* a requester signifies its possession of the bus and control may not be taken back until it releases BBSY*. Note that this situation contrasts with the prioritization of interrupt requests. A low-priority interrupt may be serviced if no other interrupt is pending. A higher-level interrupt will always interrupt one with a lower priority. The arbitration bus functions differently. An active DTB master cannot be forced off the bus. BBSY* must be asserted by a requester for at least 90 ns and remain asserted for at least 30 ns *after* the requester has released the bus. Furthermore, BBSY* must be asserted until the requester's bus grant is negated in order to assure that the arbiter has seen the BBSY* transition.

The bus clear line, BCLR*, from the arbiter informs the current DTB master that another master with a higher priority now wishes to access the bus. As stated previously, the current master does not have to relinquish the bus within a pre-scribed time limit. Typically, the master will release the bus at the first convenient instant, releasing the bus by negating BBSY*.

Bus clear is driven only by option PRI arbiters. Because the bus request lines have no fixed priority in a round robin arbitration scheme, an RRS arbiter does not drive bus clear, BCLR*. In this case BCLR* will be driven inactive-high by the bus termination network.

Figure 10.30 shows how the arbiter module communicates with requester modules. The task of the arbiter is to prioritize incoming bus requests and to grant access to the appropriate requester. When operating in the fixed priority mode (PRI), the arbiter also informs any master currently in control of the DTB that a higher level of request is pending by asserting BCLR*.

Bus requester operation   A bus requester module receives an indication from its DTB master (via the master_wants_bus signal in figure 10.30) that the latter wishes to access the DTB. The requester then asserts the appropriate bus request.

After the arbitration has taken place, the requester reads the incoming bus grant signals, BGxIN*, and passes them unchanged on BGxOUT*. If the on-board master wants the DTB and the requester's priority is equal to that on BGxIN*, the bus grant is latched internally and a master_granted_bus signal is passed to the master. BBSY* is asserted by the requester as long as the master indicates its intention to use the bus.

The requester may implement one of two options for releasing the DTB. One is called option RWD (release when done) and the other option ROR (release on request). The simpler of the options is RWD, which requires that the requester will release the bus as soon as the on-board master stops indicating bus busy. In

FIGURE 10.30   Relationship between VMEbus, arbiter, and requester

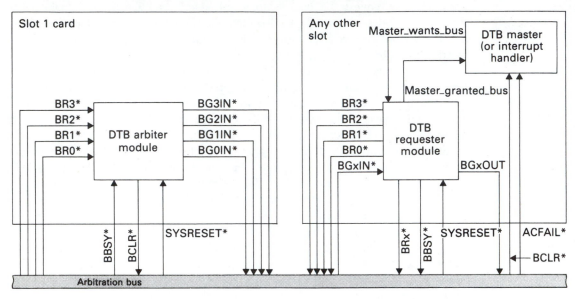

other words, the master remains in control of the bus until its task has been completed. This situation can, of course, lead to undue *bus hogging*. In systems where granting unlimited access of the bus to a master is unreasonable, the ROR option is more suitable. In this case, the requester monitors the four bus request lines. If the requester sees that another requester has requested service, it releases its BBSY* output and defers to the other request. The ROR option also reduces the number of arbitrations requested by a master, as the bus is frequently cleared voluntarily.

Arbitration process   We will now briefly look at the arbitration sequence. Figure 10.31 demonstrates one possible sequence of events taking place during arbitration between two requests at different levels of priority. Further examples are found in the VME system manual.

The sequence of events begins when both requester A and requester B assert their request outputs simultaneously. Requester A asserts BR1* and requester B asserts BR2*. Assuming that the arbiter detects BR1* and BR2* low simultaneously, it will assert only BG2IN* on slot 1, because BR2* has a higher priority than BR1*. When this signal has propagated down the daisy-chain to requester B, requester B will respond to BG2IN* low by asserting BBSY*. Requester B then releases BR2* and informs its own master that the DTB is now available.

After detecting that BBSY* has been asserted, the arbiter negates BG2IN*. At this point both BR2* and BG2IN* are inactive-high because BBSY* and the bus grants are interlocked, as shown in figure 10.31. The arbiter is not permitted to negate a bus grant until it detects BBSY* low. When master B completes its

FIGURE 10.31 Arbitrating between two requests on different levels. (Reprinted by permission of Motorola Limited)

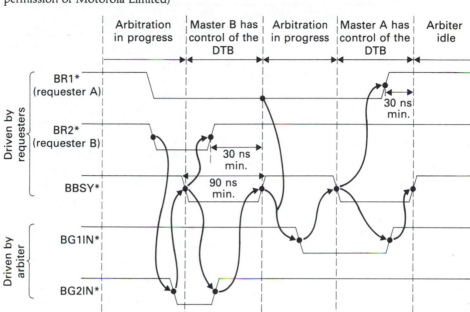

data transfer or transfers, requester B releases BBSY∗. The negation of BBSY∗ is conditional on BG2IN∗ remaining high and at least 30 ns having elapsed since the release of BR2∗. The 30-ns delay ensures that the arbiter will not interpret the old active-low value of BR2∗ as another request. Requester B will wait until the 30-ns interval has elapsed and will then release BBSY∗.

The arbiter interprets the release of BBSY∗ as a signal to arbitrate bus requests once more. Since BR1∗ is active-low and is the only bus request line asserted, the arbiter grants access to the DTB to request A by asserting BG1IN∗. Requester A responds by asserting BBSY∗. When master A has completed its data transfer, requester A releases BBSY∗, provided BG1IN∗ has been received and 30 ns have elapsed since the release of BR1∗. In this example, since no bus request lines are asserted when requester A releases BBSY∗, the arbiter remains idle until a new request is made.

The preceding description is equally valid for both PRI and RRS option arbiters. The arbitration bus has been dealt with only superficially and the reader is directed to the VMEbus manual for a definitive treatment. The 68000 systems designer must provide logic to interface between the 68000 bus master and the arbitration bus.

Priority Interrupt Bus

The priority interrupt bus enables modules connected to the VMEbus to request service from a DTB master. In general, this bus is closely associated with the

TABLE 10.11   VMEbus J1 priority interrupt bus

PIN/ROW	MNEMONIC	NAME
24b	IRQ7*	Interrupt request 7
25b	IRQ6*	Interrupt request 6
26b	IRQ5*	Interrupt request 5
27b	IRQ4*	Interrupt request 4
28b	IRQ3*	Interrupt request 3
29b	IRQ2*	Interrupt request 2
30b	IRQ1*	Interrupt request 1
20a	IACK*	Interrupt acknowledge
21a	IACKIN*	Interrupt acknowledge input
22a	IACKOUT*	Interrupt acknowledge output

68000's interrupt-handling scheme described in chapter 6. The ten lines of the priority interrupt bus are given in table 10.11. Two types of module are associated with the interrupt bus: the interrupt requester ("interrupter") that requests service and the interrupt handler that receives the request.

Interrupt bus lines   Seven of the lines of the interrupt bus are devoted to interrupt requests, IRQ1* to IRQ7*, from the interrupters. Three lines, IACK*, IACKIN*, and IACKOUT*, carry out the interrupt acknowledge sequence that is initiated by the interrupt handler. The IACK* line is asserted by an interrupt handler. IACK* runs the full length of the bus and is connected to the IACKIN* pin of slot 1. When asserted, IACK* initiates a low-going transition that propagates down the interrupt acknowledge daisy-chain.

Each of the seven interrupt request lines, IRQ1* to IRQ7*, may be shared by two or more interrupter modules. Therefore, when IRQx* is asserted, the interrupt handler cannot positively identify the source of the interrupt. However, the interrupt acknowledge daisy-chain solves the problem by making certain that only one interrupter receives an acknowledgment.

When an interrupt is acknowledged, IACKIN* is asserted at slot 1. Each module driving an interrupt request line low must wait for the low level to arrive at its own board slot (i.e., be propagated down the chain) before accepting the acknowledge. The module accepting the acknowledge does not pass the active-low level on down the daisy-chain, guaranteeing that only one interrupt requester will be acknowledged. Figure 10.32 shows how the interrupt bus lines are arranged.

Figure 10.33 shows the relationship between the modules of the VMEbus and the priority interrupt subbus. The two types of module taking part in the interrupt process, the interrupter and the interrupt handler, are now described.

Interrupt handler   The interrupt handler is responsible for dealing with the interrupts originating from interrupters and performs the following four functions:

FIGURE 10.32   IACKIN∗—IACKOUT∗ daisy-chain structure. (Reprinted by permission of Motorola Limited)

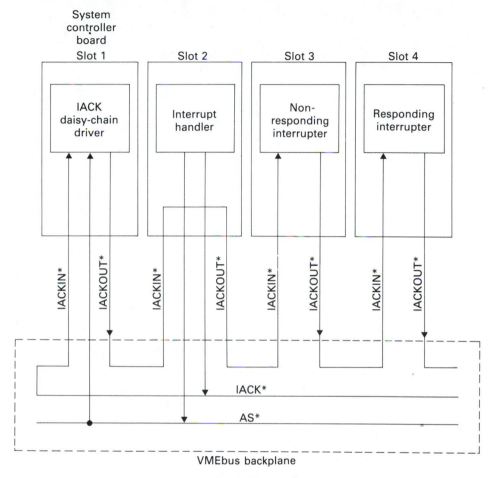

1. It prioritizes the incoming interrupt requests within its assigned range (maximum range IRQ1∗ to IRQ7∗) from the interrupt bus.

2. It uses its associated requester to access the DTB and, when granted use of the DTB, it acknowledges the interrupt.

3. It reads the status (i.e., ID byte) from the interrupter being acknowledged.

4. Based on the information received in the status/ID byte, it initiates the appropriate interrupt servicing routine.

The VMEbus specification has nothing to say about the way in which the interrupt handler actually services the interrupts. This action is device dependent and the users are left to write their own appropriate interrupt-handling routines.

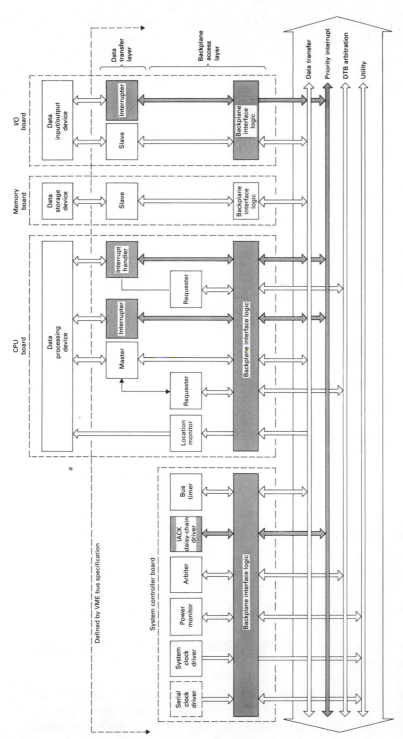

FIGURE 10.33 Modules of the VMEbus and the priority interrupt bus. (Reprinted by permission of Motorola Limited)

Interrupt handlers may be identified by an option code IH(a–b), where "a" is the lowest interrupt request level serviced and "b" is the highest; for example, an IH(3–5) option interrupt handler may service interrupts on IRQ3*, IRQ4*, and IRQ5* only. Notice that this option demands that the interrupt handler service a contiguous sequence of interrupt levels.

When the interrupt handler receives more than one interrupt request on IRQ1* to IRQ7*, it uses the DTB requester to service the highest priority interrupter.

Interrupter   The interrupter is the source of interrupt requests and is used to accomplish three tasks:

1.   It requests an interrupt from the interrupt handler. The interrupt handler monitors the interrupt request line from the interrupter.

2.   It supplies a status/ID byte to the interrupt handler when its interrupt request is acknowledged.

3.   It passes through an interrupt acknowledge daisy-chain signal if it is not requesting that level of interrupt.

Interrupts can be identified by the level of the interrupt request line that they assert to request service. The option notation is I(n), where n is the interrupt request line number; for example, I(4) means that the interrupter asserts IRQ4*. Note that more than one interrupter module may appear on any given card. Each of these interrupters may have a different option number.

An interrupter monitors the address bus of the DTB, IACK*, and the IACKIN*/IACKOUT* daisy-chain to determine when its interrupt is being acknowledged. When the acknowledgement is received, the interrupter places a status/ID byte on the lower eight lines (D_{00} to D_{07}) of the data bus and signals the byte's validity to the interrupt handler via the DTACK* line.

Slaves and interrupts   Although both a DTB slave and an interrupter may access the system data transfer bus, four important distinctions are made between a DTB slave and an interrupter:

1.   The interrupter ignores the contents of the address modifier bus, AM0 to AM5. Equally, the DTB slave ignores the IACK* signal and never responds when IACK* is asserted.

2.   The slave decodes the contents of the address bus (A_{01} to A_{15}, A_{01} to A_{23}, or A_{01} to A_{31}) together with AM0 to AM5 and responds accordingly. The interrupter decodes only the lowest-order address lines, A_{01} to A_{03}, when it detects an interrupt acknowledge. However, the interrupter responds only if it has an interrupt request pending, if the interrupt acknowledge on A_{01} to A_{03} matches the level of the pending request, and if it is receiving a low level on its IACKIN*.

Unless all of the above three conditions are met, the interrupter does not respond to the acknowledge sequence. If IACKIN* is asserted but the other conditions are not met, the interrupter passes on the low level on IACKIN* to the next module in the daisy-chain via IACKOUT*.

3. The interrupter is required to drive only the lowest eight data bits in response to an acknowledgment. Therefore, it is not required to monitor DS1*. The interrupter is also not required to monitor the state of WRITE* as it is never written to.

Centralized distributed interrupt handlers   In single-handler VMEbus systems, the seven interrupt request lines are all monitored by a single interrupt handler module. Interrupts are prioritized by levels 1 to 7 and by position along the interrupt daisy-chain. In a distributed interrupt-handling system up to seven independent interrupt handlers may be allocated to interrupt processing.

No real problems are introduced by distributed interrupt handling. Each interrupt handler is assigned one or more interrupt request lines. An interrupt handler in a distributed system operates exactly as in its single-handler counterpart. Interrupts are prioritized on IRQ1* to IRQ7* and by their positions along the daisy-chain.

Should two or more interrupt handlers respond to interrupts at the same time, a bus contention problem exists. This problem is resolved by an arbiter module. Each interrupt handler asserts a bus request line (BR0* to BR3*) in order to gain control of the DTB, and the arbiter determines which handler gets access to the DTB according to the priority option in force.

VMEbus Utilities

The VMEbus supports the four miscellaneous signal lines presented in table 10.12.

SYSCLK   The system clock is a master timing signal, free running at 16 MHz, and serves as a source of timing for all VME modules. It is not necessarily of the same frequency or phase as the processor's own clock; that is, the SYSCLK clock has no fixed phase relationship with any other VMEbus signal.

SYSRESET*   System reset is an open-collector line driven by either a power monitor module or a manual reset switch. This signal is normally identical to the 68000's RESET* input/output (see chap. 6) and its effect is to place the

TABLE 10.12   VMEbus utilities

PIN/ROW	MNEMONIC	NAME
10a	SYSCLK	System clock—16-MHz clock
3b	ACFAIL*	A.C. failure (power-down)
12c	SYSRESET*	System reset
10c	SYSFAIL*	System fail—indicates failure mode

processor and/or all other modules in a known state on initial power-up or following a manual reset. SYSRESET* must be asserted for a minimum period of 200 ms.

SYSFAIL* System fail is a general-purpose signal whose function is to indicate that the system has failed in some sense. What constitutes a failure and what action is to be taken when SYSFAIL* is asserted is not defined by the VMEbus standard.

We recommend that all cards within the VMEbus system drive SYSFAIL* active-low on power-up and maintain SYSFAIL* low until they have all passed their self-tests. In systems with nonintelligent cards (i.e., without an on-board processor), we recommended that they hold SYSFAIL* low until a master on another card has completed a test on them. SYSFAIL* can be asserted at any instant during normal (i.e., non-power-up) operation of the system when the failure of one of the modules is detected.

SYSFAIL* and SYSRESET* are related. After SYSRESET* is negated (i.e., released), all cards enter their self-test mode and hold SYSFAIL* low until each test has been successfully completed. Once SYSFAIL* has been negated, the system enters its normal operating mode.

ACFAIL* The ACFAIL* line is driven by open-collector circuits and, when asserted, indicates that the a.c. power supply to the VMEbus card frame has either failed or is no longer within its specified operating range. Once ACFAIL* has been asserted, the master may use the period of time between the negative transition of ACFAIL* and the point at which the system 5 V supply falls below its minimum specification to force an orderly power-down sequence; for example, sufficient time may be given to carry out a "core dump" and store all working memory on disk so that an orderly restart may be made later.

Summary

In this chapter, we have looked at the bus that distributes information between the various parts of a computer. We have examined the electrical characteristics of buses and the bus drivers and receivers needed to interface modules to the bus. The final part of this chapter has provided an overview of the VMEbus that adds value to the 68000's own bus. In particular, the VMEbus provides all the facilities necessary to implement a multiprocessor system. By means of its SYSFAIL*, SYSRESET*, and ACFAIL* lines, the VMEbus is able to provide a limited measure of automatic self-test and recovery from certain forms of failure.

The only feature of the 68000 CPU lacking in the VMEbus is the 68000's synchronous bus. Fortunately, this feature is not absolutely necessary, as a pseudo-synchronous bus can be derived from the existing VMEbus signals. Although the data transfer bus part of the VMEbus is almost identical to that of the 68000 itself, the system designer must provide his or her own interface to the arbitration and interrupt buses.

Problems

1. Explain the meaning of the following terms as they are applied to bus technology.
   a. Bus driver
   b. Bus receiver
   c. Static bus contention
   d. Dynamic bus contention
   e. Bus protocol
   f. Passive bus driver
   g. Active bus driver
   h. Bus arbiter
   i. Reflection
   j. Bus termination

2. A manufacturer decides to produce a 68000-based personal computer. All on-board memory, interface, and peripherals are located on a single card. The designer wishes to keep the cost to an absolute minimum and decides not to include an external bus. However, the designer does wish to offer a range of add-on peripherals that do not require to take advantage of the 68000's full operating speed. Therefore, a compromise is chosen that exploits the 68000's asynchronous interface but is very cheap to implement.

   The proposed bus uses an 8-bit parallel interface (plus ground return paths) to take advantage of low-cost connectors. This bus uses a 4-bit control word and a 4-bit data word to move data between the computer and a peripherals module.
   a. Design a 4-bit control bus, C0, C1, C2, C3, to control the flow of data on the 4-bit data bus, I0 to I3. The control signals should permit the bus to mimic the 68000's asynchronous bus.
   b. For the 8-bit bus you have designed, construct a protocol flowchart and a timing diagram for both a read (word) cycle and a write (word) cycle.

3. For the diagram of figure 10.18 calculate:
   a. The write-to-read bus to memory contention time
   b. The write-to-read data bus driver to data bus driver contention time
   c. The read-to-write bus to memory contention time
   d. The read-to-write data bus driver to data bus driver contention time

4. Like most microprocessors, the 68000 uses special-purpose control lines to augment the data transfer bus. These control lines include FC0 to FC2, BR*, etc., IPL0* to IPL2*, etc. An alternative approach is to employ a *message bus* that carries encoded system control messages; for example, a device requiring attention may inject a suitable message onto this bus.

   Devise a method of implementing such an arrangement in a 68000-based environment. Note that a suitable protocol is needed to determine which device may access the message bus. This situation can be achieved by using a special-purpose control line or by time-division multiplexing. The IEEE-488 bus has some of the characteristics of this type of control bus.

5. Derive a general expression for the maximum rate (bits per second) at which a bus can operate, stating any assumptions you make. HINT: Consider the time taken for a message (e.g., address) to be transmitted from a master to a slave and the time taken for the transmitter to receive a reply.

6. Design an interface between a 68000 module and the VMEbus. Assume that the module is to go in slot 1 of the bus.

7. We stated previously that the SYSFAIL* line of the VMEbus is driven low by modules during their "self-test" mode immediately following the initial application of power. Describe how a 68000 module can be forced into a self-test mode and indicate the hardware and software necessary to perform this task.

Chapter 11

Designing a

Microcomputer System

We are now going to apply some of the lessons learned in earlier chapters and design a modest 68000-based microcomputer. This chapter is divided into three parts:

1. An examination of some of the ways in which microcomputers are designed in order to make their testing relatively easy. A brief discussion then follows of the equipment and techniques commonly used in debugging digital systems.

2. The design of a 68000-based microcomputer with an expansion bus.

3. The design of a monitor and loader that permits information to be transferred to the 68000 system from a host computer. This monitor is written in assembly language and includes the routines necessary to drive a serial interface, to convert between ASCII strings and numeric quantities, and to interpret commands input from the console.

11.1 Designing for Reliability and Testability

Once upon a time, an engineer designed a system to work, and to work as well as possible within its economic limitations. Design engineers were very important people and lived in castles (or at least mansions). Sometimes, due to faulty components or to the general perversity of nature, the apparatus that the designer had created stopped working. When this happened, the repairman or troubleshooter was called in to pinpoint the source of the problem and to repair it. Unlike the designer, the troubleshooter lived in a cottage in the grounds of the castle, if he was lucky, or in a hut if he was not.

We now live in the age of realism and have banished such fairy stories. Design is no longer the only major factor in the production of complex digital equipment. Today, the cost of debugging and testing a microcomputer can be more than designing or building it in the first place. In other words, we can see little point in designing a system if it is almost impossible to test when it fails.

The designer and the test engineer now have to form an equal partnership and work together. The designer must produce a system with testability as one of its main criteria. To make this situation possible, designers must understand the limitations of the components they use, know their failure modes, and include facilities to help the test engineer to pinpoint the source of failure.

Before we can consider how to design testable equipment and examine fault-finding procedures, we need to look at some of the reasons why equipment fails. These reasons are as follows:

1.   *The blunder.* A blunder is an act of folly that could have been avoided; for example, a designer may specify an OR gate instead of a NOR gate or may connect two or more gates with totem-pole outputs to the DTACK* line. Such blunders should not occur and are entirely due to human error. Blunders can be eliminated by double-checking circuits and systems before they reach production.

   Sometimes blunders can be discovered at the prototype or "bread-board" stage, or when the system is emulated in software. The latter approach is popular with the designer of digital circuits, and software packages are available for the emulation of digital systems.

2.   *The subtlety.* A subtlety is a sort of "gentle blunder," and is a human design error that does not stick out like the blunder. A subtlety may be missed when the circuit is double-checked or when it is emulated in software. A typical subtlety is a timing error, which appears when a system is expanded by, say, the addition of a memory module. Without the module, the system works and passes its initial tests. With the module, the system fails because the additional signal delays through bus transmitters and receivers cannot be tolerated.

3.   *The "stuck-at" fault.* A logic element may fail internally so that its output becomes independent of its input and remains either stuck-at-one or stuck-at-zero. A stuck-at fault is relatively easy to locate, provided that the inputs of the logic elements can be modified to permit outputs to toggle between states. We will return to this topic when we consider the design of testable systems. Note that a stuck-at fault may also be due to a short-circuit between adjacent tracks of a printed circuit.

4.   *The faulty IC.* Sometimes an IC is faulty in some other way than the stuck-at fault described previously. This fault can always be detected or cleared by substituting the suspected device with another of the same type

that is known to function. Unfortunately, we are no longer able to test all ICs before they are used as the number of internal states in a complex device is so great. Moreover, a faulty IC sometimes produces spectacularly obscure faults. For example, a microprocessor may execute an instruction correctly unless it is preceded by a particular instruction that causes it to fail; such a fault might be discovered only after the device has been in production for several months.

5.   *The faulty PCB.* Many faults are caused by defects in the mechanical components of a digital system. In particular, the tracks of a printed circuit board may be shorted together or left open-circuit because of a break in a trace. The worst type of fault is a blob of solder under an integrated circuit socket that short-circuits two pins but cannot be detected by optical inspection. These defects often produce symptoms identical to the "stuck-at" fault already mentioned.

6.   *The intermittent fault.* The intermittent fault is one of the nastiest of faults because it is difficult to find, apparently inexplicable, and seemingly malicious! The origin of this fault may lie in any of the mechanisms already mentioned, although intermittent faults are most closely associated with mechanical problems. The intermittent fault is there one minute and gone the next, making it very difficult to trace. I have heard of engineers dealing with particularly frustrating intermittent faults by placing the board on the floor, jumping on it, and then reporting the defect as "too extensive to warrant further investigation."

Testability

Influence of Testability at the Design Stage

Testing a system is like detective work—the source of the fault has to be deduced from the evidence it leaves behind. The test engineer is, however, better off than the detective. A system can be designed in such a way that a fault either automatically "points to itself" or is made to "show up" (with a little prompting). We will soon see how this objective is achieved.

Two things are necessary to achieve testability: the ability to monitor activity within a system and to influence this activity. Figure 11.1 illustrates both these points with a simple circuit, a logic module driven by an on-card clock.

In figure 11.1a, the clock is connected directly to the system on the card. No convenient way exists to observe the action of the clock or to determine whether it is working according to its specification. At best, a probe can be attached to some pin carrying the clock signal.

In figure 11.1b, the clock is buffered and brought off the card via one of the pins on the PCB. We can now use external equipment to monitor the state of the

FIGURE 11.1   Example of a testable circuit

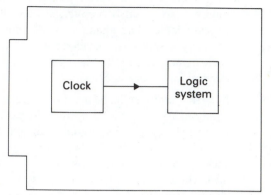

(a) Clock generator connected directly to the logic circuit

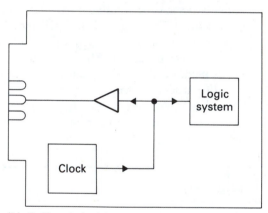

(b) Buffered clock brought off-card

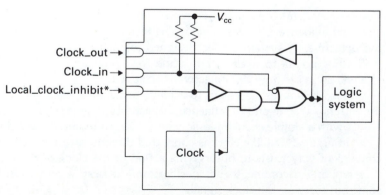

(c) On-card clock with facility for external clock input

clock without disturbing (i.e., loading) the system on the PCB. Note that two prices have been paid: an economic price (i.e., the cost of the additional buffer and pin on the connector) and a reduction in overall reliability (an extra component is needed on the board).

In figure 11.1c, not only has the buffered clock been brought off the board but two inputs have been provided to modify the operation of the system. The clock is gated through an AND gate and a control signal, local_clock_inhibit*, can be forced low to inhibit the on-card clock, effectively disconnecting it from the logic system. An external clock may be injected into the clock_in terminal once the local clock has been inhibited, thus permitting the system to be synchronized with an external clock that may be slowed or stopped for test purposes.

Figure 11.2 illustrates another path to enhanced testability. In figure 11.2a, the two control signals, PRESET and HALT*, are permanently strapped to V_{cc} or ground, as appropriate, because their particular control functions are not required by the system. By using pull-up or pull-down resistors, these control lines can be brought out to test pins and employed to test the system by operating it in special modes (e.g., halted). This procedure can be extended to permit the injection of other stimuli and goes a long way to making stuck-at faults easier to detect.

FIGURE 11.2   Increasing testability by making control signals accessible

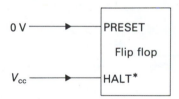

(a) Control signals permanently connected to a logical zero or a one

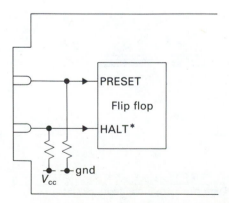

(b) Control signals brought out to pins on a connector for testing

In general, a digital system should be designed so that as many internal signals as possible (address, data, control) are available for examination off-card. Sometimes an additional connector can be added to the card and used solely for test purposes. Similarly, test inputs for the generation of control stimuli should also be provided. Apart from making testing digital equipment easier, such provisions facilitate automatic testing. In an automatic testing system, a digital computer applies preprogrammed signals via the test inputs and computer-controlled test equipment monitors the response at the test outputs.

Testability and Feedback Paths

The greatest obstacle to the effective testability of a computer system is its closed-loop nature. Consider first the open-loop circuit of figure 11.3a. An input is successively operated on by a number of processes to yield an output. At no stage does any feedback path exist between the output and input—hence the

FIGURE 11.3   Open-loop and closed-loop systems

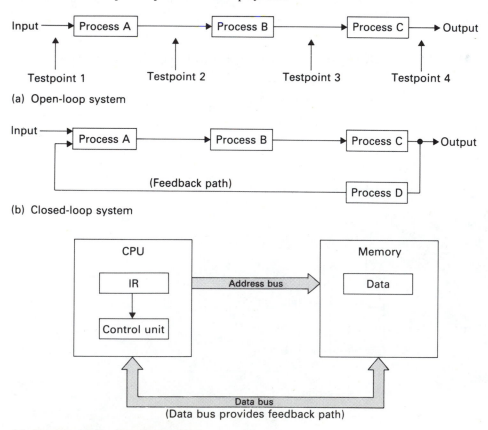

(a) Open-loop system

(b) Closed-loop system

(c) Computer as a closed-loop system

term *open-loop*. To debug such a system, a known signal is injected into the input and traced through the various processes. If the input to a process is known and the nature of the process is known, the output of a process can be calculated. Whenever the measured output of a process differs from its expected value, we can confidently say that the process is faulty. Televisions, radios, and hifi equipment are largely examples of open-loop systems (although even these use closed-loop techniques in some circuits).

Consider now the closed-loop system of figure 11.3b. The input is combined with some function of the output and applied to process A. The output of process A is fed to processes B and C, and the output of process C fed back to process A. Such a system is called a *closed-loop* system because information circulates round the loop, from output to input. Localizing the source of a fault is now very difficult. The effects of a fault propagate through the system, are fed back to the input, and flow round the circuit. Thus, the effect of a fault at one point may be detected at an entirely different point—even "upstream" of the actual fault.

Figure 11.3c shows the computer as a closed-loop system. The computer calculates an address internally and uses it to read the next instruction from memory. The op-code flows along the data bus to the computer, where it is interpreted. The result of this interpretation eventually leads to the generation of a new address and the sequence repeats ad infinitum.

Suppose the contents of a memory cell have been corrupted. The data read from the cell may cause the address of the next instruction to differ from that intended, and, say, a spurious jump made, leading to unpredictable behavior. Because all aspects of the behavior of the system appear faulty, we find great difficulty in pinpointing the source of the failure; for example, all the faults below could have produced the same observed effect:

1.   The address from the computer is wrong because of a fault in the CPU. Equally, the CPU may be functionally perfect but its support circuitry (reset, clock, interrupt, etc.) may be faulty.

2.   The address at the memory is wrong due to a fault on the address bus. Included here are the effects of errors in the address decoding circuitry.

3.   The data on the data bus is wrong due to a fault in the memory (the actual fault in our example).

4.   The data on the data bus is wrong due to a fault on the data bus. Data bus errors also arise from faults in the address bus buffers and their associated control.

There are two ways of dealing with this problem. One method is to monitor the operation of the system at several points over a period of time and then analyze its behavior to determine the cause of the fault. Complex and expensive test equipment (the logic analyzer) is involved, a subject dealt with later in this chapter. The other method is to break the feedback path. Without feedback, the digital system can be tested by the same techniques available to the television repair person.

Static Testing

Static testing is the name given to tests on a digital system that break the feedback loop between input and output. Basically, in a static test the result of one operation is not permitted to lead to the next operation; that is, only one cycle at a time is permitted.

A static tester replaces the CPU by a *CPU emulator* and is illustrated in figure 11.4. The CPU emulator mimics certain aspects of a CPU. A test circuit has a number of switches enabling address, data, and control signals to be set up manually. From this module, a 64-pin header at the end of a length of ribbon cable is plugged into the 68000 socket of the system under test.

The circuit details of a possible static emulator are given in figure 11.5. Address information is set up on twenty-three switches and applied to the inputs of twenty-three tristate bus drivers. When enabled, these bus drivers place a user-selectable address onto the address bus of the system under test. As this address is static, we are able to examine address lines and address decoder outputs on the module under test with an oscilloscope or even a voltmeter. Of course, static emulation is not very helpful in debugging dynamic memory circuits!

In a similar way, control lines AS*, UDS*, LDS*, BG*, FC0 to FC2 can all be set up from switches on the emulator. Note that control lines should all be debounced by RS flip-flops, as shown in figure 11.5. The emulator must be able to both provide a source of data to emulate a write cycle and to read data from memory to emulate a read cycle. In figure 11.5, sixteen bus drivers place data from switches on the data bus whenever $R/\overline{W} = 0$ and another sixteen bus receivers drive LEDs to indicate the state of the data bus.

To use the static emulator in the read mode, the appropriate address is set up, $R/\overline{W}$ set to a logical one, and AS* plus UDS* or LDS* set to a logical zero.

FIGURE 11.4   Static emulator

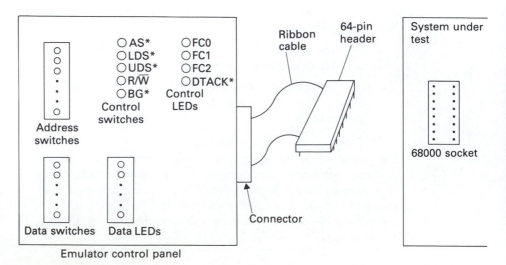

FIGURE 11.5   Circuit diagram of a simple static emulator

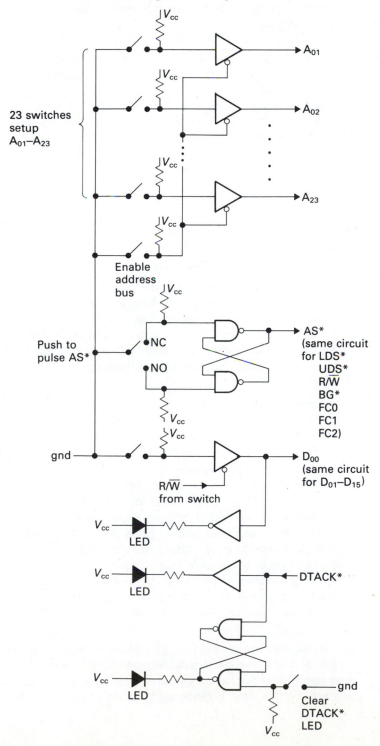

The contents of the data bus are then displayed on the data LEDs. As the DTACK∗ pulse from the system under test may be very short, a latch is necessary to catch its leading edge.

If the system has a ROM with known data, we are able to test the address and data buses by applying an address and examining the resulting data. Should this data not be the one expected, the address and data paths can be traced until the fault has been located.

It would be wrong to suggest that this type of static emulation is anything other than a relatively crude error detector/locator; for example, the static emulator might not detect two address lines shorted together if the test address includes both the faulty address lines at the same level. However, such a circuit should prove quite effective for use in university and polytechnic laboratories.

Good Circuit Design

In a book on microprocessor systems we are not able to become involved with the detailed design of digital circuits. However, some of the points that the engineer should bear in mind are worth listing when designing a circuit:

1. *Maximize access to the inputs and outputs.* Whenever possible, the inputs and outputs of circuits and submodules within the system under test should be accessible; that is, test points and test input paths should be liberally provided in the system. This is particularly true of systems with complex integrated circuits with inaccessible internal test points. The next best thing is to provide facilities to monitor the input and output pins of complex ICs.

2. *Adopt a modular approach to systems design.* As we have already seen, when we decompose a system into a number of subsystems, we can easily test the whole system by testing the subsystems one by one. Note that this approach generally requires that feedback paths be broken for the duration of the test. Sometimes modularity conflicts with economics. We may find expediency in using several components, spread throughout the card, to carry out a given logical operation; for example, the reset function (power-on-reset, manual reset, etc.) may be implemented by using a gate here, a gate there. In other words, unused gates at various points in the system are combined to provide a reset circuit for very little additional cost. While this procedure may be good from an economic point of view, it runs counter to the principle expressed previously. Using dedicated circuits to perform a single task makes it easier to test the circuit in isolation. Sometimes the function can be carried out by test hardware external to the system under test.

3. *Avoid asynchronous logic.* Asynchronous circuits are arranged so that the output of one element triggers the next element, and so on. An asynchronous circuit does not have a global clock to determine the instant when each element changes state. Because the behavior of an asynchronous circuit may

change if the signal delay incurred by an element is greater or less than that expected and because the asynchronous circuit is prone to race conditions, this circuit is not popular with some designers. Therefore, designers should, wherever possible, choose fully clocked synchronous circuits.

4. *Avoid monostables.* The monostable is a classic digital circuit that generates a pulse of fixed duration whenever it is triggered. A resistor-capacitor network (figure 11.6a) determines the duration of the pulse. The monostable is not popular with either the test engineer or the designer. The test engi-

FIGURE 11.6   Monostable

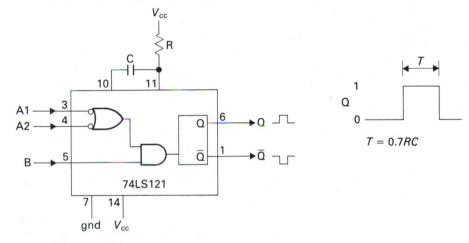

(a) Monostable controlled by a CR network

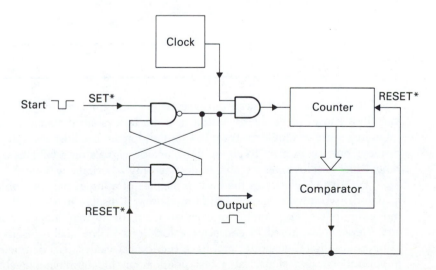

(b) Monostable controlled entirely by digital components

neer is unhappy because observation of the output of a monostable is often difficult—especially if the pulse is very short. The designer does not like the monostable because it is inflexible (the timing delay is determined by analog components) and is also prone to trigger from noise on the power lines or other spurious inputs. An alternative to the conventional monostable is the purely digital circuit of figure 11.6b. When the RS flip-flop is set, the AND gate is enabled and the counter counts up. When the output of the counter reaches a preset value, the output of the comparator resets the flip-flop and the counter is cleared. The advantage of this circuit is its absence of analog components and its flexibility—the pulse width is modified by changing the clock rate or by reprogramming the counter. These facilities are very useful in testing the system.

5. *Place "important" devices in sockets.* Some designers believe that important (or even *all*) digital elements should be plugged into sockets rather than soldered directly to the board. Testing ICs becomes very easy as they can be unplugged and tested off-card. This approach is very controversial, because integrated circuit sockets are relatively unreliable and intermittent faults due to poor pin-socket contacts are common. However, without sockets, the testing of integrated circuits by substitution is a rather difficult task. Unsoldering ICs often damages PC boards.

6. *Do not use marginal design.* Never design a system that operates outside its guaranteed parameters. We all know that a gate with a fanout of ten will drive twelve loads because worst-case parameters are just that. In "normal" operation these parameters can be exceeded, but no designer should ever rely on this fact. Cases have been reported where manufacturers have had a working model on the test bed and then gone into full-scale production, with disastrous results.

Logic Analyzer

The logic analyzer continues from where the static emulator left off. The analyzer examines and displays the operation of a digital system dynamically and in real-time. In principle, a logic analyzer is a digital-domain oscilloscope. An oscilloscope displays one, two (or up to about eight) analog signals on a CRT as a function of time. Most oscilloscopes are able to display only a periodic waveform.

Figure 11.7 illustrates the basic principles of a logic analyzer, which operates in one of two modes: an acquisition mode and a display mode. In the acquisition mode (figure 11.7a), a number of channels from the system under test are sampled and the samples stored in consecutive locations in the analyzer's memory. The samples are digital quantities and have the logical values zero or one. This fact is important, because signals at a test point at an indeterminate level are always recorded as a logical zero or a logical one by the analyzer. The analyzer is trig-

FIGURE 11.7   Logic analyzer

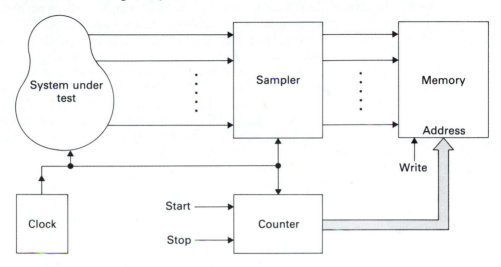

(a) Signal acquisition mode

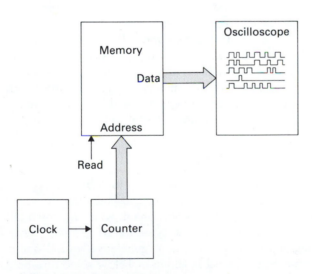

(b) Signal display mode

gered by a start signal and stops on receipt of a stop signal. During this time, the counter counts successively upward as each sample is taken and stored.

In the display mode (figure 11.7b), the counter free-runs and periodically steps through each memory location containing data collected during the acquisition phase. This data is fed to the inputs of a multichannel oscilloscope and displayed as a series of traces, one for each channel.

From the preceding comments, we can clearly see that the logic analyzer provides a snapshot of the state of the system under test over a period of time. If sufficient channels exist, we are able to sit down and analyze the activity on the buses and therefore to determine whether or not the system is functioning correctly. From the observed data, the cause of a fault can frequently be localized. Note that the logic analyzer can debug both hardware and software, and that some logic analyzers are able to deal with asynchronous events such as interrupts.

Many logic analyzers offer a number of display options. Figure 11.8 shows the four most popular display formats. Figure 11.8a and b illustrates the waveform and binary modes, respectively. The waveform is reconstructed from the digital data stored in the analyzer memory. Unlike the oscilloscope, these waveforms are purely digital and are *idealized* versions of the waveforms from the actual system under test. Because the original signals are sampled periodically, timing relationships cannot *accurately* be measured from the logic analyzer display. The binary mode displays the data as a table (octal and hexadecimal modes are also common).

Figure 11.8c illustrates the disassembly mode, in which the information from the system under test comes from the processor's address and data buses and is displayed in mnemonic form. In order to do this, the logic analyzer must include a "personality module" to disassemble the code of the particular microprocessor under test. The display mode is very effective in software debugging—particularly for real-time and interrupt-driven systems.

Figure 11.8d illustrates the rather curious looking point-plotting display. An n-channel logic analyzer plots each n-bit sample as a single point on the screen, by dividing the screen into 2^n points. Therefore, as the digital system changes from one state to another, a sequence of points is displayed on the screen. Interpreting such a display is an art form! Some people would say that reading the display is comparable to reading the future in tea leaves.

Logic Analyzer Characteristics

Before we look at how logic analyzers help us to debug microprocessor systems, we need to think about their characteristics and limitations. Possibly the key part of a logic analyzer is its signal-acquisition circuit, which is shown in block diagram form in figure 11.9. The input signals, typically 16 to 64 or more channels, are applied to analog signal comparators that generate a logical one or zero output depending on whether the signal is above or below some threshold. This threshold may be switch selectable to suit TTL or ECL logic levels, or continuously variable to permit the acquisition of an arbitrary binary signal in the range (typically) -3 to $+12$ V.

Because the input goes through a comparator, it is always interpreted as a true or false level. Therefore, a logic analyzer cannot readily be used to detect faults due to incorrect signal levels. That procedure is the province of the oscilloscope.

The outputs of the comparators are then captured by a latch. Figure 11.10 provides a timing diagram of a synchronously clocked logic analyzer operating

FIGURE 11.8   Logic analyzer display formats

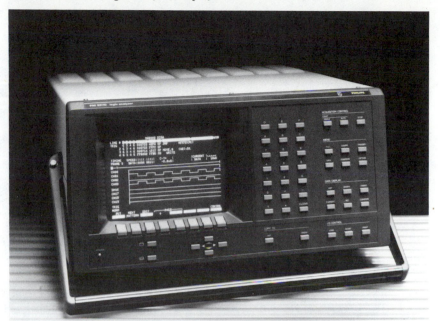

(a) The waveform display mode. (Reprinted by permission of Philips Limited)

(b) The binary display mode. (Reprinted by permission of Thurlby Electronics Limited)

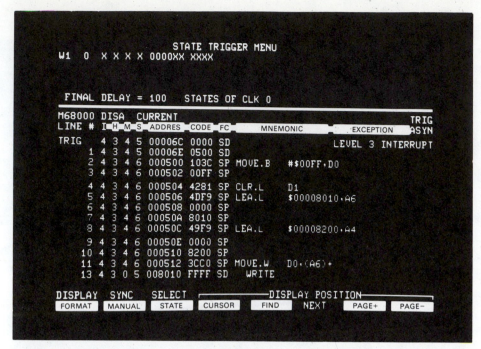

(c) The disassembly display mode. (Reprinted by permission of Philips Limited)

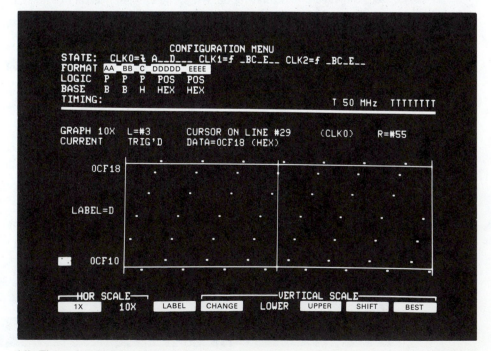

(d) The point-plotting display mode. (Reprinted by permission of Philips Limited)

FIGURE 11.9   Signal acquisition circuit of a logic analyzer

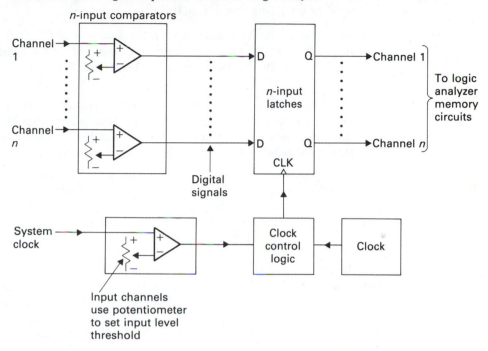

FIGURE 11.10   Effect of sampling a signal synchronously

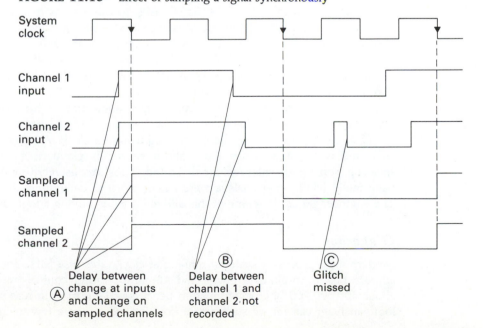

from, say, the system clock. To keep things simple, only two channels of input are shown. Three points are noted from this diagram:

1.   At point A, the signals on channels 1 and 2 change state. The change is not displayed until the signals have been sampled by the falling edge of the clock. Therefore, the logic analyzer does not record input changes instantaneously.

2.   At point B, channel 1 makes a negative transition before channel 2. As both channels are not sampled until the next falling edge of the clock, the displayed data shows them making a negative transition simultaneously; that is, the relative delay between traces in not preserved.

3.   At point C, a short pulse, or glitch, occurs on channel 2. Because this pulse falls between two successive sampling clocks, it is not recorded and does not appear on the display. Therefore, short-term events that play havoc with the system under test may go unnoticed when subjected to investigation by a logic analyzer.

The above points present a more gloomy picture than is actually the case. Remember that a real microprocessor-based system is itself clocked synchronously. Moreover, the setup- and hold-times of the logic analyzer are likely to be smaller than those of many components in a microprocessor system. However, if a glitch does occur in a microprocessor system, *some* logic analyzers will most probably miss it.

Logic analyzers with asynchronously clocked data-acquisition latches are also available. Here the latch is triggered by the analyzer's own clock. The phase relationship between channels becomes easier to observe, as the number of sampling clock pulses per system clock is increased. The sampling clock frequency should be at least four times the system clock frequency and a factor of ten to twenty is not uncommon. The use of such a high clock ratio also makes the capture of glitches much easier. Figure 11.11 illustrates the advantages of asynchronous clocking.

Some logic analyzers have a special glitch-detection feature. As a glitch is missed entirely if it falls between two sampling points, a latch can be used to detect a glitch by applying the channel input to its clock. A glitch triggers the latch and is displayed when the analyzer enters its playback mode. Generally speaking, some logic analyzers are dedicated almost exclusively to detecting hardware faults while other analyzers are aimed more at debugging software errors. The engineer should be aware of this difference when buying a logic analyzer.

Triggering

Modern microprocessor systems, running at clock rates of 8 MHz and with 24-bit address buses, 16-bit data buses, and 10-bit (or more) control buses, generate about 400,000,000 bits of information per second! Clearly, no reasonably priced logic analyzer can record such a data flow for more than a few microseconds. A

FIGURE 11.11   Effect of sampling a signal asynchronously

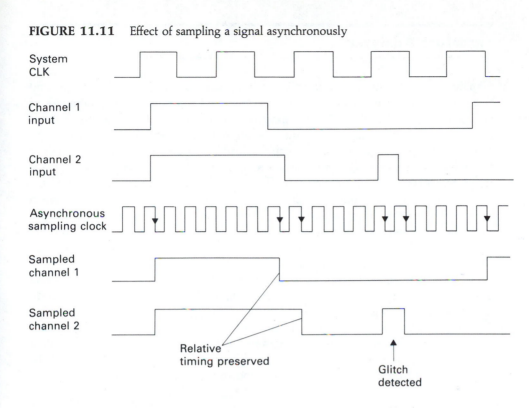

method of starting the recording process and terminating it at suitable times must be found.

Logic analyzers are invariably triggered by an *event* that is defined by the operator. The event corresponds to some pattern of data on the input channels and/or a particular data pattern at the *qualifier inputs*. A logic analyzer has inputs (qualifier inputs) that are employed by the analyzer to trigger the recording of data, but are not themselves displayed. We should note that a signal employed for the purposes of triggering the display may be defined as 1, 0, or X (i.e., don't care); for example, an address in the range $4500 to $450F may be used as a trigger by selecting the trigger to be 0100 0101 0000 XXXX. Early logic analyzers had their trigger conditions entered from front panel switches. Modern devices use a keyboard or a keypad to enter the trigger conditions.

The analyzer may also be triggered *before* the specified event. This apparent exercise in time travel is achieved by letting the analyzer record input data freely; that is, at any instant the analyzer's buffer contains the last N samples recorded, where N is the length of the buffer. The input is stored in a circular buffer and, once the buffer is full, new data overwrites the oldest data in the buffer. The recording is halted by the trigger, at which point the analyzer memory contains a record of the data flow from the system under test leading up to the trigger event.

Signature Analyzer

Signature analysis offers a quick, effective, low-cost troubleshooting technique and is aimed at the manufacturer of digital systems who produces large numbers of similar systems rather than at the engineer who builds a single prototype. A logic analyzer produces a snapshot of the operation of a system, which can later be examined to deduce the cause of a fault. Clearly, complex equipment and highly trained personnel are required. Signature analysis simply gives the equipment under test a task to perform and then offers a "go/no go" analysis of the results.

At any point, or node, in a digital circuit, the signal level switches between logic states as information passes through the node. If the equipment executes a given task, the sequence of pulses observed at the node is the same each time the task is carried out. The node may be an address, data, or control line or an intermediate point such as a chip select.

The signal analysis condenses the complex sequences of pulses at a node into a single *fingerprint* or *signature*, which is similar to the cyclic redundancy code found in data transmission systems.

Figure 11.12 illustrates the principle and the great simplicity of the signature analyzer. A 16-bit shift register is clocked by the system under test. The data moved into the least-significant bit of the shift register is the EXCLUSIVE OR of the data input from the system under test and four outputs from the shift register; that is,

$$D_0 = D_{in} \oplus Q_6 \oplus Q_8 \oplus Q_{11} \oplus Q_{15}$$

Sixteen stages are used because a 16-bit shift register detects a multibit error in the data stream with a probability of 99.998 percent and a single-bit error with a probability of 100 percent. Fewer stages do not give such a large probability of detecting an error and more stages increase the cost of the signature analyzer.

Figure 11.13 provides an idea of the circuitry of a signature analyzer (albeit

FIGURE 11.12   Principle of the signature analyzer

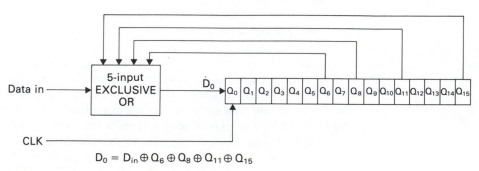

$$D_0 = D_{in} \oplus Q_6 \oplus Q_8 \oplus Q_{11} \oplus Q_{15}$$

FIGURE 11.13   Highly simplified circuit of a signature analyzer

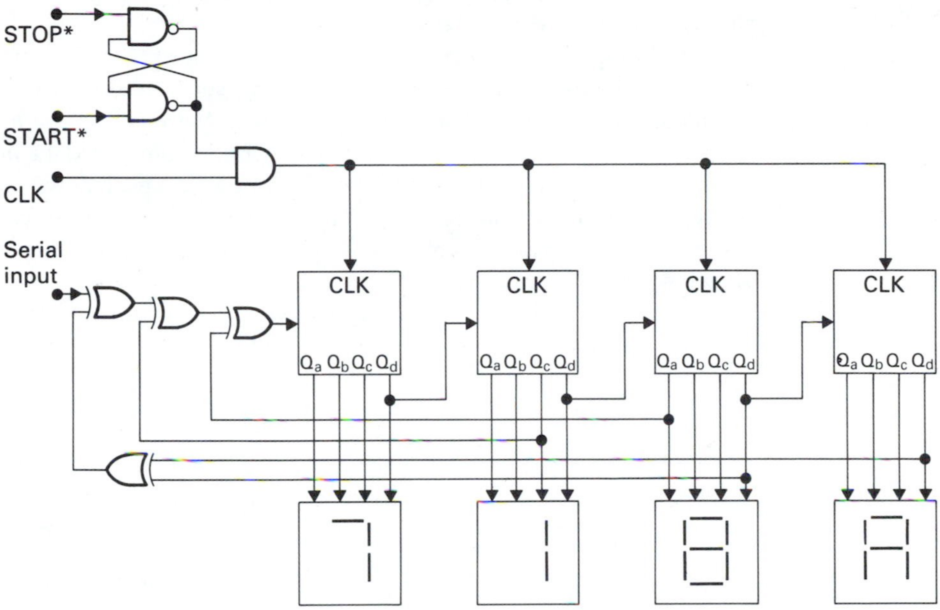

a highly simplified circuit). Four inputs to the analyzer exist: a clock, a data input, a start, and a stop. To use the analyzer, the four leads are attached to the system under test. Suppose that the start signal makes an active transition. Data is clocked into the shift register until the stop signal is asserted. The displayed signature then represents the outcome of the test.

The signature is totally arbitrary and is not amenable to analysis. The operator compares the measured signature with that recorded in the troubleshooting manual for the system under test. If the signatures are the same, the equipment has passed the test. If they differ, it has failed.

In order to apply signature analysis usefully, the system under test should be placed in some cyclical free-running mode; for example, the operating system ROM may be replaced by a test ROM that executes a software loop. The start and stop signals are obtained from suitable points within the system under test; for example, A16 may be toggled after every hundredth cycle of the loop to generate a start signal. The data input may come from any point in the system that is not at a static signal level. For each node at which the probe is placed, the expected signature is recorded in the system manual—just as voltages are provided at test points in analog circuits.

As the system is operating in a cyclic mode, the signature is constantly updated—each new signature being the same as the previous signature. If the signature is unstable, an intermittent fault or a problem caused by asynchronous events (e.g., interrupts, DMA, DRAM refresh cycles) interfering with the test may result. Sometimes an unstable signature is caused by the choice of unsuitable clock, data, start, or stop signals. Clearly, the data input should make its transitions when the clock is stable.

Although the preceding method of forcing the system under test into a repeatable, known, cyclic mode involves the substitution of a test ROM, other techniques are available. It is possible to break the feedback path within a digital system by disconnecting the CPU's data inputs from the data bus by means of some test fixture. Then the data lines can be pulled up or down to force the CPU to execute an infinite series of NOPs or some other operation code. As with the test ROM, the signature is measured at various points in the circuit and compared with the published values.

Signature analysis is obviously suited to production line testing, where fault finding is turned into a flowchart procedure that test staff can learn in a very short time.

Microprocessor Development System

The microprocessor development system, MDS, is designed to facilitate both the design and production of a microprocessor system and to debug it. Inside the MDS lies a general-purpose digital computer, frequently (but not always) based on the microprocessor in the system to be developed. The general-purpose computer is disk based and offers comprehensive software development facilities. Combined with this computer is a built-in logic analyzer to test the hardware of the system under development. Unlike all other test equipment, the MDS can be used to debug a system from its paper implementation phase to its production-line testing.

Software Development

The software development system runs under an operating system, which may be a proprietary operating system such as UNIX or may originate from the manufacturer of the MDS. Software running under the operating system normally includes an editor, assembler, linker, emulator, and possibly one or more compilers.

As a microcomputer consists of two fundamental components (its hardware and its software) and one component is useless without the other, a microprocessor system is inherently difficult to develop. The MDS solves this dilemma by providing a framework within which the software can be constructed and debugged, entirely independently of the target system on which it will eventually run.

Once the hardware environment of the target system has been specified, the software development can begin. The MDS offers an editor and an assembler so that the necessary object code can be produced. Alternatively, a compiler may be provided that generates the object code for the appropriate CPU in the system being developed. If this system were all an MDS offered in the way of software development, it would hardly be worth the large price tag attached to it.

The MDS is also able to run the software under its emulation mode. Usually three levels of emulation are offered—levels 0, 1, and 2. In level 0, the target hardware is not available and the software runs entirely on the MDS system. All the usual debug-package software tools are supplied and we are able to examine and modify memory locations, to insert breakpoints, and to trace through the program; for example, keyboard input can be simulated as a file that returns a character wherever it is interrogated.

Under level 1 emulation, the target hardware is present and an emulation probe from the MDS is inserted in the socket of the CPU in the target hardware. The actual CPU is, of course, in the MDS. Partitioning the processor's memory space is possible between the target and MDS system.

Figure 11.14 shows how the memory is partitioned between the MDS and target hardware. The 68000 itself is part of the MDS hardware. Its address bus is connected to both the MDS and the external target hardware. Consequently, the same location is accessed in both systems. The data bus and associated control signals are multiplexed between the MDS memory and the target hardware. Whenever the CPU generates an address, it is applied to a mapping table to determine whether that address belongs in the MDS or the target hardware. The output of the mapping table controls the multiplexer and routes signals between the CPU and the MDS or between the CPU and the target hardware.

During the software emulator initialization phase, the address table is set up by the programmer when he or she allocates address space to the MDS or to the target hardware. Suppose that the software has been successfully debugged and that the target hardware contains a serial I/O port. We are now able to assign all

FIGURE 11.14 Partitioning the memory space between the CPU and the MDS

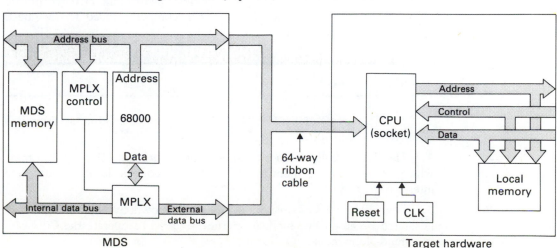

memory to the MDS and map only the serial interface address space to the target hardware. In this state, only the I/O port together with its address and data paths on the target system are being tested. The I/O port can, of course, be used normally even though its associated ROM and RAM are all in the MDS.

If the preceding test works, more features of the target hardware can be mapped onto the CPU address space—including the RAM. At this stage, all peripherials are operating in the target hardware rather than being emulated in the MDS and all data is located in the target's own memory. All the MDS's debug features can still be used.

By now, only the CPU and the ROM portion of the target system are in the MDS. The last stage in the development process is to transfer the program developed on the MDS to EPROM or even to mask-programmed ROM. When this stage is completed and the EPROM plugged into the target hardware, the MDS runs in emulation mode 2.

In emulation mode 2, the MDS monitors the operation of the target hardware. Indeed, we can safely say that the MDS is now operating as a logic analyzer. MDSs offering this facility have additional channel inputs (usually as an option to the basic model) that can be connected to various points of the target system to permit the usual logic analyzer triggering modes.

The MDS is one of the most expensive and complex pieces of test equipment available (neglecting the computer-controlled automatic test station found on a production line) and is intended for use by system design and development engineers who follow the design of equipment from its original concept to prototype.

11.2 Design Example Using the 68000

In this section we examine the design of a modest microcomputer based on the 68000 CPU. Before we consider the design of this computer, called TS2, we need to provide it with a specification.

Specification of the TS2

1.   The TS2 uses a 68000 CPU. (I'd get funny looks if I used an 8086 in a book about the 68000.)

2.   The TS2 is built on an extended, double Eurocard (233.4 × 220 mm), which provides ample room for the CPU, bus control, local memory, and interface circuitry.

3.   The CPU card is capable of operating on its own. System testing is thus facilitated because other modules are not required to operate the CPU card in a stand-alone mode.

4. An external bus is used to connect other modules to the CPU card. An interface between the 68000 on the CPU module and the backplane is essential.

5. The VMEbus itself is not used, as the full functionality of the VMEbus is not necessary. Therefore, a relatively low cost backplane can be implemented.

6. The memory on the CPU card is static RAM and EPROM to avoid the difficulty in debugging the CPU system together with its DRAM. This author does not have a microprocessor development system that would permit the debugging of DRAM *independently* of the CPU and its software.

7. Full seven-level interrupt facilities are provided.

8. No on-card facility limits the capability of the system.

9. Full address decoding is provided. The address space is to be compatible with the Motorola MEX68KECB (ECB for short) development system in order to facilitate the transport of software between TS2 and the ECB.

10. The vector number table at $00 0000 to $00 03FF is implemented in RAM. Therefore, the reset vectors are overlaid as described in chapter 6.

11. The RAM is implemented by 8K × 8 CMOS devices to minimize the component count.

12. The ROM is implemented by 2764 type 8K × 8 EPROMs.

13. The terminal (console) interface is through a serial port. A secondary serial port is also provided. Configuration is to be the same as in the ECB development system.

The block diagram of the arrangement of a single board computer satisfying the design criteria is given in figure 11.15, which is a very general diagram and serves as a "checklist" for the various parts of the system to be elaborated. Only one design decision has been taken at this stage. For the sake of simplicity, the module's local address and data buses have not been buffered. This fact implies that care should be taken not to load the local address and data buses too heavily.

Basic CPU Control Circuitry

Every CPU requires a certain amount of basic control circuitry to enable it to operate—this circuitry includes its clock, reset, halt, and similar functions. Such circuitry can be designed largely independently of the rest of the system and is needed to perform even the simplest tests on the CPU. Therefore, we will design these circuits first.

Figure 11.16 gives the diagram of the control circuitry surrounding the

FIGURE 11.15   Block diagram of a single board computer

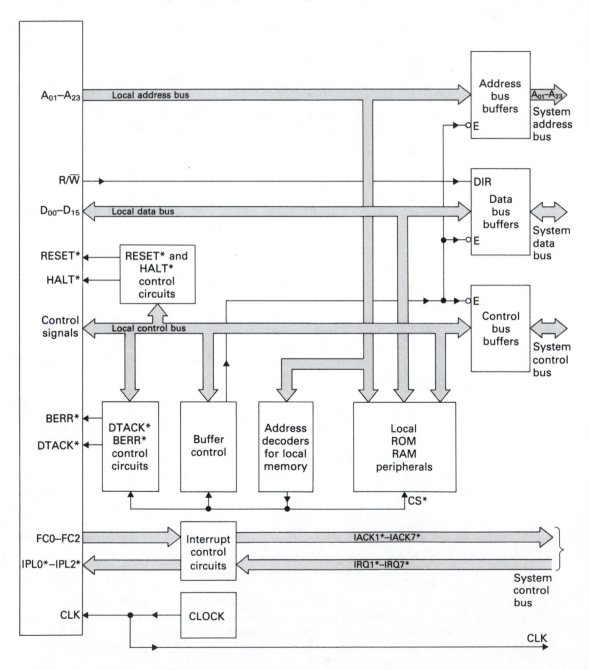

FIGURE 11.16   Circuit diagram of the 68000 reset, halt, and clock control circuits

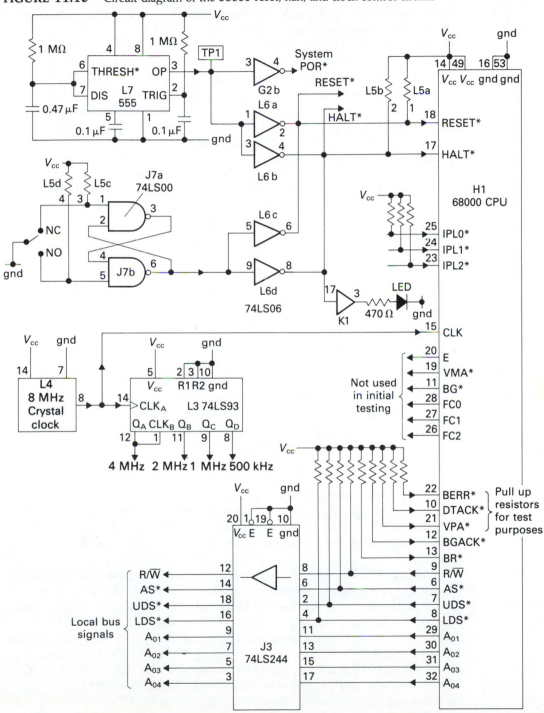

68000, excluding the interrupt request inputs. The control of HALT* and RESET* is conventional (see chapter 4). At power-on, a 555 timer configured as a monostable, L7, generates a single active-high pulse.

The position of each integrated circuit, or to be more precise each DIL package, on the double Eurocard is indicated by a letter and a number. The letter denotes the row in which the IC is found and the number denotes its position in that row. I have used this method to allow spaces on the board to be populated with ICs later, without altering the numbering (i.e., sequence) of existing ICs. Had I called them 1, 2, ..., the addition of a new IC in a previously empty location would have given it an out-of-sequence number.

Open-collector inverting buffers, L6a and L6b, apply the reset pulse to the 68000's RESET* and HALT* inputs, respectively. A manual reset generator is formed from two cross-coupled NAND gates, J7a and J7b, and applied to the reset lines by a further two open-collector buffers, L6c and L6d. An inverting buffer, G2b, gates the reset pulse from L7 onto the system bus as the active-low POR* (power_on_reset). This signal can be used by other modules to clear circuits on power-up.

An LED is connected to the HALT* pin via a buffer. This LED is fitted to the front panel and confirms the reset operation. It also shows if the CPU has asserted HALT* because of a double bus fault.

The 68000 clock input is provided by an 8-MHz crystal-controlled clock in a DIL package. L3, a 74LS93 divide-by-sixteen counter, provides submultiples of the basic clock frequency for other functions. When performing initial tests, I usually run the CPU from a 4-MHz clock.

The high impedence control inputs shown in figure 11.16 are pulled up to the V_{cc} by resistors. Although pull-up resistors are necessary on BR* and DTACK*, etc., the reader may be surprised to find them on AS*, UDS*, LDS*, and R/$\overline{W}$. They are required here because these pins are driven by tristate outputs in the 68000. When the 68000 relinquishes the bus, all tristate lines are floated. To leave the state of these bus lines undefined is unwise, as a spurious bus cycle might possibly be generated in certain circumstances. A better course is to be safe rather than sorry. During the testing phase, some of the pull-up resistors were temporary and used only for test purposes, because they were connected to lines that will later be pulled up or down by totem-pole outputs. They appear in figure 11.16 so that the circuit can be tested independently of the rest of the system.

Testing the CPU control circuitry is very easy. The power_on_reset circuit is tested by attaching an oscilloscope probe to test point 1 (TP1), switching on the V_{cc} power supply, and observing the positive-going pulse. A negative-going pulse should be observed at the CPU's RESET* and HALT* pins. The manual reset pulse generator should force HALT* and RESET* low whenever the reset button is pushed.

An 8-MHz square wave should be observed at the CLK input to the CPU. All inputs pulled up to a logical one should be at a logical one state.

The next step is to install the 68000 and to force the CPU to free-run. As no memory components have yet been fitted, the CPU must be fooled into thinking that it is executing valid bus cycles. To do this DTACK* is temporarily connected to the AS* output. Whenever the 68000 starts a memory access by asserting AS*, DTACK* is automatically asserted to complete the cycle.

The 68000 is a tricky beast to test in a free-running mode, because it generates an exception if a nonvalid op-code is detected. Should the 68000 then generate a second exception, the resulting bus fault will cause it to halt. Therefore, the 68000 must always see a valid op-code on its data bus. One way of doing this is to pull up (or down) the data bus lines with resistors to V_{cc} (or ground). Traditionally, CPUs are tested by placing a NOP (no operation) op-code on the data bus. The 68000 NOP code is $4E71 (i.e., %0100 1110 0111 0001). If this code is jammed onto the data bus, the 68000 will also use it for the stack pointer and reset vectors during the reset exception processing! Sadly, this code will lead to an address error. When the CPU reads the stack pointer from addresses $00 0000 and $00 0002 at the start of its reset exception processing, it obtains $4E71 4E71. Unfortunately, this value is *odd* and generates an address exception. We need to use a dummy op-code that is even to allow the CPU to free-run.

When a suitable op-code has been jammed onto D_{00} to D_{15}, the 68000 should free-run and a square wave be observed on address pins A_{01} to A_{23}. The frequency at pin A_i should be one half that at pin A_{i-1}.

Interrupt Circuit

The interrupt control circuitry surrounding the 68000 is entirely conventional and does not depart from that described in chapter 6. In figure 11.17 a 74LS148 eight-line to three-line priority encoder, J4, converts the seven levels of interrupt request input into a 3-bit code on IPL0* to IPL2*. Note that each interrupt request input must have a pull-up resistor.

The function code from the 68000 is decoded by J5, a 74LS138, and the resulting IACK* output used to enable a second decoder, J6. J6 is also strobed by AS* and converts the information on A_{01} to A_{03} during an IACK cycle into one of seven levels of interrupt acknowledge output (IACK1* to IACK7*). Other function code information supplied by J5 that may be useful in debugging the system is the "user/supervisor" memory access codes and the "program/data" bus cycle codes.

The interrupt control circuitry can be tested by periodically pulsing IRQ7* (the nonmaskable interrupt) and observing the response on IACK7*. A suitable source of pulses for IRQ7* can be found on the address lines during the free-running mode—for example, A_{05}. Note that other levels of interrupt cannot be tested yet as the 68000 sets its mask bits to level 7 during its reset. In general, detailed testing of interrupt control circuits is not possible until exception-handling routines have been written.

FIGURE 11.17   The 68000 interrupt control circuitry

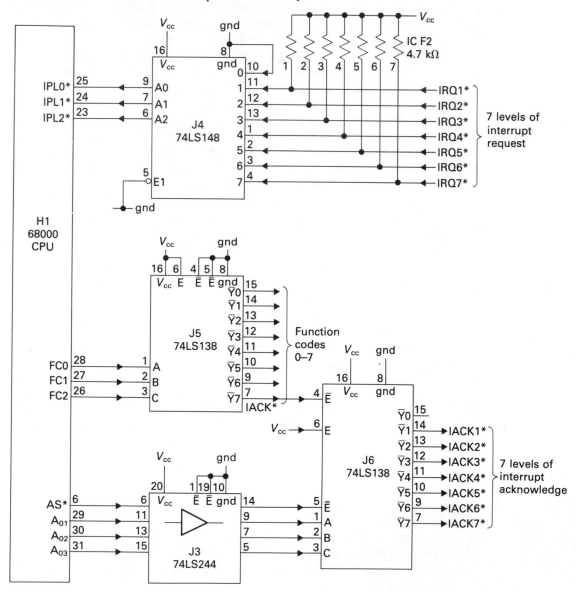

Address Decoder Circuitry on the CPU Module

The specification of the TS2 CPU module calls for up to 32K bytes of static RAM and up to 32K bytes of EPROM at the bottom of the processor's 16M-byte memory space. Immediately above the RAM memory space sits the peripheral

TABLE 11.1 Memory map of the TS2 CPU module

	SIZE (bytes)	DEVICE	ADDRESS SPACE
1	8	EPROM1	00 0000–00 0007
2	16K	RAM1	00 0008–00 3FFF
3	16K	RAM2	00 4000–00 7FFF
4	16K	EPROM1	00 8000–00 BFFF
5	16K	EPROM2	00 C000–00 FFFF
6	64	Peripheral 1	01 0000–01 003F
7	64	Peripheral 2	01 0040–01 007F
8	64	Peripheral 3	01 0080–01 00BF
9	64	Peripheral 4	01 00C0–01 00FF
10	64	Peripheral 5	01 0100–01 013F
11	64	Peripheral 6	01 0140–01 017F
12	64	Peripheral 7	01 0180–01 01BF
13	64	Peripheral 8	01 01C0–01 01FF

address space, permitting up to eight memory-mapped components, each occupying 64 bytes. Table 11.1 gives the memory map of the TS2 CPU module. The address decoding table corresponding to the memory map of table 11.1 is given in table 11.2.

The diagram of a possible implementation of table 11.2 is given in figure 11.18. A five-input NOR gate, K3a, generates an active-high output, G1, whenever A_{19} to A_{23} are all low. Together with $A_{18}*$ and $A_{17}*$, this gate enables a three-line to eight-line decoder, K5, that divides the lower 128K bytes of memory space from $00 0000 to $01 FFFF into eight blocks of 16K. The first four blocks decode the address space for the read/write memory and ROM. We deal with the selection of the reset vector memory space in ROM later.

The active-low peripherals_group_select* output of K5 (i.e., the address range $01 0000 to $01 3FFF) enables a second three-line to eight-line decoder, K6. K6 is a 25LS2548 that has two active-low and two active-high enable inputs. It also has an active-low open-collector output, ACK*, that is asserted whenever the device is enabled *and* is strobed by a negative-going pulse on its RD* or WR* inputs.

K6 is also enabled by G3 from K4a, which is high when A_{09} to A_{13} are all low, and by AS* from the CPU. Thus, whenever a valid address in the range $01 0000 to $01 01FF appears on the address bus, one of K6's active-low outputs is asserted. When either UDS* or LDS* go low in the same cycle, the ACK* of the decoder is asserted, indicating a synchronous access to a peripheral by asserting the processor's VPA* input. Note that this arrangement is intended to be used in conjunction with 6800-series peripherals.

An access to the reset vectors in the range $00 0000 to $00 0007 is detected by gates K3a, K3b, K4a, K4b, H4c, and H3a. When the output of each NOR gate

TABLE 11.2 Address decoding table for the TS2 CPU module memory map

	DEVICE	A_{23}	A_{22}	...	A_{16}	A_{15}	A_{14}	A_{13}	A_{12}	A_{11}	A_{10}	A_{09}	A_{08}	A_{07}	A_{06}	A_{05}	A_{04}	A_{03}	A_{02}	A_{01}
1	EPROM1	0	0	⋮	0	0	0	0	0	0	0	0	0	0	0	0	0	0	×	×
2	RAM1	0	0	⋮	0	0	0	×	×	×	×	×	×	×	×	×	×	×	×	×
3	RAM2	0	0	⋮	0	0	1	×	×	×	×	×	×	×	×	×	×	×	×	×
4	EPROM1	0	0	⋮	0	1	0	×	×	×	×	×	×	×	×	×	×	×	×	×
5	EPROM2	0	0	⋮	0	1	1	×	×	×	×	×	×	×	×	×	×	×	×	×
6	PERI1	0	0	⋮	1	0	0	0	0	0	0	0	0	0	0	×	×	×	×	×
7	PERI2	0	0	⋮	1	0	0	0	0	0	0	0	0	0	1	×	×	×	×	×
8	PERI3	0	0	⋮	1	0	0	0	0	0	0	0	0	1	0	×	×	×	×	×
9	PERI4	0	0	⋮	1	0	0	0	0	0	0	0	0	1	1	×	×	×	×	×
10	PERI5	0	0	⋮	1	0	0	0	0	0	0	0	1	0	0	×	×	×	×	×
11	PERI6	0	0	⋮	1	0	0	0	0	0	0	0	1	0	1	×	×	×	×	×
12	PERI7	0	0	⋮	1	0	0	0	0	0	0	0	1	1	0	×	×	×	×	×
13	PERI8	0	0	⋮	1	0	0	0	0	0	0	0	1	1	1	×	×	×	×	×

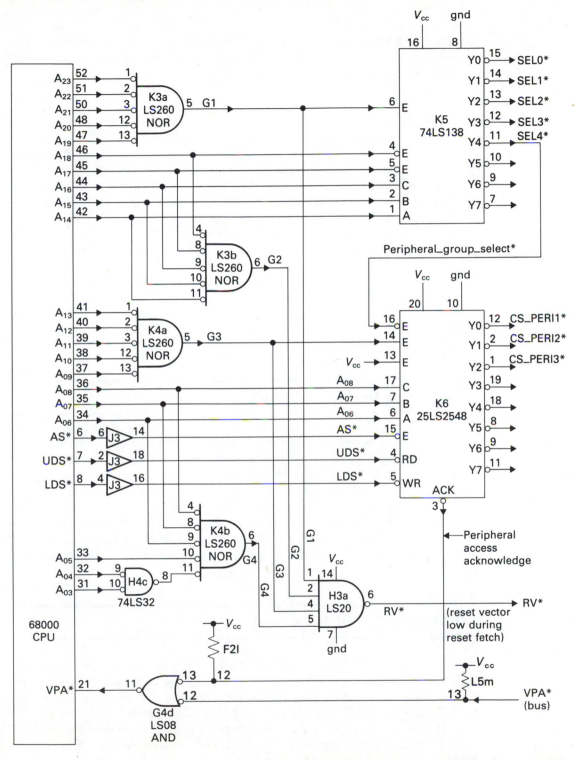

FIGURE 11.18 Arrangement of TS2's address decoding circuits on the CPU module

is high, signifying a zero on A_{03} to A_{23}, the output of the NAND gate H3a, RV∗, goes active-low; that is, RV∗ is low whenever a reset vector is being accessed and is used to overlay the exception table in read/write memory with the reset vectors in ROM.

The address decoder of figure 11.18 can be tested to a limited extent by free-running the CPU and detecting decoding pulses at the outputs of the address decoder. A better technique is to insert a test ROM and to execute an infinite loop which periodically accesses the reset vector space. This makes it easy to observe the operation of the circuit on an oscilloscope.

The selection of the individual RAM and EPROM components from the address decoder outputs is carried out by the circuit of figure 11.19. Two-input NOR gates combine one of the four device-select signals (SEL0∗ to SEL3∗) from the address decoder with the appropriate data strobe (UDS∗ or LDS∗) to produce the actual active-low chip-select inputs to the eight memory components on the CPU module.

The circuit of figure 11.19 is also responsible for overlaying the reset vector space onto the ROM memory space. The technique used in figure 11.19 is exactly as described in chapter 6. When the RV∗ signal goes active-low while a reset vector is being fetched, the read/write memory at $00 000 to $00 3FFF is disabled and the EPROM at $00 8000 to $00 BFFF substituted.

Memory on the CPU Module

The use of 8K × 8 memory components permits the design of a relatively large memory with a very low component count and virtually no design effort. Figure 11.20 gives the circuit diagram of half the memory components on the CPU module—the others are arranged in exactly the same fashion but are enabled by different chip-select signals from the address decoder.

No further comment is required other than to point out that the EPROMs have their active-low output enables (OE∗) driven by R/$\overline{W}$ from the processor via an inverter. This action is necessary to avoid a bus conflict if a write access is made to EPROM memory space.

DTACK∗ and BERR∗ Control

Each memory access cycle begins with the assertion of AS∗ by the 68000 and ends with the assertion of DTACK∗ (or VPA∗) by the addressed device or with the assertion of BERR∗ by a watchdog timer. Figure 11.21 gives the diagram of the DTACK∗ and BERR∗ control circuitry on the CPU module.

Whenever a block of 16K bytes of memory is selected on the CPU module, one of the four select signals, SEL0∗ to SEL3∗, goes active-low. The output, MSEL, of the NAND gate H3b is then forced active-high. MSEL becomes the

FIGURE 11.19   Selecting RAM and ROM on the CPU module

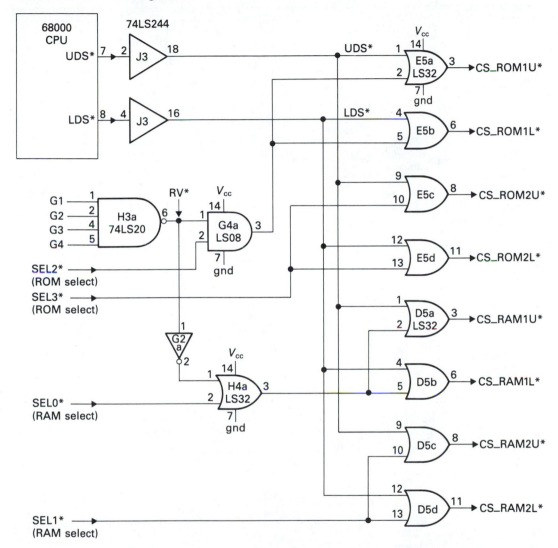

ENABLE/LOAD* control input of a 74LS161 4-bit counter, H2. When MSEL = 0 (i.e., on-board memory not accessed), the counter is held in its load state and the data inputs on D_a to D_d are preloaded into the counter—in this example 1100. The Q_d output from the counter is gated, uninverted, through G4b, H4b, and G4c to form the processor's DTACK* input.

When MSEL goes high the counter is enabled. The counter is clocked from the 68000's clock and counts upward from 1100. After four clock pulses, the counter folds over from 1111 to 0000 and Q_d (and therefore DTACK*) goes low to provide the handshake required by the 68000 CPU. At the end of the cycle,

FIGURE 11.20 RAM and ROM on the CPU module

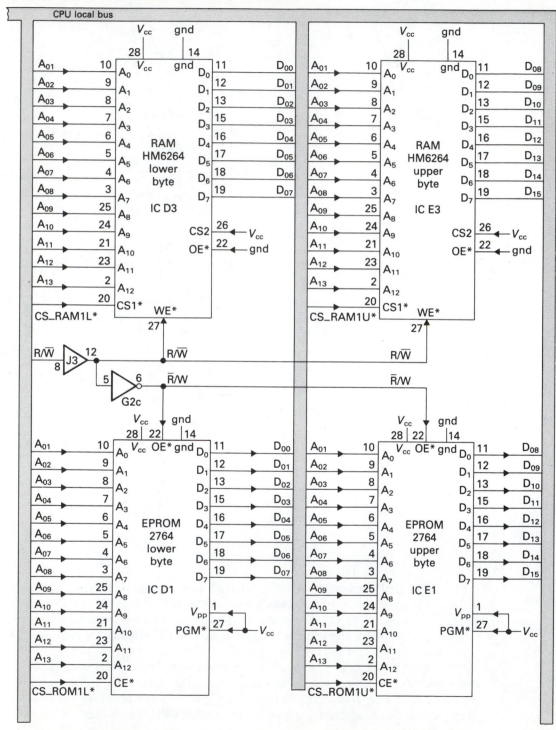

FIGURE 11.21   DTACK* and BERR* control circuitry

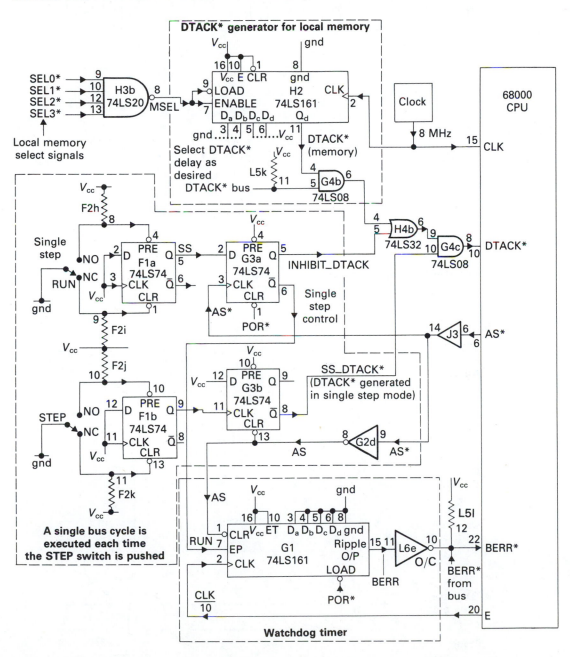

FIGURE 11.22   Timing diagrams for DTACK∗ and BERR∗ control

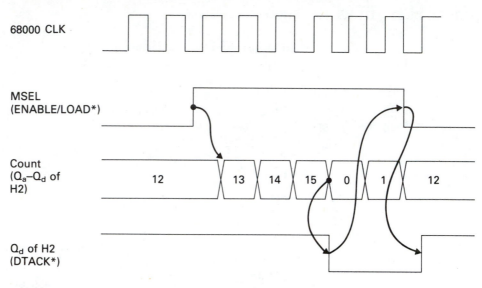

(a) DTACK* delay generator

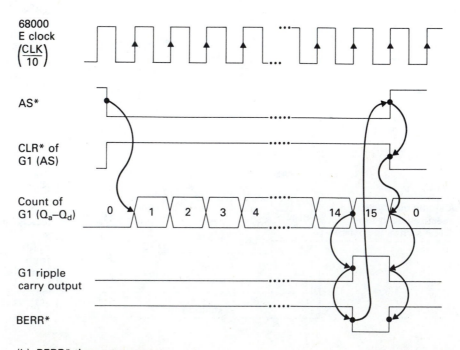

(b) BERR* timeout generator

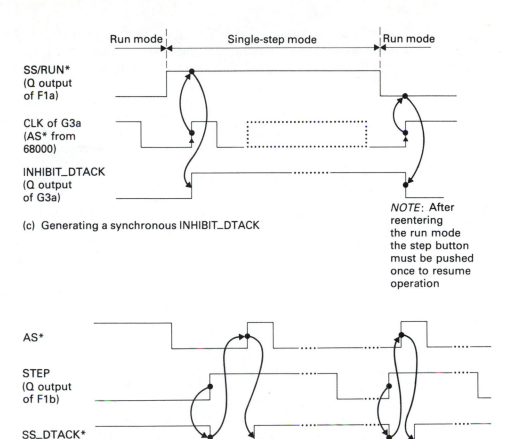

(c) Generating a synchronous INHIBIT_DTACK

NOTE: After reentering the run mode the step button must be pushed once to resume operation

(d) Producing a single-step DTACK* signal

AS* is negated and MSEL goes low to preload the counter with 1100 and negate DTACK*. Figure 11.22a gives the timing diagram of this circuit.

At the same time that H2 begins counting, a second timer, G1 (another 74LS161), also begins to count upward. The count clock is taken from the 68000's E output which runs at CLK/10. This counter is cleared to zero whenever AS* is negated. The ripple output from the counter goes high after the fifteenth count from zero and is inverted by the open-collector gate L6e to provide the CPU with a BERR* input. Therefore, unless AS* is negated within fifteen E-clock cycles of the start of a bus cycle, BERR* is forced low to terminate the cycle. Note that the counter is disabled (EP = 0) in the single-step mode (discussed later) to avoid a spurious bus error exception. Figure 11.22b provides a timing diagram of the watchdog timer.

A useful feature of the DTACK* circuit is the addition of a single-step mode, allowing the execution of a single bus cycle (note bus cycle *not* instruction) each time a button is pushed. This facility can be used to debug the system by freezing the state of the processor.

One of the inputs to the OR gate H4b is INHIBIT_DTACK. If this is active-high, the output of the OR gate is permanently true and the generation of DTACK* by the DTACK* delay circuit (or from the system bus) is inhibited. Therefore, a bus cycle remains frozen with AS* asserted, forcing the CPU to generate an infinite stream of wait states.

Two positive-edge triggered D flip-flops, F1a and G3a, control INHIBIT_DTACK. F1a acts as a debounced switch and produces an SS/RUN* signal from its Q output, depending only on the state of the single-step/run switch. Unfortunately, it would be unwise to use the output of F1a to inhibit DTACK*, because changing from run to single-step mode in mid bus cycle might lead to unpredictable results. Instead, the output of F1a is synchronized with AS* from the processor by a second flip-flop, G3a. Figure 11.22c shows how the INHIBIT_DTACK signal from G3a is forced high only when AS* is negated at the end of a bus cycle. The 68000 always enters its single-step mode at the start of a new cycle before AS* is asserted.

In the single-step mode, DTACK* pulses are generated manually by depressing the "step" switch. The output of this switch is debounced by flip-flop F1b. A second flip-flop, G3b, generates a single, active-low pulse, SS_DTACK*, each time the step button is pushed. SS_DTACK* is gated in G4c to produce the DTACK* input needed to terminate the current bus cycle. Figure 11.22d gives the timing diagram of the SS_DTACK* generator.

There are two simple ways of testing the DTACK* control circuits. One is in the free-run mode and is done by connecting, say, SEL0* to AS*, so that a delayed DTACK* is produced for each bus cycle. The single-step circuit can also be tested in this mode. Another procedure is to construct a special test rig for the circuit, which simulates the behavior of the 68000 by providing AS*, CLK, and SEL0* signals.

Buffering and Bus Control on the CPU Module

The interface between the CPU module and other modules is via its backplane bus. This bus can be divided into three components: the address bus, the control bus, and the data bus. Figure 11.23 gives the circuit of the address and control signal paths and figure 11.24 gives the circuit of the data bus buffers and their control.

Three 74LS244 octal tristate bus drivers buffer the address from the 68000 onto the system bus (figure 11.23). The address buffers are all enabled by the complement of the BGACK* input to the 68000. BGACK* is pulled up to V_{cc} by a resistor and the address bus buffers are normally enabled (even when the 68000

FIGURE 11.23   Address and control buffers on the CPU module

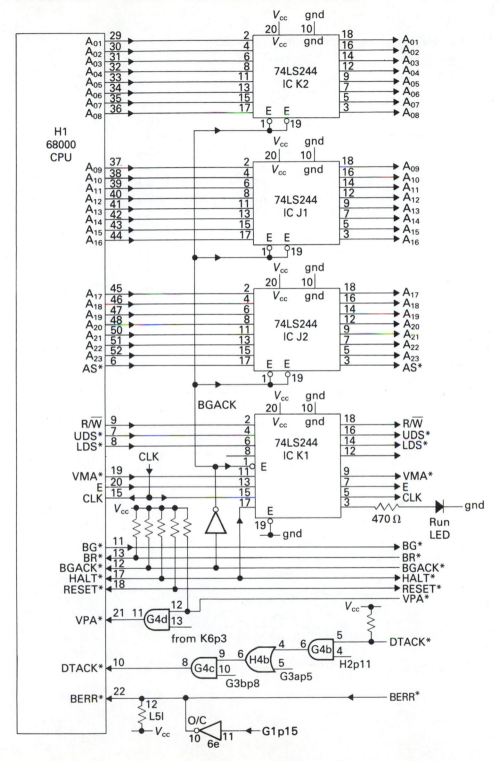

FIGURE 11.24   Data buffers and their control on the CPU module

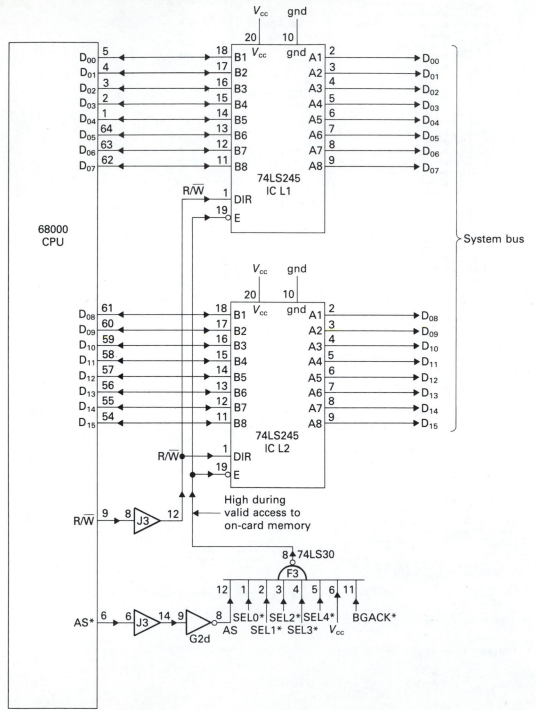

FIGURE 11.25 ACIAs on the CPU module

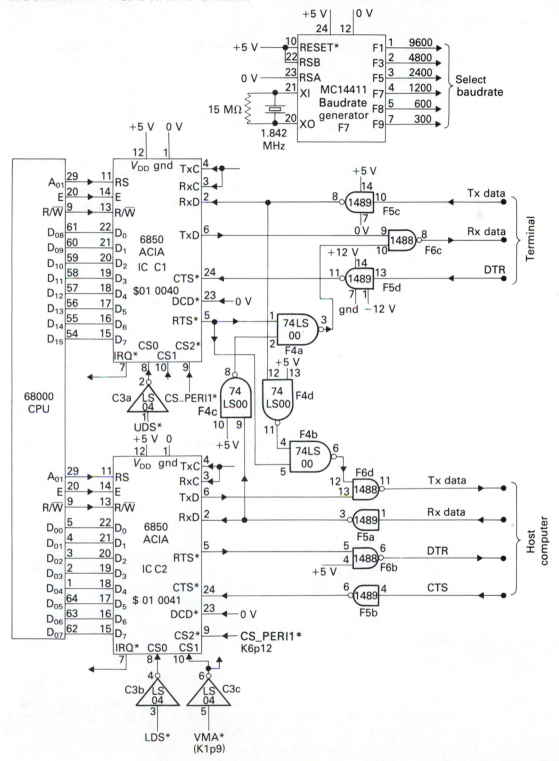

535

is addressing local memory). Whenever a module on another card wishes to use the system bus, it asserts BR∗, waits for BG∗ to be asserted, and then asserts BGACK∗. This situation causes the address bus buffers on the CPU module to float, leaving the bus free for the new bus master.

The asynchronous bus control signals from the 68000 (AS∗, UDS∗, LDS∗, R/$\overline{W}$) are buffered in exactly the same way as the address by one half of an octal bus transceiver. Three control signals, CLK, VMA∗, and E, from the CPU are buffered by permanently enabled bus drivers, as we do not anticipate that another CPU will implement synchronous bus cycles from the system bus.

The remaining bus control signals have been dealt with elsewhere and are included in figure 11.23 for the sake of completeness. All inputs to the 68000 have pull-up resistors.

The data bus buffers of figure 11.24 are implemented by two 74LS245 octal bus transceivers. Both transceivers have their data direction controlled by R/$\overline{W}$ from the CPU and are enabled only when the 68000 executes a valid bus cycle to nonlocal memory. If local memory is accessed, one of SEL0∗ to SEL4∗ goes active-low and the logical one at the output of the eight-input NAND gate, F3, disables the data bus transceivers.

If the 68000 gives up the bus in response to the assertion of BR∗, execution of the bus cycles is stopped and AS∗ is not asserted until the 68000 is once more in control. By making the BGACK∗ input to the 68000 a necessary condition to enable the data bus transceivers, the transceivers are automatically turned off whenever the on-board CPU has relinquished the bus.

I/O Ports on the CPU Module

The only I/O ports implemented on the TS2 CPU module are the two 6850 ACIAs illustrated in figure 11.25 (see p. 535). This circuit is almost identical to that found in the ECB module described in chapter 9. One port is dedicated to the terminal (IC C1 at address $01 0040) and the other (IC C2 at address $01 0041) is dedicated to the host computer interface. Whenever RTS∗ from C1 is made electrically high, the terminal interface is connected directly to the host port.

11.3 Monitors

When microprocessors first began to appear in the mid 1970s, their initial markets were relatively small because few engineers, designers, or even academics had any practical experience with programmable digital systems. Semiconductor manufacturers were quick to realize that the key to microprocessor sales was education.

Accordingly, they produced a number of single board microcomputers that could be connected to a VDT or teletype. These microcomputers also provided the user with an introduction to programming and to the control of external systems, because all boards had some form of parallel I/O port.

A whole generation of engineers learned to program—often in machine code, as some engineers did not even have access to an assembler. Early SBCs had tiny memories. My first microcomputer had less than 1,024 bytes of read/write memory. In order to get such a primitive system to do anything useful, the single board computers were supplied with a program in read-only memory, called a monitor. The monitor was the microcomputer's "operating system." The words are in quotes because the operating system of the SBC was often so primitive that few computer scientists would recognize it as such. A monitor provided the user with at least three basic functions:

1. The ability to input data or instructions (normally in machine code form) into the computer's memory.

2. The ability to execute a program starting at a given address.

3. The ability to read the contents of a memory location and to display them on the terminal.

The preceding facilities did at least enable many engineers to come to terms with the microprocessor. As time passed, the monitor grew more sophisticated and many functions were added. However, the monitor did not grow and grow without limit. Once the cost of read/write memory had declined to a small fraction of its original price and the floppy disk system became affordable, the monitor was not often needed and was replaced by the *bootstrap loader*. Following a reset, the bootstrap loader in ROM reads the operating system off a disk, places it in RAM, and runs it. Now, instead of the primitive monitor, the engineer has access to a full operating system with assemblers, compilers, editors, debuggers, and system utilities.

Today, the monitor has not disappeared entirely. It is not found in expensive, industrial microprocessor development systems. Nor is it found in low-cost, high-volume personal computers, where the scale of production permits a more comprehensive operating system and its associated secondary storage. The monitor is, however, found in some educational systems, where the cost of a disk-based operating system is prohibitive and the volume of production does not warrant a tailor-made operating system in ROM. One such monitor is called TUTOR and occupies 16K bytes of ROM in Motorola's ECB. We will examine some of TUTOR's facilities later.

There have been several noticeable trends in the facilities offered by modern monitors. The greatest change reflects the environment in which they are now used. Originally, the single board development system was the only computer in the laboratory or classroom. Now it is often surrounded by many relatively sophisticated systems. Therefore, monitors are frequently designed to allow software to be developed on a larger machine (the host computer) and then transferred (or downline-loaded) into the single board computer (the target machine).

Such monitors place more emphasis on the debugging of programs than on their creation. If the initial editing and assembly is done on the host computer, only the machine code (i.e., object code) needs to be transferred to the SBC. Then the programmer can set up initial conditions and run the code in the environment for which it was intended.

The TS2 microcomputer described earlier in this chapter needs a monitor to permit it to be tested and to allow programs to be entered and executed. Development of a monitor similar to TUTOR would be unrealistic here as that would represent a major design effort and consume a book of its own. A more tractable approach is to design a monitor capable of performing the three basic functions listed earlier in this section. Such a monitor is able to transfer programs and data between itself and an external host. The monitor to be presented also gives the reader an introduction to 68000 assembly language programming and a collection of useful subroutines dealing with input/output transactions. Before designing this monitor, we look at the structure of a monitor and at some of the facilities it offers.

Structure of a Monitor

A monitor is a program, resident in ROM, whose minimal function is to enter a program into the microprocessor's RAM and then transfer control to that program. In order to do this, the monitor must provide procedures to control the microcomputer's input/output port, which is connected to a display device (the console or terminal). Most monitors communicate with a VDT by means of an asynchronous serial interface.

When we consider the design of a practical monitor, three points must be appreciated:

1. The monitor must be in read-only memory and located in the CPU's memory space where it is activated following a reset.

2. The monitor must control at least the terminal I/O interface. Therefore, the type of I/O port and its physical location within the processor's memory space is fixed.

3. A monitor should provide some facility for dealing with interrupts and exceptions. The structure of a monitor can be described in terms of PDL.

```
Module_Monitor
                Initialize_system_constants
                Set_up_console_I/O_port
                Set_up_interrupt_vector_table
                Display_heading_on_VDT
```

```
REPEAT
        Clear_input_buffer
        Get Command
        CASE Command OF
                Memory: Display/modify_memory_contents
                Breakpoint: Set/clear_breakpoint
                GO: GO_and_execute instructions
                LOAD: Load formatted data into memory
                DUMP: Output formatted data from memory
                TM: Enter transparent mode
        END CASE
UNTIL system reset
END module
```

Although many possible commands may be included in a monitor, a few of the most important commands and their effects can be identified. Some of these commands are now detailed. As the TUTOR monitor on the MEX68KECB is so widely available and is also based on debugging facilities offered by Motorola's EXORMACS MDS, the following commands are related to TUTOR where necessary.

Memory display/modify   The display/modify command allows the contents of a selected memory location to be examined and, if necessay, modified. Although found on all monitors, the memory display/modify function exhibits a wide spread of facilities from system to system. A primitive monitor permits the examination of a byte at a specified address and its replacement by a new value, if desired. More sophisticated monitors allow byte, word, or longword operations and may even permit data to be displayed or entered in mnemonic form; that is, the contents of the specified location are disassembled.

TUTOR has two separate memory display/modify functions: MD (memory display), which displays the contents of one or more memory locations, and MM (memory modify), which displays the contents of a memory location and permits new data to be entered. Both commands allow data display and data entry to be in mnemonic form.

Memory block move   The block move command allows a block of memory to be moved (i.e., copied) from one part of the memory space to another. It is frequently used in conjunction with EPROM programmers, where the data to be written into the EPROM is copied from its source destination to the EPROM buffer, or vice versa.

Memory block fill   The block fill command presets the contents of a region of memory space to a given value, which is frequently done to initialize data storage areas before running a program. Clearly, if the data is initialized to, say $00, before executing a program, any change from $00 (after the execution of the program) can be detected by means of the memory display functions.

Memory search   Sometimes location of a particular data item in a region of memory space is necessary. The memory search command allows the user to seek the first occurrence of a given byte (word, longword) or a given string within a region of memory.

Load a block of data into memory The load command transfers a block of data from a terminal, secondary storage device, or host processor into the read/write memory space of the computer. The data to be loaded must be formatted in the exact way expected by the monitor; that is, the data is in the form of records with a header, byte count, data field, and error-detecting code.

TUTOR's load function has the form LO[⟨port number⟩][;options][=text]. The port number defines the source of the data to be loaded; the options (specified by the contents of the square brackets) permit checksums to be ignored or the data to be echoed back to the console terminal. The "=text" field causes the message "text" to be transmitted to the specified port before the data is loaded; for example, the command LO2; X=LIST MYPROG.BIN causes the string LIST MYPROG.BIN to be transmitted to the host computer via port 2 and the resulting data from the host to be displayed on the console terminal as well as stored in memory.

The data loaded by the LO function of TUTOR must conform to the S-record format that is widely used to record binary data. S-record data represents binary data in packets with five fields, as shown in figure 11.26. All binary data is represented in ASCII-encoded hexadecimal form. This representation is, of course, very inefficient, and originates from the time when many data-storage devices (e.g., papertape) did not support pure binary, 8-bit characters.

Dump a block of data This command is the complementary function of the load command. A specified block of data is formed into S records and transmitted to a storage device (e.g., a cassette in low-cost systems) or to a host processor. Some monitors call this the PUNCH command—a term belonging to the days of papertape.

TUTOR's dump command has the form

DU[⟨port number⟩]⟨address 1⟩⟨address 2⟩[⟨text⟩].

If present, the optional text field is used to create an S0 header; for example, the command DU4 86C0 87FF CLEMENTS1 transmits to port 4 (the cassette port) an S0 message containing the data field CLEMENTS1, and a sequence of S1 messages with the data in memory locations $86C0 through $87FF. TUTOR follows this with an S9 or an S8 termination record.

Set/remove breakpoints This command allows users to place (or to remove) breakpoints in their programs. A breakpoint is a memory location that, when accessed by the processor, forces some specific action to take place. Normally, a breakpoint is a software exception operation code that is inserted in a program in place of a normal instruction. TUTOR uses the illegal op-code $4AFB to force an exception whenever it is encountered. Once the resulting exception has been raised, the contents of the processor's registers can be displayed on the console device. Execution is continued by replacing the illegal op-code with the

FIGURE 11.26   S-record format

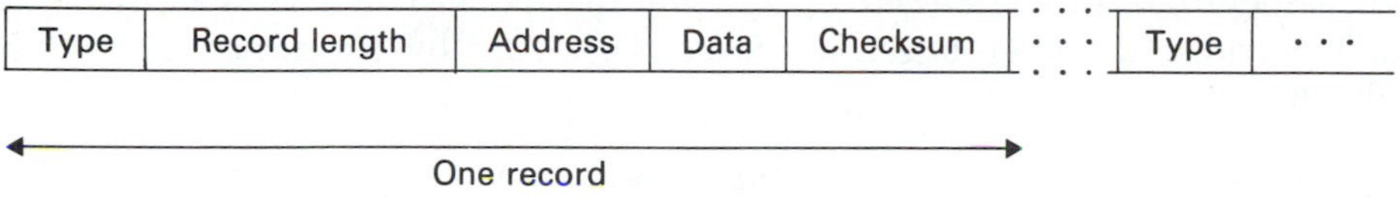

Type	Record length	Address	Data	Checksum	· · · · · · · · ·	Type	· · ·

←——————————— One record ———————————→

Field	Field width	Field contents
Type	2 characters	S-record type – S0, S1, . . . , S9
Record length	2 characters	Total number of character pairs in the record, excluding type and record length fields
Address	4, 6, 8 characters	The 2-, 3-, or 4-byte address at which the data field is to be loaded into memory
Data	$0-2n$	From 0 to n bytes of data to be loaded in memory, starting at the specified address
Checksum	2 characters	The least-significant byte of the one's complement sum of the values represented by the pairs of characters making up the record length, address, and data fields

Although there are ten types of S record, the records of most interest are:

S0   An optional record defining succeeding records. The address field is normally all zeros.

S1   A record with a data field and a 2-byte address at which the data is to be loaded.

S2   As S1 but with a 3-byte address field.

S3   As S1 but with a 4-byte address field.

S7   A termination record for a block of S records. The address field contains the 4-byte address to which control is to be passed. There is no data field.

S8   Same as S7. The S8 record provides a terminator for S records, but the address field is 3 bytes.

S9   Same as S7. The S9 record provides a terminator for S records, but with a 2-byte address field.

saved instruction originally at that address. Some systems permit the use of one breakpoint, while others allow multiple simultaneous breakpoints. All monitors supporting a breakpoint also provide a command to clear existing breakpoints.

Execute a program   Once a program has been entered and, if necessary, modified, it can be executed, which is done by loading the program counter with the address of the first instruction to be executed. Sometimes, this address is called the program's transfer address (TA). Simple monitors provide a single EXECUTE or GO function. TUTOR has three variations on this command: GD, GO, GT. Before continuing, note that the term PC in what follows does not mean the 68000's program counter. PC is a "synthetic register" and contains the next address in the *user program* that is to be executed when this program is run.

GD   The GD (GO Direct) command has the form GD ⟨address⟩ and causes a program to be executed, starting at the specified address. If an address is not provided, execution begins at the point specified by the current contents of the PC.

GO   The GO command has the form GO ⟨address⟩ and is similar to GD, thereby causing a program to be executed from the specified address. However, the GO command starts by tracing one instruction, setting any breakpoints, and then continuing.

GT   The GT (GO until breakpoint) command has the form GT ⟨breakpoint⟩, thereby causing the processor to continue executing from the address currently in the PC until it encounters the temporary breakpoint address specified by the GT command.

Set trace mode   When a program runs in the trace mode, an exception is raised after each instruction has been executed and the contents of the CPU's internal registers dumped on the console display. This action permits a program to be monitored line by line. TUTOR supports a trace command with the format TR [⟨count⟩]. The optional parameter, count, determines the number of instructions that are to be executed before the registers are dumped.

Transparent mode   The so-called transparent mode permits the console device to communicate directly with the host computer, thereby bypassing the target machine entirely. TUTOR supports this command with the syntax TM [⟨exit character⟩], where ⟨exit character⟩ specifies the character to be used to force a return to the TUTOR command level.

This command is used when the target computer is connected to both a console (on one port) and a host computer (on another port). By entering the transparent mode, the programmer is able to edit and assemble a program on the host machine. Then the exit character is entered (the default is control A) and a return to TUTOR control made. The DU (dump) function of TUTOR can then be employed to transfer the object program from the host to the target computer. Without the transparent mode, we would need to physically switch the console device from the target to the host processor and back.

Monitor Input/Output

Most monitors communicate with the outside world through a serial data link. How this communication is actually achieved varies widely from monitor to monitor. Such diversity is necessary if the functions provided by the monitor are to be made as versatile as possible. Here we consider four variations on the theme of input/output: I/O procedure, parameter-driven procedures, input/output and the device control block, and channel I/O.

I/O Procedure

Some of the earliest and most primitive monitors simply provided a subroutine (procedure) that either transmitted a character to the console (output) or received a character from the console (input). What more could one ask of an input/output routine? The answer is, "A lot." Predefined I/O routines are reasonable only when the nature of the I/O, its associated data path, and far-end (i.e., remote) terminal are all known in advance and never change.

Such an approach is very inflexible; for example, if the predefined I/O routine works with 7-bit ASCII characters, it can never be used to read 8-bit characters. Moreover, simple I/O routines do not have sophisticated built-in error-recovery procedures. What happens if the input data is faulty? What happens if the I/O is to be directed to a different port? In some of the early systems, the secondary storage device needed to be connected to the SBC by unplugging the console terminal and then plugging in the storage unit.

Parameter-Driven Procedures

The parameter-driven procedure still performs I/O transactions via predefined subroutines, but permits the operational characteristics to be modified by changing parameters stored in read/write memory. During the running of the monitor's initialization routine, these parameters are set up to reflect the expected characteristics of the console terminal. A user can later alter them to modify the I/O characteristics of the SBC and to redirect I/O to an auxiliary port if necessary.

Consider an example of parameter-driven input expressed in PDL. The console input device is an ACIA whose address is stored in a variable called Console_ACIA. Another pointer, Secondary_ACIA, holds the address of an alternative ACIA through which I/O can be directed. A flag bit, User_ACIA, is clear when I/O is performed by the console ACIA, and is set when it is performed by the secondary ACIA. By setting or clearing User_ACIA, we are able to switch I/O between ACIAs under software control.

Four other single-bit flags control the operation of the procedure. If Input_direction is set, the normal ACIA driver routine is not used and a jump is made to the subroutine, whose address is in the variable User_routine. This procedure permits the redirection of input to any device driver.

A parity strip flag is tested and, if clear, the input is to be regarded as 7-bit character-encoded data and the eighth (parity) bit stripped. Another flag (Case_conversion) determines whether lower-case characters should be converted to their upper-case equivalents. If Case_conversion is clear, upper- to lower-case conversion is carried out; for example, a lower-case "f" (110 0110) is converted into its upper-case equivalent "F" (100 0110) if Case_conversion is clear. Finally, the Echo_mode flag determines whether the input character is to be echoed on the console output device. If Echo_mode is clear, any input is echoed on the display device. All pointers and parameters are set up during the initialization phase of the monitor. Note that the default state of all single-bit flags is zero.

Module Input

```
        DEFINE POINTER: Console_ACIA {Points to console ACIA}
        DEFINE POINTER: Secondary_ACIA {Points to alternate ACIA}
        DEFINE POINTER: User_routine {Points to address of
                                alternate I/O routine}
        DEFINE BYTE: Input_flag {Composite byte of 5 control bits of
                                user supplied input}
        DEFINE BIT: Input_direction {If clear get data from console
                                else from user routine}
        DEFINE BIT: User_ACIA {If set use Secondary_ACIA}
        DEFINE BIT: Parity_strip {If clear strip parity from input}
        DEFINE BIT: Case_conversion {If clear convert lower-case to
                                upper-case}
        DEFINE BIT: Echo_mode {If clear echo input character
                                on console}

        IF Input_direction = 0   THEN InConsole ELSE InUser END_IF
        IF Parity_strip = 0      THEN Strip_parity_bit END_IF
        IF Case_conversion = 0 THEN Convert_LC_to_UC END_IF
        IF Echo_mode = 0         THEN Output END_IF
```

END Input

InConsole

```
        MOVE.B    Input_flag,D1         Get input flag byte
        BTST      #User_ACIA,D1         Input from console?
        BEQ.S     InC1                  If clear then console
        MOVEA.L Secondary_ACIA,A0 Load address of secondary
        BRA.S     InC2                  Skip load console ACIA
InC1    MOVEA.L Console_ACIA,A0   Load console ACIA address
InC2    BTST      #0,(A0)               Test ACIA status
        BNE       InC2                  Loop until ACIA ready
        MOVE.B  2(A0),D0                Read input
        RTS
```

END InConsole

InUser

```
        MOVEA.L User_routine,A0   Call user-supplied input
        JMP       (A0)
```

End InUser

Parameter-driven I/O is a great step forward over I/O provided by the rigid, embedded I/O procedures described previously. Unfortunately, this is a rather ad hoc approach to I/O and does not lend itself to generality; that is, the operating modes still have to be built into the monitor's software. If a radically different mode of operation were necessary, parameter-driven I/O would probably not prove sufficiently flexible. A better technique involves the more general concept of the device control block (DCB).

FIGURE 11.27   Device control block (DCB)

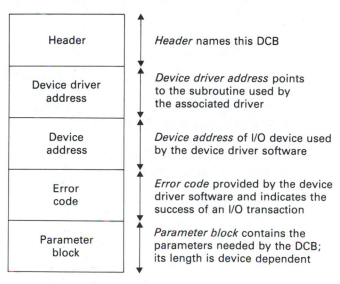

Header	*Header* names this DCB
Device driver address	*Device driver address* points to the subroutine used by the associated driver
Device address	*Device address* of I/O device used by the device driver software
Error code	*Error code* provided by the device driver software and indicates the success of an I/O transaction
Parameter block	*Parameter block* contains the parameters needed by the DCB; its length is device dependent

Input/Output and the Device Control Block

As its name suggests, a device control block (DCB) is a collection of parameters that completely defines the characteristics of an input/output transaction; that is, all the I/O procedure needs to know is the address of the appropriate DCB. All device-dependent information is stored in the DCB. Figure 11.27 illustrates a possible DCB for a console input device. The DCB is a data structure that, in the example of figure 11.27, has five fields.

The *header* supplies the name of the DCB. The header may be a logical device number or an ASCII string. The *device driver address* is a pointer to the subroutine that actually performs the input or output transaction. The *device address* provides the device driver with the location of the physical I/O device. The device *error code* is a status word returned by the device driver and reflects, for example, device_not_ready or parity errors. Finally, the DCB includes a *parameter block* that contains other information associated with the actual type of I/O being performed.

I/O by means of the DCB allows a greater degree of device independency; that is, the programmer can write programs that need to know nothing about the nature of the actual I/O devices. During the monitor's initialization phase, the console DCBs are set up in RAM using a table of default parameters held in ROM or on disk. The user can later redirect I/O by writing to the appropriate DCB, or a pointer can be set up to a new DCB.

The data structure forming the DCB is employed by a generalized I/O procedure. The programmer requests an input or an output transaction and passes the address of the DCB to the procedure; for example, in 68000 terminology, I/O may be performed by the following four steps:

1. Load D0 with the code of the operation to be performed (e.g., input, output, get_device_status, etc.).

2. Load D1 with any parameter needed to perform the desired operation.

3. Load A0 with the address of the DCB.

4. Call the generalized I/O handler (e.g., BSR IO_REQUEST).

Consider the following example of the use of a device control block in inputting data. To keep matters simple, the IO_REQUEST automatically inputs a byte. A real system would require the passing of a parameter to determine the nature of the operation to be performed. The example is in four parts: a call to the output handler (IO_REQUEST), the device control block appropriate to the input, the IO_REQUEST routine, and the device handler (IN_CON) used to obtain a character from the console ACIA.

```
CON_ACIA     EQU       $010040         Physical address of console ACIA
                :
*            Perform   I/O here
             LEA. L    CON_DCB, A0     A0 points at the DCB to be used
             BSR       IO_REQUEST      Perform the input
                :                      Continue
                :
*            Device control block for the console ACIA
CON_DCB      DC.B      'CON_ACIA'      8-byte header
             DC.L      CON_DRIVER      Address of console driver
             DC.L      CON_ACIA        Address of console ACIA
             DC.B      ERROR1          Error status 1 (logical error)
             DC.B      ERROR2          Error status 2 (physical error)
             DC.W      PARAM           Parameters needed by driver
                :
*            Entry point for standard I/O request
IO_REQUEST   JMP       8(A0)           Call input handler in DCB
                :
*            Actual device driver routine for the console ACIA
CON_DRIVER   MOVE.L    A1,—(SP)        Save A1 on stack
             LEA.L     12(A0),A1       Get address of ACIA from DCB
             CLR.B     16(A0)          Clear ERROR1 status
LOOP         MOVE.B    (A1),D0         Get ACIA status
             BTST      #0,D0           Test RDRF bit of status
             BEQ       LOOP            IF RDRF clear then repeat
             MOVE.B    D0,17(A0)       Store device status in ERROR2 of DCB
             ANDI.B    #$70,D0         Mask to error bits of device status
             BEQ.S     READ_DATA       If remaining bits clear, get data
             MOVE.B    #1,16(A0)       Else set logical error flag in DCB
READ_DATA    MOVE.B    2(A1),D0        Get input data from ACIA
             MOVEA.L   (SP)+,A1        Restore A1
             RTS
```

In this example, two error status bytes are associated with the DCB. ERROR1 is a logical error message and may be assigned codes to indicate: no_error, device_not_ready, etc. ERROR2 is a physical error message and is the status returned by the actual I/O device. The meaning of the bits in ERROR2 varies from DCB to DCB, while the bits of ERROR1 indicate one of a number of preassigned device-independent messages. For the sake of simplicity, ERROR2 is clear if there is no error and set to $01 otherwise.

Note that no processing is performed on the input (e.g., parity stripping, lower- to upper-case conversion). This processing could be done by using the PARAM field of the DCB to determine the type of processing to be applied to the input.

It should now be clear that the application-level programmer does not have to know about the details of the actual I/O routines and their associated hardware. Furthermore, simply by altering the DCB address, the I/O can easily be redirected to some other channel.

Channel I/O

For the purpose of this discussion, channel I/O is considered as an application level form of I/O using device control blocks. Channel I/O is built on the DCB mechanism and offers the programmer an even greater degree of freedom than that provided by the DCB alone.

Each I/O device is given a logical name, such as CON, PRNTR, MODEM, DISK, etc. This name is used by the programmer and forms the header of the appropriate DCB. Channel I/O does not require the programmer to know the address of the DCB. When I/O is executed, the DCBs are searched until the DCB whose name matches that supplied by the programmer is found. To do this, each DCB contains a pointer to the next DCB in the chain. Figure 11.28 illustrates such a linked list.

As an example, in one possible arrangement the programmer simply creates an ASCII string in memory, or provides a pointer to it and then calls a trap. The trap-handling routine searches each DCB for a header that matches the one provided. When the appropriate DCB has been located, the information in it is used to execute the appropriate I/O transaction. In order to avoid searching for a DCB each time a particular I/O transaction is executed, an alternative procedure is to "open" a channel. In this case, the DCB chain is searched once for the location of the appropriate DCB and the address of this DCB is "attached" to the current channel. The monitor written for the TS2 uses this form of I/O.

Monitors for the 68000 System

Now that we have designed the hardware of a 68000 system, the next step is to provide it with a monitor. The monitor presented here is a very simple monitor and is intended to achieve only two objectives: it provides an extended example of a 68000 assembly language program and it allows the hardware described earlier to be tested and downline-loaded from a host processor.

FIGURE 11.28   Linked list of DCBs used by I/O channels

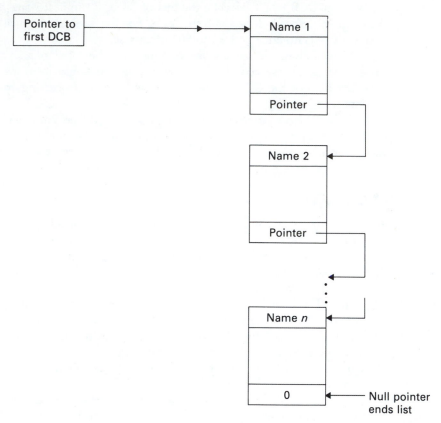

In designing such a monitor, the author is faced with conflicting goals—the monitor should be as simple as possible, yet it should illustrate a number of interesting or important features. Consequently, the monitor to be described is somewhat lop-sided and, although very primitive, includes facilities normally associated with more sophisticated monitors. The monitor described is called TS2MON.

Specification of TS2MON

1.   TS2MON is an EPROM-based monitor for a 68000 system and supports three functions: memory modify/examine, load a program from a host processor using S-formatted data, execute a program from some specified address.

2.   TS2MON is a flexible monitor whose subroutines are capable of being used by other programs easily and efficiently. TS2MON is constructed so

that additional commands may be added to its repertoire with little difficulty.

3. The command input is assembled into a buffer and then interpreted. A
command line interpreter of the type described in chapter 3 is required.

4. Input/output is handled by means of device control blocks. Following a
reset, two DCBs are set up by TS2MON: a DCB for the console and a DCB
for the host processor. Both I/O devices are ACIAs.

5. TS2MON implements a very basic form of breakpoint mechanism. A
program may be executed to a breakpoint and then run from the breakpoint.

Design of TS2MON

We are now going to discuss some of the features of TS2MON before presenting
its listing. A detailed design is not given, as the listing is well endowed with
comments. The basic structure of TS2MON is presented in PDL form.

```
Module: TS2MON
        Setup all pointers
        Setup ACIAs
        Setup exception table
        Setup DCB table
        Display heading
        REPEAT
            Get_command
            Execute_command
        END_REPEAT
End TS2MON
```

Following a reset, TS2MON sets up its operating environment, which involves
creating device control blocks for the console ACIA and the auxiliary ACIA and
loading the exception vector table with the addresses of all appropriate exception-
handling routines.

Once the DCBs have been set up, the programmer is free to modify them in
order to redirect I/O. Similarly, the exception vector table can be modified to
provide alternative exception routines. Note that any exception not explicitly
required by TS2MON is treated as an uninitialized interrupt.

In what follows, the names of subroutines are given in upper-case characters
(usually in parentheses). The main part of the program is an infinite loop which
assembles a line of text into a buffer (GETLINE), removes leading and multiple
embedded spaces from the input (TIDY), and then matches the first string in the
buffer with commands in the command table (EXECUTE). Before the built-in
command table is searched, a user command table pointed at by a longword in
UTAB is examined. This feature enables user-supplied commands to be added to
TS2MON's instruction set.

The commands provided by TS2MON are self-explanatory (see the listing).

Only two features are worthy of special mention: the DCB structure and exception-handling facilities.

During the initialization process, the monitor sets up the appropriate DCBs in RAM (SET_DCB). Input/output is performed by loading register A0 with a pointer to the name of the desired DCB and then calling IO_OPEN. This searches the linked list of DCBs for the one whose name matches that pointed at by A0. On returning from IO_OPEN, A0 contains the address of the DCB itself.

Actual I/O is performed by calling IO_REQ, which reads the address of the device handler routine from the DCB pointed at by A0 and executes that routine. As all I/O carried out by TS2MON is in character form, two routines have been included to control the console device (still using DCBs). GETCHAR reads a character, strips the parity bit, converts lower case to upper case, and echoes the input to the console. Similarly PUTCHAR displays a character on the console.

Exceptions handled by TS2MON are: illegal instructions, bus error, address errors, and breakpoints. The breakpoint exception uses the TRAP #14 vector.

Group 1 exceptions (bus and address errors) are handled by displaying the appropriate error message and then calling GROUP1, which reads the program counter from the stack and the instruction being executed at the time of the exception. As the PC on the stack is not the actual value of the PC at the time of the exception (due to the 68000's pre-fetch facility), a search is made in the area pointed at by the saved PC until the op-code corresponding to the saved instruction is located. The address of this instruction is taken as the "correct" value of the PC. The GROUP1 stack frame is then cleaned up to make it look like a group 2 exception and the group 2 exception-handling routine is called.

GROUP2 handles all group 2 exceptions and group 1 exceptions after "preprocessing" by GROUP1. The action carried out by GROUP2 is to make a copy of all the 68000's registers and the program counter/status register in a data structure called TSK_T. Two commands operate on this data structure. EX_DIS displays the contents of these registers and REG permits any register to be updated within the table; for example, the command REG PC FF0A has the effect of altering the program counter stored in the data structure to $FF0A.

Up to eight breakpoints are set up by the command BRGT ⟨address⟩. This command only stores the user-supplied address in the breakpoint table (BP_TAB). Similarly, NOBR ⟨address⟩ deletes the appropriate breakpoint from the table. A NOBR command without an address clears all breakpoints.

A program may be executed by the command GB ⟨address⟩ or by GB. If an address is supplied, a jump to that address is made; otherwise the program counter is loaded from the value stored in TSK_T. In the latter case, all address and data registers (except SSP) are loaded from the TSK_T. In both cases, the breakpoints are set prior to execution. A TRAP #14 is placed at the address pointed at by each breakpoint and the instruction that was at the address is saved in the breakpoint table.

When a breakpoint is encountered, the volatile environment is displayed and all breakpoints are cleared. Execution can be continued from the breakpoint by entering the command GB.

Listing of TS2MON

```
                        X                               Symbol equates
        00000008  BS      EQU     $08             Back_space
        0000000D  CR      EQU     $0D             Carriage_return
        0000000A  LF      EQU     $0A             Line_feed
        00000020  SPACE   EQU     $20             Space
        00000057  WAIT    EQU     'W'             Wait character (to suspend output)
        0000001B  ESC     EQU     $1B             ASCII escape character (used by TM)
        00000001  CTRL_A  EQU     $01             Control_A forces return to monitor
                        X                               Device addresses
        00000800  STACK   EQU     $00000800       Stack_pointer
        00010040  ACIA_1  EQU     $00010040       Console ACIA control
        00010041  ACIA_2  EQU     ACIA_1+1        Auxilary ACIA control
        00000008  X_BASE  EQU     $08             Start of exception vector table
        00004E4E  TRAP_14 EQU     $4E4E           Code for TRAP #14
        00000040  MAXCHR  EQU     64              Length of input line buffer
        0000003F  BUFFEND EQU     LNBUFF+MAXCHR-1 End of line buffer
                        X
        00000C00  DATA    EQU     $00000C00       Data origin
000000            LNBUFF  DS.B    MAXCHR          Input line buffer
000040            BUFFPT  DS.L    1               Pointer to line buffer
000044            PARAMTR DS.L    1               Last parameter from line buffer
000048            ECHO    DS.B    1               When clear this enable input echo
000049            U_CASE  DS.B    1               Flag for upper case conversion
00004A            UTAB    DS.L    1               Pointer to user command table
00004E            CN_IVEC DS.L    1               Pointer to console input DCB
000052            CN_OVEC DS.L    1               Pointer to console output DCB
000056            TSK_T   DS.W    37              Frame for D0-D7, A0-A6, USP, SSP, SW, PC
0000A0            BP_TAB  DS.W    24              Breakpoint table
0000D0            FIRST   DS.B    512             DCB area
0002D0            BUFFER  DS.B    256             256 bytes for I/O buffer
                        X
        XXXXXXXXXXXXXXXXXXXXXXXXXXXXXXXXXXXXXXXXXXXXXXXXXXXXXXXXXXXXXXXXXXXXXXXXXXXXXXX
                        X
                        X  This is the main program which assembles a command in the line
                        X  buffer, removes leading/embedded spaces and interprets it by matching
                        X  it with a command in the user table or the built-in table COMTAB
                        X  All variables are specified with respect to A6
                        X
008000                    ORG     $00008000       Monitor origin
008000 0000 0800          DC.L    STACK           Reset stack pointer
008004 0000 8008          DC.L    RESET           Reset vector
        00008008  RESET   EQU     X               Cold entry point for monitor
008008 4DF8 0C00          LEA.L   DATA,A6         A6 points to data area
```

```
00800C 42AE 004A              CLR.L    UTAB(A6)        Reset pointer to user extension table
008010 422E 0048              CLR.B    ECHO(A6)        Set automatic character echo
008014 422E 0049              CLR.B    U_CASE(A6)      Clear case conversion flag (UC<-LC)
008018 6136      >008050      BSR.S    SETACIA         Setup ACIAs
00801A 6100 05D8>0085F4       BSR      X_SET           Setup exception table
00801E 6100 044E>00846E       BSR      SET_DCB         Setup DCB table in RAM
008022 49FA 09D0>0089F4       LEA.L    BANNER(PC),A4   Point to banner
008026 6164      >00808C      BSR.S    HEADING         and print heading
008028 207C 0000 C000         MOVE.L   #$0000C000,A0   A0 points to extension ROM
00802E 2010                   MOVE.L   (A0),D0         Read first longword in extension ROM
008030 0C80 524F 4D32         CMP.L    #'ROM2',D0      If extension begins with 'ROM2' then
008036 6604      >00803C      BNE.S    NO_EXT          call the subroutine at EXT_ROM+8
008038 4EA8 0008             JSR      8(A0)           else continue
00803C 4E71         NO_EXT    NOP                      Two NOPs to allow for a future
00803E 4E71                   NOP                      call to an initialization routine
008040 4287         WARM      CLR.L    D7              Warm entry point - clear error flag
008042 6128      >00806C      BSR.S    NEWLINE         Print a newline
008044 614C      >008092      BSR.S    GETLINE         Get a command line
008046 6100 0080>0080C8       BSR      TIDY            Tidy up input buffer contents
00804A 6100 00BE>00810A       BSR      EXECUTE         Interpret command
00804E 60F0      >008040      BRA      WARM            Repeat indefinitely
                         x
            xxxxxxxxxxxxxxxxxxxxxxxxxxxxxxxxxxxxxxxxxxxxxxxxxxxxxxxxxxxxxxxxxxxxxxxxxxxxxxxxxxxxxxxxx
                         x
                         x   Some initialization and basic routines
                         x
            00008050     SETACIA EQU      x              Setup ACIA parameters
008050 41F9 0001 0040       LEA.L    ACIA_1,A0       A0 points to console ACIA
008056 10BC 0003            MOVE.B   #$03,(A0)       Reset ACIA1
00805A 117C 0003 0001       MOVE.B   #$03,1(A0)      Reset ACIA2
008060 10BC 0015            MOVE.B   #$15,(A0)       Set up ACIA1 constants (no IRQ,
008064 117C 0015 0001       MOVE.B   #$15,1(A0)      RTS* low, 8 bit, no parity, 1 stop)
00806A 4E75                 RTS                      Return
                         x
            0000806C     NEWLINE EQU      x              Move cursor to start of newline
00806C 48E7 0008            MOVEM.L  A4,-(A7)        Save A4
008070 49FA 099C>008A0E      LEA.L    CRLF(PC),A4     Point to CR/LF string
008074 6106      >00807C      BSR.S    PSTRING         Print it
008076 4CDF 1000            MOVEM.L  (A7)+,A4        Restore A4
00807A 4E75                 RTS                      Return
                         x
            0000807C     PSTRING EQU      x              Display the string pointed at by A4
00807C 2F00                 MOVE.L   D0,-(A7)        Save D0
00807E 101C         PS1     MOVE.B   (A4)+,D0        Get character to be printed
008080 6706      >008088      BEQ.S    PS2             If null then return
```

```
008082 6100 050C)008590          BSR      PUTCHAR        Else print it
008086 60F6     )00807E          BRA      PS1            Continue
008088 201F             PS2      MOVE.L   (A7)+,D0       Restore D0 and exit
00808A 4E75                      RTS
                            x
00808C 61DE     )00806C HEADING  BSR      NEWLINE        Same as PSTRING but with newline
00808E 61EC     )00807C          BSR      PSTRING
008090 60DA     )00806C          BRA      NEWLINE
                            x
          xxxxxxxxxxxxxxxxxxxxxxxxxxxxxxxxxxxxxxxxxxxxxxxxxxxxxxxxxxxxxxxxxxxxxxxxxxxx
                            x
                            x  GETLINE  inputs a string of characters into a line buffer
                            x           A3 points to next free entry in line buffer
                            x           A2 points to end of buffer
                            x           A1 points to start of buffer
                            x           D0 holds character to be stored
                            x
008092 43EE 0000 GETLINE LEA.L    LNBUFF(A6),A1   A1 points to start of line buffer
008096 47D1             LEA.L    (A1),A3         A3 points to start (initially)
008098 45E9 0040        LEA.L    MAXCHR(A1),A2   A2 points to end of buffer
00809C 6100 04C0)00855E GETLN2 BSR      GETCHAR        Get a character
0080A0 0C00 0001        CMP.B    #CTRL_A,D0     If control_A then reject this line
0080A4 671E     )0080C4          BEQ.S    GETLN5         and get another line
0080A6 0C00 0008        CMP.B    #BS,D0         If back_space then move back pointer
0080AA 660A     )0080B6          BNE.S    GETLN3         Else skip past wind-back routine
0080AC B7C9             CMP.L    A1,A3          First check for empty buffer
0080AE 67EC     )00809C          BEQ      GETLN2         If buffer empty then continue
0080B0 47EB FFFF        LEA      -1(A3),A3      Else decrement buffer pointer
0080B4 60E6     )00809C          BRA      GETLN2         and continue with next character
0080B6 16C0             GETLN3 MOVE.B   D0,(A3)+       Store character and update pointer
0080B8 0C00 000D        CMP.B    #CR,D0         Test for command terminator
0080BC 6602     )0080C0          BNE.S    GETLN4         If not CR then skip past exit
0080BE 60AC     )00806C          BRA      NEWLINE        Else new line before next operation
0080C0 B7CA             GETLN4 CMP.L    A2,A3          Test for buffer overflow
0080C2 66D8     )00809C          BNE      GETLN2         If buffer not full then continue
0080C4 61A6     )00806C GETLN5 BSR      NEWLINE        Else move to next line and
0080C6 60CA     )008092          BRA      GETLINE        repeat this routine
                            x
          xxxxxxxxxxxxxxxxxxxxxxxxxxxxxxxxxxxxxxxxxxxxxxxxxxxxxxxxxxxxxxxxxxxxxxxxxxxx
                            x
                            x  TIDY cleans up the line buffer by removing leading spaces and multiple
                            x       spaces between parameters. At the end of TIDY, BUFFPT points to
                            x       the first parameter following the command.
                            x       A0 = pointer to line buffer, A1 = pointer to cleaned up buffer
                            x
```

```
0080C8 41EE 0000        TIDY     LEA.L    LNBUFF(A6),A0      A0 points to line buffer
0080CC 43D0                      LEA.L    (A0),A1            A1 points to start of line buffer
0080CE 1018             TIDY1    MOVE.B   (A0)+,D0           Read character from line buffer
0080D0 0C00 0020                 CMP.B    #SPACE,D0          Repeat until the first non-space
0080D4 67F8    >0080CE           BEQ      TIDY1              character is found
0080D6 41E8 FFFF                 LEA.L    -1(A0),A0          Move pointer back to first char
0080DA 1018             TIDY2    MOVE.B   (A0)+,D0           Move the string left to remove
0080DC 12C0                      MOVE.B   D0,(A1)+           any leading spaces
0080DE 0C00 0020                 CMP.B    #SPACE,D0          Test for embedded space
0080E2 660A    >0080EE           BNE.S    TIDY4              If not space then test for EOL
0080E4 0C18 0020        TIDY3    CMP.B    #SPACE,(A0)+       If space skip multiple embedded
0080E8 67FA    >0080E4           BEQ      TIDY3              spaces
0080EA 41E8 FFFF                 LEA.L    -1(A0),A0          Move back pointer
0080EE 0C00 000D        TIDY4    CMP.B    #CR,D0             Test for end_of_line (EOL)
0080F2 66E6    >0080DA           BNE      TIDY2              If not EOL then read next char
0080F4 41EE 0000                 LEA.L    LNBUFF(A6),A0      Restore buffer pointer
0080F8 0C10 000D        TIDY5    CMP.B    #CR,(A0)           Test for EOL
0080FC 6706    >008104           BEQ.S    TIDY6              If EOL then exit
0080FE 0C18 0020                 CMP.B    #SPACE,(A0)+       Test for delimiter
008102 66F4    >0080F8           BNE      TIDY5              Repeat until delimiter or EOL
008104 2D48 0040        TIDY6    MOVE.L   A0,BUFFPT(A6)      Update buffer pointer
008108 4E75                      RTS
                        X
                        XXXXXXXXXXXXXXXXXXXXXXXXXXXXXXXXXXXXXXXXXXXXXXXXXXXXXXXXXXXXXXXXXXXXXXXXXXX
                        X
                        X  EXECUTE matches the first command in the line buffer with the
                        X  commands in a command table. An external table pointed at by
                        X  UTAB is searched first and then the in-built table, COMTAB.
                        X
00810A 4AAE 004A        EXECUTE  TST.L    UTAB(A6)           Test pointer to user table
00810E 670C    >00811C           BEQ.S    EXEC1              If clear then try built-in table
008110 266E 004A                 MOVE.L   UTAB(A6),A3        Else pick up pointer to user table
008114 6120    >008136           BSR.S    SEARCH             Look for command in user table
008116 6404    >00811C           BCC.S    EXEC1              If not found then try internal table
008118 2653                      MOVE.L   (A3),A3            Else get absolute address of command
00811A 4ED3                      JMP      (A3)               from user table and execute it
                        X
00811C 47FA 0A46>008B64 EXEC1    LEA.L    COMTAB(PC),A3      Try built-in command table
008120 6114    >008136           BSR.S    SEARCH             Look for command in built-in table
008122 6508    >00812C           BCS.S    EXEC2              If found then execute command
008124 49FA 09CF>008AF5          LEA.L    ERMES2(PC),A4      Else print "invalid command"
008128 6000 FF52>00807C          BRA.L    PSTRING            and return
00812C 2653             EXEC2    MOVE.L   (A3),A3            Get the relative command address
00812E 49FA 0A34>008B64          LEA.L    COMTAB(PC),A4      pointed at by A3 and add it to
008132 D7CC                      ADD.L    A4,A3              the PC to generate the actual
```

```
008134 4ED3                      JMP      (A3)          command address. Then execute it.

               X
         00008136  SEARCH EQU     X             Match the command in the line buffer
008136 4280                      CLR.L    D0            with command table pointed at by A3
008138 1013                      MOVE.B   (A3),D0       Get the first character in the
00813A 6734   >008170            BEQ.S    SRCH7         current entry. If zero then exit
00813C 49F3 0006                 LEA.L    6(A3,D0.W),A4 Else calculate address of next entry
008140 122B 0001                 MOVE.B   1(A3),D1      Get number of characters to match
008144 4BEE 0000                 LEA.L    LNBUFF(A6),A5 A5 points to command in line buffer
008148 142B 0002                 MOVE.B   2(A3),D2      Get first character in this entry
00814C B41D                      CMP.B    (A5)+,D2      from the table and match with buffer
00814E 6704   >008154            BEQ.S    SRCH3         If match then try rest of string
008150 264C           SRCH2      MOVE.L   A4,A3         Else get address of next entry
008152 60E2   >008136            BRA      SEARCH        and try the next entry in the table
008154 5301           SRCH3      SUB.B    #1,D1         One less character to match
008156 670E   >008166            BEQ.S    SRCH6         If match counter zero then all done
008158 47EB 0003                 LEA.L    3(A3),A3      Else point to next character in table
00815C 141B           SRCH4      MOVE.B   (A3)+,D2      Now match a pair of characters
00815E B41D                      CMP.B    (A5)+,D2
008160 66EE   >008150            BNE      SRCH2         If no match then try next entry
008162 5301                      SUB.B    #1,D1         Else decrement match counter and
008164 66F6   >00815C            BNE      SRCH4         repeat until no chars left to match
008166 47EC FFFC      SRCH6      LEA.L    -4(A4),A3     Calculate address of command entry
00816A 003C 0001                 OR.B     #1,CCR        point. Mark carry flag as success
00816E 4E75                      RTS                    and return
008170 023C 00FE      SRCH7      AND.B    #$FE,CCR      Fail - clear carry to indicate
008174 4E75                      RTS                    command not found and return

               X
               XXXXXXXXXXXXXXXXXXXXXXXXXXXXXXXXXXXXXXXXXXXXXXXXXXXXXXXXXXXXXXXXXXXXXXX
               X
               X  Basic input routines
               X  HEX    = Get one   hexadecimal character  into D0
               X  BYTE   = Get two   hexadecimal characters into D0
               X  WORD   = Get four  hexadecimal characters into D0
               X  LONGWD = Get eight hexadecimal characters into D0
               X  PARAM  = Get a longword from the line buffer into D0
               X  Bit 0 of D7 is set to indicate a hexadecimal input error
               X
008176 6100 03E6>00855E HEX      BSR      GETCHAR       Get a character from input device
00817A 0400 0030                 SUB.B    #$30,D0       Convert to binary
00817E 6B0E   >00818E            BMI.S    NOT_HEX       If less than $30 then exit with error
008180 0C00 0009                 CMP.B    #$09,D0       Else test for number (0 to 9)
008184 6F0C   >008192            BLE.S    HEX_OK        If number then exit - success
008186 5F00                      SUB.B    #$07,D0       Else convert letter to hex
008188 0C00 000F                 CMP.B    #$0F,D0       If character in range "A" to "F"
```

```
00818C 6F04    }008192           BLE.S    HEX_OK           then exit successfully
00818E 0007 0001    NOT_HEX OR.B  #1,D7           Else set error flag
008192 4E75           HEX_OK RTS                    and return
                        x
008194 2F01           BYTE   MOVE.L   D1,-(A7)         Save D1
008196 61DE    }008176           BSR      HEX              Get first hex character
008198 E900                      ASL.B    #4,D0            Move it to MS nybble position
00819A 1200                      MOVE.B   D0,D1            Save MS nybble in D1
00819C 61D8    }008176           BSR      HEX              Get second hex character
00819E D001                      ADD.B    D1,D0            Merge MS and LS nybbles
0081A0 221F                      MOVE.L   (A7)+,D1         Restore D1
0081A2 4E75                      RTS
                        x
0081A4 61EE    }008194 WORD   BSR      BYTE             Get upper order byte
0081A6 E140                      ASL.W    #8,D0            Move it to MS position
0081A8 60EA    }008194           BRA      BYTE             Get LS byte and return
                        x
0081AA 61F8    }0081A4 LONGWD BSR      WORD             Get upper order word
0081AC 4840                      SWAP     D0               Move it to MS position
0081AE 60F4    }0081A4           BRA      WORD             Get lower order word and return
                        x
                        x  PARAM reads a parameter from the line buffer and puts it in both
                        x  PARAMTR(A6) and D0. Bit 1 of D7 is set on error.
                        x
0081B0 2F01           PARAM  MOVE.L   D1,-(A7)         Save D1
0081B2 4281                      CLR.L    D1               Clear input accumulator
0081B4 206E 0040                 MOVE.L   BUFFPT(A6),A0    A0 points to parameter in buffer
0081B8 1018           PARAM1 MOVE.B   (A0)+,D0         Read character from line buffer
0081BA 0C00 0020                 CMP.B    #SPACE,D0        Test for delimiter
0081BE 6720    }0081E0           BEQ.S    PARAM4           The permitted delimiter is a
0081C0 0C00 000D                 CMP.B    #CR,D0           space or a carriage return
0081C4 671A    }0081E0           BEQ.S    PARAM4           Exit on either space or C/R
0081C6 E981                      ASL.L    #4,D1            Shift accumulated result 4 bits left
0081C8 0400 0030                 SUB.B    #$30,D0          Convert new character to hex
0081CC 6B1E    }0081EC           BMI.S    PARAM5           If less than $30 then not-hex
0081CE 0C00 0009                 CMP.B    #$09,D0          If less than 10
0081D2 6F08    }0081DC           BLE.S    PARAM3           then continue
0081D4 5F00                      SUB.B    #$07,D0          Else assume $A - $F
0081D6 0C00 000F                 CMP.B    #$0F,D0          If more than $F
0081DA 6E10    }0081EC           BGT.S    PARAM5           then exit to error on not-hex
0081DC D200           PARAM3 ADD.B    D0,D1            Add latest nybble to total in D1
0081DE 60D8    }0081B8           BRA      PARAM1           Repeat until delimiter found
0081E0 2D48 0040      PARAM4 MOVE.L   A0,BUFFPT(A6)    Save pointer in memory
0081E4 2D41 0044                 MOVE.L   D1,PARAMTR(A6)   Save parameter in memory
0081E8 2001                      MOVE.L   D1,D0            Put parameter in D0 for return
```

```
0081EA 6004      >0081F0          BRA.S    PARAM6         Return without error
0081EC 0007 0002 PARAM5  OR.B     #2,D7          Set error flag before return
0081F0 221F      PARAM6  MOVE.L   (A7)+,D1       Restore working register
0081F2 4E75              RTS                     Return with error
                 *
                 *********************************************************************
                 *
                 *  Output routines
                 *  OUT1X  = print one   hexadecimal character
                 *  OUT2X  = print two   hexadecimal characters
                 *  OUT4X  = print four  hexadecimal characters
                 *  OUT8X  = print eight hexadecimal characters
                 *  In each case, the data to be printed is in D0
                 *
0081F4 1F00      OUT1X   MOVE.B   D0,-(A7)       Save D0
0081F6 0200 000F         AND.B    #$0F,D0        Mask off MS nybble
0081FA 0600 0030         ADD.B    #$30,D0        Convert to ASCII
0081FE 0C00 0039         CMP.B    #$39,D0        ASCII = HEX + $30
008202 6302      >008206         BLS.S    OUT1X1         If ASCII <= $39 then print and exit
008204 5E00              ADD.B    #$07,D0        Else ASCII := HEX + 7
008206 6100 0388>008590 OUT1X1 BSR   PUTCHAR        Print the character
00820A 101F              MOVE.B   (A7)+,D0       Restore D0
00820C 4E75              RTS
00820E E818      OUT2X   ROR.B    #4,D0          Get MS nybble in LS position
008210 61E2      >0081F4         BSR      OUT1X          Print MS nybble
008212 E918              ROL.B    #4,D0          Restore LS nybble
008214 60DE      >0081F4         BRA      OUT1X          Print LS nybble and return
                 *
008216 E058      OUT4X   ROR.W    #8,D0          Get MS byte in LS position
008218 61F4      >00820E         BSR      OUT2X          Print MS byte
00821A E158              ROL.W    #8,D0          Restore LS byte
00821C 60F0      >00820E         BRA      OUT2X          Print LS byte and return
                 *
00821E 4840      OUT8X   SWAP     D0             Get MS word in LS position
008220 61F4      >008216         BSR      OUT4X          Print MS word
008222 4840              SWAP     D0             Restore LS word
008224 60F0      >008216         BRA      OUT4X          Print LS word and return
                 *
                 *********************************************************************
                 *
                 * JUMP causes execution to begin at the address in the line buffer
                 *
008226 6188      >0081B0 JUMP BSR      PARAM          Get address from buffer
008228 4A07              TST.B    D7             Test for input error
00822A 6608      >008234         BNE.S    JUMP1          If error flag not zero then exit
```

```
00822C 4A80                   TST.L    D0              Else test for missing address
00822E 6704      >008234      BEQ.S    JUMP1           field. If no address then exit
008230 2040                   MOVE.L   D0,A0           Put jump address in A0 and call the
008232 4ED0                   JMP      (A0)            subroutine. User to supply RTS!!
008234 49FA 08A1>008AD7 JUMP1 LEA.L    ERMES1(PC),A4   Here for error - display error
008238 6000 FE42>00807C       BRA      PSTRING         message and return
                       X
              XXXXXXXXXXXXXXXXXXXXXXXXXXXXXXXXXXXXXXXXXXXXXXXXXXXXXXXXXXXXXXXXXXXXXXXXXXXXXXX
                       X
                       X  Display the contents of a memory location and modify it
                       X
00823C 6100 FF72>0081B0 MEMORY BSR    PARAM           Get start address from line buffer
008240 4A07                   TST.B    D7              Test for input error
008242 6634      >008278      BNE.S    MEM3            If error then exit
008244 2640                   MOVE.L   D0,A3           A3 points to location to be opened
008246 6100 FE24>00806C MEM1  BSR      NEWLINE
00824A 612E      >00827A      BSR.S    ADR_DAT         Print current address and contents
00824C 6140      >00828E      BSR.S    PSPACE          update pointer, A3, and O/P space
00824E 6100 030E>00855E       BSR      GETCHAR         Input char to decide next action
008252 0C00 000D             CMP.B    #CR,D0          If carriage return then exit
008256 6720      >008278      BEQ.S    MEM3            Exit
008258 0C00 002D             CMP.B    #'-',D0         If "-" then move back
00825C 6606      >008264      BNE.S    MEM2            Else skip wind-back procedure
00825E 47EB FFFC             LEA.L    -4(A3),A3       Move pointer back 2+2
008262 60E2      >008246      BRA      MEM1            Repeat until carriage return
008264 0C00 0020       MEM2  CMP.B    #SPACE,D0       Test for space (= new entry)
008268 66DC      >008246      BNE.S    MEM1            If not space then repeat
00826A 6100 FF38>0081A4       BSR      WORD            Else get new word to store
00826E 4A07                   TST.B    D7              Test for input error
008270 6606      >008278      BNE.S    MEM3            If error then exit
008272 3740 FFFE             MOVE.W   D0,-2(A3)       Store new word
008276 60CE      >008246      BRA      MEM1            Repeat until carriage return
008278 4E75            MEM3  RTS
                       X
00827A 2F00            ADR_DAT MOVE.L D0,-(A7)        Print the contents of A3 and the
00827C 200B                   MOVE.L   A3,D0           word pointed at by A3.
00827E 619E      >00821E      BSR      OUT8X           and print current address
008280 610C      >00828E      BSR.S    PSPACE          Insert delimiter
008282 3013                   MOVE.W   (A3),D0         Get data at this address in D0
008284 6190      >008216      BSR      OUT4X           and print it
008286 47EB 0002             LEA.L    2(A3),A3        Point to next address to display
00828A 201F                   MOVE.L   (A7)+,D0        Restore D0
00828C 4E75                   RTS
                       X
00828E 1F00            PSPACE MOVE.B  D0,-(A7)        Print a single space
```

```
008290 103C 0020            MOVE.B    #SPACE,D0
008294 6100 02FA)008590     BSR       PUTCHAR
008298 101F                 MOVE.B    (A7)+,D0
00829A 4E75                 RTS
                      X
                      XXXXXXXXXXXXXXXXXXXXXXXXXXXXXXXXXXXXXXXXXXXXXXXXXXXXXXXXXXXXXXXXXXXXX
                      X
                      X  LOAD  Loads data formatted in hexadecimal "S" format from Port 2
                      X         NOTE - I/O is automatically redirected to the aux port for
                      X         loader functions. S1 or S2 records accepted
                      X
00829C 2F2E 0052    LOAD      MOVE.L    CN_OVEC(A6),-(A7) Save current output device name
0082A0 2F2E 004E              MOVE.L    CN_IVEC(A6),-(A7) Save current input device name
0082A4 2D7C 0000 8C22        MOVE.L    #DCB4,CN_OVEC(A6) Set up aux ACIA as output
0082AC 2D7C 0000 8C10        MOVE.L    #DCB3,CN_IVEC(A6) Set up aux ACIA as input
0082B4 522E 0048             ADD.B     #1,ECHO(A6)       Turn off character echo
0082B8 6100 FDB2)00806C      BSR       NEWLINE           Send newline to host
0082BC 6100 015A)008418      BSR       DELAY             Wait for host to "settle"
0082C0 6100 0156)008418      BSR       DELAY
0082C4 286E 0040             MOVE.L    BUFFPT(A6),A4     Any string in the line buffer is
0082C8 101C         LOAD1    MOVE.B    (A4)+,D0          transmitted to the host computer
0082CA 6100 02C4)008590      BSR       PUTCHAR           before the loading begins
0082CE 0C00 000D             CMP.B     #CR,D0            Read from the buffer until EOL
0082D2 66F4     )0082C8      BNE       LOAD1
0082D4 6100 FD96)00806C      BSR       NEWLINE           Send newline before loading
0082D8 6100 0284)00855E LOAD2 BSR      GETCHAR           Records from the host must begin
0082DC 0C00 0053             CMP.B     #'S',D0           with S1/S2 (data) or S9/S8 (term)
0082E0 66F6     )0082D8      BNE.S     LOAD2             Repeat GETCHAR until char = "S"
0082E2 6100 027A)00855E      BSR       GETCHAR           Get character after "S"
0082E6 0C00 0039             CMP.B     #'9',D0           Test for the two terminators S9/S8
0082EA 6706     )0082F2      BEQ.S     LOAD3             If S9 record then exit else test
0082EC 0C00 0038             CMP.B     #'8',D0           for S8 terminator. Fall through to
0082F0 662A     )00831C      BNE.S     LOAD6             exit on S8 else continue search
       000082F2 LOAD3        EQU       X                 Exit point from LOAD
0082F2 2D5F 004E             MOVE.L    (A7)+,CN_IVEC(A6) Clean up by restoring input device
0082F6 2D5F 0052             MOVE.L    (A7)+,CN_OVEC(A6) and output device name
0082FA 422E 0048             CLR.B     ECHO(A6)          Restore input character echo
0082FE 0807 0000             BTST.B    #0,D7             Test for input errors
008302 6708     )00830C      BEQ.S     LOAD4             If no I/P error then look at checksum
008304 49FA 07D1)008AD7      LEA.L     ERMES1(PC),A4     Else point to error message
008308 6100 FD72)00807C      BSR       PSTRING           Print it
00830C 0807 0003   LOAD4     BTST.B    #3,D7             Test for checksum error
008310 6708     )00831A      BEQ.S     LOAD5             If clear then exit
008312 49FA 07F3)008B07      LEA.L     ERMES3(PC),A4     Else point to error message
008316 6100 FD64)00807C      BSR       PSTRING           Print it and return
```

```
00831A 4E75           LOAD5   RTS
                x
00831C 0C00 0031      LOAD6   CMP.B   #'1',D0         Test for S1 record
008320 671E    )008340        BEQ.S   LOAD6A          If S1 record then read it
008322 0C00 0032              CMP.B   #'2',D0         Else test for S2 record
008326 66B0    )0082D8        BNE.S   LOAD2           Repeat until valid header found
008328 4203                   CLR.B   D3              Read the S2 byte count and address,
00832A 613C    )008368        BSR.S   LOAD8           clear the checksum
00832C 5900                   SUB.B   #4,D0           Calculate size of data field
00832E 1400                   MOVE.B  D0,D2           D2 contains data bytes to read
008330 4280                   CLR.L   D0              Clear address accumulator
008332 6134    )008368        BSR.S   LOAD8           Read most sig byte of address
008334 E180                   ASL.L   #8,D0           Move it one byte left
008336 6130    )008368        BSR.S   LOAD8           Read the middle byte of address
008338 E180                   ASL.L   #8,D0           Move it one byte left
00833A 612C    )008368        BSR.S   LOAD8           Read least sig byte of address
00833C 2440                   MOVE.L  D0,A2           A2 points to destination of record
00833E 6012    )008352        BRA.S   LOAD7           Skip past S1 header loader
008340 4203          LOAD6A   CLR.B   D3              S1 record found - clear checksum
008342 6124    )008368        BSR.S   LOAD8           Get byte and update checksum
008344 5700                   SUB.B   #3,D0           Subtract 3 from record length
008346 1400                   MOVE.B  D0,D2           Save byte count in D2
008348 4280                   CLR.L   D0              Clear address accumulator
00834A 611C    )008368        BSR.S   LOAD8           Get MS byte of load address
00834C E180                   ASL.L   #8,D0           Move it to MS position
00834E 6118    )008368        BSR.S   LOAD8           Get LS byte in D2
008350 2440                   MOVE.L  D0,A2           A2 points to destination of data
008352 6114    )008368 LOAD7  BSR.S   LOAD8           Get byte of data for loading
008354 14C0                   MOVE.B  D0,(A2)+        Store it
008356 5302                   SUB.B   #1,D2           Decrement byte counter
008358 66F8    )008352        BNE     LOAD7           Repeat until count = 0
00835A 610C    )008368        BSR.S   LOAD8           Read checksum
00835C 5203                   ADD.B   #1,D3           Add 1 to total checksum
00835E 6700 FF78)0082D8       BEQ     LOAD2           If zero then start next record
008362 0007 0008              OR.B    #%00001000,D7   Else set checksum error bit,
008366 608A    )0082F2        BRA     LOAD3           restore I/O devices and return
                x
008368 6100 FE2A)008194 LOAD8 BSR     BYTE            Get a byte
00836C D600                   ADD.B   D0,D3           Update checksum
00836E 4E75                   RTS                     and return
                x
                xxxxxxxxxxxxxxxxxxxxxxxxxxxxxxxxxxxxxxxxxxxxxxxxxxxxxxxxxxxxxxxxxxxxxxxxxxxxxxxxxxxxxx
                x
                x DUMP   Transmit S1 formatted records to host computer
                x        A3 = Starting address of data block
```

```
                    x           A2 = End address of data block
                    x           D1 = Checksum, D2 = current record length
                    x
008370 6100 0096>008408 DUMP   BSR      RANGE            Get start and end address
008374 4A07                    TST.B    D7               Test for input error
008376 6708     >008380        BEQ.S    DUMP1            If no error then continue
008378 49FA 075D>008AD7        LEA.L    ERMES1(PC),A4    Else point to error message,
00837C 6000 FCFE>00807C        BRA      PSTRING          print it and return
008380 B08B            DUMP1   CMP.L    A3,D0            Compare start and end addresses
008382 6A08     >00838C        BPL.S    DUMP2            If positive then start < end
008384 49FA 07D1>008B57        LEA.L    ERMES7(PC),A4    Else print error message
008388 6000 FCF2>00807C        BRA      PSTRING          and return
00838C 2F2E 0052     DUMP2     MOVE.L   CN_OVEC(A6),-(A7) Save name of current output device
008390 2D7C 0000 8C22          MOVE.L   #DCB4,CN_OVEC(A6) Set up Port 2 as output device
008398 6100 FCD2>00806C        BSR      NEWLINE          Send newline to host and wait
00839C 617A     >008418        BSR.S    DELAY
00839E 286E 0040               MOVE.L   BUFFPT(A6),A4    Before dumping, send any string
0083A2 101C            DUMP3   MOVE.B   (A4)+,D0         in the input buffer to the host
0083A4 6100 01EA>008590        BSR      PUTCHAR          Repeat
0083A8 0C00 000D               CMP.B    #CR,D0           Transmit char from buffer to host
0083AC 66F4     >0083A2        BNE      DUMP3            Until char = C/R
0083AE 6100 FCBC>00806C        BSR      NEWLINE
0083B2 6164     >008418        BSR.S    DELAY            Allow time for host to settle
0083B4 528A                    ADD.L    #1,A2            A2 contains length of record + 1
0083B6 240A            DUMP4   MOVE.L   A2,D2            D2 points to end address
0083B8 948B                    SUB.L    A3,D2            D2 contains bytes left to print
0083BA 0C82 0000 0011          CMP.L    #17,D2           If this is not a full record of 16
0083C0 6502     >0083C4        BCS.S    DUMP5            then load D2 with record size
0083C2 7410                    MOVE.L   #16,D2           Else preset byte count to 16
0083C4 49FA 064C>008A12 DUMP5  LEA.L    HEADER(PC),A4    Point to record header
0083C8 6100 FCB2>00807C        BSR      PSTRING          Print header
0083CC 4201                    CLR.B    D1               Clear checksum
0083CE 1002                    MOVE.B   D2,D0            Move record length to output register
0083D0 5600                    ADD.B    #3,D0            Length includes address + count
0083D2 612E     >008402        BSR.S    DUMP7            Print number of bytes in record
0083D4 200B                    MOVE.L   A3,D0            Get start address to be printed
0083D6 E158                    ROL.W    #8,D0            Get MS byte in LS position
0083D8 6128     >008402        BSR.S    DUMP7            Print MS byte of address
0083DA E058                    ROR.W    #8,D0            Restore LS byte
0083DC 6124     >008402        BSR.S    DUMP7            Print LS byte of address
0083DE 101B            DUMP6   MOVE.B   (A3)+,D0         Get data byte to be printed
0083E0 6120     >008402        BSR.S    DUMP7            Print it
0083E2 5302                    SUB.B    #1,D2            Decrement byte count
0083E4 66F8     >0083DE        BNE      DUMP6            Repeat until all this record printed
0083E6 4601                    NOT.B    D1               Complement checksum
```

```
0083E8 1001                      MOVE.B    D1,D0                   Move to output register
0083EA 6116      )008402         BSR.S     DUMP7                   Print checksum
0083EC 6100 FC7E)00806C          BSR       NEWLINE
0083F0 B7CA                      CMP.L     A2,A3                   Have all records been printed?
0083F2 66C2      )0083B6         BNE       DUMP4                   Repeat until all done
0083F4 49FA 0622)008A18          LEA.L     TAIL(PC),A4             Point to message tail (S9 record)
0083F8 6100 FC82)00807C          BSR       PSTRING                Print it
0083FC 2D5F 0052                 MOVE.L    (A7)+,CN_OVEC(A6)       Restore name of output device
008400 4E75                      RTS                                          and return
                        X
008402 D200             DUMP7    ADD.B     D0,D1                   Update checksum, transmit byte
008404 6000 FE08)00820E          BRA       OUT2X                   to host and return
                        X
       00008408         RANGE    EQU       X                      Get the range of addresses to be
008408 4207                      CLR.B     D7                      transmitted from the buffer
00840A 6100 FDA4)0081B0          BSR       PARAM                   Get starting address
00840E 2640                      MOVE.L    D0,A3                   Set up start address in A3
008410 6100 FD9E)0081B0          BSR       PARAM                   Get end address
008414 2440                      MOVE.L    D0,A2                   Set up end address in A2
008416 4E75                      RTS
                        X
       00008418         DELAY    EQU       X                      Provide a time delay for the host
008418 48E7 8008                 MOVEM.L   D0/A4,-(A7)            to settle. Save working registers
00841C 203C 0000 4000            MOVE.L    #$4000,D0              Set up delay constant
008422 5380             DELAY1   SUB.L     #1,D0                   Count down          (8 clk cycles)
008424 66FC      )008422         BNE       DELAY1                 Repeat until zero  (10 clk cycles)
008426 4CDF 1001                 MOVEM.L   (A7)+,D0/A4            Restore working registers
00842A 4E75                      RTS
                        X
        XXXXXXXXXXXXXXXXXXXXXXXXXXXXXXXXXXXXXXXXXXXXXXXXXXXXXXXXXXXXXXXXXXXXXXXXXXXXXXXXXXXXXXX
                        X
        X  TM  Enter transparant mode (All communication to go from terminal to
        X  the host processor until escape sequence entered). End sequence
        X  = ESC, E. A newline is sent to the host to "clear it down".
                        X
00842C 13FC 0055 0001   TM       MOVE.B    #$55,ACIA_1            Force RTSX high to re-route data
008434 522E 0048                 ADD.B     #1,ECHO(A6)            Turn off character echo
008438 6100 0124)00855E TM1      BSR       GETCHAR                Get character
00843C 0C00 001B                 CMP.B     #ESC,D0                Test for end of TM mode
008440 66F6      )008438         BNE       TM1                   Repeat until first escape character
008442 6100 011A)00855E          BSR       GETCHAR                Get second character
008446 0C00 0045                 CMP.B     #'E',D0                If second char = E then exit TM
00844A 66EC      )008438         BNE       TM1                   Else continue
00844C 2F2E 0052                 MOVE.L    CN_OVEC(A6),-(A7)     Save output port device name
008450 2D7C 0000 8C22            MOVE.L    #DCB4,CN_OVEC(A6)     Get name of host port (aux port)
```

```
008458 6100 FC12>00806C      BSR      NEWLINE         Send newline to host to clear it
00845C 2D5F 0052             MOVE.L   (A7)+,CN_OVEC(A6) Restore output device port name
008460 422E 0048             CLR.B    ECHO(A6)        Restore echo mode
008464 13FC 0015 0001        MOVE.B   #$15,ACIA_1     Restore normal ACIA mode (RTS* low)
00846C 4E75                  RTS
                        X
          XXXXXXXXXXXXXXXXXXXXXXXXXXXXXXXXXXXXXXXXXXXXXXXXXXXXXXXXXXXXXXXXXXXXXXXXXXXXXX
                        X
                        X  This routine sets up the system DCBs in RAM using the information
                        X  stored in ROM at address DCB_LST. This is called at initialization.
                        X  CN_IVEC contains the name "DCB1" and IO_VEC the name "DCB2"
                        X
00846E 48E7 F0F0   SET_DCB  MOVEM.L  A0-A3/D0-D3,-(A7) Save all working registers
008472 41EE 00D0             LEA.L    FIRST(A6),A0    Pointer to first DCB destination in RAM
008476 43FA 0774>008BEC      LEA.L    DCB_LST(PC),A1  A1 points to DCB info block in ROM
00847A 303C 0005             MOVE.W   #5,D0           6 DCBs to set up
00847E 323C 000F   ST_DCB1  MOVE.W   #15,D1          16 bytes to move per DCB header
008482 10D9        ST_DCB2  MOVE.B   (A1)+,(A0)+     Move the 16 bytes of a DCB header
008484 51C9 FFFC>008482      DBRA     D1,ST_DCB2      from ROM to RAM
008488 3619                  MOVE.W   (A1)+,D3        Get size of parameter block (bytes)
00848A 3083                  MOVE.W   D3,(A0)         Store size in DCB in RAM
00848C 41F0 3002             LEA.L    2(A0,D3.W),A0   A0 points to tail of DCB in RAM
008490 47E8 0004             LEA.L    4(A0),A3        A3 contains address of next DCB in RAM
008494 208B                  MOVE.L   A3,(A0)         Store pointer to next DCB in this DCB
008496 41D3                  LEA.L    (A3),A0         A0 now points at next DCB in RAM
008498 51C8 FFE4>00847E      DBRA     D0,ST_DCB1      Repeat until all DCBs set up
00849C 47EB FFFC             LEA.L    -4(A3),A3       Adjust A3 to point to last DCB pointer
0084A0 4293                  CLR.L    (A3)            and force last pointer to zero
0084A2 2D7C 0000 8BEC        MOVE.L   #DCB1,CN_IVEC(A6) Set up vector to console input DCB
0084AA 2D7C 0000 8BFE        MOVE.L   #DCB2,CN_OVEC(A6) Set up vector to console output DCB
0084B2 4CDF 0F0F             MOVEM.L  (A7)+,A0-A3/D0-D3 Restore registers
0084B6 4E75                  RTS
                        X
          XXXXXXXXXXXXXXXXXXXXXXXXXXXXXXXXXXXXXXXXXXXXXXXXXXXXXXXXXXXXXXXXXXXXXXXXXXXXXX
                        X
                        X  IO_REQ handles all input/output transactions. A0 points to DCB on
                        X  entry. IO_REQ calls the device driver whose address is in the DCB.
                        X
0084B8 48E7 00C0   IO_REQ   MOVEM.L  A0-A1,-(A7)     Save working registers
0084BC 43E8 0008             LEA.L    8(A0),A1        A1 points to device handler field in DCB
0084C0 2251                  MOVE.L   (A1),A1         A1 contains device handler address
0084C2 4E91                  JSR      (A1)            Call device handler
0084C4 4CDF 0300             MOVEM.L  (A7)+,A0-A1     Restore working registers
0084C8 4E75                  RTS
                        X
```

```
                 XXXXXXXXXXXXXXXXXXXXXXXXXXXXXXXXXXXXXXXXXXXXXXXXXXXXXXXXXXXXXXXXXXXXXXXXXXXXX
                 X
                 X   CON_IN handles input from the console device
                 X   This is the device driver used by DCB1. Exit with input in D0
                 X
0084CA 48E7 4040      CON_IN   MOVEM.L  D1/A1,-(A7)        Save working registers
0084CE 43E8 000C               LEA.L    12(A0),A1          Get pointer to ACIA from DCB
0084D2 2251                    MOVE.L   (A1),A1            Get address of ACIA in A1
0084D4 4228 0013               CLR.B    19(A0)             Clear logical error in DCB
0084D8 1211           CON_I1   MOVE.B   (A1),D1            Read ACIA status
0084DA 0801 0000               BTST.B   #0,D1              Test RDRF
0084DE 67F8    >0084D8         BEQ      CON_I1             Repeat until RDRF true
0084E0 1141 0012               MOVE.B   D1,18(A0)          Store physical status in DCB
0084E4 0201 00F4               AND.B    #%011110100,D1     Mask to input error bits
0084E8 6706    >0084F0         BEQ.S    CON_I2             If no error then skip update
0084EA 117C 0001 0013          MOVE.B   #1,19(A0)          Else update logical error
0084F0 1029 0002     CON_I2    MOVE.B   2(A1),D0           Read input from ACIA
0084F4 4CDF 0202               MOVEM.L  (A7)+,A1/D1        Restore working registers
0084F8 4E75                    RTS
                 X
                 XXXXXXXXXXXXXXXXXXXXXXXXXXXXXXXXXXXXXXXXXXXXXXXXXXXXXXXXXXXXXXXXXXXXXXXXXXXXX
                 X
                 X   This is the device driver used by DCB2. Output in D0
                 X   The output can be halted or suspended
                 X
0084FA 48E7 6040     CON_OUT   MOVEM.L  A1/D1-D2,-(A7)     Save working registers
0084FE 43E8 000C               LEA.L    12(A0),A1          Get pointer to ACIA from DCB
008502 2251                    MOVE.L   (A1),A1            Get address of ACIA in A1
008504 4228 0013               CLR.B    19(A0)             Clear logical error in DCB
008508 1211          CON_OT1   MOVE.B   (A1),D1            Read ACIA status
00850A 0801 0000               BTST.B   #0,D1              Test RDRF bit (any input?)
00850E 6716    >008526         BEQ.S    CON_OT3            If no input then test output status
008510 1429 0002               MOVE.B   2(A1),D2           Else read the input
008514 0202 005F               AND.B    #%01011111,D2      Strip parity and bit 5
008518 0C02 0057               CMP.B    #WAIT,D2           and test for a wait condition
00851C 6608    >008526         BNE.S    CON_OT3            If not wait then ignore and test O/P
00851E 1411          CON_OT2   MOVE.B   (A1),D2            Else read ACIA status register
008520 0802 0000               BTST.B   #0,D2              and poll ACIA until next char received
008524 67F8    >00851E         BEQ      CON_OT2
008526 0801 0001     CON_OT3   BTST.B   #1,D1              Repeat
00852A 67DC    >008508         BEQ      CON_OT1            until ACIA Tx ready
00852C 1141 0012               MOVE.B   D1,18(A0)          Store status in DCB physical error
008530 1340 0002               MOVE.B   D0,2(A1)           Transmit output
008534 4CDF 0206               MOVEM.L  (A7)+,A1/D1-D2     Restore working registers
008538 4E75                    RTS
```

```
                    x
                    xxxxxxxxxxxxxxxxxxxxxxxxxxxxxxxxxxxxxxxxxxxxxxxxxxxxxxxxxxxxxxxxxxxxxx
                    x
                    x   AUX_IN and AUX_OUT are simplified versions of CON_IN and
                    x   CON_OUT for use with the port to the host processor
                    x
00853A 43E8 000C    AUX_IN  LEA.L   12(A0),A1        Get pointer to aux ACIA from DCB
00853E 2251                 MOVE.L  (A1),A1          Get address of aux ACIA
008540 0811 0000    AUX_IN1 BTST.B  #0,(A1)          Test for data ready
008544 67FA   )008540       BEQ     AUX_IN1          Repeat until ready
008546 1029 0002            MOVE.B  2(A1),D0         Read input
00854A 4E75                 RTS
                    x
00854C 43E8 000C    AUX_OUT LEA.L   12(A0),A1        Get pointer to aux ACIA from DCB
008550 2251                 MOVE.L  (A1),A1          Get address of aux ACIA
008552 0811 0001    AUX_OT1 BTST.B  #1,(A1)          Test for ready to transmit
008556 67FA   )008552       BEQ     AUX_OT1          Repeat until transmitter ready
008558 1340 0002            MOVE.B  D0,2(A1)         Transmit data
00855C 4E75                 RTS
                    x
                    xxxxxxxxxxxxxxxxxxxxxxxxxxxxxxxxxxxxxxxxxxxxxxxxxxxxxxxxxxxxxxxxxxxxxx
                    x
                    x   GETCHAR gets a character from the console device
                    x   This is the main input routine and uses the device whose name
                    x   is stored in CN_IVEC. Changing this name redirects input.
                    x
00855E 2F08         GETCHAR MOVE.L  A0,-(A7)         Save working register
008560 206E 004E            MOVE.L  CN_IVEC(A6),A0   A0 points to name of console DCB
008564 6154   )0085BA       BSR.S   IO_OPEN          Open console (get DCB address in A0)
008566 0807 0003            BTST.B  #3,D7            D7(3) set if open error
00856A 6620   )00858C       BNE.S   GETCH3           If error then exit now
00856C 6100 FF4A)0084B8      BSR     IO_REQ           Else execute I/O transaction
008570 0200 007F            AND.B   #$7F,D0          Strip msb of input
008574 4A2E 0049            TST.B   U_CASE(A6)       Test for upper -> lower case conversion
008578 660A   )008584       BNE.S   GETCH2           If flag not zero do not convert case
00857A 0800 0006            BTST.B  #6,D0            Test input for lower case
00857E 6704   )008584       BEQ.S   GETCH2           If upper case then skip conversion
008580 0200 00DF            AND.B   #%11011111,D0    Else clear bit 5 for upper case conv
008584 4A2E 0048    GETCH2  TST.B   ECHO(A6)         Do we need to echo the input?
008588 6602   )00858C       BNE.S   GETCH3           If ECHO not zero then no echo
00858A 6104   )008590       BSR.S   PUTCHAR          Else echo the input
00858C 205F         GETCH3  MOVE.L  (A7)+,A0         Restore working register
00858E 4E75                 RTS                      and return
                    x
                    xxxxxxxxxxxxxxxxxxxxxxxxxxxxxxxxxxxxxxxxxxxxxxxxxxxxxxxxxxxxxxxxxxxxxx
```

```
                       X
                       X  PUTCHAR sends a character to the console device
                       X  The name of the output device is in CN_OVEC.
                       X
008590 2F08    PUTCHAR MOVE.L   A0,-(A7)      Save working register
008592 206E 0052       MOVE.L   CN_OVEC(A6),A0 A0 points to name of console output
008596 6122    >0085BA BSR.S    IO_OPEN       Open console (Get address of DCB)
008598 6100 FF1E>0084B8 BSR     IO_REQ        Perform output with DCB pointed at by A0
00859C 205F            MOVE.L   (A7)+,A0      Restore working register
00859E 4E75            RTS
                       X
                       XXXXXXXXXXXXXXXXXXXXXXXXXXXXXXXXXXXXXXXXXXXXXXXXXXXXXXXXXXXXXXXXXXXXXX
                       X
                       X  BUFF_IN and BUFF_OUT are two rudimentary input and output routines
                       X  which input data from and output data to a buffer in RAM. These are
                       X  used by DCB5 and DCB6, respectively.
                       X
0085A0 43E8 000C BUFF_IN LEA.L  12(A0),A1     A1 points to I/P buffer
0085A4 2451            MOVE.L   (A1),A2       A2 gets I/P pointer from buffer
0085A6 1022            MOVE.B   -(A2),D0      Read char from buffer and adjust A2
0085A8 228A            MOVE.L   A2,(A1)       Restore pointer in buffer
0085AA 4E75            RTS
                       X
0085AC 43E8 000C BUFF_OT LEA.L  12(A0),A1     A1 points to O/P buffer
0085B0 2469 0004       MOVE.L   4(A1),A2      A2 gets O/P pointer from buffer
0085B4 14C0            MOVE.B   D0,(A2)+      Store char in buffer and adjust A2
0085B6 228A            MOVE.L   A2,(A1)       Restore pointer in buffer
0085B8 4E75            RTS
                       X
                       XXXXXXXXXXXXXXXXXXXXXXXXXXXXXXXXXXXXXXXXXXXXXXXXXXXXXXXXXXXXXXXXXXXXXX
                       X
                       X  Open - opens a DCB for input or output. IO_OPEN converts the
                       X  name pointed at by A0 into the address of the DCB pointed at
                       X  by A0. Bit 3 of D7 is set to zero if DCB not found
                       X
0085BA 48E7 F870 IO_OPEN MOVEM.L A1-A3/D0-D4,-(A7) Save working registers
0085BE 43EE 00D0       LEA.L    FIRST(A6),A1  A1 points to first DCB in chain in RAM
0085C2 45D1    OPEN1   LEA.L    (A1),A2       A2 = temp copy of pointer to DCB
0085C4 47D0            LEA.L    (A0),A3       A3 = temp copy of pointer to DCB name
0085C6 303C 0007       MOVE.W   #7,D0         Up to 8 chars of DCB name to match
0085CA 181A    OPEN2   MOVE.B   (A2)+,D4      Compare DCB name with string
0085CC B81B            CMP.B    (A3)+,D4
0085CE 6608    >0085D8 BNE.S    OPEN3         If no match try next DCB
0085D0 51C8 FFF8>0085CA DBRA    D0,OPEN2      Else repeat until all chars matched
0085D4 41D1            LEA.L    (A1),A0       Success - move this DCB address to A0
```

```
0085D6 6016    >0085EE         BRA.S   OPEN4           and return
       000085D8 OPEN3   EQU     X               Fail - calculate address of next DCB
0085D8 3229 0010        MOVE.W  16(A1),D1       Get parameter block size of DCB
0085DC 43F1 1012        LEA.L   18(A1,D1.W),A1  A1 points to pointer to next DCB
0085E0 2251             MOVE.L  (A1),A1         A1 now points to next DCB
0085E2 B3FC 0000 0000   CMP.L   #0,A1           Test for end of DCB chain
0085E8 66D8    >0085C2  BNE     OPEN1           If not end of chain then try next DCB
0085EA 0007 0008        OR.B    #8,D7           Else set error flag and return
0085EE 4CDF 0E1F OPEN4  MOVEM.L (A7)+,A1-A3/D0-D4 Restore working registers
0085F2 4E75             RTS
                 X
                 XXXXXXXXXXXXXXXXXXXXXXXXXXXXXXXXXXXXXXXXXXXXXXXXXXXXXXXXXXXXXXXXXXXX
                 X
                 X  Exception vector table initialization routine
                 X  All vectors not setup are loaded with uninitialized routine vector
                 X
0085F4 41F8 0008 X_SET  LEA.L   X_BASE,A0       Point to base of exception table
0085F8 303C 00FD        MOVE.W  #253,D0         Number of vectors - 3
0085FC 20FC 0000 89E4 X_SET1 MOVE.L #X_UN,(A0)+  Store uninitialized exception vector
008602 51C8 FFF8>0085FC  DBRA  D0,X_SET1        Repeat until all entries preset
008606 91C8             SUB.L   A0,A0           Clear A0 (points to vector table)
008608 217C 0000 87B4   MOVE.L  #BUS_ER,8(A0)   Setup bus error vector
008610 217C 0000 87C2   MOVE.L  #ADD_ER,12(A0)  Setup address error vector
008618 217C 0000 879E   MOVE.L  #IL_ER,16(A0)   Setup illegal instruction error vect
008620 217C 0000 8898   MOVE.L  #TRACE,36(A0)   Setup trace exception vector
008628 217C 0000 8652   MOVE.L  #TRAP_0,128(A0) Setup TRAP #0 exception vector
008630 217C 0000 87D0   MOVE.L  #BRKPT,184(A0)  Setup TRAP #14 vector = breakpoint
008638 217C 0000 8040   MOVE.L  #WARM,188(A0)   Setup TRAP #15 exception vector
008640 303C 0007        MOVE.W  #7,D0           Now clear the breakpoint table
008644 41EE 00A0        LEA.L   BP_TAB(A6),A0   Point to table
008648 4298     X_SET2  CLR.L   (A0)+           Clear an address entry
00864A 4258             CLR.W   (A0)+           Clear the corresponding data
00864C 51C8 FFFA>008648 DBRA   D0,X_SET2        Repeat until all 8 cleared
008650 4E75             RTS
                 X
                 XXXXXXXXXXXXXXXXXXXXXXXXXXXXXXXXXXXXXXXXXXXXXXXXXXXXXXXXXXXXXXXXXXXX
                 X
       00008652 TRAP_0  EQU     X               User links to  TS2BUG via TRAP #0
008652 0C01 0000        CMP.B   #0,D1           D1 = 0 = Get character
008656 6606    >00865E  BNE.S   TRAP1
008658 6100 FF04>00855E BSR     GETCHAR
00865C 4E73             RTE
00865E 0C01 0001 TRAP1  CMP.B   #1,D1           D1 = 1 = Print character
008662 6606    >00866A  BNE.S   TRAP2
008664 6100 FF2A>008590 BSR     PUTCHAR
```

```
008668 4E73                          RTE
00866A 0C01 0002        TRAP2        CMP.B     #2,D1         D1 = 2 = Newline
00866E 6606      )008676             BNE.S     TRAP3
008670 6100 F9FA)00806C              BSR       NEWLINE
008674 4E73                          RTE
008676 0C01 0003        TRAP3        CMP.B     #3,D1         D1 = 3 = Get parameter from buffer
00867A 6606      )008682             BNE.S     TRAP4
00867C 6100 FB32)0081B0              BSR       PARAM
008680 4E73                          RTE
008682 0C01 0004        TRAP4        CMP.B     #4,D1         D1 = 4 = Print string pointed at by A4
008686 6606      )00868E             BNE.S     TRAP5
008688 6100 F9F2)00807C              BSR       PSTRING
00868C 4E73                          RTE
00868E 0C01 0005        TRAP5        CMP.B     #5,D1         D1 = 5 = Get a hex character
008692 6606      )00869A             BNE.S     TRAP6
008694 6100 FAE0)008176              BSR       HEX
008698 4E73                          RTE
00869A 0C01 0006        TRAP6        CMP.B     #6,D1         D1 = 6 = Get a hex byte
00869E 6606      )0086A6             BNE.S     TRAP7
0086A0 6100 FAF2)008194              BSR       BYTE
0086A4 4E73                          RTE
0086A6 0C01 0007        TRAP7        CMP.B     #7,D1         D1 = 7 = Get a word
0086AA 6606      )0086B2             BNE.S     TRAP8
0086AC 6100 FAF6)0081A4              BSR       WORD
0086B0 4E73                          RTE
0086B2 0C01 0008        TRAP8        CMP.B     #8,D1         D1 = 8 = Get a longword
0086B6 6606      )0086BE             BNE.S     TRAP9
0086B8 6100 FAF0)0081AA              BSR       LONGWD
0086BC 4E73                          RTE
0086BE 0C01 0009        TRAP9        CMP.B     #9,D1         D1 = 9 = Output hex byte
0086C2 6606      )0086CA             BNE.S     TRAP10
0086C4 6100 FB48)00820E              BSR       OUT2X
0086C8 4E73                          RTE
0086CA 0C01 000A        TRAP10       CMP.B     #10,D1        D1 = 10 = Output hex word
0086CE 6606      )0086D6             BNE.S     TRAP11
0086D0 6100 FB44)008216              BSR       OUT4X
0086D4 4E73                          RTE
0086D6 0C01 000B        TRAP11       CMP.B     #11,D1        D1 = 11 = Output hex longword
0086DA 6606      )0086E2             BNE.S     TRAP12
0086DC 6100 FB40)00821E              BSR       OUT8X
0086E0 4E73                          RTE
0086E2 0C01 000C        TRAP12       CMP.B     #12,D1        D1 = 12 = Print a space
0086E6 6606      )0086EE             BNE.S     TRAP13
0086E8 6100 FBA4)00828E              BSR       PSPACE
0086EC 4E73                          RTE
```

```
0086EE 0C01 000D        TRAP13  CMP.B   #13,D1          D1 = 13 = Get a line of text into
0086F2 6606     >0086FA         BNE.S   TRAP14          the line buffer
0086F4 6100 F99C>008092         BSR     GETLINE
0086F8 4E73                     RTE
0086FA 0C01 000E        TRAP14  CMP.B   #14,D1          D1 = 14 = Tidy up the line in the
0086FE 6606     >008706         BNE.S   TRAP15          line buffer by removing leading
008700 6100 F9C6>0080C8         BSR     TIDY            leading and multiple embeded spaces
008704 4E73                     RTE
008706 0C01 000F        TRAP15  CMP.B   #15,D1          D1 = 15 = Execute the command in
00870A 6606     >008712         BNE.S   TRAP16          the line buffer
00870C 6100 F9FC>00810A         BSR     EXECUTE
008710 4E73                     RTE
008712 0C01 0010        TRAP16  CMP.B   #16,D1          D1 = 16 = Call RESTORE to transfer
008716 6606     >00871E         BNE.S   TRAP17          the registers in TSK_T to the 68000
008718 6100 015A>008874         BSR     RESTORE         and therefore execute a program
00871C 4E73                     RTE
00871E 4E73            TRAP17   RTE
                        x
                        xxxxxxxxxxxxxxxxxxxxxxxxxxxxxxxxxxxxxxxxxxxxxxxxxxxxxxxxxxxxxxxxxxxxxxxxxxxx
                        x
                        x  Display exception frame (D0 - D7, A0 - A6, USP, SSP, SR, PC)
                        x  EX_DIS prints registers saved after a breakpoint or exception
                        x  The registers are saved in TSK_T
                        x
008720 4BEE 0056        EX_DIS  LEA.L   TSK_T(A6),A5    A5 points to display frame
008724 49FA 0313>008A39         LEA.L   MES3(PC),A4     Point to heading
008728 6100 F962>00808C         BSR     HEADING         and print it
00872C 3C3C 0007                MOVE.W  #7,D6           8 pairs of registers to display
008730 4205                     CLR.B   D5              D5 is the line counter
008732 1005            EX_D1    MOVE.B  D5,D0           Put current register number in D0
008734 6100 FABE>0081F4         BSR     OUT1X           and print it
008738 6100 FB54>00828E         BSR     PSPACE          and a space
00873C 5205                     ADD.B   #1,D5           Update counter for next pair
00873E 2015                     MOVE.L  (A5),D0         Get data register to be displayed
008740 6100 FADC>00821E         BSR     OUT8X           from the frame and print it
008744 49FA 0311>008A57         LEA.L   MES4(PC),A4     Print string of spaces
008748 6100 F932>00807C         BSR.L   PSTRING         between data and address registers
00874C 202D 0020                MOVE.L  32(A5),D0       Get address register to be displayed
008750 6100 FACC>00821E         BSR     OUT8X           which is 32 bytes on from data reg
008754 6100 F916>00806C         BSR     NEWLINE
008758 4BED 0004                LEA.L   4(A5),A5        Point to next pair (ie Di, Ai)
00875C 51CE FFD4>008732         DBRA    D6,EX_D1        Repeat until all displayed
008760 4BED 0020                LEA.L   32(A5),A5       Adjust pointer by 8 longwords
008764 6100 F906>00806C         BSR     NEWLINE         to point to SSP
008768 49FA 02C6>008A30         LEA.L   MES2A(PC),A4    Point to "SS ="
```

```
00876C 6100 F90E>00807C        BSR      PSTRING        Print it
008770 201D                    MOVE.L   (A5)+,D0       Get SSP from frame
008772 6100 FAAA>00821E        BSR      OUT8X          and display it
008776 6100 F8F4>00806C        BSR      NEWLINE
00877A 49FA 02A2>008A1E        LEA.L    MES1(PC),A4    Point to 'SR ='
00877E 6100 F8FC>00807C        BSR      PSTRING        Print it
008782 301D                    MOVE.W   (A5)+,D0       Get status register
008784 6100 FA90>008216        BSR      OUT4X          Display status
008788 6100 F8E2>00806C        BSR      NEWLINE
00878C 49FA 0299>008A27        LEA.L    MES2(PC),A4    Point to 'PC ='
008790 6100 F8EA>00807C        BSR      PSTRING        Print it
008794 201D                    MOVE.L   (A5)+,D0       Get PC
008796 6100 FA86>00821E        BSR      OUT8X          Display PC
00879A 6000 F8D0>00806C        BRA      NEWLINE        Newline and return
                               X
        XXXXXXXXXXXXXXXXXXXXXXXXXXXXXXXXXXXXXXXXXXXXXXXXXXXXXXXXXXXXXXXXXXXXXXXXXXXXXXXXXXXXXX
                               X
                               X  Exception handling routines
                               X
          0000879E  IL_ER      EQU      X              Illegal instruction exception
00879E 2F0C                    MOVE.L   A4,-(A7)       Save A4
0087A0 49FA 02DF>008A81        LEA.L    MES10(PC),A4   Point to heading
0087A4 6100 F8E6>00808C        BSR      HEADING        Print it
0087A8 285F                    MOVE.L   (A7)+,A4       Restore A4
0087AA 6176     >008822        BSR.S    GROUP2         Save registers in display frame
0087AC 6100 FF72>008720        BSR      EX_DIS         Display registers saved in frame
0087B0 6000 F88E>008040        BRA      WARM           Abort from illegal instruction
                               X
          000087B4  BUS_ER     EQU      X              Bus error (group 1) exception
0087B4 2F0C                    MOVE.L   A4,-(A7)       Save A4
0087B6 49FA 02A9>008A61        LEA.L    MES8(PC),A4    Point to heading
0087BA 6100 F8D0>00808C        BSR      HEADING        Print it
0087BE 285F                    MOVE.L   (A7)+,A4       Restore A4
0087C0 602C     >0087EE        BRA.S    GROUP1         Deal with group 1 exception
                               X
          000087C2  ADD_ER     EQU      X              Address error (group 1) exception
0087C2 2F0C                    MOVE.L   A4,-(A7)       Save A4
0087C4 49FA 02A9>008A6F        LEA.L    MES9(PC),A4    Point to heading
0087C8 6100 F8C2>00808C        BSR      HEADING        Print it
0087CC 285F                    MOVE.L   (A7)+,A4       Restore A4
0087CE 601E     >0087EE        BRA.S    GROUP1         Deal with group 1 exception
                               X
          000087D0  BRKPT      EQU      X              Deal with breakpoint
0087D0 48E7 FFFE                MOVEM.L D0-D7/A0-A6,-(A7) Save all registers
0087D4 6100 0180>008956        BSR      BR_CLR         Clear breakpoints in code
```

```
0087D8 4CDF 7FFF            MOVEM.L  (A7)+,D0-D7/A0-A6 Restore registers
0087DC 6144      }008822    BSR.S    GROUP2           Treat as group 2 exception
0087DE 49FA 02B7}008A97     LEA.L    MES11(PC),A4     Point to heading
0087E2 6100 F8A8}00808C     BSR      HEADING          Print it
0087E6 6100 FF38}008720     BSR      EX_DIS           Display saved registers
0087EA 6000 F854}008040     BRA      WARM             Return to monitor
                       X
                       X     GROUP1 is called by address and bus error exceptions
                       X     These are "turned into group 2" exceptions (eg TRAP)
                       X     by modifying the stack frame saved by a group 1 exception
                       X
0087EE 48E7 8080   GROUP1   MOVEM.L  D0/A0,-(A7)      Save working registers
0087F2 206F 0012            MOVE.L   18(A7),A0        Get PC from group 1 stack frame
0087F6 302F 000E            MOVE.W   14(A7),D0        Get instruction from stack frame
0087FA B060                 CMP.W    -(A0),D0         Now backtrack to find the "correct PC"
0087FC 670E      }00880C    BEQ.S    GROUP1A          by matching the op-code on the stack
0087FE B060                 CMP.W    -(A0),D0         with the code in the region of the
008800 670A      }00880C    BEQ.S    GROUP1A          PC on the stack
008802 B060                 CMP.W    -(A0),D0
008804 6706      }00880C    BEQ.S    GROUP1A
008806 B060                 CMP.W    -(A0),D0
008808 6702      }00880C    BEQ.S    GROUP1A
00880A 5588                 SUB.L    #2,A0
00880C 2F48 0012   GROUP1A  MOVE.L   A0,18(A7)        Restore modified PC to stack frame
008810 4CDF 0101            MOVEM.L  (A7)+,D0/A0      Restore working registers
008814 4FEF 0008            LEA.L    8(A7),A7         Adjust stack pointer to group 1 type
008818 6108      }008822    BSR.S    GROUP2           Now treat as group 1 exception
00881A 6100 FF04}008720     BSR      EX_DIS           Display contents of exception frame
00881E 6000 F820}008040     BRA      WARM             Exit to monitor - no RTE from group 2
                       X
       00008822   GROUP2   EQU      X                Deal with group 2 exceptions
008822 48E7 FFFF            MOVEM.L  A0-A7/D0-D7,-(A7) Save all registers on the stack
008826 303C 000E            MOVE.W   #14,D0           Transfer D0 - D7, A0 - A6 from
00882A 41EE 0056            LEA.L    TSK_T(A6),A0     the stack to the display frame
00882E 20DF       GROUP2A  MOVE.L   (A7)+,(A0)+      Move a register from stack to frame
008830 51C8 FFFC}00882E     DBRA     D0,GROUP2A       and repeat until D0-D7/A0-A6 moved
008834 4E6A                 MOVE.L   USP,A2           Get the user stack pointer and put it
008836 20CA                 MOVE.L   A2,(A0)+         in the A7 position in the frame
008838 201F                 MOVE.L   (A7)+,D0         Now transfer the SSP to the frame,
00883A 0480 0000 000A       SUB.L    #10,D0           remembering to account for the
008840 20C0                 MOVE.L   D0,(A0)+         data pushed on the stack to this point
008842 225F                 MOVE.L   (A7)+,A1         Copy TOS (return address) to A1
008844 30DF                 MOVE.W   (A7)+,(A0)+      Move SR to display frame
008846 201F                 MOVE.L   (A7)+,D0         Get PC in D0
008848 5580                 SUB.L    #2,D0            Move back to current instruction
```

```
00884A 20C0                         MOVE.L    D0,(A0)+           Put adjusted PC in display frame
00884C 4ED1                         JMP       (A1)               Return from subroutine
                          X
          XXXXXXXXXXXXXXXXXXXXXXXXXXXXXXXXXXXXXXXXXXXXXXXXXXXXXXXXXXXXXXXXXXXXXXXXXXXXXXXX
                          X
                          X   GO executes a program either from a supplied address or
                          X   by using the data in the display frame
00884E 6100 F960>0081B0 GO   BSR       PARAM              Get entry address (if any)
008852 4A07                  TST.B     D7                 Test for error in input
008854 6708      >00885E     BEQ.S     GO1                If D7 zero then OK
008856 49FA 027F>008AD7      LEA.L     ERMES1(PC),A4      Else point to error message,
00885A 6000 F820>00807C      BRA       PSTRING            print it and return
00885E 4A80             GO1  TST.L     D0                 If no address entered then get
008860 670A      >00886C     BEQ.S     GO2                address from display frame
008862 2D40 009C             MOVE.L    D0,TSK_T+70(A6)    Else save address in display frame
008866 3D7C 2700 009A        MOVE.W    #$2700,TSK_T+68(A6) Store dummy status in frame
00886C 6006      >008874 GO2  BRA.S     RESTORE            Restore volatile environment and go
                          X
>00886E 6100 007A>0088EA GB   BSR       BR_SET             Same as go but presets breakpoints
 008872 60DA     >00884E      BRA.S     GO                 Execute program
                          X
                          X       RESTORE moves the volatile environment from the display
                          X       frame and transfers it to the 68000's registers. This
                          X       re-runs a program suspended after an exception
                          X
008874 47EE 0056        RESTORE LEA.L   TSK_T(A6),A3       A3 points to display frame
008878 47EB 004A             LEA.L     74(A3),A3          A3 now points to end of frame + 4
00887C 4FEF 0004             LEA.L     4(A7),A7           Remove return address from stack
008880 303C 0024             MOVE.W    #36,D0             Counter for 37 words to be moved
008884 3F23             REST1 MOVE.W   -(A3),-(A7)        Move word from display frame to stack
008886 51C8 FFFC>008884      DBRA      D0,REST1           Repeat until entire frame moved
00888A 4CDF 00FF             MOVEM.L   (A7)+,D0-D7        Restore old data registers from stack
00888E 4CDF 7F00             MOVEM.L   (A7)+,A0-A6        Restore old address registers
008892 4FEF 0008             LEA.L     8(A7),A7           Except SSP/USP - so adjust stack
008896 4E73                  RTE                          Return from exception to run program
                          X
          00008898        TRACE EQU     X                  TRACE exception (rudimentary version)
008898 287A 020B>008AA5       MOVE.L   MES12(PC),A4       Point to heading
00889C 6100 F7EE>00808C       BSR      HEADING            Print it
0088A0 6100 FF4C>0087EE       BSR      GROUP1             Save volatile environment
0088A4 6100 FE7A>008720       BSR      EX_DIS             Display it
0088A8 6000 F796>008040       BRA      WARM               Return to monitor
                          X
          XXXXXXXXXXXXXXXXXXXXXXXXXXXXXXXXXXXXXXXXXXXXXXXXXXXXXXXXXXXXXXXXXXXXXXXXXXXXXXXX
          X  Breakpoint routines: BR_GET gets the address of a breakpoint and
```

```
                         X  puts it in the breakpoint table. It does not plant it in the code.
                         X  BR_SET plants all breakpoints in the code. NOBR removes one or all
                         X  breakpoints from the table. KILL removes breakpoints from the code.
                         X
0088AC 6100 F902>0081B0  BR_GET  BSR      PARAM            Get breakpoint address in table
0088B0 4A07                      TST.B    D7               Test for input error
0088B2 6708    >0088BC           BEQ.S    BR_GET1          If no error then continue
0088B4 49FA 0221>008AD7          LEA.L    ERMES1(PC),A4    Else display error
0088B8 6000 F7C2>00807C          BRA      PSTRING          and return
0088BC 47EE 00A0         BR_GET1 LEA.L    BP_TAB(A6),A3    A6 points to breakpoint table
0088C0 2A40                      MOVE.L   D0,A5            Save new BP address in A5
0088C2 2C00                      MOVE.L   D0,D6            and in D6 because D0 gets corrupted
0088C4 3A3C 0007                 MOVE.W   #7,D5            Eight entries to test
0088C8 201B             BR_GET2  MOVE.L   (A3)+,D0         Read entry from breakpoint table
0088CA 660C    >0088D8           BNE.S    BR_GET3          If not zero display existing BP
0088CC 4A86                      TST.L    D6               Only store a non-zero breakpoint
0088CE 6710    >0088E0           BEQ.S    BR_GET4
0088D0 274D FFFC                 MOVE.L   A5,-4(A3)        Store new breakpoint in table
0088D4 3695                      MOVE.W   (A5),(A3)        Save code at BP address in table
0088D6 4286                      CLR.L    D6               Clear D6 to avoid repetition
0088D8 6100 F944>00821E BR_GET3 BSR      OUT8X            Display this breakpoint
0088DC 6100 F78E>00806C         BSR      NEWLINE
0088E0 47EB 0002         BR_GET4 LEA.L    2(A3),A3         Step past stored op-code
0088E4 51CD FFE2>0088C8          DBRA     D5,BR_GET2       Repeat until all entries tested
0088E8 4E75                      RTS                       Return
                         X
       000088EA          BR_SET  EQU      X                Plant any breakpoints in user code
0088EA 41EE 00A0                 LEA.L    BP_TAB(A6),A0    A0 points to BP table
0088EE 45EE 009C                 LEA.L    TSK_T+70(A6),A2  A2 points to PC in display frame
0088F2 2452                      MOVE.L   (A2),A2          Now A2 contains value of PC
0088F4 303C 0007                 MOVE.W   #7,D0            Up to eight entries to plant
0088F8 2218            BR_SET1   MOVE.L   (A0)+,D1         Read breakpoint address from table
0088FA 670A    >008906           BEQ.S    BR_SET2          If zero then skip planting
0088FC B28A                      CMP.L    A2,D1            Don't want to plant BP at current PC
0088FE 6706    >008906           BEQ.S    BR_SET2          location, so skip planting if same
008900 2241                      MOVE.L   D1,A1            Transfer BP address to address reg
008902 32BC 4E4E                 MOVE.W   #TRAP_14,(A1)    Plant op-code for TRAP #14 in code
008906 41E8 0002        BR_SET2  LEA.L    2(A0),A0         Skip past op-code field in table
00890A 51C8 FFEC>0088F8          DBRA     D0,BR_SET1       Repeat until all entries tested
00890E 4E75                      RTS
                         X
       00008910          NOBR    EQU      X                Clear one or all breakpoints
008910 6100 F89E>0081B0         BSR      PARAM            Get BP address (if any)
008914 4A07                      TST.B    D7               Test for input error
008916 6708    >008920           BEQ.S    NOBR1            If no error then skip abort
```

```
008918 49FA 01BD>008AD7        LEA.L    ERMES1(PC),A4       Point to error message
00891C 6000 F75E>00807C        BRA      PSTRING             Display it and return
008920 4A80            NOBR1   TST.L    D0                  Test for null address (clear all)
008922 6720    >008944         BEQ.S    NOBR4               If no address then clear all entries
008924 2240                    MOVE.L   D0,A1               Else just clear breakpoint in A1
008926 41EE 00A0               LEA.L    BP_TAB(A6),A0       A0 points to BP table
00892A 303C 0007               MOVE.W   #7,D0               Up to eight entries to test
00892E 2218            NOBR2   MOVE.L   (A0)+,D1            Get entry and
008930 41E8 0002               LEA.L    2(A0),A0            skip past op-code field
008934 B289                    CMP.L    A1,D1               Is this the one?
008936 6706    >00893E         BEQ.S    NOBR3               If so go and clear entry
008938 51C8 FFF4>00892E        DBRA     D0,NOBR2            Repeat until all tested
00893C 4E75                    RTS
00893E 42A8 FFFA      NOBR3    CLR.L    -6(A0)              Clear address in BP table
008942 4E75                    RTS
008944 41EE 00A0      NOBR4    LEA.L    BP_TAB(A6),A0       Clear all 8 entries in BP table
008948 303C 0007               MOVE.W   #7,D0               Eight entries to clear
00894C 4298           NOBR5    CLR.L    (A0)+               Clear breakpoint address
00894E 4258                    CLR.W    (A0)+               Clear op-code field
008950 51C8 FFFA>00894C        DBRA     D0,NOBR5            Repeat until all done
008954 4E75                    RTS

             x
        00008956 BR_CLR EQU    x                            Remove breakpoints from code
008956 41EE 00A0               LEA.L    BP_TAB(A6),A0       A0 points to breakpoint table
00895A 303C 0007               MOVE.W   #7,D0               Up to eight entries to clear
00895E 2218          BR_CLR1   MOVE.L   (A0)+,D1            Get address of BP in D1
008960 2241                    MOVE.L   D1,A1               and put copy in A1
008962 4A81                    TST.L    D1                  Test this breakpoint
008964 6702    >008968         BEQ.S    BR_CLR2             If zero then skip BP clearing
008966 3290                    MOVE.W   (A0),(A1)           Else restore op-code
008968 41E8 0002     BR_CLR2   LEA.L    2(A0),A0            Skip past op-code field
00896C 51C8 FFF0>00895E        DBRA     D0,BR_CLR1          Repeat until all tested
008970 4E75                    RTS

             x
             x  REG_MOD modifies a register in the display frame. The command
             x  format is REG <reg> <value>. E.g. REG D3 1200
             x
008972 4281          REG_MOD   CLR.L    D1                  D1 to hold name of register
008974 41EE 0040               LEA.L    BUFFPT(A6),A0       A0 contains address of buffer pointer
008978 2050                    MOVE.L   (A0),A0             A0 now points to next char in buffer
00897A 1218                    MOVE.B   (A0)+,D1            Put first char of name in D1
00897C E159                    ROL.W    #8,D1               Move char one place left
00897E 1218                    MOVE.B   (A0)+,D1            Get second char in D1
008980 41E8 0001               LEA.L    1(A0),A0            Move pointer past space in buffer
008984 2D48 0040               MOVE.L   A0,BUFFPT(A6)       Update buffer pointer
```

```
008988 4282                    CLR.L    D2               D2 is the character pair counter
00898A 41FA 0122>008AAE        LEA.L    REGNAME(PC),A0   A0 points to string of character pairs
00898E 43D0                    LEA.L    (A0),A1          A1 also points to string
008990 B258           REG_MOD1 CMP.W    (A0)+,D1         Compare a char pair with input
008992 6712    >0089A6         BEQ.S    REG_MOD2         If match then exit loop
008994 5282                    ADD.L    #1,D2            Else increment match counter
008996 0C82 0000 0013          CMP.L    #19,D2           Test for end of loop
00899C 66F2    >008990         BNE      REG_MOD1         Continue until all pairs matched
00899E 49FA 0137>008AD7        LEA.L    ERMES1(PC),A4    If here then error
0089A2 6000 F6D8>00807C        BRA      PSTRING          Display error and return
0089A6 43EE 0056      REG_MOD2 LEA.L    TSK_T(A6),A1     A1 points to display frame
0089AA E582                    ASL.L    #2,D2            Multiply offset by 4 (4 bytes/entry)
0089AC 0C82 0000 0048          CMP.L    #72,D2           Test for address of PC
0089B2 6602    >0089B6         BNE.S    REG_MOD3         If not PC then all is OK
0089B4 5582                    SUB.L    #2,D2            else dec PC pointer as Sr is a word
0089B6 45F1 2000      REG_MOD3 LEA.L    (A1,D2),A2       Calculate address of entry in disptable
0089BA 2012                    MOVE.L   (A2),D0          Get old contents
0089BC 6100 F860>00821E        BSR      OUT8X            Display them
0089C0 6100 F6AA>00806C        BSR      NEWLINE
0089C4 6100 F7EA>0081B0        BSR      PARAM            Get new data
0089C8 4A07                    TST.B    D7               Test for input error
0089CA 6708    >0089D4         BEQ.S    REG_MOD4         If no error then go and store data
0089CC 49FA 0109>008AD7        LEA.L    ERMES1(PC),A4    Else point to error message
0089D0 6000 F6AA>00807C        BRA      PSTRING          print it and return
0089D4 0C82 0000 0044 REG_MOD4 CMP.L    #68,D2           If this address is the SR then
0089DA 6704    >0089E0         BEQ.S    REG_MOD5         we have only a word to store
0089DC 2480                    MOVE.L   D0,(A2)          Else store new data in display frame
0089DE 4E75                    RTS
0089E0 3480          REG_MOD5 MOVE.W    D0,(A2)          Store SR (one word)
0089E2 4E75                    RTS
                               x
                               xxxxxxxxxxxxxxxxxxxxxxxxxxxxxxxxxxxxxxxxxxxxxxxxxxxxxxxxxxxxxxxxxxxxxxxxxx
                               x
      000089E4         X_UN     EQU      x                Uninitialized exception vector routine
0089E4 49FA 0157>008B3D        LEA.L    ERMES6(PC),A4    Point to error message
0089E8 6100 F692>00807C        BSR      PSTRING          Display it
0089EC 6100 FD32>008720        BSR      EX_DIS           Display registers
0089F0 6000 F64E>008040        BRA      WARM             Abort
                               x
                               xxxxxxxxxxxxxxxxxxxxxxxxxxxxxxxxxxxxxxxxxxxxxxxxxxxxxxxxxxxxxxxxxxxxxxxxxx
                               x
                               x  All strings and other fixed parameters here
                               x
0089F4 5453 4255 4720 BANNER   DC.B     'TSBUG 2 Version 23.07.86',0,0
008A0E 0D0A 3F00     CRLF      DC.B     CR,LF,'?',0
```

```
008A12 0D0A 5331 0000    HEADER  DC.B    CR,LF,'S','1',0,0
008A18 5339 2020 0000    TAIL    DC.B    'S9 ',0,0
008A1E 2053 5220 203D    MES1    DC.B    ' SR = ',0
008A27 2050 4320 203D    MES2    DC.B    ' PC = ',0
008A30 2053 5320 203D    MES2A   DC.B    ' SS = ',0
008A39 2020 4461 7461    MES3    DC.B    '  Data reg       Address reg',0,0
008A57 2020 2020 2020    MES4    DC.B    '            ',0,0
008A61 4275 7320 6572    MES8    DC.B    'Bus error    ',0,0
008A6F 4164 6472 6573    MES9    DC.B    'Address error   ',0,0
008A81 496C 6C65 6761    MES10   DC.B    'Illegal instruction ',0,0
008A97 4272 6561 6B70    MES11   DC.B    'Breakpoint ',0,0
008AA5 5472 6163 6520    MES12   DC.B    'Trace    ',0
008AAE 4430 4431 4432    REGNAME DC.B    'D0D1D2D3D4D5D6D7'
008ABE 4130 4131 4132            DC.B    'A0A1A2A3A4A5A6A7'
008ACE 5353 5352                 DC.B    'SSSR'
008AD2 5043 2020 00              DC.B    'PC ',0
008AD7 4E6F 6E2D 7661    ERMES1  DC.B    'Non-valid hexadecimal input ',0
008AF5 496E 7661 6C69    ERMES2  DC.B    'Invalid command ',0
008B07 4C6F 6164 696E    ERMES3  DC.B    'Loading error',0
008B15 5461 626C 6520    ERMES4  DC.B    'Table full ',0,0
008B23 4272 6561 6B70    ERMES5  DC.B    'Breakpoint not active  ',0,0
008B3D 556E 696E 6974    ERMES6  DC.B    'Uninitialized exception ',0,0
008B57 2052 616E 6765    ERMES7  DC.B    ' Range error',0
                         X
                         X  COMTAB is the built-in command table. All entries are made up of
                         X       a string length + number of characters to match + the string
                         X       plus the address of the command relative to COMTAB
                         X
008B64 0404              COMTAB  DC.B    4,4             JUMP <address> causes execution to
008B66 4A55 4D50                 DC.B    'JUMP'          begin at <address>
008B6A FFFF F6C2                 DC.L    JUMP-COMTAB     n
008B6E 0803                      DC.B    8,3             MEMORY <address> examines contents of
008B70 4D45 4D4F 5259            DC.B    'MEMORY  '      <address> and allows them to be changed
008B78 FFFF F6D8                 DC.L    MEMORY-COMTAB
008B7C 0402                      DC.B    4,2             LOAD <string> loads S1/S2 records
008B7E 4C4F 4144                 DC.B    'LOAD'          from the host. <string> is sent to host
008B82 FFFF F738                 DC.L    LOAD-COMTAB
008B86 0402                      DC.B    4,2             DUMP <string> sends S1 records to the
008B88 4455 4D50                 DC.B    'DUMP'          host and is preceeded by <string>.
008B8C FFFF F80C                 DC.L    DUMP-COMTAB
008B90 0403                      DC.B    4,3             TRAN enters the transparant mode
008B92 5452 414E                 DC.B    'TRAN'          and is exited by ESC,E.
008B96 FFFF F8C8                 DC.L    TM-COMTAB
008B9A 0402                      DC.B    4,2             NOBR <address> removes the breakpoint
008B9C 4E4F 4252                 DC.B    'NOBR'          at <address> from the BP table. If
```

```
008BA0 FFFF FDAC                DC.L     NOBR-COMTAB         no address is given all BPs are removed.
008BA4 0402                     DC.B     4,2                 DISP displays the contents of the
008BA6 4449 5350                DC.B     'DISP'              pseudo registers in TSK_T.
008BAA FFFF FBBC                DC.L     EX_DIS-COMTAB
008BAE 0402                     DC.B     4,2                 GO <address> starts program execution
008BB0 474F 2020                DC.B     'GO '               at <address> and loads regs from TSK_T
008BB4 FFFF FCEA                DC.L     GO-COMTAB
008BB8 0402                     DC.B     4,2                 BRGT puts a breakpoint in the BP
008BBA 4252 4754                DC.B     'BRGT'              table - but not in the code
008BBE FFFF FD48                DC.L     BR_GET-COMTAB
008BC2 0402                     DC.B     4,2                 PLAN puts the breakpoints in the code
008BC4 504C 414E                DC.B     'PLAN'
008BC8 FFFF FD86                DC.L     BR_SET-COMTAB
008BCC 0404                     DC.B     4,4                 KILL removes breakpoints from the code
008BCE 4B49 4C4C                DC.B     'KILL'
008BD2 FFFF FDF2                DC.L     BR_CLR-COMTAB
008BD6 0402                     DC.B     4,2                 GB <address> sets breakpoints and
008BD8 4742 2020                DC.B     'GB '               then calls GO.
008BDC FFFF FD0A                DC.L     GB-COMTAB
008BE0 0403                     DC.B     4,3                 REG <reg> <value> loads <value>
008BE2 5245 4720                DC.B     'REG '              into <reg> in TASK_T. Used to preset
008BE6 FFFF FE0E                DC.L     REG_MOD-COMTAB      registers before a GO or GB
008BEA 0000                     DC.B     0,0
                             x
                             xxxxxxxxxxxxxxxxxxxxxxxxxxxxxxxxxxxxxxxxxxxxxxxxxxxxxxxxxxxxxxxxxxxxxxxxxxxxxxx
                             x
                             x  This is a list of the information needed to setup the DCBs
                             x
                  00008BEC   DCB_LST EQU       x
008BEC 434F 4E5F 494E DCB1    DC.B     'CON_IN '           Device name (8 bytes)
008BF4 0000 84CA 0001         DC.L     CON_IN,ACIA_1       Address of driver routine, device
008BFC 0002                   DC.W     2                   Number of words in parameter field
008BFE 434F 4E5F 4F55 DCB2    DC.B     'CON_OUT '
008C06 0000 84FA 0001         DC.L     CON_OUT,ACIA_1
008C0E 0002                   DC.W     2
008C10 4155 585F 494E DCB3    DC.B     'AUX_IN '
008C18 0000 853A 0001         DC.L     AUX_IN,ACIA_2
008C20 0002                   DC.W     2
008C22 4155 585F 4F55 DCB4    DC.B     'AUX_OUT '
008C2A 0000 854C 0001         DC.L     AUX_OUT,ACIA_2
008C32 0002                   DC.W     2
008C34 4255 4646 5F49 DCB5    DC.B     'BUFF_IN '
008C3C 0000 85A0 0000         DC.L     BUFF_IN,BUFFER
008C44 0002                   DC.W     2
008C46 4255 4646 5F4F DCB6    DC.B     'BUFF_OUT'
```

```
008C4E 0000 85AC 0000          DC.L    BUFF_OT,BUFFER
008C56 0002                    DC.W    2
                        X
                        XXXXXXXXXXXXXXXXXXXXXXXXXXXXXXXXXXXXXXXXXXXXXXXXXXXXXXXXXXXXXXXXXXXXXXXXXXXXXXXXXXXX
                        X
                        X  DCB structure
                        X
                        X                 ------------------------
                        X        0 ->    | DCB   name           |
                        X                |----------------------|
                        X        8 ->    | Device driver        |
                        X                |----------------------|
                        X       12 ->    | Device address       |
                        X                |----------------------|
                        X       16 ->    |Size of param block   |
                        X                |----------------------| ---
                        X       18 ->    |        Status        |   |
                        X                | logical  | physical  |   | S
                        X                |----------------------|   |
                        X                 .                    .    .
                        X                |----------------------| ---
                        X     18+S ->    | Pointer to next DCB  |
                        X
                                 END

0 ERROR(S) DETECTED

SYMBOL TABLE:

ACIA_1   010040   ACIA_2   010041   ADD_ER   0087C2   ADR_DAT  00827A
AUX_IN   00853A   AUX_IN1  008540   AUX_OT1  008552   AUX_OUT  00854C
BANNER   0089F4   BP_TAB   0000A0   BRKPT    0087D0   BR_CLR   008956
BR_CLR1  00895E   BR_CLR2  008968   BR_GET   0088AC   BR_GET1  0088BC
BR_GET2  0088C8   BR_GET3  0088D8   BR_GET4  0088E0   BR_SET   0088EA
BR_SET1  0088F8   BR_SET2  008906   BS       000008   BUFFEND  00003F
BUFFER   0002D0   BUFFPT   000040   BUFF_IN  0085A0   BUFF_OT  0085AC
BUS_ER   0087B4   BYTE     008194   CN_IVEC  00004E   CN_OVEC  000052
COMTAB   008B64   CON_I1   0084D8   CON_I2   0084F0   CON_IN   0084CA
CON_OT1  008508   CON_OT2  00851E   CON_OT3  008526   CON_OUT  0084FA
CR       00000D   CRLF     008A0E   CTRL_A   000001   DATA     000C00
DCB1     008BEC   DCB2     008BFE   DCB3     008C10   DCB4     008C22
DCB5     008C34   DCB6     008C46   DCB_LST  008BEC   DELAY    008418
DELAY1   008422   DUMP     008370   DUMP1    008380   DUMP2    00838C
DUMP3    0083A2   DUMP4    0083B6   DUMP5    0083C4   DUMP6    0083DE
DUMP7    008402   ECHO     000048   ERMES1   008AD7   ERMES2   008AF5
ERMES3   008B07   ERMES4   008B15   ERMES5   008B23   ERMES6   008B3D
```

ERMES7	008B57	ESC	00001B	EXEC1	00811C	EXEC2	00812C
EXECUTE	00810A	EX_D1	008732	EX_DIS	008720	FIRST	0000D0
GB	00886E	GETCH2	008584	GETCH3	00858C	GETCHAR	00855E
GETLINE	008092	GETLN2	00809C	GETLN3	0080B6	GETLN4	0080C0
GETLN5	0080C4	GO	00884E	GO1	00885E	GO2	00886C
GROUP1	0087EE	GROUP1A	00880C	GROUP2	008822	GROUP2A	00882E
HEADER	008A12	HEADING	00808C	HEX	008176	HEX_OK	008192
IL_ER	00879E	IO_OPEN	0085BA	IO_REQ	0084B8	JUMP	008226
JUMP1	008234	LF	00000A	LNBUFF	000000	LOAD	00829C
LOAD1	0082C8	LOAD2	0082D8	LOAD3	0082F2	LOAD4	00830C
LOAD5	00831A	LOAD6	00831C	LOAD6A	008340	LOAD7	008352
LOAD8	008368	LONGWD	0081AA	MAXCHR	000040	MEM1	008246
MEM2	008264	MEM3	008278	MEMORY	00823C	MES1	008A1E
MES10	008A81	MES11	008A97	MES12	008AA5	MES2	008A27
MES2A	008A30	MES3	008A39	MES4	008A57	MES8	008A61
MES9	008A6F	NEWLINE	00806C	NOBR	008910	NOBR1	008920
NOBR2	00892E	NOBR3	00893E	NOBR4	008944	NOBR5	00894C
NOT_HEX	00818E	NO_EXT	00803C	OPEN1	0085C2	OPEN2	0085CA
OPEN3	0085D8	OPEN4	0085EE	OUT1X	0081F4	OUT1X1	008206
OUT2X	00820E	OUT4X	008216	OUT8X	00821E	PARAM	0081B0
PARAM1	0081B8	PARAM3	0081DC	PARAM4	0081E0	PARAM5	0081EC
PARAM6	0081F0	PARAMTR	000044	PS1	00807E	PS2	008088
PSPACE	00828E	PSTRING	00807C	PUTCHAR	008590	RANGE	008408
REGNAME	008AAE	REG_MOD	008972	REG_MOD1	008990	REG_MOD2	0089A6
REG_MOD3	0089B6	REG_MOD4	0089D4	REG_MOD5	0089E0	RESET	008008
REST1	008884	RESTORE	008874	SEARCH	008136	SETACIA	008050
SET_DCB	00846E	SPACE	000020	SRCH2	008150	SRCH3	008154
SRCH4	00815C	SRCH6	008166	SRCH7	008170	STACK	000800
ST_DCB1	00847E	ST_DCB2	008482	TAIL	008A18	TIDY	0080C8
TIDY1	0080CE	TIDY2	0080DA	TIDY3	0080E4	TIDY4	0080EE
TIDY5	0080F8	TIDY6	008104	TM	00842C	TM1	008438
TRACE	008898	TRAP1	00865E	TRAP10	0086CA	TRAP11	0086D6
TRAP12	0086E2	TRAP13	0086EE	TRAP14	0086FA	TRAP15	008706
TRAP16	008712	TRAP17	00871E	TRAP2	00866A	TRAP3	008676
TRAP4	008682	TRAP5	00868E	TRAP6	00869A	TRAP7	0086A6
TRAP8	0086B2	TRAP9	0086BE	TRAP_0	008652	TRAP_14	004E4E
TSK_T	000056	UTAB	00004A	U_CASE	000049	WAIT	000057
WARM	008040	WORD	0081A4	X_BASE	000008	X_SET	0085F4
X_SET1	0085FC	X_SET2	008648	X_UN	0089E4		

Summary

Throughout this book, we have looked at various aspects of the 68000, from its programming model to its exception-handling mechanism. In this chapter, we have considered some of the practical problems of systems design and test, and have applied the lessons learned elsewhere to design a basic single board, 68000-based microcomputer. This microcomputer, the TS2, has a monitor that permits it to receive input from a terminal, modify the input, debug it, and then run it.

The monitor presented in this chapter is not intended as an optimum monitor for the 68000 microprocessor but as an extended tutorial in 68000 assembly language programming. In particular, it is designed to demonstrate one of the more interesting ways of executing input or output transactions. The monitor provides a strong measure of device-independent I/O by means of device control blocks, DCBs.

Problems

1. What facilities or attributes make a microcomputer easy to test?

2. What facilities or attributes make a microcomputer difficult to test?

3. Why are closed-loop systems harder to test and debug than open-loop systems?

4. What additional logic and circuitry would be required to make a single board 68000 microcomputer testable by turning it into an open-loop system? Assume that the SBC has a 96-pin connector that can be connected to external test equipment.

5. A microcomputer card can be designed to be "self-testing." For example, the CPU runs a program that tests its instruction set by executing a section of code in ROM, using only internal read/write storage, and then compares the result with a prestored value. Then the CPU tests the read/write memory and finally any peripherals.
   a. Design a program to test the 68000's instruction set.
   b. Write a program to test read/write memory.
   c. How do you think that peripherals may be self-tested?
   d. What additional hardware is required for these tests?

6. Describe how a logic analyzer is used to test and debug a 68000-based single board computer. What are the limitations of a logic analyzer?

7. Signature analysis is used in production-line testing because it provides only a go/no-go result. Show how a signature analyzer can be built into a single board computer to perform a test following a reset. If the test fails, it is repeated twice (by reasserting RESET*). If the test continues to fail, a front panel LED is lit.

8. Suppose that the single board computer, TS2, is to be mass produced and that it is necessary to reduce the parts count. If the single-step feature is omitted and fusible logic (PAL, etc.) used wherever possible, how far can the chip count of TS2 be reduced?

9. A designer wishes to produce an entirely general-purpose 68000 board and one of the design specifications requires that the memory (both ROM and read/write) and per-

ipherals should have software programmable addresses; that is, all addressible devices must be capable of being relocated under software control. To do this, the address decoders must be reprogrammable. Of course, ROM must be assigned to the reset vector area following a reset in order to set up the system. Design the logic required to implement this system.

10. A watchdog circuit generates an interrupt every T seconds. However, the system executes a program that resets the watchdog timer at least once every T seconds. Because the timer is reset before it times-out and generates an interrupt, the processor is never interrupted by the watchdog timer. If, however, the processor hangs up for any reason, the timer times-out and the processor is reset. In this way, it is forced out of its hang-up state. Design a watchdog timer for a 68000 system.

11. The bus interface of TS2 is designed to make TS2 a master in a 68000 system. Consequently, the TS2 module can access the bus or it can be forced off the bus whenever its BGACK* input is asserted. TS2 cannot act as a slave and be accessed by another master. Redesign TS2 so that it can be a slave and its ROM/RAM and peripherals accessed from the system bus.

12. Some of the functions not implemented by TS2MON are:
  (1) A move command that copies a block of memory from Address_1 through Address_2 to start at Address_3.
  (2) A fill command that fills a block of memory from Address_1 through Address_2 with a constant. The command should be able to use byte, word, or longword constants.
  (3) A test command that tests read/write memory in the region from Address_1 through Address_2.
Design a subroutine to implement these functions.

13. Design a simple monitor that runs itself continually as a background task and will also execute a task as a background job; that is, executing GO⟨address⟩ invokes a multitasking kernel that switches between the monitor itself and the task invoked by the GO command. Assume that a constant stream of interrupts is available from a timer.

Appendix A

Summary of the 68000

Instruction Set

Effective Addressing Mode Categories

Type	Mode	Register	Generation	Assembler Syntax
Data Register Direct	000	reg. no.	EA = Dn	Dn
Address Register Direct	001	reg. no.	EA = An	An
Register Indirect	010	reg. no.	EA = (An)	(An)
Postincrement Register Indirect	011	reg. no.	EA = (An), An ← An + N	(An)+
Predecrement Register Indirect	100	reg. no.	An ← An − N, EA = (An)	−(An)
Register Indirect With Offset	101	reg. no.	EA = (An) + d_{16}	d_{16}(An)
Indexed Register Indirect With Offset	110	reg. no.	EA = (An) + (Xn) + d_8	d_8(An, Xn)
Absolute Short	111	000	EA = (Next Word)	xxx
Absolute Long	111	001	EA = (Next Two Words)	xxxxxx
PC Relative With Offset	111	010	EA = (PC) + d_{16}	d_{16}(PC)
PC Relative With Index and Offset	111	011	EA = (PC) + (Xn) + d_8	d_8(PC + Xn)
Immediate	111	100	Data = Next Word(s)	#xxx
Quick Immediate	—	—	Inherent Data	#xxx (1–8)
Implied Register	—	—	EA = SR, USP, SP, PC	

NOTES:
EA = Effective Address
An = Address Register
Dn = Data Register
Xn = Address or Data Register used as Index Register
SR = Status Register
PC = Program Counter

d_8 = Eight bit Offset (displacement)
d_{16} = Sixteen bit Offset (displacement)
N = 1 for Byte, 2 for Words and 4 for Long Words
( ) = Contents of
← = Replaces

Condition Code Computations

Operations	X	N	Z	V	C	Special Definition
ABCD	*	U	?	U	?	C = Decimal Carry; $Z = Z \cdot \overline{Rm} \cdot \ldots \cdot \overline{R0}$
ADD, ADDI, ADDQ	*	*	*	?	?	$V = Sm \cdot Dm \cdot \overline{Rm} + \overline{Sm} \cdot \overline{Dm} \cdot Rm$; $C = Sm \cdot Dm + \overline{Rm} \cdot Dm + Sm \cdot \overline{Rm}$
ADDX	*	*	?	?	?	$V = Sm \cdot Dm \cdot \overline{Rm} + \overline{Sm} \cdot \overline{Dm} \cdot Rm$; $C = Sm \cdot Dm + \overline{Rm} \cdot Dm + Sm \cdot \overline{Rm}$
AND, ANDI, EOR, EORI, MOVEQ, MOVE, OR, ORI, CLR, EXT, NOT, TAS, TST	—	*	*	0	0	
CHK	—	*	U	U	U	
SUB, SUBI, SUBQ	*	*	*	?	?	$V = \overline{Sm} \cdot Dm \cdot \overline{Rm} + Sm \cdot \overline{Dm} \cdot Rm$; $C = Sm \cdot \overline{Dm} + Rm \cdot \overline{Dm} + Sm \cdot Rm$
SUBX	*	*	?	?	?	$V = \overline{Sm} \cdot Dm \cdot \overline{Rm} + Sm \cdot \overline{Dm} \cdot Rm$; $C = Sm \cdot \overline{Dm} + Rm \cdot \overline{Dm} + Sm \cdot Rm$
CMP, CMPI, CMPM	—	*	*	?	?	$V = \overline{Sm} \cdot Dm \cdot \overline{Rm} + Sm \cdot \overline{Dm} \cdot Rm$; $C = Sm \cdot \overline{Dm} + Rm \cdot \overline{Dm} + Sm \cdot Rm$
DIVS, DIVU	—	*	*	?	0	V = Division Overflow
MULS, MULU	—	*	*	0	0	
SBCD, NBCD	*	U	?	U	?	C = Decimal Borrow; $Z = Z \cdot \overline{Rm} \cdot \ldots \cdot \overline{R0}$

NOTES:
Sm = Source Operated — most significant bit
Dm = Destination operated — most significant bit
? = See Special Definition

Operations	X	N	Z	V	C	Special Definition
NEG	*	*	*	?	?	$V = Dm \cdot Rm, C = Dm + Rm$
NEGX	*	*	?	?	?	$V = Dm \cdot Rm, C = Dm + Rm$; $Z = Z \cdot \overline{Rm} \cdot \ldots \cdot \overline{R0}$
BTST, BCHG, BSET, BCLR	—	—	?	—	—	$Z = \overline{Dn}$
ASL	*	*	*	?	?	$V = Dm \cdot (\overline{Dm-1} + \ldots + \overline{Dm-r}) + \overline{Dm} \cdot (Dm-1 + \ldots + Dm-r)$; $C = Dm-r+1$
ASL (r = 0)	—	*	*	0	0	
LSL, ROXL	*	*	*	0	?	$C = Dm-r+1$
LSR (r = 0)	—	*	*	0	0	
ROXL (r = 0)	—	*	*	0	?	C = X
ROL	—	*	*	0	?	$C = Dm-r+1$
ROL (r = 0)	—	*	*	0	0	
ASR, LSR, ROXR	*	*	*	0	?	$C = Dr-1$
ASR, LSR (r = 0)	—	*	*	0	0	
ROXR (r = 0)	—	*	*	0	?	C = X
ROR	—	*	*	0	?	$C = Dr-1$
ROR (r = 0)	—	*	*	0	0	

NOTES:
Rm = Result operand — most significant bit
n = bit number
r = shift count

Addressing Modes

The page contains a large, densely printed reference table summarizing the 68000 instruction set. The table lists instructions (Mnemonic, Size, Address Mode) against various addressing modes with timing/cycle counts and opcode bit patterns, Boolean operations, and Condition Codes.

Mnemonic	Size	Address Mode	Dn	An	(An)	(An)+	−(An)	d₁₆(An)	d₈(An,Xn)	Abs.W	Abs.L	d₁₆(PC)	d₈(PC,Xn)	s = Imm/d = SR/CC	Opcode Bit Pattern (15–0)	Boolean	Condition Codes X N Z V C
ABCD	B	s = Dn	6												1100 RRR1 0000 0rrr	d10 + s10 + X → d	* U * U *
ABCD	B	s = −(An)					18								1100 RRR1 0000 1rrr		
ADD	B W L	s = Dn	4		12	12	14	16	18	16	20			8	1101 DDD1 SSEE EEEE	d + Dn → d	* * * * *

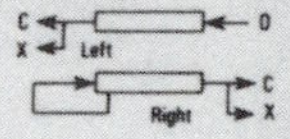

[The full table on this page is an extremely dense, multi-page reference chart (Appendix A, "Summary of the 68000 Instruction Set") printed sideways, containing dozens of instructions (ABCD, ADD, ADDA, ADDX, ADDQ, AND, ANDI, AND CCR/SR, ASL/ASR, Bcc, BCHG, BCLR, BRA, BSET, BSR, BTST, CHK, CLR, CMP, CMPA, CMPM, etc.) each with multiple rows for size and addressing-mode variants, columns of cycle-count/byte values across all addressing modes, opcode bit patterns, Boolean operation descriptions, and condition-code effects. The image resolution does not permit a reliable cell-by-cell reading of all the numeric timing values.]

Mnemonic	Size	Address Mode	Boolean	Opcode Bit Pattern (1111 11 / 5432 1098 7654 3210)	Condition Codes X N Z V C
DBcc	W	d16 = Imm	If cc true, then NOP; else Dn − 1 → Dn; if Dn = −1, then PC + disp → PC	0101 CCCC 1100 1DDD	– – – – –
DIVS	W	d = Dn	Dn32/s16 ÷ Dnr : q	1000 DDD1 11ee eeee	– * * * 0
DIVU	W	d = Dn	Dn32/s16 ÷ Dnr : q	1000 DDD0 11ee eeee	– * * * 0
EOR	B/W/L	s = Dn	d ⊕ Dnr → d	1011 rrr1 SSEE EEEE	– * * 0 0
EORI	B/W/L	s = imm	d ⊕ #Imm → d	0000 1010 SSEE EEEE	– * * 0 0
EORI CCR	B	s = imm	s ⊕ CCR → CCR	0000 1010 0011 1100	* * * * *
EORI SR	L	s = imm	s ⊕ SR → SR	0000 1010 0111 1100	* * * * *
EXG	L	s = Dn / d = Dn	s → d	1100 DDD1 0100 0DDD	– – – – –
EXT	W		bit 7 → bits 15..8	0100 1000 1000 0DDD	– * * 0 0
EXT	L		bit 15 → bits 31..16	0100 1000 1100 0DDD	– * * 0 0
ILLEGAL			(Illegal vector) → PC	0100 1010 1111 1100	– – – – –
JMP			d → PC	0100 1110 11EE EEEE	– – – – –
JSR			PC → −(SSP); d → PC	0100 1110 10EE EEEE	– – – – –
LEA	L	d = An	An → An	0100 AAA1 11EE EEEE	– – – – –
LINK		d16 = imm	An → −(SP); SP → An; SP + disp → SP	0100 1110 0101 0AAA	– – – – –
LSL, LSR	B/W			1110 rrrr SS10 1DDD	* * * 0 *
MOVE	B/W/L		s → d	00XX RRRM MMee eeee	– * * 0 0
MOVE	L		s → d	0010 RRRM MMee eeee	– * * 0 0
MOVE CCR	W	d = CCR	s → CCR	0100 0100 11ee eeee	* * * * *
MOVE SR	W	d = SR	SR → d	0100 0110 11EE EEEE	* * * * *
MOVE USP	L	s = An / s = USP	USP → An; An → USP	0100 1110 0110 0AAA	– – – – –
MOVEA	W	d = An	s → An	0011 AAAG 01ee eeee	– – – – –
MOVEA	L	d = An	s → An	0010 AAAG 01ee eeee	– – – – –
MOVEM	W		Xn → d	0100 1000 10EE EEEE	– – – – –
MOVEM	L		s → Xn	0100 1100 11ee eeee	– – – – –
MOVEP	W	s = Dn / s = d16(An)	Dn → d by bytes	0000 DDD1 1000 1AAA	– – – – –
MOVEP	L	s = Dn / s = d16(An)	s → Dn by bytes	0000 DDD1 1100 1AAA	– – – – –

Opcode Bit Pattern / Condition Codes Summary

Mnemonic	Size	Address Mode	Boolean	Condition Codes (X N Z V C)
MOVEP	L	s = Imm8	# → Dn	- - - - -
MULS	W	d = Dn	Dn × s → Dn	- * * 0 0
MULU	W	s = Dn	Dn × s → Dn	- * * 0 0
NBCD	B	d = Dn	0 - d10 - X → d	* U * U *
NEG	B W	d = Dn	0 - d → d	* * * * *
NEGX	B W	d = Dn	0 - d - X → d	* * * * *
NOP			none	- - - - -
NOT	B W	d = Dn	d → d	- * * 0 0
OR	B W	s = Dn / d = Dn	d · or · s → Dn	- * * 0 0
ORI	B W	s = Imm	d · or · # → D	- * * 0 0
ORI CCR	B	s = Imm	s · or · CCR → CCR	* * * * *
ORI SR	W	s = Imm	s · or · SR → SR	* * * * *
PEA	L		s → - (SP)	- - - - -
RESET			assert RESET pin	- - - - -
ROL ROR	B W	count = Dn / count = #1–8		* * * 0 *
ROXL ROXR	B W	count = Dn / count = #1–8		* * * 0 *
Memory	W	count = 1		* * * 0 *
RTE			(SP)+ → SR; (SP)+ → PC	* * * * *
RTR			(SP)+ → CC; (SP)+ → PC	* * * * *
RTS			(SP)+ → PC	- - - - -
SBCD	B	s = Dn / s = - (An)	d10 - s10 - X → d	* U * U *
Scc	B	cc = True / cc = False	If cc true, then 1s → d else 0s → d	- - - - -
STOP	W		# → SR; wait for interrupt	* * * * *
SUB	B W	s = Dn / d = Dn	d - s → d	* * * * *
SUBA	W L	d = An	d - s → An	- - - - -
SUBI	B W	s = Imm	d - # → d	* * * * *
SUBQ	B W	s = Imm3	d - # → d	* * * * *
SUBX	B W	s = Dn / s = - (An)	d - s - X → d	* * * * *
SWAP	W		Dn[31:16] ←→ Dn[15:0]	- * * 0 0
TAS	B		test d → cc; 1 → bit 7 of d	- * * 0 0
TRAP			PC → -(SSP); SR → -(SSP)	- - - - -
TRAPV			If V = 1, then PC → -(SSP); SR → -(SSP) else NOP	- - - - -
TST	B W L	d = Dn	test d → cc	- * * 0 0
UNLK			An → SP; (SP)+ → An	- - - - -

General Notes:

- * Word Only
- \# Number of Bytes in Instruction
- \$ Execution Time in Clock Periods
- \$ Source (s10 = base 10 operand)
- \$ Destination (d10 = base 10 operand)
- V Value is Maximum Number

- Complement (invert)
- d8 8-Bit Displacement
- d16 16-Bit Displacement
- Imm Immediate Data
- Imm3 Immediate Data, 3 Bits
- Imm8 Immediate Data, 8 Bits

Opcode Bit Pattern Codes:

- A Address Register Number
- C Test Condition
- D Data Register Number
- e Source Effective Address
- I Direction
  - 0 = Right   1 = Left
- M Destination EA Mode
- P Displacement
- Q Quick Immediate Data
- R Destination Register
- S Source Register
- Size
  - 00 = Byte   01 = Word
  - 10 = Long
- V Vector Number
- XX Move size:
  - 01 = Byte
  - 11 = Word

Condition Code Notation:

- * Set according to result of operation.
- - Not affected by operation.
- 0 Cleared
- U Undefined after operation
- ? Other — See Special Definition

Status Register

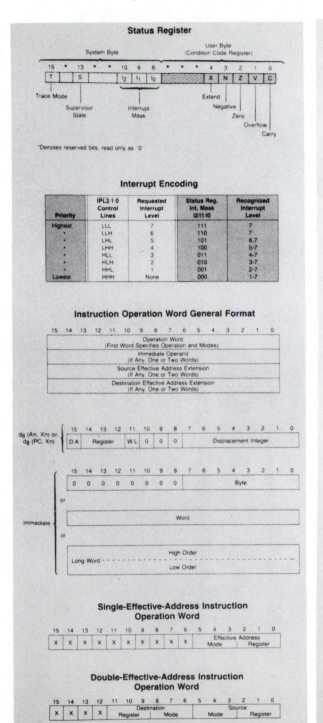

*Denotes reserved bits, read only as '0'

Interrupt Encoding

Priority	IPL2 1 0 Control Lines	Requested Interrupt Level	Status Reg. Int. Mask I2/I1/I0	Recognized Interrupt Level
Highest	LLL	7	111	7
·	LLH	6	110	7
·	LHL	5	101	6,7
·	LHH	4	100	5-7
·	HLL	3	011	4-7
·	HLH	2	010	3-7
·	HHL	1	001	2-7
Lowest	HHH	None	000	1-7

Instruction Operation Word General Format

Single-Effective-Address Instruction Operation Word

Double-Effective-Address Instruction Operation Word

Reference Classification

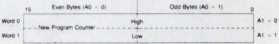

FC2	FC1	FC0	Reference Class		FC2	FC1	FC0	Reference Class
0	0	0	(Unassigned)		1	0	0	(Unassigned)
0	0	1	User Data		1	0	1	Supervisor Data
0	1	0	User Program		1	1	0	Supervisor Program
0	1	1	(Unassigned)		1	1	1	Interrupt Acknowledge

Exception Vector Format

Peripheral Vector Number Format

Where
v7 is the MSB of the Vector Number
v0 is the LSB of the Vector Number

Address Translated from 8-Bit Vector Number

Supervisor Stack Order for Bus or Address Error Exception

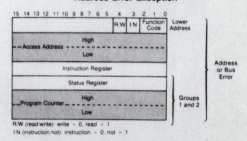

R/W (read/write): write = 0, read = 1
I/N (instruction/not): instruction = 0, not = 1

Exception Grouping and Priority

Group	Exception	Processing
0	Reset, Address Error, Bus Error	Exception processing begins within two clock cycles.
1	Trace, Interrupt, Illegal, Privilege	Exception processing begins before the next instruction.
2	TRAP, TRAPV, CHK, Zero Divide	Exception processing is started by normal instruction execution.

Exception Vector Assignment

Vector Number(s)	Address			Assignment
	Dec	Hex	Space[6]	
0	0	000	SP	Reset: Initial SSP[2]
1	4	004	SP	Reset: Initial PC[2]
2	8	008	SD	Bus Error
3	12	00C	SD	Address Error
4	16	010	SD	Illegal Instruction
5	20	014	SD	Zero Divide
6	24	018	SD	CHK Instruction
7	28	01C	SD	TRAPV Instruction
8	32	020	SD	Privilege Violation
9	36	024	SD	Trace
10	40	028	SD	Line 1010 Emulator
11	44	02C	SD	Line 1111 Emulator
12[1]	48	030	SD	(Unassigned, Reserved)
13[1]	52	034	SD	(Unassigned, Reserved)
14	56	038	SD	Format Error[5]
15	60	03C	SD	Uninitialized Interrupt Vector
16-23[1]	64	040	SD	(Unassigned, Reserved)
	95	05F		—
24	96	060	SD	Spurious Interrupt[3]
25	100	064	SD	Level 1 Interrupt Autovector
26	104	068	SD	Level 2 Interrupt Autovector
27	108	06C	SD	Level 3 Interrupt Autovector
28	112	070	SD	Level 4 Interrupt Autovector
29	116	074	SD	Level 5 Interrupt Autovector
30	120	078	SD	Level 6 Interrupt Autovector
31	124	07C	SD	Level 7 Interrupt Autovector
32-47	128	080	SD	TRAP Instruction Vectors[4]
	191	0BF		
48-63[1]	192	0C0	SD	(Unassigned, Reserved)
	255	0FF		—
64-255	256	100	SD	User Interrupt Vectors
	1023	3FF		—

NOTES:
1. Vector numbers 12, 13, 16 through 23, and 48 through 63 are reserved for future enhancements by Motorola. No user peripheral devices should be assigned these numbers.
2. Reset vector (0) requires four words, unlike the other vectors which only require two words, and is located in the supervisor program space.
3. The spurious interrupt vector is taken when there is a bus error indication during interrupt processing.
4. Trap #n uses vector number 32 + n.
5. MC68010/MC68012 only.
   This vector is unassigned, reserved on the MC68000, and MC68008.
6. SP denotes supervisor program space, and SD denotes supervisor data space.

Exception Processing Execution Times

Exception	Periods
Address Error	50(4/7)
Bus Error	50(4/7)
CHK Instruction	44(5/4) +
Divide by Zero	42(5/4)
Illegal Instruction	34(4/3)
Interrupt	44(5/3)*
Privilege Violation	34(4/3)
RESET**	40(6/0)
Trace	34(4/3)
TRAP Instruction	38(4/4)
TRAPV Instruction	34(4/3)

+ Add effective address calculation time.
*The interrupt acknowledge cycle is assumed to take four clock periods.
**Indicates the time from when RESET and HALT are first sampled as negated to when instruction execution starts.

Conditional Tests

Mnemonic	Condition	Encoding	Test
T	true	0000	1
F	false	0001	0
HI	high	0010	$\bar{C} \cdot \bar{Z}$
LS	low or same	0011	$C + Z$
CC(HS)	carry clear	0100	$\bar{C}$
CS(LO)	carry set	0101	C
NE	not equal	0110	$\bar{Z}$
EQ	equal	0111	Z
VC	overflow clear	1000	$\bar{V}$
VS	overflow set	1001	V
PL	plus	1010	$\bar{N}$
MI	minus	1011	N
GE	greater or equal	1100	$N \cdot V + \bar{N} \cdot \bar{V}$
LT	less than	1101	$N \cdot \bar{V} + \bar{N} \cdot V$
GT	greater than	1110	$N \cdot V \cdot \bar{Z} + \bar{N} \cdot \bar{V} \cdot \bar{Z}$
LE	less or equal	1111	$Z + N \cdot \bar{V} + \bar{N} \cdot V$

Pin Assignments

64-Pin Dual-in-Line Package

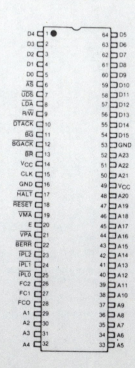

D4	1	64	D5
D3	2	63	D6
D2	3	62	D7
D1	4	61	D8
D0	5	60	D9
$\overline{AS}$	6	59	D10
$\overline{UDS}$	7	58	D11
$\overline{LDA}$	8	57	D12
$R/\overline{W}$	9	56	D13
$\overline{DTACK}$	10	55	D14
$\overline{BG}$	11	54	D15
$\overline{BGACK}$	12	53	GND
$\overline{BR}$	13	52	A23
V_{CC}	14	51	A22
CLK	15	50	A21
GND	16	49	V_{CC}
$\overline{HALT}$	17	48	A20
$\overline{RESET}$	18	47	A19
$\overline{VMA}$	19	46	A18
E	20	45	A17
$\overline{VPA}$	21	44	A16
$\overline{BERR}$	22	43	A15
$\overline{IPL2}$	23	42	A14
$\overline{IPL1}$	24	41	A13
$\overline{IPL0}$	25	40	A12
FC2	26	39	A11
FC1	27	38	A10
FC0	28	37	A9
A1	29	36	A8
A2	30	35	A7
A3	31	34	A6
A4	32	33	A5

Operation Code Map

Bits 15 through 12	Operation	Bits 15 through 12	Operation
0000	Bit Manipulation/MOVEP/Immediate	1000	OR/DIV/SBCD
		1001	SUB/SUBX
0001	Move Byte	1010	(Unassigned)
0010	Move Long	1011	CMP/EOR
0011	Move Word	1100	AND/MUL/ABCD/EXG
0100	Miscellaneous	1101	ADD/ADDX
0101	ADDQ/SUBQ/Scc/DBcc	1110	Shift/Rotate
0110	Bcc/BSR	1111	(Unassigned)
0111	MOVEQ		

Pin Assignments
68-Pin Grid Array

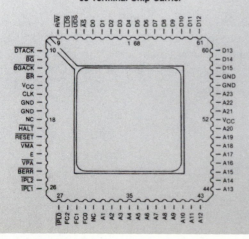

	1	2	3	4	5	6	7	8	9	10
K	NC	FC2	FC0	A1	A3	A4	A6	A7	A9	NC
J	$\overline{\text{BERR}}$	$\overline{\text{IPL0}}$	FC1	NC	A2	A5	A8	A10	A11	A14
H	E	$\overline{\text{IPL2}}$	$\overline{\text{IPL1}}$					A13	A12	A16
G	$\overline{\text{VMA}}$	$\overline{\text{VPA}}$						A15	A17	
F	$\overline{\text{HALT}}$	$\overline{\text{RESET}}$		BOTTOM				A18	A19	
E	CLK	GND		VIEW				Vcc	A20	
D	$\overline{\text{BR}}$	Vcc						GND	A21	
C	$\overline{\text{BGACK}}$	$\overline{\text{BG}}$	R/$\overline{\text{W}}$				D13	A23	A22	
B	$\overline{\text{DTACK}}$	$\overline{\text{LDS}}$	$\overline{\text{UDS}}$	D0	D3	D6	D9	D11	D14	D15
A	NC	$\overline{\text{AS}}$	D1	D2	D4	D5	D7	D8	D10	D12

68-Terminal Chip Carrier

Powers of 16, Powers of 2

16^m m=	2^n n=	Value		16^m m=	2^n n=	Value
0	0	1		4	16	65,536
	1	2			17	131,072
	2	4			18	262,144
	3	8			19	524,288
1	4	16		5	20	1,048,576
	5	32			21	2,097,152
	6	64			22	4,194,304
	7	128			23	8,388,608
2	8	256		6	24	16,777,216
	9	512			25	33,554,432
	10	1,024			26	67,108,864
	11	2,048			27	134,217,728
3	12	4,096		7	28	268,435,456
	13	8,192			29	536,870,912
	14	16,384			30	1,073,741,824
	15	32,768			31	2,147,483,648
				8	32	4,294,967,296

ASCII Character Set (7-Bit Code)

LS Dig. \ MS Dig.	0	1	2	3	4	5	6	7
0	NUL	DLE	SP	0	@	P	`	p
1	SOH	DC1	!	1	A	Q	a	q
2	STX	DC2	"	2	B	R	b	r
3	ETX	DC3	#	3	C	S	c	s
4	EOT	DC4	$	4	D	T	d	t
5	ENQ	NAK	%	5	E	U	e	u
6	ACK	SYN	&	6	F	V	f	v
7	BEL	ETB	'	7	G	W	g	w
8	BS	CAN	(	8	H	X	h	x
9	HT	EM	)	9	I	Y	i	y
A	LF	SUB	*	:	J	Z	j	z
B	VT	ESC	+	;	K	[	k	{
C	FF	FS	,	<	L	\	l	|
D	CR	GS	-	=	M	]	m	}
E	SO	RS	.	>	N	^	n	~
F	SI	US	/	?	O	_	o	DEL

Hexadecimal and Decimal Conversion

How to use:

Conversion to Decimal: Find the decimal weights for corresponding hexadecimal characters beginning with the least significant character. The sum of the decimal weights is the decimal value of the hexadecimal number.

Conversion to Hexadecimal: Find the highest decimal value in the table which is lower than or equal to the decimal number to be converted. The corresponding hexadecimal character is the most significant. Subtract the decimal value found from the decimal number to be converted. With the difference repeat the process to find subsequent hexadecimal characters.

23	Byte		16	15	Byte		8	7	Byte		0
23 Char		20	19 Char		16	15 Char		12	11 Char		8	7 Char		4	3 Char		0

Hex	Dec	Hex	Dec	Hex	Dec	Hex	Dec	Hex	Dec	Hex	Dec
0	0	0	0	0	0	0	0	0	0	0	0
1	1,048,576	1	65,536	1	4,096	1	256	1	16	1	1
2	2,097,158	2	131,072	2	8,192	2	512	2	32	2	2
3	3,145,728	3	196,608	3	12,288	3	768	3	48	3	3
4	4,194,304	4	262,144	4	16,384	4	1024	4	64	4	4
5	5,242,880	5	327,680	5	20,480	5	1280	5	80	5	5
6	6,291,456	6	393,216	6	24,576	6	1536	6	96	6	6
7	7,340,032	7	458,752	7	28,672	7	1792	7	112	7	7
8	8,388,608	8	524,288	8	32,768	8	2048	8	128	8	8
9	9,437,184	9	589,824	9	36,864	9	2304	9	144	9	9
A	10,485,760	A	655,360	A	40,960	A	2560	A	160	A	10
B	11,534,336	B	720,896	B	45,056	B	2816	B	176	B	11
C	12,582,912	C	786,432	C	49,152	C	3072	C	192	C	12
D	13,631,488	D	851,968	D	53,248	D	3328	D	208	D	13
E	14,680,064	E	917,504	E	57,344	E	3584	E	224	E	14
F	15,728,640	F	983,040	F	61,440	F	3840	F	240	F	15

Appendix B

Differences between the

68000 and the 68010

Microprocessors

For most practical purposes the 68000 and the 68010 are effectively identical and nearly all object code written for the 68000 will also run on the 68010 to produce the same results. In short, the 68010 is an enhanced version of the 68000. However, some important differences exist between the 68000 and the 68010. The manufacturers of the 68010 have modified the 68000 in three ways:

1. Performance. The 68010 executes some instructions much faster than the 68000 at the same clock speed.

2. Virtual machine support. The 68010 makes life a little easier for the designer of operating systems.

3. Virtual memory support. The 68010 supports virtual memory by allowing a bus cycle to be continued after a bus error exception; that is, a page fault can be generated by a memory management unit, the relevant page replaced in RAM by the operating system, and then the faulted instruction continued.

Improving the 68000's Performance

Apart from one or two new instructions, the 68010 has the same instruction set as the 68000, but its internal microprogramming has been improved to give it a useful increase in speed over the 68000.

Although most of the 68010's instructions require as many clock cycles as the same instructions on the 68000, some instructions show marked improvements; for example, the MULU instruction requires 70 clock cycles on a 68000 but only 40 cycles on a 68010.

A major improvement in the 68010's performance results from its loop mode operation. The 68010 implements the DB_{cc} instruction in a special way that enhances its operation. Consider the following fragment of code:

```
        LEA.L    SOURCE,A0          A0 points at the source of data to be moved
        LEA.L    DESTINATION,A1     A1 points at the destination of the data
        MOVE.W   #BLOCK_SIZE,D0     D0 holds the size of the block to move −1
*
LOOP    MOVE.W   (A0)+,(A1)+        Move a word from source to destination
        DBEQ     D0,LOOP            Repeat loop until all data moved
```

The work of the loop is performed by the MOVE.W (A0)+,(A1)+ and the DBEQ D0,LOOP instructions. Because the 68010 has a two-word, tightly coupled instruction prefetch mechanism, these two instructions are read only *once* when the loop is first executed; that is, the 68010 performs only source *operand* fetch and destination *operand* store operations, while the loop is being executed. The loop mode is, of course, invisible to the programmer.

Architectural Enhancements of the 68010

From the point of view of a task running in the user mode, the 68010 is identical to the 68000 (apart from the MOVE from SR to be described later). Improvements in the 68010's architecture are visible only to the operating system that runs in the supervisor mode. The supervisor mode model of the 68010 consists of the following five registers:

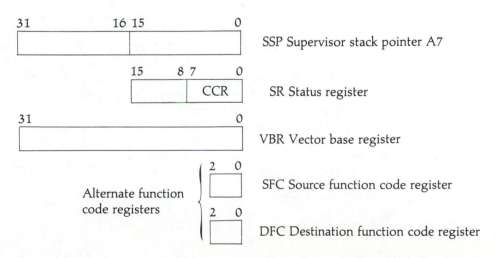

The 68010's new registers are the vector base register, VBR, and the alternate function code registers, SFC and DFC. We consider the VBR first. Whenever the 68000 responds to an exception, it reads the exception vector from the appropriate location in the exception vector table in the region $00 0000 to $00 03FF. The 68010 calculates the address of an exception vector in *exactly* the same way as the 68000, but the 68010 adds the address of the exception vector to the contents of the VBR to give the actual address of the exception vector. The following diagram illustrates this action:

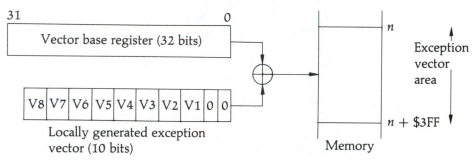

Locally generated exception
vector (10 bits)   Memory

The advantage of the VBR is its ability to support multiple exception vector tables. Simply reloading the VBR selects a new exception vector table anywhere in the 68010's address space. Of course, such a facility is only really useful in certain classes of multitasking systems, where each task maintains its own copy of the exception vector table. For example, the various tasks may treat, say, a divide_by_zero exception in different ways. If each task shared the *same* exception vector table, the exception handler would have to determine which task generated the current divide_by_zero exception, and then call the corresponding procedure. By changing the exception vector table each time a new task is run, exceptions are automatically vectored to the handler appropriate to the task now running. A VBR avoids the problems of locating read/write memory in the region $00 0000 to $00 03FF and then overlaying the first two longwords at $00 0000 to $00 0007 with the supervisor stack pointer and initial program counter value in ROM. The 68010 also facilitates the use of ROM at the top end of memory, because the exception vector table can be relocated in any suitable block of read/write memory by modifying the contents of the VBR. Note that the VBR is cleared (loaded with zero) following a hardware reset. Therefore, the 68010 automatically emulates the 68000's mode of exception vector generation until the operating system explicitly loads an offset into the VBR.

New registers require new instructions to access them. The 68010 has a move to and a move from control register instruction, MOVEC, to access the VBR or the SFC or DFC registers. MOVEC is a privileged instruction with the assembly language form

        MOVEC Rc,Rn

or

        MOVEC Rn,Rc

where Rn is a general register (A0 to A7 or D0 to D7) and Rc is a control register (VBR, SFC, or DFC).

For example, the exception vector table can be relocated to $8000 by the sequence,

```
MOVE.L     #$8000, D0
MOVEC.L    D0,VBR
```

The alternate function code registers are used in conjunction with the new 68010 instruction MOVES (move to or from address space). Before continuing, we have to make it clear that the alternate function code registers have a meaning only in systems with memory management units that distinguish between user address space and supervisor address space. The 68000 uses its function code outputs on FC0 to FC2 to indicate to an MMU the type of address space being accessed (user or supervisor). If the type of address space accessed does not match the type of address space determined by FC0 to FC2, the MMU issues a bus error exception by asserting BERR*. This arrangement has a subtle flaw! When the 68000 is in the supervisor mode, it cannot make a memory access to user address space, because all its accesses are to supervisor address space. What we need is a method of fooling the MMU into thinking that the microprocessor is operating in the user mode when it is, in fact, operating in the supervisor mode. Such a facility permits the operating system to transfer data to user data space. Equally, it allows the operating system to perform diagnostic tests on user address space.

The 68010 is able to execute an access to *any* address space when it is in the supervisor mode by means of the privileged instruction MOVES, which has the assembly language forms

```
MOVES  Rn,〈ea〉
```

and

```
MOVES  〈ea〉,Rn
```

where Rn is a general register and 〈ea〉 is an effective address. Legal addressing modes are: (An), (An)+, −(An), d(An), d(An, Xi), Abs.W, and Abs.L. Note that MOVES permits byte, word, and longword operands.

The address space used by the MOVES instruction is determined by the source function code (SFC) register, if the source operand is in memory. Similarly, the address space is determined by the destination function code (DFC) register, if the MOVES instruction specifies a destination operand. For example, suppose the operating system wishes to read the contents of location $40000 which is in user address space. The following sequence of operations will perform this task:

```
MOVE.L     #%001,D0     Load D0 with user data function code
MOVEC.L    D0,SFC       Copy user space code into the SFC register
MOVES.W    #$40000,D1   Read data from user data space
```

The 68010 and Virtual Machine Support

The 68010 has one new instruction to access the status register and treats the existing 68000 MOVE from SR in a different way to the 68000. Before we look at these instructions, we should describe the virtual machine. It is sometimes necessary to run two (or more) operating systems on the *same* machine *concurrently*. Such a situation might be found in circumstances where users require such diverse facilities (e.g., business and scientific) that no one operating system is sufficient. When two operating systems are run concurrently, each operating system provides a virtual environment for the programs running under it; that is, each user program sees its operating system as the real (i.e., virtual) operating system of the machine itself. In fact, the operating systems are themselves *user tasks* running under the actual operating system of the machine. A similar situation exists when a programmer is developing an operating system. The operating system being developed cannot run in the user mode because it is an operating system and requires access to the privileged operations associated with the supervisor mode. Equally, it cannot run in the supervisor mode because it is a user task running under the real (i.e., the actual) operating system.

The solution to this dilemma is to run the operating system under test in the user mode but to make it *appear* to this operating system as if it were really running in the supervisor mode. Whenever the operating system under test attempts to use a supervisor mode facility, an exception is generated and the actual operating system emulates in software the requested facility. In this way, the operating system under test appears to run on a virtual machine.

Although the 68000 implements some of the facilities required by a virtual machine, a major flaw exists in the 68000's structure. A 68000 program running in the *user* mode can access the status word by means of a MOVE SR,⟨ea⟩ operation. A virtual machine should not allow a user task to "see" the status register that reflects the activity of the real machine. Consequently, the 68010 makes the MOVE SR,⟨ea⟩ instruction a privileged operation, so that any attempt by a program in the user mode to access the status register results in a privilege violation exception.

The 68010 introduces a new instruction, MOVE CCR,⟨ea⟩, to enable user tasks to access the condition code register byte of the status word. Clearly, it is perfectly reasonable for a user task to access the condition code register. The MOVE CCR,⟨ea⟩ is not privileged and has the effect of copying the CCR into the lower byte of the word specified by the given effective address. The upper byte of this word is filled with zeros.

The 68010 and the Bus Error

For all practical purposes, the 68010's most significant advance over the 68000 is the 68010's ability to rerun bus cycles terminated by a bus error exception. Whenever the BERR∗ input to the 68000 is asserted (and HALT∗ not asserted), a bus error exception is forced and the bus error exception handler executed in software. If the bus error is due to a page fault, the instruction that caused the fault must be rerun once the appropriate page in read/write memory has been loaded from disk by the operating system. Unfortunately, the 68000 does not store sufficient information on the stack to permit the faulted memory access to be rerun.

The 68010 saves more information on the stack following an interrupt than the 68000. The 68010 stack frame is as follows:

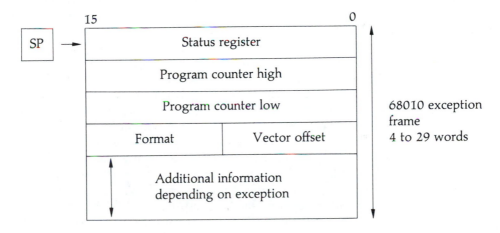

The 68010 saves the most volatile portion of the current processor status in a variable-length stack frame. The most-significant four bits of the word saved immediately before the low-order word of the program counter provide the *format* of the current stack frame. The 68010 currently defines two values of the format code:

    0000 = short format (stack frame = 4 words)
    1000 = long format (stack frame = 29 words)

The RTE, return from exception, instruction uses the format code to determine whether the current exception has a 4-word or a 29-word stack frame.

The 29 words of the 68010 long format stack frame saved when a bus error exception is processed provide *all* the information needed to continue an instruction. Notice the word *continue* in the previous sentence. The 68010 does not rerun or restart an instruction interrupted by a bus error exception. Instead, it saves sufficient information in the stack frame to continue the instruction from the point at which it was interrupted.

After a bus error (or an address error) exception has been processed, an RTE can be used to complete the interrupted instruction. If the faulted bus cycle was a read-modify-write cycle, the entire cycle will be rerun whether the fault occurred during the read or the write operation.

Breakpoint Instructions

The 68000 generates an illegal instruction exception if ever it attempts to execute an op-code that is not part of the 68000's instruction set. However, the designers of the 68000 have *reserved* a special illegal instruction with the assembly language form ILLEGAL and with the op-code $4AFC. The ILLEGAL instruction can be used to generate an illegal instruction exception for test purposes (or for any other purpose desired by the programmer). The special bit pattern $4AFC will always be an illegal op-code in all future enhancements of the 68000.

In addition to the illegal op-code $4AFC, the 68010 defines eight other reserved illegal instructions with the bit patterns $4848 to $484F. These instructions are called *breakpoint* illegal instructions and are treated in a special way. When a breakpoint illegal instruction is encountered by the 68010, it begins an illegal instruction exception in the normal fashion. However, the 68010 executes a special bus cycle, called a *breakpoint* cycle, before the normal stacking operations are carried out. A breakpoint cycle is a dummy read cycle in which FC0 to FC2 are all set high and the address lines are all set low. The 68010 does not execute a read or a write operation during the breakpoint cycle and the 68010 continues with normal exception handling irrespective of whether the cycle is terminated by a DTACK*, BERR*, or VPA*. The purpose of the breakpoint cycle is to provide a trigger for external hardware. For example, the breakpoint cycle can be used in system testing. The breakpoint is detected by looking for 1, 1, 1 on FC0 to FC2 and 0 on A_{01} to A_{23}. When the breakpoint is executed, the hardware detects it and triggers, say, a signature analyzer. A second breakpoint can be used to stop the signature analyzer.

The RTD Instruction

The only new user mode instruction available to the 68010 programmer is the return and deallocate instruction, RTD. The assembly language form of RTD is RTD #⟨displacement⟩, where the displacement is a 16-bit twos complement value which is sign extended to 32 bits before use. The effect of an RTD is

$$[PC] \leftarrow [[SP]] \qquad [SP] \leftarrow [SP] + 4$$
$$[SP] \leftarrow [SP] + d$$

In plain English, the longword at the top of the stack is pulled and deposited in the program counter (i.e., just like an RTS instruction) and then the contents of the stack pointer are increased by d bytes. An example should make this clearer. Suppose a procedure receives three parameters that have been passed via the stack. The following diagram shows the stack immediately after the subroutine call:

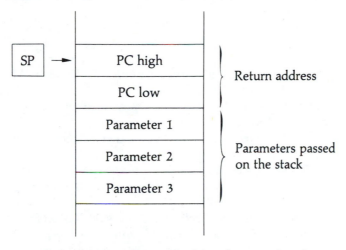

A 68010 can either return from the procedure by executing an RTS and then clean up the stack by executing an LEA 6(SP),SP in the calling code, or it can return and clean up the stack within the procedure by executing the following sequence:

```
MOVE.L   (A7)+,A0   Get the return address in A0
LEA.L    6(A7),A7   Clean up the stack
JMP      (A0)       Return from subroutine
```

The 68010 is able to return from the subroutine *and* clean up the stack (i.e., deallocate parameters) at the same time by executing RTD #6.

Bibliography

Bacon, J. *The Motorola MC68000: An Introduction to Processor, Memory and Interfacing*. Prentice-Hall, 1986.

Brown, G., and Harper, K. *MC68008 Minimum Configuration System*. Application Note AN897, Motorola Inc., 1984.

Carter, E.M., and Bonds, A.B. "A 68000-based system for only $200." *Byte* (January 1984): 403–416.

Clements, A. *Microcomputer Design and Construction*. Prentice-Hall, 1982.

———. "A Microprocessor for Teaching Computer Technology." *Computer Bulletin (UK)* 2, Part 1 (March 1986), 14–16.

Coffron, J.W. *Using and Troubleshooting the MC68000*. Reston Publishing, 1982.

Davis, R. *Prioritized Individually Vectored Interrupts for Multiple Peripheral Systems with the MC68000*. Application Note AN819, Motorola Inc., 1981.

Eccles, W.J. *Microprocessor Systems: A 16-bit Approach*. Addison-Wesley, 1985.

Fischer, W. "IEEE P1014—A Standard for the High-Performance VME Bus." *IEEE Micro* (February 1985), 31–41.

Foster, C.C. *Real Time Programming—Neglected Topics*. Addison-Wesley, 1981.

Gillet, W.D. *An Introduction to Engineered Software*. Holt-Saunders, 1982.

Groves, S. "Balancing RAM Access Time and Clock Rate Maximizes Microprocessor Throughput." *Computer Design* (July 1980), 118–126.

Hilf, W., and Nausch, A. *M68000 Familie*. Teil 1, "Grundlagen und Architekture." Munich: Te-wi Verlag, 1984.

Jaulent, P. *Circuits Périphériques de la Famille 68000*. Paris: Editions Eyrolles, 1985.

——— *The 68000 Hardware and Software*. Macmillan (UK), 1985.

Kane, G., Hawkins, D., Cramer, W., and Leventhal, L. *68000 Assembly Language Programming*. Osborne/McGraw-Hill, 1986.

King, T., and Knight, B. *Programming the M68000*. Addison-Wesley, 1986.

Laws, D.A., and Levy, R.J. *Use of the Am26LS29, 30, 31 and 32 Quad Driver/Receiver Family in EIA RS-422 and 423 Applications*. Advanced Micro Devices Application Note, June 1978.

Lenk, J.D. *How to Troubleshoot and Repair Microcomputers*. Reston Publishing, 1980.

MacGregor, D., and Mothersole, D.S. "Virtual Memory and the MC68010." *IEEE Micro* 3 (June 1983), 24–39.

Morton, M. "68000 Ticks and Traps." *Byte* 11, No. 9 (September 1986), 163–172.

Motorola Inc. *High Performance Memory Design Technique for the MC68000*. Application Note AN838, Motorola Inc., 1982.